INSTITUTIONS, POLICIES, AND GOALS

INSTITUTIONS, POLICIES, AND GOALS

A Reader in American Politics

Editors

Kenneth M. Dolbeare
University of Washington

Murray J. Edelman
University of Wisconsin

with

Patricia Dolbeare

D. C. HEATH AND COMPANY
Lexington, Massachusetts Toronto London

CONTENTS

Introduction

PART I
POLICY-MAKING: NATIONAL GOVERNMENT
INSTITUTIONS AMIDST THE PRESSURES
OF THE 1970s 1

1   The National Security Managers and the National Interest   5
    Richard J. Barnet

2   The State System and the State Elite   17
    Ralph Miliband

3   The Threat of World Depression   43
    Lyn Marcus

4   The Making of a Majority: Safeguard and the Senate   68
    Nathan Miller

5   The War-Making Machinery   83
    Robert J. Bresler

6   Eulogies and Evasions   91
    Robert Sherrill

7   The Committee System   98
    Charles L. Clapp

8   Taken—by Train   114
    Robert Sherrill

9   The Lockheed Scandal   119
    James G. Phillips

10   Decision-Making in a Democracy: The Supreme Court
    as a National Policy Maker   128
    Robert A. Dahl

11   The End of American Party Politics   145
    Walter Dean Burnham

PART II

PROBLEMS AND POLICIES: FROM CONSTRASTING PERSPECTIVES 161

12 Capitalism, Colonialism, and Racism 164
     William K. Tabb

13 The Artificial Universe 180
     Vine Deloria, Jr.

14 Crisis of the Cities 191
     Nancy Spannaus

15 Watershed of the American Economy 204
     David Deitch

16 Public Policy and the White Working Class 212
     John Howard

17 Income Distribution in the United States 227
     *Frank Ackerman, Howard Birnbaum, James Wetzler,
     and Andrew Zimbalist*

18 Looking at Poverty from a Radical Perspective 248
     Howard M. Wachtel

PART III

POLITICAL CHANGE: APPROACHES TO ANALYSIS AND ACTION 267

19 The Possibilities for Political Change 271
     Michael Parenti

20 On Political Belief: The Grievances of the Poor 283
     Lewis Lipsitz

21 Power and Pluralism: A View from the Bottom 305
     Michael Parenti

22 Blue Ridge: The History of Our Struggle Against
     Levi-Strauss 332
     Brenda C. Mull

23 Party Programs—Serving the People 345
     Bobby Seale

24 Conscience of a Steelworker 352
     Barbara and John Ehrenreich

PART IV

POLITICAL CHANGE: GOALS AND PRESCRIPTIONS 359

25　The Strategy of Sexual Struggle　362
　　Caroline Hennessey

26　Toward an Ecological Theory of Value　382
　　Arthur and Stephanie Pearl

27　Chicano Manifesto: New Strategies for the Seventies　395
　　Armando B. Rendón

28　Black Awakening: Toward a Transitional Program　414
　　Robert L. Allen

29　Toward a New America　422
　　New American Movement

30　Strategies for Socialism: Tasks and Perspectives　441
　　National Caucus of Labor Committees

INTRODUCTION

Let us quickly say what is so distinct about this collection as to justify still another introductory reader in American politics. We begin with what it is *not,* and move promptly to what it *is.*

This is *not* a collection of three articles each about the Congress, the President, the Supreme Court, political parties, interest groups, public opinion, voting, and so on. It is not cast in any elaborate framework such as systems analysis or functional theory; integration is achieved by a focus on social problems and efforts to solve them. It is not limited to the scholarly research of political scientists, although several are among the various social scientists represented. It is not merely topical, although it deals with vital current issues and problems. And it has no single theme or point of view to put forward, although its premise is that the 1970s are an era of pervasive conflict, probable crisis, and possible change.

The collection *is* a rather wide-ranging synthesis of social science and good journalism, organized in three basic blocks: (1) policy-making amidst the legacies of the past and other pressures, (2) the "fit" between pressing social problems and existing public policies, and (3) prospects and prescriptions for change. It emphasizes the integration of politics and economics in the United States. It emphasizes the problems, actions, and goals of various minority groups, women, and the white working class. It focuses first on the workings of the major American institutions, their burdens and limitations. Then, after exploring the policies they have generated to deal with current problems, it shifts to the second major focus: the values, goals, and specific prescriptions of key contemporary social movements.

To more fully illustrate our purposes here, we shall offer a more detailed explanation of our design and identify the assumptions and intentions that lie behind it. Our original goal was to develop a collection of readings that would serve to accompany and supplement our textbook in this field (*American Politics: Policies, Power, and Change.*) But this collection quickly acquired an independent character and rationale. It will readily stand alone, or serve with other texts and interpretations, as well as with our own book. This does mean, however, that we are obliged to state the organizing principles and criteria of selection that have led to this particular collection.

Part I is the first major focus of the collection. In a variety of ways, and with attention to each of the major institutions in turn, we examine the ways in which decisions are made in American government. The context established for this consideration is that of multiple pressures—stemming in part from those elements within the society which are able to mobilize such pressure upon decision-makers, and in part from the characteristics of the major social problems themselves. Our concern is initially with the conceptual frame in which the analyst seeks to understand the actions of political institutions, because there are many different ways to look at the relationship between elements of power in the society and political decision-making. Too often, the assumption is made that the only question at issue is the relationship between the people and their elected representatives; too complete a focus on this "democratic" imagery may preclude recognition that there are other types of forces at work to shape decision-making. Once the issue has been presented, however, we invest most of our time and selections in exploring the dynamics of the policy-making process at the national level. The important issues are who makes decisions, in what ways, and to whose benefit. What emerges from this collection, not surprisingly, is a sense that our institutions are hard-pressed by volume, complexity, and intransigence of issues—and that they are not very well prepared to deal with such problems. Their own rules and procedures and traditions, to say nothing of their electoral arrangements, add to the problem of achieving timely and appropriate response. The suggestion remains, moreover, that the needs and imperatives—and the key decision-makers—coming out of the economic system have a large part to play in shaping the ultimate policies of the national government.

The second Part examines some major social problems, and looks at current governmental policies which try to cope with them. There are three broad problems considered: minorities' relationship to the larger society, the problems of the cities, and the economic situation, particularly that of the majority of Americans—the white working class and the poor. In each case, selections are designed to portray the assumptions and goals involved in existing policies, and to provide contrasting perspectives on what should be done with each problem. The contrasting perspectives are those which imply change in the same direction as recent changes have gone; we have not included arguments urging elimination of government programs or drastic curtailment of the opportunities of citizens to enjoy social services or increasing "equality," because space demands forced concentration on the most viable and likely options.

Parts III and IV are the second major focus of the collection. In them, we try to accomplish two primary tasks. The first is to explore the meaning of change, and the manner in which various groups have sought to achieve it. Here we are obliged to take up some of the major elements in the conventional wisdom of political science: the apathy and withdrawal of some voters, the nature of pluralism, and so on. The selections are designed to suggest that these elements of received wisdom may not be conclusively established, and to invite further inquiry. Additional selections seek to provide a sense of the character of efforts to achieve change, and of the obstacles in the way of accomplishing even relatively limited goals. The second task (Part IV) is to provide an idea of the types of goals and programs which various change-seeking movements have in mind. We believe that the ideologies and prescriptions of contemporary social movements contain much of the dynamism of American politics today, and that they must be understood in their own terms before an analyst can hope to understand contemporary politics. We have therefore included several excerpts and articles, in an effort to cover a wide range of change-seeking movements and arguments. Most of these are unorthodox—that is, not movements committed exclusively to legal or electoral means of change. The empirical fact is that, if people are unable to attain their goals through the existing political institutions of a society, they will in many cases seek redress of what they perceive as injustice through other means. By now, it is a commonplace of American politics that several groups assert that the legal/electoral systems do not provide real opportunities for them to achieve their goals. The varieties of extra-legal supplementation of the traditional political remedies are many, and these excerpts provide a sense of the determination and prospects of several of these movements.

This last section can also be viewed as the culmination of the book because it brings together the alternative ways of organizing to achieve different levels of change. Some of the advocates seek only that change which would serve rather limited group goals. Others have in mind changes which would revise certain aspects of national policy or certain conditions of life, but leave nearly all others virtually untouched. And then there are some which believe that there must be fundamental reconstruction of all basic values and the nature of the economic and social systems as well. These are differences in the *scope* of change sought, ranging from quite marginal and specific matters, to society-wide issues and practices, to the very basic organizing principles of the society, economy, and polity themselves. These selections also embody differences in the *means* by which change is to be achieved, ranging from voting and persuasion to revolution. Several face the question of how a large enough and coherent enough movement for change is to be built. This is surely one of the crucial issues confronting those who believe that large-scale changes are necessary, and we think it belongs at the center of a collection of this sort.

More specific analyses of individual selections may be found in the essays preceding each Part. But we have no intent to weave a particular analysis or argument out of the selections included. The purpose of a collection of readings in a field such as this is to provide the raw materials out of which teachers and students may draw several of the vital dimensions of politics. This book will have served its purpose if it contains elements which can be the subject of serious analysis and discussion, and if it nudges readers toward determination to become independent, autonomous thinkers about the major questions of politics.

Kenneth M. Dolbeare
Murray J. Edelman

INSTITUTIONS, POLICIES, AND GOALS

PART I
POLICY-MAKING: NATIONAL GOVERNMENT INSTITUTIONS AMIDST THE PRESSURES OF THE 1970s

The special problems and conditions of the 1970s have placed new strains on the already burdened institutions of government. This group of 11 selections explores some of the highlights of decision-making within the major institutions of the national government—the Presidency and the executive departments and agencies, the Congress, the Supreme Court, and the political parties. It combines problem-focused analyses with case studies and descriptions of rules and patterns of performance on the part of particular institutions. Out of it we expect readers to draw a clearer sense of the procedures involved in decision-making, and the difficulties which confront those responsible. Naturally, we shall be concerned also with just who those responsible officials are, and with the question of who benefits from their decisions.

The first three selections form a distinctive group. They employ different approaches to raise the question of how an analyst should look at government decision-makers. Richard Barnet's article focuses on the specific individuals who exercised power in regard to foreign-policy-making from 1940 to 1967. He finds that they did not arise through elections, but rather through appointments from business or professional careers. This implies that the standards and preferences of their private careers, most of which were in major corporations and banks, may have had more to do with their actions in government than any democratically-determined policies. Moreover, Barnet sees a shared image of the world, and of the interests of the United States, being held by this homogeneous group of officials. His evidence regarding their attitudes may be less convincing than his data on their backgrounds. But the important point to see in his article is its basic approach: he is suggesting that one way to look at and try to understand institutions of government is to ask, who are the decision-makers and what interests do they serve?

The second selection in this first group is part of a larger work by Ralph Miliband. He does not employ evidence concerning the backgrounds and career experiences of specific decision-makers, but he argues that essentially all decision-makers come from the upper social class, and that they therefore have certain narrow interests in common. His approach is to see government itself as a reflection not of the society's democratic aspirations, but of its existing social order. In other words, one understands government and its actions by looking at the class structure of the society and seeing how the upper echelons of that class structure employ government to serve their ends. In the latter part of this excerpt, Miliband goes on to argue that, regardless of who actually holds office, they must act in accordance with the needs and imperatives of the economic system of their society. They must do so, he says, in order to maintain employment and increase production. Thus, he suggests that the range of decision-makers' alternatives and actions is fixed, and that government may best be understood as the agent of the economic order carrying out the policies required to keep it healthy.

The last selection in this group takes this point somewhat further, viewing the actions of the government in terms of the specific economic policy needs and immediate past experience of the United States. Lyn Marcus attributes the behavior of men in government not to their specific backgrounds or to their shared images of the world so much as to the profit-seeking needs of the U.S. economy. These are analyzed in a world context, and the actions of men in government seen as rational and predictable responses to profit needs under these conditions.

The usual approach to analysis of the decision-makers' actions is to view them as acting in a setting where the rules of their respective institutions establish certain constraints, where the demands of groups within the society are strongly felt, and where legislators and executives must decide issues on the basis of the merits of the specific case before them. Some of the selections which follow approach their subjects in exactly these ways. But this first group of selections presents three somewhat different ways of trying to understand the behavior of men in government, and some of the subsequent selections will follow these approaches more than the traditional ones. The reason for this is that we think the traditional approaches may omit some of the important factors involved in political decision-making. Government decision-makers do not act in a vacuum. They act in a context which includes more than just recognizedly "political" factors. They cannot help but be concerned with whether their actions promote economic well-being, for example, and thus we must explore the extent to which such concerns affect decisions. The question immediately raised, of course, is whether the economic well-being that is considered is that of the nation as a whole, or of special segments of the population.

The second, and principal, body of selections in this section is made up of case studies of the interactions of various national government institutions, and some insightful reflections on the workings of certain of them. Several selections consider the extent to which changes in institutional procedures would make it possible for better or more timely decisions to emerge from those institutions. The first four deal principally with the Congress, the Presidency, and executive agencies. Nathan Miller's article on the Senate's consideration and ultimate passage of the Safeguard missile defense system neatly captures much of the flavor of the Senate in action. The process of bargaining, pressuring, compromising, and debating is well portrayed; the President's capacity to apply pressure is emphasized, and the personal character of much Senate decision-making is evident. The unstated question raised by the account, of course, is whether this system provides for effective consideration of the merits of the issue involved.

Perhaps the central source of tension in the Congress, and particularly in the Senate, during the last decade was the matter of the Vietnam War. In the next article, Robert Bresler shows how much difficulty the Senate has had in recent years in playing a part in the foreign policy-making process, together with the President and various executive agencies and departments. Bresler asks whether the answer to the problem of making better policy lies in institutional changes to increase the relative power and responsibility of the Congress. Robert Sherrill's article, however, shows how difficult it is for the Congress to do things differently from the past. Traditions and long-established procedures are supported by the fact that members of the Congress need to have predictable standards of behavior, and by the hope on the part of rising members that they too someday will enjoy the special influence and power that comes from holding key positions. In any social group, the pressure is strong to conform to group norms, and members do not wish to be viewed as outcasts by the group, or even a majority of them, with whom they must continue to do business.

What holds the key to the Congress, its operating characteristics and its resistance to reform, is the committee system. Charles Clapp's essay here is drawn from an important larger work in which he described what it is like to be a Congressman. Notice how important the major positions on the Congressional committees are, and how seniority determines influence. The Congress must divide its responsibility in some fashion, in order to cope with the range and diversity of problems it faces; but by doing so it places special responsibility (and power) in the hands of a relatively few (and perhaps unrepresentative) people.

The next two articles explore the role of business interests and government decision-making in somewhat more focused fashion. Robert Sherrill's analysis of the government loan obtained by the Penn Central Railroad in order to stave off bankruptcy, and James Phillips' study of Lockheed's similar success, combine to suggest that the government considers the survival of such businesses so important that it is willing to step in to support them when they experience difficulties. Each may be considered on its own merits as special interest legislation, but the more important question is more general: to what extent are many businesses, not just Penn Central and Lockheed, dependent on government support? What does this suggest about the integration of economics and politics?

The final pair of selections here takes up two other major institutions. Dahl's article on the Supreme Court is often reprinted, for it shows clearly how fully the Supreme Court takes part in national policy-making. At the same time, it indicates something about the nature of this participation. Much has been written about an "activist" Supreme Court, or a "conservative" Court. Dahl argues that the Court essentially follows majority trends, at least insofar as they are reflected in the election results in the Presidency and the Congress. The article by Burnham confronts the question of change within the political parties. He proceeds from the premise that the parties have not been performing their representing function in recent years. Burnham is pessimistic about the future role of political parties, but his analysis incisively reviews much of the development and recent experiences of the parties, and his assessment seems well worth serious consideration.

In conclusion, it might be well to keep in mind the extent to which analyses of the workings of national institutions proceed on the basis of (often unstated) assumptions about the relationship between the people and the actions of the government. Even Dahl's article on the Court, a non-elective body, deals with the extent to which popular preferences are inserted into public policy. Burnham views the parties as crucial links between the people and government action. But much of what we have seen suggests that there are many intervening or mediating factors between the people's preferences and the policies enacted by government decision-makers. And the approaches taken by the first three authors in this section insist that these intervening forces and factors are the *real* ones shaping public policies. To what extent is this true? Is it all a matter of what approach to analysis one chooses to take? Or are there types of evidence that would help to resolve the question?

1.
THE NATIONAL SECURITY MANAGERS AND THE NATIONAL INTEREST

Richard J. Barnet

"Foreign policies are not built on abstractions. They are the result of practical conceptions of the national interest . . .," Charles Evans Hughes once noted when he was secretary of state. The key word of course is *practical*. Like the flag, the national interest can mean many different things to different people. The term in itself is the classic abstraction. It has virtually no inherent meaning. It acquires meaning only through interpretation. Those who play the role of interpreting the national interest are the priests of the modern state. Their values, their analysis of events, and their faith in the future determine what is deemed to be in the nation's interest and how it is to respond to the world political environment.

This, of course, has always been so. In times past those who managed the affairs of a great nation invariably defined the national interest in terms of power and glory. Whatever accrued to the majesty of the state was in its interest. It mattered little how much the people had to be taxed for it or how many had to die. The realization that a leader's conception of the national interest may be self-serving or fallible lay behind the attempt in the American Constitution to subject the foreign relations power to some form of democratic control. As Abraham Lincoln put it at the time of the Mexican War:

> The provision of the Constitution giving the warmaking power to Congress, was dictated, as I understand it, by the following reasons: Kings had always been involving and impoverishing their people in wars, pretending generally, if not always, that the good of the people was the object. This, our Convention understood to be the most oppressive of all kingly oppressions: and they resolved to so frame the Constitution that no one man should hold the power of bringing this oppression upon us.[1]

From Richard J. Barnet, "The National Security Managers and the National Interest," *Politics and Society*, vol. 1, no. 2 (February 1971), pp. 257–268 © 1971 by Geron-X, Inc. Reprinted by permission of the publisher. Portions of this paper are excerpted from the *Economy of Death* published by Atheneum Publishers in October 1969.

The Vietnam catastrophe has dramatized the reality that democratic control of foreign policy has failed. The executive has been given extraordinary powers to commit the United States to military intervention abroad and has simply taken others. Congressmen lack the information on which to make informed judgments about the national interest, and they are not encouraged to obtain it. It has generally been assumed that there is no alternative to vesting life and death power over the society in the hands of a few men. In the Cuban missile crisis of 1962 about 10 individuals made the decisions which by their modest contemporary estimates could have resulted in 150,000,000 casualties. Their analysis of the national interest was the only guide. That fact is taken as an inevitable consequence of the nuclear age. Whether, indeed, the advent of nuclear weapons has rendered democratic control of foreign policy obsolete or merely made it more essential is beyond the argument of this paper.

The extraordinary concentration of power in the hands of the executive does, however, make the question of recruitment of the National Security Managers a particularly crucial one. These are the men who occupy the top foreign policy and national security positions (assistant secretary and higher) in the Departments of State, Defense, the Army, Navy, and Air Force, the Central Intelligence Agency, the Atomic Energy Commission, and the White House staff. It is their collective picture of the outside world which has formed the basis for official judgments of the national interest. Their job has been to simplify the kaleidoscopic experience of the last generation for the rest of us. They have defined the threats to the national interest, made the commitments that were supposed to meet the threats, and, in most cases, have been the sole judges of their own performance.

I have examined the backgrounds and careers of the 400 individuals who held these positions from 1940 to 1967. Certain patterns revealed by the study may help to explain why the United States has defined the national interest in the way that it has.[2]

The men who have designed the bipartisan foreign policy have for the most part been without experience in the politics or administration of domestic affairs. They have been above electoral politics. Fewer than 20 individuals of the group have held elective office of any kind. Only Harold Stassen, Chester Bowles, Averell Harriman, and G. Mennen Williams held high office. (It is noteworthy that the first three were the leading mavericks among the National Security Managers during the last generation. Stassen and Bowles both lost their high posts for bucking official orthodoxy.) Their skills have not been those of the politician who must at least give the appearance of solving problems or reconciling competing interests if he hopes to be re-elected, but those of the crisis manipulator. Dean Rusk characterized his personal goal in office as secretary of state as handing the Berlin Crisis over to his successor in no worse shape than he found it. This the managerial or "keep the balls bouncing" view of statecraft characteristic of those who count on being somewhere else when the ball drops.

Since National Security Managers have been recruited outside the electoral process, they do not expect to have to defend their policies before the electorate. Public opinion therefore plays a marginal role in the formulation of their concept of the national interest.

Fewer than 10 percent of the top national security bureaucrats have held appointive positions in agencies that deal with domestic problems of American life. The lack of experience with public domestic problems characteristic of almost all National Security Managers has helped to perpetuate the artificial separation between the national security institutions and the rest of the government. A generation of National Security Managers has asserted that we can have a military machine "second to none" and can do everything that needs to be done at the same time. This assertion, which rests on the premise that there isn't much that needs doing in American society is an easy one for those without firsthand knowledge of America's domestic crisis or responsibility for dealing with them. Thus national priorities have become seriously distorted for two reasons. First, we have no institutional machinery for evaluating competing demands on the tax dollar from the Military Establishment, on the one hand, and from the rest of the country, on the other. Second, for a generation we have put in charge of the national security bureaucracy men who by virtue of career, training, and interests have little sensitivity to public problems in domestic society.

Since the National Security Managers are remarkably insulated from public opinion and are responsive to a far narrower range of domestic pressures than are the managers of the domestic agencies, the process by which they are recruited is particularly significant. During the last generation National Security Managers have been primarily recruited from the world of big business and high finance.

If we take a look at the men who have held the very top positions, the secretaries and under-secretaries of State and Defense, the secretaries of the three services, the chairman of the Atomic Energy Commission, and the director of the CIA, we find that out of 91 individuals who held these offices during the period 1940–67, 70 of them came from major corporations and investment houses. This includes eight out of ten secretaries of Defense, seven out of eight secretaries of the Air Force, every secretary of the Navy, eight out of nine secretaries of the Army, every deputy secretary of Defense, three out of five directors of the CIA, and three out of five chairmen of the Atomic Energy Commission.

The historian, Gabriel Kolko, investigated 234 top foreign policy decision makers and found that "men who came from big business, investment and law held 59.6 percent of the posts."[3] The Brookings Institution volume *Men Who Govern*, a comprehensive study of the top federal bureaucracy from 1933 to 1965, reveals that before coming to work in the Pentagon 86 percent of the secretaries of the Army, Navy, and the Air Force were either businessmen or lawyers (usually with a business practice).[4] In the Kennedy Administration 20 percent of all civilian executives in defense-related agencies came from defense contractors.[5] Defining the national interest and protecting national security have been deemed to be the proper province of business. Indeed, as President Coolidge used to say, the business of America is business.

The collection of investment bankers and legal advisors to big business who designed the national security bureaucracies and helped to run them for a generation came to Washington in 1940. Dr. New Deal was dead, President Roosevelt announced, and Dr. Win the War had come to take his place. Two men, Henry L. Stimson, Hoover's secretary of state and a leading member of the Wall Street bar, and James V. Forrestal, president of Dillon Read Company, one of the biggest investment bankers, were responsible for recruiting many of their old friends and associates to run the war. In the formative postwar years of the Truman Administration when the essential elements of United States foreign and military policy were laid down, these recruits continued to act as the nation's top National Security Managers. Dean Acheson, James V. Forrestal, Robert Lovett, John McCloy, Averell Harriman, all of whom became acquainted with foreign policy through running a war, played the crucial roles in deciding how to use America's power in peace.

Once again it was quite natural to look to their own associates, each an American success story, to carry on with the management of the nation's military power. Thus, for example, Forrestal's firm, Dillon Read, contributed such key figures as Paul Nitze, who headed the State Department Policy Planning Staff in the Truman Administration and ran the Defense Department as deputy to Clark Clifford in the closing year of the Johnson Administration. William Draper, an architect of United States postwar policy toward Germany and Japan, came from the same firm. In the Truman years 22 key posts in the State Department, 10 in the Defense Department, and five key national security positions in other agencies were held by bankers who were either Republicans or without party affiliation. As Professor Samuel Huntington has pointed out in his study, *The Soldier and the State*, "They possessed all the inherent and real conservatism of the banking breed."[6] Having built their business careers on their judicious management of risk, they now become expert in the management of the crisis. Their interest lay in making the system function smoothly—conserving and expanding America's power. They were neither innovators nor problem solvers. Convinced from their encounter with Hitler that force is the only thing that pays off in international relations, they all operated on the assumption that the endless stockpiling of weapons was the price of safety.

The Eisenhower Administration tended to recruit its National Security Managers from the top manufacturing corporations rather than from the investment banking houses. To be sure, bankers were not exactly unwelcome in the Eisenhower years. Robert Cutler, twice the president's special assistant for national security affairs, was chairman of the board of the Old Colony Trust Company in Boston; Joseph Dodge, the influential director of the Bureau of the Budget, was a Detroit banker; Douglas Dillon, of Dillon Read, was under-secretary of state for economic affairs; Thomas Gates, the last Eisenhower secretary of defense, was a Philadelphia banker and subsequently head of the Morgan Guaranty Trust Company.

But most of the principal figures of the era were associated with the leading industrial corporations, either as chief executives or directors; many of these corporations ranked among the top 100 defense contractors. Eisenhower's first secretary of defense was Charles Wilson, president of General Motors; his second was Neil McElroy, a public relations specialist who became president of Procter and Gamble. One deputy secretary of defense was Robert B. Anderson, a Texas oilman. Another was Roger Kyes, another General Motors executive, and third was Donald Quarles of Westinghouse.

When President Kennedy was elected on his campaign promise to "get the country moving again," the first thing he did was to reach back eight years for advice on national security. Many of the men he appointed as top National Security Managers of the New Frontier were the old faces of the Truman Administration. In addition to Dean Rusk, a strong Mac-Arthur supporter in the Korean War who wrote the memorandum urging the UN forces to cross the 38th parallel in Korea, Kennedy's State Department appointments also included George McGhee, a successful oil prospector and principal architect of Truman's Middle East policy. Adolf Berle, Averell Harriman, Paul Nitze, John McCone, John McCloy, William C. Foster, and other experienced hands from the national security world also made it clear that the new administration would follow familiar patterns.

The Kennedy Administration brought in a few new faces as well. The appointment of McGeorge Bundy as special assistant to the president for national security affairs inaugurated what has come to be a tradition of giving that crucial staff position to men holding academic chairs. Bundy, Rostow, and Kissinger are hardly typical professors nor were their appointments recognition of independent academic work. Each had been unofficial consultant or insider for years before his appointment. (In an interview Rostow once noted that he had not spent a year outside the government since 1946.) Each rose in the national security bureaucracy by becoming the protégé of powerful men such as Acheson, Stimson, and Rockefeller or by working directly for the election of the presidential candidate. The other Kennedy innovation was to bring in a group of young economists from the Rand Corporation to introduce systems analysis and cost effectiveness into the Pentagon.

But with the exception of Bundy's, the principal positions were filled according to old specifications.

Robert McNamara was president of Ford instead of General Motors; Roswell Gilpatric, appointed deputy secretary of defense, was a partner in a leading Wall Street law firm. In career experience he differed from his immediate Republican predecessor, James Douglas, in three principal respects. His law office was in New York rather than in Chicago. He had been under-secretary of the Air Force, while Douglas had been secretary. He was a director of Eastern Airlines instead of American Airlines.

The recruitment patterns in the key positions in the Department of Defense relating to procurement, research, development, and other contracting functions are particularly significant.

Recently Senator William Proxmire brought up the case of Thomas Morris, the former assistant secretary of defense for procurement who became vice-president of Litton Industries. In his last year as procurement chief Litton contracts jumped from $180 million to $466 million, an increase of almost 250 percent. Senator Proxmire charged the firm with "buying influence with the Pentagon and plenty of it" through a "payoff."[7] Morris had indeed been "integrally and powerfully involved with every Pentagon decision" on procurement, as Proxmire charged, but his case was by no means unique. A generation of engineer-entrepreneurs, high-level systems managers, and procurement specialists have been shuttling back and forth between defense contractors and strategic positions in the Department of Defense.

This trend began in the early 1950s, with the Korean rearmament and the beginning of the missile program. In 1950, William Burden, a partner of Brown Brothers, Harriman and a director of Lockheed Aircraft Company, was made special assistant for research and development to Air Force Secretary Finletter. A month after he resigned in 1952, one of his partners, James T. Hill, who later was active in Itek (a Rockefeller-financed defense corporation) became assistant secretary for management. Burden was followed in the research and development job by Trevor Gardner, president and majority stockholder of Hycon Corporation. Gardner, who had been put in charge of a committee "to eliminate interservice competition in development of guided missiles," resigned in 1956 in protest over the Defense Department's refusal to give the Air Force exclusive control of the missile program. During his years in Washington, his company tripled its government contracts. His successor was Richard Horner, a career scientist who had worked for the military. In less than two years Horner managed to land a senior vice-presidency with the Northrop Aircraft Company. His successor, Joseph V. Charyk, did even better. He came from Lockheed, and after four years of advising on what the Air Force should buy and build, became head of Ford's space technology division and later, after another stint at the Pentagon, president of the Communications Satellite Corporation. His three successors, Brockway McMillan, Courtland D. Perkins, and Alexander Flax, managed to combine similar patriotic service with careers as managers or directors of the Bell Telephone Laboratories, Fairchild Stratosphere Corporation, and Cornell Aeronautics Laboratory, all major defense contractors.

Many principal officials of the Air Force either had a home in the aircraft industry or found one on leaving office. Malcolm MacIntyre, under-secretary in the Eisenhower Administration, for example, was a Wall Street lawyer who moved up after his Pentagon service to the presidency of Eastern Airlines and later to a vice-presidency of Martin Marietta, another leading contractor. Robert H. Charles, a Johnson appointee who handled the C-5A cargo plane and was prepared to pay Lockheed almost $2 billion more than the contract price, had been executive vice-president of McDonnell Aircraft. Philip B. Taylor, appointed by Eisenhower to be assistant secretary in charge of material, had been with both Curtis Wright and Pan American. Roger Lewis, another Eisenhower assistant secretary in charge of material, had also been a vice-president of Pan American World Airways and finally president of General Dynamics. Another assistant secretary, Joseph Imirie, became yet another vice-president of Litton Industries.

The principal officers in charge of research, development, and procurement for the Army have included William Martin (Bell Laboratories), Finn Larsen (Minneapolis Honeywell), Willis M. Hawkins, Jr. (Lockheed), and Earl D. Johnson, who, like Frank Pace, a former secretary of the Army, climbed from the Pentagon into the presidency of General Dynamics. The Navy research and development officers, James Wakelin, Robert W. Morse, Albert Pratt, have been associated with such leading defense contractors as Itek, Chesapeake Instruments, Ryan Aeronautics, and Simplex Wire and Cable. From 1941 until 1959, the Navy had an assistant secretary in charge of its own separate air force. Two of them were Wall Street lawyers and directors of aviation corporations: Artemus Gates (Boeing) and John L. Sullivan (Martin Marietta). Two others were connected with the airline industry: James H. Smith (Pan American) and Dan A. Kimball (Continental Airlines). Kimball later became president of Aerojet General.

Many of the most important decisions on research, development, and procurement have been made at the Defense Department level. Here also the recruitment patterns are the same: in the Eisenhower Administration, Frank Newbury (Westinghouse), Donald Quarles (Western Electric, Sandia Corporation), Clifford Furnas (Curtis Wright), to give three examples. In the Kennedy and Johnson administrations, John Rubel (Lockheed, Litton), Eugene Fubini (IBM, Airborne Instruments Laboratory), Harold Brown and John Foster (Livermore Laboratories).

Why are these recruitment patterns important? Why do they raise problems? There is a certain superficial plausibility in recruiting Pentagon managers from the weapons professionals in industry. But the practice builds into the operations of government a commitment to an escalating arms race. For the men who sustain the weapons research, development, and procurement process, service in the Pentagon is an essential element of career building. In virtually every case the individuals in charge of these functions have used their tenure at the Department of Defense to better themselves. Many have come as vice-presidents and left as presidents. Quite apart from the question of conflict of interest which is a serious one, there is the larger problem of biased judgment. In discussing the Morris case, noted earlier, Senator Proxmire pointed out that almost 90 percent of defense contracting is by negotiation and not by competitive bid. Thus "whether Litton or some other firm gets a particular contract will be determined very largely by the subjective attitude of Pentagon officials toward Litton officials."[8] The real problem, however, is not so much a matter of corrupt practice as distorted perception. The men on the Litton Industries-Pentagon shuttle have no incentive to look for or to find an alternative to the arms race. Indeed, they need continued psychological assurance that there is no alternative to stockpiling instruments of death. When virtually the only people who make the crucial initial decisions whether new weapons systems are needed, whether they cost too much, or who should make them, are those men who directly and personally stand to gain from big defense budgets, a national policy of escalating military budgets has already been established.

However, the recruitment of the National Security Managers primarily from the world of business raises some larger issues which are even more significant. First, it should be said that this practice is typical of other great nations. The dominant interest group or class in a society normally takes control of its foreign relations. Since the business of America is business, what could be more natural than that businessmen should decide the national interest?

The first problem is that the homogeneous backgrounds and virtually identical careers of the National Security Managers produce a standard way of looking at the world, a set of shared, unchallengeable assumptions. It has often been asked during the Vietnam War how almost everybody in the upper reaches of government could be so wrong about the underlying premises of United States policy. Most of the men who have set these assumptions and have operated over the last generation from them have been drawn from executive suites and law offices within shouting distance of each other in about 15 city blocks in New York, Washington, Detroit, Chicago, and Boston. Their reference group for deciding the national interest is narrow. When planning a decision of national security policy they do not normally solicit the views of civil rights leaders, farmers, laborers, mayors, artists, or small businessmen. Nor do people from these areas of national life become National Security Managers. In almost 30 years there has been one woman and no Negro appointed to the top national security positions. Indeed, when Martin Luther King expressed opposition to the Vietnam War, he was told that it was "inappropriate" for someone in the civil rights movement to voice his views on foreign policy. The opinions which the National Security Manager values are those of his friends and colleagues. They have power, which is often an acceptable substitute for judgment, and since they view the world much as he does, they must be right. They are also the men with whom he will most likely have to deal when he lays down the burdens of office. "What will my friends on Wall Street say?" the director of the Arms Control and Disarmament Agency once exclaimed when asked to endorse a disarmament proposal that would limit the future production of missiles.

There are of course differing policy views among the National Security Managers. There is rivalry among the military services and differing attitudes within bureaus of the State Department. But the consensus on premises and ends has been remarkably secure. Keeping ahead in the arms race is the key to security. The solution of urgent domestic problems must be deferred until some undetermined point at which ideal security will have been achieved. Given an imperfect world, the country is doing as well as can be expected in developing its own resources and in guiding the world to a stable order.

The National Security Manager is likely to be among the most shrewd, energetic, and often engaging men in America, but he has little feel for what is happening or should happen in his country. When Charles Wilson, the former president of General Motors who became Eisenhower's secretary of defense, blurted out his delightful aphorism, "What is good for General Motors is good for America and vice-versa" he was merely restating the basic national security premise. Using national power, including military forces if necessary, to create a "good business climate" at home and abroad is more important than a good social climate in lower-class or middle-class America. An excited stock market rather than the depletion rate of the nation's human and natural resources is the index of America's progress. The National Security Manager sees his country from a rather special angle because despite the thousands of miles he has logged, he is something of an emigré in his own society. The familiar itinerary takes him from one air-conditioned room to another across the continent, his office on Wall Street or LaSalle Street, his temporary office at the Pentagon or in the White House basement, a visit to a London or a Texas client, a dinner at the Council on Foreign Relations and so forth. The closest he ever comes to seeing a hungry American is when his dinner companion is treated to bad service at one of Manhattan's declining French restaurants.

Under the stimulus of defense spending the American economy has boomed, but its benefits have not been equitably shared. The disparity between rich and poor in America has widened. The National Security Managers have not regarded the redistribution of wealth as a priority concern, for they have had neither the experience nor the incentive to understand the problems of the poor. Their professional and personal interest are with the business and commercial concerns whom they serve and with whom they identify.

By recruiting the National Security Managers from those who have been successful as conservators and managers in the booming domestic economy, we have built into the system a powerful bias in favor of a dynamic status quo—that is, preservation of America's pre-eminent economic and military position by the continually increasing and projecting American power abroad. Just as a corporation can stay in place only by moving ahead, so a nation must expand its power. Again, this is hardly an exceptional philosophy for a great nation nor one limited to men from business backgrounds. The party bureaucrats who are the National Security

Managers in the Soviet Union have a remarkably similar outlook as to the proper role of a great nation. The point is that at a moment in history when technology has altered the meaning of national security fundamentally and the problems of human survival are utterly different from anything facing mankind before, the men who define the American national interest are by virtue of temperament, background, and class interest those with the least incentive to make changes. Looking at the world from where they do, they see little urgency for radical alternative political and social solutions to the problems of how men live in their own country, much less in the outside world.

The National Security Managers have measured their triumphs and failures in terms of their ability to use national power to compel other governments to yield to America's will. Security they have defined as keeping open as many options as possible through the skillful manipulation of the political environment. But the purpose of this vast managerial effort has been lost. Skillful management leading to the acquisition of more power has become an end in itself.

We know that social organisms survive only if they are capable of learning from their experience and adapting to changing circumstances. As the nation prepares to enter the twenty-first century, it is clear that we need new definitions of national interest. There can be no national security until international relations are seen not as a competitive game but as a strategy for creating a world environment in which the central question is not the acquisition of power but the use of power to make the world livable for man. To do this we need radically different institutions for defining and implementing the national interest. And very different sorts of men, with different allegiances and interests, to manage the problem of survival.

Notes

1. Abraham Lincoln quoted in Roy P. Basler and others (eds.), *The Collected Works of Abraham Lincoln*, vol. 1 (New Brunswick: Rutgers University Press, 1953), pp. 451–452, and cited in Merlo J. Pusey, *The Way We Go To War* (Boston: Houghton Mifflin Co., 1969), p. 61.

2. Study of 400 career backgrounds:

> Shortly after the Cuban missile crisis I decided that I wanted to know more about the men who were my defenders. Where did they come from? Who picked them? Where did they go when they laid down what they like to call their "awesome responsibilities"? Whom do they represent? Who gets to be a National Security Manager and who

doesn't? To try to find answers to these questions I collected information from *Who's Who in America* or official biographies issued by their departments about all the individuals who held the following positions from 1940 until a cutoff date in July 1967: secretary, under-secretary, and assistant secretary of the Departments of State, Defense, the Army, Navy, and Air Force; the commissioners and the general manager of the Atomic Energy Commission; the director and deputy director of the Central Intelligence Agency; the special assistant to the president for national security affairs; and the assistant director of the Bureau of the Budget for International Affairs. In looking at the group as a whole I was particularly interested in their geographical distribution, religious background, political affiliations, and educational attainments. The results rather conclusively confirm the John Birch Society view of the foreign policy establishment in at least one respect. The majority are easterners. Fifty-four percent (215 members) of the group came from the Atlantic seaboard. Fifty-two members come from the South, 40 from the Far West, and 63 from the Midwest.

Of the 148 who indicated a religious affiliation, 132 listed themselves as Protestant, 14 as Catholic, and two as Jewish. It is a fact, however, that the religious and ethnic background of the group which did not disclose such information is also overwhelmingly Anglo-Saxon and Protestant.

Only a third of the group disclosed a past political affiliation. Thirty-nine National Security Managers admitted to being Democrats. There were 33 identifiable Republicans. Seventeen individuals held some elective office during their career as Democrats, eight as Republicans.

To confirm my impression that the National Security Managers were far less involved in electoral politics than the non-national security bureaucrats, we made a survey of 85 individuals appointed secretary, under-secretary, and assistant secretary in the Departments of Commerce, Agriculture, Labor, Interior, and Health, Education, and Welfare during the last 15 years. Within this sample 26.3 percent had been elected to public office and another 16.2 percent identified themselves as having been active in working for their respective parties.

The National Security Managers as a group attended our best schools. About 39 percent attended Ivy League colleges as undergraduates. In the years examined in the study, only 14.5 percent of the top domestic policy bureaucrats were graduates of Ivy League schools. Over 60 percent of the National Security Managers had graduate training. About one-third of the group are law school graduates. Another 10 percent were trained as scientists or engineers and most of the rest have advanced degrees in the social sciences and business administration.

The national security establishment boasts a high concentration of Rhodes scholars. Fifteen of the 397 noted in their autobiographies that they had been judged as typifying the ideals of Cecil Rhodes and had been selected for a year at Oxford. Among the lawyers, a number found their way to the State Department and the Pentagon by way of Supreme Court clerkships, and a majority of the group have been editors of law reviews. The world of national security has been a congenial home for the legal mind.

3. Gabriel Kolko, *The Roots of American Foreign Policy: An Analysis of Power and Purpose* (Boston: Beacon Press, 1969), p. 19.

4. David T. Stanley *et al.*, *Men Who Govern* (Washington: Brookings Institution, 1967), p. 141.

5. Ibid., p. 142.

6. Samuel Huntington, *The Soldier and the State* (Cambridge: Harvard University Press, Belknap Press, 1957), p. 380.

7. U.S. *Congressional Record* (May 5, 1969), p. S4543.

8. U.S. *Congressional Record* (May 5, 1969), p. S4543.

2.
THE STATE SYSTEM AND THE STATE ELITE

Ralph Miliband

Writing in 1902, Karl Kautsky observed that "the capitalist class rules but does not govern," though he added immediately that "it contents itself with ruling the government."[1] This is the proposition which has to be tested. But it is obviously true that the capitalist class, as a class, does not actually "govern." One must go back to isolated instances of the early history of capitalism, such as the commercial patriciates of cities like Venice and Lübeck, to discover direct and sovereign rule by businessmen.[2] Apart from these cases, the capitalist class has generally confronted the state as a separate entity—even, in the days of its rise to power, as an alien and often hostile element, often under the control and influence of an established and landowning class, whose hold upon the state power had to be broken by revolution, as in France, or by erosion, as in England in the nineteenth century,[3] that process of erosion being greatly facilitated, in the English case, by the constitutional and political changes wrought by violence in the seventeenth century.[4]

Nor has it come to be the case, even in the epoch of advanced capitalism, that businessmen have themselves assumed the major share of government. On the other hand, they have generally been well represented in the political executive and in other parts of the state system as well; and this has been particularly true in the recent history of advanced capitalism.

This entry of businessmen into the state system has often been greatly underestimated. Max Weber, for instance, believed that industrialists had neither the time nor the particular qualities required for political life;[5] and Schumpeter wrote of the "industrialist and merchant" and "there is surely no trace of any mystic glamour about him which is what counts in the ruling of men. The stock exchange is a poor substitute for the Holy Grail . . . A genius in the business office may be, and often is, utterly unable outside of it to say boo to a goose—both in the drawing-room and

Excerpted from Chapters 3 and 4 of *The State in Capitalist Society: An Analysis of the Western System of Power* by Ralph Miliband. © 1969 by Ralph Miliband. Basic Books, Inc., Publishers, New York.

17

on the platform. Knowing this he wants to be left alone and to leave politics alone."[6] Less dramatically but no less definitely, Raymond Aron has more recently written of businessmen that "they have governed neither Germany, nor France, nor even England. They certainly played a decisive role in the management of the means of production, in social life. But what is characteristic of them as a socially dominant class is that, in the majority of countries, they have not themselves wanted to assume political functions."[7]

Businessmen themselves have often tended to stress their remoteness from, even their distaste for, "politics"; and they have also tended to have a poor view of politicians as men who, in the hallowed phrase, have never had to meet a payroll and who therefore know very little of the *real* world—yet who seek to interfere in the affairs of the hard-headed and practical men whose business it is to meet a payroll, and who therefore do know what the world is about. What this means is that businessmen, like administrators, wish to "depoliticise" highly contentious issues and to have these issues judged according to the criteria favored by business. This may look like an avoidance of politics and ideology: it is in fact their clandestine importation into public affairs.

In any case, the notion of businessmen as remote from political affairs, in a direct and personal way, greatly exaggerates their reluctance to seek political power; and equally underestimates how often the search has been successful.

In the United States, businessmen were in fact the largest single occupational group in cabinets from 1889 to 1949; of the total number of cabinet members between these dates, more than 60 percent were businessmen of one sort or another.[8] Nor certainly was the business membership of American cabinets less marked in the Eisenhower years from 1953 to 1961.[9] As for members of British cabinets between 1886 and 1950, close to one-third were businessmen, including three prime ministers—Bonar Law, Baldwin, and Chamberlain.[10] Nor again have businessmen been at all badly represented in the Conservative cabinets which held office between 1951 and 1964. And while businessmen have, in this respect, done rather less well in some other advanced capitalist countries, nowhere has their representation been negligible.

But the government itself is by no means the only part of the state system in which businessmen have had a direct say. Indeed, one of the most notable features of advanced capitalism is precisely what might be called without much exaggeration their growing colonization of the upper reaches of the administrative part of that system.

State intervention has gone further and assumed more elaborate institutional forms in France than anywhere else in the capitalist world.[11] But both in the elaboration of the French Plans and in their execution, men belonging to the world of business, and particularly of big business, have enjoyed a marked, almost an overwhelming preponderance over any other occupational or "sectional" group. As Mr. Schonfield notes, "in some ways, the development of French planning in the 1950s can be viewed as an act of voluntary collusion between senior civil servants and the senior managers of big business. The politicians and the representatives of organised labour were both largely passed by."[12]

Much the same kind of business predominance over other economic groups is to be found in the financial and credit institutions of the state,[13] and in the nationalized sector.[14] The creation of that sector has often been thought of as removing an important area of economic activity from capitalist control and influence. But quite apart from all the other forces which prevent a subsidiary nationalized sector from being run on other than orthodox lines, there is also the fact that business has carved out an extremely strong place for itself in the directing organs of that sector; or rather, that business has been invited by governments, whatever their political coloration, to assume a major role in the management and control of the public sector.[15] In comparison, representatives of labor have appeared as very poor parents indeed—not, it should be added, that the entry of a greater number of "safe" trade union leaders would make much difference to the orientation of institutions which are, in effect, an integral part of the capitalist system.

The notion that businessmen are not directly involved in government and administration (and also in parliamentary assemblies[16]) is obviously false. They are thus involved, ever more closely as the state becomes more closely concerned with economic life; wherever the state "intervenes," there also, in an exceptionally strong position as compared with other economic groups, will businessmen be found to influence and even to determine the nature of that intervention.

It may readily be granted that businessmen who enter the state system, in whatever capacity, may not think of themselves as representatives of business in general or even less of their own industries or firms in particular.[17] But even though the *will* to think in "national" terms may well be strong, businessmen involved in government and administration are not very likely, all the same, to find much merit in policies which appear to run counter to what they conceive to be the interests of business, much less to make themselves the advocates of such policies, since they are almost by definition most likely to believe such policies to be inimical to the "national interest." It is much easier for businessmen, where required, to divest themselves of stocks and shares as a kind of *rite de passage* into government service than to divest themselves of a particular view of the world, and of the place of business in it.

Notwithstanding the substantial participation of businessmen in the business of the state, it is however true that they have never constituted, and do not constitute now, more than a relatively small minority of the state elite as a whole. It is in this sense that the economic elites of advanced capitalist countries are not, properly speaking, a "governing" class, comparable to preindustrial, aristocratic, and landowning classes. In some cases, the latter were able, almost, to dispense with a distinct and fully articulated state machinery and were themselves practically the state.[18] Capitalist economic elites have not achieved, and in the nature of capitalist society could never achieve, such a position.

However, the significance of this relative distance of businessmen from the state system is markedly reduced by the social composition of the state elite proper. For businessmen belong, in economic and social terms, to the upper and middle classes—and it is also from these classes that the members of the state elite are predominantly, not to say overwhelmingly, drawn. The pattern is monotonously similar for all capitalist countries and applies not only to the administrative, military, and judicial elites, which are insulated from universal suffrage and political competition, but to the political and elective ones as well, which are not. Everywhere and in all its elements the state system has retained, socially speaking, a most markedly upper- and middle-class character, with a slowly diminishing aristocratic element at one end, and a slowly growing working-class and lower-middle-class element at the other. The area of recruitment is much more narrow than is often suggested. As Professor Dahrendorf notes, "the 'middle class' that forms the main recruiting ground of the power elite of most European countries today, often consists of the top 5 per cent of the occupational hierarchy in terms of prestige, income and influence."[19]

One main reason for this bourgeois predominance in the appointive institutions of the state system has already been discussed in relation to the economic and social hierarchies outside that system, namely that children born of upper- and middle-class parents have a vastly better chance of access than other children to the kind of education and training which is required for the achievement of elite positions in the state system. Greatly unequal opportunities in education also find reflection in the recruitment to the state service, since qualifications which are only obtainable in institutions of higher education are a *sine qua non* for entry into that service.

Thus in France the main means of entry to top administrative positions is the Ecole Nationale d'Administration. But Professor Meynaud notes that in the year 1962, 56 out of 71 university students who were successful in the examinations for admission to the ENA belonged by social origin to "la partie la plus favorisée de la population"; and of the 22 successful candidates from the civil service itself, 10 belonged to the same class. Of the university students who presented themselves, there was not a single one whose parents were workers or peasants. "Dans l'ensemble," Meynaud comments, "la sélection sociale de la haute fonction publique reste essentiellement inégalitaire. Autrement dit, malgré la réforme de 1945, la 'démocratisation' demeure très limitée."[20] The same is also true of the French military[21] and of the French judiciary.[22]

Not of course that France is notably more "undemocratic" in this respect than other capitalist countries. Thus the bulk of British higher civil servants has to a remarkable degree continued to be drawn from a narrowly restricted segment of the population, much of it public school and Oxbridge educated;[23] and the same marked upper- and middle-class bias has remained evident in the higher reaches of the British army[24] and the judiciary.[25]

The picture is not appreciably different for the United States, where the kind of inequality of educational opportunity which was mentioned in the last chapter has also helped to narrow the area of recruitment to the state service. As Professor Matthews notes:

> Those American political decision-makers[26] *for whom this information is available* are, with very few exceptions, sons of professional men, proprietors and officials, and farmers. A very small minority were sons of wage-earners, low salaried workers, farm labourers or tenants . . . the narrow base from which political decision-makers appear to be recruited is clear.[27]

In the case of the United States military it has also been noted that:

> . . . on the whole, the high officers of the army and navy have been men of the upper-middle rather than truly higher or definitely lower classes. Only a very small percentage of them are of working-class origin.[28]

As for Supreme Court Justices, it has been remarked that:

> . . . throughout American history there has been an overwhelming tendency for presidents to choose nominees for the Supreme Court from among the socially advantaged families . . . In the earlier history of the Court he very likely was born in the aristocratic gentry class, although later he tended to come from the professional upper-middle class.[29]

The same kind of upper- and middle-class preponderance is yet again encountered in Federal Germany:

> . . . while less than 1 per cent of the present population of the Federal republic [one writer notes] carries a "von" in the family name, the bearers of aristocratic titles may actually have increased among senior civil servants. Senior civil servants claiming descent from working-class families remain as conspicuous by their absence as ever.[30]

Similarly, Professor Dahrendorf notes that:

> . . . despite the break up of the old monopoly and the consequent dwindling significance of nobility, German elite groups from 1918 to the present [including the state elite] have been consistently recruited to a disproportionately great extent from middle and higher groups of the service class and the middle class as well as from their own predecessors in elite positions.[31]

And much the same story is told for Sweden[32] and Japan.[33]

While inequality of educational opportunity, based on social class, helps to account for this pattern, there are other factors which contribute to its formation. Here too, as in the case of access to elite positions outside the state system, there is also the matter of connections. Certainly, the more spectacular forms of nepotism and favoritism associated with an unregenerate aristocratic and pre-industrial age are not part of the contemporary, middle-class, competitive state service: the partial liberation of that service from the aristocratic grip was indeed one of the crucial aspects of the extension of bourgeois power in the state and society. But it would, all the same, be highly unrealistic to think that even in an examination-oriented epoch membership of a relatively narrow segment of the population is not a distinct advantage, not only in terms of entry into the higher levels of the state service, but also, and hardly less important, of chances of upward movement inside it. Such membership affords links of kinship and friendship, and generally enhances a sense of shared values, all of which are helpful to a successful career. Two French authors put the point well, and what they say can scarcely be thought to apply exclusively to France:

> If a student of modest origin has successfully negotiated his university course, the entrance examination of the E.N.A. and even, why not, the final examination where the "cultural" sifting is perhaps more severe than on entry, he will not, nevertheless, be on the same level as the offspring of great bourgeois families or of high officials: the spirit of caste and personal family relations will constantly work against him when promotions are made (at the highest level, promotion is more uncertain than at lower ones).[34]

Those who control and determine selection and promotion at the highest level of the state service are themselves most likely to be members of the upper and middle classes, by social origin or by virtue of their own professional success, and are likely to carry in their minds a particular image of how a high-ranking civil servant or military officer ought to think, speak, behave and react; and that image will be drawn in terms of the class to which they belong. No doubt, the recruiters, aware of the pressures and demands of a "meritocratic" age, may consciously try to correct their bias; but they are particularly likely to overcome it in the case of working-class candidates who give every sign of readiness and capacity to adapt and conform to class-sanctioned patterns of behavior and thought. "Rough diamonds" are now more acceptable than in the past, but they should preferably show good promise of achieving the right kind of smoothness.

Max Weber claimed that the development of bureaucracy tended "to eliminate class privileges, which include the appropriation of means of administration and the appropriation of authority as well as the occupation of offices on an honorary basis or as an avocation by virtue of wealth."[35]

But this singularly underestimates the degree to which existing class privileges help to restrict this process, even though they do not arrest it altogether.

It is undoubtedly true that a process of social dilution has occurred in the state service, and has brought people born in the working classes, and even more commonly in the lower-middle classes, into elite positions inside the state system. But to speak of "democratisation" in this connection is somewhat misleading. What is involved here is rather a process of "bourgeoisification" of the most able and thrusting recruits from the subordinate classes. As these recruits rise in the state hierarchy, so do they become part, in every significant sense, of the social class to which their position, income and status gives them access. As was already noted about working-class recruitment into the economic elite, this kind of dilution does not materially affect the class character of the state service and may indeed strengthen it. Moreover, such recruitment, by fostering the belief that capitalist societies are run on the principle of "the career open to the talents" usefully obscures the degree to which they are not.

Given the particular hierarchies of the existing social order, it is all but inevitable that recruits from the subordinate classes into the upper reaches of the state system should, by the very fact of their entry into it, become part of the class which continues to dominate it. For it to be otherwise, the present intake would not only have to be vastly increased: the social order itself would have to be radically transformed as well, and its class hierarchies dissolved.

Social dilution of an even more pronounced kind than in the appointive institutions of the state system has also occurred in those of its institutions whose staffing depends, directly or indirectly, on election, namely the political executive and parliamentary assemblies. Thus, men of working-class or lower-middle-class origin have not uncommonly made their way into the cabinets of advanced capitalist countries—some of them have even become presidents and prime ministers; and an enormous amount of personal power has on occasion been achieved by altogether déclassé individuals like Hitler or Mussolini.

What significance this has had for the politics of advanced capitalism will be considered later. But it may be noted at this stage that men drawn from the subordinate classes have never constituted more than a minority of those who have reached high political office in these countries: the large majority has always belonged, by social origin and previous occupation, to the upper and middle classes.[36]

To a somewhat lesser degree, yet still very markedly, this has also been the pattern of the legislatures of advanced capitalist countries. The growth in representation of working-class parties (save of course in the United States) has brought into these assemblies, though still as a minority, men (and occasionally women) who were not only born in the working classes but who, until their election, were themselves workers or at least

closely involved in working-class life; and even bourgeois parties have undergone a certain process of social dilution. Nevertheless, these latter parties,
which have generally dominated parliamentary assemblies, have remained
solidly upper and middle class in their social composition, with businessmen
and others connected with various kinds of property ownership constituting
a sizable and often a very substantial part of their membership.[37] In terms
of class, national politics (and for that matter, sub-national politics as well)[38]
has continued to be an "activity" in which the subordinate classes have
played a distinctly subsidiary role. Mr. Guttsman writes for Britain that:

> . . . if we ascend the political hierarchy from the
> voters upwards, we find that at each level—the membership of
> political parties, party activists, local political leaders, M.P.'s,
> national leaders—the social character of the group is slightly
> less "representative" and slightly more tilted in favour of those
> who belong to the middle and upper levels of our society.[39]

The tilt is in fact much more than slight; and the point does not
apply any the less to other countries than to Britain.

What the evidence conclusively suggests is that in terms of social
origin, education and class situation, the men who have manned all command positions in the state system have largely, and in many cases overwhelmingly, been drawn from the world of business and property, or from
the professional middle classes. Here as in every other field, men and women
born into the subordinate classes, which form of course the vast majority
of the population, have fared very poorly—and not only, it must be
stressed, in those parts of the state system, such as administration, the
military and the judiciary, which depend on appointment, but also in those
parts of it which are exposed or which appear to be exposed to the vagaries
of universal suffrage and the fortunes of competitive politics. In an epoch
when so much is made of democracy, equality, social mobility, classlessness
and the rest, it has remained a basic fact of life in advanced capitalist countries that the vast majority of men and women in these countries has been
governed, represented, administered, judged, and commanded in war by
people drawn from other, economically and socially superior and relatively
distant classes.

The Purpose and Role of Governments

The reason for attaching considerable importance to the social
composition of the state elite in advanced capitalist countries lies in the
strong presumption which this creates as to its general outlook, ideological
dispositions, and political bias. In the case of the governments of these
countries, however, we can do much more than merely presume: after all,
hardly a day goes by in which political leaders in charge of the affairs of
their country do not press upon the public their ideas and beliefs. Much of

this may conceal as much as it reveals. But a great deal remains which, together with much other evidence, notably what governments actually do, affords a clear view of what, in large terms, they are about.

At first sight, the picture is one of endless diversity between succeeding governments, and indeed inside each of them; as also between governments of different countries. Presidents, prime ministers, and their colleagues have worn many different political labels (often wildly misleading), and belonged to many different parties, or occasionally to none.

This diversity of views, attitudes, programs and policies, on an infinite number of subjects, is certainly very striking and makes for live political debate and competition. And the impression of diversity and conflict is further enhanced by the insistence of party leaders, particularly at election time, on the wide and almost impassable, or actually impassable, gulf which separates them from their opponents and competitors.

The assertion of such profound differences is a matter of great importance for the functioning and legitimation of the political system, since it suggests that electors, by voting for one or other of the main competing parties, are making a choice between fundamental and incompatible alternatives, and that they are therefore, as voters, deciding nothing less than the future of their country.

In actual fact however, this picture is in some crucial ways highly superficial and mystifying. For one of the most important aspects of the political life of advanced capitalism is precisely that the disagreements *between those political leaders who have generally been able to gain high office* have very seldom been of the fundamental kind these leaders and other people so often suggest. What is really striking about *these* political leaders and political officeholders, in relation to each other, is not their many differences, but the extent of their agreement on truly fundamental issues— as they themselves, when occasion requires, have been wont to recognize, and as large numbers of people among the public at large, despite the political rhetoric to which they are subjected, recognize in the phrase "politicians are all the same."[40] This is an exaggeration, of course. But it is an exaggeration with a solid kernel of truth, at least in relation to the kind of men who tend to succeed each other in office in advanced capitalist countries. Marxists put the same point somewhat differently when they say that these men, whatever their political labels or party affiliations, are bourgeois politicians.

The basic sense in which this is true is that the political officeholders of advanced capitalism have, with very few exceptions, been agreed over what Lord Balfour, in a classical formulation, once called "the foundations of society," meaning above all the existing economic and social system of private ownership and private appropriation—Marx's "mode of production." Balfour was writing about Britain, and about the Whig and Tory administrations of the nineteenth century. But his point applies equally well to other capitalist countries, and to the twentieth century as well as to the nineteenth.

For it is no more than a matter of plain political history that the governments of these countries have mostly been composed of men who beyond all their political, social, religious, cultural, and other differences and diversities, have at least had in common a basic and usually explicit belief in the validity and virtues of the capitalist system, though this was not what they would necessarily call it; and those among them who have not been particularly concerned with that system, or even aware that they were helping to run a specific economic system, much in the way that they were not aware of the air they breathed, have at least shared with their more ideologically-aware colleagues or competitors a quite basic and unswerving hostility to any socialist alternative to that system.

There have, it is true, been occasions, whose significance will be considered presently, when men issued from working-class and formally socialist parties have occupied positions of governmental power, either alone or more commonly as members of coalitions, in many capitalist countries. But even though these men have quite often professed anti-capitalist convictions, they have never posed—and indeed have for the most part never wished to pose—a serious challenge to a capitalist system (or rather, as most of them would have it, a "mixed economy"), whose basic framework and essential features they have accepted much more readily than their pronouncements in opposition, and even sometimes in office, would have tended to suggest.

In this sense, the pattern of executive power has remained much more consistent than the alternation in office of governments bearing different labels and affecting different colorations has made it appear: capitalist regimes have mainly been governed by men who have either genuinely believed in the virtues of capitalism, or who, whatever their reservations as to this or that aspect of it, have accepted it as far superior to any possible alternative economic and social system, and who have therefore made it their prime business to defend it. Alternatively, these regimes have been governed by men who, even though they might call themselves socialists, have not found the commitment this might be thought to entail in the least incompatible with the ready, even the eager, acceptance of all the essential features of the system they came to administer.

In fact, it could even be said that this basic acceptance of the capitalist order has been more pronounced in this century than in any previous epoch in the history of capitalism. This is not only because it is mainly conservative politicians who have dominated the political executive of their country; or because formally socialist politicians who have occupied office have been content to work the system; but also because the virtual disappearance of the landed interest and of aristocracy as a powerful economic, social and political force, and their assimilation into the ranks of business, has removed one strongly discordant voice from the councils of government. This does not mean that aristocrats themselves have ceased to occupy office; but rather that with the "bourgeoisification" of aristocracy, a greater degree of basic consensus on the nature of the economic and social order than ever before became possible.

However, even if we leave out for the present the particular role of formally socialist power-holders, it must be stressed again that this basic consensus between bourgeois politicians does not preclude genuine and important differences between them, not only on issues other than the actual management of the economic system, but on that issue as well.

Thus, it has always been possible to make an important distinction between parties and leaders, however committed they might be to the private enterprise system, who stood for a large measure of state intervention in economic and social life, and those who believed in a lesser degree of intervention; and the same distinction encompasses those parties and men who have believed that the state must assume a greater degree of responsibility for social and other kinds of reform; and those who have wished for less.

This quarrel between strong interventionists and their opponents has been and remains a perfectly genuine one. No doubt, no serious politician—however bourgeois and convinced of the virtues of private enterprise—would now wish or be able to dismantle the main structure of state intervention; and indeed it is often the most capitalist-oriented politicians who see most clearly how essential that structure of intervention has become to the maintenance of capitalism. Even so, sufficient differences endure about the desirable extent, the character, and the incidence of intervention, to make the debate around such questions (and around many other ones as well) a serious and meaningful one, upon whose outcome depends much which affects many aspects of public policy and many individual lives. From this point of view at least, competition between these men is by no means a complete sham.

But the fact nevertheless remains that these differences and controversies, even at their most intense, have never been allowed by the politicians concerned to bring into question the validity of the "free enterprise" system itself; and even the most determined interventionists among them have always conceived their proposals and policies as a means, not of eroding—let alone supplanting—the capitalist system, but of ensuring its greater strength and stability. To a much larger extent than appearance and rhetoric have been made to suggest, the politics of advanced capitalism have been about different conceptions of how to run the same economic and social system, and not about radically different social systems. This debate has not so far come high on the political agenda.

This consensus between political officeholders is clearly crucial. The ideological dispositions which make the consensus possible may not, because of various counter-pressures, finally determine how governments will act in every particular situation. But the fact that governments accept as beyond question the capitalist context in which they operate is of absolutely fundamental importance in shaping their attitudes, policies, and actions in regard to the specific issues and problems with which they are confronted, and to the needs and conflicts of civil society. The general commitment deeply colors the specific response, and affects not only the solution envisaged for the particular problem perceived, but the mode of perception itself; indeed, ideological commitment may and often does prevent perception at all, and makes impossible not only prescription for the disease, but its location.

However, political officeholders themselves do not at all see their commitment to capitalist enterprise as involving any element of class partiality. On the contrary, they are the most ardent and eloquent exponents of the view of the state, and of themselves, as above the battles of civil society, as classless, as concerned above all to serve the whole nation, the national interest, as being charged with the particular task of subduing special interests and class-oriented demands for the supreme good of all. In their thoughts and words, Hegel's exalted view of the state as the embodiment and the protector of the whole of society, of its higher reason, and of its permanent interests, lives again—particularly when they rather than their opponents are in office. "I belong to everyone and I belong to no one," General de Gaulle said shortly after coming to power in 1958, and it would be absurd to doubt that this is indeed how the general does see himself—far, far above the interests of lesser men, be they capitalists, wage earners, farmers, shopkeepers, the sick, the poor, the young or the old. Other political leaders may not find it easy to present themselves in quite such grandiose terms; but they do their best, and see themselves in much the same guise as the general does, even when they appear to others to exhibit the most blatant class bias in their policies and actions.

That most political leaders in positions of power do hold this view of their office, and of themselves, with sincerity and conviction need not, in general, be doubted. Indeed, to dismiss their proclamations of freedom from class bias as mere hypocrisy leads to a dangerous underestimation of the dedication and resolution with which such leaders are likely to pursue a task of whose nobility they are utterly persuaded. Men so persuaded are not easily deflected from their purpose by appeals to reason or sentiment or evidence, particularly when matters of great moment are at stake.

Opponents of capitalism believe it to be a system whose very nature nowadays makes impossible the optimum utilization of resources for rational human ends; whose inherent character is one of compulsion, domination, and parasitical appropriation; whose spirit and purpose fatally corrode all human relations; and whose maintenance is today the major obstacle to human progress.

Bourgeois politicians and governments view the system in precisely opposite terms—as most closely congruent with "human nature," as uniquely capable of combining efficiency, welfare, and freedom, as the best means of releasing human initiative and energy in socially beneficent directions, and as providing the necessary and only possible basis for a satisfactory social order.

Anyway, why speak of "capitalism" at all, with its emotive and propagandistic evocations of a system which no longer *really* exists, and which has been replaced by an "industrial system" in which private enterprise, though still the essential motor of the economy, is now much more "responsible" than in the past, and whose purposes are now in any case closely supervised by the democratic state?

"Liberal democracy," Robert Lynd wrote 25 years ago, "has never dared face the fact that industrial capitalism is an intensely coercive form of organisation of society that cumulatively constrains men and all of their institutions to work the will of the minority who hold and wield economic power; and that this relentless warping of men's lives and forms of association becomes less and less the result of voluntary decisions by 'bad' men or 'good' men and more and more an impersonal web of coercions dictated by the need to keep 'the system' running."[41] This is even more true today than when it was first written; but the governments which manage "liberal democracy" are mostly composed of men who *cannot* see the system in this guise, who attribute the deficiencies in it which they perceive as separate and specific "problems," remediable within its confines—in fact *only* remediable within its confines. This is what makes it possible for politicians who are, in this fundamental respect, extreme doctrinaires, to claim that theirs is an essentially empirical, undogmatic, pragmatic, *practical* approach to affairs.

A French writer recalls de Gaulle's famous phrase, "Toute ma vie, je me suis fait une certaine idée de la France," and comments that "quand l'idée de la France prend corps et devient réalité, elle se confond dans son esprit tout naturellement prisonnier de son milieu avec la France des Trusts."[42]

The comment may not be exactly accurate, since de Gaulle's "idea" of France is certainly more complex than is allowed here. But it is quite true that this "idea" includes, as the general's policies during and immediately after the war clearly showed and as his conduct of affairs since 1958 has also demonstrated, economic and social arrangements in which large-scale capitalist enterprise, no doubt under the watchful eye of a strong state, must play a crucially important role. With greater or lesser qualifications, other political leaders and governments have taken the same view, and seen capitalist enterprise as a necessary, desirable, to-be-assumed element of their society. They wish, without a doubt, to pursue many ends, personal as well as public. But all other ends are conditioned by, and pass through the prism of, their acceptance of and commitment to the existing economic system.

Given their view of that system, it is easy to understand why governments should wish to help business in every possible way, yet do not at all feel that this entails any degree of bias toward particular classes, interests, and groups. For if the national interest is in fact inextricably bound up with the fortunes of capitalist enterprise, apparent partiality toward it is not really partiality at all. On the contrary, in serving the interests of business and in helping capitalist enterprise to thrive, governments are really fulfilling their exalted role as guardians of the good of all. From this standpoint, the much-derided phrase "What is good for General Motors is good for America" is only defective in that it tends to identify the interests of one particular enterprise with the national interest. But if General Motors is taken to stand for the world of capitalist enterprise as a whole, the slogan is one to which governments in capitalist countries do subscribe, often explicitly. And they do so because they accept the notion that the economic rationality of the capitalist system is synonymous with rationality itself, and that it provides the best possible set of human arrangements in a necessarily imperfect world.

In this sense, the attitude of political officeholders to businessmen as a class or as a social type is of relatively minor importance. Their circle of relations, friends, former associates, and acquaintances is much more likely to include businessmen than, say, trade union leaders; and the favorable view they take of capitalist enterprise is also likely to make them take a sympathetic view of the men who run it. Thus President Eisenhower in 1952:

> I believe in our dynamic system of privately owned businesses and industries. They have proven that they can supply not only the mightiest sinews of war, but the highest standard of living in the world for the greatest number of people. . . . But it requires someone to take these things and to produce the extraordinary statistics that the United States with 7 per cent of the world's population produces 50 per cent of the world's manufactured goods. If that someone is to be given a name, I believe that his name is the American business-man.[43]

Political leaders in countries less steeped in the business creed are not often quite so naively gushing; and even in the United States, presidents have on occasion taken a less enthusiastic view of those whom one of them (admittedly long ago, and not very seriously) denounced as "malefactors of great wealth." It may well be, indeed, that many political leaders have taken a very poor view of this or that section of business, or even considered business as an inferior activity, from which they felt themselves far removed.

All this, however, is of no serious consequence, given a fundamental commitment to the system of which businessmen are an intrinsic and major part.[44] Because of that commitment, and because of their belief that the national interest is inextricably bound up with the health and strength of capitalist enterprise, governments naturally seek to help business—and businessmen. Thorstein Veblen once wrote that "the chief—virtually sole— concern of the constituted authorities in any democratic nation is a concern about the profitable business of the nation's substantial citizens."[45] This is quite true, but not necessarily or at all because of any particular predilection of the "constituted authorities" for substantial citizens. The concern goes with the general commitment.

The first and most important consequence of the commitment which governments in advanced capitalist countries have to the private enterprise system and to its economic rationality is that it enormously limits their freedom of action in relation to a multitude of issues and problems. Raymond Aron has written that "il va de soi qu'en régime fondé sur la propriété des moyens de production, les mesures prises par les législateurs et les ministres ne seront pas en opposition fondamentale avec les intérêts des propriétaires."[46] This proposition, he comments, is too obvious to be instructive. It *should* perhaps be obvious. But it does not appear to be so to most Western political scientists who view the state as free from the inherent bias in favor of capitalist interests which Professor Aron's proposition implies.

That bias has immense policy implications. For the resolution, or at least the alleviation of a vast range of economic and social problems requires precisely that governments *should* be willing to act in "fundamental opposition" to these interests. Far from being a trivial matter, their extreme reluctance to do so is one of the largest of all facts in the life of these societies. Were it to be said about a government that though faced with a vast criminal organization it could not be expected to act in fundamental opposition to it, the observation would not be thought uninstructive about its character and role. The same is true of the proposition which Professor Aron so casually puts forward and tosses aside.

On the other hand, that proposition tends to obscure a basic aspect of the state's role. For governments, acting in the name of the state, have in fact been compelled over the years to act against *some* property rights, to erode *some* managerial prerogatives, to help redress *somewhat* the balance between capital and labor, between property and those who are subject to it. This is an aspect of state intervention which conservative writers who lament the growth of "bureaucracy" and who deplore state "interference" in the affairs of society regularly overlook. Bureaucracy is indeed a problem and a danger, and the experience of countries like the Soviet Union has amply shown how greatly unrestrained bureaucratic power can help to obstruct the creation of a socialist society worthy of the name. But concentration upon the evils of bureaucracy in capitalist countries obscures (and is often intended to obscure) the fact that "bureaucratic" intervention has often been a means of alleviating the evils produced by unrestrained private economic power.

The state's "interference" with that power is not in "fundamental opposition" to the interests of property: it is indeed part of that "ransom" of which Joseph Chamberlain spoke in 1885 and which, he said, would have to be paid precisely for the purpose of *maintaining* the rights of property in general. In insisting that the "ransom" be paid, governments render property a major service, though the latter is seldom grateful for it.

Even so, it would not do to ignore the fact that even very conservative governments in the regimes of advanced capitalism have often been forced, mainly as a result of popular pressure, to take action against *certain* property rights and capitalist prerogatives.

As against this, however, must be set the very positive support which governments have generally sought to give to dominant economic interests.

Capitalist enterprise, as was noted in Chapter 1, *depends* to an ever greater extent on the bounties and direct support of the state, and can only preserve its "private" character on the basis of such public help. State intervention in economic life in fact largely *means* intervention for the purpose of helping capitalist enterprise. In no field has the notion of the "welfare state" had a more precise and apposite meaning than here: there are no more persistent and successful applicants for public assistance than the proud giants of the private enterprise system.

Nor need that assistance be of a direct kind to be of immense value to capitalist interests. Because of the imperative requirements of modern life, the state must, within the limits imposed upon it by the prevailing economic system, engage in bastard forms of socialization and assume responsibility for many functions and services which are beyond the scope and capabilities of capitalist interests. As it does so, however, what Jean Meynaud calls "the bias of the system" ensures that these interests will automatically benefit from state intervention. Because of the private ownership and control of a predominant part of economic life, Professor Meynaud writes:

> . . . all the measures taken by the state to develop and improve the national economy always end up by being of the greatest benefit to those who control the levers of command of the production-distribution sector: when the state cuts tunnels, builds roads, opens up highways or reclaims swamps, it is first of all the owners of the neighbouring lands who reap the rewards . . . the concept of the "bias of the system" makes it also possible to understand that the measures taken to remedy the derelictions, shortcomings and abuses of capitalism result ultimately, where successful, in the consolidation of the regime. It matters little in this respect that these measures should have been undertaken by men sympathetic or hostile to capitalist interests: thus it is that laws designed to protect the workers and directed against their exploitation by employers will be found useful to the latter by inducing them to make a greater effort to rationalise or mechanise the productive process.[47]

Governments may be solely concerned with the better running of "the economy." But the description of the system as "the economy" is part of the idiom of ideology, and obscures the real process. For what is being improved is a *capitalist* economy; and this ensures that whoever may or may not gain, capitalist interests are least likely to lose.

The "bias of the system" may be given a greater or lesser degree of emphasis. But the ideological dispositions of governments have generally been of a kind to make more acceptable to them the structural constraints imposed upon them by the system; and these dispositions have also made it easier for them to submit to the pressures to which they have been subjected by dominant interests.

Taxation offers a ready illustration of the point. As was noted in Chapter 2, the economic system itself generates extremely powerful tendencies toward the maintenance and enhancement of the vast inequalities of income and wealth which are typical of all advanced capitalist societies. Given that economic system, no government can achieve redistributive miracles. But the limits of its powers in this field are nevertheless not finally fixed—despite the system's tendencies to inequality and the fierce opposition of the forces of wealth to redistributive taxation. And the fact that taxation has not, over the years, affected more deeply than it has the disparities of income and wealth in these societies must to a major extent be attributed to the attitude of governments toward inequality, to the view they take of the conflicting claims of the rich and the poor, and to their acceptance of an economic orthodoxy which has, at any particular moment of time, declared additional burdens on the rich to be fatal to "business confidence," "individual initiative," the propensity to invest, and so on.

The same considerations apply to government intervention in "industrial relations," the consecrated euphemism for the permanent conflict, now acute, now subdued, between capital and labor.

Whenever governments have felt it incumbent, as they have done more and more, to intervene directly in disputes between employers and wage earners, the result of their intervention has tended to be disadvantageous to the latter, not the former. On innumerable occasions, and in all capitalist countries, governments have played a decisive role in defeating strikes, often by the invocation of the coercive power of the state and the use of naked violence; and the fact that they have done so in the name of the national interest, law and order, constitutional government, the protection of "the public," and so on, rather than simply to support employers, has not made that intervention any the less useful to these employers.

Moreover, the state, as the largest of all employers, is now able to influence the pattern of "industrial relations" by the force of its own example and behavior: that influence can hardly be said to have created new standards in the employer-employee relationship. Nor could it have been expected to do so, given the "business-like" spirit in which the public sector is managed.

Governments are deeply involved, on a permanent and institutionalized basis, in that "routinisation of conflict," which is an essential part of the politics of advanced capitalism. They enter that conflict in the guise of a neutral and independent party, concerned to achieve not the outright defeat of one side or the other but a "reasonable" settlement between them. But the state's intervention in negotiations occurs in the shadow of its known and declared propensity to invoke its powers of coercion, against one of the parties in the dispute rather than the other, if "conciliation" procedures fail. These procedures form, in fact, an additional element of restraint upon organized labor, and also serve the useful purpose of further dividing the trade union ranks. The state does interpose itself between the "two sides of industry"—not, however, as a neutral but as a partisan.

Nor is this nowadays only true when industrial disputes actually occur. One of the most notable features in the recent evolution of advanced capitalism is the degree to which governments have sought to place new and further inhibitions upon organized labor in order to prevent it from exercising what pressures it can on employers (and on the state as a major employer) in the matter of wage claims. What they tend to achieve, by such means as an "incomes policy," or by deflationary policies which reduce the demand for labor, is a *general* weakening of the bargaining position of wage earners.[48] Here too, the policies adopted are proclaimed to be essential to the national interest, the health of the economy, the defense of the currency, the good of the workers, and so on. And there are always trade union leaders who can be found to endorse both the claims and the policies. But this does not change the fact that the main effect of these policies is to leave wage earners in a weaker position *vis-à-vis* employers than would otherwise be the case. The *purpose*, in the eyes of political officeholders, may be all that it is said to be; but the *result*, with unfailing regularity, is to the detriment of the subordinate classes. This is why the latter, in this as in most other instances, have good reason to beware when the political leaders of advanced capitalist countries invoke the national interest in defense of their policies—more likely than not they, the subordinate classes, are about to be done. Wage earners have always had to reckon with a hostile state in their encounter with employers. But now more than ever they have to reckon with its antagonism, in practice, as a direct, pervasive, and constant fact of economic life. Their immediate and daily opponent remains the employer; but governments and the state are now much more closely involved in the encounter than in the past.

Quite naturally, this partiality of governments assumes an even more specific, precise and organized character in relation to all movements, groupings, and parties dedicated to the transformation of capitalist societies into socialist ones. The manner in which governments have expressed this antagonism has greatly varied over time, and between countries, assuming here a milder form, there a harsher one; but the antagonism itself has been a permanent fact in the history of all capitalist countries. In no field has the underlying consensus between political officeholders of different political affiliations, and between the governments of different countries, been more substantial and notable—the leaders of all governmental parties, whether in office or in opposition, and including nominally "socialist" ones, have always been deeply hostile to the socialist and militant left, of whatever denomination, and governments themselves have in fact been the major protagonists against it, in their role of protectors and saviors of society from the perils of left-wing dissidence.

In this instance too, liberal-democratic and pluralist theorists, in their celebration of the political competition which prevails in their societies, and in their insistence on the political neutrality of the state, quite overlook the fact that the governments of advanced capitalist societies, far from taking a neutral view of *socialist* competition, do their level best to make it more difficult. In some countries, for instance Federal Germany, Communist and other left-wing parties and organizations are suppressed altogether, and membership made a crime punishable by law; in others, such as the United States, left-wing organizations, of which the Communist Party is only one, operate in conditions of such harassment as to narrow rather drastically, in their case, the notion of free political competition.

Nor is the state's hostility less marked in other countries, though it may assume different forms—for instance electoral manipulation as in France and Italy for the purpose of robbing their Communist parties of the parliamentary representation to which their electoral strength entitles them; the engineering of bias in the mass media, in so far as lies in the considerable and growing power of governments; and also episodic but quite brutal repression of left-wing dissenters.

Governments, in other words, are deeply concerned, whatever their political coloration, that the "democratic process" should operate within a framework in which left-wing dissent plays as weak a role as possible.

The argument is not whether governments should or should not be neutral as between conservative and anti-conservative ideologies, movements, parties, and groups. That question is not susceptible to resolution in terms of such imperatives. The argument is rather that the governments of advanced capitalist countries have never been thus neutral, and that they have for the most part used the state power on the conservative as against the anti-conservative side. And the further argument is that in so doing they have, whatever other purposes they might have wished to serve, afforded a most precious element of protection to those classes and interests whose power and privileges socialist dissent is primarily intended to undermine and destroy. Those who believe in the virtues of a social order which includes such power and privileges will applaud and support governmental partiality, and may even ask for more of it. Those who do not will not. The important point is to see what so much of political analysis obscures, often from itself, namely that this *is* what governments, in these countries, actually do.

The argument so far has centered on some of the main *internal* consequences which flow from the commitment of governments to the capitalist system. But the *external* consequences of that commitment are no less direct and important.

Here, perhaps even more than in other fields, the purposes which governments proclaim their wish to serve are often made to appear remote from specific economic concerns, let alone capitalist interests. It is the national interest, national security, national independence, honor, greatness, and so on that is their concern. But this naturally includes a sound, healthy, thriving economic system; and such a desirable state of affairs depends in turn on the prosperity of capitalist enterprise. Thus, by the same mechanism which operates in regard to home affairs, the governments of capitalist countries have generally found that their larger national purposes required the servicing of capitalist interests; and the crucial place which these interests occupy in the life of their country has always caused governments to make their defense against foreign capitalist interests, and against the foreign states which protect them, a prime consideration in their conduct of external affairs.[49]

The whole history of Western (and Japanese) imperialism is a clear case in point. It is certainly not true that these governments went into Africa or Asia *simply* to serve powerful economic interests. Nor did they embark upon imperialist expansion *simply* because they were "compelled" to do so by such interests. Vast historical movements of this kind cannot be reduced to these simplicities. But here too the many other purposes which governments have wished to serve in their quest for empire have involved, pre-eminently, the furtherance of private economic interests. They may *really* have been concerned with national security, the strengthening of the economic and social fabric, the shouldering of the white man's burden, the fulfillment of their national destiny, and so forth. But these purposes required, as they saw it, the securing by conquest of lands which were already or which could become zones of exploitation for their national capitalist interests, whose implantation and expansion were thus guaranteed by the power of the state. In this case too the fact that political officeholders were seeking to achieve many other purposes should not obscure the fact that, *in the service of these purposes*, they became the dedicated servants of their business and investing classes.

The same considerations apply to the attitude of capitalist governments toward the formally independent countries of the Third World in which their national capitalist interests have a stake, or might acquire one.

Thus, the attitude of the government of the United States toward, say, Central and Latin America is not exclusively determined by its concern to protect American investments in the area or to safeguard the opportunity of such investments in the future. When for instance the government of the United States decided in 1954 that the Arbenz government in Guatemala must be overthrown,[50] it did so not merely because that government had taken 225,000 acres of land from the American-owned United Fruit Company but because that action, in the eyes of the government of the United States, provided the best possible proof of "Communist" leanings, which made the Arbenz regime a threat to "American security."[51] But what this and many other similar episodes mean is that "American security" is so interpreted by those responsible for it as to require foreign governments to show proper respect for the rights and claims of American business. This may not be the only test of a government's "reliability"; but it is a primary one nevertheless. As a general rule, the American government's attitude to governments in the Third World, or for that matter in the whole non-socialist world, depends very largely on the degree to which these governments favor American free enterprise in their countries or are likely to favor it in the future.[52] The governments of other advanced capitalist countries are moved by a similar concern. The difference between them and the government of the United States is not in basic approach but in the scale of their foreign investments and enterprises and in their capacity to act in defense of these interests.

In this perspective, the supreme evil is obviously the assumption of power by governments whose main purpose is precisely to abolish private ownership and private enterprise, home and foreign, in the most important sectors of their economic life or in all of them. Such governments are profoundly objectionable not only because their actions adversely affect foreign-owned interests and enterprises or because they render future capitalist implantation impossible; in some cases this may be of no great economic consequence. But the objection still remains because the withdrawal of any country from the world system of capitalist enterprise is seen as constituting a weakening of that system and as providing encouragement to further dissidence and withdrawal.

Here also lie the roots of the fierce hostility toward the Bolshevik Revolution which led the capitalist powers to try to crush it in blood—long before, incidentally, the notion of "Soviet aggression" had become the standard justification for their policies. And here too lies the main clue to the foreign policies of these powers since the end of World War II, indeed during that war as well.[53] The purpose, always and above all else, has been to prevent the coming into being, anywhere, of regimes fundamentally opposed to capitalist enterprise and determined to do away with it.

Western officeholders have justified their attitude to socialist regimes and movements in terms of their love of freedom, their concern for democracy, their hatred of dictatorship, and their fear of aggression. In this instance, as in most others, it is not very useful to ask whether in these proclamations they were "sincere" or not. The important point is rather that they defined freedom in terms which made capitalist enterprise one of its main and sometimes its sole ingredient. On this basis, the defense of freedom does become the defense of free enterprise: provided *this* is safe, all else, however evil, can be condoned, overlooked and even supported.[54] Almost by definition, no regime which respects capitalist interests can be deemed hopelessly bad and must in any case be considered as inherently superior to any regime which does not. Given this attitude, it is not of major consequence that capitalist governments should have been concerned, in external relations, with more than the interests of their businessmen and investors. However that may be, *these* are the interests which their policies have most consistently served.

Notes

1. K. Kautsky, *The Social Revolution*, 1903, p. 13.

2. See, for example, O. C. Cox, *The Foundations of Capitalism*, 1959.

3. See, for example, J. D. Kingsley, *Representative Bureaucracy*, 1944.

4. On which see, for example, Barrington Moore, Jr., *Social Origins of Dictatorship and Democracy*, chap. 1.

5. R. Bendix, *Max Weber: An Intellectual Portrait*, 1960, p. 436.

6. J. Schumpeter, *Capitalism, Socialism and Democracy*, 1950, pp. 137–8.

7. R. Aron, *La Lutte des Classes*, 1964, p. 280.

8. H. D. Lasswell, et al., *The Comparative Study of Elites*, 1952, p. 30.

9. See, for example, Mills, *The Power Elite*, pp. 232ff.

10. Lasswell, *et al.*, *The Comparative Study of Elites*, p. 30. See also Guttsman, *The British Political Elite*, pp. 92ff.

11. Even here, however, the notion of "planning" ought not to be invested with too positive a meaning: see, for example, J. Sheahan, *Promotion and Control of Industry in Post-War France*, 1963, who notes that "throughout the 1950's, the French technique of planning used a mild system of differential favours to secure cooperation, but attached no direct penalties to the refusal to cooperate" (p. 181); the same author also describes French "planners" as a "group of well intentioned and intelligent people trying to help clarify alternatives for government and business" (p. 181).

12. Schonfield, *Modern Capitalism*, p. 128.

13. For Britain see, for example, S. Wilson and T. Lupton, "The Social Background and Connections of 'Top Decision-Makers,'" in *The Manchester School of Economic and Social Studies*, vol. 27, 1959.

14. See, for example, *Universities and Left Review, The Insiders* (no date); C. Jenkins, *Power at the Top*, 1959; and J. Hughes, *Nationalised Industries in the Mixed Economy*, 1960.

15. A typical recent example being the appointment by the Wilson government of an eminent businessman, with no Labour connections, to head the newly-nationalized (or rather re-nationalized) Steel Corporation.

16. See note 38.

17. Note, however, the conclusion reached by a Senate investigating committee that, in World War II, "dollar-a-year men (as they were then called) were 'persons with axes to grind' and 'lobbyists' " (D. C. Blaisdell: *American Democracy under Pressure*, 1950), p. 190.

18. Thus, Professor Habbakuk writes of England in the eighteenth century that "the English landowners were the governing class of the country. Ministers were drawn usually from the great families and though the property qualifications imposed by the Act of 1711 were easily evaded, the normal social and political processes ensured that most MPs came from landed families. Local government likewise was in the hands, not of a bureaucracy, but of Justices of the Peace, who were generally land-owners. The land tax was administered by the same class, and even in those departments which were staffed by professionals, the more important and dignified posts were often filled from landowning families" (H. J. Habbakuk, "England," in A. Goodwin (ed.), *The European Nobility in the 18th Century*, 1953, pp. 11–12). Landed families, it should also be noted, predominated in the Army, the Navy, and the Church.

19. Dahrendorf, "Recent Changes in the Class Structure of European Socie-ties," p. 238.

20. Meynaud, *La Technocratie*, p. 51. Another writer notes that for the years 1952–58, about 60 percent of the 547 successful candidates for admis-sion to the ENA belonged to "les milieux à la fois les moins nombreux et les plus élevés dans la hiérarchie sociale, fonctionnaires des catégories A1 et 2, cadres et chefs d'entreprise" (A. Girard, *La Réussite Sociale en France*, 1961, p. 308). See also F. Bon and M. A. Burnier, *Les Nouveaux Intellectuels*, 1966; T. B. Bottomore, "Higher Civil Servants in France," in *Transactions of the Second World Congress of Sociology*, 1953; and P. Lalumière, *L'Inspection des Finances*, 1959.

21. See, for example, R. Girardet, *La Crise Militaire Française 1945–1962*, 1964, pp. 39–46. Another writer notes, however, that "in regard to social origins the centre of gravity for the army officer corps as a whole, follow-ing a pattern typical for a period of low military prestige, had probably sunk to the lower-middle class by the late 1950s. Yet in the higher grades the middle and upper bourgeoisie, and to a lesser degree the noble aristocracy, were still well represented, though in decline" (J. S. Ambler, *The French Army in Politics 1945–1962*, p. 134).

22. See, for example, Girard, *La Réussite Sociale en France*, p. 336.

23. See, for example, R. K. Kelsall, *The Higher Civil Servants in Britain*, 1955; Wilson and Lupton, "Top Decision Makers," in *The Manchester School of Economics and Social Studies*, vol. 27, 1959; and "Recruit-ment to the Civil Service," 6th Report of the Committee on Estimates, H. C. 308, 1964–65.

24. See, for example, J. Harvey and K. Hood, *The British State*, 1958, pp. 112ff.

25. No less than 76 percent of judges in 1956 had been educated at public schools (Glennerster and Pryke, *The Public Schools*, p. 17). See also "Well-Bred Law" in *The Sunday Times*, August 18, 1963.

26. "Political decision makers" here includes "high level civil servants."

27. D. R. Matthews, *The Social Background of Political Decision-Makers*, 1954, pp. 23–24 (italics in text).

28. Mills, *The Power Elite*, p. 192. Professor Janowitz also notes that "American military leaders traditionally have come from the more privileged strata" (M. Janowitz, *The Professional Soldier*, 1960, p. 69). He also adds that "however, recent trends in their social background supply striking confirmation of the decline of the relatively high social origins of the military, and its transformation into a more socially heterogeneous group" (p. 89). But this "more socially heterogeneous group" still leaves men born in the "business, professional and managerial" classes with a crushing preponderance over those born in the "white collar" and "worker" class (see *ibid.*, Table 14, p. 91).

29. J. R. Schmidhauser, "The Justices of the Supreme Court—A Collective Portrait," in *Midwest Journal of Political Science*, 1959, vol. 3, p. 45.

30. L. J. Edinger, "Continuity and Change in the Background of German Decision-Makers," in *Western Political Quarterly*, 1961, vol. 14, p. 27.

31. Dahrendorf, *Society and Democracy in Germany*, p. 228.

32. "The number of workers' sons among the politico-bureaucratic top echelons has diminished from 10 per cent in 1949 to 9 per cent in 1961, whereas the percentage of sons of big businessmen went up from 12 per cent to 17 per cent" (Therborn, *Power in the Kingdom of Sweden*, p. 59).

33. See, for example, Abegglen and Mannari, "Leaders of Modern Japan: Social Origins and Mobility."

34. Bon and Burnier, *Les Nouveaux Intellectuels*, p. 165.

35. M. Weber, *The Theory of Social and Economic Organisation*, 1947, p. 340.

36. See Lasswell et al., *The Comparative Study of Elites*, p. 30; Guttsman, *The British Political Elite*, pp. 79ff; Matthews, *The Social Background of Political Decision-Makers*, pp. 23–24; D. Lerner, *The Nazi Elite*, 1951, p. 6; L. D. Edinger, "Post-Totalitarian Leadership: Elites in the German Federal Republic," in *American Political Science Review*, 1960, vol. 54, no. 1, p. 70; Abegglen and Manari, "Leaders of Modern Japan: Social Origins and Mobility" in *Economic Development and Cultural Change*, vol. 9, no. 1, Part 2 (October 1960), p. 116.

37. See, for example, Guttsman, *The British Political Elite*, pp. 97ff; H. Berrington and S. E. Finer, "The British House of Commons," in *International Social Science Journal*, 1961, vol. 13, no. 4, pp. 601ff; J. Blondel, *Voters, Parties and Leaders*, 1963, chap. 5; M. Dogan,

"Political Ascent in a Class Society: French Deputies 1870–1958," in D. Marvick (ed.), *Political Decision-Makers*, 1961; G. Braunthal, *The Federation of German Industry in Politics*, 1961, pp. 152ff; T. Fuku-taki, *Man and Society in Japan*, 1962, p. 117.

38. See below, pp. 171ff.

39. Guttsman, *The British Political Elite*, p. 27.

40. As witnessed, for instance, by the number of people in countries like Britain and the United States who, when asked whether they believe that there are important differences between the main competing parties, tend to answer in the negative.

41. Foreword to R. A. Brady, *Business as a System of Power*, 1943, p. xii.

42. H. Claude, *Le Gaullisme*, 1960, p. 76.

43. S. E. Harris, *The Economics of Political Parties*, 1962, p. 5. On coming to office, President Johnson put the same point somewhat differently but, it may be surmised, with no less feeling: "We think we have the best system. We think that where a capitalist can put up a dollar, he can get a return on it. A manager can get up early to work and with money and men he can build a better mousetrap. A laborer who is worthy of his hire stands a chance of getting attention and maybe a little profit-sharing system, and the highest minimum wages of any nation in the world" (R. Evans and R. Novak, *Lyndon B. Johnson: The Exercise of Power*, 1966, p. 347).

44. Note, for example, President Kennedy's lack of enthusiasm for businessmen in general (A. M. Schlesinger, Jr., *A Thousand Days: John F. Kennedy in the White House*, 1965, pp. 631ff), but also his almost desperate concern to reach accommodation with the "business community," for which see below, chap. 6.

45. T. Veblen, *Absentee Ownership*, 1923, pp. 36–37.

46. R. Aron, "Classe Sociale, Classe Politique, Classe Dirigeante," in *Archives Européennes de Sociologie*, 1960, vol. 1, no. 2, pp. 272–273.

47. J. Meynaud, *Rapport sur la Classe Dirigeante Italienne*, 1964, pp. 190–191.

48. See, for example, Kidron, *Western Capitalism Since the War*, pp. 190ff; "Incomes Policy and the Trade Union," in *International Socialist Journal*, 1964, vol. 1, no. 3; and "The Campaign Against the Right to Strike," in *ibid.*, 1964, vol. 1, no. 1.

49. As an American Secretary of State put it in May 1914 to the National Council of Foreign Trade, in words which have remained highly ap-posite: "I can say, not merely in courtesy—but as a fact—my Depart-ment is your department; the ambassadors, the ministers and the consuls are all yours. It is their business to look after your interests and to guard your rights." (Quoted in W. A. Williams, *The Tragedy of American Diplomacy*, 1959, p. 51).

50. See, for example, D. Wise and T. B. Ross, *The Invisible Government*, chap. 11, 1964.

51. "In the era of the Cold War, keeping Soviet power and influence out of the hemisphere, and particularly out of the Panama Canal area, was far more important to Washington than old-fashioned style banana diplomacy. But certainly the seizure of United Fruit's holdings without adequate compensation forced Eisenhower to take action" (*ibid.*, p. 170).

52. Nor of course is this a *new* feature of American foreign policy. For its permanent importance in American history, see, for example W. A. Williams, *The Tragedy of American Diplomacy*, and, by the same author, *The Contours of American History*, 1961.

53. See, for example, J. Bagguly, "The World War and the Cold War," in D. Horowitz (ed.), *Containment and Revolution*, 1967.

54. In October 1961, President Kennedy told Cheddi Jagan, then prime minister of British Guiana, that "we are not engaged in a crusade to force free enterprise on parts of the world where it is not relevant. If we are engaged in a crusade for anything, it is national independence. That is the primary purpose of our aid. The secondary purpose is to encourage individual freedom and political freedom. But we can't always get that; and we have often helped countries which have little personal freedom, if they maintain their national independence. This is the basic thing. So long as you do that, we don't care whether you are socialist, capitalist, pragmatist, or whatever. We regard ourselves as pragmatists" (A. M. Schlesinger, Jr., *A Thousand Days*, pp. 775–776). The trouble with such sentiments is not only that they are belied by American support across the world for regimes whose "national independence" consists in subservience to the United States, and about which the notion of "individual freedom and political freedom" is a grotesque if not an obscene joke. Equally important is the fact that the *real* test is always a regime's attitude to capitalist and notably American enterprise. Aid to Yugoslavia, or to any other dissident Communist country, comes within the sphere of Cold War politics, and scarcely affects the main point.

3.
THE THREAT OF WORLD DEPRESSION

Lyn Marcus

U.S. Imperialism's world economy is now in the opening phase of a probable new general crisis. That is to suggest a threatened repetition of the 1929–31 bang, only on an augmented scale more appropriate to the atomic age. No exact date can be set, nor is a bust yet a certainty for the immediate future. At this stage of the process, the depression itself is not the point; it is the *threat* of such a crisis that is determining the course of present world history.

The views expressed here have nothing in common with conceptions falsely attributed to Marx, such as the vulgar "Marxist" view that "inevitable" depressions "spontaneously" transform workers into socialists. On the contrary, as Lenin emphasized, the ruling class never faces an absolutely insoluble economic crisis. As long as workers and colonial peoples consent, the U.S. financiers have the possibility of finding a solution agreeable to their interests—through some radical change in existing institutions. It is the history of this century that imperialists have been successful on balance in so overcoming each new economic threat. Whether through wars, ferocious witch hunts, struggles against real wages of workers, or in the last resort, fascism itself, the main centers of imperialism have kept their capitalist banners aloft through every economic storm.

Dramatic turns in the course of world history, including great revolutions, are not automatically brought about by depressions, but through the upheavals, such as wars, great labor struggles, which are *initiated* by the efforts of the ruling class to prevent or get out of economic crisis.

So, today's signs of an early probable economic crisis do not mean an inevitable bust. Rather, such portents impel U.S. ruling circles to seek solutions to their economic problems at the expense of real wages, through wars, and through a whole assortment of innovations in the domain of social relations, in official morality, and in political institutions.

Now, as in each prior such crisis (for example 1914, 1939), it is

From L. Marcus, *The Third Stage of Imperialism* (New York: National Caucus of Labor Committees), pp. 9–46. Reprinted by permission of the publisher.

the imperialists themselves who unsettle the established institutions of class collaboration ("wage guidelines"), who initiate wars (Vietnam), trample today on the moral sentiments which they yesterday inculcated in all layers of the population (diminishing credibility of Kennedy, Johnson regimes). It is the tendency for a general increase in such radicalizing actions by the ruling circles, today as in the case of the French Revolution, which those circles have no more option than Louis XVI but to undertake, that transform periods of impending crisis into the breaking points of history. It is this which makes a period such as our own one of wars, great socialist struggles, and even revolutions.

This view is in contrast, of course, to those schools which attempt to establish a mechanical correlation between "radicalizing factors" and popular unrest. The key to history is the conservatism of the oppressed, the ruled; their stubborn reluctance to institute change in their own interest, their prolonged devotion to the old regime to a point long after reasonable self-interest demands revolution. It is only when an economic crisis is transformed into a social, political crisis, that the floodgates of history are opened and overdue social change unloosed with a violence which is in proportion to the depth and duration of its prior suppression.

Socialist Rhetoric and the "New Reality"   Granted, most socialists have so far declined to adopt such a view of present events. During the late forties and early fifties the shards of the old socialist parties, disappointed by the failure of a postwar depression to appear, went over to the prevailing liberal myth, that the postwar U.S. economy, with its "built-in stabilizers," had become a virtually depression-proof autarchy.

To the degree that many disheartened old radicals remained active socialists, they based their perspective on revolutions in the colonial countries; they had given up hope that "it could happen here." Ironically, they have generally defined contemporary U.S. Imperialism as "something new," something "unknown to Marx," incomprehensible to Marxist analysis, *in the same fundamental terms* as Eduard Bernstein did in his analysis of the German economy in 1897–99. So, with respect to the scientific merit of such prevailing "socialist" views, it suffices to cite Rosa Luxemburg's *Reform or Revolution*,[1] which has almost as much relevance on this point, *as a scientific work*, today as it did in the first decade of this century. Suffice to say, most socialists are taken absolutely unaware by the history-making developments now emerging from the economic basis of contemporary U.S. world imperialism.

1958—A Turning Point   Unlike these socialists, the leading layer of financial intelligentsia is not astonished. The public record shows that these circles have been acutely aware of the danger to imperialism since the late forties, when they narrowly escaped an explosion of the inflationary forces of that period. The more or less inevitable onset of the present crisis was forseen not later than 1958. It was evident at that latter time that the investment miracles in Western Europe, Japan, and elsewhere in advanced capitalist sectors, would run their course by the mid-sixties. When that happened, U.S. imperialism would face—as it does at this moment—the kind of threatened general monetary crisis which follows any period of prolonged credit-expansion.[2]

This very foresight has impelled leading financial circles to develop some appropriate new strategy to replace the tottering basis of postwar prosperity. The general form of such solution on which all leading imperialist thought necessarily converges would be described by an economic historian as a "Third Stage of Imperialism." That is to say, a fundamental change in the general form of exploitation of the underdeveloped sectors by the advanced, to forced combined industrial development of both advanced and underdeveloped. That is the strategic outlook of official U.S. imperialist policy since at least Eisenhower's 1960 State of the Union address on foreign policy.

How Policy is Made

This is not to counterpose to "economic determinism" a "conspiratorial" account of history. Examining the way in which leading circles develop and implement new policies and tactics, their course seems to justify the account of history peculiar to pragmatism.

The desired new imperialist order of things emerges as the prescience of a narrow fraction of the leading bourgeois intelligentsia. Such broadly conceived new strategies tend to be comprehended only by a narrow layer of financiers whose everyday life compels them to take a world view on all important questions of their self-interest. Guided by such hazy foresights, encumbered by the awkwardness and cretinism of the legislative and executive bureaucracies through which policies are implemented, the ruling circles stumble, fumble, and bungle, combating not only objective difficulties but also the parochialism and conceptual impotence of the more numerous and backward layers of their own class.

At every turn, they are burdened further by the inertia inherent in that motley collection of diverse class and caste interests out of which they have assembled a broader social base for their regimes. Through wild groping activity, policies and strategies are constantly modified. An experiment backfires, such as the extremely short-lived pro-Castro policy: an about face; another experiment flounders, such as the gerry-rigged "Alliance for Progress": a retreat; then a new thrust, and so on. Through such zigs and zags they are kept to a definite secular course not so much by intent as by the buffets of impatient self-interest.

Laws of Bureaucratic Response   It is just this character of the state bureaucracy which disorients most "expert" observers of the political process. That is to say, most contemporary commentators attempt to find a lawful account of the course of current history in the inner structure of bureaucratic life or in the rationalizations of position papers, and so on. Their very factual premises show that they have overlooked the most fundamental things. While examining this or that leg or perhaps the tail of the elephantine bureaucracy, even with the most exacting scholarship, they miss such essential points as the nature of the bureaucracy as a social formation, and the contradictions between the dictates of its bureaucratic interest and the interest of the system it has been constructed to serve.

That is to say that the bourgeois state bureaucracy, a corporate bureaucracy, the Soviet bureaucracy, or a trade union bureaucracy have immediate interests, each as a distinct social formation, which are seldom symmetrical with and often antagonistic to those of the larger social formation, the base, on which the existence of the bureaucracy depends. From day to day, it might seem that the inner laws of bureaucracy are leading toward a repudiation of the social basis for its own existence. Yet, with few exceptions, in the final analysis, they are seen to respond, however crudely, to the interests of the base. So, for example, Stalin butchered the leadership of the Red Army which wished to prepare for a war with Nazi Germany, made deals with Hitler which seemed—and were—contrary to the interests of the Soviet nation, and yet, having betrayed the interests of the USSR bloodily up to that point, marshaled the defense of the Soviet Union. It is the same with a trade-union bureaucracy, which may sell out its membership through sweetheart contracts and whatnot, but, even though reluctantly, will lead a militant strike *to defend the existence of its base*. In a general way, these principles also apply to the bourgeois state bureaucracy.

The reality of the process is determined in the interactions of state bureaucracy and the economy. The economy throws up a problem to be solved by the bureaucracy. The bureaucracy, perhaps in this instance acting according to its bureaucratic interests as such rather than the interests of the imperialist economy, may supply no answer or provide a mistaken policy. The matter does not end there. The inactions or actions of the bureaucracy themselves have material consequences in the economy, which in turn present the bureaucracy with new crises to solve, and so on. That is to say, the lawful historic course of the bureaucracy does not arise from the internal processes of the bureaucracy per se, but from the interrelationship between the executive and the economy.

Internal Bureaucratic Development This foregoing account still leaves one issue to be settled before we can attribute to imperialism a definite policy, a "Third Stage of Imperialism" strategy.

Non-Marxists, dealing with the subject of the origins of state policy, have argued that in fact the government bureaucracy's decisions are not *usually* premised on a conscious grasp of imperialism's relevant historic economic interest. Up to this point the empiricist scholar is factually correct. The same can be said for the corporate bureaucracy, whose premises and mode of decision making do not correspond *intensionally* (sic) to the corporate long-term economic interest. But, after noting this, the non-Marxist commits a flagrant error of extrapolation; "therefore," he reasons, "U.S. policy is not determined by imperialist historic economic interest."

To this empiricist error our own argument thus far fails to supply a complete alternative. The question remains: if the internal criteria of the state bureaucracy are not immediately, at least, those of imperialism's economic interest, how do the buffets of circumstance ultimately impose the dictates of such a lawful expression of interest upon it?

For a first approximation of the answer one can conveniently turn his attention to the corporate bureaucracy, a phenomenon closely akin to the state bureaucracy, but affording the empiricist case-method worker the advantage of "repeatability" of the lawfulness exhibited. In such cases we see that a corporate bureaucracy whose internal premises are contrary to the corporate interest, actually functions according to a general line dictated by objective assessment of the corporation's lawful self-interest.

A corporation's executive is composed of departments, such as sales and marketing, manufacturing, purchasing, accounting, finance, and so on. In the workings of the bureaucracy, each of these separate functions proceeds from a point of view which is mostly antagonistic to that of its brother departments. Consider, for example, the matter of merchandise and inventory policies, on which the interests of sales are violently antagonistic to manufacturing's interest, and the interests of both run violently counter to the interest represented by finance. If the "natural" point of view of any one department were to prevail for long, the corporation would go bankrupt. Yet the actual functioning of the executive lies not in what bureaucrats think or know concerning corporate interest, but in the "effective interaction" of contending departmental tendencies.

That is not the end of the matter, of course. The bureaucracy, as a social formation, naturally tends to seek to increase itself, to divert increased surplus to itself—at the expense of even stockholders and financiers, to aggrandize itself. The corrective to this tendency and to other dysfunctions emerging from the bureaucracy itself is obtained from financial processes. Contrary to the popular current myths of "corporate capitalism," the corporation is by no means autonomous. Its existence, and its internal sources of funds depend in most cases on outside sources of credit.

Even in those few instances where corporations seem financially independent of Wall Street—and that is only an appearance—they are subject to the rule of finance. They are consumers of credit issued by vendors and others, and are themselves creators of credit afforded to customers and vendors; some are financiers, in the sense that they are major exporters of financial capital into the general capital funds market. They are all today exactly, in principle, what Rosa Luxemburg saw them to be 60 years ago.

Slight variations in rate of return on investment and prevailing interest rates cause masses of capital and credit to flow in or out of any corporation, thus settling in a most unarguable fashion the issue of merchandising, inventory policies, of bureaucratic staff-stockpiling, additions of new executive office suites, and so forth. Finance ultimately determines the flow, in or out of the firm, of means of payment through which the bureaucracy, as a social formation, reproduces itself, adds to or eliminates functions, and pursues the investment activities which represent the outcome of its executive judgment.

How Bureaucracy Evolves   The development of a bureaucracy appropriate to the corporate interest did not arise by pre-design; it evolved. How that process of evolution proceeds is seen in connection with the growth of the computer industry. Since the main use of the computer today is administrative, the design of a computer system should be determined by the function it ought to serve in the executive. Yet, the introduction of computer technology to the firm itself portends devastating changes in the internal structure of the bureaucracy.

At first, following the path of least resistance, computer systems were aimed to continue the lines of existing corporate accounting and related practices. This approach was, in the main, a failure; then, it began to be recognized that the computer necessitated changes in the conception of corporate organization, and with that the notion of *total* computerized corporate systems began to be hatched, to the end that the fruits of technology were adapted to the needs of an emerging, changed form of corporate organization. The development of computers in this direction tends now to bring such changes in organization into being.

However, computer use and applications design involve massive expenditures which, in corporate jargon, have to be "justified." So, computer systems and applications design development must follow the line of corporate economic interest, and so the implied organizational revolution in the corporate bureaucracy in turn follows the same lines.

In a similar way, each developed "function" of the bureaucracy emerged and evolved a distinct relation to the bureaucracy as a whole. It is in this constant effort to throw up new "functions," to redefine relations among functions, that the bureaucracy adapts itself to the line of lawful economic interest.

The government bureaucracy is of the same general form, not as a result of any accident. Its line of development has been to provide first of all a massive instrumentality of public finance and credit, to create credit for sustaining the capitalist market through massive hocking of the future tax-income powers and expectations of the state. It provides this resource not only for domestic use, but for foreign as well, and develops, parallel to this, the other essential instrumentalities, military, intelligence apparatuses, "built-in stabilizers" both economic and social-political, to support the purely economic side of those ventures, just as corporate sales, manufacturing, labor relations, and so on cohere indispensably with finance. The inter-relation of central banking systems with the public treasury (Federal Reserve Act), instituted in the wake of the 1907 panic and developed further in the wake of the 1929–31 crisis, offers one side of this evolution. The military establishment, whose main effect on the economy is the subsidy of private capital's profits through public funds, grew out of U.S. capitalism's inability to get out of the thirties' depression by private means. Or, so particular a development as the Civil Rights decision of 1954, which happened to occur at just that peculiar point of national economic development when investors in runaway shops in the South were concerned with the fact that cheap Negro labor there was insufficiently educated to provide effective labor-power for modern industry. (Compare Winthrop Rockefeller versus Faubus.) It is in this way that the state apparatus acquires new functions, interacting with the modified old, to yield in balance, a characteristic response to imperialism's economic interests.

Methods of Political Analysis   The consequences and lawful behavior of social formations lie not in the intentions of the individuals who are their members, but in the structure of the social formation as a whole. The beliefs of the individual members generally correspond only in a fantastic way to the function which they serve. Occasionally, in the case of an exceptional individual, particularly one with an overview of the bureaucracy, we may encounter a statement of purpose filled with Machiavellian candor; but for the rank and file of the bureaucratic intelligentsia, their own statements respecting premises and objects have mainly the significance of a purely religious utterance, a rationalization.

The only solution to the problems of scientific investigation thus presented is, first of all, to know the dictates of imperialist historic economic interest, and then to trace the process through which the bureaucracy responds to the imperatives thrust upon it by problems reflecting manifest imperialist self-interest.

Our tasks, in attempting to adduce the new policy toward which they are impelled, are mainly threefold. Firstly, to define the problem which compels imperialism to seek a new general strategy for its further existence. Secondly, to summarize the main features of the indicated solution, "The Third Stage of Imperialism." Finally, to show that in imperialism's attempted passage from the present strategy to the new, a breaking-point in history is created, at which the question of socialism in the advanced countries is again transferred from the domain of contemplation to become an issue of practice.

Postwar Boom—Western Europe

The failure of most American socialists to grasp the basis for postwar prosperity flowed generally from their ignorance of economics, or in cases where there was economic practice, the approach to this issue on the mistaken premise of "national" economies. Even today, this latter error is pursued in some of the most credible socialist circles; that is the case with the Baran-Sweezy *Monopoly Capital,* in which the authors mistakenly abstract the question of U.S. corporate surplus and surplus rates from their basis in a U.S. imperialist *world* economy. So they attain particular conclusions which are, in fact, opposite to the larger reality. This, in itself, is a most relevant point of our immediate inquiry, which we shall take up a short space ahead.

The first approach to a correct view is given in Harry Magdoff's paper on imperialism.[3] The postwar prosperity of the U.S. economy has been most directly based on U.S. investment in the advanced capitalist sectors abroad. Of course, but for passing observations in the appropriate direction, Magdoff does not attempt to go further, that is to show the dependency of all advanced sector's capitalist development on its relations with the underdeveloped sector. On account of the limited scope of Magdoff's brief paper, some socialist scholars have mistakenly contended that he did not actually deal with imperialism, since they misconstrue "imperialism" to mean "colonialism." In any case, Magdoff proved his point phenomenologically, that the profitability of U.S. Imperialism at home today depends immediately on its growing postwar investment in the advanced capitalist sectors abroad. It is the exhaustion of those investment opportunities, *symptomized* by the British crisis and the present West German recession, which is turning the postwar boom into a threatened general crisis.

War-ruined Western Germany, France, Italy, Japan, with their masses of cheap, unemployed, skilled labor, provided the objective basis for massive U.S. credit-expansion and overseas investment. Foreign aid of various kinds, motivated by "Marshall Plan" policy, provided the so-called "infrastructural development" necessary to the private capital investment which followed the aid dollar.

Socialist Victory Was Possible   Britain, too, was "conquered" by U.S. Imperialism through World War II, although not in quite the same way as the Continental economies. In the Continental economic satrapies of postwar U.S. Imperialism, enormous masses of obsolete capital were written off, thereby freeing those economies for a kind of "fresh start" development based on the most modern plant and equipment. Britain's essential obsolescence was preserved. This difference, in respect to which colonial France lies midway between colonial Britain and colonyless Germany and Italy, flowed from the fact that the British pound, with its far-flung colonial resources and colonial currency reserves, was an indispensable bulwark for the dollar. Since Britain's obsolete capital at home was part of the value of the pound, ancient plants could not be easily written off; instead the average value of the pound with respect to the dollar was ultimately reduced, at the expense of British workers and colonial peoples, making the obsolescence-rotten pound a harder currency, to prop up its inflated master, the dollar.

This was not the inevitable outcome of that war. It was when the French Maquis surrendered their weapons to de Gaulle—on the friendly advice of Stalin, when French Communists entered the provisional Gaullist government as "strikebreakers" (until they were ungratefully dismissed by the French bourgeoisie), that France, and German's flank, was secured to U.S. Imperialism. The same process is seen in postwar Italy. A socialist revolution in Western Europe at that time, when striking GIs thus exhibited their disinterest in putting down such revolutions, would have swept all Europe and brought the capitalist world system promptly to an end. But the French and Italian communist leaders betrayed socialism, and the rest is history.

Postwar Boom—Colonial World

Formal international accounting grossly understates the dependency of U.S. Imperialist prosperity in the advanced countries on the growing misery in the underdeveloped. Magdoff points to the accounting side of the matter in his reference to the general outflow of capital from the under-developed to advanced sectors.[4] A greater exploitation, not shown in the accounts, occurs through the low prices at which underdeveloped countries sell and the relatively high prices at which they buy. If colonial labor were paid on the basis of simple labor time at a European scale—which is not the basis for wages under capitalism—there would be a monstrous rise in the price of mineral and plantation exports from the underdeveloped to the advanced countries, a direct deduction from the gross national product of those countries and a ferocious deduction from profits. A similar, if far smaller deduction from U.S. and Western European GNP would occur if colonial labor were paid even on the basis of its labor-power (that is relative productivity) at Western European scales. This gives us some first approximation of the general relationship between the two sectors, but not yet the answer.

The fact of the underdeveloped countries is that they are rich in labor but extraordinarily poor in labor power; they lack skills, they lack the modern means of production with which to "compete" with U.S. or Western European labor. Thus, a product requiring many hours of labor-time by colonial peoples is exchanged for the money equivalent of a product requiring a few hours or less of labor-time in the advanced countries. Some indication of this is given in comparative figures on gross national product and national income per capita among the economies of the various sectors. How many working-lives of how many hundred laborers in Latin America or India are required to buy the modern machinery required to employ one native worker under modern productive conditions?

Comparing England and India, for example, in the seventeenth century, we see that this discrepancy was by no means as great at the start of the bringing of the "benefits of capitalism" to the "underprivileged heathen." This present misery is in fact the principal "blessing of civilization" which Europeans and Americans have bestowed upon their dark-skinned brothers. This discrepancy, in fact, embodies the concentrated history of capitalism in the presently underdeveloped sectors: primitive accumulation. Capitalist colonial looting and trade, imperialist investment, have systematically stripped those sectors of their social capital, the natively-produced social product which could have supplied the means of production for these people to keep pace with the advanced capitalist nations.

The Falling Rate of Profit

This phenomenon is exacerbated by a tendency of capitalism known as "the falling rate of profit." That is to say, as the organic composition of capital (ratio of cost of means of production to wages) increases, the rate of profit on combined capitalist investment must tend to fall. It is the apparent "violation" of this law in the "national" U.S. economy that is the centerpiece of Baran and Sweezy's Monopoly Capital.

Contrary to the implications of Monopoly Capital, the tendency of the rate of profit to fall is not a short-term affair (of a mere decade or two), nor is it a "national" economic phenomenon. Since the world market has become, in the late nineteenth century, a completely interconnected economic whole, the law of the falling rate expresses itself, like the average rate of surplus value, only on a world scale. Any isolated national examination of the phenomenon must produce findings which are necessarily contrary to the reality, as in Monopoly Capital.

As Marx showed, the price of commodities is not determined in particular by their value,[5] but by their price of production, that is to say by an average rate of profit on invested capital. (The notion of average rate is not a mere percentage figure, but varies from industry to industry and sector to sector to equalize itself to correspond to realizable profit: for example liquidity, risk, long-term—short-term, and so on.) The "investment decision" which leads to an increase in the organic composition of capital locally is predicated upon considerations of increased productivity and other essentials of expected profit-rate. Furthermore, the more general becomes the flow of capital, as through the development of world money markets and international credit, the more freely capital and credit flow from one sector or sub-sector of that world economy to another. The gradient of these shifts is, of course, the rate of profit.

Thus, at the level of the individual firm or sector, the limit of expansion of production is determined by the point at which the resulting rate of profit on investment falls below the "average," such that capital ceases to flow into that sector and instead tends to flow to other sectors. If prices in any sector make the rate of profit higher, capital flows in until expansion—overproduction, for example—causes an equalization of effective profit rates, and so forth.

In this process the rate of increase of profit to wages is far greater in general than the rate of increase of profit to total capital invested—for reasons beyond the technical scope of this paper. The result is that a local increase in investment rates *tends* to reduce the rate of profit in the world as a whole, however, not necessarily in that sub-sector in which the augmentation of organic composition occurs. Since higher investment ratios are governed by "investment decisions" bearing on the productivity of labor, what happens is that the advanced sectors take the consequences of their capital investment out of the hides of the less-developed sectors.

To understand how this occurs, we have only to recognize the contradiction between the individual firm, or foreign investment sector, of an underdeveloped sector of the economy, and the economy as a whole. The falling rate of profit tendency, generated mainly in the advanced sector, does not transmit itself so much to the foreign investments in the underdeveloped sectors as through those investments in the local economy which lie outside the foreign investment sector. In a word, *primitive accumulation;* the capitalist sector controlled by foreign investors maintains its profits by milking the "native" sector. The more capitalism develops in the advanced, the more ferociously it transmits the penalties of its advancement to the semi-colonial native sector.

The result is that these populations generally are stripped not only of the means of creating "native" capital, but of their very means of existence. So, we have the picture of growing populations—undergoing a population explosion produced significantly by capitalist influences, but deprived of the means of production wherewith to produce the material means of its own existence, starvation. This achievement, starvation, is not to be credited to the falsely alleged genius of parson Malthus, but to the direct effects of imperialism.[6]

What *Monopoly Capital*, thus, fails to take into account is that the profits raked in by U.S. leading corporations depend immediately on the cheap, skilled labor of other advanced capitalist countries and the mass of literal starvation among billions of people. Without directly relating U.S. corporate surplus to starvation in the Southern Hemisphere no scientific judgments can be advanced respecting surplus or tendencies in "surplus" rates.

This is not to suggest that imperialism thus escapes the consequences of the falling rate of profit. It only, so to speak, has exacted from its poorest subjects the price of the bondsman's fee, wherewith it enjoys a certain period of freedom up to the day of its inevitable trial.

Exactly as U.S. Imperialism begins to exhaust a sufficiency of investment opportunities in Western Europe and other advanced sectors, it is compelled to turn for new investment opportunities to the underdeveloped sector. Its needs in this matter are not to be measured in terms of its investment appetites of 1946 or 1950, but embody the greatly augmented and desperate financial needs of both itself and its foreign advanced-capitalist satrapies. It has nowhere to turn for this purpose but to those very underdeveloped sectors it has already depleted as investment markets for industrial investment. The means of its former prosperity now threatens to become the instrument of its collapse. So, the imperialist world economy, like Riemannian space, proves to be circular.

Inevitably, U.S. leading intelligentsia seek a solution to the new problem in the same general terms which seemed to produce such spectacular success at the last crisis. The notion of overcoming the backwardness of depleted economies by "Marshall Plan" schemes is the institutionalized response of the leading layers of state bureaucracy as it has been constituted under the past 20 years of the "Marshall Plan" prosperity.

Postwar Boom—Credit Expansion

Modern imperialism circumvents the short-term threats of "overproduction" by, first, turning the unsold production into security for credit —indeed by hocking all real and fictitious values in sight in order to create more credit. This credit, in turn, is transformed into money through the state treasury and central banking system, money which is also mortgaged to create new credit—and so on the process continues, upward toward a seemingly endless prosperity.

Up to a point of reckoning.

The accumulation of an ever-growing public and private debt in this way creates an additional item of cost in the capitalist's accounts: debt service. This, debt service, is the combined interest, service charges, and currently due repayments of principal advanced which are the current costs created by any debt. For a number of reasons, some to be cited for illustration here, this item of cost, debt service, tends to grow more rapidly than the means for paying it off. When, after any prolonged period of credit-expansion—like that of the past 25 years—debt service overtakes or exceeds the existing means for its payment, a balance of payments—liquidity—crisis appears in the world economy.

A Balance of Payments Crisis   The natural reaction of the world market to such a balance of payments crisis is to discount the value of instruments of indebtedness, such as stocks, mortgages, acceptances, and even the securities of central banking systems and national governments. Obviously, if a debtor's ability to meet current payment due on a debt is reduced, then the value of that debt, as an investment purchase by another party, is also reduced. However, since this debt represents, in large part, the main constituent of assets held by central bankers, and since this debt has been used as security for printed currency and other means of payment, a balance of payments crisis threatens to bring about a devaluation of such currencies themselves. It is therefore those principal currencies which are responsible for the largest portion of the world's created credit—such as the dollar and sterling today—which tend to suffer the most immediate balance of payments pressures.

Such a crisis does not mean that the book value, so to speak, of the capitalists' mortgaged properties and paper are insufficient for the amount owed. The problem is that the capitalists' current incomes are insufficient to meet payments due without curtailing other expenditures indispensable to maintaining the capitalist system. In any bankruptcy, for example, the book value of buildings, inventories, equipment, and portfolio may far exceed the amount owed to creditors. The debtor is nonetheless bankrupt; he cannot meet his bills as they fall due, so his *long-term* assets must be auctioned off to pay his *short-term* debt. It is the same with national economies suffering a balance of payments crisis; no matter what the value of long-term assets, the debtor is bankrupt unless he can satisfy the current demands for payment advanced by his creditors.

Debtor and Creditor the Same Person   The irony of such a crisis is that the debtor and creditor are, so to speak, the same person, the capitalist class. It is not merely a matter of capitalist, John, failing to pay capitalist, Paul. If John is unable to pay Paul, Paul is in reduced circumstances for paying Peter, who in turn, is thus impaired in his ability to pay John, thus compelling John to auction his assets off to pay Paul, eliminating himself as a customer for Paul and as a supplier to Peter, which reduces Paul's income thereafter, thus forcing Paul into the position John occupied a moment before. The problem is not that John is unable to produce at a current profit; it is that held-over mass of debt, which somehow must be rid of.

Property Forms A Fetter on Production   The root of this problem is the capitalist system, that is to say the connection between property forms in the means of production and production itself. If a capitalist ceases to be a capitalist in terms of property forms, titles of ownership, he ceases to function as a capitalist, irrespective of his abilities as an organizer of production, the productive capacities of the workers he employs or the need for the product of his plant. So, productive relations are made into capitalist property relations, with the result that production ceases with the extinction of the title to property in those means of production—on penalty of law.

So we have a situation in which the need for certain commodities, the productivity of workers (rate of surplus value), have nothing to do with the continuation of production. While it might seem that a writing down of capitalists to their true, bankrupt value should have no effect on the continuing operation of the means of production itself, it does, and it must—for that is the basis on which production proceeds under capitalist property relations. It is for that reason that a general auctioning off of debt-ridden capitalists at their true value produces a depression.

Why, then should we permit the process of production on which our material means of existence depend, to be periodically shut down or curtailed by the mere anomalies of capitalist property forms? That is, of course, the question raised in a particularly acute way by every actual or threatened depression, as it is by every war launched in an effort to perpetuate those same property forms.

It is most relevant at this point to consider some of the ways in which debt service overtakes the available allocated means for its own payment.

Cancerous Speculative Growth   A substantial part of the gain in debt service charges over allocated means for its payment arises through capitalists' speculation. Any financier knows the elementary principle of prudent borrowing: the use of borrowed money must yield a greater increased income than the debt service so incurred. No financier would borrow on any other basis. Yet, in practice, without any financier necessarily violating that principle for his own part, through just such prudent borrowing *individually*, financiers *as a whole* absolutely repudiate that, their own sacred principle of thrift.

A real estate financier, for example, will borrow on the basis of a just expectation of an inflationary rise in the resale price of old properties. This flow of capital into real estate speculation, while it agrees with the *individual financier's* dictum of prudent borrowing on his own part, does not contribute to any increase in value produced by the capitalist system as a whole. Resale of stocks, bonds, and other forms of speculative investment have that same character; they increase the aggregate debt service which must be ultimately paid out of useful production's income without increasing productive output in the slightest.

Such speculation is inherent to the capitalist system. One might mistakenly assume that the calamity of sixteenth century Antwerp and Ausgburg bankers would have warned them of the consequences (inevitably, the bankrupt debtor must repudiate his debt, with or without the sanction of canon law, and then the banker must himself become bankrupt). However, the anarchy of capitalism prevents such individual capitalist precautions. While the individual financier may bewail, as through the voice of the *Wall Street Journal*, the horrible prospect implicit in mounting state debt, he is the first in line to demand the fruits of federal, debt-based spending to his own account.

Since speculative gains in stocks, bonds, real estate, government securities, depend upon an increased flow of capital, credit and exactions from workers (as through rents for inflated real properties), and each new flood of such speculative capital into these areas tends to increase the rate of appreciation of purely paper values. Thus the tendency is to attract still further credit and capital into these same areas—away from useful investment in the means of production. If, in order to sustain this bubble of speculation, the state and central banking system continue to supply a flood of cheap credit, eventually the rate of gain in speculation must overtake the rate of realized profit of industry, so that production constricts for want of capital, while masses of real capital and credit flow into a deadly inflationary spiral in pure speculation. So much for the collective wisdom and sanity of the capitalist class.

Just because, in fact, the financiers have *collectively* learned the evil outcome of their own uncontrollable individual impulses, they have collectively encouraged the central banking system and state apparatus to regulate them to a limited extent. The very statism concerning which they howl in their peculiar organs is an instrument of their own creation, and their shrieking and gnashing of teeth is but an expression of the contradiction between their collective interest and individual suicidal urges.

This point is of some importance both to the matter at hand and to the general thesis advanced at the outset. Consider the uninformed view of Kennedy's role in the steel price increase affair. Kennedy was being, it was misconstrued, "liberal," even anti-capitalist. Not the dutiful son of Joseph Kennedy! The capitalists do not convene at something like an NAM conference to decree that the government shall regulate them in such and such a way. On the contrary, their leaders, coming to recognize such a need for regulation, as Teddy Roosevelt's "liberal" Republicans, create an institution, a function of the bureaucracy—such as Department of Justice anti-trust activities—to deal with such matters. It may be that the particular actions of these agencies, in pursuit of their narrowly assigned function, will deviate from time to time from actual capitalist interests. That is no matter, these functions of government, as in the Kennedy steel case, are in the general interest of the capitalist system, just as are the reserve ratio and other regulative actions of the Federal Reserve System, the explicit agency of the leading U.S. financiers.

Obviously, the mass of "values" accounted in speculative paper are not real capital in the sense of investments in means of production; the gains embodied in those titles are purely fictitious, represent *fictitious capital*. As these titles themselves, stocks, mortgages, and so on, become security for new credit, and ultimately for the creation of new masses of currency itself, money itself is devalued in content by the increasing proportion of speculative "hot air" in each dollar bill.

Parasitism and Waste   Credit is also piped into wasteful forms of investment connected to the means of production and distribution. The number of government and corporate clerks per productive worker are increased; the number of salesmen per productive worker rises. Large masses of capital flow into redundant sales offices, financial institution establishments, purely redundant "dealerships," supermarkets, and so forth, all of which adds not one penny's worth to the real output of production itself.

The federal government creates a debt for war production. State, federal and local governments hock their future tax receipts for largely wasteful "public trough" expenditures, or to employ capitalists in wasteful public projects. So, more debt piles up, creating new debt service demands against current income without contributing to any increase in the current real wealth out of which payment must be rendered.

If we inspect the history of the postwar domestic economy, especially since 1957–58, we find stagnation in the employment of productive workers, semi-stagnation in the rate of new investment, and the bulk of the rise in employment in outright parasitical (government bureaucracy) or redundant elements of the social division of labor. If we deduct from real productive employment and investment, that portion attributable to military spending, to redundant commercial investment, to growth of plant and staff for financial institutions, and compare this with the growth of public and private debt, we see how the domestic picture of credit-expansion corresponds to that outlined above.

Debt service incurred by capitalists in this way must be paid mainly out of surplus value, out of specifically that *portion* of surplus value which corresponds to interest in the current structural norms of capital flows. That is to say, there is an allocable portion of total surplus which can be used to pay debt service without disturbing the general equilibrium. When that amount is exceeded, as debt service overtakes this allocable portion of surplus value, the crisis appears.

Is A Crisis Inevitable?   A balance of payments deficit is not in itself a crisis. If the capitalist system has any immediate long-term prospect of investments in real production which might increase its ability to pay off debt service, the capitalists can negotiate terms with themselves (for example International Monetary Fund, informal agreements among central bankers directly, and so on) through which to defer a certain portion of short-term deficits in the form of a longer-term debt. What makes the immediate threat from the balance of payments crisis so severe is the exhaustion of opportunities for real investment in the advanced sector.

This is not to suggest that there are no remaining investment opportunities in Europe, for example. On the contrary, as with American interests' taking over of the French computer industry, or Chrysler's take over of British Rootes, or Ford's take over of its British subsidiary, there are many such *essentially speculative* investment opportunities. Nor is there any absolute want of some real further investment opportunities, a situation which might be improved slightly by some rationalization of Common Market arrangements. The problem is that the mass of real investment opportunities has fallen way behind the mass of needs of capitalists for such investments. It is this that turns the 10-year crisis of sterling and the 10-year U.S. balance of payments run-out into the threat of an early depression.

Short-Term Imperialist Alternatives

The first reaction of the insolvent imperialist is, of course, to see how much his grandmother will bring at the nearest pawnshop. Who can be tapped to meet the capitalists' debts? The imperialists' short-term solution to their crisis is exemplified by the present case of Britain, which, in U.S. Imperialist interests (through the mediation of a "Labour" government), is exacting the needed funds from the workers' wage envelope. Otherwise, in this country we already see wages lagging behind inflationary rises (guidelines), and capitalists' state debts at all levels being met through increased state and local as well as federal sales and income taxes.

This is exemplified by the case of the New York City Lindsay administration, rushed into the breach by the financiers to solve the threatened municipal insolvency developed under the previous administration. Rising City debt service, a product of Democrats' frequent trips to the more respectable pawnshop, was one of the major, growing items of City deficit. Financiers postponed the impending financial crisis through increased sales taxes and a newly instituted city income tax. The introduction of that tax on wages reduced the contributions of real estate financial interests to half of the total city tax revenue. In other words, a shift of the burden of debt from financiers, who cause the debt, to wage-earners. The same pattern may be expected to continue in new city income taxes and in federal tax rises.

However, such short-term measures are just that. They suffice only to delay the sheriff's auction on the bankers' premises.

Without sources of investment for profit, capital ceases to be capital. So, the point at which newly formed capital loses the opportunity to become capital invested for profit, the profit-system as a whole threatens to break down. So, paying off current debt service with sums taken from wages solves nothing, since the accumulated payment is only added to the fund of capital demanding investments for profit.

The apparent solution, and institutionalized response, is to increase war production, that is, for the federal, state and local government to go further into hock to maintain an already cancerous credit-expansion. Of course, despite this, the inevitable reaction of imperialism, under more intensive blows from the balance of payments crisis, must be to take more out of labor, to the point of straining in the extreme, if not breaking, the coalition of financiers and labor bureaucrats on which the stability of the present political system depends. In the final analysis, that still solves nothing.

"Third Stage of Imperialism"

The form of the long-term solution sought by the capitalists is suggested by the runaway shop. Already, capital created by the production of skilled U.S. workers has run away to build shops employing only less skilled but much cheaper labor in Europe. In this way the average profit on a world scale is sustained and average profit at home also increased in particular.

There is an abundance of cheap labor below the equator, but a shortage of *labor power*. That is to say, a runaway shop, if it is to be competitive, must find labor with a certain level of skill in general, literate labor, labor that is not only the product of modern education, but also latently educated through *something* of a "Western" standard of living. And plants cannot be simply dumped into the middle of an undeveloped savanna or jungle; plants require power, efficient transportation, communications systems, proximity to suppliers and customers, and so forth. The population must also be susceptible to "Western" ways of doing things, to capitalist notions of property relations, family, order, and so forth; it must be assimilable into the modern capitalist culture as reflected in relations between line workers and foremen. That is to say, in addition to the more obvious objective prerequisites for investment, there are, equally important, the subjective preconditions, juridical notions of human relations, and so on. All of these conditions together are loosely termed "infrastructure" by brain-trusters in the state bureaucracy.

It is in that direction that imperialists see their longer-term solution to the presently impending economic crisis. Since they move through a bureaucracy, not as scientists, they do not discover such a solution by advancing, discussing, proving some general theory, but pragmatically, through the concepts embodied in the institutions left over from the past. They see the solution not in scientific terms, but through the precedent of the "Marshall Plan" and "Fomento" development of Puerto Rico, in terms of "Food for Peace" and Fulbright funds, in terms of the International Monetary Fund, and through foreign institutions, such as Latin American juntas, or the Nehru bureaucracy or Ky regime, which are their existing institutionalized relations with underdeveloped sectors. They approach something new mainly by attempting to patch up the old instruments, by turning their instrumentalities into a Rube Goldberg device of gadgets affixed hither and yon, each attachment grafted on to "solve" a problem discovered through some particular experience.

Such a new policy was first officially presented to the general public, as we have stated, by former President Eisenhower, in his 1960 State of the Union address on Foreign Policy. In order to open up the Southern Hemisphere for direct internal market investment, a new "Marshall Plan" would have to be launched, this time with the burden assumed proportionately by Western Europe and Japan. Massive public aid and loans would develop the infrastructure, after which private capital, finding the economic and political climate agreeably air-conditioned for its comfort, would move in. Of course, Eisenhower pointed out that colonial peoples desiring to harvest such largesse from imperialism would have to learn to discipline themselves, a point which was later clarified by the assassination of Patrice Lumumba.

At the instant Eisenhower was delivering this policy statement, Douglas Dillon, then an underling at the State Department, was negotiating a treaty along those very lines with that late great "socialist," Nehru. Under the terms of this treaty, India became, economically at least, in the same relationship to the U.S., Western Europe, and Japan as Puerto Rico to the U.S. Under the provisions of this treaty since, while British India investment has stagnated, West German and Japanese investment leaped ahead, a process interrupted by the current famine.

Kennedy's abortive "Alliance for Progress" was a miserably inadequate, gerry-rigged "fomento" scheme, in all probability hastily scrounged for the occasion from the drafting boards of the leftover Eisenhower bureaucracy. But it was also, in principle, consistent with a policy Kennedy had set forth in a 1958 Senate address. Kennedy's half-baked "land reform" program in Vietnam, continued recipes of the same sort now afoot, Daddy Bird Johnson's occasional mumblings about a "managed social revolution" for Latin America, are aspects of a bureaucratically bungled thrust toward implementation of the policy enunciated by Eisenhower in 1960.

"Third Stage" If it could be launched, this policy would represent a third stage of imperialism. The first stage is represented by British colonialist rape of India, by Britain's military effort to push the opium habit on Chinese people, and other picaresque colonial adventures of buccaneering commercial capital. The second stage is that characterized by Lenin and Hilferding, of monopoly capital's investment in the extra-active industries, the use of masses of virtually slave colonial labor to work the plantations and mines. Under this second stage of imperialism, under which we have lived to this point, foreigners, like the unlamented Leopold of Belgium, or the interests of our own Rockefeller operated abroad with policies which respected not the least how many natives were butchered or worked to death, as long as there remained sufficient "slave" labor to man the imperialist workings. That is the continuing situation, under which our leading press indulges us with its ritual tears of ink over massive misery abroad, without troubling to suggest any alteration in that U.S. policy causing this suffering. In the new stage of imperialism—if it is launched—the lot of colonial peoples will be more fortunate in one respect. It happens that starving illiterates do not represent labor power for today's industrialists. That is to say that U.S. imperialists *will* regard colonial peoples as productive labor, as workers whose human virtues are acknowledged in direct proportion to their qualities of cheapness and servility. The Southern Hemisphere is intended to become the happy hunting ground of the runaway shop in this period as Puerto Rico has been in the last.

"Could It Work?" A number of socialist commentators, basing themselves substantially on the "Alliance for Progress" experience, deny

that such a "Third Stage of Imperialism" policy could work even if the colonial peoples permitted it. On the contrary, if not prevented, it could work quite well for some period of time, provided only that the imperialists themselves are prepared to undertake the risks, the massive and revolutionary measures required to get such a program under way.

We must grant the cited socialist doubters that, "All things being equal," those very difficulties of starting up would ordinarily prevent imperialists from undertaking such a hazardous venture. The same could be said, of course, for the past two world wars. It happens that, as on the verge of a world war, "all other things" are by no means equal. Imperialism is impelled to any desperate resort the policy demands; it has no other long-term basis on which to predicate its existence.

The first obstacle to industrial development of the Southern Hemisphere is the plantation system. For any sector of the world economy to maintain an industrial working class, it must have a ready and ample supply of cheap food. "Cheap food" is a relative matter; that is to say, there must be a relative abundance at prices which represent only a fraction of the workers' pay for his family's needs. U.S. food "surpluses" do not suffice for this purpose; they are only useful supplemental means or part of an initial "pump-priming," to get local industrialization going under its own power. In order to have local food prices scaled to the wage-levels of local workers, this need must be mainly met out of agricultural surpluses from relatively low-wage areas. It is mainly to ample local food production that the plantation system is an obstacle.

In order to provide plantation owners with cheap labor, there has been created a layer of landless, proletarianized peasants without skills or opportunities for any other kind of employment—as we see in the case of migrant agricultural labor in the U.S. itself. The latifundist is therefore violently opposed to any "Homestead Act" which will raise the price of agricultural labor by affording peasants the opportunity to take up idle land and put it into modern farm production. In the Southern Hemisphere, the proletarianization of large masses of peasantry is accomplished almost automatically by the draining of the internal economy of the social capital which would be required to develop agriculture. This result of primitive accumulation is augmented by juridical measures including landlordism which prevent peasants from freely occupying and developing fertile plots.

Before stable industrialization can take place, this latifundist *system* must be largely destroyed. This does not mean, generally, a distribution of banana and coffee lands for potato or corn farming. It means mainly a program of distributing *idle* arable plots to peasants, together with technological and financial assistance from the state. This will drive up the price of plantation labor, forcing the plantations to shift from labor-intensive to mechanized methods of production.

The present system is sometimes clumsily called "feudal." In fact, the latifundist system—a system of producing masses of agricultural output for the money market—is a product of capitalism, and has not occurred anywhere in the history of man except through the development of mercantile capitalism (for example, Hellenism generally, ancient Rome in particular, Southern slave-system). So, the question of social revolution in Latin America, for example, is not a matter of capitalists settling accounts with feudal remnants, but of capitalism reforming itself.

The imperialists' difficulty in Latin America at this point is that plantation interests there are not an isolated group within the capitalist system. Plantations are only the agricultural extremity in that part of the world of the central banking system in the advanced. To institute land reform, to force latifundists to mechanize, and so on, is to wipe out a source of profits of the imperialist home countries.

Furthermore, the *compradore* class in these countries, rooted in the latifundist families and system, forms the "loyal" native governing class, the officer cadres of the police and armies servile to imperialist interests. To overturn the present latifundist interests in these countries is to attack major imperialist profits and investments in that sector and also to alienate and impoverish that caste of dons and colonels on which Coca-Colaization is presently based.

However, these consequences will ultimately be risked and the solution found, if the need is sufficiently desperate—as it is.

Actually, the latifundists will be offered no more than "psychological" hardships. The procedure to be used is in principle the same as that employed in Northern U.S. cities' slum clearance programs. A tax collection is taken up from wage earners; these funds are used to compensate slumlords or latifundists at top dollar. "Here's your money; go and invest it in industrial development." The objective transition from serf-owner to financier, like that from gangster to successful businessman, requires only sufficient ready cash.

A Variation—The Case of India One major leg of imperialism's future is India, which requires a slightly different approach than that due for Latin America. The tired soil of that unhappy country does not admit of the land reform solutions feasible in much of Latin America. Decades of soil development, of technological work, must pass before that portion of the subcontinent can feed itself and also provide a surplus to sustain a growing cheap industrial proletariat.

The old British Raj provided for its industrial investment in India with rice imports from Burma. Such resources are insufficient for the collective investment appetites of the U.S., Western Europe, and Japan. It is the Southeast Asian rice bowl as a whole that can provide just such needed agricultural surpluses—that is to speak of such regions as the Mekong River area. (Obviously, there is no direct investment, present or prospective, in Vietnam itself which would explain the present costly war; but when the importance of the rice bowl as a whole is weighed against imperialism's present and future desperate interest in India, the Vietnam War appears in its proper focus in terms of U.S. imperialist interests.)

Planned imperialist investment in the underdeveloped sector is divided into two main parts, *public* and *private*. Massive public assistance, in the form of government grants, World Bank loans, and so forth, are intended to build up what contemporary bureaucrats term the "infra-structure" of the economy. This is to provide education, highways, railways, power, and so forth. These are elements which do not represent profitable investments themselves, but which are indispensable to private investment as they provide labor with skills and otherwise create the facilities on which modern plants depend. Then, private investment follows. This is the "Marshall Plan" on a larger scale, adapted to the special enormous difficulties of these sectors.

The role of the military should not be overlooked in this process of developing a capitalist infrastructure. Marx remarked on the expression of concentrated production relations in the capitalist army; Engels researched some of the actual connections by which such a result is produced. The organization of a large-scale local army of a U.S. model is the most direct way of educating large numbers of colonial peoples, of drilling them in the customs and technology of capitalist life. The army as an economic entity in its own right, also provides, in addition to a massive prostitution industry, a host of camp-followers who soon learn the elements of modern capitalism—cheating, price-gouging, misleading packaging. In the wake of the army appear those wealthy pimps, gangsters, black-marketeers, and so on who have small capital and some knowledge of business, together with a mass of demobilized soldiers who have been drilled in following foremen's orders, in maintaining mechanical tools, and so on. (Compare Vietnam today.)

With the colonial economies already running at a capital deficit, the public and private capital must come from the product of labor in the advanced countries. To turn India, parts of Africa and Latin America around, from primitive accumulation resources to sectors of industrial development, public aid alone must be advanced on a war-spending scale. Unless financier profits are to be reduced for this purpose, war-economy scale increases in profits and in employee taxes must provide the bulk of these funds.

The general scheme for accomplishing this funding is seen in the "wage guidelines" recipe. That is, to hold real wages down to a fraction of the gains in potential real wages attained through productivity, to hold wage increases behind the combined effect of inflation and major increases in productivity. Thus, at best the material standard of living of the worker in the U.S., Europe, and so on, may remain about the same while his portion of the product of labor is rapidly reduced.

As for the effect of this scheme on the U.S. economy, it should not be imagined that U.S. foreign aid represents the slightest bit of charity on the part of financiers here. Most U.S. aid dollars need never leave a New York bank; these deposits in U.S. banks will be used to purchase from U.S. corporations the capital goods exported—the U.S. financier will immediately be paid for his "largesse," while the foreign economy will be in a greater amount of debt to the U.S. bankers! If a small amount of this money does actually leak into colonial native economies, no matter; it will only be used to prime the local pump to further assist U.S. direct investment.

"Neo-Colonialism"   The "Third Stage of Imperialism" should not be confused with "neo-colonialism," a term which only reflects the confusion with which many observers regard U.S. take over of the colonial world from the old colonial powers. Economically, there is nothing very new in what these observers term "neo-colonialism"; these forms are only a part of the old "Second Stage of Imperialism."

Neo-colonialism signifies chiefly that U.S. Imperialism has at last succeeded in extending its 1899 "Open Door To China" policy to the entire colonial world. That "Open Door" policy, it should be remembered, was simply a kind of declaration of war on the old colonial powers, in which a bumptious, nascent U.S. Imperialism threw down the gauntlet: "Tear down your customs fences around those colonies we Americans intend to make our property." The granting of national independence to former colonies by old colonial powers—often at the explicit insistence of U.S. Imperialism—merely shows that the U.S. has finally compelled those old powers to knuckle under, to turn the colonial world over to the unhampered exploitation of the dollar.

In the case of the Belgian Congo, for example, it was the U.S. which pressured a reluctant Belgium into granting Congo independence, the same U.S. which backed Belgium's invasion of that former colony to the hilt immediately thereafter. The White House does not object to Belgian paratroopers shooting down colonial women and children on an Eichmann scale, merely to Belgian customs officials annoying the emissaries of U.S. capital.

Still "neo-colonialism," occurring at the fulfillment of the "Second Stage of Imperialism," does represent the point at which the "Third Stage" begins to emerge. The famous CIA flair shows itself in the recently established counterrevolutionary regimes now in the saddle in Algeria, Congo, Ghana, and Indonesia. U.S. and "allied" agents seek out among the nationalists those who show a proper understanding for the capitalist way of life, just as any slumlord might seek out some ambitious lad to take on the problem of dealing directly with the tenants. As the slumlord "sells" the slum building (with, of course, a usurious second mortgage) to the ambitious lad, assuring him that he is now a "financier," so the U.S. agent or one of his ilk paints the delights of capitalist status to the upcoming "boy." "Of course, this will be your very own native industry; we will be content with no more than a first and second mortgage, plus a fair share of any profits which manage to miraculously survive our financial rates."

From Economics to Politics

The main difficulties facing the "Third Stage" enterprise are not economic but political.

The "managed social revolution" involves a radical transformation of institutions and social relations in both the advanced and underdeveloped sectors of the world economy. Any such change is hazardous to the ruling class as it upsets the fabric of established ideologies and institutions on which the social and political stability of the previous period was predicated. Furthermore, the imperialists are compelled to undertake such measures just at the time when the authority of prevailing ideologies and institutions are already being questioned on account of economic disturbances, intensified labor struggles, unpopular wars, and an enormously diminished credibility of their regimes. With the illusions of two decades wearing thin in the advanced sector and the super-exploited sector already aboil, the imperialist is in the position of escaping from a burning house through a pond of boiling oil.

This has been portended in the short-term effects of the Cuban revolution on radicalization throughout the colonial world and, to some extent, in the U.S. itself. It is shown in the wake of the Vietnam War today.

Some significant risk arises for imperialism from its own capitalist factions and from cleavages in the state bureaucracy and political machines. These forces do not represent by any means a conscious monolith, for reasons we have already shown. The polarization of the capitalists and their bureaucracy into a "liberal" and right faction can be the basis for violent cleavages in the imperialist ranks. The present imperialist regime in the U.S. is based on a conscious coalition of financiers, politicians, and treacherous trade union bureaucrats; imperialist interests now impel them toward breaking the trade union bureaucracy coalition, a break which cannot be successfully carried through without drastic changes in existing political institutions—laws, forms of government. At every important turn, the most conscious leading layer is hampered by the cretinism of its own social base, creating the danger for it of indecision just at the point when a clear course of policy might be most urgently required.

In the state bureaucracy—as in the corporate bureaucracy—a dramatic change in policy can be accomplished only under conditions of crisis. The leadership that is "ahead of its time" will find its efforts sabotaged by the bureaucracy's rank and file. This phenomenon, bureaucratic cretinism, plays a decisive short-term role in the making of history, tending to cause the leading circles to delay indicated new policies until the latest stages of a crisis, when such innovations are introduced almost too late. This same consideration may reduce the leading circles for a brief period to a condition of indecision, vacillation, in which they are unable to rule effectively. So, it follows, it is almost a law that every such general economic crisis creates at some point an interval of discontinuity in capitalist hegemony at which an effective socialist leadership and movement can intervene successfully to change the course of history. That is the imperialists' greatest hazard.

Large socialist or Communist parties are no guarantee in themselves of such an effective leadership, as history since the end of World War I shows in the case of Germany (several times: 1918, 1923, 1933), France (1945), Italy (1945), Britain (1945). The issue is one of *quality* of socialist leadership, of program. The question, What will be the result of the present threat of general economic crisis? can thus be answered: either we, in the U.S., for example, will create a leadership of revolutionary intelligentsia and develop programs of socialist reindustrialization which win the support of a majority of wage earners, or U.S. Imperialism or Imperialist-Fascism will succeed in establishing its survival through a "Third Stage of Imperialism" for another historic period.

Notes

1. Rosa Luxemburg, *Social Reform or Revolution*, Tr. Integer, Young Socialist Publications, Colombo, Ceylon, 1966.

2. Karl Marx, *Capital*, Vol. *III*, Kerr, pp. 523–611.

3. Harry Magdoff, "Economic Aspects of Imperialism," *Monthly Review*, vol. 18, no. 6, November 1966.

4. Magdoff, "Economic Aspects of Imperialism," *Monthly Review*, vol. *18*, no. 6, November 1966.

5. If commodities were sold at their value, the price of an article would be the sum of: (1) The direct "outside" cost of materials, machinery, plant, and so on, consumed in its production, *plus* (2) a fixed multiple (for example, 150 percent, 200 percent) of its direct productive labor cost. This fixed multiple would be approximately constant for all commodities in the economy.

6. This involves a kind of exploitation which cannot be treated as an extreme case of wage-exploitation. The latter scrapes wealth from the sweat of a man's back; the former sucks his blood—for example literal starvation. For obvious reasons, I term this latter process *negative accumulation*.

4.
THE MAKING OF A MAJORITY: SAFEGUARD AND THE SENATE

Nathan Miller

In the late summer of 1969, two days before the Senate approved President Nixon's plan to deploy the Safeguard anti-ballistic-missile system by a single vote, Senator James B. Pearson, a thoughtful Kansas Republican, discussed the significance of the marathon debate.

"You know, this issue will come as close as any to turning on the quiet consciences of the individual Senators," he told a visitor. "The Senate would be a powerful instrument if all the issues were debated in this manner."

Not since the summer of 1941, when the House approved continuation of the draft by one vote, had a President's decision on an issue of national security been so narrowly supported. Opponents were to talk of a Pyrrhic victory, but just as the draft could be continued or suspended by a single vote, so could an ABM system.

How was this one-vote victory won? What were the forces brought to bear on the "quiet consciences" of the individual senators? How much influence did those forces have on the result?

Shortly before the President announced his decision to deploy Safeguard on March 14, 1969, a small group of men met with Bryce N. Harlow, the Administration's chief congressional lobbyist, in his office down the corridor from Nixon's own Oval Office. Their job was to sell the ABM to a reluctant nation and a recalcitrant Senate. Independent polls indicated an Administration defeat, or at least a stand-off. Forty-five senators were opposed to the ABM; only 25 favored it; 30 were uncommitted. For a year, ABM opponents had been building an effective network of grass-roots organizations, many of them based on opposition to the Vietnam War. "We all knew we had a long road and a hill ahead," Harlow was to say later.

From Nathan Miller, "The Making of a Majority: Safeguard and the Senate," in *Inside the System*, edited by Charles H. Peters and Timothy J. Adams (New York: Praeger Publishers) pp. 158–182. © 1970 by The Washington Monthly Company. Reprinted by permission of the publisher.

Ironically, the Administration regarded Safeguard as a compromise. Unlike the Sentinel system approved by President Johnson for deployment in the suburbs, Safeguard was to protect the nation's nuclear deterrent out on the Great Plains.

But, as everyone at the meeting was aware, far more than the fate of another weapons system was at stake. Nixon had called the ABM "absolutely essential" to the nation's security. To many senators, however, it had become the symbol of misplaced priorities—priorities that allocated $79 billion for military spending while civilian needs went begging. Under the bipartisan leadership of Senators John Sherman Cooper, the highly respected Kentucky Republican, and Philip A. Hart, the liberal Michigan Democrat, opposition to the ABM had grown rapidly during 1968 and the first two months of 1969. Backed by scientific briefings and staff memoranda, aided by the growing outcry from the suburbs, their support had widened to the point where it approached a majority of the Senate.

But this White House meeting was to produce a carefully orchestrated campaign directed by Herbert G. Klein, the Administration's director of communications. Even opponents were to call it "one of the most sophisticated and professional jobs of lobbying we've ever seen." Before the battle was over, the President, the White House staff, the Pentagon, individual senators, the scientific community, defense contractors, and the public participated in what became the most passionate struggle in recent legislative history.

Administration lobbyists quickly wrote off the opponents; energies and arguments must concentrate on the uncommitted, they agreed, and the approach must be soft sell.

"Twisting arms and wrenching sockets would leave too much scar tissue," said one of the men who attended the White House staff meeting. "We decided that if the system was worth anything at all it would sell itself—but we had to make sure that our side of the story got told."

That was Herb Klein's job. Within hours of the President's announcement of his Safeguard plan, newspapers all over the country received thick packets of information supporting Mr. Nixon's stand. Such ABM supporters as Vice President Spiro T. Agnew and Secretary of Defense Melvin R. Laird followed up with television appearances. But before long, Senator Edward M. Kennedy (D-Mass.) was organizing a national movement against deployment of Safeguard.

The first dividends of the Administration's campaign were not long in accruing. Immediately after the Presidential announcement, Senator Hugh A. Scott (R-Pa.), the newly named minority whip, switched from opposition to support of the ABM. His defection was to provide the majority of one—although no one knew it at the time.

Party loyalty, rather than the issue itself, persuaded Senator Scott. Although he was to remain open to compromise, he felt it improper for one of the Administration's own floor leaders to oppose the President on an issue of national security.

Within four days, nine other senators switched from the undecided column to support of the ABM, including the late Everett M. Dirksen (D-Ill.), then minority leader. Now, an Associated Press poll showed 44 senators firmly opposed to Safeguard, 35 for it, and 21 uncommitted.

The opponents picked up a vote, too. Jim Pearson, who had originally voted for Sentinel, joined the opposition, saying deployment would be inconsistent with the spirit of the nuclear nonproliferation treaty and would make "only a marginal contribution" to security.

Even though the polls favored the opposition, their leaders were cautious. The Senate majority leader, Mike Mansfield (D-Mont.), said that if the President decided to use the full weight of his office, it was his guess that "as of now there would be enough votes to uphold the President's decision." But Mansfield emphasized that a vote was still months away.

Both sides laid plans for a long campaign, with their most effective propaganda timed to take effect at the tail end of the debate. Scientific witnesses appeared before various committees, where they gave conflicting views based on the same evidence. Secretary Laird produced the claim that the Russians were trying for "a first strike" that would knock out unprotected Minuteman missiles in their silos.

With the Nixon Administration being given a respite on Vietnam, such prominent "doves" as Senators J. William Fulbright (D-Ark), Albert Gore (D-Tenn.), Jacob K. Javits (R-N.Y.), and Stuart Symington (D-Mo.) joined in the fight against the ABM. Already in the works since February was what was to be known as the "Kennedy report," a compendium of 16 articles by leading scientists and other experts, all contesting the necessity and feasibility of the ABM. A proposed Sentinel site in the Boston suburbs had brought Senator Kennedy into the fight, along with volunteers recruited from the Harvard-MIT complex.

Although he was ostensibly looking out for the interests of his constituents, nothing that Kennedy did could be divorced from national politics. Furthermore, he had just been elected assistant majority leader. Some members of the new Administration were convinced that his anti-ABM activities were part of a grand design leading to the Presidential election of 1972. The expectation that he might well be the next President had no small influence on potential recruits to the anti-ABM forces.

To combat anti-ABM organizations, the Administration set up its own lobbying groups, the most prominent being the Citizens Committee for Peace and Security, headed by William J. Casey, a New York lawyer with White House connections.

President Nixon maintained a low profile during this stage of the maneuvering, limiting himself to a few telephone calls and personal chats with uncommitted senators. But other members of his Administration were active.

Determined to hold on to the dozen or so Republicans who were against the ABM, the opposition had carefully nurtured a bipartisan approach. But Representative Rogers C. B. Morton (R-Md.), the vigorous new chairman of the Republican National Committee, moved to drive a wedge between the opponents by raising the issue of party loyalty.

The move drew quick protests from Republican opponents of Safeguard. It particularly angered Senator Charles H. Percy (R-Ill.), one of the earliest ABM foes, who declared that "this is not a clear-cut case of party loyalty but a national issue. There cannot and must not be a loyalty test." Vice-President Spiro T. Agnew traveled the country trying to persuade GOP dissidents to come to the aid of the party. Senator Percy's staff reported that there was considerable "heat" on him from home. Morton denied pressuring anybody, but, following the Percy protest, there was a noticeable decline in overt action by the national committee.

However, this caution did not extend to some middle-level government officials, who took up free-lance lobbying for the ABM on their own. The experience of Senator William B. Saxbe, a freshman Republican from Ohio who opposed Safeguard, was typical. One day a federal official telephoned to warn him that his anti-ABM stand was going to cost him some patronage. "At first, I was burned up about it, but I later put it down to general ineptitude," the Senator said. "I checked on this guy and he didn't have a damn thing to do with patronage."

Another freshman, Senator Charles McC. Mathias, Jr. (R-Md.), disclosed that when he called a regulatory agency about a problem, he was told: "We might give more attention to your ideas if you would get on the team."

Senator Pearson also had several brushes with the Administration. First, an Army general informed an aircraft manufacturer in Kansas that the Pentagon might not be able to go through with a contract if Safeguard was defeated. Then he was not given advance notice—a standard courtesy for senators—when the Administration acted favorably on his request that some federal offices not be moved out of Kansas. So he lost the chance to take credit at home. Finally, the Department of Agriculture, after having given its private blessing to a bill Pearson had proposed, abruptly changed its mind.

By early May, the polls showed that the Administration was rapidly gaining votes. Forty-three senators now favored the ABM, 47 were opposed, and 10 remained uncommitted. Three previously uncommitted Republican freshmen swung behind the President at this point—Robert W. Packwood of Oregon, Robert Dole of Kansas, and Henry Bellmon of Oklahoma.

Bellmon's support turned on the forced resignation of a young Treasury Department tax expert, accused by the Senator of being a "highly partisan" Democrat who should be replaced by a deserving Republican. Treasury officials had fought Bellmon's demands for the removal of Paul R. McDaniel, an Oklahoman accused of "leaking" information to Fred Harris, the state's senior senator and chairman of the Democratic National Committee. But they finally yielded when the White House passed the word that Bellmon was threatening to vote against Safeguard.

Senator Packwood's decision was interpreted as a declaration of his independence of Oregon's senior senator, Mark O. Hatfield, a leading Republican foe of the ABM. Senator Hatfield had given at least tacit support to Wayne L. Morse, Packwood's Democratic opponent in 1968.

While Harlow and his deputy, Kenneth Belieu, a former Army colonel who lost a leg in Korea, prospected for votes on Capitol Hill, President Nixon was becoming by far the most effective Administration lobbyist. He began scurrying from senator to senator, applying his own brand of friendly persuasion. A steady stream of senators had breakfast, lunch, dinner, and countless cups of coffee with him.

Mr. Nixon was personally involved in the lobbying effort much more deeply than most people realize. He saw many members in private—many of them alone, without even a staff member present, so that the senator involved was free to keep the conversation to himself if he chose.

The locus of such talks varied, but most of them occurred in the President's office, or in the family dining room on the second floor of the White House, or in the East Room after Sunday services, or on evening cruises down the Potomac on the Presidential yacht, *Sequoia*. Nixon stated and restated this chief argument: that ABM deployment would carry weight in arms-limitation talks with the Russians and in dealing with the Chinese over the next decade.

"He pointed out that a plan can't progress until you try it, and this thing (the ABM) has been researched to death," Harlow recounted. "He emphasized the flexibility of his approach to the ABM."

Meanwhile, with a small staff of his own and an array of Pentagon people, Belieu operated what he called "an educational effort" at the Capitol. Material was prepared for senators who wanted clarification of various points. Administration witnesses were coached. Pentagon briefings were arranged.

This team operated out of Senator Dirksen's inner office, just down the hall from the Senate chamber. The room came with a private entrance, leather club chairs, a yellow sofa of faintly Empire antecedents, a well-stocked bar, and a large picture of the host with his hair as tangled as if he had just stepped out of a speeding convertible.

Since almost every senator favored continued research and development, the Administration emphasized to the uncommitted that deployment of Safeguard at missile sites in Montana and North Dakota should be considered "applied research." With senators confused by conflicting technical arguments, the lobbyists used the argument that it would weaken the President's hand to go to disarmament talks without the ABM. If that failed to persuade, they told the waverers that it is always the best policy to follow the lead of the President on security matters.

These turned out to be effective arguments, especially with the older members. Thus, the ABM further underscored the widening generation gap in the Senate: of the 21 newest senators, 12 were to oppose the ABM; but of the 19 most senior, only five would.

Paper Warfare

Now both sides began to set off the propaganda salvos they had been preparing for months. First out was the so-called Kennedy report, which concluded that the ABM "cannot perform effectively the missions suggested for it" but could launch a new arms race. Published in book form under the title ABM,[1] it was to sell 13,000 copies in hardback and 150,000 in paperback within two months.

On the other side, William J. Casey's pro-ABM lobby began to swing into action, with full-page newspaper advertisements proclaiming that "84 percent of all Americans support an ABM system." Although Casey denied knowledge of it, an inquiry showed that defense industries were well represented among the ad's sponsors. Angry ABM foes, hotly contending that the poll results were loaded, got an unexpected crack at Casey when the President nominated him to be a member of the General Advisory Committee of the Arms Control and Disarmament Agency. Since such a nomination requires Senate confirmation, Casey had to appear before Senator Fulbright's Foreign Relations Committee, where the anti-ABM sentiment was strong. The committee ultimately confirmed the Casey nomination, but not until its members had discredited the advertisement.

During the hearing, Senator Symington reported that he had received a letter from a business acquaintance questioning his opposition to the ABM. Then he told Casey:

> It was, I thought, a very unusual letter. So I called him up and said, "Why do you write me a letter about this? You do not know anything more about the ABM than I know about the products you sell. It's not your line of work." He said, "Well, I have been slugged into writing a few people," and I said, "Who slugged you?" and your name was mentioned first.

George D. Aiken (R-Vt.), the Senate's senior Republican, told Casey he had received 58 letters after the ad had appeared in three Vermont papers. Fifty-three opposed the ABM and only five favored it, he told Casey.

"I'd say since then probably the percentage has dropped to maybe five or six to one, but it is overwhelming in opposition," said the old Yankee, who was still uncommitted. "You are costing the taxpayers a lot of money, because I have to answer all these letters."

Twenty-two companies in 16 states had a financial stake in the ABM, and most were careful to avoid open congressional lobbying. But three major ABM contractors—Motorola, General Electric, and Lockheed—

contributed to the American Security Council, a conservative organization financed by private industry that took an active part in the fight for the ABM.

At almost the exact time the Kennedy report came out, the ASC issued its own analysis of the ABM, contending that Safeguard was part of a system "designed to give the American people a seamless garment of security in an age of nuclear danger." It distributed 20,000 copies of the report. But even more important to the pro-ABM campaign, the ASC mounted a massive direct-mail operation that flooded Senate offices with thousands of letters.

The ever-tightening struggle for votes continued. In early June a poll showed 48 votes against Safeguard and 47 for it. The months of strain began to tell on those involved. As one senatorial staff member muttered at the time: "We're deluged by the ABM; sickened by the ABM; drowned by the ABM."

Part of the folklore of Capitol Hill is that Congress abhors a confrontation. It was not surprising, then, that some members became seriously concerned by the prospect of the Senate and the White House drifting out of control toward a collision. They began to search for a way out.

"The Administration can win by one or two or three votes," said Mike Mansfield, "but that's what they called in Roman days a Pyrrhic victory. It would be better to compromise."

Senator Scott, a reluctant ABM supporter, agreed. Although he maintained that the President would win, Scott suggested that Nixon might compromise if he wanted unified congressional support—the type Scott felt was needed "from the standpoint of influencing world opinion."

From up in New England, where Senator Thomas J. McIntyre (D-N.H.) had gone on a speaking trip among his constituents, came a proposal that looked like a workable compromise—deployment of the computers and radars at the sites in Montana and North Dakota, but an indefinite delay on establishing missile launchers and acquiring land for 10 other planned ABM complexes.

The response was less than enthusiastic. The White House said the President rejected the notion of a compromise. ABM opponents, who saw the McIntyre plan as "a disguised deployment," said they would vote funds only for continued research and development at the Kwajalein test area in the Pacific—and not for deployment of any kind.

Senator McIntyre philosophically brushed off these responses. He sat back to wait until one side or the other realized that it was going to lose if it refused to compromise.

The Uncommitted Five

At long last, floor debate on the ABM got under way on July 8. According to all of the informal tabulations, the Senate was almost equally divided. That morning, Senator John C. Stennis (D-Miss.), floor manager of the military-procurement authorization bill, which contained $759.1 million for the first phase of Safeguard, came to the press gallery for the first time in 22 years. "Boys," he said, "I feel like I'm going to war."

Two days after the debate began, the opponents received their biggest psychological lift. Senator Aiken announced his opposition to immediate deployment of the ABM and urged the President to compromise to save his plan from defeat.

With the canny old Yankee saying that Safeguard was dead without modification, observers believed that a compromise was now just a matter of time. Without such a proposal, Aiken said, he favored an amendment by Cooper and Hart that would limit spending to research and development at Kwajalein but bar deployment.

A worried Senator Barry M. Goldwater (R-Ariz.) went to the White House to urge President Nixon to make a televised plea for Safeguard. Administration lobbyists began calling defense contractors around the country urging them to put in a word for the ABM with uncommitted senators.

Now there appeared to be just five: Senators Mike Gravel (D-Alaska), Warren G. Magnuson (D-Wash.), Clinton P. Anderson (D-N.M.), John J. Williams (R-Del.), and McIntyre.

One of the surprising things about the running series of nose counts taken by both sides was that some potential votes were based on assumptions. Senate lore had much to do with these assumptions, for one of the unwritten rules is that you do not ceaselessly importune a senator for his vote.

One assumption gone awry, as it turned out, involved the vote of Senator Winston L. Prouty (R-Vt.). After Aiken stated his position, the ABM opponents began to take Prouty's vote for granted. He had voted against Sentinel, was thought to be under the senior senator's influence, and could therefore be counted upon to vote against Safeguard. Or so the assumption went.

But Senator Prouty had problems of his own. He had the prospect of a tough fight for re-election ahead in 1970. Senator John G. Tower (R-Tex.), a major ABM proponent, was chairman of the Republican Senatorial Campaign Committee, which has a large campaign kitty at its disposal. Besides, President Nixon was popular in Vermont, and a strong endorsement from him would help. The schoolmasterish-looking Vermonter visited Belieu's command post with greater frequency. He received a briefing at the Pentagon, and, more importantly, he accepted invitations to four Potomac cruises with the President.

The opponents finally got wind of this. On July 13, Senator Cooper tried to call Prouty at home to persuade him to hold off a decision until later in the week, when the opposition would present its arguments at a secret session of the Senate. But it was Sunday morning, and Senator Prouty was out. He had gone to the White House for church services. The sermon that day was "The Great Adventure," linking the imminent moon shot with President Nixon's upcoming Asian tour. Over coffee in the State Dining Room after the service, Senator Prouty told the President he had made up his mind: he was going to vote for the ABM.

The news engulfed the ABM opponents in gloom. One of them put their situation in baseball terms: "If we had Prouty, the ball game would be over. Without him, it's extra innings."

At this point, the opposition was counting on 47 solid votes and figured that the Administration had 45 certain votes, with three others leaning its way. To win, then, the opposition needed four of the five publicly uncommitted votes.

But on the weekend after Senator Prouty announced his decision to the President, the opponents suffered an even less predictable blow. Senator Kennedy's car plunged into a Cape Cod pond under bizarre circumstances, taking the life of a young secretary—and much of the Senator's influence—with it. "It's difficult to say that things would have been different if Kennedy had been here," an anti-ABM strategist said of the crucial week following the accident. "But he did miss seven or eight days of the debate, and the loss of his influence just might have made the difference."

Baptism of Gravel

"I'm the only freshman who is still uncommitted, and everybody seems to think that because I'm a freshman I can be muscled around."

This was Senator Mike Gravel, a 39-year-old Alaskan, describing his misadventures as the only new senator who had taken no position on the ABM. (Pressure on older members was never so strong. As Senator Magnuson put it, "I've been around here for 33 years. It's pretty hard to exert pressure on me.")

The heat on Gravel came partly from Alaska oil men who thought a vote for Safeguard would ensure federal authorization to exploit Alaska's extremely valuable oil reserves. Some sources say that the oil men came into the picture at the behest of oil men from Texas, Senator Tower's home state.

In any case, the most important pro-ABM influence on Gravel was Senator Henry M. Jackson (D-Wash.), an expert on military affairs, a "hawk" on Safeguard, and President Nixon's first choice for Secretary of Defense. Jackson had long since adopted the role of mentor to his young colleague. After Gravel won the Democratic nomination for the Senate in 1968, both Jackson and Magnuson held a fund-raising affair for him in Seattle. When he came to Washington to be sworn in, it was "Scoop" Jackson who escorted him down the aisle of the Senate.

Thus, it was natural for Jackson to try to persuade Gravel to vote for Safeguard. He took him to the White House and provided briefcases bulging with information supporting deployment. But there were increasingly clear indications that Gravel, while still giving the impression of neutrality, had already made up his mind to vote against it.

On August 4, he and Jackson met in the Senate cloakroom. After an angry discussion, Senator Jackson declared: "If you vote against the ABM, it's going to cause you problems around here." As one witness put it: "That's about as strong as one senator ever gets with another senator—maybe stronger."

The next day, Gravel formally announced his intention to oppose deployment by supporting the Cooper-Hart amendment.

Gravel still refuses to discuss his encounter with Jackson. But, in talking about the effect his decision may have on his relations with the Administration, he shrugs and says, "I can see the situation where I will want something badly and reach out for it—and then the meat cleaver will come down on my hand."

Gravel's decision left four uncommitted senators. A secret session of the Senate, which turned into a noisy duel of charts between Jackson and Symington, changed no minds.

Then There Were Two

The opposition received one last boost: McIntyre and Magnuson came out against the ABM. Unable to get the Administration, now sensing victory, to accept his plan, McIntyre said he would vote for the Cooper-Hart proposal.

Magnuson had been under strong pressure to vote for Safeguard to ensure continued funding for the SST being built by the Boeing Company, the largest employer in his home state. Yet he remained one of the few senators to resist the President's moonlit arguments on the *Sequoia*.

"The President told me to 'let me know how you feel and I want to let you know how I feel.' I told him," the gruff old veteran said. He went on to vote against Safeguard, he said, because the weight of scientific opinion suggested that "it may never work."

This narrowed down the "uncommitted" to only two: the ailing and uncommunicative Senator Anderson and lame-duck Senator Williams of Delaware, who had already said he would not run for re-election in 1970. Opponents expected Williams to vote with the Administration, but they had some hope about Anderson. After all, Anderson had expressed concern that an issue of such importance would be decided on such a close vote.

With the voting only two days away, Senator Hart was saying the Senate was split 50–50, even if both uncommitted members turned out to be pro-ABM. A tie would give the Administration a victory—but it would be a moral victory for the opposition.

"We don't count moral victories around here," snapped Senator Tower. "It's the final vote that counts." And he confidently predicted that the final vote would be 51 to 49 in favor of the Administration. If his tally were correct, it meant that one of the members being counted upon to vote for the Cooper-Hart amendment was actually opposed to it.

Observers combed their lists in search of a likely suspect.

Cherchez la Femme

Could it be Senator Edward W. Brooke (R-Mass.)? To him, the threat to peace of the ABM was secondary to the multiple warhead (MIRV). He wanted the Administration to declare a moratorium on testing. Could the President have secured his vote with such a promise?

What about Senator Howard W. Cannon (D-Nev.)? He had originally voted for Sentinel but had voted against Safeguard in the Armed Services Committee. Nevada voters were worried that ABM deployment could mean continued nuclear testing in the state, which might frighten away tourist business. There were reports that $11 million trimmed from a Nevada water project might be restored if he voted right.

That night, Senator Margaret Chase Smith (R-Maine), the ranking minority member of the Armed Services Committee, who had consistently opposed the ABM in any form for over a year, quietly met with William C. Lewis, her administrative assistant, and drew up what she was later to call "a simple amendment" to the procurement bill.

The next afternoon, as Herb Klein was making a final call to newsmen to tell them George Meany, President of the AFL-CIO, was willing to make a pro-ABM statement if asked, Mrs. Smith came to the Senate floor.

Senator Fulbright was addressing a nearly empty chamber. Mrs. Smith, a 71-year-old widow known for her independence and the fresh rose she wears every day, chatted briefly with Senator Stennis. Then she asked Senator Fulbright for "thirty seconds" of his time, quickly dropped her amendment on the clerk's desk, and walked out.

Senator Hart took a quick look at it and was "confused and distressed." The amendment, he discovered, went much further than the Cooper-Hart proposal. It would prevent any funds at all from being spent on Safeguard, including research and development.

"The Republicans had been telling me all along that they had thirty votes on their side, but I could count only twenty-nine," said an elated "Scoop" Jackson. "As soon as she put in that amendment I knew she was the thirtieth."

Senators Cooper and Hart professed to be unalarmed. They said her amendment was "consistent" with Mrs. Smith's previous position. She had sponsored an anti-ABM amendment in committee, and, in 1968, contending that the system wouldn't work, had voted to strike all funds for deployment of Sentinel.

Had she taken a stand on Cooper-Hart?

No.

Had anyone asked her to take a stand?

No: her position was understood. (Later Mrs. Smith was to express surprise that no one from the opposition had been in touch with her.)

By nightfall, there was a gnawing fear among anti-ABM partisans that their chances for any kind of victory—either the moral victory of a tie vote or the actual victory that Senator Anderson's vote would bring—were evaporating.

Four of the leading anti-ABM strategists met privately to try to determine what Mrs. Smith would do. There appeared to be a strong possibility that she would vote for her amendment—which under the rules would be taken up before Cooper-Hart—and then, out of some twist of feminine logic, vote against Cooper-Hart because she was opposed to research and development, even if this meant approval of deployment.

But they broke up in disagreement over her motives. Two of the strategists said her intentions were good, if misguided. The others speculated that the Administration had been unhappy with her anti-ABM vote in committee and that Mrs. Smith wanted to vote *against* the ABM and *for* the Administration.

A seat on the Maritime Commission may also have been involved. The five-year term of James V. Day, a Maine man supported by Senator Smith, had expired, and the West Coast, which was unrepresented, was demanding the spot. A month after the vote, the President nominated Day for another five-year term.

The Vote

Finally, on August 6, the Senate prepared to vote. At 11 o'clock, the session opened with a prayer by the Rev. Dr. Edward L. R. Elson, the chaplain, "to deploy the strength of our true character, so that as a people we may send forth missiles of friendship and goodwill to all mankind."

Over in the New Senate Office Building, Senator Anderson's telephone rang with a call from President Nixon. Former Vice-President Hubert H. Humphrey, an ABM foe, had called earlier. So had at least six senators.

The day before, Averell Harriman, an old friend from Truman days, had dropped by in an attempt to persuade him to oppose Safeguard. So had another old friend, Walter Reuther, President of the United Auto Workers. Senators Cooper and Hart had spent an hour with him.

This visit was to be critical. The main point under discussion was a proposal drafted by Anderson but never introduced. It would have approved funds for research and development but blocked deployment until a special blue-ribbon commission had conducted a six-month inquiry into the feasibility of the ABM. It was to include all former secretaries of Defense as well as others to be designated by the President.

Senator Anderson's aim was to produce a substantial majority on the ABM—somewhere in the 60s or 70s—rather than the bare majority anticipated. Senators Cooper and Hart said they saw merit in the proposal— but in the words of Senator Hart, "we were not sure what Senator Anderson was going to do when we left his office."

On the other side, Senator Jackson exerted the most influence on the old man. Their relationship was also close; it extended back to the days when Jackson had come to the Capitol as an Anderson protégé. In 1961, moreover, Jackson had married Miss Helen Hardin, a secretary in Anderson's office. And when Jackson had taken over the Interior Committee from Anderson, he had kept Anderson appointees on the payroll.

On the morning of the vote, Senator Anderson drafted a brief statement saying that the ABM should be deployed "but that does not mean deployment in the next day, week, or month . . . from my point of view, there must be some program controlled by our military which could check carefully what other nations were doing and keep us fully safeguarded."

What had he received in exchange? Long-time observers of Anderson's activities speculated that he had won an IOU from the Administration that would fall due when he wanted some specific program for his constituency.

On the Senate floor, ABM opponents, unaware that their battle had been lost, struggled to keep Senator Smith's vote for Cooper-Hart. One observer, listening to the flattery directed at her, commented: "Not since Cleopatra have so many senators listened to one woman's proposition with such interest."

A newsman ran into Senator Gore under the steps of the Capitol where he was awaiting a luncheon guest. Did anyone have any plans to deal with Mrs. Smith, he was asked. "No-o-o," the Senator drawled, but his eyes flashed.

Mrs. Smith distributed a letter to her colleagues, saying (a) that she had "no confidence in Safeguard" and (b) that Cooper-Hart, by supporting research and development on the project, "merely postpones the time of decision."

By now it was late afternoon. The Senate was readying itself to vote on her amendment. Almost as if it were on the spur of the moment, Senator Gore rose with a small piece of paper in his hand and turned toward the only woman in the Senate.

Would she accept an amendment to her amendment, clearly spelling out that funds for radar and other components for ABM systems *other than Safeguard* would not be barred? Mrs. Smith looked thoughtfully across the chamber at Senator Gore for a few moments, then agreed.

Pandemonium. Now it was the Administration team's turn to show distress, for they realized that the Gore stratagem would save her vote for a proposal similar to Cooper-Hart. Barry Goldwater sprang to his feet to protest; he tried to block the addition of new language to the existing Smith amendment. Stennis and Richard B. Russell (D-Ga.) huddled on the floor; Jackson's face looked gray.

Then came a breathing space. Almost as if by design, Senator John Sparkman (D-Ala.), an ABM supporter, moved to suspend debate so that he could introduce to his colleagues Horace Maybray King, Speaker of the British House of Commons, who was a guest on the Senate floor.

Taking advantage of the line of senators forming in the back of the chamber to greet the visitor, Smith, Hart, Cooper, Symington, and Javits moved off the floor to a small room behind the rostrum to draft a new amendment.

Senator Gore came out to talk with the press. Seeing him in the lobby, Mary McGrory, of the *Washington Evening Star*, asked: "Are they working something out in there?"

"Why, yes," Gore replied.

"Then get back in there, man!" she shouted. Meekly, Senator Gore rejoined the small group.

When the session resumed, the senators voted down the original Smith motion, 89 to 11, and the new Smith-Gore proposal was called up. It stated that no funds could be used for any work on Safeguard but that research and development would be permitted on other advanced ABM systems.

The Administration forces, trying to reorganize, endeavored to raise doubts in the minds of some Cooper-Hart supporters about the meaning and extent of the new amendment.

Taking over for the pro-ABM forces, Senator Russell contended that the new language "will kill all the research and development of the so-called Safeguard system after senators have stood here on the floor day after day and stated they were in favor of research and development . . . that strangles it in its crib."

The Georgian's argument had an effect on two Cooper-Hart supporters, Senators Joseph Montoya (D-N.M.) and Cannon. Senators Hart and Symington moved in with quick explanations, holding them in line.

There are reports that at this point Senator Anderson privately told Mrs. Smith he would support the Smith-Gore amendment but that the word leaked out and Senator Jackson had a quick conversation with the New Mexican in the cloakroom. As they returned to the floor, they shook hands and smiled.

"This is a tragedy!" thundered Senator Stennis. "Some who say they're for research, they're going to have red faces when they see what they've done. Tragedy! It compounds tragedy!"

Senator Russell, who sits beside Senator Magnuson, tried to engage him in conversation. In a stage whisper, Magnuson turned to Senator Mansfield and asked: "How are you going to vote, Mike?"

"I'm voting for it."

"Well, I guess I am, too," Magnuson said.

"This system is not aimed at people," declared an irate Senator Tower. "It will not harm the hair on one Russian's head—even if it were fired off."

Senator John O. Pastore (D-R.I.), an ABM supporter known as the Senate's "screaming eagle," unburdened himself of a speech that seemed to be aimed at only one man—Senator Anderson, who sits beside him.

Finally, the clerk began to call the roll. There was no stretching out of names so that members could get to the floor. There was no need for it this time: all 99 men and one woman were in their places.

"Mr. Aiken!"

"Aye!"

"Mr. Allen!"

"No!"

"Mr. Allott!"

"No!"

"Mr. Anderson!"

A pause. And then, "No!"

The drama had ended. The vote, with the Vice-President joining in, was 51 to 50 against the quickly fashioned compromise.

The next time around, on Cooper-Hart, Mrs. Smith switched, amid a gasp from the gallery that sounded like air being sucked out of the chamber. Senator Tower had gotten his 51 to 49 vote.

The next day, Senator Hart sat in a brown leather chair in the President's Room off the Senate chamber and discussed the implications of the vote.

"It was one of the Senate's finest hours," he said. "We made the system work."

On the floor, the same coalition that had come within a vote of defeating Safeguard was winning a single-vote victory on an amendment introduced by several younger members to set up an auditing system for major military contracts.

Amendments to curtail testing and transport of chemical and biological warfare agents were to be approved and plans laid for a massive re-evaluation of Pentagon programs. The day in which a Defense Department request for a weapons system meant automatic approval had clearly passed.

In 1968, Senator Hart noted, he had failed in an attempt to reduce the Pentagon's research budget to the level of the previous year. In 1969, the Armed Services Committee itself had cut it by more than $1 billion.

In 1968, the Senate had spent only three days on the military procurement bill. In 1969, it had spent six weeks and the end was not in sight.

"If that's not progress," he said, "I don't know what is."

Note

1. Abram Chayes and Jerome B. Wiesner (eds.), *ABM* (New York: Harper & Row and Signet, 1969).

5.
THE WAR-MAKING MACHINERY

Robert J. Bresler

Soon after American troops moved into Cambodia, Sen. Jacob Javits warned his Senate colleagues: "The constitutional powers of Congress will remain hypothetical unless we take appropriate steps now to exercise our authority." Proposals soon followed to prohibit the future use of American troops in Cambodia, to repeal the Gulf of Tonkin Resolution, and to require the withdrawal of all American troops from Indo-China by mid-1971. Already Congressional legislation forbids the introduction of American ground combat troops into Laos or Thailand.

Thus, having followed Mr. Johnson into Vietnam and Mr. Nixon into Cambodia, Americans and their political representatives are, for the first time in a generation, seriously questioning the President's role in foreign policy. However, to deal effectively with so profound an issue, Americans will have to go far beyond current mild proposals for restrictions on Executive war making and recall an older tradition for dismantling (not merely limiting) this war-making power. That tradition is rooted in a history of radical and conservative criticism at least two generations old.

The first glimmers of Congressional restiveness were apparent in the summer of 1969. At that time, the Senate passed the National Commitments Resolution calling for Congressional approval of the commitment of troops and financial assistance to any foreign country. The odd coalition of dovish liberals and legalist conservatives which passed the resolution employed arguments similar in tone to those used by Sen. Robert Taft against President Truman's intervention in Korea and deployment of troops to Western Europe. These sentiments were the beginning of a revision of basic concepts of liberal internationalism. The Senate Foreign Relations Committee in its Report on the National Commitments Resolution, for instance, derided "the new generation of foreign policy experts who [encourage] the belief that foreign policy is an occult science which ordinary citizens, including members of Congress, are simply too stupid to grasp."

From Robert J. Bresler, "Illusions of Control: The War-Making Machinery," *The Nation*, August 17, 1970, pp. 105–109. © 1970 by Nation Associates, Inc. Reprinted by permission of the publisher.

The report condemned the use of crisis diplomacy to place "tremendous pressures upon members of Congress to set aside apprehensions as to the exercise of power by the executive, lest they cause some fatal delay or omission in the nation's foreign policy." In the Senate debate on the resolution, Senator Church denounced bipartisanship as a means "to gather more power into the hands of the President by eliminating between elections any semblance of organized opposition in Congress." Sen. Sam Ervin, a Southern conservative and strict constructionist, declared that the revolt against Executive war making meant simply "that the people will not support forever a policy which is made for them but without them."

The implication of such challenges stands on their heads the old arguments for a powerful Executive. For 30 years, American Presidents have exploited the notions of "expertise," "bipartisanship," and "crisis diplomacy" to secure their own supremacy. Presidential control of experts and information has deprived Congress of resources vital to its formation of independent judgments. Bipartisanship, a liberal canon once used quite skillfully to quarantine Congressional isolationists, has fudged the lines of political responsibility, baffled voters, and immobilized serious and sustained Congressional opposition. But the most potent of these weapons, crisis diplomacy, has frightened a Congress reluctant to risk decisions involving war or peace.

Examples abound. The preamble to the Tonkin Resolution speaks of a "deliberate and systematic campaign of aggression that the Communist regime of North Vietnam has been waging against its neighbors." Yet the Congress made no such finding, nor did the State Department until early 1965. What *did* happen in Tonkin in 1964? Or at the 38th parallel in 1950? Or in Santo Domingo in 1965? Were there threats to our national interest in Formosa in 1955, in the Middle East in 1957, in Cuba in 1961 serious enough to justify the sweeping grants of discretionary power Congress delegated to the President? Historians and ambitious journalists may be able to piece together these events months or years after they occurred, but while they were happening the only facts available were certified by an Executive stamp.

In addition to fearing a recalcitrant and parochial Congress, liberal internationalists and supporters of the Executive state have long feared the vagaries of an aroused public opinion. What if American opinion should one day weary of its global responsibilities and choose "the easy path"? Henry Kissinger, W. W. Rostow, and Walter Lippmann, all prominent liberal internationalists of the 1950s, indicated precisely such anxieties. In *Necessity for Choice*, Kissinger warned of Americans' "penchant for choosing the interpretation of current trends which implies the least effort"; Rostow (*The United States in the World Arena*) considered the American people "self-indulgent" because they were apparently so attracted by President Eisenhower's slogan of "peace and prosperity" in the 1956 election; and Lippmann, writing in *The Public Philosophy* in 1955, called public opinion "destructively wrong at the critical junctures . . . and a dangerous master of decision when the stakes are life and death."

These suspicions of the popular mind led to the establishment of institutional arrangements for shaping national security policy in ways which would insulate the "wisdom" of the few from the opinions of the many. Conflicts would be resolved at the top level of leadership and, in the words of V. O. Key, "clusters of public opinion in conflict [would] gradually dissolve because of lack of encouragement from prestigious givers of cues." (*Public Opinion and American Democracy.*)

Dissatisfied with Eisenhower's sluggish leadership, out-of-power liberals argued in the late 1950s for a national security state strengthened through tighter Presidential control, public sacrifice, and a revitalization of the chain of command. When they returned to power in the 1960s, there followed the McNamara reforms in the Pentagon and the Churchillian tone of the Kennedy administration. Democracy would be saved, despite itself, from the easy path.

In Vietnam and Cambodia lies bankrupt this elitist thinking and the notion that foreign policy is, at its best a product of secrecy and expert opinion. Since the Gulf of Tonkin, Americans have been public witness to the indiscriminate and arbitrary use of force, the manipulation of information and the unlimited waste of resources—all in the name of global responsibility and all justified by the transcendent wisdom of Presidential leadership. As Sen. Frank Church recently lamented: "The myth that the Chief Executive is the fount of all wisdom in foreign affairs today lies shattered on the shoals of Vietnam."

Now, after a generation of Executive war making, it begins to be apparent that the major political arguments for Executive domination of foreign policy can be turned against themselves: The destructive force of technology *requires* severe controls on its use rather than its immediate application in time of crisis; the need for expert guidance *requires* its detachment from Executive controls and its use as a public resource. The policy process must be opened up to public scrutiny so as to protect mankind from the "wisdom" of the few.

How did this fascination with Executive power flourish? Americans, especially liberals, should be embarrassed to recall, as Richard Neustadt, author of *Presidential Power*, has acknowledged, that they helped to create the myth which so loosely equated Presidential greatness with the exercise of war powers. A major point of the cold-war consensus, voiced particularly by liberalism and conventional political science, saw a dominant Executive as essential to a modern state and the conduct of contemporary diplomacy. Great Presidents would have to be strong Presidents, and for liberals it was no more than coincidence that strong Presidents invariably became war Presidents.

The liberal academic tradition contributed studies which treated the war-making adventures of our Presidents (be it Theodore Roosevelt's exploits in Panama, Wilson's in Mexico, Franklin Roosevelt's in the North Atlantic, or Truman's in Korea) as creative examples of the use of Executive power.

What this point of view neglected was the fact that these dominant Executives accepted public opinion, particularly in relation to war making, as something to be manipulated or structured, and that they treated Congress as an institution to be circumvented or co-opted. For example: after the negative public reaction to his quarantine-the-aggressor speech, Franklin Roosevelt adjusted only the timing of his policy, not its substance. Harry Truman's landmark decisions to build the H-bomb, rearm Germany, intervene in Korea, and cross the 38th parallel were all made within the insulated and rarified atmosphere of the National Security Council, with Congress offering only some advice and little consent, and the public offering only its prayers. John Kennedy's decisions to sponsor the Bay of Pigs invasion and to increase troop support in Southeast Asia were made unilaterally, if not surreptitiously. Lyndon Johnson's invasions of Vietnam and the Dominican Republic were willed by Executive decree and presented to Congress and the public at large as faits accomplis.

Liberal internationalists consistently (as during the troops-to-Europe and the Bricker Amendment debates) brushed aside attempts by Congressional conservatives to place strong constitutional and legal controls upon the President's conduct of foreign policy. Liberal rhetoric, such as that which permeated the campaigns of Adlai Stevenson and John Kennedy, spoke of national sacrifice and of the Presidential obligation to make the hard choices and to avoid the easy path. The easy path became inevitably equated with peace and compromise; the hard choices involved sustaining costly military programs and unpopular military adventures. This rhetoric, however, never clearly stated that those hard choices required that the Executive be protected from effective Congressional and public scrutiny.

As liberal internationalism became the dominant theme of foreign policy, the President became the capstone of policy and the Congress merely an ornament. It assumed that only the Executive could command the necessary scientific and military advice, determine military requirements, formulate appropriate responses to enemy threats, and thus orchestrate diplomatic and military policy. America's global interests, so the argument ran, needed a decision-making apparatus that would operate with secrecy and dispatch. This required unity of command and a policy determined solely by Presidential control and guidance.

In the face of this internationalism, constitutional arguments for the separation of powers and democratic controls upon foreign policy became irrelevant, if not obstructionist. Congressmen were merely annoying kibitzers who, as Kenneth Waltz has aptly put it in Foreign Policy and Democratic Politics, "may harry the officials and the diplomats who need time to think, may frighten them into timidity where boldness is required and block their attempts to move with subtlety to meet complex and shifting situations whose implications most Congressmen are not equipped to comprehend."

The slow and open deliberations of the democratic legislature constituted a threat to an Executive involved in the complicated and clandestine moves of nuclear diplomacy or counterinsurgency warfare. The personification of the disdain of internationalists toward Congress was Secretary of State Dean Acheson. When a Congressional committee began investigating the constitutional propriety of President Truman's decision to garrison troops indefinitely in Western Europe, Acheson admonished them: "The argument as to who has the power to do this, that or the other thing is not exactly what is called for from Americans in this critical juncture." Acheson was hardly alone. George Kennan, often in sharp disagreement with him on substantive matters of policy, shared his impatience with democratic procedures. Upon retiring, Kennan concluded that Congressmen should leave the policy makers and experts "unmolested." Lest we forget the breadth of this consensus, Senator Fulbright in 1961 warned Congress that "for the existing requirements of American foreign policy we have hobbled the President by too niggardly a grant of power." Thus the conventional wisdom of liberal internationalism assumed that American obligations abroad should not be fettered by strict constitutionalism at home.

From this perspective it was required that Congress disregard the concept of checks and balances, as it applied to foreign affairs, and become in fact an appendage of the Executive and an accomplice in an illicit process of constitutional revision. Congressmen who felt moved to dissent should do so quietly and privately, lest they become heretics. In a classic example, Senator Fulbright lost his influence with President Johnson only when he became a public rather than a private critic of the Vietnamese policy. In *American Political Institutions and Public Policy*, Eugene Eidenburg quotes this frank admission by a White House aide to Johnson:

> Fulbright decided unilaterally to leave the team and take his differences of opinion to the public forum. That is not the way the game is played. The President and his Administration can tolerate differences of opinion but within a structure of dissent that is quietly approached.

By publicly questioning the President's judgment in a moment of assumed emergency and violating "a structure of dissent that is quietly approached," legislators such as Fulbright forfeit any influence they may have on Executive policy.

Where do we go from here? Perhaps a new appreciation for Congress is upon us. Congress remains an anomaly. It is the one major American institution to resist the bureaucratic-managerial norms which pervade our political system and have proven disastrous when applied to foreign affairs. Our bureaucratic foreign policy spawned clandestine wars, as in Laos; and the managerial mentality found the path to Vietnam through its counterinsurgency calculations. Legislative openness, deliberation, and delay—characteristic of democratic assemblies and the bane of managerial efficiency—may be the best hope of those who desire a saner foreign policy.

"What would have been on my mind," Senator Church has conjectured, "if President Johnson had said to a joint session of Congress that the government of North Vietnam had by stealth invaded and attacked the government of South Vietnam on a day that would live in infamy? I would have said, 'Where is the evidence?' "

Yet it must be acknowledged that Congressional acquiescence in the expansion of Executive war making stems in large part from the desire *not* to be held politically responsible for crucial decisions. And in spite of the growing new consensus against national commitments made secretly and independently by the Executive, Congressional leadership remains openly in complicity with the national security bureaucracy. Congressional committees on the armed services and on atomic energy jealously guard the privileges of those agencies they are assigned to oversee. In major cold-war crises Congress may continue to shrink from the risks of decision making and permit the President to define both the problem and its solution—invariably in military terms.

Thus, those who hope for a radical redirection of American foreign policy will find little solace in simply transferring the war-making power to Congress. With Executive power lying often within their grasp, liberal Congressmen have been reluctant to challenge its use; and conservatives, single-minded on the question of anti-communism, have been blinded to their own libertarian traditions. It is problematical that the dilemma of Executive war making could be resolved merely by passing new laws, resolutions, or even constitutional amendments. In fact, laws restricting Executive discretion in foreign policy already exist in abundance, and the Constitution itself clearly places the war-making power with Congress.

The arguments for legal controls assume naively that the Executive can be granted all the instruments of war making and then, simply because he lacks the legal authority, be constrained in their use. Again and again we have seen Presidents acting in haste—Korea, Cuba, Santo Domingo, Vietnam, Cambodia—and then sending their legal staffs to serve up some rationale to appease public and Congressional opinion. Power cannot be lavishly granted with one hand and hedged by legal restrictions with the other. Once power configurations are so imbalanced, constitutional guarantees alone cannot reset them.

Public officials often fail to understand this fact. One as knowledgeable in the ways of policy making as Senator Fulbright insists that the Congress should prevent the President "from believing that he has the authority to intervene because we have provided some kind of instrumentality that will enable him to do so." With the same naïveté, the Senate can, in one month, vote overwhelmingly for the National Commitments Resolution inhibiting Presidential power and, in the next month, by similar margin, vote funds for the C-5A transport to provide, according to Sen. John Stennis, "the total for maximum mobility which is an essential element of all our military planning."

Merlo Pusey, author of an otherwise perceptive study of war making, *The Way We Go To War*, betrays a similar myopia. After a careful review of Presidential usurpation from the Greer incident to Tonkin, Pusey concludes that what is needed is a new War Powers Act, which would begin "a new order of teamwork [between President and Congress] in the awful business of committing the country to armed conflict." This would in substance do no more than affirm the constitutional principle that establishes the right of Congress to move troops into combat, and would leave intact the vast military-intelligence machinery that created the disasters of Tonkin and the Bay of Pigs. The recommendations neglect the sorry history of similar legislative controls such as the United Nations Participation Act of 1945. That act, passed as enabling legislation for the United Nations Treaty, requires Congressional approval prior to any authorized use of American troops under United Nations command. When he dispatched American troops to Korea, President Truman simply ignored it and allowed both the act and the Constitution itself to evaporate "in a puff of rhetoric." Other American Presidents, with much the same arrogance, have brushed aside the legal commitments of the Rio Treaty, the United Nations Charter, and the SEATO Pact in order to send troops to the Congo, the Dominican Republic, Laos, Thailand, Vietnam, and now Cambodia.

While Congress can on occasion expose the Executive to embarrassing public scrutiny, it unfortunately remains an institution encrusted by the seniority system and special-interest politics. Therefore any effort for constitutional revision must simultaneously view with those institutional pressures which propagate our state of protracted conflict—the corporate linkages with reactionary elites from Greece to Brazil, profligate defense profiteering, and the bureaucratic corruption of expert knowledge.

The solution, then, is evident. If the Congress is to reclaim its war-making *authority*, it must seek to control the war-making *machinery* and to slow down the process of decision making. The challenge then is to develop procedures which insinuate Congress deep into the very fabric of policy making and, in a sense, force it to accept its constitutional mandate. To do this requires making expert opinion a public resource and information a public commodity. Defense laboratories such as the Lincoln Lab at MIT could be made responsible to Congress, as is the General Accounting Office; it could then provide the legislators with an independent means to evaluate weapons systems.

In the American experience there is a tradition which eschews large standing armies, foreign entanglements, entrenched centralized power, and asserts the Congressional prerogative. Possibly a new vision of an open and democratic foreign policy can be defined out of that tradition, so as to hedge power with strong institutional constraints, expose it to public scrutiny and make its application deliberative. Still needed are new public avenues of participation and clear institutional obstacles to Executive domination.

In William Borah and Robert Taft may be found the strands of such a tradition, combining the Populist Left and libertarian Right and confronting directly the problem of war making. It was Senator Taft's amendment to the Selective Service Act of 1940 that restricted the deployment of conscripts beyond the Western Hemisphere; Sens. Gerald Nye and Robert La Follette, Jr., proposed in 1941 a national advisory referendum on whether Congress should approve the use of land, naval, and air forces outside the Western Hemisphere; and Sen. Arthur Vandenberg suggested in 1932 a constitutional amendment clearly defining the power of Congress to prevent defense profiteering.

These thoughts—from the Right and Left—went beyond legalism. This legacy and our grim cold-war past should leave no doubt that if we are to avoid the drift into a Napoleonic state, the assignment will be not simply to relocate the war-making power but rather to dismantle it.

6.
EULOGIES AND EVASIONS

Robert Sherrill

When Richard Russell died, the Ninety-second Congress got a swell chance early in the session to limber up its rhetorical pipes. If one recalls that the Senator, by chairing the Armed Services Committee from 1951 to 1968, was a principal creator of the cold-war disaster and of our hysterical anti-Communist militarism, one may not be inclined to agree with Sen. Quentin Burdick that Russell's departure was "a great loss to the nation," or with Sen. Vance Hartke, that a suitable epitaph for Russell is "the greatest man I have ever known in public life, beyond comparison," or with Sen. Milton Young, that "Dick Russell was a part of God's plan . . . his silver beams did pierce far into the gleam of America's night"; or with Sen. Frank Church, that "His passing is like the felling of a great tree in a small forest." And when one considers that for the past two years Russell chaired the Senate Appropriations Committee, which gave little assistance to the needy and much assistance to the wealthy special interests, one might be especially hard pressed to agree with Rep. William Colmer's assessment of Russell's career: "Rising like a huge mountain above the undulating plain of humanity," which a future historian will be able to see only by lifting "his eyes high toward heaven to catch its summit."

Such rhetoric on the death of a colleague, especially one who packed plenty of clout during his lifetime, is to be expected. Unfortunately, there is some evidence that in this instance both liberals and conservatives meant it, for the Ninety-second Congress has already shown its determination to go down the same old racist Southern path (much beloved by Mr. Russell) which just about every previous Congress has trod so faithfully. There were some signs of this in the Senate, and many more in the House.

The House played another act in the roadshow tragedy that for six years has been billed as "The Mississippi Challenge." The curtain went up in 1964 when the Mississippi Freedom Democratic Party (MFDP) showed up at the Democratic National Convention and demanded that they be

From Robert Sherrill, "92nd Congress: Eulogies and Evasions," *The Nation,* February 15, 1971, pp. 197–200. © 1971 by Nation Associates, Inc. Reprinted by permission of the publisher.

seated in place of the all-white delegation on the ground that the whites
had been illegally chosen via a Jim Crow election. Nobody at the convention doubted it, but still the blacks were offered only two meaningless
"roving delegate" positions; the MFDP refused.

Then, you will remember, that great thespian Hubert Humphrey,
fearing that if the plantation hands became too boisterous they might queer
his chances to play Vice-President, tried to get the MFDP to accept the
compromise.

Mrs. Fannie Lou Hamer, the legendary civil rights fighter from
Ruleville, Mississippi, recalled the embarrassing episode: "Mr. Humphrey,
he kept telling us to compromise for two votes. He seemed very upset, very
upset. Our attorney at the time [Joseph Rauh, an intimate Humphrey sup-
porter] told us if we didn't go for the two votes, if we didn't slow down,
Mr. Humphrey wouldn't get the nomination. I declare it was Mr. Rauh,
and that's what he said. Mr. Humphrey was sitting right there when Mr.
Rauh said that and he had tears in his eyes—I mean Humphrey had tears in
his eyes—when Joe Rauh said it. I declare that is the truth. I asked [Hum-
phrey] if his position was more important than the lives of 400,000 black
people in Mississippi."

Mr. Humphrey was too much of a gentleman to answer the question. But the Mississippi blacks were herded aside in 1964 and told to come
back four years later and everything would be fixed up just fine.

And sure enough, in 1968, the Aaron Henry-Charles Evers delegation was seated at the Democratic National Convention and the old white
Mississippi crowd was excluded. Loyalists were named to the national
committee, and the loyalist wing of the Mississippi party—now calling itself
not just the Democratic Party but the Democratic Party of the State of
Mississippi (DPSM), as if the new label would wipe out the old racist
taint—went into operation with the full stamp of approval of the national
Democratic headquarters. The great day had arrived at last: the Mississippi
Democrats were actively operating within the national party.

Well, not quite. Theoretically, perhaps, but not practically. Came
the elections of 1970 and the new, integrated DPSM tried to get on the
ballot and couldn't. Twice it tried, and twice the Mississippi Secretary of
State sent back the application with a note saying that there already was a
Democratic Party on the ballot—the Democratic Party of Gov. John Bell
Williams, Sens. Jim Eastland and John Stennis, and Reps. Thomas Gerstle
Abernethy, Jamie L. Whitten, Charles H. Griffin, Gillespie V. (Sonny)
Montgomery, and William Meyers Colmer—and that was good enough for
him.

Stennis and, of course, all the Congressmen were up for re-election
that year and the DPSM invited them all to file for office under the DPSMs
auspices, or at least to file jointly through the new loyalist party. They
refused.

Instead, they ran for office under a party label that was not recognized by the national Democratic headquarters; they ran in a party whose leadership was the same as had been refused seating at the 1968 national convention, and which since then had continued racism unabated, as best illustrated when Governor Williams cleared the state highway patrol of any guilt in the massacre at Jackson State College.

If the proudly racist Mississippi Congressional delegation could run a wildcat race and still be seated as bona fide Democrats with full seniority, then the question would be: is there really a national Democratic Party?

This was the question behind the 1970 Mississippi Challenge. Heading it on the inside was Rep. John Conyers of Detroit, who at least momentarily seems to be the spokesman for his fellow 11 blacks in the House. He would raise the question at the Democratic caucus at the beginning of Congress, hoping—though not hoping with much hope—to strip the Mississippians of their seniority.

What would this have meant? Most important, it would have meant dumping Colmer as chairman of the Rules Committee, which has been the graveyard of progressive legislation since New Deal days.

Other enormous benefits would have accrued to the nation from the deposing of the Mississippians. Representative Whitten would no longer have throttled farm reforms from the chair of the House Appropriations Subcommittee on Agriculture, and that other advocate of agri-business interests, Rep. Thomas G. Abernethy, would have lost his chairmanship of a House Agriculture subcommittee. And if the House had taken the step, the Senate would have had a hard time explaining why it didn't follow suit and depose Senator Stennis from his chairmanship of the Senate Armed Services Committee.

The Democratic Study Group (DSG), the House liberals, issued a special report in which the legal proprieties were laid out. Since the Mississippians hadn't run as national Democrats or as Republicans but as their own homespun variety of a party called "Democratic," they were clearly third-party candidates, and the DSG reported that there was ample precedence for putting third-party politicians at the bottom of the seniority list. It had been done to eight third-party Congressmen since 1930: three from the Progressive Party, three from the Farmer-Labor Party, one from the Independent Party and one from the American Labor Party. As the names of those parties indicate, they were on the left. So the question in 1971 was: would Congress do to right wingers what it had done to left wingers in the past?

Among other benefits to be had from deposing them, said the DSG, was party discipline: "The precedent would strengthen the Democratic Party in Congress by denying leadership posts to those—such as Representatives Colmer, Whitten and Abernethy—whose use the posts conferred on them by the Democrats to subvert the Democratic Party in their home states and in Congress."

As for Representative Conyers, he saw the issue much more simply and perhaps more accurately: "What we were really answering Congressionally was what we thought of blacks in the Democratic Party. And secondly, we were deciding whether we would allow any gang of political thugs to steal the Democratic Party label in a state." Naturally, Conyers first sought the support of the leadership. He went to the Speaker-to-be Carl Albert, who comes from what is quite appropriately known as the "Little Dixie" section of Oklahoma. Conyers recalls:

> I sat down with Carl, and Carl and I started out—
> this was on a Thursday, I shall never forget it—and Carl was as
> sympathetic as he could be. As a matter of fact, Carl and I
> have always had very good relations. Friendly. I could always
> go into the Majority Leader's office all the time. And so I was
> in there explaining this thing to him, the legal difficulties, and
> oh man, he sympathized with me totally. He understood the
> necessity that forced and compelled me to bring this thing,
> but no support would I get from him.
> He just *couldn't*. You know, how's a guy going to rip
> off five Mississippi Congressmen with a total of 114 years
> seniority? In other words, it didn't matter what the merits
> were—this was out. But he understood that I had to do it.

As Conyers sat there listening to Albert's pious fraternalism, he began to get mad. "Something happened to me," he says. "Just two weeks before, I had been on national hookup, *Issues and Answers*, and I had said there would be new winds of change with Carl Albert. Oh, yes, I had said things were going to be different. And all of a sudden I realized that nothing was going to change."

Conyers might have been more sympathetic if Albert had had to play it cool in order to win the speakership, but,

> Here was this guy unanimously elected—nobody in sight to
> challenge him. He couldn't have been defeated if he had
> wanted to be, and he sat there telling he was going to counte-
> nance the precedent that sanctions the most vicious form of dis-
> crimination that is practiced politically in any of the fifty states
> of the union. He couldn't be defeated. He was undefeatable,
> but he wouldn't support me.

So Conyers on the spot told Albert he was withdrawing his support, and after thinking it over all night he decided to run against Albert. Why not? "Look at my programs," says Conyers, "my votes, my statements—they make far more sense than his do. If I was the Speaker, I could heal the Democratic Party and break up this Southern Democratic-Republican coalition by putting my finger on what was the biggest, single point of reform— knocking out the Mississippi delegation."

So Conyers started calling colleagues he thought might be interested in dumping Albert, who, at best, represents the last withered branch of the Sam Rayburn line. He says he found "the liberals were afraid of the

Mississippi Challenge. They honestly were. And they were afraid of the logic of somebody running against Carl Albert. The standard response was, 'Jesus, John, you know I'd vote for you but I'm committed. Carl Albert pinned me down—what am I supposed to do? Go back on my word?' "

> And I began to realize that what we were doing was just going through the motions. Here we are in the 92nd Congress talking about what we're going to do to Nixon in 1972, and these guys are still holding on to Colmer, who is out of the past. The only thing he can do is hurt us, and the question is, how much are we going to let him hurt us?
>
> And then you think of poor Aaron Henry and these guys who for twenty years have been fighting to get in the Democratic Party! What the hell for? You know, it's just a ridiculous circumstance here—we're now asked to ratify the Democratic Convention Posture and these guys say, no, no, our friendship, our loyalty, our camaraderie over these last twenty to thirty years are far more important than us unifying the party, for speaking out definitely to blacks and oppressed— hell, no. We're going to beat Nixon, and screw the blacks at the same time. And you know, I say, Carl Albert and Hale Boggs made a mistake. It's my bet that they're not going to be able to do that. I just don't have confidence that they can put this kind of game together. They're going to have to go into the black community and explain why Conyers' motion to challenge these guys couldn't win their support and approval.

Conyers didn't get much help lobbying for the Mississippi Challenge. The United Auto Workers said they were for it, but if they lobbied they did it mighty quietly. The AFL-CIO was also conspicuously quiet, and reportedly the NAACP was also. The only outfit actively pushing with him, says Conyers, was the momentarily revived Americans for Democratic Action.

Inside the caucus, only two other Congressmen, one white, Bob Eckhardt of Texas, and one black, Charles Diggs of Michigan, joined Conyers in arguing for stripping seniority from the Mississippians.

Most of the heavy arguments on behalf of the whites-only Mississippi Democratic Party came from Wilbur Mills, Wayne Hays, and Jim Wright. Wright of Fort Worth—one of LBJ's protégés—was especially mean and especially corny. Rather than exclude the Mississippi segregationists, he said (quoting that old poem), the party should draw a circle and pull people in. We can't afford these divisions and animosities. We're off to a new start, fellows. Let's put these black-white hatreds behind! The Democratic party is big enough for everybody!

Conyers thought he would perhaps get 100 votes for the Mississippi Challenge. He got 55. In his race for the speakership, he received 20 votes. So if you want to know how many Democrats there are in the U.S. House of Representatives who want to throw off the Southern yoke and free the Rules Committee, there's your answer: 55.

And what are the House reformers going to do about their defeat? Nothing. They'll just go on meeting in little groups, saying nice things to one another. There are enough blacks in the House—12—to get together and call themselves a black caucus. Some are cautious and some are militant, and the militant ones say they will try to convert the cautious ones. So there's that way to pass the time. And then there's an even smaller group of blacks and whites—Ryan, Conyers, Kastenmeier, Eckhardt, Rosenthal, Mikva, Fraser, Burton, and others—who get together and say liberal things to one another from time to time.

Abner Mikva, that remarkable fellow from the Second Ward of Chicago, perhaps because he has been in Washington only a couple of years, appraises the situation clearly:

> The biggest single disappointment to a new man is the intransigence of the system. You talk to people and they say, "You're absolutely right, something ought to be done about this." And yet, somehow we go right on ducking the hard issues. We slide off the necessary confrontations with problems. This place has a way of grinding you down.
>
> Some people around here still quote Sam Rayburn's "go along to get along" thesis as an ethical way of life, not just a pragmatic way of life. They quote that as the way a good Congressman should act. I've had it quoted to me innumerable times, including by people who are genuinely concerned about the issues I'm concerned about and who are genuinely concerned about my own welfare. They tell me, "You've got a great career here." And every time I finish that kind of a conversation I go back and ask myself, why do they think I have a great career here? I'm one of the worst go-along guys in politics. They seem to be elevating to an ethical level the politician's impulse to get re-elected. But I don't know anything in the Constitution or the Bible that says everyone who has been elected should do everything he can to be re-elected.
>
> I wouldn't be so perturbed if they would say, "Here's some practical advice." But they always try to raise it to an ethical level. They say the seniority system isn't so bad because it benefits some good guys. They say it is important to be elected if you are a good guy because Congress needs you.
>
> Well, the way I feel, it's sometimes important to be defeated, too. Al Lowenstein was defeated because he stood for the right things, and so his loss will nourish the Republic. There were dozens of other guys who were defeated, too, last year, but if you asked what defeated them, nobody could tell you. We know what defeated Al Lowenstein. His constituency didn't agree with his views on civil liberties and the war in Vietnam.

There aren't many in the Ninety-second Congress who would agree with Mikva. (In fact, it's pretty easy to see why the Army selected him as one to investigate.) The attitude of the Ninety-second Congress is the old traditional one: play it safe in caucus, play it safe on the floor, play it safe in committee. Go along to get along, and when you kick off after 30 or 40 years, your colleagues will pile into an Air Force plane and go to your home town and say nice things over your grave, as they did for Richard Russell, or they'll fill the *Congressional Record* with remarks about how you were a huge mountain above an undulating plain or a part of God's plan. The United States Congress has its own measure of things.

7.
THE COMMITTEE SYSTEM

Charles L. Clapp

"No one will be able to understand Congress unless he understands the committee system and how it functions," said one congressman at the opening session of the Brookings round table conference. The House and Senate must, of course, work their will on legislative proposals that are cleared by committees, but it is in the committee rooms that the real work is done. There, choices are made between alternative proposals, and decisions are reached to pigeonhole or kill outright other bills. The latter actions virtually eliminate the possibility of further consideration by the House or Senate; the former involve determinations that generally govern the reception of the measure in the parent body. By weighting a measure with unpalatable items though reporting it, a committee can hasten its demise. By amending a bill so as to weaken the opposition it can almost guarantee success. By endorsing a measure strongly, a committee increases significantly the likelihood that it will be accepted. Close House and Senate adherence to committee recommendations is the practice, although recommended legislation in controversial fields, such as agricultural policy, may face defeat on the floor. Normally, few substantive changes are made during floor debate. The volume and complexity of legislative proposals, the strong tradition of deferring to the "specialist," the search for ways to reconcile often conflicting pressures on congressmen, the very size of Congress—all conspire to enhance the authority of committee action. According to a congressional committee study, 90 percent of all the work of the Congress on legislative matters is carried out in committee.

The influence of committees in the legislative process is bolstered by the practice, particularly prevalent in the Appropriations Committee, of confining efforts to defeat or modify a proposal to activities within the committee itself. Once the battle has been fought and resolved there, those in the committee minority often do not press their case on the House floor. If they do intend to press it, they are careful, at the time of the committee

From Charles L. Clapp, *The Congressman: His Work as He Sees It*, pp. 241–59. © 1963 by The Brookings Institution. Reprinted by permission of the publisher.

vote, to "reserve" the right to do so. But the emphasis is on closing ranks and presenting a united front.

Committee pre-eminence and the difficulties involved in setting aside measures receiving committee endorsement have led party leaders on occasion to ignore seniority in making assignments to committees handling crucial or controversial legislation, as has been illustrated in Chapter 5. They also have led the executive and the interest groups to concern themselves with the assignment process.

The central role of committees in the legislative process has also underscored the importance of strategic referral of bills to committee: by careful attention to the wording, a congressman may have his bill sent to a committee more favorably disposed to it than the one to which it might otherwise have been referred.

Powers and Procedures

Committees are virtually autonomous bodies, hiring their own staffs, establishing their own rules of procedure, proceeding at their own pace for the most part, and resisting on occasion the urgings of the party. Chairmen may openly and successfully flaunt the party leadership, or they may have such stature that they are seldom requested to follow specific courses of action. And the reports of committees or their subcommittees may become as binding on executive departments as if they were law.

Committees differ tremendously in composition and method of operation, and may change significantly from one year to the next. As one congressman said, "Each committee tends to be unique in its unwritten rules—an organism in itself. The character changes with different chairmen and with different congresses." Some rely heavily on staff, interest groups, or the executive; others are relatively free from all such influences. Some are characterized by a lack of partisanship and generally report measures to the House floor by unanimous or nearly unanimous vote; strong partisanship is typical of others. In view of the central role of committees in the legislative process, an understanding of the working relationships that exist within the various committees is very helpful—often indispensable—to those who desire to influence legislation.

Just as different personalities alter procedures, the impact of a committee on the outlook of its members may be perceptible also. For example, service on the Appropriations Committee seems to make members more conservative. This is true in part because the membership is recruited carefully from the ranks of representatives likely to be susceptible to the socialization process. Although their attitudes toward issues vary, they are considered "reasonable" and "responsible," capable of adjusting easily to committee procedures and committee thinking. The fact that there is little turnover in committee membership tends to promote a group identity that is unusual and that aids in the assimilation of new members. Explained one liberal who sits on the committee:

The Appropriations Committee develops a strange sort of breed. As soon as you get on the committee somehow you become more responsible as a member of Congress. You find you have to justify expenditures and you cannot pass over any situation very lightly. As a result you become more conservative. I think it is fair to say that on the whole the members of the Appropriations Committee are more conservative than most members of Congress. Committee members pause long before they support various programs. They are always thinking of what additional taxes are necessary to carry these programs out. Most congressmen, on the other hand, are just thinking how worthwhile the program would be, neglecting the point of how much additional taxes would be required.

The important work of committees takes place in closed rather than open sessions. It has been estimated that in recent years from 30 percent to 40 percent of committee meetings have been held in executive session. While House committees dealing with money matters and unusually technical or sensitive legislation, such as the Appropriations, Ways and Means, and Foreign Affairs committees are concerned with, are more disposed to meet in private than most other groups, nearly every committee makes fairly extensive use of this procedure. Closed sessions facilitate compromise, promote candor and serious discussion, and eliminate the temptation to "play to the spectators," which occasionally overcomes members of Congress. Party representatives may have met together prior to a "mark-up" session in order to determine strategy and the party stand on a bill. But partisan stances are often sublimated and an atmosphere conducive to thoughtful consideration of legislation is more likely to prevail. Here representatives whose names the general public would not recognize may develop reputations among their colleagues based on their insights and their capacity for hard work. Despite the obvious advantages of holding executive sessions on many kinds of problems, there are persistent complaints, particularly from the press, that too many committee sessions are conducted behind closed doors. Far from promoting better legislation, these critics assert, closed sessions are often detrimental since, there, decisions are reached that would not be tolerated were the proceedings conducted in public.

Majority-Minority Relationships   The degree of cooperation existing between majority and minority members of a committee may be more dependent on the personal relationships between the chairman and ranking minority member than on the subject matter area involved. These two individuals usually have served together on the committee for an extended period and may have learned to work together comfortably. Retirement of one of them may alter intracommittee relationships. As one congressman illustrated:

> We had excellent relationships in our committee between the chairman and _____ [long-time ranking minority member]. But since the latter's retirement last year things have changed. I have sensed a strained relationship between the chairman and _____ [the new ranking minority member]. I don't look for close liaison to continue. I think a sharp clash is going to develop very shortly.

Intracommittee relationships may be changed in other ways, too. The leadership may seek to alter the kind of legislation reported by a committee by deliberately "packing" it with people of different philosophy than those who have long held control. A single issue may so solidify party lines that years of cooperation and harmony will be swept aside. Or interference by the Executive in the normal committee operation may have drastic effects. One Democratic congressman described such an incident:

> _____, who heads one of our subcommittees, doesn't always support our Democratic party's position. When the _____ bill came along, he supported President Eisenhower's proposal, and we had to maneuver for months and months to get him straightened out. That was the start, really, of unity among the committee Democrats. The Republicans had to be for Ike's plan because pressure was put on them. They finally stood with the administration on all parts of the bill instead of going along with the old procedure whereby we took care of committee members and other individuals. There were so many weaknesses in administration policy that we were able to unify all of the Democrats to vote against everything in the bill. In the course of considering it, interparty relationships got so bad that they have carried over into other programs. Recently, every vote on an important measure in the committee has been almost a straight party vote. That is fine with us because it is much easier when you can write the legislation among the Democrats. The Republicans started having caucuses and we started having them too.

That statement led to the following discussion regarding the cooperation between majority and minority on committees:

> On our committee we have a close relationship with the ranking minority member. In House tradition the minority member is consulted in scheduling legislation, but I wonder how many committees do this. I have been critical of consultation because I think we fail to get legislation passed if we try to iron it out with the minority ahead of time. In your committee, the minority isn't consulted at all about legislation, I suppose.

> *

> It is consulted to a degree. But last year we didn't tell them in advance that we were going to vote on the TVA bill.

> They had hundreds of amendments to offer to it, and we suggested that they offer them all en bloc. So we had ten minutes to consider the bill. That's democracy in action! It is all contrary to the textbooks, but it is the only way we ever could have gotten a bill out of the committee.

As the first speaker noted, consultation between leading majority and minority members of a committee is not uncommon. Members of some committees and subcommittees work in such close harmony that even the questions the chairman and staff intend to put to witnesses are furnished to the minority prior to hearings.

A Republican was sharply critical of one House committee, attributing what is generally regarded as an undistinguished record on legislation to excessive partisanship and domination by the chairman.

> Everything that could be wrong with a committee is wrong with that one. The chairman has all the power to schedule legislation; he won't schedule anything. He makes trades on things in which he is interested. When hearings are scheduled, he is abusive to departmental witnesses. He and the ranking member on his side take up the time; anyone below the ranking one or two members on our side has no opportunity to say anything. The committee is nothing but a propaganda agency. That is demonstrated by the fact that no substantive legislation in the areas of its jurisdiction has been passed in the time I have been in Congress. More of that committee's bills are defeated on the floor than those of any other committee. There is no discussion between Democrats and Republicans on the committee, and the Republicans never know what is going to happen.

Another Republican told of one way in which committee staffs may be used for partisan purposes.

> I am on two committees which practice a good deal of partisanship. The chief clerk of one of them kept a record of how many subcommittee meetings I attended. It included not only the subcommittee on which I served but those to which I did not belong. It included the amount of time I spent in each, and what I said. The information was forwarded to my opponent. I couldn't figure how my opponent knew so much about my activities last session, or why the chairman of the committee made snide remarks about me during meetings. Finally I found out. I was in the district talking about southern domination of our committee, and it got back to the chairman.

Problems of Jurisdiction and Intercommittee Coordination   Many thoughtful members of the House are concerned about problems of overlapping jurisdiction, intercommittee coordination, lack of proper liaison and exchange of information, and situations in which committees hearing testimony and presumed to possess special competence do not actually make the decisions. Matters relating to defense and national security, foreign policy, and science are among those for which it is often difficult to determine jurisdiction. Rivalry may develop between committees with common interests as they seek to establish their primacy in a certain field or to undertake hearings or investigations which promise to arouse widespread interest and publicity. Committees are jealous of their prerogatives and resent intrusion. Information gained may not be shared with competitors. When there is duplication of effort, prospective witnesses suffer too.

The following discussion illuminates some of the jurisdictional questions that plague the House:

> Conflicting committee jurisdiction is a real problem. Take the missile field, for example. The Armed Services Committee, the Appropriations Committee, the Military Affairs Subcommittee of the Government Operations Committee all have had jurisdiction. Then the Space Committee was organized this year and began questioning all the military leaders about the missile program. As a consequence, people from the Pentagon are testifying before four different House committees and then going over to the Senate and doing the same thing. That is time consuming and unnecessary.
>
> *
>
> Another kind of problem arises when two committees share interests, and there is no liaison between them. For example, railroad retirement and unemployment insurance for railroad workers was brought to the floor by the Interstate and Foreign Commerce Committee although Ways and Means has the bulk of unemployment insurance programming and social security. There was no liaison between the committees' staffs. It is important to have the committees in agreement on some fundamental propositions so whatever is passed on railroad retirement will be somewhat in conformity with other unemployment insurance programs and social security.
>
> *
>
> Another example is foreign trade. The Foreign Affairs Committee has an interest, as has Interstate and Foreign Commerce by its very definition. Yet I dare say Ways and Means does the bulk of the legislating in that field because it gets reciprocal trade within its jurisdiction. There is no liaison between committees. In addition to overlapping jurisdiction you have piracy. Foreign Affairs developed the idea of distributing surplus foods abroad as a means of furthering good foreign relations. The Agriculture Committee took it over.

As a result of the confusion and overlap, there is much feeling among representatives that there should be more coordination of committee activity within the House itself, even though they express little enthusiasm for joint House-Senate committees. A coordinating body is sometimes suggested, though the point is made that much of the coordination could be accomplished by the committees concerned if attention could be directed to the problem. "It wasn't by accident," said one congressman, "that when the highway bill was before the Public Works Committee, Ways and Means people sat in. Liaison was necessary, and we made sure it occurred."

Another lawmaker observed that there was very little exchange of information between the Appropriations Committee and the Government Operations Committee, "yet Government Operations' job is to follow federal expenditures to see whether they are in accordance with the law and spent efficiently. The testimony and information they get is very valuable to Appropriations." In corroboration of this observation one member of the Appropriations Committee said: "There still isn't enough of that. We seldom get members of a Government Operations subcommittee appearing before us to give us the benefit of their work. Nor do we get any staff liaison. I think it is unfortunate."

The Appropriations Committee is often resented by legislators assigned to other committees, in part because of its power over the congressional purse. Some congressmen who do not themselves take the initiative to ensure that the results of the deliberations of their committees are, where relevant, made available to the Appropriations Committee believe the latter group is negligent in failing to seek out such information. And some believe that members of other standing committees should be invited to sit in on appropriations subcommittee meetings where appropriate, as is the practice in the Senate. Commented one legislator:

> Theoretically the weapons system is authorized by the Committee on Armed Services, but that is only in theory. On the missile programs that have been permitted to go ahead, decision is made by the Appropriations Committee through the language of reports and through riders. The committee which heard all the testimony and is presumed to have special competence is not the one which makes the decision. If we are going to take the trouble to develop men with specialized knowledge in a given field, then we should give them the right to sit in and second guess on Appropriations. There is no point in having hearings before Armed Services and then have the final decision made by Appropriations.

That statement led to the following comment:

> Isn't it a little more complicated than that? Isn't it a fact that the Armed Services Committee doesn't really make decisions on major problems, that it involves itself more with housekeeping and peripheral matters? I suspect that if we had an Armed Services Committee that made substantial policy decisions rather than accommodations between the weapons systems, then the Appropriations Committee would not be in a position to do what it now does.

While many House members resent the Appropriations Committee and believe it to be somewhat arrogant in its attitude, there is wide recognition that its members work diligently. Membership on the committee is eagerly sought, but it is realized that the committee has a heavy workload which successful applicants must help to shoulder. There is, therefore, sympathy within the House for the heavy responsibilities of the committee and even for the committee itself when it is bypassed.

> Wouldn't it be better to require that bills for which there is overlapping jurisdiction be re-referred to another committee before they come to the floor? Agriculture passed a bill increasing the authorization for special school milk programs by $3,000,000, and it went directly to the floor, bypassing Appropriations. How can Appropriations have control over total government expenditures without having every bill involving expenditures re-referred to them before coming to the floor? Another ridiculous thing is that although the Foreign Affairs committee sits for weeks deciding what to put in the Mutual Security bill, the proceeds used for local currency under Public Law 480 is under Agriculture. Appropriations is bypassed.

Committee Chairmen

Committee chairmen rank high among the most influential members of Congress. Sometimes respected, sometimes feared, often criticized by their colleagues, the majority have learned well the traditional privileges of their station. As men of authority and power, they are fair game for detractors who charge they often fail to discharge their duties in responsible fashion. Some appear unmoved by such criticism, regarding it as the inevitable result of power; most, at times at least, regard their actions as "misunderstood." Even House members who have words of praise for their own chairman are quick to document the "arbitrary actions" of others. As one congressman said: "All committee chairmen are despots. Some of them are benevolent despots, as is the case of my chairman, but in any event they are despotic. They can run their committees as they see fit, and they usually do." In the face of such comments, it is not surprising that chairmen have a reputation in the House for moving to each other's defense if their power is threatened.

Characteristics of Success An effective chairman is much respected in the House, earning even the grudging admiration of those who oppose him on legislative issues. In analyzing the success of one Democratic chairman, a Republican commented:

> The prime requirement for any chairman who wants to be an effective leader is to demonstrate that he is informed about the subject matter of his committee, and clearly this

committee chairman is informed. And in demonstrating that he is, he commands the respect of the committee and of the House.

But knowledge of his subject is only one of the essential attributes of a successful chairman. Realism in perceiving his support and skill in exploiting it can make a chairman strong. An awareness of the realities of a given situation—of what is possible and what is not possible—is basic. Observes one representative:

> The really skillful chairman understands where he stands on the floor. Judge Smith seems, perhaps more than anyone else among the chairmen, skillful in manipulating this relationship. He works in relation to the House as a whole. He is aware, or thinks he is aware, that he can get away with stalling a bill quietly when the House is not for it. He is aware he cannot stall a bill indefinitely if the majority is for it.
> Some chairmen have virtually no influence in the House and very little influence in committees. Others have influence out of all importance to their committees because of their personal prestige. So you have an incredible variety in the role, the position, and the power of the chairman.

The chairmen who are best liked by their committee colleagues are usually those who consult their associates on important matters, follow regularly established procedures, are amenable to reason, are not disposed to retain all committee perquisites for themselves, and do not discriminate against junior members by denying them adequate opportunity to participate fully—almost equally—in committee activities.

Sources and Uses of Power   The power of a committee chairman is impressive, varying somewhat according to committee tradition and the personal impact of the incumbent. He calls committee meetings and presides at them, exercising discretion in the recognition of his colleagues when they desire to speak. He decides the order in which bills are to be considered in the committee and when hearings should be held. Committee staffing is largely his prerogative. It is he who creates subcommittees, selects their membership, designates the chairman, and determines which legislative proposals shall be heard by each. He passes on requests for committee travel, initiates or approves special projects, acts as floor manager of legislative proposals voted out of his committee (a responsibility which carries with it the often crucial decision as to which members share in the limited debate), or designates the manager and, should such proposals go to conference, generally functions as head of the managers representing the House.

If he does not choose to have his committee governed by formal rules, his resistance may be sufficient to overcome efforts to provide for them. Should he determine to ignore established rules, it is only rarely and with great difficulty that his opponents can succeed in forcing him to acknowledge them.

In the last analysis he is, of course, responsible to his committee colleagues and can be called to account by them. Yet he often successfully avoids and sometimes flouts established procedures. Discontent may smoulder, but it seldom erupts in victorious rebellion. A freshman member of Congress says:

> I knew committee chairmen were powerful, but I didn't realize the extent of the power or its arbitrary nature. Recently, when my chairman announced he planned to proceed in a particular way, I challenged him to indicate under what rules he was operating. "My rules," he said. That was it, even though there were no regularly authorized rules permitting him to function in that manner. There is great reluctance to challenge committee chairmen even though you don't agree with them. Everyone seems fearful; all members have pet projects and legislation they want passed. No one wants to tangle too much because they realize what the results would be.

Primarily, a chairman's strength rests on personal relationships undergirded by tradition. As chairman, time and again he is in a position to grant special consideration to the request of a committee member—a request which, were normal procedures to be followed, might not be acted on promptly if at all. His power is cumulative: association with his colleagues over a period of years enables him to build a strong residue of personal good will and IOUs in the face of which open revolt is most difficult.

Colleagues are grateful when he assigns them a subcommittee of their own and the right to staff it, and they want to retain this power. They know, too, that the chairman, by virtue of his position, possesses influence and leverage with other committee chairmen that on occasion, may prove helpful. In short, they recognize it is within his power to bestow certain privileges, and they hesitate to antagonize him. One Democrat describes the problem faced by would-be reformers:

> The toughest kind of a majority to put together is one to reform a committee in the face of opposition from the chairman. As you get closer to the top of the hierarchy, the pressures on people who normally would be counted on to aid reformers are enormous and even people who would be classified as among the "good guys" rather than the "bad guys" tend to chicken out. It is the second and third termers who really have to lead the rebellion. The new fellows are still in a dream world and after you get beyond two or three terms you are part of the team and begin to see some merit in the system.

Another representative describes a recent attempt to bring about reform:

> Our chairman is a lovable fellow but we have had no rules and no subcommittees. Inspired by the examples of some other committees last session, a number of us drew up some rules, setting up subcommittees and so on, and moved their adoption. The matter was brought to a vote after much anguish and finagling, and we were voted down. How? A couple of freshmen who had been interested in reform were "detained" in their district on this particular occasion. Some of the older people near the chairman in seniority, who nevertheless were spiritually on our side, voted against us because they had received pap from the chairman and there was more coming.
>
> I should add a happy sequel. With this Congress came some changes in membership, and the chairman saw the handwriting. So now for the first time in history, we have a few subcommittees and a much better situation.
>
> Majorities are Pickwickian things. You really have to have about a two-thirds majority like we now have in order to get results. Last session we had a simple majority spiritually in our favor, but they would not stand up and be counted.

A third member confirmed that many chairmen are resourceful in maintaining their power:

> One chairman calls freshmen into his office and points out "if you vote for this set of rules, the chairmanships will all go to the senior members, but if you play along with me, you, as a first termer, will be selected as chairman of an important subcommittee." That gimmick has worked now for I don't know how many years. And he does appoint first termers as subcommittee chairmen.

Yet there is evidence that when contrasted with the authority of predecessors of several decades ago, the outside limits of power of today's chairmen are declining. The process has been gradual—so gradual as to be imperceptible to some congressmen. One leader in the movement to curtail the unrestricted freedom of chairmen by providing regularized procedures for committee operation explained the difference in this way:

> When talking about a chairman's powers, one can differentiate between negative and positive power. Prior to the Reorganization Act when there were thirty or forty committees, you had the classical picture of what I call the negative chairman. A chairman, functioning within a system of smaller committees with narrower jurisdiction, was able to pigeonhole any bill referred to his committee to which he was opposed, provided there was not overwhelming sentiment in the House that action had to be taken. He could simply say, "There will be no hearings. We are not going to take up this bill."
>
> This negative power of chairmen still exists today in the sense that chairmen can employ delaying tactics, by failing

to call hearings, for example. But it is much more limited than it used to be, although the political scientists haven't completely caught up with that fact.

When we talk about the positive power of a chairman, we are talking about the chairman who not only is influential in his committee, but who has tremendous power and prestige on the floor. He will seldom be overruled. But the great power of pigeonholing legislation that chairmen once exercised simply by saying autocratically, "I am against this bill and there will be no hearings," has all but disappeared. Minor bills have been stalled in this fashion, but I challenge anyone to name a major bill that any chairman has killed in that way, except at the very end of a session when the time factor becomes important.

While there is considerable agreement with the views expressed above, there also is vigorous dissent. One congressman said he thought the speaker "a little too charitable and too satisfied with things as they are." He continued:

Look at all the committees that prevent consideration of legislation. Ways and Means will not consider any fiddling with oil depletion allowance. You can go on with example after example where there are taboos because of the chairman, very largely. The fact is that most of the committees, despite the valiant efforts of some members, are not reformed and the chairman is, if not omnipotent, at least the wielder of a tremendous negative influence.

In support of the position that chairmen still exert autocratic influence one lawmaker said:

The _____ committee offers a good example of complete and total dictatorship in action. The chairman runs the committee with an iron hand. He puts people on subcommittees, takes them off, and announces transfers at will. About a year ago a subcommittee was considering something to which he was strongly opposed, but which seemed likely to pass. Just as the meeting opened, in walked four additional members of the full committee two Democrats and two Republicans. Without forewarning the subcommittee chairman, the chairman of the full committee had added four men to the group. In less than an hour there was to be a vote on a very important issue about which the four could not possibly have been fully informed. The chairman assumed that all four additions would vote with him against the legislation. It looked as though he had won until much to his distress one of the four broke ranks. But the action in increasing the subcommittee size was taken solely and arbitrarily by the chairman. Subcommittee chairmen do a lot of grumbling, but when the chips are down they vote with the chairman.

Consensus appears to be that while it probably is true that a chairman could not so flagrantly defy the will of the House today as formerly, efforts to proceed in the face of his objection depend primarily on the intensity of the pressure which can be brought to bear to get him to act, the nature of the majority aligned against him, and his own personality and conviction. Even today, opposition from a committee chairman to a proposal coming before his committee can be extremely detrimental, and sometimes fatal, to the measure. To overcome the obstinancy of a recalcitrant chairman requires a firm and determined majority strongly and skillfully led. Yet it is also true that legislators feel that fewer chairmen execute their responsibilities in the fashion of the stereotype of the autocratic committee head of old who kept his own counsel and regarded "his" committee as completely subject to his will. A definite trend in the other direction is discernible, though it would be erroneous to conclude that all chairmen are "reformed."

Today's delaying tactics are likely to be more subtle ("The judge is a much shrewder man than _____. He uses a bowie knife where _____ uses a meat axe.") and less irritating than those of the past, but the results may be the same. Observed one member, "I don't think there is a chairman in the House who will say, 'I won't give you a hearing.' They don't need to say that. A skillful chairman will schedule hearings and action on a bill in such a way that by the time it gets out of committee, it won't have time to get by the House." One chairman is drawn in this fashion:

> _____ is one of the most charming and delightful chairmen in the House, and highly skillful. He doesn't sidetrack us by ever refusing anything. He just schedules a workload in other areas which makes it impossible for us to get our legislation heard. He always keeps us busy, never refusing anyone a hearing on legislation, always holding out hope. I have eternal hope. But he has one of the fullest schedules you will ever encounter.

A chairman is sometimes also criticized on the grounds that, in the words of one congressman: "Often he is trying to squirrel away information. He doesn't even want some of the committee members to be well informed, much less the average member of Congress." It is charged, too, that many of them have a lien on committee staff members, requiring them to perform assignments which should be undertaken by the chairman's personal office staff, thereby diverting hard-pressed committee aides from their primary responsibilities. Although the House itself is reluctant to interfere in the activities of its committees or in committee expenditures, on occasion it has done so, generally as a rebuke to individual chairmen. For example, it reduced sharply requests of two committees for funds in the Eighty-eighth Congress, and, in one case, even specified the allocation of the funds authorized and required that the appropriate subcommittee chairman co-sign all authorizations for spending.

Preference for a Strong Chairman   As critical as some congressmen are of chairmen who seek to dominate committee proceedings and decisions, most of them seem to prefer a "strong" chairman to a "weak" one. For example, one representative stated, "I sometimes think I would prefer a despot to a man who is a pile of jelly." Another lawmaker agreed, and although a member of the minority party, had high praise for his chairman:

> The chairman of my committee is often considered a despot. I think he is a strong leader. He runs what is called in the Navy a taut ship. You know where you are headed. Sometimes you have to fight to get your point across, but if it is a good point you can get it across. I would prefer to have a committee run like that to one functioning without real leadership. Our chairman is responsible to the committee and we are very loyal to him because of the quality of his leadership. He has a record that is unparalleled for getting legislation through. Seniority, experience, and responsible leadership are the basis of his power.

Seniority and the Choice of Chairmen   There is no evidence of significant support in the House for modifying the present system for selecting committee chairmen by seniority. Though some freshmen express dissatisfaction with seniority as a test for capacity to lead a committee, nearly all of their more experienced colleagues assert there is no more satisfactory alternative. Even many freshmen support the present system. Indeed, there is some feeling that opposition to selecting chairmen by seniority is concentrated among those who write about the Congress, many of whom, it is said, possess little understanding of it. Acceptance by the Congress of seniority does not signify that members are enthusiastic about it. They are not. Rather they fear that the alternatives involve even more disadvantages. As one liberal House Democrat has written, "It is not that Congress loves seniority more but the alternatives less."

It is admitted that the present impersonal and automatic system for designating committee chairmen fails to distinguish between outstanding and mediocre House members, occasionally elevating a man incapable of leading or who possesses a record of inattention to committee responsibilities. It is also agreed that the system is not conducive to the maintenance of party discipline and that committee chairmen as a group are neither ideologically nor geographically representative of the House as a whole.

The characteristic congressional response to these criticisms is that seniority avoids the "politicking," logrolling, and factionalism that would accompany any system likely to replace it. It promotes stability by providing for an orderly transfer of authority to an heir apparent whose selection is assured. It is also suggested that to substitute another method might result in the loss of valuable talent. Said one congressman:

> Suppose you picked the number four man on a committee as a chairman. Wouldn't you immediately do away with the usefulness of the first three? They would be unhappy that

they hadn't been picked and the chairman would always be regarding them as possible rivals and probably wouldn't want to give them stature. You are dealing with people, and human nature must be considered in deciding the method to be used.

Selection of a chairman by vote of committee members—more precisely, by the majority members—is thus regarded as unsatisfactory: the present impersonal system avoids the rivalries likely to develop among the more experienced committee members. In rewarding experience, the seniority system, it is asserted, generally places in positions of power men and women who through long exposure to the subject matter and to the process by which committee work is carried forward have become alert to the technicalities of legislation and its possible ramifications, and to the kinds of sources of pressures affecting the key issues before the committee. They are adept at handling relationships with the executive branch and with their own colleagues. From the minority's point of view, the present practice may result in the designation of an individual less motivated by partisanship and therefore more amenable to "reason," than election procedures would bring forward. It seems clear that many congressmen are not anxious to replace seniority with a system in which adherence to party would become a major determinant. They enjoy the flexibility of voting and degree of independence which seniority promotes. When it was suggested by one representative that where the Congress and Presidency are controlled by the same party, it is important to have committee chairmanships in the hands of legislators sympathetic to the President's program, another congressman said firmly:

> I think you make a basic mistake when you assume that it is desirable for the committee chairman to be in harmony with the administration on every issue. Don't forget this is a tripartite form of government. I think it is a healthy thing sometimes to have competition if not conflict between the legislative branch and the executive branch.

An influential liberal Democrat has said that when he first was elected to Congress he shared the public image of "aging tyrannical chairmen ruling their committees with iron hands, pigeonholing bills willy-nilly and generally running Congress the way Henry VIII ran England." Eventually, however, he came to realize there was "a wide discrepancy between political folklore about the seniority system and fact about [it]."[1] He and other members believe seniority has become a popular whipping boy, unfairly charged with responsibility for many weaknesses of the committee system. Seniority, it is observed, does no more than designate the chairman; his powers and duties depend on rules of procedure adopted by the committee on which he serves. Committee inertia may produce too strong a chairman, but the remedy is clear: reform rests with the committee itself.

The tendency for committees to establish formal rules of procedure ("one man rule is on the way out") is but one of many influences that may mitigate the sometimes undesirable results of seniority. As has been demonstrated elsewhere in this volume, the seniority principle is not firmly applied in making committee assignments when there are strong reasons pointing to another choice. And the proliferation of subcommittees and select committees provides an unusual opportunity to grant early recognition to able and restive junior members of Congress who might otherwise be required to wait years to assume positions of leadership.

Though the general principle of seniority is well established as one of the basic tenets of the congressional system, there is nothing in the existing rules of the Congress to cloak it with legitimacy. It is a custom of convenience. It is clear that the elements of stability it lends to a system otherwise noted for its uncertainties and maneuverings have increased the reluctance to cast it aside.

Note

1. Emanuel Celler, "The Seniority Rule in Congress," *Western Political Quarterly*, vol. *14* (March 1961), pp. 160–67.

8.
TAKEN—BY TRAIN

Robert Sherrill

Out of respect for Richard K. Mellon, who had for years been a director of the Pennsylvania Railroad, other board members attended his funeral in Pittsburgh on June 5. Not wanting to spend all their time frivolously, they used the graveside get-together to plan how they might persuade the federal government to bail the nation's largest railroad out of it present financial difficulties.

Sen. Hugh Scott, the Republican minority leader, was also at the funeral, and the directors agreed to meet the following Tuesday in his Washington office. By the time this august group of businessmen assembled in the Senate Office Building on June 9, they had the procedure well arranged, for shortly after leaving Mellon's mortal remains, they were on the telephone to David Rockefeller at Chase Manhattan Bank, and shortly thereafter David was on the telephone to brother Nelson, and he quickly passed the word on to the White House.

So the meeting in Scott's office went off like clockwork. At 9:30 the Congressional fall guys trooped in: Mike Mansfield; Wright Patman, and John Sparkman, chairmen of the banking committees; Warren Magnuson and Harley Staggers, chairmen of the commerce committees. Transportation Secretary John Volpe and his Under Secretary James M. Beggs were ostensibly in charge of the meeting, and they did participate with a passion, but the fellow who *really* ran the show was Treasury Under Secretary Paul A. Volcker.

The purpose of the meeting was to sell everyone present on the idea that the Pennsylvania Railroad—or rather the Pennsylvania Central, as it became with the merger in 1968—should be given a $200 million loan under the Defense Production Act. Now, inasmuch as the Treasury Department has nothing whatsoever to do with the Defense Production Act, you may wonder what business this was of Treasury Under Secretary Volcker. On a sentimental basis, if nothing else, he had every reason not only to be there but to dominate the meeting: he was a vice-president of Chase Manhattan before he came to the Treasury Department, and Chase Manhattan owns 5.6 percent of the stock of Penn Central—believed to be the biggest bloc of that stock held by any person or corporation, except for the 7.2 percent held by Morgan Guaranty Trust Co.

Using some large colored flip cards (supplied by Penn Central) to lecture from, Volcker ran swiftly through a maze of statistics to prove that the railroad was very probably on its deathbed. One who was there said: "I noticed that Volcker seldom had to look at the flip cards. He seemed to know the Penn Central data by heart." Volcker's tone was panicky. Without exactly saying it, he told his audience: "You men hold the entire free enterprise system in your hands. You can walk out of here having said 'no' to us, and the system will crumble." He topped that requiem by saying, "Unless we can go back to the banks with some kind of agreement this afternoon, the Penn Central will have to take bankruptcy by the end of the week."

It was clear that the White House and the Defense Department had agreed to "help our friends at the Pennsy," and had ordered their underlings to "find some law we can use." The law dredged up for the occasion was the Defense Production Act, which normally has been used to give loans to small businesses that are needed for defense work and can't float large enough loans through normal channels. Never before has the Defense Production Act been used to salvage one of the corporate giants.

On cue from Volcker, Assistant Secretary of Defense Barry Shillito sprang to his feet and delivered a lecture on what absolutely essential defense work the Pennsy did for the nation. But an observer of the session said later that Senator Magnuson interrupted at that point and got Shillito to admit that actually the Penn Central earned only bout $100 million a year from the Pentagon, or about 5 percent of the railroad's $2 billion income, which hardly would qualify the Penn Central to call itself a major cog in the Pentagon machinery.

The banker-controlled Treasury Department's interest in Penn Central is much broader than merely Chase and Morgan. Seventy-seven banks have in recent years loaned a total of $500 million to the Penn Central management, and of course they all would much prefer to get paid in full rather than take 60¢ on the dollar, which is what they would get if Penn Central went into bankruptcy.

To understand just how fully this is a banker problem—not a railroad problem—one should scan the interlocking ties between the Penn Central and financial institutions at the time of these negotiations. For example, these are Penn directors:

- S. T. Saunders, director of Chase Manhattan, First National Exchange Bank of Virginia, Philadelphia Savings Fund, First Pennsylvania Banking and Trust Co. and its holding company.
- A. E. Perlman, a director of Marine Midland Grace Trust Co.

- D. C. Bevan, director of Provident National Bank.
- P. A. Gorman, Bankers Trust Co., and its holding company.
- L. W. Cabot, New England Merchants National Bank and Suffolk Franklin Savings Bank.
- W. L. Day, Philadelphia Savings Fund and First Pennsylvania Corp.
- J. T. Dorrance Jr., Morgan Guaranty Trust Co., and its holding company.
- S. H. Knox, Marine Midland Grace Trust Co., and its holding company.
- W. A. Marting, Bankers Trust Co., and its holding company, and National City Bank of Cleveland.
- R. S. Odell, Wells Fargo Bank.
- T. L. Perkins, Morgan Guaranty Trust Co.
- R. G. Rincliffe, Philadelphia National Bank and Philadelphia Savings Fund.
- R. S. Rauch, Girard Trust Bank and Philadelphia Savings Fund.
- J. M. Seabrook, director of Provident National Bank.

Three directors—Cabot, Perkins and Dorrance—subsequently resigned from Penn Central on the ground that they wanted to allay public suspicion of "dividend interests." (It isn't good business to be too obvious.)

With banker clout like that on its board, one would think Penn Central could float another loan, or as many loans as it needed, whenever it needed them. But at the skull session in Scott's office, Volcker claimed that the railroad had actually gone into the market the week before with debentures carrying 10.5 percent interest and couldn't raise a measly $120 million loan.

As Rep. William A. Barrett later observed: "The very fact that the big banks were beginning to cut Penn Central off from credit should have given the Nixon Administration reason to doubt the advisability of backing new loans to the corporation. When banks won't lend to a $7-billion corporation, then something is drastically wrong and I question whether it is proper for the federal government to become involved in an apparently open-ended guarantee of credit in such a situation."

The mechanics of the loan as agreed on will see the same 77 banks already into Pennsy supplying the railroad with the $200 million at 8 percent interest, the loan guaranteed by the government. That means a saving of at least 2.5 percentage points over what the railroad would have had to pay for a normal commercial loan—if it had found one. Other loans of $300 million are anticipated in the next few months at the same interest rate and with the same government guarantee. At first glance the lower interest may seem to be a disadvantage to the lending banks. But if the rail line *should* go bust at some future time, the government—you and I—will have to pay off the half-billion-dollar bank loans at face value, rather than at the bankruptcy percentage that would hold for a normal commercial loan. Thus the public is lifting that much burden of risk from Chase and Morgan and the other fat cats who own this road.

There are other ways the Penn Central directors could have taken care of their problem, if they had wanted to go the free-enterprise route rather than come crying to the government. They could have sold off some of their assets and paid their loans as they fell due. The Penn Central doesn't own just railroad equipment and roadbeds. Its owns many millions of dollars worth of oil wells, real estate property (including some of the choicest in New York City), pipelines, hotels and amusement parks, and other Americana. When you get hopelessly in debt, you sell your second car and pay up. But not the Pennsy. It doesn't like to do anything that might disturb the luxurious atmosphere in which its immediate past president, Stuart T. Saunders, and its new president, Paul T. Gorman, earn quarter-million-dollar incomes. Rather than tighten up on that kind of expenditure, it runs to the government.

Another thing that these great believers in the free-enterprise system could have done, if they had wanted to play by the rules they demand of everyone else, was to have gone bankrupt like good sports. Volcker kept wailing that the bankruptcy of the line "would mean no coal would be delivered to utility companies in critical areas," and "needed chemicals would not be delivered to industry in critical areas." Everyone who was listening knew that was nonsense.

Railroads that go bankrupt don't stop running. The New Haven line, bankrupt and in receivership for years, kept rolling along. A number of lines were bankrupt during the depression of the 1930s, but they kept rolling—until the big free-enterprise champions like the Pennsy gobbled them up.

There might be some argument for using public funds to save the Pennsy if it were a power for good, but it isn't. It has done everything it could do suppress needed competition. For example, Ben Heineman, perhaps the most imaginative railroad man of this generation, tried to put together a line that would bypass Chicago and St. Louis, offering an alternate east-west railroad that would get away from those notable traffic bottlenecks. Although it would not have posed damaging competition to rail networks in which the Pennsylvania had an interest, it would have offered competition of a sort, and the management of the Pennsylvania and of the Santa Fe joined forces with the Morgan Guaranty Trust and other major money interests to block Heineman.

The Pennsy has not survived because it was the most efficient road; it has survived and prospered out of financial bullying. As a matter of fact, its reputation for the last 10 or 15 years has been that of one of the least competent railroads, and it has got progressively worse since its merger with the New York Central. Its annual financial statements—symptomatic of the sickness that besets the line—have become notorious in the railroad industry for their inaccuracies and what appears to be outright deception.

On this point *Forbes* magazine, May 15, noted sarcastically: "If there were a prize for the annual report that goes furthest in trying to put a good face on a bad situation, the prize would go to Penn Central. The company had a simply disastrous year in 1969. Nevertheless, it managed to report a small ($4 million) net profit before an extraordinary loss of $125 million. It did so by imaginative bookkeeping and tax offsets."

The financial difficulties of the Penn Central have been talked about by railroad men for years. A. Scheffer Lang, who was Federal Railroad Administrator in the Department of Transportation (DOT) under the Johnson administration and now is on the faculty at MIT, says that the present crisis was anticipated and discussed by DOT officials in his day and that they agreed the railroad should receive no federal help and should be allowed to go bankrupt.

Shortly after leaving that office, Lang said in an interview with *Railway Age* that while "in the early years, the Pennsylvania Railroad was by all odds the best managed and most progressive railroad in the world," now "in almost any technical or management area you want to name, you can find one or more roads that do a better job." He said the Penn Central was operating simply with a caretaker philosophy, the ultimate and most disastrous example of which would be found in the New Haven line (owned by the Penn Central).

Asked if he meant that the Pennsylvania was taking itself and the rest of the industry down the New Haven path, Lang answered: "Not exactly. I'm sure none of the responsible people in Penn Central management are consciously willing to take the industry as a whole, let alone their own company, down the kind of road the New Haven has traveled. That would mean, of course, nationalization—because while you can pawn the New Haven off on Penn Central, you can't pawn Penn Central off on anybody except the federal government."

A year after Lang made that observation the Penn Central is being pawned off on the federal government, but not, however, with any honest admission of nationalization.

9.
THE LOCKHEED SCANDAL

James G. Phillips

Air Force Col. Joe Warren, a crusty cost-efficiency expert, was unmoved by Lockheed Aircraft's attempt to snow him over its C-5A jet transport program. Lockheed's briefing, he wrote Air Force headquarters almost four years ago, was "like seeing the rerun of an old movie—the plot still has drama and suspense, the script was excellent, the acting superb, but the outcome will be the same as it was the first, second or tenth time it was shown. The contract costs will be exceeded." Warren was right. With the Air Force refusing to impose tough cost discipline on a favored aerospace contractor, Lockheed has run up one of the most whopping cost overruns ever experienced on a weapons procurement program. Worse still, there's been no change in the inner workings of the military-industrial complex, which precipitated the C-5 disaster.

New evidence I have obtained indicates that at least $1.5 billion of the $2-billion C-5A overrun was clearly avoidable. In the first place, the Air Force gave Lockheed the contract (probably for the sole reason of keeping the company in business) despite known deficiencies in its design proposal that were sure to lead—and did—to expensive redesign work. Even then, much of the overrun might have been salvaged if the Air Force had clamped down on excessive plant overhead rates and blatant inefficiency on the production line. But despite the early warnings by Colonel Warren and other cost experts, top Air Force brass and bureaucrats swept these problems under the rug. At every stage, the Air Force's primary interest was in concealing the problem, not solving it.

The C-5 program was destined for trouble from the beginning, and here's why: the contract, signed in October 1965, contained a novel provision permitting Lockheed to come in with a low bid to land the program, with the virtual assurance of getting bailed out later by the government in the event of trouble. This provision was called the "repricing formula" by the Air Force and later the "golden handshake" by critics. It allowed the

From James G. Phillips, "What Really Happened? The Lockheed Scandal," *The New Republic*, August 1, 1970, pp. 19–23. Reprinted by permission of *The New Republic*. © 1970 Harrison-Blaine of New Jersey, Inc.

company to offset at least part of its losses on Production Run A of 58 aircraft by recomputing the price agreed on earlier for Run B of 57 planes. Although the second run would be undertaken at the option of the government, it appeared almost certain that the Air Force would want the extra planes and more. Air Force long-range airlift plans called for a 120-plane, six-squadron program. The other five planes would be procured from Run C—another option for the purchase of up to 85 planes at a price to be negotiated later.

The "handshake" clause, based on an extremely complicated mathematical formula, provided essentially that if actual costs of Run A exceeded the original contract "target cost" (contract price less profits) by more than 40 percent, target cost of Run B (set at $490 million in 1965) would be increased by approximately $1.25 for every additional dollar spent on Run A above the 40-percent cost growth mark. Cost increases of less than 40 percent would be financed as follows: for increases of 30 percent or less, Lockheed and the government would share responsibility, with the government paying 70 percent. Lockheed's share would be applied against its projected Run A profits of $128 million, which would be evaporated once costs rose by more than 30 percent. If the Run B option weren't exercised, Lockheed would bear full responsibility for all cost growth over 30 percent. But if the Air Force bought Run B, the "golden handshake" would go into effect once cost growth passed that mark. For cost increases of 30 to 40 percent, the handshake would reimburse Lockheed 87 cents on every additional dollar it spent, and above 40 percent, Lockheed would get back $1.25. (Both the 87-cents and $1.25 formulas, however, were pegged to the number of aircraft ordered under Run B, and lesser amounts than these would be paid if the government bought less than 32 of the Run B planes.)

Once a 40-percent cost increase appeared likely, the handshake loomed as a reverse incentive encouraging Lockheed to be less efficient. At this point, it would be in the company's interest to run up even greater costs on the initial production run in order to make 25 cents profit on every additional dollar it spent. Because of the sharing formula on the first 40 percent of extra costs, the cost growth would have to be astronomical before the handshake could turn Run A losses into an overall profit on the program. (The original target profit agreed to for the Run B option was only $49 million.) But at the same time, catastrophic losses would be impossible unless the Air Force decided not to buy Run B or the company actually lost money on its Run B operation—a prospect that appeared unlikely because aircraft costs per unit characteristically decline as a contractor gains experience with a program. Undoubtedly, this protection against big losses was an important factor in Lockheed's decision to cut corners on its bid.

Desperate for new business, Lockheed's management in early 1965 ordered its staff's lowest cost estimate reduced by 10 percent in order to undercut its competitors—Douglas Aircraft (now McDonnell-Douglas) and the Boeing Co. Lockheed's bid of $1.9 billion for research and production, including Run B if ordered, was $79 million less than Douglas' and $300 million less than Boeing's. The Lockheed proposal expressed a high degree of technical optimism that was unfounded under the circumstances. It also made little allowance for inflation though the Air Force had warned all three contractors to take that factor into account as a normal business risk over the first two years of the contract (after that, the contract provided that inflationary increases would be covered largely by the government). Nor did the Lockheed proposal make allowance for the fact that the C-5 award was the first of a new type of contract called "Total Package Procurement," under which the contractor would commit himself to a fixed price ahead of time for both research and production—a risky proposition that might have given Lockheed pause had it not been for the protection afforded by the golden handshake provision. Although an Air Force Source Selection Board found Boeing's proposal superior in its technical aspects, Lockheed won the contract on the basis of its low cost bid. The entire program was to cost $3.4 billion, including the airframe, engines, and spare parts.

In a move to narrow the technical edge held by Boeing, Lockheed had hurriedly adopted certain design changes suggested by the Air Force just before submitting its bid. It had vastly underpriced the cost of these changes, increasing its bid by only $48 million. At least one high-ranking Air Force official told company management that its allowance for the changes was far too low, but Lockheed ignored his advice.

Almost from the start of development work in early 1966, Air Force cost experts assigned to a top-level headquarters management group began citing evidence of a big cost overrun in the making. A. E. Fitzgerald, the deputy for management systems who later was to lose his job after testifying to Congress on the C-5's problems, noted early in the year that overhead rates at the company's production facility in Marietta, Georgia, were vastly exceeding target. Col. Larry M. Killpack, chief of the Air Force's Cost and Economic Information Bureau, found by year's end that several key parts of the program were overrun by more than 100 percent. On December 8, Killpack concluded in a memo to Air Force Headquarters that "Lockheed is in serious difficulty on the C-5A." Five days later, Colonel Warren penned his memo. All these reports fell on deaf ears.

As Lockheed admitted later, the reason for its early overspending was a massive redesign effort related partly to the last-minute technical changes the company had squeezed into its contract proposal. The most significant of these changes had been enlargement of the wing to meet Air Force requirements for the plane's short-field landing capability. But reconfiguration of the wing brought on weight problems, which required a new round of redesign work. After Fitzgerald learned of the extent of the redesign effort, he reported that these engineering problems almost certainly would mean a heavy cost impact when the plane moved from research to production.

By late 1966, the C-5's Systems Program Office (SPO), the office charged with day-to-day monitoring of the C-5 contract, joined the efficiency experts in their concern over the C-5's mounting costs. The SPO had become alarmed at indications from Lockheed management that the company did not intend to make good on the full contract performance specifications. One of the developments that bothered the SPO was Lockheed's proposal for a "tradeoff," as the company described it, relaxing the weight requirements in exchange for increased engine thrust, to be provided at government expense. The proposal was rejected.

In an extraordinary move, the SPO on February 1, 1967, sent Lockheed a "cure notice" indicating the contract would be cancelled unless Lockheed presented a satisfactory plan for improvement within the next 30 days. It was the first such action ever taken by the Air Force on a major weapons program. Although Air Force Headquarters questioned the advisability of the action, the SPO prevailed. Standby press releases announcing the move were prepared both at Wright-Patterson Air Force Base, Ohio, where the SPO is located, and at Air Force Headquarters in Washington. But both were marked for use only in the event of press inquiry, and when press questions failed to develop, neither was ever released. This was one of the most blatant of all the Air Force's cover-ups and one of the most costly in terms of the public interest. Since the plane had not yet moved into production, disclosure of its problems at this stage might have led to enough pressure to induce the Air Force to switch the contract to Boeing or at least bear down on costs.

The cure notice evoked tremendous concern at Lockheed, which was then preparing a public offering of $125 million in convertible debentures. Within the next three weeks, Lockheed met repeatedly with the SPO but to no avail. With time running out, Lockheed finally swayed the SPO on February 21, by promising to dispatch a top-level technical team from corporate headquarters in California to help the foundering Lockheed-Georgia management resolve the plane's technical problems. The cure notice was rescinded.

Despite the presence of the headquarters technical team, it was business as usual on the production line. Col. Jack W. Tooley, a former Army airlift expert working as a civilian adviser to Lockheed, reported that he observed incredible inefficiency in the plant. "From time to time," he recalled recently, "since I had nothing better to do, I would walk through the main plant, observing what was going on. The number of workers loafing on the job was absolutely unbelievable. In fact, my major contributions to Lockheed probably were these trips through the production line, since workers seeing me without a badge and in a suit and white shirt went back to work, as they were not sure of who I was."

Tooley added that he talked at some length with one of the supervisors on the production line, who told him that he had "40 more men in his department than he needed; that he was getting about six hours' work out of eight hours; that when he went to ten hours and over, the production dropped to five hours." Tooley also said he knew "personally of two cases where the individual was making $10 an hour, did not have a degree, was not doing anything, and yet spent 60 hours a week doing it because that is what the contract called for. This can be multiplied by many hundreds of times."

The situation was not much better at General Electric's plant in Evendale, Ohio, where the C-5's engines were under production. Here Fitzgerald also found excessive overhead rates and a large part of the work force loafing. After one trip to the facility in early 1967, Fitzgerald wrote Air Force Headquarters: "I observed a total of 134 people, of whom 35, or 26 percent, appeared to be working. The modal pace of work was quite low, approximately 70 percent of normal. Machine utilization appeared to be about 50 percent on the day shift and lower still on the swing shift." Fitzgerald later told Congress that at least $1 billion of the C-5 overrun could have been saved if the Air Force had required reasonable efficiency and economy of work forces at the Lockheed and GE plants.

Annoyed by the continuous appearance of cost analysts, Lockheed and their sympathizers in the Pentagon began seeking their systematic exclusion from the program. Orders were cut sending Warren to Addis Ababa as Air Attaché. Fitzgerald and other friends of Warren at Air Force Headquarters were able to block that appointment, but Warren was still removed from the program and assigned to a Pentagon computer manager job. Killpack was transferred to Vietnam, and Tooley quit Lockheed-Georgia in disgust.

With its technical problems mounting, Lockheed turned to costly and exotic materials such as titanium to help pare down the excess weight. By now the company had found it was useless to try to wiggle out of contract specifications. Despite some expressions of unhappiness at higher levels, the SPO refused to budge.

Without doubt, the SPO's adherence to the contract dealt Lockheed a stunning blow. When the company had run into production problems on earlier programs, the Air Force would often waive specifications or provide enough contract change orders (sometimes called "contract nourishment" in the trade) to ensure that the company came out well. Lockheed's chief development engineer on the program later told Securities and Exchange Commission investigators that he never suspected the C-5 contract would be enforced: "As is so frequently the case with multi-layer management," he said, "someone at the top can say do it this way to avoid this, that and another, and these people down below say here's the contract, but that's just a lot of boiler plate and we'll work together." In its 1969 report to stockholders, the company said the Air Force's strict insistence on performance specifications and delivery dates "resulted in expenses by contractor far beyond the original estimate to avoid ever-present threats of cancellation for default. . . . Contract terms were regarded as sacrosanct even though a relaxation of specifications and delivery dates could have greatly lessened costs."

In May 1967, Lockheed moved from research to the production phase of the program with the plane's technical problems far from resolved. At a meeting of the top-level Air Force management group, at least one official complained that more time should have been spent on development. "This is the first major aircraft system," he said, "to begin operational systems development after completing an extensive contract definition phase. The central idea of contract definition is to define achievable performance and to develop realistic schedules and credible cost estimates in relation thereto. Clearly, Lockheed flunks the course on this basis."

Despite continuing SPO concern over the technical difficulties, Lockheed characterized the problems as nonrecurring and refused to acknowledge their potential impact on costs. Late in 1967, Lockheed-Georgia notified corporate headquarters that "the bulk of the program remains before us, giving us ample opportunity for cost savings. . . ." Although Lockheed added a $90 million contingency fund to its cost estimates by the end of 1967, it explained to its auditor, Arthur Young Co., that it was merely being conservative and that the funds would not be needed. Arthur Young's notes indicate unbounded optimism on Lockheed's part. The first indication of a really disastrous overrun on the Lockheed program came in April 1968, when the SPO estimated costs of $2.9 billion through Run B, a $1 billion overrun. The SPO figured Lockheed had known about the cost situation since the early part of the year, since the company at that time had "intensified their efforts to maneuver within the contract framework to get the Air Force to pay for work we contend is already on contract. In addition, they started attempting to limit our visibility on program cost."

Nonetheless, Lockheed insisted the SPO projections were far too high, and it pressured the SPO to change them. SEC investigators found later that Lockheed had threatened to follow the SPO briefing team wherever it went, to shoot down their figures.

But with a decision soon due on the Run B option, Lockheed decided to adopt a low profile and hope that, as before, Air Force Headquarters would not become unduly alarmed at another pessimistic SPO estimate. As the SEC staff put it, the rebuttal package was ready if needed "to help protect Lockheed's position in this respect, but would not be used unless necessary because of the danger of focusing attention on the cost increase." The SPO apparently recognized this same motive in June when it wrote that it was definitely in Lockheed's favor to keep the Air Force "in the dark" on the costs of Run A, because of their potentially adverse impact on a decision to exercise the Run B option.

At this point, however, even the SPO, which had been relatively tough on Lockheed, became concerned over the effect that disclosure of its cost projections might have on the company's liquidity position. Its reports to higher headquarters contained the following notation: "Security considerations. You will see we are estimating that Lockheed will overrun the ceiling price of the contract by a significant margin, that is, they will incur large monetary losses on the program. The SPO has treated this information as extremely sensitive in view of the adverse publicity and stock market implications." SPO said there was no pressure from Lockheed or higher headquarters to insert this warning in its report. It said the suggestion was made "purely and simply because the cost figures . . . were estimates and were not concurred in by the contractor. There was a wide variation between the estimate contained in this report and the contractor's estimate. It was felt that should the Air Force prove to be inaccurate subsequent to wide public disclosure, the Air Force would be accused of acting irresponsibly."

Instead, the SPO decided to err on the side of the contractor and let the public be damned. Air Force Headquarters moved quickly to close off possible leaks by directing that the information be limited to top-level reports and be excluded from any document receiving wide circulation. Although Congress had been notified of the SPO's August 1967 estimate of a $331 million overrun, it was not informed of the new projection. Neither was it told of a follow-up study in October, which placed the overrun on the entire program at $2 billion, including $1.5 billion on the Lockheed program. The SEC staff revealed that the Air Force considered rewriting performance specifications at this point to give Lockheed a better break. (Some of the performance specifications were relaxed later, and the Air Force now is planning significant further relaxation in order to avoid another costly redesign of the wing.)

The next episode came in early November, when Richard Kaufman, staff economist for the Joint Congressional Economic Committee's Economy in Government Subcommittee, was setting up a subcommittee hearing on "The Economics of Military Procurement." Kaufman had followed the C-5 program closely and knew of the latest overrun estimate. Although no subcommittee member or staffer had yet contacted Fitzgerald, several Pentagon associates recommended him.

When Kaufman invited Fitzgerald to testify, bedlam broke loose in the Pentagon. Defense Department Comptroller Robert Moot, the Pentagon's top financial officer, warned Fitzgerald that his testimony "would leave blood on the floor." The Pentagon sought to substitute a more manageable witness, but the subcommittee chairman, Sen. William Proxmire (D-Wis.), insisted that Fitzgerald appear. Finally, the Pentagon agreed to let Fitzgerald attend as a backup witness. At the hearing November 13, Proxmire ignored the Pentagon's hand-picked witness and called Fitzgerald immediately to the stand. Fitzgerald confirmed Proxmire's estimate of the $2-billion overrun, leading to his immediate removal from the program and eventual dismissal from his job.

With Congress and the public enraged about the overrun, the Pentagon flatly repudiated Proxmire's figures. Its Public Affairs Office put out a release contending that current estimates for the program were only $4.3 billion instead of the $5.3 billion Proxmire had revealed. Supplementary material requested of Fitzgerald for the hearing record was altered by the

Pentagon to show the lower figure. The difference turned out to be the Air Force's omission of some $900 million for spare parts—another item that was badly overrun. The spares were mostly engines and ground equipment—items the Air Force classifies as an operating cost and not as original investment. The Pentagon news release failed to make this distinction however, thus conveying the impression that Proxmire was overstating costs.

Despite opposition from the Defense Department's Systems Analysis Office, which sought to limit the C-5 program to three squadrons, the Air Force on January 14, 1969, exercised the Run B option, but instructed Lockheed for the time being to limit production to long-leadtime items for only 23 more planes. On grounds of budgetary restraints, the Air Force announced last October that it would curtail the program after completion of 81 planes. With the effect of the golden handshake formula now blunted (because the Air Force was ordering less than 90 planes), Lockheed stood to lose more than $500 million. Contending the Pentagon's exercise of the Run B option required purchase of all 57 Run B planes, Lockheed sued the government for default. (Lockheed now figures it would have broken even on the full 115-plane program.)

The cozy relationships of the military-industrial complex came to light again this spring when Lockheed requested $640 million in emergency financing and Pentagon officials, backed by military enthusiasts in Congress, sought to expedite the company's claim. Even when the Pentagon learned that Lockheed's immediate cash problem had resulted from its commercial program—the L-1011 "airbus"—it still maintained its support of the proposed bailout money. Lockheed was a national asset like the redwood tree.

Even the Securities and Exchange Commission (but not its tough-minded staff) has shown sympathy for the embattled contractor. At the completion of the SEC staff's year-long investigation of Lockheed's cost disclosures on the C-5 program and alleged illegal dumping of company stock by corporate insiders, the Commission announced June 2 that the investigation "did not disclose evidence of unlawful insider trading." The Commission's terse announcement seemed at odds with the findings of the staff's report. Citing specific instances of heavy selling by top corporate officers at critical junctures in the program, the staff raised the "possibility that this was done on the basis of inside information." Rumors abounded that the staff had recommended indictments; the SEC denied it.

Although the SEC release announced the Commission's decision to study cost disclosures on a number of weapon contracts, including the C-5A, it gave no indication of the staff's considerable misgivings over Lockheed's disclosure policy on the C-5 program. In its report, the staff raised the question of "the adequacy of disclosure in annual and interim filings with the Commission and with the [New York Stock] Exchange, as well as information prepared for public distribution." The staff also raised questions as to the adequacy of Lockheed's description of the cure notice in a registration statement it filed with the SEC in March 1967, covering the $125 million debenture issue. The Commission at first put the staff report under wraps but later made it public under stiff pressure from Congress.

As I said earlier, much of the C-5 overrun could have been avoided if the Air Force had really cracked down. Of the $2-billion overrun, less than $200 million can be attributed to inflation. The rest is due entirely to Lockheed's redesign effort and pure inefficiency on the Lockheed and GE production lines. Even if Lockheed had charged an extra $200–$250 million in the beginning to get its design up to a par with Boeing's (or by that same token if the contract had gone to Boeing), the whole program should have cost no more than $3.8 billion, given reasonable efficiency. Thus about $1.5 billion of the overrun should have been saved. As it is, the Air Force estimates that even the 81-plane program is going to cost $4.6 billion—$1.2 billion more than the original contract estimate for 115 planes. Thus far, the Air Force has spent $2.5 billion on the program and has received one operable plane!

Defense Secretary Melvin R. Laird has sought to prevent recurrence of C-5 type fiascos by setting "milestones" which a contractor must reach before he moves on to the next phase of a weapons program. This policy means little, however, unless Pentagon bureaucrats clamp down on contractor boondoggling. Signs are thus far that they haven't. Pentagon studies already are predicting a $1-billion overrun on Lockheed's S-3A anti-submarine aircraft program, the first major weapons purchase initiated by Laird. Deputy Secretary of Defense David Packard recently succeeded in pre-empting headlines about that overrun by issuing a non-story that he had warned the Navy to keep close tabs on program costs. Packard acknowledged only a $100-million overrun on the current portion of the contract and did not reveal the present estimate for total cost at competion.

It is too much to expect that Pentagon bureaucrats will move voluntarily to shape up military procurement. That would involve harsh measures against favored contractors and, for the less efficient among them, a bankruptcy or two. The ties that bind Pentagon bureaucrats and the giant contractors—the mutual interest in huge defense budgets, the promise of lucrative jobs in industry for former military and civilian officials, and the feeling that they must stand four-square against an unappreciative public—are simply too strong for that.

Perhaps the only answer is a series of taxpayer suits against government officials who breach the public trust, particularly with respect to concealment of cost problems that could lead to gigantic expenditures later if not brought under control. Not too long ago, the public wouldn't have stood for the C-5 affair. In 1956, T. Lamar Caudle, an assistant attorney general under President Truman, was convicted and sentenced to two years in prison for failing to prosecute tax fraud cases that came under his jurisdiction. The charge on which he was convicted was conspiracy to deprive the government "of the fair services of Caudle." That law ought to be applied to Pentagon bureaucrats.

10.
DECISION-MAKING IN A DEMOCRACY: THE SUPREME COURT AS A NATIONAL POLICY-MAKER

Robert A. Dahl

To consider the Supreme Court of the United States strictly as a legal institution is to underestimate its significance in the American political system. For it is also a political institution, an institution, that is to say, for arriving at decisions on controversial questions of national policy. As a political institution, the Court is highly unusual, not least because Americans are not quite willing to accept the fact that it *is* a political institution and not quite capable of denying it; so that frequently we take both positions at once. This is confusing to foreigners, amusing to logicians, and rewarding to ordinary Americans who thus manage to retain the best of both worlds.

I

A policy decision might be defined as an effective choice among alternatives about which there is, at least initially, some uncertainty. This uncertainty may arise because of inadequate information as to (a) the alternatives that are thought to be "open"; (b) the consequences that will probably ensue from choosing a given alternative; (c) the level of probability that these consequences will actually ensue; and (d) the relative value of the different alternatives, that is, an ordering of the alternatives from most preferable to least preferable, given the expected consequences and the expected probability of the consequences actually occurring. An *effective* choice is a selection of the most preferable alternative accompanied by measures to insure that the alternative selected will be acted upon.

No one, I imagine, will quarrel with the proposition that the Supreme Court, or indeed any court, must make and does make policy decisions in this sense. But such a proposition is not really useful to the

From Robert Dahl, "Decision-Making in a Democracy: The Supreme Court as a National Policy-Maker," *Journal of Public Law*, vol. 6, 1958, pp. 279–95. © 1958 by Emory University Law School. Reprinted by permission of the publisher.

question before us. What is critical is the extent to which a court can and does make policy decisions by going outside established "legal" criteria found in precedent, statute, and constitution. Now in this respect the Supreme Court occupies a most peculiar position, for it is an essential characteristic of the institution that from time to time its members decide cases where legal criteria are not in any realistic sense adequate to the task. A distinguished associate justice of the present Court has recently described the business of the Supreme Court in these words:

> It is essentially accurate to say that the Court's preoccupation today is with the application of rather fundamental aspirations and what Judge Learned Hand calls "moods," embodied in provisions like the due process clauses, which were designed not to be precise and positive directions for rules of action. The judicial process in applying them involves a judgment. . . . that is, on the views of the direct representatives of the people in meeting the needs of society, on the views of Presidents and Governors, and by their construction of the will of legislatures the Court breathes life, feeble or strong, into the inert pages of the Constitution and the statute books.[1]

Very often, then, the cases before the Court involve alternatives about which there is severe disagreement in the society, as in the case of segregation or economic regulation; that is, the setting of the case is "political." Moreover, they are usually cases where competent students of constitutional law, including the learned justices of the Supreme Court themselves, disagree; where the words of the Constitution are general, vague, ambiguous, or not clearly applicable; where precedent may be found on both sides; and where experts differ in predicting the consequences of the various alternatives or the degree of probability that the possible consequences will actually ensue. Typically, in other words, although there may be considerable agreement as to the alternatives thought to be open [(a)], there is very serious disagreement as to questions of fact bearing on consequences and probabilities [(b) and (c)], and as to questions of value, or the way in which different alternatives are to be ordered according to criteria establishing relative preferability [(d)].

If the Court were assumed to be a "political" institution, no particular problems would arise, for it would be taken for granted that the members of the Court would resolve questions of fact and value by introducing assumptions derived from their own predispositions or those of influential clienteles and constituents. But, since much of the legitimacy of the Court's decisions rests upon the fiction that it is not a political institution but exclusively a legal one, to accept the Court as a political institution would solve one set of problems at the price of creating another. Nonetheless, if it is true that the nature of the cases arriving before the Court is sometimes of the kind I have described, then the Court cannot act strictly as a legal institution. It must, that is to say, choose among controversial alternatives of public policy by appealing to at least some criteria of acceptability on questions of fact and value that cannot be found in or deduced from precedent, statute, and Constitution. It is in this sense that the Court is a national policy-maker, and it is this role that gives rise to the problem of the Court's existence in a political system ordinarily held to be democratic.

Now I take it that except for differences in emphasis and presentation, what I have said so far is today widely accepted by almost all American political scientists and by most lawyers. To anyone who believes that the Court, is not, in at least some of its activities, a policy-making institution, the discussion that follows may seem irrelevant. But to anyone who holds that at least one role of the Court is as a policy-making institution in cases where strictly legal criteria are inadequate, then a serious and much debated question arises, to wit: Who gets what and why? Or in less elegant language: What groups are benefited or handicapped by the Court and how does the allocation by the Court of these rewards and penalties fit into our presumably democratic political system?

II

In determining and appraising the role of the Court, two different and conflicting criteria are sometimes employed. These are the majority criterion and the criterion of Right or Justice.

Every policy dispute can be tested, at least in principle, by the majority criterion, because (again: in principle) the dispute can be analyzed according to the numbers of people for and against the various alternatives at issue, and therefore according to the proportions of the citizens or eligible members who are for and against the alternatives. Logically speaking, except for a trivial case, every conflict within a given society must be a dispute between a majority of those eligible to participate and a minority or minorities; or else it must be a dispute between or among minorities only.[2] Within certain limits, both possibilities are independent of the number of policy alternatives at issue, and since the argument is not significantly affected by the number of alternatives, it is convenient to assume that each policy dispute represents only two alternatives.[3]

If everyone prefers one of two alternatives, then no significant problem arises. But a case will hardly come before the Supreme Court unless at least one person prefers an alternative that is opposed by another person. Strictly speaking, then, no matter how the Court acts in determining the legality or constitutionality of one alternative or the other, the outcome of the Court's decision must either (1) accord with the preferences of a minority of citizens and run counter to the preferences of a majority; (2) accord with the preferences of a majority and run counter to the preferences of a minority; or (3) accord with the preferences of one minority and run counter to the preferences of another minority, the rest being indifferent.

In a democratic system with a more or less representative legislature, it is unnecessary to maintain a special court to secure the second class of outcomes. A case might be made out that the Court protects the rights of national majorities against local interests in federal questions, but so far as I am aware, the role of the Court as a policy-maker is not usually defended in this fashion; in what follows, therefore, I propose to pass over the ticklish question of federalism and deal only with "national" majorities and minorities. The third kind of outcome, although relevant according to other criteria, is hardly relevant to the majority criterion, and may also be passed over for the moment.

One influential view of the Court, however, is that it stands in some special way as a protection of minorities against tyranny by majorities. In the course of its 167 years, in 78 cases, the Court has struck down 86 different provisions of federal law as unconstitutional,[4] and by interpretation it has modified a good many more. It might be argued, then, that in all or in a very large number of these cases the Court was, in fact, defending the rights of some minority against a "tyrannical" majority. There are, however, some exceedingly serious difficulties with this interpretation of the Court's activities.

III

One problem, which is essentially ideological in character, is the difficulty of reconciling such an interpretation with the existence of a democratic polity, for it is not at all difficult to show by appeals to authorities as various and imposing as Aristotle, Locke, Rousseau, Jefferson, and Lincoln that the term democracy means, among other things, that the power to rule resides in popular majorities and their representatives. Moreover, from entirely reasonable and traditional definitions of popular sovereignty and political equality, the principle of majority rule can be shown to follow by logical necessity.[5] Thus to affirm that the Court supports minority preferences against majorities is to deny that popular sovereignty and political equality, at least in the traditional sense, exist in the United States; and to affirm that the Court *ought* to act in this way is to deny that popular sovereignty and political equality *ought* to prevail in this country. In a country that glories in its democratic tradition, this is not a happy state of affairs for the Court's defenders; and it is no wonder that a great deal of effort has gone into the enterprise of proving that, even if the Court consistently defends minorities against majorities, nonetheless it is a thoroughly "democratic" institution. But no amount of tampering with democratic theory can conceal the fact that a system in which the policy preferences of minorities prevail over majorities is at odds with the traditional criteria for distinguishing a democracy from other political systems.[6]

Fortunately, however, we do not need to traverse this well-worn ground; for the view of the Court as a protector of the liberties of minorities against the tyranny of majorities is beset with other difficulties that are not so much ideological as matters of fact and logic. If one wishes to be at all rigorous about the question, it is probably impossible to demonstrate that any particular Court decisions have or have not been at odds with the preferences of a "national majority." It is clear that unless one makes some assumptions as to the kind of evidence one will require for the existence of a set of minority and majority preferences in the general population, the view under consideration is incapable of being proved at all. In any strict sense, no adequate evidence exists, for scientific opinion polls are of relatively recent origin, and national elections are little more than an indication of the first preferences of a number of citizens—in the United States the number ranges between about 40 and 60 percent of the adult population—for certain candidates for public office. I do not mean to say that there is no relation between preferences among candidates and preferences among alternative public policies, but the connection is a highly tenuous one, and on the basis of an election it is almost never possible to adduce whether a majority does or does not support one of two or more policy alternatives about which members of the political elite are divided. For the greater part of the Court's history, then, there is simply no way of establishing with any high degree of confidence whether a given alternative was or was not supported by a majority or a minority of adults or even of voters.

In the absence of relatively direct information, we are thrown back on indirect tests. The 86 provisions of federal law that have been declared unconstitutional were, of course, initially passed by majorities of those voting in the Senate and in the House. They also had the president's formal approval. We could, therefore, speak of of a majority of those voting in the House and Senate, together with the president, as a "law-making majority." It is not easy to determine whether any such constellation of forces within the political elites actually coincides with the preferences of a majority of American adults or even with the preferences of a majority of that half of the adult population which, on the average, votes in congressional elections. Such evidence as we have from opinion polls suggests that Congress is not markedly out of line with public opinion, or at any rate with such public opinion as there is after one discards the answers of people who fall into the category, often large, labeled "no response" or "don't know." If we may, on these somewhat uncertain grounds, take a "lawmaking majority" as equivalent to a "national majority," then it is possible to test the hypothesis that the Supreme Court is shield and buckler for minorities against national majorities.

Under any reasonable assumptions about the nature of the political process, it would appear to be somewhat naive to assume that the Supreme Court either would or could play the role of Galahad. Over the whole history of the Court, on the average one new justice has been appointed every 22 months. Thus a president can expect to appoint about two new justices during one term of office; and if this were not enough to tip the balance on a normally divided Court, he is almost certain to succeed in two terms. Thus, Hoover had three appointments; Roosevelt, nine; Truman, four; and Eisenhower, so far, has had four. Presidents are not famous for appointing justices hostile to their own views on public policy nor could they expect to secure confirmation of a man whose stance on key questions was flagrantly at odds with that of the dominant majority in the Senate. Justices are typically men who, prior to appointment, have engaged in public life and have committed themselves publicly on the great questions of the day. As Mr. Justice Frankfurter has recently reminded us, a surprisingly large proportion of the justices, particularly of the great justices who have left their stamp upon the decisions of the Court, have had little or no prior judicial experience.[7] Nor have the justices—certainly not the great justices—been timid men with a passion for anonymity. Indeed, it is not too much to say that if justices were appointed primarily for their "judicial" qualities without regard to their basic attitudes on fundamental questions of public policy, the Court could not play the influential role in the American political system that it does in reality play.

The fact is, then, that the policy views dominant on the Court are never for long out of line with the policy views dominant among the lawmaking majorities of the United States. Consequently it would be most unrealistic to suppose that the Court would, for more than a few years at most, stand against any major alternatives sought by a lawmaking majority. The judicial agonies of the New Deal will, of course, quickly come to mind; but Mr. Roosevelt's difficulties with the Court were truly exceptional. Generalizing over the whole history of the Court, the chances are about one out of five that a president will make one appointment to the Court in less

TABLE 1

The Interval Between Appointments to the Supreme Court

Interval in years	Percent of total appointments	Cumulative Percent
Less than 1	21	21
1	34	55
2	18	73
3	9	82
4	8	90
5	7	97
6	2	99
—	—	—
12	1	100
Total	100	100

NOTE: The table excludes the six appointments made in 1789. Except for the four most recent appointments, it is based on data in the *Encyclopedia of American History*, 461–462 (R. B. Morris, ed., 1953). It may be slightly inaccurate because the source shows only the year of appointment, not the month. The 12-year interval was from 1811 to 1823.

than a year, better than one out of two that he will make one within two years, and three out of four that he will make one within three years. Mr. Roosevelt had unusually bad luck: he had to wait four years for his first appointment; the odds against this long an interval are four to one. With average luck, the battle with the Court would never have occurred; even as it was, although the "court-packing" proposal did formally fail, by the end of his second term Mr. Roosevelt had appointed five new justices and by 1941 Mr. Justice Roberts was the only remaining holdover from the Hoover era.

It is to be expected, then, that the Court is least likely to be successful in blocking a determined and persistent lawmaking majority on a major policy and most likely to succeed against a "weak" majority; for example, a dead one, a transient one, a fragile one, or one weakly united upon a policy of subordinate importance.

IV

An examination of the cases in which the Court has held federal legislation unconstitutional confirms, on the whole, our expectations. Over the whole history of the Court, about half the decisions have been rendered more than four years after the legislation was passed.

TABLE 2
Percentage of Cases Held Unconstitutional Arranged by
Time Intervals Between Legislation and Decision

Number of years	New Deal legislation	Other	All legislation
2 or Less	92	19	30
3–4	8	19	18
5–8	0	28	24
9–12	0	13	11
13–16	0	8	6
17–20	0	1	1
21 or More	0	12	10
Total	100	100	100

TABLE 3
Cases Holding Legislation Unconstitutional Within Four Years After
Enactment

Interval in years	New Deal		Other		Total	
	No.	Percent	No.	Percent	No.	Percent
2 or Less	11	29	13	34	24	63
3 to 4	1	3	13	34	14	37
Total	12	32	26	68	38	100

Of the 24 laws held unconstitutional within two years, 11 were measures enacted in the early years of the New Deal. Indeed, New Deal measures comprise nearly a third of all the legislation that has ever been declared unconstitutional within four years after enactment.

It is illuminating to examine the cases where the Court has acted on legislation within four years after enactment—where the presumption is, that is to say, that the lawmaking majority is not necessarily a dead one. Of the 12 New Deal cases, two were, from a policy point of view, trivial; and two, although perhaps not trivial, were of minor importance to the New Deal program.[8] A fifth[9] involved the NRA, which was to expire within three weeks of the decision. Insofar as the unconstitutional provisions allowed "codes of fair competition" to be established by industrial groups, it is fair to say that President Roosevelt and his advisers were relieved by the Court's decision of a policy they had come to find increasingly embarrassing. In view of the tenacity with which Mr. Roosevelt held to his major program, there can hardly be any doubt that had he wanted to pursue the major policy objective involved in the NRA codes, as he did, for example, with the labor provisions, he would not have been stopped by the Court's special theory of the Constitution. As to the seven other cases,[10] it is entirely correct to say, I think, that whatever some of the eminent justices might have thought during their fleeting moments of glory, they did not succeed in interposing a barrier to the achievement of the objectives of the legislation; and in a few years most of the constitutional interpretation on which the decisions rested had been unceremoniously swept under the rug.

The remainder of the 38 cases where the Court has declared legislation unconstitutional within four years of enactment tend to fall into two rather distinct groups: those involving legislation that could reasonably be regarded as important *from the point of view of the lawmaking majority* and those involving minor legislation. Although the one category merges into the other, so that some legislation must be classified rather arbitrarily, probably there will be little disagreement with classifying the specific legislative provisions involved in 11 cases as essentially minor from the point of view of the lawmaking majority (however important they may have been as constitutional interpretations).[11] The specific legislative provisions involved in the remaining 15 cases are by no means of uniform importance, but with one or two possible exceptions it seems reasonable to classify them as major policy issues from the point of view of the lawmaking majority.[12] We would expect that cases involving major legislative policy would be propelled to the Court much more rapidly than cases involving minor policy, and, as Table 4 shows, this is in fact what happens.[13]

Thus a lawmaking majority with major policy objectives in mind usually has an opportunity to seek for ways of overcoming the Court's veto. It is an interesting and highly significant fact that Congress and the president do generally succeed in overcoming a hostile Court on major policy issues. It is particularly instructive to examine the cases involving major

TABLE 4
Number of Cases Involving Legislative Policy (Other
Than Those Arising Under New Deal Legislation)
Holding Legislation Unconstitutional Within Four
Years After Enactment

Interval in years	Major policy	Minor Policy	Total
2 or Less	11	2	13
3 to 4	4	9	13
Total	15	11	26

policy. In two cases involving punitive legislation enacted by Radical
Republican Congresses against supporters of the Confederacy during the
Civil War, the Court faced a rapidly crumbling majority whose death knell
as an effective national force was sounded with the election of 1876.[14]
Three cases are difficult to classify and I have labeled them "unclear." Of
these, two were decisions made in 1921 involving a 1919 amendment to the
Lever Act to control prices.[15] The legislation was important, and the provision in question was clearly struck down, but the Lever Act terminated
three days after the decision and Congress did not return to the subject
of price control until World War II, when it experienced no constitutional
difficulties arising from these cases (which were primarily concerned with
the lack of an ascertainable standard of guilt). The third case in this
category successfully eliminated stock dividends from the scope of the
Sixteenth Amendment, although a year later Congress enacted legislation
taxing the actual income from such stock.[16]

The remaining 10 cases were ultimately followed by a reversal of
the actual policy results of the Court's action, although not necessarily of
the specific constitutional interpretation. In four cases,[17] the policy consequences of the Court's decision were overcome in less than a year. The
other six required a long struggle. Workmen's compensation for longshoremen and harbor workers was invalidated by the Court in 1920;[18] in 1922
Congress passed a new law which was, in its turn, knocked down by the
Court in 1924;[19] in 1927 Congress passed a third law, which was finally
upheld in 1932.[20] The notorious income tax cases[21] of 1895 were first somewhat narrowed by the Court itself;[22] the Sixteenth Amendment was recommended by President Taft in 1909 and was ratified in 1913, some 18 years
after the Court's decisions. The two child labor cases represent the most
effective battle ever waged by the Court against legislative policy-makers.
The original legislation outlawing child labor, based on the commerce
clause, was passed in 1916 as a part of Wilson's New Freedom. Like Roosevelt later, Wilson was somewhat unlucky in his Supreme Court appointments; he made only three appointments during his eight years, and one
of these was wasted, from a policy point of view, on McReynolds. Had
McReynolds voted "right," the subsequent struggle over the problem of
child labor need not have occurred, for the decision in 1918 was by a Court

TABLE 5

Type of Congressional Action Following Supreme Court Decisions Holding Legislation Unconstitutional Within Four Years After Enactment (Other Than New Deal Legislation)

Congressional action	Major policy	Minor policy	Total
Reverses Court's policy	10[a]	2[d]	12
Changes own policy	2[b]	0	2
None	0	8[e]	8
Unclear	3[e]	1[f]	4
Total	15	11	26

NOTE: For the cases in each category, see footnote 13.

divided five to four, McReynolds voting with the majority.[23] Congress moved at once to circumvent the decision by means of the tax power, but in 1922 the Court blocked that approach.[24] In 1924 Congress returned to the engagement with a constitutional amendment that was rapidly endorsed by a number of state legislatures before it began to meet so much resistance in the remaining states that the enterprise miscarried. In 1938, under a second reformist president, new legislation was passed, 22 years after the first; this a chastened Court accepted in 1941,[25] and thereby brought to an end a battle that had lasted a full quarter-century.

The entire record of the duel between the Court and the lawmaking majority, in cases where the Court has held legislation unconstitutional within four years after enactment, is summarized in Table 6.

Thus the application of the majority criterion seems to show the following: First, if the Court did in fact uphold minorities against national majorities, as both its supporters and critics often seem to believe, it would be an extremely anomalous institution from a democratic point of view. Second, the elaborate "democratic" rationalizations of the Court's defenders and the hostility of its "democratic" critics are largely irrelevant, for lawmaking majorities generally have had their way. Third, although the Court seems never to have succeeded in holding out indefinitely, in a very small number of important cases it has delayed the application of policy up to as much as 25 years.

V

How can we appraise decisions of the third kind just mentioned? Earlier I referred to the criterion of Right or Justice as a norm sometimes invoked to describe the role of the Court. In accordance with this norm, it might be argued that the most important policy function of the Court is to protect rights that are in some sense basic or fundamental. Thus (the argument might run) in a country where basic rights are, on the whole, respected, one should not expect more than a small number of cases where the Court has had to plant itself firmly against a lawmaking majority. But majorities may, on rare occasions, become "tyrannical"; and when they do, the Court intervenes; and although the constitutional issue may, strictly speaking, be technically open, the Constitution assumes an underlying fundamental body of rights and liberties which the Court guarantees by its decisions.

Here again, however, even without examining the actual cases, it would appear, on political grounds, somewhat unrealistic to suppose that a Court whose members are recruited in the fashion of Supreme Court justices would long hold to norms of Right or Justice substantially at odds with the rest of the political elite. Moreover, in an earlier day it was perhaps easier to believe that certain rights are so natural and self-evident that their fundamental validity is as much a matter of definite knowledge, at least to all reasonable creatures, as the color of a ripe apple. To say that this view is unlikely to find many articulate defenders today is, of course, not to disprove it; it is rather to suggest that we do not need to elaborate the case against it in this essay.

In any event the best rebuttal to the view of the Court suggested above will be found in the record of the Court's decisions. Surely the six cases referred to a moment ago, where the policy consequences of the Court's decisions were overcome only after long battles, will not appeal to many contemporary minds as evidence for the proposition under examination. A natural right to employ child labor in mills and mines? To be free of income taxes by the federal government? To employ longshoremen and harbor workers without the protection of workmen's compensation? The Court itself did not rely upon such arguments in these cases, and it would be no credit to their opinions to reconstruct them along such lines.

So far, however, our evidence has been drawn from cases in which the Court has held legislation unconstitutional within four years after enactment. What of the other 40 cases? Do we have evidence in these that the Court has protected fundamental or natural rights and liberties against the dead hand of some past tyranny by the lawmakers? The evidence is not impressive. In the entire history of the Court there is not one case arising

TABLE 6
Type of Congressional Action After Supreme Court Decisions Holding Legislation Unconstitutional Within Four Years After Enactment (Including New Deal Legislation)

Congressional action	Major policy	Minor policy	Total
Reverses Court's policy	17	2	19
None	0	12	12
Other	6*	1	7
Total	23	15	38

* In addition to the actions in Table 5 under "Changes Own Policy" and "Unclear," this figure includes the NRA legislation affected by the *Schechter Poultry* case.

under the First Amendment in which the Court has held federal legislation unconstitutional. If we turn from these fundamental liberties of religion, speech, press and assembly, we do find a handful of cases—something less than 10—arising under Amendments Four to Seven in which the Court has declared acts unconstitutional that might properly be regarded as involving rather basic liberties.[26] An inspection of these cases leaves the impression that, in all of them, the lawmakers and the Court were not very far apart; moreover, it is doubtful that the fundamental conditions of liberty in this country have been altered by more than a hair's breadth as a result of these decisions. However, let us give the Court its due; it is little enough.

Over against these decisions we must put the 15 or so cases in which the Court used the protections of the Fifth, Thirteenth, Fourteenth, and Fifteenth Amendments to preserve the rights and liberties of a relatively privileged group at the expense of the rights and liberties of a submerged group: chiefly slaveholders at the expense of slaves,[27] white people at the expense of colored people,[28] and property holders at the expense of wage earners and other groups.[29] These cases, unlike the relatively innocuous ones of the preceding set, all involved liberties of genuinely fundamental importance, where an opposite policy would have meant thoroughly basic shifts in the distribution of rights, liberties, and opportunities in the United States—where, moreover, the policies sustained by the Court's action have since been repudiated in every civilized nation of the Western world, including our own. Yet, if our earlier argument is correct, it is futile—precisely because the basic distribution of privilege was at issue—to suppose that the Court could have possibly acted much differently in these areas of policy from the way in which it did in fact act.

VI

Thus the role of the Court as a policy-making institution is not simple; and it is an error to suppose that its functions can be either described or appraised by means of simple concepts drawn from democratic or moral theory. It is possible, nonetheless, to derive a few general conclusions about the Court's role as a policy-making institution.

National politics in the United States, as in other stable democracies, is dominated by relatively cohesive alliances that endure for long periods of time. One recalls the Jeffersonian alliance, the Jacksonian, the extraordinarily long-lived Republican dominance of the post–Civil War years, and the New Deal alliance shaped by Franklin Roosevelt. Each is marked by a break with past policies, a period of intense struggle, followed by consolidation, and finally decay and disintegration of the alliance.

Except for short-lived transitional periods when the old alliance is disintegrating and the new one is struggling to take control of political institutions, the Supreme Court is inevitably a part of the dominant national alliance. As an element in the political leadership of the dominant alliance, the Court of course supports the major policies of the alliance. By itself, the Court is almost powerless to affect the course of national policy. In the absence of substantial agreement within the alliance, an attempt by the Court to make national policy is likely to lead to disaster, as the *Dred Scott* decision and the early New Deal cases demonstrate. Conceivably, the cases of the last three decades involving the freedom of Negroes, culminating in the now famous decision on school integration, are exceptions to this generalization; I shall have more to say about them in a moment.

The Supreme Court is not, however, simply an *agent* of the alliance. It is an essential part of the political leadership and possesses some bases of power of its own, the most important of which is the unique legitimacy attributed to its interpretations of the Constitution. This legitimacy the Court jeopardizes if it flagrantly opposes the major policies of the dominant alliance; such a course of action, as we have seen, is one in which the Court will not normally be tempted to engage.

It follows that within the somewhat narrow limits set by the basic policy goals of the dominant alliance, the Court *can* make national policy. Its discretion, then, is not unlike that of a powerful committee chairman in Congress who cannot, generally speaking, nullify the basic policies substantially agreed on by the rest of the dominant leadership, but who can, within these limits, often determine important questions of timing, effectiveness, and subordinate policy. Thus the Court is least effective against a current lawmaking majority—and evidently least inclined to act. It is most effective when it sets the bounds of policy for officials, agencies, state governments or even regions, a task that has come to occupy a very large part of the Court's business.[30]

Few of the Court's policy decisions can be interpreted sensibly in terms of a "majority" versus a "minority." In this respect the Court is no different from the rest of the political leadership. Generally speaking, policy at the national level is the outcome of conflict, bargaining, and agreement among minorities; the process is neither minority rule nor majority rule but what might better be called *minorities* rule, where one aggregation of minorities achieves policies opposed by another aggregation.

The main objective of presidential leadership is to build a stable and dominant aggregation of minorities with a high probability of winning the presidency and one or both houses of Congress. The main task of the Court is to confer legitimacy on the fundamental policies of the successful coalition. There are times when the coalition is unstable with respect to certain key policies; at very great risk to its legitimacy powers, the Court can intervene in such cases and may even succeed in establishing policy. Probably in such cases it can succeed only if its action conforms to and reinforces a widespread set of explicit or implicit norms held by the political leadership; norms which are not strong enough or are not distributed in such a way as to ensure the existence of an effective lawmaking majority but are, nonetheless, sufficiently powerful to prevent any successful attack on the legitimacy powers of the Court. This is probably the explanation for the relatively successful work of the Court in enlarging the freedom of Negroes to vote during the past three decades and in its famous school integration decisions.[31]

Yet the Court is more than this. Considered as a political system, democracy is a set of basic procedures for arriving at decisions. The operation of these procedures presupposes the existence of certain rights, obligations, liberties and restraints; in short, certain patterns of behavior. The existence of these patterns of behavior in turn presupposes widespread agreement (particularly among the politically active and influential segments of the population) on the validity and propriety of the behavior. Although its record is by no means lacking in serious blemishes, at its best the Court operates to confer legitimacy, not simply on the particular and parochial policies of the dominant political alliance, but upon the basic patterns of behavior required for the operation of a democracy.

Notes

1. Frankfurter, *The Supreme Court in the Mirror of Justices*, 105 U. of Pa. L. Rev. 781, 793 (1957).

2. Provided that the total membership of the society is an even number, it is technically possible for a dispute to occur that divides the membership into two equal parts, neither of which can be said to be either a majority or minority of the total membership. But even in instances where the number is even (which should occur on the average only half the time), the probability of an exactly even split, in any group of more than a few thousand people, is so small that it may be ignored.

3. Suppose the number of citizens, or members eligible to participate in collective decisions, is n. Let each member indicate his "most preferred alternative." Then it is obvious that the maximum number of most preferred alternatives is n. It is equally obvious that if the number of most preferred alternatives is more than or equal to $n/2$, then no majority is possible. But for all practical purposes those formal limitations can be ignored, for we are dealing with a large society where the number of alternatives at issue before the Supreme Court is invariably quite small. If the number of alternatives is greater than two, it is theoretically possible for preferences to be distributed so that no outcome is consistent with the majority criterion, even where all members can rank all the alternatives and where there is perfect information as to their preferences; but this difficulty does not bear on the subsequent discussion, and it is disregarded. For an examination of this problem, consult Arrow, *Social Choice and Individual Values* (1951).

4. Actually, the matter is somewhat ambiguous. There appear to have been 78 cases in which the Court has held provisions of federal law unconstitutional. Sixty-four different acts in the technical sense have been construed, and 86 different provisions in law have been in some respects invalidated. I rely here on the figures and the table given in Library of Congress, Legislative Reference Service, *Provisions of Federal Law Held Unconstitutional by the Supreme Court of the United States*, 95, 141–47 (1936), to which I have added *United States v. Lovett*, 328 U.S. 303 (1946), and *United States ex rel. Toth v. Quarles*, 350 U.S. 11 (1955). There are some minor discrepancies in totals (not attributable to the differences in publication dates) between this volume and *Acts of Congress Held Unconstitutional in Whole or in Part by the Supreme Court of the United States*, in Library of Congress, Legislative Reference Service, *The Constitution of the United States of America, Analysis and Interpretation* (Corwin ed., 1953). The difference is a result of classification. The latter document lists 73 acts held unconstitutional (to which *Toth v. Quarles*, supra, should be added) but different sections of the same act are sometimes counted separately.

5. Dahl, *A Preface to Democratic Theory*, c. 2 (1956).

6. Compare Commager, *Majority Rule and Minority Rights* (1943).

7. Frankfurter, *op. cit.* supra note 1, at 782–84.

8. *Booth v. United States*, 291 U.S. 339 (1934), involved a reduction in the pay of retired judges. *Lynch v. United States*, 292 U.S. 571 (1934), repealed laws granting to veterans rights to yearly renewable term insurance; there were only 29 policies outstanding in 1932. *Hopkins Federal Savings & Loan Ass'n v. Cleary*, 296 U.S. 315 (1935), granting permission to state building and loan associations to convert to federal ones on a vote of 51 percent or more of votes cast at a legal meeting. *Ashton v. Cameron County Water Improvement District*, 298 U.S. 513 (1936), permitting municipalities to petition federal courts for bankruptcy proceedings.

9. *Schechter Poultry Corp. v. United States*, 295 U.S. 495 (1935).

10. *United States v. Butler*, 297 U.S. 1 (1936); *Perry v. United States*, 294 U.S. 330 (1935); *Panama Refining Co. v. Ryan*, 293 U.S. 388 (1935); *Railroad Retirement Board v. Alton R. Co.*, 295 U.S. 330 (1935); *Louisville Joint Stock Land Bank v. Radford*, 295 U.S. 555 (1935); *Rickert Rice Mills v. Fontenot*, 297 U.S. 110 (1936); *Carter v. Carter Coal Co.*, 298 U.S. 238 (1936).

11. *United States v. Dewitt*, 9 Wall. (U.S.) 41 (1870); *Gordon v. United States*, 2 Wall. (U.S.) 561 (1865); *Monongahela Navigation Co. v. United States*, 148 U.S. 312 (1893); *Wong Wing v. United States*, 163 U.S. 228 (1896); *Fairbank v. United States*, 181 U.S. 283 (1901); *Rassmussen v. United States*, 197 U.S. 516 (1905); *Muskrat v. United States*, 219 U.S. 346 (1911); *Choate v. Trapp*, 224 U.S. 665 (1912); *Evans v. Gore*, 253 U.S. 245 (1920); *Untermyer v. Anderson*, 276

U.S. 440 (1928); *United States v. Lovett,* 328 U.S. 303 (1946). Note
that although the specific legislative provisions held unconstitutional
may have been minor, the basic legislation may have been of major
policy importance.

12. *Ex parte Garland,* 4 Wall. (U.S.) 333 (1867); *United States v. Klein,* 13
Wall. (U.S.) 128 (1872); *Pollock v. Farmers' Loan & Trust Co.,* 157
U.S. 429 (1895), rehearing granted 158 U.S. 601 (1895); *Employers'
Liability Cases,* 207 U.S. 463 (1908); *Keller v. United States,* 213 U.S.
138 (1909); *Hammer v. Dagenhart,* 247 U.S. 251 (1918); *Eisner v.
Macomber,* 252 U.S. 189 (1920); *Knickerbocker Ice Co. v. Stewart,*
253 U.S. 149 (1920); *United States v. Cohen Grocery Co.,* 255 U.S.
81 (1921); *Weeds, Inc. v. United States,* 255 U.S. 109 (1921);
Bailey v. Drexel Furniture Co., 259 U.S. 20 (1922); *Hill v. Wallace,*
259 U.S. 44 (1922); *Washington v. Dawson & Co.* 264 U.S. 219
(1924); *Trusler v. Crooks,* 269 U.S. 475 (1926).

13a. *Pollock v. Farmers' Loan & Trust Co.,* 157 U.S. 429 (1895); *Employers'
Liability Cases,* 207 U.S. 463 (1908); *Keller v. United States,* 213
U.S. 138 (1909); *Hammer v. Dagenhart,* 247 U.S. 251 (1918);
Bailey v. Drexel Furniture Co., 259 U.S. 20 (1922); *Trusler v. Crooks,*
269 U.S. 475 (1926); *Hill v. Wallace,* 259 U.S. 44 (1922); *Knickerbocker Ice Co. v. Stewart,* 253 U.S. 149 (1920); *Washington v. Dawson & Co.,* 264 U.S. 219 (1924).

b. *Ex parte Garland,* 4 Wall. (U.S.) 333 (1867); *United States v. Klein,*
13 Wall. (U.S.) 128 (1872).

c. *United States v. Cohen Grocery Co.,* 255 U.S. 81 (1921); *Weeds, Inc. v.
United States,* 255 U.S. 109 (1921); *Eisner v. Macomber,* 252 U.S.
189 (1920).

d. *Gordon v. United States,* 2 Wall. (U.S.) 561 (1865); *Evans v. Gore,* 253
U.S. 245 (1920).

e. *United States v. Dewitt,* 9 Wall. (U.S.) 41 (1870); *Monongahela Navigation Co. v. United States,* 148 U.S. 312 (1893); *Wong Wing v. United
States,* 163 U.S. 228 (1896); *Fairbank v. United States,* 181 U.S. 283
(1901); *Rassmussen v. United States,* 197 U.S. 516 (1905); *Muskrat v. United States,* 219 U.S. 346 (1911); *Choate v. Trapp,* 224 U.S.
665 (1912); *United States v. Lovett,* 328 U.S. 303 (1946).

f. *Untermyer v. Anderson,* 276 U.S. 440 (1928).

14. *Ex parte Garland,* 4 Wall. (U.S.) 333 (1867); *United States v. Klein,* 13
Wall. (U.S.) 128 (1872).

15. *United States v. Cohen Grocery Co.,* 255 U.S. 81 (1921), *Weeds, Inc. v.
United States,* 255 U.S. 109 (1921).

16. *Eisner v. Macomber,* 252 U.S. 189 (1920).

17. *Employers' Liability Cases,* 207 U.S. 463 (1908); *Keller v. United States,*
213 U.S. 138 (1909); *Trusler v. Crooks,* 269 U.S. 475 (1926); *Hill v.
Wallace,* 259 U.S. 44 (1922).

18. *Knickerbocker Ice Co. v. Stewart,* 253 U.S. 149 (1920).

19. *Washington v. Dawson & Co.*, 264 U.S. 219 (1924).

20. *Crowell v. Benson*, 285 U.S. 22 (1932).

21. *Pollock v. Farmers' Loan & Trust Co.*, 157 U.S. 429 (1895).

22. *Nicol v. Ames*, 173 U.S. 509 (1899); *Knowlton v. Moore*, 178 U.S. 41 (1900); *Patton v. Brady*, 184 U.S. 608 (1902); *Flint v. Stone Tracy Co.*, 220 U.S. 107 (1911).

23. *Hammer v. Dagenhart*, 247 U.S. 251 (1918).

24. *Bailey v. Drexel Furniture Co.*, 259 U.S. 20 (1922).

25. *United States v. Darby*, 312 U.S. 100 (1941).

26. The candidates for this category would appear to be *Boyd v. United States*, 116 U.S. 616 (1886); *Rassmussen v. United States*, 197 U.S. 516 (1905); *Wong Wing v. United States*, 163 U.S. 228 (1896); *United States v. Moreland*, 258 U.S. 433 (1922); *Kirby v. United States*, 174 U.S. 47 (1899); *United States v. Cohen Grocery Co.*, 255 U.S. 81 (1921); *Weeds, Inc. v. United States*, 255 U.S. 109 (1921); *Justices of the Supreme Court v. United States ex rel. Murray*, 9 Wall. (U.S.) 274 (1870); *United States ex rel. Toth v. Quarles*, 350 U.S. 11 (1955).

27. *Dred Scott v. Sandford*, 19 How. (U.S.) 393 (1857).

28. *United States v. Reese*, 92 U.S. 214 (1876); *United States v. Harris*, 106 U.S. 629 (1883); *United States v. Stanley* (Civil Rights Cases), 109 U.S. 3 (1883); *Baldwin v. Franks*, 120 U.S. 678 (1887); *James v. Bowman*, 190 U.S. 127 (1903); *Hodges v. United States*, 203 U.S. 1 (1906); *Butts v. Merchants & Miners Transportation Co.*, 230 U.S. 126 (1913).

29. *Monongahela Navigation Co. v. United States*, 148 U.S. 312 (1893); *Adair v. United States*, 208 U.S. 161 (1908); *Adkins v. Children's Hospital*, 261 U.S. 525 (1923); *Nichols v. Coolidge*, 274 U.S. 531 (1927); *Untermyer v. Anderson*, 276 U.S. 440 (1928); *Heiner v. Donnan*, 285 U.S. 312 (1932); *Louisville Joint Stock Land Bank v. Radford*, 295 U.S. 555 (1935).

30. "Constitutional law and cases with constitutional undertones are of course still very important, with almost one-fourth of the cases in which written opinions were filed [in the two most recent terms] involving such questions. Review of administrative action . . . constitutes the largest category of the Court's work, comprising one-third of the total cases decided on the merits. The remaining . . . categories of litigation . . . all involve largely public law questions." Frankfurter, *op. cit.* supra note 1, at 793.

31. *Rice v. Elmore*, 165 F.2d 387 (C.A. 4th, 1947), cert. denied 333 U.S. 875 (1948); *United States v. Classic*, 313 U.S. 299 (1941); *Smith v. Allwright*, 321 U.S. 649 (1944); *Grovey v. Townsend*, 295 U.S. 45 (1935); *Brown v. Board of Education*, 347 U.S. 483 (1954); *Bolling v. Sharpe*, 347 U.S. 497 (1954).

11.
THE END OF AMERICAN PARTY POLITICS

Walter Dean Burnham

American politics has clearly been falling apart in the past decade. We don't have to look hard for the evidence. Mr. Nixon is having as much difficulty controlling his fellow party members in Congress as any of his Democratic predecessors had in controlling theirs. John V. Lindsay, a year after he helped make Spiro Agnew a household word, had to run for mayor as a Liberal and an Independent with the aid of nationally prominent Democrats. Chicago in July of 1968 showed that for large numbers of its activists a major political party can become not just a disappointment, but positively repellant. Ticket-splitting has become widespread as never before, especially among the young; and George C. Wallace, whose third-party movement is the largest in recent American history, continues to demonstrate an unusually stable measure of support.

Vietnam and racial polarization have played large roles in this breakdown, to be sure; but the ultimate causes are rooted much deeper in our history. For some time we have been saying that we live in a "pluralist democracy." And no text on American politics would be complete without a few key code words such as "consensus," "incrementalism," "bargaining" and "process." Behind it all is a rather benign view of our politics, one that assumes that the complex diversity of the American social structure is filtered through the two major parties and buttressed by a consensus of middle-class values which produces an electoral politics of low intensity and gradual change. The interplay of interest groups and public officials determines policy in detail. The voter has some leverage on policy, but only in a most diffuse way; and, anyway, he tends to be a pretty apolitical animal, dominated either by familial or local tradition, on one hand, or by the charisma of attractive candidates on the other. All of this is a good thing, of course, since in an affluent time the politics of consensus rules out violence and polarization. It pulls together and supports the existing order of things.

There is no doubt that this description fits "politics as usual," in the United States, but to assume that it fits the whole of American electoral politics is a radical oversimplification. Yet even after these past years of turmoil, few efforts have been made to appraise the peculiar rhythms of American politics in a more realistic way. This article is an attempt to do so by focusing upon two very important and little celebrated aspects of the dynamics of our politics: the phenomena of critical realignments of the electorate and of decomposition of the party in our electoral politics.

As a whole and across time, the reality of American politics appears quite different from a simple vision of pluralist democracy. It is shot through with escalating tensions, periodic electoral convulsions, and repeated re-definitions of the rules and general outcomes of the political game. It has also been marked repeatedly by redefinitions—by no means always broaden-ing ones—of those who are permitted to play. One other very basic char-acteristic of American party politics that emerges from an historical over-view is the profound incapacity of established political leadership to adapt itself to the political demands produced by the losers in America's stormy socioeconomic life. As is well known, American political parties are not instruments of collective purpose, but of electoral success. One major im-plication of this is that, as organizations, parties are interested in control of offices but not of government in any larger sense. It follows that once suc-cessful routines are established or re-established for office-winning, very little motivation exists among party leaders to disturb the routines of the game. These routines are periodically upset, to be sure, but not by adaptive change within the party system. They are upset by overwhelming external force.

It has been recognized, at least since the publication of V. O. Key's "A Theory of Critical Elections" in 1955, that some elections in our history have been far more important than most in their long-range consequences for the political system. Such elections seem to "decide" clusters of sub-stantive issues in a more clear-cut way than do most of the ordinary varieties. There is even a consensus among historians as to when these turning points in electoral politics took place. The first came in 1800 when Thomas Jeffer-son overthrew the Federalist hegemony established by Washington, Adams, and Hamilton. The second came in 1828 and in the years afterward, with the election of Andrew Jackson and the democratization of the presidency. The third, of course, was the election of Abraham Lincoln in 1860, an elec-tion that culminated a catastrophic polarization of the society as a whole and resulted in civil war. The fourth critical election was that of William McKinley in 1896; this brought to a close the "Civil War" party system and inaugurated a political alignment congenial to the dominance of industrial capitalism over the American political economy. Created in the crucible of one massive depression, this "System of 1896" endured until the collapse of the economy in a second. The election of Franklin D. Roosevelt in 1932 came last in this series, and brought a major realignment of electoral politics and policy-making structures into the now familiar "welfare-pluralist" mode.

Now that the country appears to have entered another period of political upheaval, it seems particularly important not only to identify the phenomena of periodic critical realignments in our electoral politics, but to integrate them into a larger—if still very modest—theory of stasis and movement in American politics. For the realignments focus attention on the dark side of our politics, those moments of tremendous stress and abrupt transformation that remind us that "politics as usual" in the United States is not politics as always, and that American political institutions and leadership, once defined or redefined in a "normal phase" seem *themselves* to contribute to the building of conditions that threaten their overthrow.

To underscore the relevance of critical elections to our own day, one has only to recall that in the past, fundamental realignments in voting behavior have always been signaled by the rise of significant third parties: the Anti-Masons in the 1820s, the Free Soilers in the 1840s and 1850s, the Populists in the 1890s, and the LaFollette Progressives in the 1920s. We cannot know whether George Wallace's American Independent Party of 1968 fits into this series, but it is certain—as we shall see below—that the very foundations of American electoral politics have become quite suddenly fluid in the past few years, and that the mass base of our politics has become volatile to a degree unknown in the experience of all but the very oldest living Americans. The Wallace uprising is a major sign of this recent fluidity; but it hardly stands alone.

Third-party protests, perhaps by contrast with major-party bolts, point up the interplay in American politics between the inertia of "normal" established political routines and the pressures arising from the rapidity, unevenness and uncontrolled character of change in the country's dynamic socioeconomic system. All of the third parties prior to and including the 1968 Wallace movement constituted attacks by outsiders, who felt they were outsiders, against an elite frequently viewed in conspiratorial terms. The attacks were always made under the banner of high moralistic universals against an established political structure seen as corrupt, undemocratic, and manipulated by insiders for their own benefit and that of their supporters. All these parties were perceived by their activists as "movements" that would not only purify the corruption of the current political regime, but replace some of its most important parts. Moreover, they all telegraphed the basic clusters of issues that would dominate politics in the next electoral era: the completion of political democratization in the 1830s, slavery and sectionalism in the late 1840s and 1850s, the struggle between the industrialized and the colonial regions in the 1890s, and welfare liberalism vs. laissez-faire in the 1920s and 1930s. One may well view the American Independent Party in such a context.

The periodic recurrence of third-party forerunners of realignment— and realignments themselves, for that matter—are significantly related to dominant peculiarities of polity and society in the United States. They point to an electorate especially vulnerable to breaking apart, and to a political system in which the sense of common nationhood may be much more nearly skin-deep than is usually appreciated. If there is any evolutionary scale of political modernization at all, the persistence of deep fault lines in our electoral politics suggests pretty strongly that the United States remains a "new nation" to this day in some important political respects. The periodic recurrence of these tensions may also imply that—as dynamically developed as our economic system is—no convincing evidence of political development in the United States can be found after the 1860s.

Nation-wide critical realignments can only take place around clusters of issues of the most fundamental importance. The most profound of these issues have been cast up in the course of the transition of our Lockeian-liberal commonwealth from an agrarian to an industrial state. The last two major realignments—those of 1893–96 and 1928–36—involved the two great transitional crises of American industrial capitalism, the economic collapses of 1893 and 1929. The second of these modern realignments produced, of course, the broad coalition on which the New Deal's welfarist-pluralist policy was ultimately based. But the first is of immediate concern to us here. For the 1896 adaptation of electoral politics to the imperatives of industrial-capitalism involved a set of developments that stand in the sharpest possible contrast to those occurring elsewhere in the Western world at about the same time. Moreover, they set in motion new patterns of behavior in electoral politics that were never entirely overcome even during the New Deal period, and which, as we shall see, have resumed their forward march during the past decade.

As a case in point, let me briefly sketch the political evolution of Pennsylvania—one of the most industrially developed areas on earth—during the 1890–1932 period. There was in this state a pre-existing, indeed, preindustrial, pattern of two-party competition, one that had been forged in the Jacksonian era and decisively amended, though not abolished, during the Civil War. Then came the realignment of the 1890s, which, like those of earlier times, was an abrupt process. In the five annual elections from 1888 through November 1892, the Democrats' mean percentage of the total two-party vote was 46.7 percent, while for the five elections beginning in February 1894 it dropped to a mean of 37.8 percent. Moreover, the greatest and most permanent Republican gains during this depression decade occurred where they counted most, numerically: in the metropolitan areas of Philadelphia and Pittsburgh.

The cumulative effect of this realignment and its aftermath was to convert Pennsylvania into a thoroughly one-party state, in which conflict over the basic political issues were duly transferred to the Republican primary after it was established in 1908. By the 1920s this peculiar process had been completed and the Democratic party had become so weakened that, as often as not, the party's nominees for major office were selected by the Republican leadership. But whether so selected or not, their general-election prospects were dismal: of the 80 state-wide contests held from 1894 through 1931, a candidate running with Democratic party endorsement won just one. Moreover, with the highly ephemeral exception of Theodore Roosevelt's bolt from the Republican party in 1912, no third parties emerged as general-election substitutes for the ruined Democrats.

The political simplicity which had thus emerged in this industrial heartland of the Northeast by the 1920s was the more extraordinary in that it occurred in an area whose socioeconomic division of labor was as complex and its level of development as high as any in the world. In most other regions of advanced industrialization the emergence of corporate capitalism was associated with the development of mass political parties with high structural cohesion and explicit collective purposes with respect to the control of policy and government. These parties expressed deep conflicts over the direction of public policy, but they also brought about the democratic revolution of Europe, for electoral participation tended to rise along with them. Precisely the opposite occurred in Pennsylvania and, with marginal and short-lived exceptions, the nation. It is no exaggeration to say that the political response to the collectivizing thrust of industrialism in this American state was the elimination of organized partisan combat, an extremely severe decline in electoral participation, the emergence of a Republican "coalition of the whole" and—by no means coincidentally—a highly efficient insulation of the controlling industrial-financial elite from effective or sustained countervailing pressures.

Irrelevant Radicalism

The reasons for the increasing solidity of this "system of 1896" in Pennsylvania are no doubt complex. Clearly, for example, the introduction of the direct primary as an alternative to the general election, which was thereby emptied of any but ritualistic significance, helped to undermine the minority Democrats more and more decisively by destroying their monopoly of opposition. But nationally as well the Democratic party in and after the 1890s was virtually invisible to Pennsylvania voters as a usable opposition. For with the ascendency of the agrarian Populist William Jennings Bryan, the Democratic party was transformed into a vehicle for colonial, periphery-oriented dissent against the industrial-metropolitan center, leaving the Republicans as sole spokesmen for the latter.

This is a paradox that pervades American political history, but it was sharpest in the years around the turn of this century. The United States was so vast that it had little need of economic colonies abroad; in fact it had two major colonial regions within its own borders, the postbellum South and the West. The only kinds of attacks that could be made effective on a nation-wide basis against the emergent industrialist hegemony—the only attacks that, given the ethnic heterogeneity and extremely rudimentary political socialization of much of the country's industrial working class, could come within striking distance of achieving a popular majority—came out of these colonial areas. Thus "radical" protest in major-party terms came to be associated with the neo-Jacksonian demands of agrarian small-holders and small-town society already confronted by obsolescence. The Democratic party from 1896 to 1932, and in many respects much later, was the national vehicle for these struggles.

The net effect of this was to produce a condition in which—especially, but not entirely on the presidential level—the more economically advanced a state was, the more heavy were its normal Republican majorities likely to be. The nostalgic agrarian-individualist appeals of the national Democratic leadership tended to present the voters of this industrial state with a choice that was not a choice: between an essentially backward-looking provincial party articulating interests in opposition to those of the industrial North and East as a whole, and a "modernizing" party whose doctrines included enthusiastic acceptance of and co-operation with the dominant economic interests of region and nation. Not only did this partitioning of the political universe entail normal and often huge Republican majorities in an economically advanced state like Pennsylvania, but the survival of national two-party competition on such a basis helped to ensure that no local reorganization of electoral politics along class lines could effectively occur even within such a state. Such a voting universe had a tendency toward both enormous inbuilt stability and increasing entrenchment in the decades after its creation. Probably no force less overwhelming than the post-1929 collapse of the national economic system would have sufficed to dislodge it. Without such a shock, who can say how, or indeed whether, the "System of 1896" would have come to an end in Pennsylvania and the nation? To ask such a question is to raise yet another. For there is no doubt that in Pennsylvania, as elsewhere, the combination of trauma in 1929–33 and Roosevelt's creative leadership provided the means for overthrowing the old order and for reversing dramatically the depoliticization of electoral politics which had come close to perfection under it. Yet might it not be the case that the dominant pattern of political adaptation to industrialism in the United States has worked to eliminate, by one means or another, the links provided by political parties between voters and rulers? In other words, was the post–1929 reversal permanent or only a transitory phase in our political evolution? And if transitory, what bearing would this fact have on the possible recurrence of critical realignments in the future?

Withering Away of the Parties

The question requires us to turn our attention to the second major dynamic of American electoral politics during this century: the phenomenon of electoral disaggregation, of the breakdown of party loyalty, which in many respects must be seen as the permanent legacy of the fourth party system of 1896–1932. One of the most conspicuous developments of this era, most notably during the 1900–20 period, was a whole network of changes in the rules of the political game. This is not the place for a thorough treatment and documentation of these peculiarities. One can only mention here some major changes in the rules of the game, and note that one would have no difficulty in arguing that their primary latent function was to ease the transition from a preindustrial universe of competitive, highly organized mass politics to a depoliticized world marked by drastic shrinkage in participation or political leverage by the lower orders of the population. The major changes surely include the following:

- The introduction of the Australian ballot, which was designed to purify elections but also eliminated a significant function of the older political machines, the printing and distribution of ballots, and eased a transition from party voting to candidate voting.

- The introduction of the direct primary, which at once stripped the minority party of its monopoly of opposition and weakened the control of party leaders over nominating processes, and again hastened preoccupation of the electorate with candidates rather than parties.

- The movement toward nonpartisan local elections, often accompanied by a drive to eliminate local bases of representation such as wards in favor of at-large elections, which produced—as Samuel Hays points out—a shift of political power from the grassroots to city-wide cosmopolitan elites.

- The expulsion of almost all blacks, and a very large part of the poor-white population as well, from the Southern electorate by a series of legal and extralegal measures such as the poll tax.

- The introduction of personal registration requirements the burden of which, in faithful compliance with dominant middle-class values, was placed on the individual rather than on public authority, but which effectively disenfranchised large numbers of the poor.

Breakdown of Party Loyalty

Associated with these and other changes in the rules of the game was a profound transformation in voting behavior. There was an impressive growth in the numbers of political independents and ticket-splitters, a growth accompanied by a sea-change among party elites from what Richard Jensen has termed the "militarist" (or ward boss) campaign style to the "mercantilist" (or advertising-packaging) style. Aside from noting that the transition was largely completed as early as 1916, and hence that the practice of "the selling of the president" goes back far earlier than we usually think, these changes too must be left for fuller exposition elsewhere.

Critical realignments, as we have argued, are an indispensable part of a stability-disruption dialectic which has the deepest roots in American political history. Realigning sequences are associated with all sorts of aberrations from the normal workings of American party politics, both in the events leading up to nominations, the nature and style of election campaigning and the final outcome at the polls. This is not surprising, since they arise out of the collision of profound transitional crisis in the socioeconomic system with the immobility of a nondeveloped political system.

At the same time, it seems clear that for realignment to fulfill some of its most essential tension-management functions, for it to be a forum by which the electorate can participate in durable "constitution making," it is essential that political parties not fall below a certain level of coherence and appeal in the electorate. It is obvious that the greater the electoral disaggregation the less effective will be "normal" party poltics as an instrument of countervailing influence in an industrial order. Thus, a number of indices of disaggregation significantly declined during the 1930s as the Democratic Party remobilized parts of American society under the stimulus of the New Deal. In view of the fact that political parties during the 1930s and 1940s were once again called upon to assist in a redrawing of the map of American politics and policy-making, this regeneration of partisan voting in the 1932–52 era is hardly surprising. More than that, regeneration was necessary if even the limited collective purposes of the new majority coalition were to be realized.

Even so, the New Deal realignment was far more diffuse, protracted, and incomplete than any of its predecessors, a fact of which the more advanced New Dealers were only too keenly aware. It is hard to avoid the impression that one contributing element in this peculiarity of our last realignment was the much higher level of electoral disaggregation in the 1930s and 1940s than had existed at any time prior to the realignment of the 1890s. If one assumes that the end result of a long-term trend toward electoral disaggregation is the complete elimination of political parties as foci that shape voting behavior, then the possibility of critical realignment would, by definition, be eliminated as well. Every election would be dominated by TV packaging, candidate charisma, real or manufactured, and short-term, ad hoc influences. Every election, therefore, would have become deviating or realigning by definition, and American national politics would come to resemble the formless gubernatorial primaries that V. O. Key described in his classic *Southern Politics.*

The New Deal clearly arrested and reversed, to a degree, the march toward electoral disaggregation. But it did so only for the period in which the issues generated by economic scarcity remained central, and the generation traumatized by the collapse of 1929 remained numerically preponderant in the electorate. Since 1952, electoral disaggregation has resumed, in many measurable dimensions, and with redoubled force. The data on this point are overwhelming. Let us examine a few of them.

A primary aspect of electoral disaggregation, of course, is the "pulling apart" over time of the percentages for the same party but at different levels of election: this is the phenomenon of split-ticket voting. Recombining and reorganizing the data found in two tables of Milton

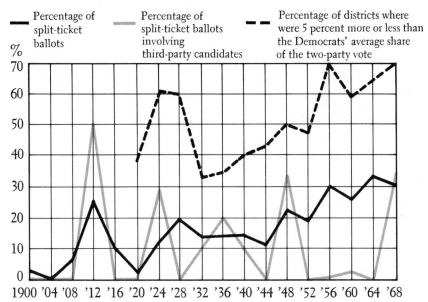

▬ Percentage of split-ticket ballots	▬ Percentage of split-ticket ballots involving third-party candidates	▬ ▬ Percentage of districts where were 5 percent more or less than the Democrats' average share of the two-party vote

The Emergent Independent Majority, 1900–1968. Third-party candidates often inspire voters to split their tickets, but the overall trend
has been for voters to ignore party labels.

Cummings' excellent study, *Congressmen and the Electorate*, and extending
the series back and forward in time, we may examine the relationship between presidential and congressional elections during this century.

Such an array captures both the initial upward thrust of disaggregation in the second decade of this century, the peaking in the middle to
late 1920s, the recession beginning in 1932, and especially the post-1952
resumption of the upward trend.

Other evidence points precisely in the same direction. It has generally been accepted in survey-research work that generalized partisan
identification shows far more stability over time than does actual voting
behavior, since the latter is subject to short-term factors associated with
each election. What is not so widely understood is that this glacial
measure of party identification has suddenly become quite volatile during
the 1960s, and particularly during the last half of the decade. In the first
place, as both Gallup and Survey Research Center data confirm, the proportion of independents underwent a sudden shift upward around 1966:
while from 1940 to 1965 independents constituted about 20 percent to 22
percent of the electorate, they increased to 29 percent in 1966. At the
present time, they outnumber Republicans by 30 percent to 28 percent.

Second, there is a clear unbroken progression in the share that
independents have of the total vote along age lines. The younger the age
group, the larger the number of independents in it, so that among the
21–29 year olds, according to the most recent Gallup findings this year, 42
percent are independents—an increase of about 10 percent over the first

half of the decade, and representing greater numbers of people than identify with either major party. When one reviews the June 1969 Gallup survey of college students, the share is larger still—44 percent. Associated with this quantitative increase in independents seems to be a major qualitative change as well. Examining the data for the 1950s, the authors of *The American Voter* could well argue that independents tended to have lower political awareness and political involvement in general than did identifiers (particularly strong identifiers) of either major party. But the current concentration of independents in the population suggests that this may no longer be the case. They are clearly and disproportionately found not only among the young, and especially among the college young, but also among men, those adults with a college background, people in the professional-managerial strata and, of course, among those with higher incomes. Such groups tend to include those people whose sense of political involvement and efficacy is far higher than that of the population as a whole. Even in the case of the two most conspicuous exceptions to this—the pile-up of independent identifiers in the youngest age group and in the South—it can be persuasively argued that this distribution does not reflect low political awareness and involvement but the reverse: a sudden, in some instances almost violent, increase in both awareness and involvement among southerners and young adults, with the former being associated both with the heavy increase in southern turnout in 1968 and the large Wallace vote polled there.

Third, one can turn to two sets of evidence found in the Survey Research Center's election studies. If the proportion of *strong* party identifiers over time is examined, the same pattern of long-term inertial stability and recent abrupt change can be seen. From 1952 through 1964, the proportion of strong Democratic and Republican party identifiers fluctuated in a narrow range between 36 percent and 40 percent, with a steep downward trend in strong Republican identifiers between 1960 and 1964 being matched by a moderate increase in strong Democratic identifiers. Then in 1966 the proportion of strong identifiers abruptly declines to 28 percent, with the defectors overwhelmingly concentrated among former Democrats. This is almost certainly connected, as is the increase of independent identifiers, with the Vietnam fiasco. While we do not as yet have the 1968 SRC data, the distribution of identifications reported by Gallup suggests the strong probability that this abrupt decline in party loyalty has not been reversed very much since. It is enough here to observe that while the ratio between strong identifiers and independents prior to 1966 was pretty stably fixed at between 1.6 to 1 and 2 to 1 in favor of the former, it is now evidently less than 1 to 1. Both Chicago and Wallace last year were the acting out of these changes in the arena of "popular theater."

Finally, both survey and election data reveal a decline in two other major indices of the relevance of party to voting behavior: split-ticket voting and the choice of the same party's candidates for President across time.

It is evident that the 1960s have been an era of increasingly rapid liquidation of pre-existing party commitments by individual voters. There

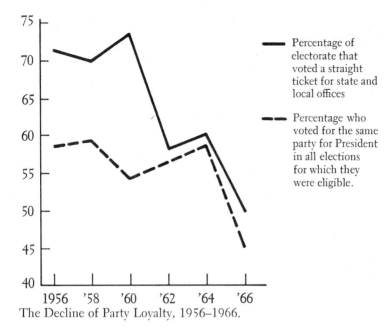

Percentage of electorate that voted a straight ticket for state and local offices

Percentage who voted for the same party for President in all elections for which they were eligible.

The Decline of Party Loyalty, 1956–1966.

is no evidence anywhere to support Kevin Phillips' hypothesis regarding an emergent Republican majority—assuming that such a majority would involve increases in voter identification with the party. More than that, one might well ask whether, if this process of liquidation is indeed a preliminary to realignment, the latter may not take the form of a third-party movement of truly massive and durable proportions.

The evidence lends some credence to the view that American electoral politics is undergoing a long-term transition into routines designed only to fill offices and symbolically affirm "the American way." There also seem to be tendencies for our political parties gradually to evaporate as broad and active intermediaries between the people and their rulers, even as they may well continue to maintain enough organizational strength to screen out the unacceptable or the radical at the nominating stage. It is certain that the significance of party as link between government and the governed has now come once again into serious question. Bathed in the warm glow of diffused affluence, vexed in spirit but enriched economically by our imperial military and space commitments, confronted by the gradually unfolding consequences of social change as vast as it is unplanned, what need have Americans of political parties? More precisely, why do they need parties whose structures, processes, and leadership cadres seem to grow more remote and irrelevant to each new crisis?

Future Politics

It seems evident enough that if this long-term trend toward a politics without parties continues, the policy consequences must be profound. One can put the matter with the utmost simplicity: political parties, with all their well-known human and structural shortcomings, are the only devices thus far invented by the wit of Western man that can, with some effectiveness, generate countervailing collective power on behalf of the many individually powerless against the relatively few who are individually or organizationally powerful. Their disappearance as active intermediaries, if not as preliminary screening devices, would only entail the unchallenged ascendancy of the already powerful, unless new structures of collective power were somehow developed to replace them, and unless conditions in America's social structure and political culture came to be such that they could be effectively used. Yet *neither* of these contingencies, despite recent publicity for the term "participatory democracy," is likely to occur under immediately conceivable circumstances in the United States. It is much more probable that the next chapter of our political history will resemble the metapolitical world of the 1920s.

But, it may be asked, may not a future realignment serve to re-crystallize and revitalize political parties in the American system?

The present condition of America contains a number of what Marxists call "internal contradictions," some of which might provide the leverage for a future critical realignment if sufficiently sharp dislocations in everyday life should occur. One of the most important of these, surely, is the conversion—largely through technological change—of the American social stratification system from the older capitalist mixture of upper or "owning" classes, dependent white-collar middle classes, and proletarians into a mixture described recently by David Apter: the technologically competent, the technologically obsolescent, and the technologically superfluous. It is arguable, in fact, that the history of the Kennedy-Johnson Administrations on the domestic front could be written in terms of a coalition of the top and bottom of this Apter-ite mix against the middle, and the 1968 election as the first stage of a "counterrevolution" of these middle strata against the pressures from both of the other two. Yet the inchoate results of 1968 raise some doubts, to say the least, that it can yet be described as part of a realigning sequence: there was great volatility in this election, but also a remarkable and unexpectedly large element of continuity and voter stability.

It is not hard to find evidence of cumulative social disaster in our metropolitan areas. We went to war with Japan in 1941 over a destruction inflicted on us far less devastating in scope and intensity than that endured by any large American city today. But the destruction came suddenly, as a sharp blow, from a foreign power; while the urban destruction of today has matured as a result of our own internal social and political processes, and it has been unfolding gradually for decades. We have consequently learned somehow to adapt to it piecemeal, as best we can, without changing our lives or our values very greatly. Critical realignments, however, also seem to require sharp, sudden blows as a precondition for their emergence.

If we think of realignment as arising from the spreading internal disarray in this country, we should also probably attempt to imagine what kinds of events could produce a sudden, sharp, and general escalation in social tensions and threatened deprivations of property, status or values.

Conceivably, ghetto and student upheavals could prove enough in an age of mass communications to create a true critical realignment, but one may doubt it. Student and ghetto rebellions appear to be too narrowly defined socially to have a *direct* impact on the daily lives of the "vast middle," and thus produce transformations in voting behavior that would be both sweeping and permanent. For what happens in times of critical realignment is nothing less than an intense, if temporary, quasi revolutionizing of the vast middle class, a class normally content to be traditionalists or passive-participants in electoral politics.

Yet, even if students and ghetto blacks could do the trick, if they could even begin, with the aid of elements of the technological elite, a process of electoral realignment left-ward, what would be the likely consequences? What would the quasi revolutionizing of an insecure, largely urban middle class caught in a brutal squeeze from the top and the bottom of the social system look like? There are already premonitory evidences: the Wallace vote in both southern and nonsouthern areas, as well as an unexpected durability in his *postelection* appeal; the mayoral elections in Los Angeles and Minneapolis this year, and not least, Lindsay's narrow squeak into a second term as mayor of New York City. To the extent that the "great middle" becomes politically mobilized and self-conscious, it moves toward what has been called "urban populism," a stance of organized hostility to blacks, student radicals, and cosmopolitan liberal elites. The "great middle" remains, after all, the chief defender of the old-time Lockeian faith; both its material and cultural interests are bound up in this defense. If it should become at all mobilized as a major and cohesive political force in today's conditions, it would do so in the name of a restoration of the ancient truths by force if necessary. A realignment that directly involved this kind of mobilization—as it surely would, should it occur—would very likely have sinister overtones unprecedented in our political history.

Are we left, then, with a choice between the stagnation implicit in the disaggregative trends we have outlined here and convulsive disruption? Is there something basic to the American political system, and extending to its electoral politics, which rules out a middle ground between drift and mastery?

The fact that these questions were raised by Walter Lippmann more than half a century ago—and have indeed been raised in one form or other in every era of major transitional crisis over the past century—is alone enough to suggest an affirmative answer. The phenomena we have described here provide evidence of a partly quantitative sort which seems to point in the same direction. For electoral disaggregation is the negation of party. Further, it is—or rather, reflects—the negation of structural and behavioral conditions in politics under which linkages between the bottom, the middle, and the top can exist and produce the effective carrying out of collective power. Critical realignments are evidence not of the presence of such linkages or conditions in the normal state of American electoral politics, but precisely of their absence. Correspondingly, they are not manifestations of democratic accountability, but infrequent and hazardous substitutes for it.

Taken together, both of these phenomena generate support for the inference that American politics in its normal state is the negation of the public order itself, as that term is understood in politically developed nations. We do not have government in our domestic affairs so much as "nonrule." We do not have political parties in the contemporary sense of that term as understood elsewhere in the Western world; we have anti-parties instead. Power centrifuges rather than power concentrators, they have been immensely important not as vehicles of social transformation but for its prevention through political means.

The entire setting of the critical realignment phenomenon bears witness to a deep-seated dialectic within the American political system. From the beginning, the American socioeconomic system has developed and transformed itself with an energy and thrust that has no parallel in modern history. The political system, from parties to policy structures, has seen no such development. Indeed, it has shown astonishingly little substantive transformation over time in its methods of operation. In essence, the political system of this "fragment society" remains based today on the same Lockeian formulation that, as Louis Hartz points out, has dominated its entire history. It is predicated upon the maintenance of a high wall of separation between politics and government on one side and the socio-economic system on the other. It depends for its effective working on the failure of anything approximating internal sovereignty in the European sense to emerge here.

The Lockeian cultural monolith, however, is based upon a social assumption that has come repeatedly into collision with reality. The assumption, of course, is not only that the autonomy of socioeconomic life from political direction is the prescribed fundamental law for the United States, but that this autonomous development will proceed with enough smoothness, uniformity and generally distributed benefits that it will be entirely compatible with the usual functioning of our antique political structures. Yet the high (though far from impermeable) wall of separation between politics and society is periodically threatened with inundations. As the socioeconomic system develops in the context of unchanging institutions of electoral politics and policy formation, dysfunctions become more and more visible. Whole classes, regions or other major sectors of the population are injured or faced with an imminent threat of injury. Finally the triggering event occurs, critical realignments follow, the universe of policy and of electoral coalitions is broadly redefined, and the tensions generated by the crisis receive some resolution. Thus it can be argued that critical realignment as a periodically recurring phenomenon is as centrally related to the workings of such a system as is the archaic and increasingly rudimentary structure of the major parties themselves.

Party vs. Survival

One is finally left with the sense that the twentieth-century decomposition of partisan links in our electoral system also corresponds closely with the contemporary survival needs of what Samuel P. Huntington has called the American "Tudor polity." Electoral disaggregation and the concentration of certain forms of power in the hands of economic, technological, and administrative elites are functional for the short-term survival of nonrule in the United States. They may even somehow be related to the gradual emergence of internal sovereignty in this country—though to be sure under not very promising auspices for participatory democracy of any kind. Were such a development to occur, it would not necessarily entail the disappearance or complete suppression of subgroup tensions or violence in American social life, or of group bargaining and pluralism in the policy process. It might even be associated with increases in both. But it would, after all, reflect the ultimate sociopolitical consequences of the persistence of Lockeian individualism into an era of Big Organization: oligarchy at the top, inertia and spasms of self-defense in the middle, and fragmentation at the base. One may well doubt whether political parties or critical realignments need have much place in such a political universe.

PART II
PROBLEMS AND POLICIES: SOME CONTRASTING PERSPECTIVES

In the last section, we examined certain characteristics of the decision-making process, with particular regard for the general kinds of problems that the institutions of the national government experience in the 1970s. In this section, we shall look more intensively at the nature of the social problems that make up the political agenda. We shall represent three important problems, not because they are the only or the most significant ones, but because they show the range and character of the problems that confront the United States today. We shall try to include selections which see problems from a variety of perspectives. The first problem is that of minority-majority relationships, the second the crisis of the cities, and the last the more general problem of the standards by which the economy should be managed.

The issue of race relations, or the status of minorities in the United States, is one that has been present ever since the first landings of white people on this continent. It did not begin in the 1960s, although it is clear that it escalated into a series of questions of high public priority in that decade. It was the insistence of the minorities themselves that placed this question on the political agenda at that time, of course, and not some generous act on the part of the dominant white society. Blacks, Asians, Puerto Ricans, Chicanos, and Indians all developed distinctive movements during that period, and self-consciously insisted upon rights of cultural and economic self-determination as the 1970s began. Each minority, however, has a particular history, a particular experience of discrimination at the hands of the dominant society, and thus each has a specific and often distinctive set of claims for redress today. Thus, the problem of the relationship of minorities to the dominant white European society is not one problem but several, and they are joined together here for convenience of organization.

The first two articles in this section deal with minority-majority relationships, and, as might be expected, they see them in different ways. William Tabb's article takes up the economic and social status of blacks as a question of colonialism. The concept of colonialism has been applied to the status of blacks as a means of characterizing their dependent and exploited status within the United States. Tabb critically examines the famous "Kerner Report" on urban riots in the 1960s, and finds it unperceptive with respect to the real causes of black deprivation. He locates these causes in the economic exploitation of blacks by predominantly white businesses and owners, many of whom are located in the ghetto. He sees this relationship as being essentially that of colonial masters to colonial subjects. Thus, for Tabb, the essential character of the exploitative process is economic rather than racist.

Vine Deloria does not employ the concept of colonialism, but he introduces one of the distinguishing features of the American Indian's situation—the appropriation and totally different use of land by the white man. Deloria maintains that Indians knew how to preserve and protect the land for future use, while the white man has ruined it through over-applications of technology and economic shortsightedness. His essay suggests at least how far contemporary land use would have to be modified in order to return to the conservation-orientation of the Indians.

The next selection shows a distinctive approach to the problems of the cities. Much has been written about the specific problems of American urban centers, such as housing or welfare or transportation. Prescriptions are often made for the "solution" of each of these problems in isolation. A more fundamental analysis of the crisis of the cities, and one which takes issue with such allegedly superficial studies, is that of Nancy Spannaus. She sees the urban crisis as grounded in predictable aspects of capitalist investment policies and profit-maximizing, and argues that only a radical restructuring of the economy along socialist lines will suffice to solve this crisis; anything less will only postpone or paper over problems, to the ultimate disadvantage of the working classes.

The last four selections in this section involve aspects of a broader problem: national management of the economy. This is a very large problem, of course, involving such questions as who should set the basic goals and operating principles of the economy, and whose interests should receive first priority in doing so. But the scope of this problem is at least addressed by these selections. David Deitch's article points out some of the issues and problems involved in President Nixon's wage-price controls of 1971, and usefully sketches some of the factual background that led to these "New Economic Policies." The problem of inflation and depression at one and the same time confounded many observers in the late 1960s and into the 1970s, and Deitch makes clear the nature of the assumptions and choices made by the administration. He points out, for example, that in the not-so-long run, the real cost of stabilization would be paid by working-class people.

In a broader survey of policies toward the working class, John Howard shows that the economic situation of such people is marginal. He goes on to relate this economic marginality to government policies, and then to compare the United States' policies with those of other advanced industrialized nations. Finally, he links political behavior to economic marginality, arguing that the American working class is more concerned with its own survival than it is affirmatively prejudiced against any other groups in the population. This article is one of the very best of a recent series that has tried to analyze the social situation of the white working class, and it strongly suggests that images of the affluent worker are quite unfounded—as, indeed, may also be the image of deep-seated racism and/or superpatriotism. The American worker is in trouble, Howard suggests, and government has contributed to that trouble.

Finally, we have included two excellent surveys and explanations of income distribution in the United States. The consequences of the nature of economic organization for people is most readily seen in terms of the way in which income is distributed throughout the society. Ackerman and his co-authors show convincingly that inequality is both substantial and permanent, they trace its causes back to the character of the economy, and then they ask whether such inequality is either necessary or desirable. Not surprisingly, they conclude that it is neither. Perhaps more importantly, they try to suggest that it is not just economics, but also politics, which causes this inequality. In other words, they too see the economy and the political system linked closely together, such that each reinforces the effects created by the other. Wachtel's article analyzes the causes of poverty in a manner that effectively supplements Ackerman. He shows how little poverty is attributable to the characteristics of individuals and how much to the role of the government and the economic system.

In exploring the roots of problems, at least as they are seen by several authors with contrasting viewpoints, we have once again seen that the dynamics of the American economy are closely involved. Not only do the practices and values of the economy play a continuing part in the problems examined, but government policies articulate with these characteristics of the economy to sustain as much as to alleviate the problems. This is part of the problem of politics: the range of possible alternatives, and the sources of power to act on them, are both limited by the structure and needs of the economy. Few American political decision makers have seen a way around this dilemma, although we shall see in the next section that some are trying.

12.
CAPITALISM, COLONIALISM, AND RACISM

William K. Tabb

In the vast array of theoretical interpretations of the structural position of black Americans in our society two viewpoints appear to dominate the thinking of economists' writing from a left perspective. The first is that of the black ghetto as an internal colony set off from the rest of the society and systematically exploited in a consistent manner to maximize the well-being of the "mother country" (white America). The second view sees blacks as a marginal working class, lacking control over the means of production and who, though forced to work longer hours for less pay than other (white) workers, are essentially members of the working class. The policy implications of these two conceptual frameworks are quite different.

In this paper it is suggested that these two viewpoints need not be seen as contradictory, but are best considered within a more comprehensive theory of exploitation. Both of these interpretations can be contrasted with what might be termed the concerned liberal viewpoint, best enunciated perhaps by the *Report of the National Advisory Commission on Civil Disorders*.[1] This paper begins with a discussion of the analysis underlying the Kerner Commission Report and the work of such scholars as Gary Becker[2] and Milton Friedman[3] whose theoretical approach to the question of discrimination greatly influences others working in this area. An interpretation of the black ghetto as an internal colony will be presented and then contrasted to, and synthesized with, the viewpoint of the black worker as a marginal producer within a competitive economic framework. A discussion of the policy implications of these two views will conclude this paper.

The Kerner Report as Conventional Wisdom

The dominant view offered by the Kerner Commission report is that blacks have been discriminated against, treated brutally, and excluded

From William K. Tabb, "Capitalism, Colonialism, and Racism," *Review of Radical Political Economics*, vol. 3, no. 3 (Summer 1971), pp. 90–105. © by the Union for Radical Political Economics, July 1971. Reprinted by permission of the publisher.

from their rightful place as equal citizens. This, the *Report* suggested, was the effect of "white racism" defined as the prejudiced attitudes whites showed toward blacks. By stressing these attitudes, the *Report* gave its attention to *personal* racism rather than *institutional* racism. "Thus the *Report* placed too much emphasis on changing white attitudes and under-played the importance of changing white behavior and the basic structure of such institutions as schools, labor unions, and political parties."[4]

The generally uncritical acceptance and praise for the *Report* in academic circles and by the informed public is in some ways easy to understand. It is almost with a sigh of relief that Americans accepted the pious generalizations that we are all guilty, we are a racist society, white attitudes are to blame, we must do more to help blacks.

The *Report* represents concerned liberal viewpoint which typically: (a) stresses moral objections to racism while underestimating the extent to which racism is a structural part of American institutions, and (b) denies that the market economy—hence, employment, housing, and so on, is *structurally* exploitative. The corollary to (a) and (b) is that "we" have "options" and can "rearrange priorities" without altering the socioeconomic structure.

> The *Kerner Report* demands no changes in the way power and wealth are distributed among the classes; it never gets beyond its indictment of "white racism" to specify the forces in the political economy which brought the black man to riot . . . To treat the *symptoms* of social dislocation (e.g., slum conditions) as the *causes* of social ills is an inversion not peculiar to the *Kerner Report*. Unable or unwilling to pursue the implications of our own data, we tend to see the effects of a problem as the problem itself. The victims, rather than the victimizers, are defined as "the poverty problem." It is like blaming the corpse for the murder.[5]

In no area is this general indictment of the concerned liberal view more well-founded than in the realm of economic policy research. Students of the "poverty problem" count the number of aged, the children, the poorly educated, and the women heading families, and suggest that demographic characteristics "cause" poverty, or are "responsible" for poverty. The effects of exclusion, deprivation, and exploitation are taken as the causes of the problem. A prime example of this type of thinking is the recent concern to "help the Negro family" become more stable. The controversy surrounding the issue is dealt with adequately elsewhere.[6] Suffice it only to point out that United States Census Bureau statistics show: "At family income levels $7,000 and above, about 90 percent of Negro children are living with both parents. At the other end of the economic scale, only about one-fourth of Negro children in families with incomes below $3,000 are living with both parents."[7]

The tendency to mistake effect for cause and to suggest remedies in accord with such analysis are not the only weaknesses of much of the current work in the field. An equally harmful tendency, also exemplified by the *Kerner Commission Report*, is the rationalization of "racism" in terms of the personal preference maps of individuals. Here economists are in the vanguard of those basing their work on such a view. They are unfortunately not alone. The Kerner Commission approaches the problem also as seeing discrimination against blacks as caused by employers' preferences not to hire blacks. In Gary Becker's phrase, employers have "a taste for discrimination." By this term Becker suggests that if the employer has a "taste for discrimination" then "he must act *as if* he were willing to pay something either directly or in the form of a reduced income, to be associated with some persons instead of others. When actual discrimination occurs, he must, in fact, either pay or forfeit income for this privilege. This simple way of looking at the matter gets at the essence of prejudice and discrimination."[8] This is highly questionable. The essential nature of research on racism is to discover why such prejudice exists.

The employer with a "taste for discrimination" prefers to seek out white workers even after equally qualified blacks apply for the position. Obviously in a period of full employment he must pay more to indulge this "taste"—but equally obviously if we define full employment as 2 percent unemployment (leaving 2 percent of the labor force to be frictionally unemployed—changing jobs at any point in time), then in normal market conditions, the United States rarely reaches full employment and so the cost of discrimination to an employer is not as great as it would be in a tighter market.

In fact, it is not at all obvious that employers always suffer pecuniary losses by not hiring equally qualified blacks. If the white workers in his employ exhibit racist attitudes, hiring blacks may create frictions on the job which may lower productivity. If the blacks are in sales positions, or otherwise visible to customers, sales may suffer. In other situations hiring blacks may bring pecuniary benefits to employers, as when blacks are hired as strike breakers, an occurrence frequently chronicled in American labor history. By re-enforcing animosities, unionization efforts may be inhibited because blacks and whites are unable to work together. Raymond Franklin suggests that: "The main weakness of Becker's theoretical approach is that it accents in a relatively static fashion the subjective aspects of discrimination and neglects the historical, institutional, and objective circumstances that operate in various types of market situations." As Franklin points out, "Becker does not seek to identify the origins of disutility. In Becker's model, disutility is given."[9] Introducing the concept of the "taste for discrimination" displays the essential nature of what is being maximized—what is at stake is usually not an employer's "taste for discrimination, but his taste for profits."[10]

This approach implicitly accepts the notion that there is justice in the view that the individual (white) is entitled to his preferences as to whom he associates with (other whites) and whom he does not wish to associate with (blacks). Put this boldly, one might think the argument would be rejected by almost all members of the academic community. Yet we find such an eminent economist as Milton Friedman explaining discrimination in the following terms:

> The man who exercises discrimination pays a price for doing so. He is, as it were, "buying" what he regards as a "product." It is hard to see that discrimination can have any meaning other than a "taste" of others that one does not share. We do not regard it as "discrimination"—or at least not in the same invidious sense—if an individual is willing to pay a higher price to listen to one singer than to another, although we do if he is willing to pay a higher price to have services rendered to him by a person of one color rather than by a person of another.[11]

Thus free choice and the rights of the individual are interfered with when government enacts equal opportunity laws.

The same type of criticism can be made of the Friedman viewpoint as has been made of Becker's. What is at stake is not freedom of choice. In the competitive system many black Americans who find themselves on the losing end have seen the matter not as a personal problem but as an institutional one and are led to dismiss the dominance of the twin concepts of freedom of choice and competition. The repercussions of this awareness are only now beginning to be felt in terms of the more militant attitudes held by some black Americans.

> In a capitalist society, discrimination against Negroes takes place under the banner of freedom to choose. The freedom of choice to the white consumer means freedom to avoid living next door to a Negro. Freedom to organize an association around your job or trade means freedom to dissociate from Negroes by keeping them out of your trade or industry. The employer's freedom to combine labor and capital in production means freedom not to hire or to promote black labor relative to white labor, or freedom to avoid the social costs of technological unemployment, or those connected with the movement of a plant from the central city . . . Hence, it requires no great powers of reason to understand why the Negro is not a natural ally of the capitalist system.[12]

As more blacks implicitly, and increasingly explicitly, come to hold essentially anti-capitalist ideology, the type of solutions to racist exploitation which they are willing to consider undergoes significant change. This expansion of options to be considered is reflected in the rise to influence of the Nation of Islam and the Black Panther Party. The separatist ideology of the Muslims is certainly not new to American black thinking, but the Panthers' stress on class analysis certainly is. The degree to which the strategy debates in the black community are keyed to an assessment of the possibilities inherent in the capitalist system is a subject which requires brief attention.

At one pole in the discussion of the place of blacks in the American capitalist system stand men like Burkeley Burrell, currently the President of the National Business League, an organization founded in 1900 by Booker T. Washington (financed by white corporate leaders, most prominently John D. Rockefeller of Standard Oil and Julius Rosenwald of Sears).

> . . . It is an article of faith with us that the free entrepreneuring system that is an American trademark is directly and indirectly responsible for all of the good things that have inured to our citizenry. *We want to become a truly meaningful part of that system.* . . .[13]

Those who accept the desirability of participation by blacks as owners in American capitalism as a major goal include many moderates and some militants—most prominently, Roy Innis of CORE.

Innis and others have been criticized in strong terms by blacks who reject American capitalism as a model of development. James Forman and his associates, for example, have charged:

> Ironically, some of the most militant black nationalists, as they call themselves, have been the first to jump on the bandwagon of black capitalism. They are pimps, black power pimps and fraudulent leaders and the people must be educated to understand that any black man or Negro who is advocating a perpetuation of capitalism inside the United States is in fact seeking not only his ultimate destruction and death, but is contributing to the continuous exploitation of black people all around the world. For it is the power of the United States government, this racist imperialist government, that is choking the life of all people around the world.[14]

The distinction between the nature of capitalist and socialist solutions is pointed out even by such leaders as Ralph Abernathy of SCLC when he suggests: "We need to organize community owned development corporations where profits will be returned to building the community . . . We want to share in the public sector of the economy through publicly controlled non-profit institutions . . . I don't believe in black capitalism. I believe in black socialism."[15]

The differences in frames of reference and the ideological presumptions of different theories of causation have been belabored in order to stress the bias in current research done by whites about blacks and to contrast them to some of the thinking being done by blacks. While generalization in this area is hazardous, all too many Americans, while they see the dimensions as past tragedies, and foresee the possibility of still worse conflict, do not see racism in its institutional framework, but rather only in its individual manifestations and harmful attitudes. What alternative analyses are available to those wishing to understand the place of the black minority in the United States? Specifically, is the colonial framework referred to earlier useful in understanding the historical experience and present reality of black Americans?

The Ghetto as Colony

There are two key relationships which must be proved to exist before the colonial analogy can be accepted: (1) economic control and exploitation, and (2) political dependence and subjugation. Both of these necessitate social separation and a superior-inferior status relationship. If these can be demonstrated to exist, then the case can be made that the ghetto must break the shackles imposed by colonial exploitation if meaningful long-run improvement is to take place.

In defining colonialism, militants argue that the spatial separation of colony and colonial power is secondary to the existence of control of the ghetto from the outside through political and economic domination by white society. An historical comparison of the forms which colonialism has taken, and a description of the place of blacks in the American economy makes clear that internal colonialism is an apt description of the place blacks hold in our society.

The vast majority of colonies were established by Western powers over technologically less-advanced peoples of Asia, Africa, and Latin America. Military supremacy, combined with judicious bribing of local leaders and a generous sprinkling of Christian missionaries, enabled an outside power to dominate an area spatially separate from the ruling state. In some colonies there was extensive settlement by Europeans. If the territory was relatively unpopulated (Canada, Australia, New Zealand, and the United States), a policy of genocide and exchanging land for beads allowed the settlers to gain control. When their numbers and strength grew, the settlers could demand independence from the mother country. Nationhood was usually followed by a continuing economic relationship, but on better terms than the colony had enjoyed before it became independent. In some of the cases where European settlement was large but still a small minority of the total population of the colony, often a long and bloody struggle for independence resulted. Algeria is a case in point.

The black experience in America was somewhat different. Here the colonized were brought to the "mother" country to be enslaved and exploited. Internal colonialism thus involves the conquest and subjugation of a people and their physical removal to the ruling state. The command of the resources of the captive people (their labor power) followed. One can find parallel cases in the ancient histories of Egypt, Greece, and Rome. In these nations slaves were also brought to the mother country to be exploited, to do the dirty work of these "great societies." The grandeur of the mother country was built on the backs of the exploited slaves.

In the United States an important part of the capital accumulated in the early nineteenth century also came from slave labor. Douglass North suggests that the timing and pace of an economy's development is determined by the success of its export sector and the disposition of the income received by the export sector. He argues that in the key years in which capital accumulation took place, "it was the growth of the cotton textile industry and the demand for cotton which was decisive. The vicissitudes of the cotton trade were the most important influence upon the varying rates of growth in the economy during the period."[16] That New England merchants, through their control over the foreign trade and commerce of the country, and over insurance and shipping, did much of the actual accumulating should not be allowed to obscure this point. Cotton was the strategic variable. It paid for our imports, and "the demand for western foodstuffs and northeastern services and manufactures was basically dependent upon the income received from the cotton trade."[17] This is not an attempt to single out one factor as providing the "key" to development. But as cotton was the "carrier" industry inducing economic growth, so slavery was the basis of cotton production. Often the terrible burden of slavery is acknowledged, but rarely is the contribution of slave labor to the capital accumulation process seen as the very sizable factor in American development that it truly was.

To bring the story quickly to the present the relevant question is: Did the freeing of the slaves make a structurally significant difference in the colonial relationship? A comparison between the black ghetto as a colony within the United States today and the typical ex-colony which has gained its nominal political independence yet remains in neo-colonial subjugation suggests that in both instances formal freedom is not to be equated with real freedom.

Introductory chapters of a standard development textbook present a description of the typical less-developed country; low per capita income, high birth rate, a small, weak middle class, low rates of increase in labor productivity, in capital formation, and in domestic savings, as well as a small monetized market. The economy of such a country is heavily dependent on external markets where its few basic exports face an inelastic demand (that is, a demand which is relatively constant regardless of price and so expanding total output may not mean higher earnings). The international demonstration effect (the desire to consume the products which are seen generally available in the wealthier nations) works to increase the quantity of foreign goods imported to the underdeveloped country, putting pressure on their balance of payments since the value of imports exceeds the value of exports. Much of the small modern sector of the underdeveloped economy is owned by outsiders. Local entrepreneurship is limited, and in the absence of intergovernmental transfers, things might be still worse.

The economic relations of the ghetto to white America closely parallel those between Third World nations and the industrially advanced countries. The ghetto also has a relatively low per capita income and a high birth rate. Its residents are for the most part unskilled. Businesses lack capital and managerial know-how. Local markets are limited. The incidence of credit default is high. Little saving takes place in the ghetto, and what is saved is usually not invested locally. Goods and services tend to be "imported" for the most part, only the simplest and the most labor-intensive being produced locally. The ghetto is dependent on one basic export—its unskilled labor power. Aggregate demand for this export does not increase to match the growth of the ghetto labor force and unemployment is prevalent. Cultural imperialism is also part of the relationship as ghetto schools traditionally teach the history of the "Mother Country" as if blacks had no part in its development, as if blacks had no identity of their own, no culture, no origins worthy of mention in the chronicles of the world's nations and peoples. The dominant culture is constantly held up as good, desirable, worthy of emulation. The destruction of the indigenous culture is an important weapon in creating dependence and reinforcing control.

Consumer goods are advertised 24 hours a day on radio and television; ghetto residents are constantly reminded of the availability of goods and services which they cannot afford to buy. Welfare payments and other governmental transfers are needed to help pay for the ghetto's requirements. Welfare however only reinforces the dependency relationship, reinforces the psychology of inferiority, keeping body barely together even as it gnaws at the soul, sapping militancy and independence. In the light of these pressures, the forcefulness, strength, and the revolutionary beauty of the militant struggles being waged by welfare mothers locally and by the National Welfare Rights Organization is even more impressive.

Local businesses are owned, in large numbers, by nonresidents, many of whom are white. Marginal, low profit businesses are more likely to be owned by blacks;[18] larger, more profitable ones are owned by whites.[19] Important jobs in the local public economy (teachers, policemen, and postmen) are held by white outsiders. The black ghetto, then, is in many ways in a position similar to that of the typical underdeveloped nation.

It has been suggested that the distortion of the local economy caused by outside ownership can be compared to the creation of underdevelopment in external colonies through processes described by Frank.[20] In this light the dishonest practices of ghetto merchants[21, 22] and the crippling effects on ghetto residents[23, 24] can be seen not as unfortunate occurrences which come about through "unfair dealings" by greedy individuals, but rather as the direct result of the unequal power relations between the internal colony and the white mother country.

The conclusion has been drawn from the colonial model that attention should be centered on attempting to create community control over the local public economy, to encourage black ownership in the private sector, and in some cases to promote collectivization of the local economy. These political and economic programs may be seen as attempts to achieve black power. This phrase, greeted only a few years back with great horror by many whites and also some blacks, has been accepted, accommodated, and increasingly used by the same forces which have long controlled the destiny of the black ghettos to impose the equivalent of neo-colonialism. The objective of indirect rule can be detected in statements such as the following by Jacob Javits, the Republican Senator from New York, addressing the United States Chamber of Commerce in 1968: "American business has found that it must develop host country management and new forms of joint ownership in establishing plants in the fiercely nationalistic less-developed countries (so too), this same kind of enlightened partnership will produce the best results in the slums of our own country."[25] It is not only the desire to continue to do business which leads to a willingness to accept blacks as junior partners; long run self-interest dictates such a policy on even more basic grounds of self-interest. For example, the final report from a conference for corporate executives held at the Graduate School of Business at Columbia University in January 1964, stresses that "practical businessmen must recognize that this (ghetto rebellion) is a deep-seated economic problem that threatens every business, perhaps even our business system."[26] Since that meeting the corporate house organs and business community journals have been flooded with articles stressing the need for corporate involvement.

The rationale for this new-found interest has not gone unnoticed by blacks who have placed "black capitalism" and "corporate involvement" in the context of neo-colonialism. Robert Allen, for example, writes:

> . . . any black capitalist or managerial class must act, in effect, as the tacit representative of the white corporations which are sponsoring that class. The task of this class is to ease corporate penetration of the black communities and facilitate corporate planning and programming of the markets and human resources in those communities. This process occurs regardless of the personal motivations of the individuals involved, because it stems from the nature of the corporate economy itself and the dependent status of the fledgling, black capitalist-managerial class.[27]

Increasingly, even the acquiring of political control of city hall in predominantly black urban areas is a "hollow prize" as the local tax base just cannot support the programs needed by the central cities. The "independent" local political administration is dependent on "foreign aid" from the external mother country—the total independence of a black nation would mean even greater poverty for blacks who would have their labor power and little else. Independence based on community control would have a less extreme, but essentially similar result, perpetuating division within the working class.

Such an analysis also suggests that black power need not finally be measured by its ability to establish black autonomy from white society. Black control over the black community brings benefits only if it is within the context of an ability to enforce demands for the transfer of significant resources. Effectiveness in this area necessitates alliances with other groups to pressure for common goals. The questions of alliance with whom and for what have generally been answered: coalition with the labor movement to redistribute resources to the working class and low income people, away from corporations and all those enjoying "unearned" income.[28] While this answer appears in accord with some strands of Marxian theory, it is an answer which has been repeatedly rejected by most white workers and their union leadership.

Robert Blauner has argued that the utility of the colonial analogy depends upon the distinction between "colonization as a process and colonialism as a social, economic, and political system," arguing that "Important as are economic factors, the power of race and racism cannot be sufficiently explained through class analysis." Blauner stresses the "common process of social oppression" which he sums up in his discussion of the "colonization complex."[29] Blauner's distinction makes the colonial analogy a more acceptable one. At the same time it points in the direction of a wider theory of exploitation in which colonization as a process can be seen as a method of class subjugation in which part of the working class—black Americans, and indeed Mexican Americans, Puerto Ricans, and others are separated out as a distinct group from the rest of the working class to serve the function of a pariah group creating division in the working class and perpetuating division within the working class.

The reasons an alliance has been difficult to forge must be investigated in more detail in terms of the objective relations between white and black workers in the historic development of American capitalism.

Blacks as a Marginal Working Class

Marxists have long recognized that some segments of the working class enjoy privileges and material gain at the expense of other workers.[30, 31] Engels saw the small minority of skilled artisans in the England of 1844 as forming "an aristocracy among the working class" (a phrase appearing in the introduction to the 1892 edition of *The Conditions of the Working Class in England in 1844*). Lenin in Chapter 8 of *Imperialism* suggests that at least some segments of the working class benefit from the exploitation of colonial labor.

The marginal working class, John Leggett has written,

> . . . refers to a sub-community of workers who belong to a subordinate ethnic or racial group which is unusually proletarianized and highly segregated. Workmen of this type fill many manual roles in heavy industry and face an inordinant

amount of economic insecurity. This is evidenced by their large concentration in marginal occupational positions, their lack of formal education, and finally and most obviously, their high rate of unemployment.[32]

The isolation of the blacks is in many respects similar to that of other workers who are forced to form their own separate communities. Kerr and Siegel describe the coal town and the logging camp as ghetto-like, worlds unto themselves, in which a sense of group solidarity develops. "These communities," they write, "have their own codes, myths, heroes, and social standards. There are few neutrals in them to mediate the conflicts and dilute the mass . . . all the members of each of these groups have the same grievances." The strike for the isolated mining town is "a kind of colonial revolt against far removed authority, an outlet for accumulated tensions, and a substitute for occupational and social mobility."[33] The ghetto rebellion can be described in similar terms.

At another level, the class conflict both in the mining town and in the black ghetto is mediated by the middle class. In the mining community the preachers, doctors, newspaper editors, and so on all were dependent on the mine owners and could be dismissed at will. This led them to offer an ideological defense of existing property relationships. In the ghetto the black bourgeoisie has traditionally played a similar role of mediating conflicts and undermining militance, suggesting that cooperation is the best way, asking, not threatening, and generally undermining potential radical movements. While a secondary division, the co-option of part of the black community by the white power structure, is an important barrier in the liberation struggle.

The extent to which the capitalist class is able to isolate segments of the working class from each other strengthens its position. By creating a marginal working class of blacks and giving white workers a relatively more privileged position, it strengthens its control. If one group of workers is able to command higher pay, to exclude others from work, and if the other group or groups of workers are limited in their employment opportunities to the worst jobs and lowest pay, then a marginal working class has been created which benefits the labor aristocracy and to an even greater extent the capitalist class. The marginal working class produces goods which are generally available below the cost which would have been obtained if they had received wages closer to those paid to the labor aristocracy which had used its bargaining position to its own advantage. Thus Eric Hobsbawm suggests that the aristocracy of labor "arises when the economic circumstances of capitalism make it possible to grant significant concessions to the proletariat, when certain strata manage, by means of their special scarcity, skill, strategic position, organizational strength, etc., to establish notably better conditions for themselves than the rest."[34] In just such a manner has black labor generally been excluded from equal status to the benefits of white society—capitalist and worker alike.

From the time black slaves were freed to sell their labor as a commodity, they came to serve both as a reserve army and as a pool of labor, ready and willing to do the "dirty work" of the society at low wages. In the first role they served as an equilibrating factor in the economy. In periods of labor shortage blacks have made important gains, but with economic downturns they have been systematically displaced. Thus the jobs that blacks were recruited for in the labor shortages of World War I and the prosperity of the twenties were taken away in the Depression. Arthur Ross writes: "There was widespread invasion of Negro jobs by unemployed whites, often with the assistance of employers, unions, and lawmakers. Municipal licensing ordinances were reviewed in the South in order to drive Negroes out of barbering, plumbing, and other new occupations Negroes had entered during recent years."[35] In the second role they were restricted to the most menial, physically exhausting, and alienating labor which the white society offered. Furthermore they allowed white society to enjoy a profusion of goods and services at prices much lower than if these commodities had been produced at prevailing white worker wages. Thus blacks served in part as the classic Marxian reserve army and also as a "non-competing group," to borrow a term from another nineteenth century scholar, John Cairnes.

Therefore, it is important to see that the position of blacks in the society is primarily a result of their position as a marginal working class. Under American capitalism someone has always played this role. Traditionally immigrant groups have served as the structural equivalent of the blacks as a white marginal working class. In England, until the arrival of great numbers of Pakistanis in recent years, the Irish were the major occupants of this position. This structural characteristic of competitive capitalist economics suggests that the elimination of discrimination, even if it be more than a mere token, would be but a minor element in any radical alteration of the income distribution of the Negro population. For it is not discrimination that causes this difference. Institutionalized discrimination contributes to particular forms of poverty among Negroes and enhances the privileges of many whites. But in the main, discrimination is the medium—in the context of U.S. economics and social history—by which a special kind of poverty and a special kind of labor reserve is maintained.

"As in the case of white poverty, Negro poverty—more clearly seen because of its extreme character—is a function of the industrial and economic structure. Elimination of discrimination will not eliminate such major sources of poverty as unemployment, casual and intermittent jobs and low-paid occupations."[36] It is within this structural framework that the place of blacks as a marginal working class becomes clearer. It is not just that blacks are often at the end of the hiring line, but also that to some extent they are standing in a different line:

> The manpower problems of the urban ghetto appear best
> defined in terms of a dual labor market: a *primary* market

offering relatively high-paying, stable employment, with good working conditions, chances of advancement and equitable administration of work rules; and a *secondary* market, to which the urban poor are confined, decidedly less attractive in all of these respects and in direct competition with welfare and crime for the attachment of the potential labor force.[37]

Race, Class, and Social Change

The possibilities for change on a class basis are constrained by forces largely beyond the control of black Americans. Obstacles include not merely the material benefits whites receive from the exploitation of blacks, but important "psychic income" as well. Whites gain in relative status if blacks are held down. Fear of blacks is an integral accompaniment to these feelings of superiority.

Whites are made to feel better off than the blacks and, consequently, less prone to demand better pay and working conditions; on the other hand, if they become militant, they can be replaced by blacks who will work for less. An economic system based on individual competition breeds a social system based on relative income and status. One fears moving down the status hierarchy and fears those below trying to move up. The degree to which the individual aspires to move up leads him to identify with the group above him.

> The net result of all this is that each status group has a deep-rooted psychological need to compensate for feelings of inferiority and envy toward those above by feelings of superiority and contempt for those below. It thus happens that a special pariah group at the bottom acts as a kind of lightning rod for the frustrations and hostilities of all the higher groups, the more so the nearer they are to the bottom. It may even be said that the very existence of the pariah group is a kind of harmonizer and stabilizer of the social structure—so long as the pariahs play their role passively and resignedly.[38]

Thus the psychic gains from racism often appear to outweigh the material losses. White workers' subjective calculations on the matter are not made without pressures of employers who encourage racism, union officials who do the same partly out of fear of new leadership groups emerging, and partly out of the recognition that if the employer can exploit black workers less he may seek to exploit whites relatively more. It seems also that both workers and their union leaders are heavily conditioned by the "scarcity consciousness" bred during the Great Depression and sustained in each downturn. The supply of union workers is to be kept down.

The point is that racism, while in and of itself an important factor, is in the final analysis only another form of class exploitation which benefits some white workers in the short-run. A wider theory of exploitation must be built which encompasses in a single model a race and class analysis. Such a theory will emerge not merely out of reflective thinking but out of revolutionary practice. Though the costs and benefits of present racist arrangements to white workers may be crucial determinants of the future of race relations, they are not the only key. The costs of perpetuating racism and the repression which accompanies this policy will be determined largely by the militancy of blacks and their white supporters.

Notes

1. *Report of the National Advisory Commission on Civil Disorders* (New York: Bantam Books, 1968).

2. Gary S. Becker, *The Economics of Discrimination* (Chicago: University of Chicago Press, 1957).

3. Milton Friedman, "Capitalism and Discrimination," from *Capitalism and Freedom* (Chicago: University of Chicago Press, 1962), reprinted in *Economics: Mainstream Readings and Radical Critiques* (New York: Random House, 1970).

4. Philip Meranto (ed.), *The Kerner Report Revisited* (University of Illinois: Institute of Government and Public Affairs, June 1970), pp. 3–4.

5. Michael Parenti, "The Possibilities for Political Change," in Philip Meranto (ed.), *The Kerner Commission Revisited* (Urbana: University of Illinois, Institute of Government and Public Affairs, 1970), pp. 145–146.

6. Lee Rainwater, *The Moynihan Report & The Politics of Controversy* (Cambridge, Mass.: The M.I.T. Press, 1968).

7. United States Bureau of the Census and the Bureau of Labor Statistics, *The Social and Economic Status of Negroes in the United States, 1969* (Washington, D.C., Government Printing Office, 1970), p. 75.

8. Becker, ibid., p. 6.

9. Raymond S. Franklin, "A Framework for the Analysis of Inter-Urban Negro-White Economic Differentials," *Industrial and Labor Relations Review* (April 1968), p. 118.

10. Morris Silver, "Employee Tastes for Discrimination, Wages and Profits," *Review of Social Economy*, September 1968.

11. Friedman, ibid., p. 110.

12. Raymond S. Franklin, "The Political Economy of Black Power," *Social Problems*, reprinted in David Mermelstein, *Economics: Mainstream*

Readings and Radical Critiques (New York: Random House, 1970), pp. 337–338.

13. William L. Henderson and Larry C. Ledebur, Economic Disparity: Problems and Strategies for Black America (New York: The Free Press, 1970), p. 51.

14. James Boggs, Manifesto for a Black Revolutionary Party (Philadelphia: Pacesetters, 1968), p. 1.

15. Henderson and Ledebur, ibid., pp. 1–4.

16. Douglass C. North, The Economic Growth of the United States, 1790–1860 (Englewood Cliffs, N.J.: Prentice-Hall, 1961), p. 67.

17. North, ibid., p. 67.

18. James Heilbrun, "Jobs in Harlem: A Statistical Analysis," Regional Science Association Papers, 1970.

19. Michael Zweig, "Black Capitalism and the Ownership of Property in Harlem," Stony Brook Working Paper No. 16 (Economic Research Bureau, State University of New York at Stony Brook, August 1970).

20. Andre Gunter Frank, Capitalism and Underdevelopment in Latin America (New York: Monthly Review Press, 1967).

21. David Caplovitz, The Poor Pay More (New York: The Free Press, 1967).

22. Frederick D. Sturdivant (ed.), The Ghetto Marketplace (New York: The Free Press, 1969).

23. William H. Grier and Price M. Cobbs, Black Rage (New York: Bantam Books, 1968).

24. Kenneth B. Clark, Dark Ghetto (New York: Harper and Row, 1965).

25. Jacob Javits, "Remarks to the 56th Annual Meeting of the United States Chamber of Commerce," in United States, Congressional Record, Ninetieth Congress, second session, May 7, 1968.

26. Eli Ginsberg (ed.), The Negro Challenge to the Business Community (New York: McGraw-Hill, 1964), p. 87.

27. Robert L. Allen, Black Awakening in Capitalist America (New York: Doubleday, 1969), pp. 187–188.

28. Bayard Rustin, "Black Power and Coalition Politics," Commentary, September 1966.

29. Robert Blauner, "Internal Colonialism and Ghetto Revolts," Social Problems, Spring 1969, pp. 393–395.

30. E. P. Thompson, The Making of the English Working Class (New York: Pantheon Books, 1964).

31. J. L. Hammond and Barbara Hammond, *Town Laborer, 1760–1832, The New Civilization* (London: Longmans Green and Co., 1928).

32. John C. Leggett, *Class, Race and Labor* (New York: Oxford University Press, 1968), p. 14.

33. Clark Kerr and Abraham Siegel, "The Interindustry Propensity to Strike—An International Comparison," in Arthur Kornhauser, Robert Dubin, and Arthur M. Rose (eds.), *Industrial Conflict* (New York: McGraw-Hill, 1954), pp. 191–192.

34. Eric Hobsbawm, "Lenin and the 'Aristocracy of Labor,'" in Paul M. Sweezy and Harry Magdoff, *Lenin Today* (New York: Monthly Review, 1970), p. 50.

35. Arthur M. Ross, "The Negro in the American Economy," in *Employment, Race and Poverty*, Arthur M. Ross and Herbert Hill (eds.) (New York: Harcourt, Brace & World, 1967), p. 15.

36. Harry Magdoff, "Problems of United States Capitalism," in Ralph Miliband and John Saville, *The Socialist Register 1965* (New York: Monthly Review Press, 1965), pp. 75–76.

37. Michael J. Piore, "Public and Private Responsibility in On-The-Job Training of Disadvantaged Workers," *Department of Economics Working Paper*, No. 23 (Cambridge, Mass.: Massachusetts Institute of Technology, June 1968), pp. 2–3.

38. Paul A. Baran and Paul M. Sweezy, "Monopoly Capitalism and Race Relations," in David Mermelstein (ed.), *Economics: Mainstream Readings and Radical Critiques* (New York: Random House, 1970), p. 309.

13.
THE ARTIFICIAL UNIVERSE

Vine Deloria, Jr.

The justification for taking lands from Indian people has always been that the needs and requirements of civilized people had to come first. Settlers arriving on these shores saw a virtual paradise untouched by the works of man. They drooled at the prospect of developing the land according to their own dictates. Thus a policy of genocide was advocated that would clear the land of the original inhabitants to make way for towns, cities, farms, factories, and highways. This was progress.

Even today Indian people hold their land at the sufferance of the non-Indian. The typical white attitude is that Indians can have land as long as whites have no use for it. When it becomes useful, then it naturally follows that the land must be taken by whites to put to a better use. I have often heard the remark "what happens to the Indian land base if we decide we need more land?" The fact that Indian rights to land are guaranteed by the Constitution of the United States, over 400 treaties, and some 6,000 statutes seems irrelevant to a people hungry for land and dedicated to law and order.

The major reason why whites have seen fit to steal Indian lands is that they feel that their method of using land is so much better than that of the Indian. It follows that God would want them to develop the land. During the Seneca fight against Kinzua Dam, sympathetic whites would raise the question of Indian legal rights and they would be shouted down by people who said that the Indians had had the land for 200 years and did nothing with it. It would be far better, they argued, to let whites take the land and develop something on it.

From the days of the earliest treaties, Indians were shocked at the white man's attitude toward land. The tribal elders laughed contemptuously at the idea that a man could sell land. "Why not sell the air we breathe, the water we drink, the animals we hunt?" some replied. It was ludicrous to Indians that people would consider land as commodity that could be owned by one man. The land, they would answer, supports all life. It is given to all people. No one has a superior claim to exclusive use of land, much less does anyone have the right to fence off a portion and deny others its use.

In the closing decades of the last century, Indian tribes fought fiercely for their lands. Reservations were agreed upon and tribes held a fragment of the once expansive hunting grounds they had roamed. But no sooner had Indians settled on the reservations, than the government, ably led by the churches, decided that the reservation areas should be divided into tiny plots of land for farming purposes. In many reservation areas it was virtually impossible to farm such lands. The situation in California was so desperate that a report was issued denouncing the government land policy for Indians. The report contained such detrimental material exposing the vast land swindles that it was pigeonholed in the Senate files and has never been released and cannot be obtained today, nearly a century later!!!

Tribe after tribe succumbed to the allotment process. After the little plots of land were passed out to individual Indians, the remainder, which should have been held in tribal hands, was declared surplus and opened to settlement. Millions of "excess" acres of land were thus casually transferred to federal title and given to non-Indian settlers. Churches rushed in and grabbed the choice allotments for their chapels and cemeteries, and in some cases simply for income-producing purposes. They had been the chief advocates of allotment—on the basis that creating greed and selfishness among the Indians was the first step in civilizing them and making them Christians.

For years the development of the land did make it seem as if the whites had been correct in their theory of land use. Cities were built, productive farms were created, the wilderness was made safe, and superhighways were built linking one portion of the nation with the others. In some areas the very landscape was changed as massive earth-moving machines relocated mountains and streams, filled valleys, and created lakes out of wandering streams.

Where Indian people had had a reverence for the productiveness of the land, whites wanted to make the land support their way of life whether it was suited to do so or not. Much of San Francisco Bay was filled in and whole areas of the city were built upon the new land. Swamps were drained in the Chicago area and large portions of the city were built on them. A great portion of Ohio had been swamp and grassland and this was drained and farmed. Land was the great capital asset for speculation. People purchased apparently worthless desert land in Arizona, only to have the cities grow outward to their doorstep, raising land prices hundreds of percents. Land worth pennies an acre in the 1930s became worth thousands of dollars a front foot in the 1960s.

The rapid increase of population, technology, and capital has produced the present situation where the struggle for land will surpass anything that can be conceived. We are now on the verge of incredible development of certain areas into strip cities that will extend hundreds of miles along the coasts, major rivers, and mountain ranges. At the same time, many areas of the country are steadily losing population. Advanced farming techniques allow one man to do the work that several others formerly did, so that the total population needed in agricultural states continues to decline without a corresponding decline in productivity.

The result of rapid industrialization has been the creation of innumerable problems. Farm surpluses have lowered prices on agricultural products so that the federal government has had to enter the marketplace and support prices to ensure an adequate income for farmers. Farm subsidies are no longer a small business. In nine wheat and feed grain-producing counties in eastern Colorado in 1968, $31.4 million was given in farm subsidies. In all of Colorado, $62.8 million was given in 1968 to support farmers. This was a state with a declining farm population. Under the Agricultural Stabilization Conservation Service, some $3.5 billion was paid out in 1968, $675 million paid to 33,395 individual farmers as farm "income maintenance," some receiving amounts in excess of $100,000.

For much of the rural farm areas the economy, the society, and the very structure of life is completely artificial. It depends wholly upon government welfare payments to landowners, a thinly disguised guaranteed annual income for the rich. If the payments were suddenly cut off, millions of acres would become idle because it would not pay to farm them and there would be no way to live on them without income. Our concern for the family farm and the rural areas is thus a desperate effort to maintain the façade of a happy, peace-loving nation of farmers, tillers of the soil who stand as the bastion of rugged individualism.

If rural areas have an artificial economy, the urban areas surpass them in everything. Wilderness transformed into city streets, subways, giant buildings, and factories resulted in the compete substitution of the real world for the artificial world of the urban man. Instead of woods, large buildings rose. Instead of paths, avenues were built. Instead of lakes and streams, sewers and fountains were created. In short, urban man lives in a world of his own making and not in the world that his ancestors first encountered.

Surrounded by an artificial universe where the warning signals are not the shape of the sky, the cry of the animals, the changing of seasons, but simply the flashing of the traffic light and the wail of the ambulance and police car, urban people have no idea what the natural universe is like. They are devoured by the goddess of progress, and progress is defined solely in terms of convenience within the artificial technological universe with which they are familiar. Technological progress totally defines the outlook of most of America, so that as long as newer buildings and fancier roads can be built, additional lighting and electric appliances can be sold, and conveniences for modern living can be created there is not the slightest indication that urban man realizes that his artificial universe is dependent on the real world.

Milk comes in cartons, and cows are so strange an animal that hunters from large cities kill a substantial number of cattle every year on their annual hunting orgies. This despite the fact that in many areas farmers paint the word COW on the side of their animals to identify them. Food comes in plastic containers highly tinged with artificial sweeteners, colors, and preservatives. The very conception of plants, growing seasons, rainfall, and drought is foreign to city people. Artificial criteria of comfort define everything that urban areas need and therefore dominate the producing rural areas as to commercial products.

The total result of this strange social order is that there has been total disregard for the natural world. The earth is considered simply another commodity used to support additional suburbs and superhighways. Plant and animal life are subject to destruction at the whim of industrial development. Rivers are no more than wasted space separating areas of the large cities. In many areas they are open sewers carrying off the millions of tons of refuge discarded by the urban consumer.

The Indian lived with his land. He feared to destroy it by changing its natural shape because he realized that it was more than a useful tool for exploitation. It sustained all life, and without other forms of life, man himself could not survive. People used to laugh at the Indian's respect for smaller animals. Indians called them little brother. The Plains Indians appeased the buffalo after they had slain them for food. They well understood that without all life respecting itself and each other no society could indefinitely maintain itself. All of this understanding was ruthlessly wiped out to make room for the white man so that civilization could progress according to God's divine plan.

In recent years we have come to understand what progress is. It is the total replacement of nature by an artificial technology. Progress is the absolute destruction of the real world in favor of a technology that creates a comfortable way of life for a few fortunately situated people. Within our lifetime the difference between the Indian use of land and the white use of land will become crystal clear. The Indian lived with his land. *The white destroyed his land. He destroyed the planet earth.*

Non-Indians have recently come to realize that the natural world supports the artificial world of which they are so fond. Destruction of nature will result in total extinction of the human race. There is a limit beyond which man cannot go in reorganizing the land to suit his own needs. Barry Commoner, Director of the Center for the Biology of Natural Systems at Washington University in St. Louis, has been adamant about the destruction of nature. He told a Senate Subcommittee on Intergovernmental Affairs that the present system of technology would destroy the natural capital, the land, air, water, and other resources within the next 50 years. He further pointed out that the massive use of inorganic fertilizers may increase crop yields for a time but inevitably changes the physical character of the soil and destroys the self-purifying capability of the rivers. Thus the rivers in Illinois have been almost totally destroyed, while the nitrate level of rivers in the Midwest and California has risen above the safe level for use as drinking water.

A conference on pollution in Brussels outlined the same problem and had a much earlier deadline in mind. Scientists there predicted the end of life on the planet within a minimum of 35 years. Elimination of the oxygen in the atmosphere was credited to jet engines, destruction of oxygen-producing forests, and fertilizers and pesticides such as DDT that destroy oxygen-producing microorganisms. Combining all of the factors that are eliminating the atmosphere, the scientists could not see any future for mankind. Realization of the situation is devastating.

Even where forests and plant life exist, the situation is critical. In southern California millions of trees are dying from polluted air. A recent aerial survey by the Forest Service in November 1969, showed 161,000 acres of conifers already dead or dying in southern California. The situation has been critical since 1955, when residents of the area discovered trees turning yellow, but no one even bothered to inquire until 1962. In the San Bernardino forest 46,000 acres of pine are already dead and close to 120,000 acres more are nearly dead.

With strip cities being developed that will belch billions of tons of pollutants skyward every day the pace will rapidly increase so that optimistic projections of 50 to 100 years more of life must be telescoped to account for the very rapid disappearance of plant life by geometrically increasing pollution. The struggle for use of land has polarized between conservationists, who understand that mankind will shortly become extinct, and developers, who continue to press for immediate short-term financial gains by land exploitation.

The Bureau of Land Management, alleged guardian of public lands, has recently been involved in several controversial incidents with regard to its policies. In one case Bureau officials reversed themselves and acceded to Governor Jack Williams' request to transfer 40,000 acres of federal range to the state "so the land could be leased to ranchers." Stewart Udall, the great conservationist, upheld the original decision of the Bureau of Land Management because he thought that federal lands closer to cities could be obtained for development purposes. The overall effect of government policies on land is to silently give the best lands to state or private development without regard for the conservation issue or the public welfare.

We can be relatively certain that the federal and state governments will not take an objective view of land use. Agencies established to protect the public interest are subject to heavy political pressure to allow land to slip away from their trusteeship for short-sighted gains by interest groups. This much is certain: at the moment there is not the slightest chance that mankind will survive the next half century. The American public is totally unconcerned about the destruction of the land base. It still believes in the infallibility of its science, technology, and government. Sporadic and symbolic efforts will receive great publicity as the future administrations carefully avoid the issue of land destruction. Indian people will find their lands under continual attack and will probably lose most of them because of the strongly held belief that progress is inevitable and good.

With the justification of progress supporting the destruction of Indian tribes and lands, the question of results becomes important. Four hundred years of lies, cheating, and genocide were necessary in order for American society to destroy the whole planet. The United States government is thus left without even the flimsiest excuse for what has happened to Indian people, since the net result of its machinations is to destroy the atmosphere, thus suffocating mankind.

There is a grim humor in the situation. People used to make fun of Indians because of their reverence for the different forms of life. In our lifetime we may very well revert to panicked superstition and piously worship the plankton of the sea, begging them to produce oxygen so that we can breathe. We may well initiate blood sacrifices to trees, searching for a way to make them productive again. In our lifetime, society as a whole will probably curse the day that white men landed on this continent, because it will all ultimately end in nothingness.

Meanwhile, American society could save itself by listening to tribal people. While this would take a radical reorientation of concepts and values, it would be well worth the effort. The land-use philosophy of Indians is so utterly simple that it seems stupid to repeat it: man must live with other forms of life on the land and not destroy it. The implications of this philosophy are very far-reaching for the contemporary political and economic system. Reorientation would mean that public interest, indeed the interest in the survival of humanity as a species, must take precedence over special economic interests. In some areas the present policies would have to be completely overturned, causing great political dislocations in the power structure.

In addition to cleaning up streams and rivers and cutting down on air pollution, a total change in land use should be instituted. Increase in oxygen-producing plants and organisms should be made first priority. In order to do this, vast land areas should be reforested and bays should be returned to their natural state. At present, millions of acres of land lie idle every year under the various farm programs. A great many more acres produce marginal farming communities. Erosion and destruction of topsoil by wind reduces effectiveness of conservation efforts. All of this must change drastically so that the life cycle will be restored.

Because this is a total social problem and the current solutions such as sporadic national and state parks and soil banks are inadequate answers, land-use plans for the entire nation should be instituted. The government should repurchase all marginal farmlands and a substantial number of farms in remote areas. This land should be planted with its original growth, whether forest or grassland sod. The entire upper midwest plains area of the Dakotas and Montana and upper Wyoming should become open-plains range with title in public hands. Deer, buffalo, and antelope should gradually replace cattle as herd animals. Outside of the larger established towns, smaller towns should be merely residences for people employed to redevelop the area as a wilderness.

Creeks and streams should be cleared of mining wastes and their banks replanted with bushes and trees. The Missouri should be returned to its primitive condition, except where massive dams have already been built. These should remain primarily as power-generating sites without the corresponding increase in industry surrounding them. Mining and tourism should be cut to a minimum and eventually prohibited. The present population could well be employed in a total conservation effort to produce an immense grasslands filled with wildlife.

The concept is not impossible. Already a rancher in Colorado has tried the idea of grazing wild animals and beef cattle on his range with excellent results. Tom Lasater has a 26,000-acre ranch east of Colorado Springs, Colorado. He has pursued a no-shooting, no-poisoning, no-killing program for his land. There has already been a substantial increase in game animals, primarily mule deer and antelope, without any disturbance to his beef animals. Lasater first decided to allow wild animals to remain on his land when his foreman remarked, after the prairie dogs had been exterminated, that the grass always grew better when the prairie dogs had been allowed to live on the land.

The result of Lasater's allowing the land to return to its primitive state has been the notable decrease of weeds. Lasater feels that the smaller animals, such as gophers, ground squirrels, badgers, and prairie dogs, that dig holes all provided a better means of aerating the ground and introducing more oxygen into it than modern farming methods of periodically turning the sod by plowing. All of the wildlife use on the land produced better grazing land and reduced the danger of overgrazing in a remarkable way. The fantastic thing about Lasater's ranch is that it returns almost double the income from beef cattle, because of the improved conditions of the soil and the better grasses, than would the average ranch of comparable acreage using the so-called modern techniques of ranching.

The genius of returning the land to its original animals is that the whole program cuts down on labor costs, maintains fertility far better than modern techniques, increases environmental stability, and protects the soil from water and wind erosion. The net result is that the land supports much more life, wild and domestic, and is in better shape to continue to support life once the program is underway. Returning the major portion of the Great Plains to this type of program would be the first step in creating a livable continental environment. But introduction of this kind of program would mean dropping the political platitudes of the rancher and farmer as America's last rugged individualists, admitting that they are drinking high on the public trough through subsidies, and instituting a new kind of land use for the areas involved.

In the East and Far West, all land that is not immediately productive of agricultural products for the urban areas should be returned to forest. This would mean purchasing substantial acreage in Wisconsin, Ohio, Michigan, New York, New Jersey, and Pennsylvania and planting new forests. With the exception of settled urban areas, the remainder of those states would probably become vast woods as they were originally. Wildlife would be brought in to live on the land since it is an irreplaceable part of the forest ecology. With the exception of highspeed lanes for transportation facilities, the major land areas of the East Coast would become forest and woodlands. The presence of great areas of vegetation would give carbon-dioxide-consuming plants a chance to contribute to the elimination of smog and air pollution.

The social structure of the East would have to change considerably. In New York City the number of taxicabs is limited because unimpeded registration of cabs would produce a city so snarled with traffic that there would be no transportation. In the same manner anyone owning a farm of substantial acreage would have to be licensed by the state. The rest of the land would become wilderness with a wildlife cycle supporting the artificial universe of the cities by producing relatively clean air and water. The countless millions now on welfare in the eastern cities could be resettled outside the cities with conservation jobs and in retirement towns to ensure that the green belt of oxygen-producing plants would be stabilized.

In the coal mining states strip mining would be banned and a substantial number of people could be employed in work to return the land to its natural state. Additional people could harvest the game animals and the food supply would partially depend upon meat from wild animals instead of DDT-bearing beef animals. Mines would be filled in and vegetation planted where only ugly gashes in the earth now exist. People disenchanted with urban society would be allowed to live in the forests with a minimum of interference. Any who might want to live in small communities and exist on hunting and fishing economies would be permitted to do so.

On the seacoasts, pollution should be cut to a minimum. Where there are now gigantic ports for world shipping, these would be limited to a select few large enough to handle the trade. Others would have to become simply ports for pleasure boats and recreation. Some of the large commercial centers on both coasts would have to change their economy to take into account the absence of world trade and shipping. Beaches would have to be cleaned and set aside as wilderness areas or used by carefully selected people as living areas. Lobster beds, oyster beds, and areas that used to produce edible seafood would have to be returned to their original condition.

The pollution crisis presents the ultimate question on tribalism. If mankind is to survive until the end of the century, a substantial portion of America's land area must be returned to its original state of forests and grasslands. This is fundamentally because these plants produce oxygen and support the life cycle at the top of which is man. Without air to breathe it is ridiculous to speak of progress, culture, civilization, or technology. Machines may be able to live in the present environment, but it is becoming certain that people cannot.

By returning the land to its original state, society will have to acknowledge that it can no longer support 200 million people at an artificial level of existence in an artificial universe of flashing lights and instantaneous communications. To survive, white society must return the land to the Indians in the sense that it restores the land to the condition it was in before the white man came. And then to support the population we now have on the land that will be available, a great number of people will have to return to the life of the hunter, living in the forests and hunting animals for food.

Whenever I broach this subject to whites, they cringe in horror at the mere prospect of such a development. They always seem to ask how anyone could consider returning to such a *savage and unhappy state*, as the government reports always describe Indian life. Yet there is a real question as to which kind of life is really more savage. Does the fact that one lives in a small community hunting and fishing for food really indicate that one has no sensitive feelings for humanity? Exactly how is this kind of life primitive when affluent white hunters pay thousands of dollars every fall merely for the chance to roam the wilderness shooting at one another in the hopes of also bringing down a deer?

In 1967 I served on the Board of Inquiry for Hunger and Malnutrition in the United States. We discovered that a substantial number of Americans of all colors and backgrounds went to bed hungry every night. Many were living on less than starvation diets and were so weakened that the slightest sickness would carry them off. The black children in the Mississippi delta lands were eating red clay every other day to fill their stomachs to prevent hunger pains. Yet the Agricultural Department had millions of tons of food in giant storehouses that went undistributed every year. Is this type of society more savage than living simply as hunters and fishermen? Is it worth being civilized to have millions of people languishing every year for lack of food while the warehouses are filled with food that cannot be distributed?

Last Christmas in California a federal judge, disgusted at the snarls of red tape that prevented distribution of food to hungry people, ordered a warehouse opened and the food distributed in spite of the pleas of bureaucrats that it was against regulations. In the field of hunger alone the government had better act before hungry people take the law into their own hands.

For years Indian people have sat and listened to speeches by non-Indians that gave glowing accounts of how good the country is now that it is developed. We have listened to people piously tell us that we must drop everything Indian as it is impossible for Indians to maintain their life style in a modern civilized world. We have watched as land was stolen so that giant dams and factories could be built. Every time we have objected to the use of land as a commodity, we have been told that progress is necessary to the American way of life.

Now the laugh is ours. After four centuries of gleeful rape, the white man stands a mere generation away from extinguishing life on this planet. Granted that Indians will also be destroyed—it is not because we did not realize what was happening. It is not because we did not fight back. And it is not because we refused to speak. We have carried our responsibilities well. If people do not choose to listen and instead overwhelm us, then they must bear the ultimate responsibility.

What is the ultimate irony is that the white man must drop his dollar-chasing civilization and return to a simple, tribal, game-hunting, berry-picking life if he is to survive. He must quickly adopt not just the contemporary Indian world view but the ancient Indian world view to survive. He must give up the concept of the earth as a divisible land area that he can market. The lands of the United States must be returned to public ownership and turned into wilderness if man is to live. It will soon be apparent that one man cannot fence off certain areas and do with the land what he will. Such activity will be considered too dangerous to society. Small animals and plants will soon have an equal and perhaps a greater value for human life than humans themselves.

Such a program is, of course, impossible under the American economic and political system at the present time. It would interfere with vested economic interests whose motto has always been "the public be damned." Government policy will continue to advocate cultural oppression against Indian tribes, thinking that the white way of life is best. This past year, five powerful government agencies fought the tiny Lummi tribe of western Washington to prevent it from developing a bay that the tribe owned as a sealife sanctuary. The agencies wanted to build massive projects for commercial use on the bay, the Indians wanted it developed as a conservation area restoring its original food-producing species such as fish, clams, and oysters. Fortunately, the tribe won the fight, much to the chagrin of the Army Corps of Engineers, which makes a specialty of destroying Indian lands.

The white man's conception of nature can be characterized as obscene, but that does not even begin to describe it. It is totally artificial and the very existence of the Astrodome with its artificial grass symbolizes better than words the world visualized by the non-Indian. In any world there is an aspect of violence that cannot be avoided; Nature is arbitrary and men must adjust to her whims. The white man has tried to make Nature adjust to his whims by creating the artificial world of the city. But even here he has failed. Politicians now speak reverently of corridors of safety in the urban areas. They are main lines of transportation where your chances of being robbed or mugged are greatly reduced. Everywhere else there is indiscriminate violence. Urban man has produced even an artificial jungle, where only the fittest or luckiest survive.

With the rising crime rate, even these corridors of safety will disappear. People will only be able to go about in the urban areas in gangs, tribes if you will. Yet the whole situation will be artificial from start to finish. The ultimate conclusion of American society will be that even with respect to personal safety it was much safer and more humane when Indians controlled the whole continent. The only answer will be to adopt Indian ways to survive. For the white man even to exist, he must adopt a total Indian way of life. That is really what he had to do when he came to this land. It is what he will have to do before he leaves it once again.

14.
CRISIS OF THE CITIES

Nancy Spannaus

The "crisis of the cities"—what is it? Why is it? What must we do about it? This paper seeks to answer these questions from the point of view that the urban crisis has arisen from the long-term, lawful unfolding of capitalist investment policies and augurs the imminence of world capitalist breakdown. In exposing the cause of the expansion of government services as well as their current deterioration, it must conclude that only an organizing approach toward total reconstruction at capitalist expense is appropriate to the budgetary failures of individual cities.

The Growth of Urban Services: Signal of Capitalist Crisis

A glance at recent history shows that the phrase "urban crisis" began to take national headlines in the late 1950s. Popularization of the fact that the cities were being overcome by slums, poverty, and general decay stemmed from two critical processes occurring at the time: (1) the aftermath and very partial recovery from the 1957–58 recession; and (2) the building of the Kennedy national political machine. The "urban crisis" was touted as a crisis for blacks and focused attention on ghetto housing, education, and the continuing massive unemployment of approximately 25 percent among black youth.

Not surprisingly, the popularizers of the "crisis of the inner city," the Kennedy machine, had "solutions" in mind and on the drawing boards. These "solutions"—a grab-bag of juvenile delinquency, anti-poverty, and community action programs—were, of course, designed to deal with another crisis as well—the political bind of a Democratic Party in need of the urban black vote. Needless to say, the ghetto programs succeeded much better in creating a loyal black Democratic apparatus than in easing the problems of unemployment and poverty. Youth unemployment stayed over 20 percent; housing and services continued to deteriorate. And, before the poverty pro-

From Nancy Spannaus, "Crisis of the Cities," *The Campaigner*, Fall 1971. (New York: National Caucus of Labor Committees), pp. 5–9. Reprinted by permission of the publisher.

gram passed its prime, it helped create a more spectacular crisis—the explosive black-white polarization that erupted as early as 1963 in the South and reached its zenith with the Newark/Detroit/Watts riots in 1965–67.

Around 1965, however, the urban crisis took on a less racial aspect. Major industrial centers in the United States which had practically doubled their expenditures since 1957, began to experience a budgetary squeeze. Higher interest rates on city bonds; the need to increase expenditures on services just to maintain previous poor standards (that is, increased costs of maintaining decrepit schools, subways, and so on); strong political pressure against skyrocketing local taxes—all contributed to the rise of anxiety, among bondholders in particular, that the cities could pay their way. The very "remedies" applied—imposing even higher taxes on working people; allowing stagnation in quantity and quality of vital services; increasing borrowing, though on a longer-term basis—have, of course, only led to greater budget crises. In 1970 these began to take the form of layoffs of thousands of public employees in major metropolitan areas, not to mention the acceleration of layoffs by attrition. Such crises now threaten, in a more obvious way than ever before, the total breakdown of education, health, and sanity throughout the entire 80 percent of the U.S. population that lives in cities—be they black, white, or green.

By now it is excruciatingly evident that the Kennedy liberals' campaign cries signified far more than a political gimmick. The Democratic Party's outreach to ghetto blacks demonstrated an inadvertent recognition that the United States would not recover from the 1957–58 recession in such a way as to reintegrate black youth into the work force, and to relieve the related problems of unemployment, growing slums, and decaying services. Manufacturing of useful civilian goods and technology began to stagnate or decline following 1957–58. No significant amount of decent low-rent housing had been built since immediately after World War II. Expansion of jobs was slated for the arenas of patchwork city services, or the development of military/aerospace, not areas of human need, where investment would threaten current profitable ventures. In a real sense the political "urban crisis" which was used by John and Robert Kennedy signaled the intensification of capitalist stagnation and decay that started in the teens, but had finally begun to move toward an inevitable world depression in the 1970s. The "crisis of the cities" is, at heart, the crisis of capitalist underproduction.

The Crisis Historically

Throughout the twentieth century, U.S. residents have experienced a relatively-continuous expansion of government services ranging from police and fire "protection" to education to public housing. The primary role played by these state services appears in bold relief when one looks at the 1930s.

In the Depression years, when employment and production had dropped by a third or more, and "private enterprise" found itself incapable of reorganizing the economy, U.S. corporations turned to the government to bail them out. They asked not only for government regulation of prices, wages, and production, but for services. These services were to mitigate pressure being applied to them by the unemployed and to reduce the costs of establishing and maintaining industry. Consequently the government undertook huge expansion of relief payments and developed such make-work, social-control programs as the Civilian Conservation Corps. Slightly later the government provided more substantive benefits to private enterprise in the form of construction of a widespread industrial infrastructure, including electric power plants, bridges, highways, hospitals, and schools. All of these projects greatly aided industry by providing it with a trained, mobile work force and with easily-available cheaper power and transport—mostly at wage earner's expense, but also by redistributing corporate profit for the benefit of the capitalist class as a whole.

Some of these services—which were largely financed by a vast extension of the federal income tax system—dried up as private industry again expanded its jobs to the point where mass political organizing no longer threatened to erupt. Welfare is the most glaring example, its decline continuing smoothly through the 1940s and becoming precipitous during the relative prosperity of 1952–57. Current levels, despite large increases, remain considerably below the 1930s. Local public expenditures for highways and police have also declined somewhat over the last four decades, indicating a relative saturation in the case of the former, and the development of less direct methods of social control in the latter case.

On the other hand, education costs, borne mostly by local governments, have skyrocketed. Business has required these expenditures in order for the work force to adapt to changing technology and the shift from manufacturing to clerical, service, and technical jobs. Education expenditures have increased especially in the areas of remedial/vocational programs for ghetto youth and of higher education—that is expansion of community colleges and state takeover of private colleges. In both these cases monies are being spent primarily to make up the deficit in basic educational services, a deficit caused as much by the low quality of housing, nutrition, jobs, and so on available to youth as to deficiencies in educational content.

While the government has not entered the housing market on any meaningful scale as a competitive builder since the late 1940s, its role in serving real estate interests has expanded over the past two decades. Urban renewal has functioned to bail out landlords and banks holding unprofitable land, but left new construction, complete with tax abatement, to private profit makers. Federal, state, and city loan programs—which guarantee up to 90 percent of the mortgages and provide interest rates in the range of 1–3 percent, have mushroomed. The difference between these interest rates and bank rates is, of course, subsidized by tax revenue. Unfortunately for the wage-earner, even these terms are insufficient to attract investment out of speculation in slums and other waste into decent low-rent housing. As a result, the housing shortage has taken center stage of the urban crisis—and been used as leverage to attack unionized construction workers. Vestiges of housing services for wage earners and home owners, instituted during the post-World War II labor upsurge, were finally strangled to death on May 26, 1971, with the formal end of rent control and its code enforcement divisions in New York City.

Contraction in the percentage of public funds spent on direct police control has been more than offset by the expansion of slightly less blatant institutions of social control, such as addiction services, correctional facilities, mental hospitals, and so forth. These "services" have grown in response to a deterioration of housing and job opportunities which makes stable human relationships and sanity less and less possible to achieve. Jails and institutional care facilities throughout the country are notoriously over-crowded. New York City's jails are operating at 120 percent to 200 percent of rated capacity, according to the City's 1970–71 executive budget message. Mental hospitals have become so full that some institutions have begun massive programs of rehabilitation to clear wards. These progressive programs often release patients who have lived in institutions 10 to 20 to 40 years and can only "return" to isolation and early death.

The basic "service" provided to private industry by the federal government, of course, is military spending, which has doubled since 1959 (as have federal interest payments). The federal contribution to other services is dwarfed by comparison, but has grown faster than military expenditures in the areas of housing, education, and health and welfare. The portion of state and municipal budgets coming from federal grants continues to grow faster than municipal expenditures as a whole; this trend will be greatly accelerated by the pending Family Assistance Plan. Yet federal assumption of the costs of underproduction has not prevented the burgeoning of predominantly local expenses, local taxes, and presently, drastic cutbacks in municipal services.

Financing

Urban services not only dispense benefits primarily in the interest of bankers and industrialists, but also are financed substantially by wage taxation, whence the bulk of revenue on all levels of government comes (75 percent of state and local revenues; two-thirds of federal revenue). Rising revenue from federal taxes has been accompanied over the past decade by a decrease in individual income tax rates—even counting the Vietnam surtax. Tax rates for states and cities have, on the contrary, climbed steadily.

City and state governments pick up most of the tab for protecting property from fire and theft (which amounts to 28 percent of the budget in cities with over a million residents), education, and health. In addition, they are providing increasingly direct subsidies to business in the form of rising debt service on city bonds and on bonds issued by semi-public authorities and funds (for transit, school facilities, and so on). The debt for municipalities—approximately $87 billion in 1968—more than doubled from 1958. Debt service payments—over 10 percent of the budget in major cities, though the average percentage comes to 3 percent nation-wide—have been aggravated by the high interest rates of the mid-sixties, as well as increased borrowing. More and more of the national per capita debt comes from state and local (as compared with federal) borrowing.

State and local tax burdens have risen at a much sharper rate than the federal since the end of World War II. The percent of large city population subject to local income taxes increased from 14 percent to over 39 percent from 1957 to 1969. The amount of city income coming from individual income taxes—which fall mostly on wage earners—more than quadrupled from 1959 to 1966/67 as individual income certainly did not. Over the same period local sales tax receipts rose by 70 percent and property taxes (in most areas paid primarily by single home owners) jumped 80 percent—both reflecting substantial rate increases. Mayor Lindsay's budget message for 1970–71 reports that the cost of city government (expense budget) is growing at rates more than double the growth of personal income in the city—making it clear that the expansion of the city budget is occurring at the expense of residents' living standards. These jumps in taxation go a long way toward explaining the rise of taxpayer groups and repeated defeats of bond issues, which are the major means of supporting school expenses as well as capital spending throughout the country, since 1965. Yet local tax increases and tax substitutes (that is transit fares, bridge tolls, and so on) continue to rise for city wage earners.

Concurrently the proportion of tax revenue coming from businesses has decreased. In New York City business taxation pays for only a quarter of the budget, while in 1915 it paid 92 percent. In New York State the corporate tax burden has decreased over the last decade. Nation-wide, corporate income taxes have supplied about 3.5 percent of local and state revenue over the past decade compared to 4 and 5 percent in the 1940s.

Most of the federal income tax burden has shifted from corporations, under all federal taxes. Banks are hardly taxed at all, at the same time they receive tax-free interest on state and local bonds. At 7 percent interest (or more)—the high for long-term bonds in the sixties, though short-term borrowing can cost much more—a city pays two to three times the original amount borrowed back to the banks.

As long as taxes can be raised, why are services being slashed? Either way living standards are being cut without the comptrollers of the government—banks and corporations—having to confront the strongly-unionized sections of the U.S. labor movement, which are concentrated in heavy industry. In many ways raising taxes seems preferable to corporate interests.

Taxpayers' movements, which require the transcendence of normal capitalist institutions like unions, community organizations, and single issue clubs in program and representation, are a much less probable threat than strikes by city unions facing layoffs or wage cuts.

But taxes cannot be raised indefinitely, especially in a recession, where incomes are decreasing and uncertain. The bankers and others cannot count on enough revenues coming in. Therefore the government now chooses to cut services as well, an act which carries the threat of public employees' strikes. In the current period of widespread labor unrest over declining real wages, the government runs the risk of a strike by public employees triggering mass ferment. But such a chance it has to take.

For what is at stake in this barrage of tax increases and service reductions is the very existence of the capitalist system. So much credit and paper—much of it government debt—has been floated through the system that capitalists must gouge wages simply to keep their heads above water. Else they face a world depression. Leery of direct onslaughts on auto or steel workers, they instead cut wages through reducing the quality and quantity of health care, transportation, education, and cultural activities. In this way the standard of living in the U.S. has deteriorated much more than is reflected in the decline in real wages since 1965, as well as rendering wages more and more meaningless in so far as what is available to buy.

The capitalists cannot avoid a depression, however. As they increase primitive accumulation through taxation and decreased real production, they are not only destroying the cities as physical entities and crippling ghetto youth, but eradicating the productive capacity of an entire generation in human terms. The costs of social control will increase further; markets will decrease. The current budgetary crisis is both a precursor and a contributor to world depression.

Alternate Views

There are two widespread popular explanations for why the budget cuts are occurring now. The first, and most popular on the Left and among liberals, is the Vietnam War. The second, most consistently articulated by Professors Cloward and Pliven, "theoreticians" of the welfare rights movement, and widespread among the working population, is attributing the crisis to the aggressiveness of welfare recipients in expanding the "public dole," and, more peripherally, to the greed of public employee unions.

Vietnam   There is a large measure of coincidence between the escalation of the Vietnamese War and war spending, and the escalation of the urban crisis. "Defense" expenditures doubled between 1959 and 1969, as did urban budgets and decay. The astronomical jump of 25 percent in military spending between 1965 and 1966 coincided with the onset of municipal budget crises. But neither Vietnam nor war spending in general caused the crisis of the cities. Instead both the war and urban crisis result from a common cause—capitalism's inability to produce and reproduce on an expanding scale.

It is beyond the scope of this paper to unravel the details of causation and continuation of the war in Vietnam. But the identification of three major processes involved with its inception and development will suffice to show its derivative character:

1. Direct military expenditures have constituted at least a third of the federal budget since 1941. Currently war (as opposed to defense in general) expenditures take slightly less than 40 percent of the budget—well within "normal" range for post-Depression U.S.
2. U.S. military presence in Southeast Asia began with the intention, among others, of opening the area to exploitation by U.S. investors.
3. Contracts for armaments and other military supplies have propped up the U.S. economy since the late 1930s by providing cost-plus provisions, tax-financed research, and other fringe benefits which provide capitalists an investment outlet that allows them to avoid less lucrative productive investment.

It is clear, then, that the Vietnam War is derived from long-term basic capitalist investment needs, needs which lead to war spending, foreign loans, and other kinds of waste spending. It should also be evident that, even without this particular war, the same tendencies toward waste spending are in operation. And, finally, we have amply demonstrated that this shift from productive to wasteful investment has resulted in the increase in unemployment, urban deterioration, and city services which have caused the urban budget crisis. There would be a budget crisis even without the war!

Is this argument too complicated or clouded for the Communist Party (CP), Socialist Workers Party (SWP), and Lindsay liberals to understand? No, not at all. They will continue to assert that the war has caused the urban crisis until the end of the war fails to result in increased spending on urban problems—because they find that linking Vietnam and urban problems allows them to put themselves at the front of, and to appear to lead, masses of people. Sheer opportunism!

In arguing that an end to the Vietnam War will mean money for the cities, Lindsay and others and the established Left join hands in a conspiracy to keep capitalists off the hook—to blame the war, not capitalism itself, for economic and social decay. If the war is the problem, they say, we must build a huge cross-class movement of everyone who is against the war: executives, Democrats, labor leaders, and so on. And in order not to alienate any of these persons who lend prestige as well as numbers to our movement, we should not attack the capitalist practices which led to the war; we must not call for reconstruction of the cities at capitalist expense, but at the expense of the workers' taxes which are presently going to the war. By omission the CP and SWP imply that the war will end—or lead to the end—of war spending; that an anti-war movement, full of liberal capitalists, is implicitly anti-capitalist.

A glance at their bedfellows Lindsay and McGovern and their sponsorship of budget cuts, tax credits, and other boondoggles clearly exposes this opportunism for what it is. Ending the war will not end the budget cuts or capitalism. Only a movement armed with understanding of what underlies the war economy can attack the war and the urban crisis in an effective, coherent way.

Welfare Crisis   A recent book by Professors Cloward and Piven, *Regulating the Poor: The Function of Public Welfare*, outlines in sophisticated form the argument which the *Daily News* sells with sensationalism: rioting, aggressive welfare clients, and poor people have pushed welfare rolls up so high that they have brought major industrial centers to the brink of bankruptcy.

As in the case of the war, the coincidence of the two events—budget crises and a 217 percent rise in families receiving Aid to Dependent Children rolls in the largest metropolitan areas since 1964—encourages one to look for a causal connection. Yet scrutiny of city finances reveals that welfare spending still takes a relatively small percentage of state and local revenue: 8 percent or less. In New York City approximately $300 million of local tax money goes for welfare, compared to over $800 million for debt service, $862.9 million for police and their accouterments, and $1.8 billion for education. In Philadelphia welfare spending has taken about 5 percent of the city general fund revenue throughout the 1960s; police and debt service absorb close to 15 percent each! A comparison of Chicago's budgets through the 1960s reveals a similar picture: relief took approximately 5 percent of the city tax revenues in 1961 and even less in 1967. While educational expenditures, among others, are financed separately in both Chicago and Philadelphia, and would surpass police and debt service expenditures, the insignificance of welfare spending in causing municipal budget crises would only be more clear if education outlays were counted in.

Taking federal aid into account, welfare costs have, of course, more than doubled since the mid-1960s. But this rise has not been what put the squeeze on local governments. In the broadest sense the social costs of unemployment and low wages may be said to be causal—in that they have produced the physical and social decay that raises the budgets for firemen, policemen, courts, narcotics, education, hospitals, sanitation—as well as welfare.

Cloward and Piven argue correctly that a rise in unemployment or decline in wages, per se, does not lead to increased demand for, much less the receipt of, welfare benefits. But they believe that the disorderly behavior by the poor in the 1967 riots and welfare demonstrations, partially fomented by federal poverty programs and partially the consequence of an increase in social anomie in the ghetto, won the increases in benefits for clients. If their argument were correct, an exacerbation of such protest tactics now would again produce higher living standards for the poor—a patent impossibility.

These social work anarchists comprehend neither the economic nor political role of welfare in a capitalist society. The welfare system is not only a way of quieting the poor and disciplining them to willingness to take marginal or scab jobs; it also serves the function of keeping a reserve labor force just healthy enough to be able to work when needed. Consequently, the Kennedy-Johnson administrations did not consider the raising of welfare standards an unintended, unfortunate side-effect of their efforts to build a ghetto machine; like civil rights legislation before it, this action was seen as instrumental in raising the standard of living of welfare clients who were being bled of all will or capacity for work, so they could be made useful to capitalism. This is not to mention the beneficial results which rising welfare budgets have for slumlords and sweatshop employers who pay wages low enough to be supplemented by welfare.

Today the liberal advocates of a $4,000–$6,000 base for the Family Assistance Plan are not merely playing for welfare votes or those of the working poor: they want to raise welfare budgets (at the expense of the working man's, to be sure) to a level where they'll produce persons capable of an 8–10 hour day, efficient work habits, and so forth. The Urban Coalition, recently joining in coalition with welfare clients in New York around housing and more income demands, has not become anti-capitalist. It seeks to make the system work by reducing some wage earners' incomes for the benefit of those who are starving, and not so incidentally, banks and businesses as well. The political benefit the capitalists reap is not only the allegiance of welfare groups, but continued exacerbation of friction between clients and working taxpayers.

By overlooking the "liberal" capitalists' policies for welfare in this period, Cloward and Piven are forced into the conclusion that militance by ghetto residents won the concessions they received by show of strength and numbers. The history of the Welfare Rights Movement since the fall of 1968 shows the fallacy of this belief. As soon as wage earners began to resist skyrocketing local taxes, the concessions ceased. Special grants were stopped; grant cuts were instituted; in some states many clients were cut off the rolls; in most the rate of acceptance began to decline. No matter that higher taxes were not very much related to increased welfare expenditures; the increase in welfare was used by politicians to divert the wrath of taxpayers toward the poor, not landlords and banks.

If the ghettoes had exploded at that point, we might have seen race riots—but no concessions. For contrary to Cloward and Piven's thesis about the 1930s, it was the political threat of a movement which combined the unemployed with the employed workers that then forced capitalists and the government to make large concessions, not just the threat of "uncontrolled masses." The welfare rights movement and the ghetto rebellions posed no such threat: on the contrary, they almost always directed their fury against white unionized workers as well as at government officials. With such an outlook, and the objective consequence of welfare meaning higher taxes on workers, the movement could only accentuate already-existing bitter divisions between the employed and unemployed.

Cloward and Piven would like to believe that the continued numerical growth of the welfare rolls represents gain for the welfare rights movement, even though these clients are receiving less and less. Such self-deception can only be described as pitiful, combined as it is with the delusion that when the rolls reach a certain number, and workers forced onto welfare have been sufficiently degraded and "radicalized" by the miserable treatment they receive, a revolution (of some undefined sort) will spontaneously occur.

Public Employees

Militancy by public employees (particularly state and local) has recently joined the welfare rights movement as a well-publicized "prime suspect" in the crime of city bankruptcies. The facts that wage gains for some city workers have equaled or surpassed those for private employees since 1965; that government employees are being more rapidly unionized than any other unorganized sector of the labor movement; and that well over 50 percent of state and local government payrolls goes to wages (as opposed to rent and capital construction)—all have been used by the government and the press to attack municipal unions. Professors Cloward and Piven helped develop the "liberal" wing of this attack as early as 1968–69, by publishing an article that branded any public employee union which fought for improved wages and working conditions as racist oppressors of the poor.

The government onslaught on state and local public employees finds easy support among burdened taxpayers. When taxpayers see state and local jobs doubling between 1959 and 1967 and payrolls rising 100 percent over the same period, they can believe—with the help of the press—that city workers are their enemies: people relaxing on "cushy" civil service, with veto power over the city government and with high salaries "stolen" from their hard-earned tax money.

The key to demolishing the myth that municipal workers are bankrupting the cities lies with destroying the lie that wages cause inflation. A certain level of wages and wage-equivalents (city and other government services) are the prerequisites for productive job performance—a level now defined by a wage of at least $10,000 a year for a family of four, and not reached by a large majority of public employees. It is what job is performed by the wage earner, not the level of his wage, which determines whether his wage is "wasted" or not from a social point of view. Since most public jobs are bureaucratic or fruitlessly attempting to compensate for a decline in major U.S. industrial production, public employee wages are in a sense wasted. But only because the government and private business have defined the role of government jobs as subsidizers and handmaidens to the private sector of the economy.

Some government services are essential, of course. And wages will inevitably take up a larger proportion of expenditures in service industries like government than in mechanized heavy industrial sectors. Sectors of the economy like public transit and hospital care, for example, must run "at a loss" so to speak. The only way to ensure that this "loss" is compensated is the constant development of productive employment—where social surplus can develop at accelerating level—in the economy as a whole. But it is the lack of just such productive employment that led to the rapid rise of "service" (largely governmental and unproductive) jobs. Service jobs cannot be "productive" while major U.S. production industries are being allowed to stagnate and decline.

Public employees have not caused the budget crisis. Instead, the decline in U.S. capitalism has led to a rapid expansion of public payrolls, whose occupiers (putting aside the unknown percentage of patronage and public relations jobs) are battling for adequate living standards.

Without the war, without the welfare crisis, and an upsurge in public employee militancy, U.S. capitalism and its urban industrial center would still be in crisis and decay.

An Urban Strategy

If one recognizes the roots of the urban crisis in world-wide capitalist decay, and understands how urban budgets serve banking and corporate interests and divide working people, one must include the following elements in an "urban strategy."

1. Proposals for reconstruction of the cities through creation of productive, well-paid jobs, not just for filling the fiscal gaps precipitating local budget crises (see Emergency Reconstruction program, NCLC, 8/70).
2. Programs of taxation which penalize capitalists for creating the current social deficit and take capital out of unproductive use.
3. Political organization of working class and related forces into institutions which unite usually competitive sections of the working class around programs and action in their common interest, helping to create the political working class for itself.

Adopting such a strategy means rejecting the capitalists' terms for battle: the terms of "every man (or group) for himself," and of addressing "obvious facts," not causes. Capitalist ideology and organization dictate such actions as the juggling of deficits by New York City's Comptroller Beame, and demonstrations which protest layoffs, but do not deal with budget cuts or taxes. Bourgeois methods of struggle confine the labor movement and unemployed, and major socialist organizations as well, from going beyond defensive, ad hoc actions around special interests. Such methods continue to leave the capitalists' right to govern unchallenged, when every move of the ruling class proclaims their ineptness to provide the basics of civilized life, much less an expanding standard of living.

The budget crisis is a harbinger of coming world depression. A movement against budget cuts and layoffs must recognize this context and begin to develop the self-consciousness and economic/political alternatives to running the economy; traditional "protest" will not suffice. Such a movement must break down people's habit of compartmentalizing themselves into "workers" in one area, and "consumers" in most areas. Workers must be organized and educated to see themselves as self-conscious directors of society.

A prime example of organizing which retains this compartmentalization is the work of the Metropolitan Council on Housing in New York City, a group strongly influenced in political direction by the Communist Party (CP). In the face of attacks by Lindsay and Rockefeller which have brought rent increases and virtually destroyed all aspects of rent control over the last year, all Met Council can advocate are squatting in vacant buildings and rent strikes. Even if its organizers were attempting to organize on a broader basis than building by building (their current tack), Met Council would not find this strategy effective in preventing rent increases and deterioration of buildings. For to prevent such gouging requires mass construction of housing, not just occupation of the several thousand livable vacant apartments in the city. Tenants must not organize themselves as "rent-payers" or "rent-withholders," a view the Met Council methods re-enforce. They must see themselves as "economic planners" and builders who dare to demand housing construction at the expense of banks and big real estate—in order to get out of their immediate bind. Yet Met Council—and the CP in general—keeps tax and construction demands low-key, or separate from "consumer issues," doing nothing to change the consciousness of their membership as to how solutions can be effected. It is easier to collect membership cards.

Such compartmentalization of "consumer" and "producer" issues recurs in most defense movements to save jobs, increase welfare checks, or stop tax increases. Each such movement seeks to relieve immediate pressures, but leaves the question of reconstruction of the economy to "others" or "later." This abdication from the responsibility of reorganizing the economy in the interests of working people insures continued depression of living standards under an increasingly repressive state. (See "Centrism, Campaigner," vol. 3, no. 1.)

To fail to take on the task of economic reconstruction means that most "socialists" and the labor movement will have no alternative to supporting liberal capitalists of the McGovern/McCloskey type, especially in 1972. Having built no independent class-wide institution around expanded production and better living standards at capitalist expense, they will follow the only "reconstruction" program around—the anti-war "reconversion" charade of the liberals. The Communist Party and Socialist Workers Party (plus labor bureaucrats like Victor Gotbaum of AFSCME and Leonard Woodcock of the UAW) will tacitly accept the cry of "tax reform," rather than expropriation of capitalist income; the end of the Vietnam War, rather than an end to all military spending; and the building of a new "Urban Coalition" with "new priorities" rather than a working class party.

It should go without saying that an adequate reconstruction program must demand financing at the expense of capitalist waste and speculation. It should also be evident that specific kinds of political organizations are required to develop and fight for such a program in relation to specific strikes and budget cuts.

Class-for-itself program; class-for-itself organization—each is the prerequisite for the other in a seeming vicious circle. Therefore it is essential that united fronts form now, initiated by those handfuls of the unemployed, trade unionists, socialists, and students ready to move on a common-interest program. Such united fronts must undertake consistent propaganda education and outreach. Under the impetus of current strikes and wildcats, which threaten to break out into mass strikes, such a nucleus alone has the ability to generate a mass-based working-class movement that can meet the needs of the class.

The socialist left in the U.S.—the CP and SWP—is essential to the building of class-wide united fronts that can deal effectively with the urban crisis. If these organizations continue to mislead their followers by tailing liberal capitalists and union bureaucrats, while refusing to join anti-capitalist united fronts, they must and can be destroyed. If the CP and SWP join such united fronts, they will help build the only kind of leadership capable of solving the "urban crisis."

15.
WATERSHED OF THE AMERICAN ECONOMY

David Deitch

A good deal of public fascination is being expressed about the notion that a Republican Administration was the one to institute wage-price controls and other forms of governmental interference in the private economy during "peace-time"—as if somehow the Republicans had some special formula for dealing with the developing economic crisis. There is no formula; the crisis is inherent in the political economy; the only "solution"— a technical one to the massive political problem represented by the conflicting requirements of large capital and of working people—is greater rationalization of the economy over the long term and the expropriation of working-class incomes in order to achieve the necessary stabilization in the short term.

It seems probable that a Democratic Administration would have resolved sooner to move toward the more managed capitalism that one finds in the Western European states, and the fact that Richard Nixon assumed this historic task rather than, say, Hubert Humphrey is of small consequence. In both cases, the working class of America, and indeed the rest of the "free world," will have its pockets picked in a more delicate fashion, now that the bludgeoning tactics of high unemployment are seen to have failed as a stabilization technique for the first time in a generation. America is now in a new stage, but it is a stage that other capitalist nations have arrived at earlier. In this sense, the Nixon economic controls can't "work," but must be seen as part of an adjustment process long under way in Europe—the development of a new "managed" capitalism, a higher order of rationalization designed to eliminate the disruptions of the inflationary struggle, the cooptation as it were, of the Socialist alternative.

The Nixon Administration, having delayed the inevitable as long as possible, has reluctantly signed the death warrant in this country of the so-called "free market" in favor of greater management and control. The

From David Deitch, "Nixon's N.E.P.: Watershed of the American Economy," *The Nation*, September 13, 1971, pp. 198–202. © 1971 by Nation Associates, Inc. Reprinted by permission of the publisher.

purpose of the three-month wage-price "freeze" is to permit time for the organization of a permanent mechanism to determine who shall get what share of the national income—an "incomes policy" linked in some way to growth in productivity. What this means is that a process has been set in motion whereby the American working class will be made to see that its own prosperity is an indissoluble function of private profit; indeed, that it can expect little unless and until private capital has its due. In order to facilitate this process, of course, the trade unions must be incorporated into the incomes policy strategy and a "consensus" established that will carry forward the new philosophy of containment of radical change by officially administered prices and wages through agreed upon norms; in short, a planned growth and strategy for economic mobilization within the competitive world capitalist system, as if peacetime economic warfare were synonymous with military conflict, and "patriotism" an integral part of the campaign to restore the pre-eminent position that America acquired largely as a result of World War II.

But how did all this come about, and why do we have an economic "crisis"—the word is used advisedly—that must be dealt with by extraordinary means? Why is it that a watershed has been reached in the American political economy requiring the most sweeping series of economic initiatives since the Great Depression?

To answer this question one must re-examine the economic behavior of the 1960s, the war in Vietnam, indeed the peculiar behavior of the entire postwar period of which the sixties were merely the distillation of the most important attributes of our capitalistic system.

The existing inflation is especially dangerous because it is associated with the reduction in liquidity of the economy during the post-World War II period, a reduction which, however persistent, did not become critical until around 1965 when the war in Asia accelerated the deterioration in liquidity and the entire inflationary process. [See "Depression Warning: Out on the Credit Limb" by Michael Tanzer, *The Nation*, June 2, 1969.] Superficially stated, liquidity is the ability to pay off debt, and its converse is the tendency toward bankruptcy. The loss of liquidity can be measured in various ways, not least of which is the fact that increased inputs of debt are required to boost gross national product, while an ever greater portion of corporate profits must be devoted to debt repayment. Both Keynesians and monetarists have been dead wrong in debating whether the economy is "depression proof" and whether "built-in stabilizers" are able to correct the course of the economy. The relatively few financial experts who paid attention to balance sheets—pointing out that increasing profits may be futile if the accumulation of debt has been rising faster—correctly predicted that the society was heading in the direction of depression, that it has been acquiring an enormously high fixed cost structure through the accumulation of debt, and that debt itself is the most important inflationary stimulus in the economy.

When liquidity becomes critically low—when the means are not sufficiently available to pay off the accumulation of debt—accelerating increases in the money supply are needed to fuel economic expansions because natural liquidity is unavailable. Forcing business to expand through government spending or through additional monetary inflation generated by the Federal Reserve Board only aggravates the deterioration in liquidity. The ratio of interest payments to corporate profits plus interest payments— that is, the proportion of income available to all security holders that is consumed by interest payments—is one measure of the debt burden plaguing corporations. This ratio, according to the Bank Credit Analyst of Montreal, was 48 percent in 1970, compared with 37 percent in 1960 and 31 percent in 1929. Meanwhile, the increase in public and private debt in 1970 was $117 billion, against a GNP increase of only $45.1 billion. In other words, it took $2.60 to boost a dollar's worth of GNP. In the previous five years, an average $1.92 of debt raised the GNP by $1. In almost every year, a heavier dose of debt is required to generate the American GNP. Interest payments of approximately $125 billion a year—rising inexorably—constitute an eighth of GNP, and must be paid off or disavowed—threatening an important break in the chain of payments, and thus depression. Several sensational bankruptcies in the last few years have indicated that a prolonged economic recession, with a consequent decline in corporate profits, could produce the circumstances that lead to profound economic dislocation.

It is not *just* the ability of giant corporations and big labor to administer prices and wages that has made the present inflation intractable. Monopoly is the means by which inflation is executed, not its *raison d'être*. Ten years ago, 15 years ago, the corporations and the unions were equally adept at maintaining the conditions which have stabilized the distribution of income since World War II. Something new has been added to the equation: a tremendously high and rising fixed cost structure that is being built into the U.S. economy—that is, debt—is causing all its elements to run ever faster in order to stay ahead of the inflationary process. For the first time in a generation, high unemployment and recessionary conditions have failed to stabilize the economy and point it toward a new expansion without important inflation.

What seems to be clear is that the American economy is not generating enough wealth to satisfy the requirements of the inflationary society. With the inflation having been extended for a prolonged period, almost everybody's real income has declined, and the ruling class is forced to seek extraordinary measures to expropriate income where it is not available through normal business expansion. Inasmuch as the corporations, collectively speaking, are unable to undertake a normal expansion because profits and borrowing must be devoted to restoring liquidity, they are more dependent on inflationary prices than on increased sales to sustain income levels. To help the corporations out of their difficulties, Washington understandably does not go out of its way now to promote a business expansion but rather offers increased depreciation allowances, a big capital investment tax credit, an import surcharge, a tax cut: in other words, measures designed to expropriate public funds for private investment purposes.

Japan has a similar debt problem, but learned earlier how to "solve" it by picking the pockets of its working class. More and more American management consultants are now saying, with Herman Kahn, that Japan's brand of managed capitalism is something to emulate. Indeed, no other capitalist country has found how to implement its method of expropriating public funds for private investment purposes. Japan's intense preoccupation with ever rising private investment has resulted in enormous productivity gains (an incredible 14.2 percent average annual increase between 1965 and 1970, compared with a thin 2.21 percent for the United States, now the lowest of all the industrialized countries), but also in tremendous pent-up demands for social investment and more equitable income distribution.

The Japanese Government's economic policies have been specifically designed to concentrate capital in areas where world demand is highest—that is, heavy machinery, chemicals, and precision products. Corporate mergers are encouraged to meet and overwhelm international competition. The Bank of Japan works overtime toward this end by stabilizing an industrial system that makes extremely high use of corporate debt to finance growth. Since Japanese companies finance expansion by borrowing in the neighborhood of 80 percent of total capital requirements, fixed costs are extremely high. Because the break-even point is so high, Japanese companies must operate facilities at near capacity and the output is moved onto world markets at competitively low prices. The extremely high use of debt has raised productivity, permitted smaller profit margins by expanding volume, and caused Japan to become the world's greatest industrial competitor.

The United States has failed to match Japan's utilization of debt financing, despite the encouragement of American management consultants, who foresaw that this was the road toward stepped-up return on equity investment and, more important, the retention of U.S. economic hegemony in world competition. Nevertheless, the United States has managed to acquire a bigger debt repayment problem simply because it lacks the kind of economic "rationalization" that Japanese capitalists benefit from. What this means is that the United States is moving toward a more managed capitalism precisely because it must find new ways to expropriate public funds for private investment purposes in an intensely competitive world.

I want to develop the idea that the intention of our economic policy in 1970–71 has been to delay a legitimate business expansion while finding other means for the corporations to acquire capital. As most economists by now realize, Mr. Nixon's new economic program is short on fiscal stimulation, since government spending and employee cuts balance out tax reductions. Recent events nevertheless indicate that the United States continues to seek inflationary solutions to inflationary problems.

The purpose of the President's economic policy is to maintain the price level despite enormous corporate overcapacity. It seeks to avoid price cutting as the means to stimulate consumption. In fact, the economic managers do not want a boom in consumption just yet, for the liquidity reasons outlined above. What they do want is to create the conditions for a restoration of liquidity that will prepare the corporations to undertake a legitimate expansion and a prolonged upswing of profits. The present period is one of preparation and transition.

While it is traditional for the corporations to want to maintain their prices despite sluggish sales, there is an added incentive this time in the form of billions of dollars of "excess" savings accumulated in the banks. The idea is to get consumers to spend this money—estimated at upward of $15 billion—on the existing price level. The economic managers are worried that a crisis of confidence is causing the American people to save rather than to spend their money. Consumers are being given the message that with expiration of the wage-price freeze prices are likely to go up, so it makes sense for them to buy now. Naturally, they are never advised to demand lower prices, given the fact that goods are in general oversupply.

Although newspaper reports trumpet that the dollar is "weak" in foreign exchange markets, the fact is that foreign currencies are going up while the dollar, in absolute terms, stays constant. This means that foreign merchandise is becoming more expensive, both relatively in terms of U.S. merchandise, and absolutely in terms of the amount of dollars they will cost. The dollar is "weak," yet prices go higher. The 10 percent import surcharge is similarly designed to raise the price of foreign merchandise relative to American goods. The obvious intention is to avoid giving American consumers the option of buying cheaper merchandise.

What the Administration has chosen not to do is try to step up consumption by raising total government spending. It does not wish to set off a new inflationary spiral, just to maintain the old inflationary price level. However, it does hope to boost consumption by causing people to spend what they already have in the banks—their savings, which have reached the highest total rate since World War II. The concept is simple indeed: while the corporations believe they have already paid out higher wages than they can well afford, they haven't yet received the full benefits of the inflated price level. In order to get those benefits in terms of profits, the corporations must induce consumers to spend what they have saved from their "catch up" wages.

In this sense, working-class savings are being expropriated by an economic policy which maintains a price level that is ultra high relative to excess capacity, in order to facilitate corporate profits. In this way, the economic technocrats hope to work off some of that tremendous expansion of the money supply that never did result in bigger industrial output of consequence. Moreover, what the corporations can rake in as profits they don't have to borrow. Savings can either be plundered via profits or borrowed, and the Washington managers don't want to set off a new corporate borrowing spree. They know that the mushrooming ball of paper credit threatens to blow wide open, and so the conditions must be created that can repay debts, not increase them more than necessary. Once the accumulated savings are skimmed off, one might expect legitimate efforts at economic stimulation through stepped-up government spending. But first, it is necessary to expropriate these savings through bigger profits, in order that the corporations can prepare themselves in terms of liquidity for the next big economic expansion. The fact that important liquidity problems still exist (94 percent of the long-term bond financing in the first half of 1971 was monopolized by the top 500 corporations) is the biggest reason why an important industrial expansion has been delayed. An economic policy designed to expand business at a time when the corporations didn't feel ready to accept a business boom would only have aggravated the liquidity situation.

The wage-price freeze, centerpiece of the stabilization package, will bring down interest rates as the inflationary component is removed from the price of credit. This is the only price that will come down; indeed, interest rates must come down if a new economic expansion is to take place. As borrowing costs drop (they haven't until now, despite the sluggish economy), so will the interest rate paid on savings accounts, and that is an added incentive for people to take savings out of the banks and spend it. Monetary policy is saying that too much money has been created, and that too much of it has gone into savings accounts. It is amusing that some critics of the Nixon stabilization plan complain that no freeze has been slapped on profits, when the purpose of the plan is precisely to facilitate a sustained upswing in corporate profits.

But for all of this to happen, the United States must become a garrison state of the world economic community. The inflationary price level at home must be protected by raising barriers to foreign competition. And other public funds must be expropriated for the sake of investment in productivity gains that will lead American corporations to victory in the world marketplace. Patriotism has already been invoked in this regard and the cooperation of labor is essential.

The initial outburst by top American labor leaders against the new economic plan of the Administration will only serve to make their ultimate capitulation that much more ludicrous. What is at stake here is not basic philosophy but the price to be paid and to whom. Big labor has already backed off from contesting the legality of the wage-price freeze, and will content itself with an attack upon the grossly unfair peripheral spending-revenue aspects, all of which are calculated to grease the transition to a new economic order.

So what we are witnessing now is the politics of the transition from the old order to the new managed capitalism in which the labor movement is fully incorporated into the tripartite arrangement with government and industry. As the old ties are dissolved and new bonds forged, there is bound to be a little friction, but the whole purpose is to increase the total rationalization of the economy, to make it work more "efficiently" while preserving the essential capitalist institutions and, most important of all, maintaining the traditional links between property and power. It is just an accident of history that the transition is taking place under a Republican Administration which tried as hard as it could to maintain the old order. The inflationary struggle enveloping the society required the ruling class to move, no matter which party was in power.

A chief exponent of the new managed capitalism is *The New York Times*, which expressed editorially on August 27 its gratitude that big labor is beginning to see the light on the wage-price freeze, and that it was O.K. if it wanted to negotiate some of the more unfair giveaways of the spending portion of the package. AFL-CIO President George Meany and UAW President Leonard Woodcock evidently found it necessary to make an initial display of militancy in order to consolidate their connections to the Democratic Party, which unquestionably will make the economy the most important issue in the 1972 campaign, and as the precondition of their representing all workers in the future wage-determining machinery. In other words, the new capitalism requires a strong, centralized trade union movement with which to bargain. But with only about a quarter of American workers organized, labor's participation in the national consensus becomes difficult. Right-wing Neanderthal talk of breaking up the unions as a way to defuse the wage-price spiral thus seems contrary to historical trends in which the working class in Western industrial states are organized into units that can be managed and bargained with.

The purpose of the political transition now under way is to get the last corporate and labor holdouts to accept the principle of the incomes policy, with the understanding that negotiation and consensus are at its core. A major effort will be made to convince all that the incomes policy is the formula for steady expansion and jobs, and that working prosperity is inextricably linked to productivity and corporate profits.

The *New York Times* perceives that labor "bellicosity" has diminished, while at the same time it grants Meany and Woodcock the moral right to protest only the peripheral aspects of the stabilization package; this indicates that the early stage of the incomes policy has begun in behavioral terms. The *Times* appears satisfied that the labor bureaucracy has accepted the critical principle.

The labor bureaucracy must ultimately silence the rank and file if it wants to join in the tripartite planning, in the same sense that the wildcat strike cannot be tolerated. It will have to assure workers that certain guarantees of income distribution can be expected. The corporations, of course, believe that the incomes policy is their own guarantee for a stabilized income distribution. The question needs to be answered, too, whether the working class ought to cooperate in this evolution even on the assumption of an improved incomes distribution. Simply negotiating the terms of an incomes policy will emasculate any hope of changing the basic relation between property and power. That is its intention. The Left must quickly come to an understanding of the issues involved and move to deal with an increasingly rapid unfolding of events.

In summary, the primary objective of current economic policy is less to facilitate an immediate expansion than to shift capital toward providing corporations with the investment they need to restore liquidity levels and productivity. The Nixon people have been forced into the belief that in the long run stabilization can be achieved by laying down the conditions for managed growth. For the short run, these conditions—the new economic plan—are the cover under which real incomes are expropriated for the purpose of subsidizing corporate treasuries. The working class continues to pay the price of stabilization.

16.
PUBLIC POLICY AND THE WHITE WORKING CLASS

John Howard

The United States lacks many types of social welfare programs taken for granted in other industrial democracies.[1] And the consequences of this are borne by broad sections of the population. Much attention in this regard has been focused on the poor, but a far larger segment of the population, including most of the white working class, feels the consequences of this lack as well, for it is at best marginal economically. Both the poor and the economically marginal would benefit enormously from social welfare programs. Paradoxically, however, the white working class, unlike nonwhites and some segments of the white intelligentsia, scarcely conceives of the need for new and more adequate social welfare programs. Consequently, as such programs come into existence they are popularly viewed as being for blacks or other minorities. This reinforces white working class resistance to them and reinforces their identification as racially-oriented programs.

In simple Marxist terms the white working class manifests "false consciousness." The political scientist Robert Lane has indicated that they moralize downward rather than upward,[2] becoming indignant about the welfare mother who receives a few dollars a year over her allotted stipend but shrugging off the price-rigging businessman who might have bilked the public of millions. This chapter discusses the foundations of this perspective, and its consequences as regards the character of social welfare policy in the United States.

Social scientists, like other Americans, have traditionally been concerned with the powerful and with social outcasts. Consequently, as Peter Schrag observed of the white worker, "there is hardly a language to describe him, or even social statistics." Poverty and affluence are the subject of endless studies and books, yet white workers are neither poor, nor, in any

From John Howard, "Public Policy and the White Working Class," pp. 52–70 in *The Use and Abuse of Social Science: Behavioral Science and National Policy-Making*, edited by Irving Louis Horowitz (New Brunswick, N.J.: Transaction Books). © 1971 by Transaction, Inc. Reprinted by permission of the publisher.

meaningful sense, affluent. Their life style can be conveyed in literature but social scientists have no adequate conceptual category to define their existence. Schrag attempted a summation: "between slums and suburbs, between Scarsdale and Harlem, between Shaker Heights and Hough, there are some eighty million people (depending on how you count them)." It is the world of American Legion posts, neighborhood bars, the Ukrainian club, and the Holy Name Society. They live in tract homes in Daly City and south San Francisco, Bay Ridge, and Canarsie, "bunting on the porch rail with the inscription 'Welcome Home Pete.' The gold star in the window."[3] This population is culturally square and traditionalist. Rock music and movies as an art form are not within their cultural purview; what the hip regard as "camp," they take seriously; what the hip take seriously they regard as boring, annoying or disgusting. It is a measure of the partial validity of the term "forgotten American" that they cannot be as precisely defined as those at the bottom or those at the top.[4]

This essay is divided into three parts, the first two of which take up the question of whether the white working class has a set of interests which might reasonably be served by changes in social welfare policy. In the first, on "comparative social welfare policy" the United States and other industrial democracies are compared. This comparison suggests that the United States lacks a number of social welfare programs commonly found in other industrial countries. In the second, the economic characteristics of the white working class are discussed, and it is indicated that they are far from being affluent. These two sections lay the foundation for the third, which identifies and analyzes those factors which generate and sustain white working class perspectives on social welfare policy and their seeming hostility despite being potential beneficiaries.

This essay rests on the assumption that public policy is formed partially in response to the constellation of pressures to which officeholders are subjected. Here, the pressures to be focused on are those of the white working class as an interest group. Their attitudes and behavior cannot be accounted for in terms of any simple Marxian model. The issue is one that has agitated American radicals for decades; it is also an important question for political sociology. And, of course, it is important in grasping the tone and direction of American society.

Comparative Social Welfare Policy

The United States is conventionally thought of as the most advanced nation in the world. It can be plausibly argued however that in many ways the country is rather backward, for it lacks a number of social welfare programs taken for granted in Western democracies. It is the thrust of my discussion that this has important consequences as regards the quality of life in the society and that it can be accounted for partially in terms of the absence of any strong sense of class interest or political consciousness on the part of white workers, those whom I have termed economically marginal.

The relative dearth of social welfare programs in this the most advanced nation in the world has been noted by several commentators. For example, Alvin Schorr has observed with regard to family allowances that "A majority of the countries of the world and all of the industrial West, except the United States, now have such programs." James Vadikan points out that family allowances ". . . constitute a means of redistributing income in such a way as to benefit the child-rearing portion of the population."[5] In most countries it is a fairly modest sum. Under the Canadian system, for example, the amount per child ranges from $6 a month to $10 a month depending on the child's age. By contrast, the French system is quite generous.[6] "The payment there varies according to region, the number of children in the family, and their ages. In Paris in 1964, for example, a family with four children received between 380 and 450 francs ($77 to $111) a month, exceeding the legal minimum wage at the time. In addition, various special payments may be made during pregnancy, at birth, (and) for improved housing."[7]

Edgar Z. Friedenberg has suggested that the United States ". . . still provides less in the way of social services, especially to the ill and aged, than an Englishman or Scandinavian would expect as a matter of right." National health insurance plans are found in one form or another in all of the industrial democracies, although the extent of benefits varies from place to place. In Great Britain complete medical, surgical, pharmaceutical, and dental services are offered. In Australia, one finds restricted pharmaceutical benefits, hospital benefits, and various other kinds of services. But there are basically three types of national health programs: the government may own facilities and hire the professionals, patients may pay fees and be reimbursed, or professionals may render services under contract to the government. Most West European countries have the latter type of program. There is a good deal of nonsense talked in the United States about the British system. No doctor is forced to join the national health service but 95 percent have chosen to do so. Their income is lower than that of doctors in the United States but higher than it was before Health Service came in and higher than that of other professionals in Great Britain.

Social welfare policy extends beyond the provision of certain kinds of services and income redistribution to embrace the creation of opportunities. All developed nations have specified policies with respect to manpower and employment. These policies vary in terms of the extent to which they sustain the worker during periods of unemployment and facilitate his reemployment. Sweden has a number of sophisticated manpower programs, leading Carl Uhr to observe that "We in the United States have not yet developed as comprehensive and coordinated a set of labor policies and institutions as have evolved in Sweden." In addition to a variety of training programs for older workers whose skills have become obsolete and younger people without marketable skills, there are mechanisms for matching up workers with jobs. "Workers living in labor-surplus areas," says Uhr, "are induced by a system of allowances to move to available jobs, known to the employment service, in labor shortage areas. Unemployed persons who need and want to move great distances to job opportunities in other locations may apply for and receive travel expenses to seek new work in these areas. If they locate jobs, they may immediately receive a 'starting allowance.' This is in substance a grant which becomes repayable in part only if they do not hold the new job for at least 90 days." Other problems associated with worker mobility are anticipated: "If housing for their families is not available in their new work location, they may receive 'family allowances' for the separate maintenance of wife and children for up to 9 months in their former location. These allowances pay the rent for the family up to a maximum figure, plus a cash allowance for the maintenance of wife and children."[8]

Few of these critics argue that the United States should simply mirror other industrial democracies with regard to social welfare policy and programs. These approaches are not ends in themselves but are designed to alleviate certain kinds of mass deprivation, deprivation that is readily visible and apparently persistent in this country, which has adopted few of these policies or programs. Some scholars have pointed to what they believe to be the tangible consequences of the paucity of comprehensive social welfare measures in the United States. Daniel Patrick Moynihan has stated that "The teeming disorganized life of impoverished slums has all but disappeared among North American democracies—save only the United States. It requires some intrepidness to declare this to be a fact, as no systematic inquiry has been made which would provide completely dependable comparisons, but it can be said with fair assurance that mass poverty and squalor, of the kind that may be encountered in almost any American city, simply cannot be found in comparable cities in Europe or Canada or Japan." Robert Heilbroner echoes this, "I maintain that to match the squalor of the worst of the American habitat one must descend to the middle range of the underdeveloped lands."[9]

Infant mortality rates in the United States are considerably higher than those in other industrial democracies. In 1968 with a rate of 22.1 infant deaths per 1,000 live births the country ranked above most other Western, industrial democracies. It is estimated that the nation ranks eighteenth in the world, just above Hong Kong. Some might argue that this is a consequence of the extraordinarily high rate among nonwhites, but even if we consider the rate among whites only (in Mississippi, for example, 23.1 among whites; in Pennsylvania 20.3; Maine, 22.8; New Hampshire, 20.1; Vermont, 21.0; Illinois, 20.3; West Virginia, 24.8), the national performance is inferior to that of other Western countries.[10]

Vadikan has observed that "Almost 40,000 babies die in America each year who would be saved if our infant mortality rate was as low as that in Sweden. In 1967, one million babies, one in four, [were] born to mothers receiving little or no obstetric care."[11]

To reiterate, whether the United States is the most developed nation in the world or underdeveloped depends upon the dimension one examines. If one looks at the number of automobiles per 1,000 of the population the United States leads the field. If one looks at infant mortality rates, or number of hospital beds per 1,000, or number of doctors per 1,000, or average rates of unemployment over time, the country lags, and along some dimensions lags badly.

Some might counter that the United States has programs that other democracies lack ("New Careers," Headstart, Upward Bound, and so forth). It is the case, however, that these programs are directed at the poor and are not intended to meet the needs and problems of those who are marginal. Secondly, although international comparisons are difficult to make, it does appear to be true that all things taken together (save education) the United States spends relatively less on social welfare than many other countries. Bert Seidman has observed that,

> It generally surprises most Americans to find out that their country, the wealthiest in the world, uses less of its natural wealth for the social welfare of its citizens than other advanced industrial nations and frequently less than many poor and developing nations which make considerable sacrifices to do so.
>
> For example, an International Labor Organization Report published in 1964 shows that West Germany, Luxemburg, Austria, and Italy used 17 percent, 16.8 percent, 14.8 percent and 14.7 percent respectively, of their gross national product for social welfare measures. None of the 15 nations in Western Europe, except Spain and Portugal, spent less than 8.9 percent. This contrasts with 7 percent of the gross national product spent by the United States for such programs.[12]

The United States spends more on education and has a much higher proportion of its college age population in college than West European countries. This is partially a consequence of having different channels of access to employment. However, the lower proportion of the European college age population in college does not mean that there is mass unemployment or that jobs go begging, rather the system of matching up man and job is different. There is a school of thought however which suggests that European technological development and entreprenurial efficiency may be hurt in the long run by not having a work force with as much formal education as that in the United States. If that occurs and European countries move to spend more on education, the relative position of the United States in terms of social welfare spending would remain unchanged.

Mike Harrington has indicated that "the American percentage of the gross national product devoted to direct social benefits has yet to achieve even half the typical European contribution." It is not a matter of course that the white working class with greater political consciousness would be demanding precisely these programs, but rather that they would be demanding something.

Let us now look more closely at the economic status of white workers.

The Poor and the Marginal

It is assumed by many observers that the white working class has become conservative because it has become affluent and therefore does not need amplified social welfare legislation. Actually about 12 percent of the white population is poor while another 55 to 60 percent is economically marginal.

Like poor nonwhites, poor whites have been clearly identified by demographers, economists, and sociologists. In 1967 of the 26,146,000 people in the country defined as poor, 17,764,000 were white.[13] Among the 384,000 young men in 1964, who were 20 to 24 years of age and unemployed, 310,000 were white and 74,000 were nonwhite; 450,000 or 554,000 unemployed young men 14 to 19 in 1964 were white.[14] In December 1969, 1,137,000 white males 16 years of age and over were unemployed and 266,000 blacks. The black rate was higher, of course—5.3 to 2.5 for whites. But the figures and the rates belied the notion that unemployment was solely or primarily a black problem.

The economically marginal white is much harder to identify. His existence defines the inadequacy of the simple dichotomy between the poor and the affluent. Below, five quantitative measures are employed to define the existence of this class: income distribution, standard of living, real income, credit status, and liquid assets.

As regards income distribution, in 1966, 31 percent of white families made less than $5,000; 39 percent made $5,000 to $9,999, while another 30 percent made more than $10,000 a year.[15] Seven families of 10 then were poor or marginal. But income figures per se mean little unless they are related to purchasing power and standard of living. An inference with regard to the meaning of the income of white workers can be made by an analysis of reports published by the Bureau of Labor Statistics, U.S. Department of Labor. The bureau regularly devises a "standard family budget" for a four person family consisting of working husband, nonworking wife, son, age 13, and daughter, age eight. This closely approximates actual family structure. The budget is derived from "scientific and technical judgment regarding health and social well-being" and is designed to indicate the cost of a "modest but adequate" standard of living in urban areas. In 1967 the required sum ranged down from $10,092 in Honolulu to $9,744 in the San Francisco-Oakland area, $9,079 in Philadelphia and $8,641 in Durham, with a low of $7,952 in Austin, Texas. The average for 39 cities and metropolitan areas was $9,243.[16]

In the same year, production and nonsupervisory workers on nonagricultural payrolls averaged just over $5,000 a year ranging from a high of $8,060 for construction workers to a low of $4,264 for those in wholesale and retail trade. All fell well below the government's own figure of the amount needed to enjoy a moderate level of living in urban areas.[17] The mean income of craftsmen and foremen was $9,310, otherwise no workers year to year even approach the average of the Standard Family Budget.

Further the effects of inflation eroded the money gains made by the blue collar class. Between 1965 and 1969 the average wage of 47 million production and nonsupervisory workers in private industry went up $14.74 from $96.21 to $110.95 per week; at the same time, the worker with three dependents saw his tax rise by $4.80 a week. The four-year increase in prices from a base of 100 in 1965 was $11.18. Adding the price rise to the tax increase and subtracting from the 1969 wage, the worker had $1.24 per week less to spend in 1969 than in 1965.[18]

None of this proves, of course, that the American blue collar and working class lives in misery and desperation. Obviously, it does not. Nonetheless, it seems undeniable that they are far from affluent, that life is probably a worrisome thing, and that the opportunity to get very far ahead seems more and more distant.

Apart from the bureau's "modest but adequate" standard, we also have to look into consumer finance to find the meaning of dollar income. The Economic Behavior Program of the Survey Research Center of the University of Michigan yearly collects detailed information on "family income, financial assets and debt, automobiles, other durable goods, and housing." Multi-stage area probability sampling is used to select a sample of dwelling units representative of the nation.

The debt status of economically marginal whites can be summed up as follows. About 55 percent of the families in the income category $5,000 to $7,449 had installment debt and 61 percent in the income category $7,500 to $9,999. Being unmarried and having no children reduced the probability of being in debt. About 65 to 70 percent of households with children were in debt. In 1967 the mean amount of debt for all families was $1,260. Payments for automobiles were most common but were closely followed by payments on other durables and for personal loans.[19]

The meaning of debt is amplified if viewed in terms of financial assets at the command of workers. About 80 percent of wage earners making $5,000 to $10,000 a year in 1967 either had no checking account or had less than $500 in an account. Sixty-three percent of families making $5,000 to $7,499 either had no savings account or had less than $500 in an account; 46 percent of those families making $7,500 to $9,999 had no account or had less than $500 in an account. The amount of liquid assets then is meager and most families are a paycheck or two away from public assistance.[20]

The life style of the marginal class is suggested by other data. Less than half take vacations and those who do rarely spend much money on it. It is not the case then that there is an affluent blue-collar or working class white-collar class. Most white families are either poor or economically marginal. If they are marginal they have not had a rise in real income since 1965 despite a rise in paper income. Federal data suggest that they may barely make a modest but adequate standard of living. They have acquired certain household goods and durables by going into debt and have the slenderest resources to sustain themselves in a crisis.

The American worker has to purchase out of his pocket services that are publicly provided in many other industrial democracies. He is taxed but there is no commensurate return as regards public services. For example, the American worker, except under highly restricted circumstances, bears out of his own pocket the cost of moving to a locale where he may find work, the cost of supporting his family while looking for work, and the cost of moving them. A whole complex of expenditures, which as we saw is a matter of public responsibility in Sweden, is paid for privately by the American worker.

Social scientists have devised a number of classificatory systems to describe the American population. To further delineate the position of economic marginals within the society I have formulated a rather gross system which does, nevertheless, make certain important distinctions.

I would, for purposes of this discussion, divide the American population into four categories.

At the bottom there are the poor (a disproportionate percentage of the black population and of Indians, Mexicans, and Puerto Ricans, a disproportionate percentage of the elderly and of families headed by a female). The poor subsist on public monies, inadequate incomes or both. They are unable to make ends meet and thus may suffer from malnutrition or a wide variety of debilitating, untreated medical conditions. A segment of the black population and, increasingly, parts of the Indian, Mexican, and Puerto Rican populations, show some degree of political consciousness and some conception of the need to develop national policy approaches to the problems of the deprived.

Then there are the marginals. Most of the white working class population falls into this category, and indeed most of the population. Their characteristics have already been described.[21]

Above them is a class that has substantial money income but does not own or control wealth (the distinction between income and wealth is important). They sell brain power and relatively uncommon skills and are handsomely rewarded. In this category are such persons as the upper echelon professors at the more prestigious universities, the new experts at information control, systems analysts, middle and upper echelon advertising and media men, most business management people, and the like. These people are affluent and some of them have influence with the powerful. Basically they are well-paid laborers however. The politics of this group spans the spectrum and it is difficult to tell what the factors are that account for value differences.

Last there are the true magnates, the corporate elites, the people who own or control the wealth of the country. The upper 5 percent of consumers in the country control 53 percent of the wealth. There is much greater inequality in the distribution of wealth than there is in the distribution of income, accounting for the class of income-affluent persons.

The marginals appear, for reasons we shall explore, to consider themselves closer to the top than to the bottom when in fact they are much closer to the bottom than to the top.

Political Values of the White Working Class

It should be clear by now that the white working class is not affluent. Neither, of course, are white workers poor. They make enough to meet daily living costs and are able to acquire appliances, durables, and some other kinds of goods through installment buying. They have little in the way of liquid assets and are highly vulnerable in the event of loss of job, illness or any of a number of other kinds of misfortunes. They would benefit enormously from a wide variety of social welfare measures that are quite conventional in other industrial democracies. But they are not politically active in the pursuit of these or other social welfare measures and have left lobbying and agitation for more effective and broadly based programs up to blacks and to white liberals and radicals. They are the people whose sons get drafted and sent to Vietnam and whose children are less likely to get into college even when they are extremely capable. Inadequate opportunity for higher education is generally seen as a problem of nonwhites. The existence of inadequate educational opportunities is widespread. With regard to higher education, Project Talent, a survey funded by the United States Office of Education revealed a "marked relationship between reported family income and college entry." Data were gathered on 60,000 students. Basically, the findings were that males in the 98th to 100th percentile were likely to go to college irrespective of family income. Below that, social class became very important, with the mediocre male at the 50th percentile whose family made $12,000 a year or more being more likely to have entered college than the talented boy at the 89th percentile whose family made $3,000 a year or less. The reality behind these data is neither perceived nor translated into political reality by poor and marginal whites.

Why are economically marginal whites not further to the left politically? Why are they not active in promoting the kinds of policy approaches and programs that would appear to serve their own interests?

To be a supporter of movements to realize the kinds of social welfare policy discussed earlier in this chapter implies that one, (a) recognizes the existence of certain kinds of problems, (b) accounts for these problems in system terms, and therefore, (c) calls for given policy approaches to cope with them. Obviously, if an individual either does not recognize the existence of particular problems, or accounts for them in personalistic terms, then he does not seek system changes or new policy approaches.

Evidence on how the white worker defines his own situation is vague and inconclusive. The data provide no basis for anything other than hypothesis and speculation. Therefore let us hypothesize and speculate.[22]

The results of public opinion polls suggest that white workers have a sense of the inadequacy of their position but are at a loss to explain it. Something is wrong but they are not clear as to what. Lloyd A. Free and Hadley Cantril, reporting on a representative national sample, indicate that personal economic conditions and employment status were cited by three out of four persons as their most pressing concerns.[23] This seems to have surprised the researchers. "Even in affluent America, the leading item mentioned under personal wishes and hopes was an 'improved or decent standard of living.' As one Arizona housewife pointed out, 'They say it's prosperous now, but I sure as heck don't notice it.'" This chapter suggests that the Arizona housewife was more nearly correct than Free and Cantril.

Alongside an appreciation of a precarious material situation was complete confusion with regard to policy and meliorative approaches. On the one hand, the overwhelming majority of respondents making $10,000 a year or less favored government programs to accomplish social ends, but only one third believed the government should more readily use its power. Less than one third believed that corporate powers should be curbed while almost half favored greater government control over labor unions.

The task then is to make sense of this, to understand it, to grasp the underlying logic and rationale. If there is an underlying logic it is probably something on the following order: "Yes," the worker says, "I would benefit from various kinds of government programs; they would help me meet real and pressing material problems. Those problems, however, are caused by other segments of the population. Therefore, alternatively, the government might force these people to stop doing the kinds of things which cause problems for me."

Enlarging on this, contemporary workers who recall the desperate and hungry souls populating "Hoovervilles" during the Depression, who use them as a kind of negative reference group, are likely to feel comparatively well off. Those too young to have experienced the Depression undoubtedly have it recalled for them by parents. Their dollar income is substantially greater, the number of household possessions is greater, they have greater job security. This relative satisfaction with having enjoyed a certain amount of mobility probably decreases the workers' proclivity to criticize the politico-economic system or view it as inequitable and unjust. It decreases any sense of a need to agitate for new policy. It is also the case, however, that the worker still has trouble making ends meet. These difficulties, implicitly, pose a question for him. "If I'm so much better off and make so much more money than guys made before, how come I'm still having a rough time?" His belief that the system has afforded him the opportunity for a better life decreases the likelihood that he will account for his difficulties in terms of system defects. If the system were not benign he would not now be in a position where he should be enjoying a better life. In absolving the system he also absolves those who, in some sense, run it.

There are a number of ready-made scapegoats the worker can focus on in attempting to account for its difficulties (blacks, Communists, hippies, liberals, "peace creeps"); of these, blacks are the most plausible and the most accessible. As blacks demand programs to deal with poverty, as they demand a guaranteed annual income, or an improved system of distribution of food to the needy and the hungry, as they demand a whole complex of social welfare legislation, they must seem to the white worker to be unwilling to take advantage of the opportunities he believes exist for any person willing to work. They seem to be making vigorous raids on his pocketbook. They appear to be cheaters, people unwilling to play by the rules, people who "want something for nothing." And he believes the something comes out of his pocket.

This kind of explanation posits genuine misperception on the part of the worker. An alternative (psychologically "deeper") approach might posit displacement of frustration and hostility onto scapegoats. Roughly, the position would be phrased as follows: the worker has some glimpse of the precariousness of his position and some sense of the reasons for it. However to consciously entertain notions of system defects of that sort, would be to admit harboring ideas that are "un-American" or "communist inspired." And for the man who pastes his American flag decal on the car windshield and puts an "Honor America" sticker on his bumper, this might be no small matter. It might in the political sphere be the equivalent of a man admitting to having fleeting sexual thoughts about other men. Rather than countenance thoughts he has come to view as subversive and immoral, it is psychologically easier to displace hostility onto outgroups—blacks, hippies, "bleeding hearts," "limousine liberals," and other freaks of nature.

Additionally, there are internal differentiations in the white working class which probably act to impede the expression of a common point of view or common sentiments with regard to problems and their solutions. The 80 million or so people who comprise the marginal class are differentiated by geography, ethnicity, and occupation. A number of students have discussed the persistence of ethnic identity in American communities. Michael Parenti has observed that "in a single weekend in New York separate dances for persons of Hungarian, Irish, Italian, German and Polish extractions are advertised in the neighborhood newspapers and the foreign language press."[24] Herbert Gans[25] and Gerald Suttles[26] have discussed the persistence of a tightly knit network of relationships among Italians living in Boston and in Chicago. Occupationally, the $5,000 to $10,000 category embraces secretaries and assembly line workers, senior clerks and cab drivers. Geographically workers spread out over the South with its racially dominated politics, the Midwest where fear of communism is a serious sentiment, and the Northeast where problems of traffic congestion and state financial support for parochial schools excite political passions.

In other words, there are a number of cross-cutting loyalties and interests that reduce any sense of common identity.

The trade unions embrace a larger portion of the American working class than any other organization. The union movement itself however is internally fragmented. Additionally (not counting about 2 million blacks who are trade union members) only about 14 million whites in a work force of over 70 million are union members. The American union movement very early fell into the trap of racism, excluding blacks and thereby creating a pool of strike breakers for employers and depressing the wage level of whites by ensuring low wage levels for blacks. The unions neither ideologically nor organizationally are prepared to define radically progressive policy alternatives.

The muted role of the trade unions has been crucial. The political interests of most citizens are mediated through organizations. This is particularly important for populations (white workers, for example) less likely to participate electorally in the political process. Thus, for example, the under-representations of blacks at the ballot box is counterbalanced somewhat by the existence of a variety of politically vigorous organizations (the NAACP and The Urban League are the oldest and most resilient). Traditionally, these organizations have been the vehicles of the black bourgeoisie, probably in large part because lower-class people in general are less likely to belong to voluntary organizations. Recently, however, a number of groups drawing their membership from street and ghetto blacks have become prominent (the Black Panthers, the Black Muslims and DRUM, an organization of black workers in automobile plants, are the most vigorous).

Many of those who have written on the white lower class suggest that they have "a deficient sociocultural milieu," that they possess undifferentiated and unsophisticated notions with regard to the nature of the socio-politico-economic system, and that they are bigoted and suspicious.[27] The lower middle class is seen as rigidly moralistic and concerned with propriety. The self-defeating definitions of the situation entertained by these two groups go unchallenged by major alternative formulations put forth by the trade unions who have not played the educational role vis-à-vis white workers that civil rights groups have played vis-à-vis blacks. The orientation of the unions has been to conserve and preserve rather than significantly expand or explore in terms of social welfare legislation.

The white worker is not wholly unmindful of his economic interests,[28] but he doesn't translate this knowledge into any consistent conception of major programmatic and policy change. This is left to a segment of the black movement, thereby decreasing further the white workers' likelihood of subscribing to such views.

One consequence of this political orientation of the white working class we have already seen in the relatively poor showing of the United States with regard to social welfare programs. Another important consequence is that the pursuit of more adequate social welfare legislation becomes equated with the pursuit of racial justice.

The black movement has focused attention on the deprived status of blacks. There has been no equivalent movement among whites to sensitize policy makers to the marginal status of most whites. While there are a variety of ethnically-based organizations—Hibernian clubs, Sons of Italy, Polish American clubs, Greek American clubs—none has a clearly formulated program with regard to the class problems of its members.[29] Many non-white groups, however, are so oriented. The black movement is too well-known to need discussion. Among Mexicans La Huelga has mobilized many Mexican-American agricultural workers in California and the Southwest, while Rijes Tijerina and "Corky" Gonzales have rallied Mexicans in New Mexico and Colorado. Recently Indians have demanded that attention be paid to their economic and social problems.[30]

Consequently, as meliorative policy is formulated, it is done so implicitly (and sometimes explicitly) in racial terms. Seligman has observed with regard to the poverty program that "Everyone [connected with its formulation] accepted the political view that the War on Poverty was mainly for Negroes." And in fact, blacks and other nonwhites do participate more extensively than poor whites in federal programs; for example, the percentages of black and other nonwhite in the following programs is: New Careers, 67 percent; Concentrated Employment Program, 72 percent; Neighborhood Youth Corps, Summer, 56 percent; in-school, 76 percent; out-of-school, 52 percent.[31] Many colleges and universities have begun to deal with the problem of educational opportunity by recruiting more heavily from among blacks and other nonwhites, ignoring the problem of lack of opportunity among poor and marginal whites precisely because poor and marginal whites have not articulated a position reflecting any grasp of their own position in the society.

Social welfare policy in the United States is discussed with the vocabulary of race rather than that of class. In addition to posing analytic problems, the excited hostilities and passions of poor and marginal whites make it difficult for even meagerly financed and minimally intrusive programs to function successfully. In the meantime they themselves do without.

Notes

1. It is a measure of American thinking that the very term "welfare" is equated with husbandless mothers receiving public assistance. In the broader sense of the term it refers to policies intended to redistribute national wealth in terms of need. Pekka Kuusi, the Finnish social scientist, Gunnar Myrdal, and other European scholars have written extensively on social welfare. See, for example, Richard Titmuss, *Commitment to Welfare* (New York: Pantheon Books, 1968).

2. Robert Lane, *Political Ideology: Why the American Common Man Believes What He Does* (Glencoe, Illinois: Free Press of Glencoe, 1962), pp. 330–331.

3. Peter Schrag, "The Forgotten American," *Harper's* vol. 239, no. 1431, August 1969, p. 27.

4. Christopher Jencks and David Riesman, "On Class in America," *The Public Interest*, no. 10, Winter 1968, pp. 65–86.

5. James Vadikan, *Children, Poverty, and Family Allowances* (New York and London: Basic Books, Inc., 1968), p. 6.

6. Some people might object to the introduction of a program of this sort into the United States on the grounds that it would have the effect of raising the birth rate. Vadikan concludes however that "Based on world wide experience over a considerable period of time, it would appear safe to conclude that a program of family allowances of modest size such as exists in Canada or such as might be considered in the United States could have no significant effects in increasing the birth rate." *Children, Poverty, and Family Allowances*, p. 101. Not even in France where family allowance benefits average one-fifth of the family budget of low-income people has it accelerated the birth rate.

7. Alvin Schorr, *Poor Children: A Report on Children in Poverty* (New York and London: Basic Books, Inc., 1966), p. 148.

8. Carl Uhr, "Recent Swedish Labor Market Policies," *The Manpower Revolution*, Garth Mangum (ed.) (Garden City, New York: Anchor Books, Doubleday and Company, Inc., 1966), p. 376.

9. Robert L. Heilbroner "Benign Neglect in the United States," *transaction*, vol. 7, 12 October, 1970, p. 16.

10. Seymour Kurtz (ed.), *The New York Times: Encyclopedic Almanac 1970*, The New York Times, Books and Educational Division (New York: 1969), pp. 245–299; and U.S. Bureau of the Census, *Statistical Abstracts of the United States (1955 edition)*, Washington, D.C., 1970, p. 5.

11. James Vadikan, *op. cit.*, p. 24.

12. Bert Seidman, "The Case for Higher Social Security Benefits," *The American Federationist*, vol. 74, 1, January 1967, p. 5.

13. *The New York Times: Encyclopedic Almanac*, p. 301.

14. Arthur Ross and Herbert Hill (eds.), *Employment, Race, and Poverty* (New York: Harcourt, Brace, and World, 1967), pp. 30–32.

15. George Katona, James N. Morgan, Joy Schmiedeskamp, and John A. Sundquist, *1967 Survey of Consumer Finances* (Ann Arbor, Michigan: University of Michigan, 1967), p. 11.

16. Department of Labor, Bureau of Labor Statistics, *Monthly Labor Review*, April 1969.

17. Department of Labor, Bureau of Labor Statistics, *Employment and Earnings*, vol. 16, 7, January 1970, p. 67.

18. Nathan Spero, "Notes on the Current Inflation," *Monthly Review*, vol. 21, 2, June 1969, p. 30.

19. Katona, in the work cited, pp. 15–43.

20. *Ibid.*

21. For an excellent discussion of this population, one roughly parallel to the discussion undertaken here see " 'Middle Class' Workers and the New Politics," Brendan Sexton in *Beyond the New Life*, Irving Howe (ed.) (New York: McCall, 1970), pp. 192–204.

22. Among the useful works on poor and marginal whites are: *Uptown: Poor Whites in Chicago*, Todd Gitlin and Nanci Hollander (New York: Harper & Row, 1970); Eli Chinoy, *Automobile Workers and the American Dream* (New York: Garden City, Doubleday, 1955); Lee Rainwater, Richard Coleman, and Gerald Handel, *Workingman's Wife* (New York: Oceana Publications, 1956); Lee Rainwater, *And the Poor Get Children* (New York: Quadrangle Books, 1960), and William F. Whyte, *Street Corner Society* (Chicago, Illinois: University of Chicago Press, 1943).

23. Lloyd A. Tree and Hadley Cantril, *The Political Beliefs of Americans*, (New York: Simon & Schuster, 1968), pp. 9–10, 96, 99, 190, 195–196, 218.

24. Michael Parenti, "Ethnic Politics and the Persistence of Ethnic Identification," *American Political Science Review*, LXI (September 1967), 719m.

25. Herbert Gans, *The Urban Villagers* (New York: Glencoe Free Press, 1962).

26. Gerald Suttles, *The Social Order of the Slums* (Chicago, Illinois: University of Chicago Press, 1968).

27. See, for example, Albert R. Cohen and Harold Hodges, "Lower Blue Collar Class Characteristics," *Social Problems* vol. 10, Spring 1963, 4, pp. 303–334. Jack L. Roach, "A Theory of Lower-Class Behavior," *Sociological Theory: Inquiries and Paradigms*, Llewellyn Gross (ed.), (New York, Evanston and London: Harper and Row, 1967), pp. 294–315.

28. See, S. M. Lipset, *Political Man* (Garden City: Doubleday, 1960), pp. 97–130 and A. M. Lipset and Earl Raab, "The Wallace Whitelash," *transaction*, vol. 7, 2, December 1969, pp. 23–36.

29. This is no longer wholly true. In both Cleveland and New York ethnically based groups have begun to stir. The major impetus has probably been the surge of the black population, but these groups may conceivably turn out to have ends and objectives which are not simply anti-black.

30. For a discussion of protest movements by these other minorities, see John Howard, *The Awakening Minorities: American Indians, Mexican Americans, and Puerto Ricans* (Chicago: Aldine, 1970).

31. *Handbook of Labor Statistics 1970* (Washington, D.C.: U.S. Department of Labor, Bureau of Labor Statistics, 1970), p. 123.

17.
INCOME DISTRIBUTION IN THE UNITED STATES

Frank Ackerman, Howard Birnbaum, James Wetzler,
and Andrew Zimbalist

Introduction

The persistence of income inequality in America is well-known. Affluence in the suburbs contrasts starkly with the slums of any major city or the numerous "pockets" of rural poverty. This inequality is embarrassing in a democracy. Perhaps for this reason, income distribution is rarely an explicit political issue in the United States.[1] The prevailing ideology seems to be that inequality is needed for economic growth and that soon the economy will be so prosperous that even the relatively poor will have a high standard of living. This argument gains some apparent plausibility from the history of Western Europe and North America: in these areas capitalism, with its great inequality, has been the agent of economic development.

For several reasons, we reject this neglect of distributional issues and its implicit toleration of existing inequality. First, it will require many decades of growth without redistribution to eliminate poverty, and there is no reason to assume that past rates of growth can be maintained this long. Economic growth is having increasingly intolerable ecological effects: either resources will be diverted to improve the environment or ecologically expensive production will be reduced. American growth, moreover, depends on consuming a disproportionate share of the world's natural resources: if currently underdeveloped countries ever begin to grow, America's share will be reduced.[2]

Second, the need for inequality to promote growth arises in our society because people are socialized to respond only to material incentives. Such responses are neither attractive nor unchangeable, and we can envision a society in which production takes place with little, if any, inequality.

From Frank Ackerman, Howard Birnbaum, James Wetzler, and Andrew Zimbalist, "Income Distribution in the United States," *Review of Radical Political Economics*, vol. 3, no. 3 (Summer 1971), pp. 20–43. © July 1971, by the Union for Radical Political Economics. Reprinted by permission of the publisher.

Third, there are several human objections to inequality. Meaningful democracy is impossible in a society where political resources, such as wealth, are unequally distributed. Inequality is wasteful since, after elemental needs have been satisfied, people consume partly to emulate others; as a result, total social welfare (including our unhappiness over our rival's goods) increases more slowly than income. Finally, differences in material conditions tend to conceal more fundamental human qualities and pervert interpersonal relations.

Considerable confusion surrounds the concept and measurement of income. The Gross National Product (GNP) is the sum of all goods and services produced in a year. We divide GNP into three principal components: after-tax income received by persons (personal disposable income); after-tax income retained by corporations (undistributed corporate profits plus depreciation allowances); and net taxes (taxes minus net transfers from government to the private sector). Most of this essay deals with inequality within the first component of GNP, personal income. However, corporations and government are closely related to the personal income distribution: the individuals at the top of the personal income distribution also control substantial corporate incomes; and, contrary to popular belief, the government does not do much to alleviate personal income inequality.

The first section of our text is an overview of inequality. We examine the personal income distribution and its stability over time; the effect of taxes and government spending; the distribution of wealth, and the definition and extent of poverty. The second section focuses on income differences between particular categories of people. We consider inequalities by class, race, sex, education, and family background. We do not claim to present a complete analysis of the American income distribution; only to have assembled widely scattered data on the subject and suggested some directions in which the analysis should proceed.

We have tried to keep the text as simple as possible in an attempt to make it useful to readers without a background in economics. The specialist and the skeptic should consult the footnotes which contain definitions and technical details as well as sources and references to related readings.

It is important to remember that different agencies and authors use different definitions of economic variables, so statistics from different sources cannot be compared exactly. The Internal Revenue Service definition of income varies considerably from that used by other agencies; the Census Bureau and Office of Business Economics income definitions, while much closer to each other than to the IRS income concept, are still not identical. Data sources differ in quality: the income figures are generally more reliable than the wealth data. We indicate in the text some of the weaker data that should be used with caution, but in each case they are, as far as we know, the best figures available.

The Distribution of Income

Personal Income Before Taxes   The best measure of ability to purchase goods and services is after-tax income. Appropriate data exist, however, only for the distribution of before-tax income, so we must look at that first and consider the tax structure separately. A good way to illustrate the income distribution is to rank the population by income and measure what percentage of total personal income accrues to the richest 20 percent of the population, the second richest 20 percent, and so forth (richest here meaning highest income). The more income going to the richest 20 percent ar d the less going to the poorest 20 percent, the more unequal is the distribution of income.

In the U.S. during the postwar period, the poorest 20 percent of all families have consistently received less than 6 percent of total personal income, while the richest 20 percent have received over 40 percent.[3]

TABLE 1
The Distribution of Before-Tax Family Income
(Percent)

	1969	1968	1964	1960	1956	1950	1947
Poorest fifth	5.6	5.7	5.2	4.9	5.0	4.5	5.0
Second fifth	12.3	12.4	12.0	12.0	12.4	12.0	11.8
Middle fifth	17.6	17.7	17.7	17.6	17.8	17.4	17.0
Fourth fifth	23.4	23.7	24.0	23.6	23.7	23.5	23.1
Richest fifth	41.0	40.6	41.1	42.0	41.2	42.6	43.0
Richest 5 percent	14.7	14.0	15.7	16.8	16.3	17.0	17.2

SOURCE: U.S. Census Bureau, *Current Population Reports*, Series P-60, 75, Table 8, p. 22.

In 1969, the richest 5 percent of all families received over 14 percent of total family income, or over twice as much as the entire bottom 20 percent. Moreover, Table 1 understates inequality since income received by people without families (see Table 2) is much more unequally distributed than family income.[4]

TABLE 2
The Distribution of Unrelated Individual
Income, 1969
(Percent)

Poorest fifth	3.4
Second fifth	7.7
Middle fifth	13.7
Fourth fifth	24.3
Richest fifth	50.9
Richest 5 percent	21.0

SOURCE: Same as Table 1.

The improvement in the relative position of the poorest fifth in 1968 is probably due to the reduction in unemployment during the Vietnam escalation (see the discussion of black incomes and unemployment, below). The apparent decline in the share of the top income groups results entirely from the exclusion of capital gains from Census Bureau income data. If capital gains are included, the share of the top fifth has been constant over the past 20 years.[5] We conclude that the entire distribution has not really changed since World War II.[6]

Taxes and Government Spending In theory, federal income taxes take a much higher percentage of income from the rich than from the poor. If this were true, the distribution of income after taxes would be much more equal than the distribution before the income tax. In reality, the

TABLE 3
Income Distribution Before and After the Federal Income Tax, 1962
(Percent)

	Poorest fifth	Second fifth	Middle fifth	Fourth fifth	Richest fifth	Richest 5 percent
Before tax	4.6	10.9	16.3	22.7	45.5	19.6
After tax	4.9	11.5	16.8	23.1	43.7	17.7

SOURCE: Edward C. Budd, *Inequality and Poverty*, 1967, p. xiii, xvi. These data consider family units and unrelated individuals together in the same income distribution.

effect of the income tax is rather modest, as is seen in Table 3.[7] In 1962, as in all years since World War II for which data are available, the share of the top 20 percent of the population is only about two percentage points lower after the income tax than before it. The federal income tax laws have nominal tax rates that increase sharply with income, but they are vitiated by various deductions which reduce taxable incomes of the rich below their actual incomes. Thus, the rich gain the political advantages of high nominal rates and the economic advantages of low effective rates.

But if the federal income tax takes only a relatively small step toward improving the income distribution, the overall tax structure takes a much smaller step. Less than 40 percent of all taxes are individual income taxes; an almost equal amount is collected in property and sales taxes. Most studies of property and sales taxes have concluded that they take a larger percentage of income from the poor than from the rich.[8] There is an involved, and still unsettled, academic debate over how completely corporations shift their income taxes onto consumers by raising prices. If the corporation income tax is shifted, it could be considered similar to a sales tax. We might tentatively conclude that taxes other than individual income taxes do not reduce, and probably increase, income inequality.

It is sometimes argued that the government improves the income distribution through its spending policies. We believe that military spending, accounting for nearly one-third of government spending (federal, state, and local), disproportionately benefits the wealthy. Many other programs appear to be of little benefit to the poor: foreign aid, space, police, interest on public debt (largely paying for past military spending), and highways which, combined with military spending, amounted to one-half of all government spending in 1966.[9] By comparison, spending of the traditional welfare-state variety, on schools, parks and recreation, health and hospitals, and welfare, amounted to just over one-fourth of government spending, and it is by no means obvious that these programs are primarily beneficial to the poor.

TABLE 4
Distribution of Tax Revenue by Type of Tax, Fiscal Year 1966–67
(Percent)

	All levels of government	Federal government	State and local governments
All taxes	100.0	100.0	100.0
Property and sales taxes	35.7	13.7	80.2
Individual income tax	38.2	53.4	9.6
Corporation income tax	20.6	29.5	3.7
Miscellaneous taxes	4.4	3.3	6.7

SOURCES: U.S. Bureau of the Census, *Census of Governments*, 1967, Vol. 4, No. 5; *Compendium of Government Finances*, Table 5. Motor vehicle license fees, 1.3 percent of all taxes, are combined with property and sales taxes. Social Security and similar programs are excluded, as explained in note 9.

Wealth   Income distribution approximates the distribution of economic welfare because consumption is usually limited by income.[10] By temporarily enabling some people to consume more than their income, personal wealth is a second source of economic well-being. More important, wealth is an important source of power in our society, especially political power. It is their superior wealth that enables managements to outlast strikes. The wealthy control virtually all mass media and thus have a disproportionate influence over public opinion. They finance political campaigns and lobby in the legislature.[11] Above all the wealthy own and control the giant corporations that make many important decisions about allocation of resources and distribution of income.[12] For instance, corporations influence state and local governments (as well as foreign governments) by their ability to locate their businesses only in places where a favorable political environment exists. We must consider, then, the distribution of various types of wealth, particularly corporate stock.

The best recent data on distribution of personal wealth are in a government-sponsored survey of over 2,500 households.[13] Ranking households by wealth, we find that the wealthiest 1 percent own 31 percent of total wealth and 61 percent of corporate stock.[14] Apologists for American

TABLE 5
Distribution of Various Types of Personal Wealth,
1962
(Percent)

	Wealthiest 20 percent	Top 5 percent	Top 1 percent
Total wealth	76	50	31
Corporate stock	96	83	61
Business and professions	89	62	39
Homes	52	19	6

SOURCE: Projector and Weiss, *Survey of Financial Characteristics of Consumers*, p. 110–114, 151; and Irwin Friend, Jean Crockett and Marshall Blume, *Mutual Funds and Other Institutional Investors: A New Perspective*, p. 113.

capitalism often refer to the statistic that over 30 million people own corporate stock, implying that this form of wealth is widely distributed. This is clearly nonsense: many people do own a little stock, but the vast bulk of corporate stock is owned by a very few people. Ownership of unincorporated businesses and professions is only slightly more equally distributed than is corporate stock. The types of wealth that are relatively more equally distributed are such things as automobiles and homes, which are not sources of power as is ownership of businesses and corporations.

Personal wealth, of course, does not tell the whole story. Wealth is also held by pension funds and charitable foundations. The foundations are largely formed by the wealthy, but many pension funds exist for workers. In 1969, total pension fund assets were $238 billion, less than 10 percent of national wealth.[15] In 1968, private non-insured pension funds held only 9.7 percent of the corporate stock held by domestic individuals, personal trusts, and private non-insured pension funds.[16] So, including individuals' shares of pension fund assets probably raised the share of the poorest 80 percent but does not alter the basic pattern of great inequality. The pension funds, moreover, are usually managed by either banks or the government, so their wealth is not a significant source of power to workers in the same sense that personal wealth is a source of power to capitalists.

A View from the Bottom   Extensive poverty accompanies the great concentrations of income and wealth. The most common figures on poverty, published by the Social Security Administration (SSA), define it as an income below $3,700 for a non-farm family of four (with different income cutoffs for different family sizes and residences). In 1969, 24.3 million people, or 12.2 percent of the population, were living in poverty by these criteria.[17] The SSA allows food expenditures of 80¢ per person per day, and assumes that food makes up one-third of the total budget.[18] We reject poverty lines in the neighborhood of $3,700, and thus most poverty figures published by government agencies, as implausibly low.

A more reasonable definition of poverty is the Bureau of Labor Statistics (BLS) subsistence budget for 1967.[19] It totals $5,900 for an urban family of four. The BLS calculates it on a much more detailed and reasonable basis than the SSA budget. They assume that, of the $5,900, taxes and social security take $700, leaving $5,200 after tax. Food, assumed to cost less than $1.20 per person per day (this requires very careful shopping and cooking and no meals away from home), takes $1,650 for the year. They assume rent, heat, and utilities for an inexpensive five-room, one bath apartment, to be under $90 per month, or $1,000 per year. House furnishings and household expenditures add another $300 per year. Clothing and personal care together total $700 for the family, or $175 per person. For transportation, assuming an eight-year-old used car except in cities with good public transportation, the family spends $450. Medical care and medical insurance cost $475. Less than $700 remains for other expenses.

Most people would agree that a family of four living on the BLS subsistence budget would feel quite poor and be consistently concerned with making ends meet. By 1969, inflation had raised the cost of the BLS budget to $6,500. In that year, 19 percent of all four-person families had incomes lower than $6,500.[20]

Apologists for capitalism remind us that even though vast numbers of Americans are poor, poverty is declining. Regardless of the guideline used, this is true.[21] While it is gratifying to learn that 1.1 million fewer people were "officially" impoverished in 1969 than in 1968[22] and that fewer people are dying of starvation, the point is that a wealthy society should do much better.

A Preliminary Analysis

Our society, then, is characterized by great inequality. We do not have a complete theory of why the United States' income and wealth distributions are so unequal; but we can document several "arbitrary" inequalities; that is, large differences in incomes received by groups with apparently equal abilities. These are class, race, sex, and the occupation of one's parents.

Class and Income Most people with very high incomes are capitalists who own substantial assets, especially corporate stock, and receive income primarily from those assets.[23]

The only source that describes capitalist income in any useful detail is the Internal Revenue Service.[24] In 1966 fewer than 2 percent of all taxpayers received 74 percent of all dividends and 76 percent of all capital gains.[25] In the following discussion we define the capitalist class as this group of large shareowners.

Tables 6 and 7 show the types of income of taxpayers at several income levels.[26] We define "small business income" as interest, rent, and income of farmers, unincorporated businesses, proprietors, and self-employed

TABLE 6
Types of Income, 1966

Taxable Income	Tax Returns	Types of Income (Billions of $)			
		All Types	Wage and Salary	Small Business	Capitalist
Total, all sizes	70,160,000	478.2	381.1	56.8	32.9
Under $20,000	68,230,000	401.1	349.1	35.1	12.3
$20,000–$50,000	1,644,000	48.0	24.7	14.8	7.0
$50,000–$100,000	218,000	15.4	5.3	5.0	4.4
Over $100,000	53,000	13.5	2.1	1.8	9.0

SOURCE: Same as Table 7.

professionals. "Capitalist income" is dividends and capital gains. Total small business income is almost twice as large as total capitalist income, but capitalist income is far more concentrated in the hands of the rich.

TABLE 7
Types of Income, 1966
(Same data as in Table 6 converted to percentage; Data are stated in percent)

Taxable Income	Types of Income			
	All Types	Wage and Salary	Small Business	Capitalist
Total all sizes	100.0	79.7	11.9	6.9
Under $20,000	100.0	87.0	8.7	3.1
$20,000–$50,000	100.0	51.4	30.8	14.5
$50,000–$100,000	100.0	34.3	32.3	28.4
Over $100,000	100.0	15.2	13.3	66.8

SOURCE: Internal Revenue Service, *Statistics of Income, 1966: Individual Income Tax Returns*, Tables 7, 11, 19. See note 26 for a full description of these data.

Taxpayers who reported under $20,000 in net taxable income (the vast majority) received 87 percent of their income from wages and salaries and only 3 percent from capitalist sources. At higher income levels, the share of wages and salaries falls steadily and that of capitalist income rises. The 53,000 taxpayers with net taxable incomes exceeding $100,000 received only 15 percent of their income from wages and salaries and 67 percent from dividends and capital gains.

Moreover, these IRS data are biased to minimize the relationship between class and income. About one-third of the capitalist income reported to the IRS was tax-exempt, and therefore excluded from net taxable income. So, many people who reported large capitalist incomes on their income tax returns were classified in Tables 6 and 7 as having small taxable income. A variety of tax loopholes also permits the wealthy to understate their taxable incomes: interest on municipal bonds is completely tax-exempt; exaggerated depreciation and depletion allowances are common; tax-exempt charitable donations can be padded and overstated.[27]

As a result of these and other loopholes, there were approximately 250 capitalists who reported zero taxable income, but over $100,000 each in capital gains or dividends. These individuals, all of whom are included in the lowest income class in Tables 6 and 7, received at least $70 million in reported capitalist income, completely tax-free. Doubtless there were others who achieved somewhat less spectacular success in reporting their incomes as tax-exempt; no comprehensive statistics are available on the extent of such behavior.[28]

So those who receive profits (capitalists) earn much higher incomes than those who receive wages and salaries (workers). Bourgeois economic theory justifies this inequality by referring to the role capitalists play in the economy: they provide capital, they innovate, they manage, they assume risks. It is argued either that capitalists will refuse to perform these roles if they are not adequately paid or that it is fair that capitalists receive such profits. Within the framework of a capitalist economy, profits certainly are necessary, but there is no reason to believe that *very high* profits are needed to induce capitalists to participate. Needless to say, no defender of high profits has ever urged that profits be reduced to test the hypothesis that high profits are esssential.

The notion that high profits are equitable is, of course, absolutely ridiculous. Suppose we believed (which we do not) that people should earn income in proportion to their natural ability. Even this belief would not justify inequality between classes. Workers and capitalists often have different abilities to be sure, but largely because they receive different upbringings and educations. A variety of skills are needed for modern production (though the services of some corporate board chairmen may be among the most superfluous). Some skills more than others require special education or working experience, but it is wrong to assume that capitalists, or highly paid employees, have any special natural ability. They have developed their useful skills from their preferential access to higher education and desirable jobs.

It is no accident that incomes from ownership of corporations are so unjustly high. Many of America's most important social and political institutions act systematically to serve capitalist interests. Laws against larceny, for example, are enforced much more vigorously than laws (when they exist) against monopolistic combinations. The corporations are allowed to pollute the air and water, to create demands for such dangerous products as cigarettes, and to offset wage increases or corporate income taxes with price increases. Military spending by the government is an important source of profits, owing to the ambiguous relationship between the Pentagon and its military contractors. American foreign policies, by trying to contain communism, protect profitable corporate foreign investments.[29] Both the mass media and the government oppose ideas and behavior that discourage individuals from doing the meaningless work offered by big business. In sum, the economic power of corporate enterprise is reinforced by the major institutions of our society.

Discrimination   A second pattern of inequality is discrimination against blacks and women. (This overlaps the class inequality discussed above because few blacks and women are in the capitalist class; but it also accounts for substantial inequality within the working class.) The labor market effectively preserves and aggravates inequality between groups of people. The inferior economic position of blacks, for instance, has survived more than a century after the abolition of slavery. Similarly, the low status of women in the traditional family structure is translated into low pay and menial jobs for those women who work.

Discrimination Against Blacks

In 1969 the median income for all black males was $3,900, compared to $6,800 for white males. For workers who held year-round, full-time jobs, the median incomes were as shown in Table 8.

TABLE 8
Median Incomes by Sex and Race, 1969 Workers with Year-Round, Full-Time Jobs

	Male	Female
Black	$5,900	$4,100
White	$9,500	$5,200

SOURCE: *Current Population Reports*, Series P-60, #70, p. 5.

Thus, even for workers with stable jobs, black male median income is only 67 percent of white male income and black female income only 80 percent of white female income.

While lack of schooling is one cause of the black-white income differential (a rather ambiguous cause, as we shall show below), discrimination persists when individuals with the same amount of schooling are compared as shown in Table 9. Finishing high school is worth $1,300 per year in higher income to a white male and only $900 per year to a black male. A college degree is worth $2,500 per year to a black man and $3,800 to a white man. Black college graduates seem to face the most discrimination, but this may result from a higher proportion of whites attending graduate schools.

During the 1960s the ratio of nonwhite to white median family income (which is about 3 percentage points higher than the ratio of black

TABLE 9
Median Income for All Males 25 Years Old and Over by Race and Education, 1969

Years of schooling	Black male	White male	Ratio
Elementary—less than eight	$3,000	$ 3,600	.82
Eight years	4,300	5,500	.79
High school one–three years	5,200	7,300	.71
High school four years	6,100	8,600	.71
College one–three years	7,100	9,600	.74
College four or more	8,600	12,400	.69

SOURCE: *Current Population Reports*, Series P-60, #75, Table 47, p. 104.

to white median family income) has narrowed considerably, as is evident from Table 10.

The ratio of nonwhite to white median family income has risen from .53 in 1963 to .63 in 1969. Recently, officials in the Nixon Administration have been using these data to suggest that the nation is in the process of eliminating economic discrimination and that the appropriate

TABLE 10
Ratio of Black to White Income and Unemployment Rate

Year	Median family income ratio	Unemployment rate (percent)
1969	.63	3.5
1968	.63	3.6
1967	.62	3.8
1966	.60	3.8
1965	.55	4.5
1964	.56	5.2
1963	.53	5.7
1962	.53	5.5
1961	.53	6.7
1960	.55	5.5
1959	.52	5.5
1958	.51	6.8
1957	.54	4.3
1956	.53	4.1
1955	.55	4.4
1954	.56	5.5
1953	.56	2.9
1952	.57	3.0
1951	.53	3.3
1950	.54	5.3
1949	.51	5.4
1948	.53	3.8

SOURCE: *Current Population Reports*, Series P-60.

policy is now "benign neglect." (Note, however, that the absolute gap between median nonwhite and white family incomes has widened since 1961 from $3,400 to $3,600, as measured in constant 1969 dollars.)

The proposition that structural changes in the economy tending to reduce discrimination have occurred during the sixties may well be true, but data on relative median incomes clearly overstate the improvement. Blacks are usually the last workers to be hired and the first to be fired; as a result they benefit disproportionately from prosperity and the resulting labor shortages. The high level of white employment during the Korean War increased the ratio of nonwhite to white median family income from .51 in 1949 to .57 in 1952, but all of this gain was lost during the 1958 recession. We cannot accurately determine how much of the recent improvement in the relative position of nonwhites has been the result of Vietnam War prosperity and how much has been the result of reduced racism. The distinction is important for two reasons: gains resulting from labor shortages only are likely to be reversed during recessions, and the inflationary effects of labor shortages limit their use as a policy instrument to reduce discrimination. To the extent that the trends toward improvement in the relative position of nonwhites result only from prosperity, it cannot be expected to continue past 1969.

Discrimination Against Women

Most working women are in the labor force not because they are bored with housework but because they must work to support themselves: 51.4 percent of all women in the 1967 labor force were either unmarried, separated from their husbands, or married to men earning less than $3,000 per year. The breakdown is shown in Table 11.

Nevertheless, the job market is segmented so that men and women compete only among themselves for different jobs, with women eligible only

TABLE 11
Marital Status of Women in the Labor Force, 1967

Status	Women in labor force	Percent
Total, all women in labor force	27.5 million	100.0
Single	5.9	21.5
Married, but husband absent	1.6	5.7
Widowed	2.5	9.0
Divorced	1.7	6.0
Married, but husband earns less than $3,000 per year	2.5	9.2
Total who must work	14.2	51.4

SOURCE: U.S. Department of Labor, *Handbook on Women Workers*, p. 23, 34.

TABLE 12
Median Income of Civilians with Year-Round, Full-Time Jobs, 1968

Years of schooling	Male income	Female income	Ratio
Elementary—less than eight	$ 5,300	$3,300	.62
Eight years	6,600	3,600	.55
High school one–three years	7,300	3,900	.53
High school four years	8,300	4,800	.58
College one–three	9,300	5,500	.59
College 4 years	11,800	6,700	.57
College five or more	12,800	8,300	.64
Total	8,100	4,700	.58

SOURCE: U.S. Department of Labor, *Handbook on Women Workers*, pp. 23, 34.

for the lowest paying jobs. For workers with year-round, full-time jobs, female median income is 58 percent of male median income.[30] This discrimination persists when we compare median incomes of men and women with the same education.[31]

Restricting our comparison to workers with full-time, year-round jobs clearly understates discrimination against women because the female unemployment rate is much higher than the male rate. In 1969, the adult female unemployment rate was 4.7 percent compared to an adult male rate of 2.8 percent.[32] Moreover, a higher proportion of women withdraw from the labor force when they cannot find jobs or are forced to accept part-time or seasonal work and, in both cases, are not counted as unemployed.[33]

Sex discrimination does not seem to be declining. The ratio of female to male median wage and salary income for full-time, year-round workers has declined from .63 in 1956 to .58 in 1968.[34] Among the major occupational groups, the relative position of women seems to be improving (slowly) only for professional and technical workers. In the past 10 years, the number of white female unrelated individuals and families headed by a woman below the poverty line has not changed, and the number of such nonwhite females and female-related families has actually increased. All of the decline in poverty referred to above has affected families headed by men or male unrelated individuals.[35]

Education and Social Mobility   The closer relation of education and income distribution is obvious from Tables 9 and 12. For men with full-time, year-round jobs, median incomes in 1968 were $11,800 with a college diploma, $8,300 with a high school diploma, and $6,600 for eight years of schooling. A similar relation is seen for both women and blacks.

The notion of social mobility through education is one of the most widespread beliefs about American society. Is your job terrible and poorly paid? Work hard, save money to put your kids through college, and they will escape into better jobs and comfortable lives. As much as any other idea, this has served to rationalize an alienated, impoverished existence for millions of Americans.

The belief that there is actual mobility through education, however, is a myth. It is true that better-educated people earn higher incomes. But it is also true that children of wealthier families become far better educated. So the effect of education is to preserve and to legitimize existing inequalities in income distribution.

Table 13 shows that high school seniors are much more likely to enter college if they come from wealthy families. A high school senior from the top income group (family income over $15,000) is over four times as likely to enter college as a senior from the bottom income group (family income under $3,000).

TABLE 13
College Attendance of High School Graduates by Income, 1966

Family income in 1965	Percentage of 1966 high school graduates who started college by February, 1967
Under $3,000	19.8
$3,000–$4,000	32.3
$4,000–$6,000	36.9
$6,000–$7,000	41.1
$7,500–$10,000	51.0
$10,000–$15,000	61.3
Over $15,000	86.7
Total, all incomes	46.9

SOURCE: *Current Population Reports*, Series P-20, #185, Table 8.

TABLE 14
Distribution of Benefits from Public Higher Education in California, 1964

	All Families	Families without children in California higher education	Families with children in		
			Junior college	State college	University of California
Median family income	$8,000	$7,900	$8,800	$10,000	$12,000
Average subsidy received	—	0	$1,700	$ 3,800	$ 4,900
Subsidy as percent of median family income	—	0	12	31	41

SOURCE: Hansen and Weisbrod, *Journal of Human Resources*, vol. IV, no. 2, Tables 5 and 6.

It is not hard to understand why wealthier students stay in school longer. Even in states where public higher education is free, students still have significant living expenses which must be paid by their families. There are not nearly enough scholarships and loans to go around.

Family income affects education at all stages. Poor children are more likely to drop out of high school before the twelfth grade or to drop out of college before graduation. Rich children attend the better and more prestigious private universities. They also receive a disproportionate share of the benefits of public higher education, as is shown by a recent study of California higher education, one of the most extensive and progressive systems in the country.

Median income for the state was $8,000, but it was $12,000 for families with children in the University of California, the top track of the educational system. The state subsidy, that is, full cost of education less fees paid by the student, was considerably greater to families with children in the higher tracks, which were also the families with higher incomes. Moreover, public higher education is financed by state and local taxes, which take a higher percentage of income from the poor than from the rich.

Public higher education is only one force tending to preserve inequality from one generation to the next. A direct (although rough) measure of intergenerational preservation of status can be seen in the data in Table 15 taken from a Census Bureau study of occupations of men working in 1962.

Seventy-one percent of the sons of white-collar workers were themselves white-collar workers, while only 37 percent of the sons of blue-collar workers and 23 percent of the sons of farm workers (farm owners and employees combined) had white-collar jobs. In other words, the chances of ending up in a white-collar job were almost twice as high for a white-collar worker's son as for a blue-collar worker's son, and three times as high for a white-collar worker's son as far a farmer's son. Of course there has been some movement from lower status jobs into white-collar jobs; there had to

TABLE 15
Occupations of Men Working in 1962 (25–64 Years Old) and of Their Fathers (Percent)

Father's occupation when son was 16 years old	Total	Son's occupation in March 1962		
		White collar	Blue collar	Farm
White collar	100.0	71.0	27.6	1.5
Blue collar	100.0	36.9	61.5	1.6
Farm	100.0	23.2	55.2	21.6
Total	100.0	40.9	51.4	7.7

SOURCE: Calculated from Blau and Duncan, *American Occupational Structure*, Table J2.1, p. 496. The data were obtained from a Census Bureau survey of 20,000 men.

be, since the proportion of the labor force in white-collar jobs has been expanding rapidly.

To some extent Table 15 reflects racial discrimination, since most nonwhites are in the blue-collar or farm categories. However, most of the men in each of the three major occupational categories are white; Table 15 suggests the existence of a hierarchy of status, preserved across generations, even within the white male working class.

Conclusion

We find, then, that American capitalism is characterized by considerable unjustifiable inequality of income and wealth, a state of affairs that is not improving over time. Causes of this inequality include social class distinctions between workers and capitalists and economic discrimination against women and minority groups. Legend has it that the United States is the land of equal opportunity; nevertheless, there is very little actual social mobility. Wealth, both personal and corporate, is perhaps the most important source of political power; and, in a vicious cycle, political power is used to preserve existing accumulations of wealth.

Notes

1. The wage-price guidepost policy in the early 1960s, for example, urged that all wages and profits increase at the rate of 3.2 percent per year, thereby freezing the existing distribution of income, presumably forever.

2. In 1968 North America, with less than 9 percent of the world's population, had the following percentage of total world consumption of energy:

natural and imported gases	67.5 percent
liquid fuel	38.6 percent
total energy	37.5 percent

In the same year the United States, with approximately 6 percent of the world's population, had the following percentages of the total world consumption of:

steel	26 percent
rubber	42 percent
tin	35 percent
fertilizer (nitrogenous, potash, and phosphate)	26 percent

SOURCE: United Nations, *Statistical Yearbook*, 1969.

3. The Census Bureau data are based on an annual sample of 50,000 households, so they are probably a good approximation of the actual figures. Table 1 uses 1947 and 1950, thus breaking the pattern of "leap years only," because 1948 and 1952 are unavailable in the source.

4. We should really consider the income distribution only of families with the same size, since larger families tend to have higher incomes as well as greater need. But the differences in incomes between families of different sizes are not nearly as great as the differences between even two-person families and unrelated individuals.

For the family distribution in 1968, a family was in the top 5 percent if it had income exceeding approximately $23,000; in the top 20 percent with income over about $13,000; and in the bottom 20 percent with income under about $4,600.

Also, incomes in any particular year are more unequally distributed than normal incomes (income averaged over several years) because different people have the high and low incomes in different years, so we are overstating inequality in normal incomes.

5. See Edward C. Budd, "Postwar Changes in the Size Distribution of Income in the U.S.," *American Economic Review*, May 1970; and John Gorman,"The Relationship Between Personal Income and Taxable Income," *Survey of Current Business*, May 1970, on the definitions of income used by various government agencies. Capital gains are commonly excluded from all figures except Internal Revenue Service data; however, there is no theoretical basis for this exclusion.

Because fully one-half of capital gains and only a portion of dividends are tax-exempt, individual stockholders generally prefer capital gains to dividends; corporations now systematically retain earnings rather than pay them out in dividends, so capital gains are a customary, almost predictable source of income for many rich people. A complete picture of money income distribution should include capital gains.

The following table is a rough adjustment of the share of the top 20 percent to include estimated capital gains.

Year	Share of top fifth without capital gains (from Table 1)	Total reported capital gains as a percent of total personal income	Share of top fifth with capital gains
1947	43.0 percent	2.2 percent	44.2 percent
1950	42.6	2.6	44.1
1956	41.2	2.8	42.8
1960	42.0	2.6	43.5
1964	41.3	3.2	43.1
1968	40.6	5.2	43.5

Reported capital gains are two times taxable capital gains, since Federal Income Tax laws consider only half of long-term capital gains as taxable income. Data on taxable capital gains are in Gorman. We are assuming that all capital gains are long-term and go to the richest 20 percent, which is approximately true.

These data, also neglect certain types of non-monetary income such as food grown at home and imputed rent on homes occupied by the owner, which are distributed more equally than money income.

6. Many discussions of income distribution begin with 1929 and show a large decrease in the share of the top income groups since that date. However, data for 1910–37 (see Gabriel Kolko, *Wealth and Power in America*, p. 14) suggest that 1929 was a peak in the share of top income groups, not equaled before or since, so starting with 1929 may be inappropriate.

7. Table 3 is based on Department of Commerce, Office of Business Economics data and is not comparable with Table 1. For income distribution before and after federal income taxes in other years, see Kolko and the source to Table 3. Unfortunately, these data are unavailable after 1962.

8. See Bishop, *Tax Burdens and Benefits of Government Expenditures by Income Class, 1961 and 1965* (Tax Foundation). Some studies, especially those using normal or "permanent" income concepts, conclude that property taxes may be proportional, not regressive. See Dick Netzer, *The Economics of the Property Tax*, chap. 3.

9. Source: *Statistical Abstract of the United States: 1967*, Table 585. Total government expenditure was 189.4 billion dollars. Expenditures of state-owned utilities and liquor stores, a total of 7.3 billion dollars, are excluded from the total.

Social Security and other self-financing social insurance programs, a total of 28.1 billion dollars in 1966, are excluded from data on both taxes and government spending in this essay. Since the people who benefit from self-financing programs are the people who pay for them, no significant redistribution occurs.

10. Economic welfare is, of course, a much broader concept than income. We must include public goods that are provided free to everybody as well as effects of one individual's income on the welfare of others.

11. On September 20, 1970, the *New York Times* reported that "Officials of 49 companies that ranked among the top 25 defense, space, and nuclear contractors in the fiscal year 1968 donated at least $1,235,402 to political campaigns during the 1968 Presidential election year . . . ." Republicans received over 80 percent of the money. This figure, moreover, excludes contributions to state elections, to primary campaigns, and to campaign committees that only operated within one state. One week later, the *Times* reported that the entire labor movement's campaign fund for 1968 totaled $1,730,000.

12. There is an involved academic debate over the extent of conflicts of interest between owners and managers of corporations. See Berle and Means, *The Modern Corporation and Private Property*; and Galbraith, *New Industrial State*. Some conflicts do exist; but both owners and the

.   managers want to maximize the value of the corporation's common stock and its profits, so their interests converge on most questions of income distribution. This view is elaborated in Baran and Sweezy, *Monopoly Capital*.

13. Dorothy S. Projector and Gertrude Weiss, *Survey of Financial Characteristics of Consumers*, Federal Reserve System, 1966. They consider six types of wealth, as of December 31, 1962: homes (less mortgage debt); automobiles (net of debt); liquid assets (such as bank accounts and government bonds); and real estate (net of debt); value of businesses and professions; and miscellaneous assets (almost entirely personal trusts). In surveys like this one, people tend to understate their wealth, but it is hard to say whether the understatement is relatively greater for rich or poor.

14. These data are linear interpolations of the data in the study and may be inaccurate by as much as one percentage point. For corporate stocks, we have added together stock owned by individuals and stock owned in personal trusts, since the latter accounted for 13.5 percent of common stock owned by households and trusts together in 1964, the earliest year for which we have data. We assume that mutual funds are distributed in the same manner as stock between households and trusts.

15. Securities and Exchange Commission, *Statistical Bulletin*, May 1970.

16. Friend, Crockett, and Blume, p. 113. Again we assume that mutual funds are distributed among the three groups in the same way as are common stocks.

17. See *Current Population Reports*, Series, P-60, No. 76.

18. These are the Social Security Administration standards that were developed by Mollie Orshansky. See her articles in *Social Security Bulletin*, January, July 1965, December 1966, and March 1968. On the problem of defining poverty, see Oscar Ornati, "The Poverty Band and the Count of the Poor," in Budd, *Inequality and Poverty*.

19. This is the lowest of the three budgets presented in Jean C. Brackett, "New BLS Budgets . . . ," *Monthly Labor Review*, April 1969. The more commonly quoted "modest, but adequate" budget is the middle of the three budgets, amounting to $9,800 for an urban family of four in 1967. For a discussion of the "modest, but adequate" budget and related problems of defining poverty, see Donald Light, "Income Distribution: The First Stage in the Consideration of Poverty," appearing in this collection of papers.

20. *Current Population Reports*, Series P-60, no. 75.

21. A caveat is appropriate here. As we suggested earlier, absolute growth in income does not mean proportional absolute growth in economic welfare. First, since World War II more people, especially blacks, have left the farm and are living in urban areas which have a higher cost of living. Second, the real costs of living in the U.S. have increased aside

from changes in the price level. More Americans need a car to get to work; more city-dwellers need air-conditioning to breathe clean air and to avoid the "oven" effects of temperature inversions; many women workers in cities are expected to spend their money keeping up with the latest fashions. People must travel farther to find a pleasant spot for swimming and relaxation. Many economic goods today satisfy needs that used to be satisfied by non-economic means.

22. See note 17.

23. In this paper "class" is defined as a group of people who play the same functional role in the economy. It is frequently used to mean much more: people in similar economic positions often (though surely not inevitably) become a socially cohesive unit with similar political ideology, and sometimes the definition of social class includes social or political unity as well as common economic roles. We believe that American capitalists form a distinct social class in both senses. See G. William Domhoff, Who Rules America?

24. See IRS, Statistics of Income, 1966: Individual Income Tax Returns (hereafter abbreviated Tax Returns).

25. The source here is Tax Returns, Tables 12 and 20. One percent of all taxpayers received 74 percent of total dividends and 1 percent 76 percent of all capital gains. We do not know how big the overlap is between these two groups, although it is probably substantial. If exactly the same taxpayers constituted the top 1 percent dividend and capital gains recipients, then 1 percent of the taxpayers received 75 percent of capitalist income; if the overlap was zero, then 2 percent of the taxpayers received 75 percent of capitalist income. This is what we mean by "less than 2 percent."

Note that these estimates of the distribution of income from corporate stock are in the same ball park as the estimates of distribution of stockholders in Table 5.

26. In Tables 6 and 7, our "size of taxable income" is what the IRS terms "adjusted gross income." This is really taxable income and excludes much tax-exempt capitalist income. Only one-half of all long-term capital gains are taxable income and a portion of dividends is also tax-exempt under the provisions of income tax legislation. Tax-exempt capital gains and dividends totaled $9.8 billion, almost one-third of total capitalist income reported in Table 6. Our category "Total Income" is "adjusted gross income" plus all tax-exempt capital gains and dividends. Capitalist income in the tables is all reported dividends plus all capital gains less capital losses.

These and other concepts are discussed in Tax Returns, pp. 163–173. There are other tax-exempt incomes which do not appear in our "Total Income" category, but these are much smaller and tend to be more equally distributed throughout the population than capitalist income. Adjusted gross income does include ordinary personal exemptions and most standard and itemized deductions.

Some minor sources of reported taxable income (the largest is pensions and annuities totaling $4 billion) are not shown in Tables 6 and 7, so wage and salary, small business, and capitalist income add up to slightly less than total income. The rows in Table 6 and 7 do not exactly add up to "Total, all sizes" owing to statistical sampling techniques used to estimate data for lower income groups. See *Tax Returns*, p. 175–180.

27. See Phillip M. Stern, *The Great Treasury Raid*.

28. The source is the same as note 26. Some 246 people reported zero net taxable income and over $100,000 in taxable capital gains; their total taxable capital gains were $58.4 million. Forty-six people reported zero net taxable income and over $100,000 in taxable dividends; their total taxable dividends were $11.8 million. There is no way to determine the overlap between these two groups, but it is probably substantial.

29. A vast literature exists on all of these relations between the political and cultural superstructure and economic infrastructure. The benefits from government foreign and military policies accrue largely to a corporate elite. Twenty of the 25 largest industrial corporations are among the Pentagon's top 80 defense contractors (See Kaufman, "We Must Guard Against Unwarranted Influence by the Military-Industrial Complex," *New York Times* magazine June 22, 1969). Six of the 9 industrial corporations with the highest net incomes earned more than 25 percent of their incomes from foreign operations in 1966: Standard Oil of New Jersey (54 percent), Mobil Oil (52 percent), Standard Oil of California (51 percent), Texaco (35 percent), IBM (33 percent), and Gulf Oil (29 percent). (We calculated these percentages from Securities and Exchange Commission Series 10-K Reports. We compare foreign profits after foreign taxes and before domestic taxes with domestic profits after taxes, because the effective domestic tax rate on foreign profits is very low.)

30. Measuring economic discrimination against women is difficult because some women prefer to work part-time or not at all. Simply comparing median incomes of men and women, therefore, is not very meaningful. Restricting the comparison to workers with year-round, full-time jobs corrects this bias, but it overlooks women who wanted but could not find full-time work.

31. These ratios are incomplete measures of discrimination because they do not allow for the possibility that men work more overtime or have more experience on their job, but adjusting for these possibilities would not alter the basic pattern of considerable discrimination.

32. See the 1970 *Economic Report of the President*.

33. See Department of Labor, *Handbook on Women Workers*.

34. See Department of Labor, *Handbook on Women Workers*.

35. See *Current Population Reports*, Series P-60, no. 68.

18.
LOOKING AT POVERTY FROM A RADICAL PERSPECTIVE

Howard M. Wachtel

If the Word was the Beginning,
Then a new beginning must need another Word.
(Carl Oglesby, from "Lemon Light")

Poverty is a condition of society, not a consequence of individual characteristics. If poverty is a condition of society, then we must look to societal institutions to discover the cause of poverty rather than to the particular individual characteristics of the poor. The societal institutions which have been of particular importance of Western industrialized countries are the institutions of capitalism—markets in labor and capital, social stratification and class, and the state.

The interaction of these institutions of capitalism manifest themselves in a set of attributes and problems that we normally associate with the condition of poverty in society. These *attributes* of poverty, however, are incorrectly viewed as the causes of poverty. For example, income distribution, the living conditions of the poor, education, health, and the personal characteristics of the poor are merely surface manifestations (the superstructure) of a systemically caused problem. It is important to differentiate between these manifestations of poverty—normally called "the poverty problem"—and their underlying causes. We return to this theme later, but first let us contrast this formulation with the orthodox view of poverty and its causes.

Since the Industrial Revolution commenced in Great Britain and spread to other Western nations, the poor have been blamed for their own poverty. The causes of poverty have been assigned to the characteristics of the individual rather than to societal institutions. In nineteenth century America this was given a crude formulation within the industrializing ideology of individualism. The New Deal provided a temporary break from

From Howard M. Wachtel, "Looking at Poverty from a Radical Perspective," *Review of Radical Political Economics*, vol. 3, no. 3 (Summer 1971), pp. 1–19. © July 1971 by the Union for Radical Political Economics. Reprinted by permission of the publisher.

this tradition. However, this ideology has reappeared in the more sophisticated mid-twentieth century liberalism in which we now reside. Public policy has mirrored these trends in social ideology, starting with the Elizabethan Poor Laws and their American counterparts down to the Great Society's poor laws.

Social science research has mirrored our social ideology. Virtually all of the past and contemporary social science research has concentrated on the characteristics of individuals who are defined as poor by the federal government. Being poor is associated with a set of individual characteristics: age, sex, race, education, marital status, and so on. But these are not causes of poverty. There have been dozens of studies of the so-called "causes of poverty"; not surprisingly, these studies merely associate the "cause" of poverty with a particular set of individual characteristics. For example, if you are poor and have low levels of education, it does not necessarily follow that low levels of education are a cause of poverty since education itself is endogenous to the system. The causes of inequality in education and their impact on incomes must be analyzed by examining social class, the role of the state, and the way in which educational markets function.[1]

There has been essentially no social science research in the last 10 years on the question of poverty which has gone beyond a mere cataloguing of the characteristics of the poor.[2] A proper formulation of the problem would start with poverty as a result of the normal functioning of societal institutions in a capitalist economy. Given the existence of poverty as a result of the functioning of societal institutions, the next question is: who is poor? Is poverty randomly distributed across the population with respect to various individual characteristics or is it nonrandomly distributed? Poverty research has demonstrated that the incidence of poverty is nonrandomly distributed in America. Blacks, Mexican-Americans, Indians, women, the old, and so on, have a higher probability of becoming poor than do individuals without these characteristics. The so-called studies of the "causes" of poverty have simply estimated the differential importance of the individual characteristics associated with the poor. The research has only demonstrated which groups of people are affected most adversely by capitalist institutions.

The orientation of this poverty research has not been accidental, and it reveals some interesting insights into the sociology of knowledge. Since the Industrial Revolution, the poor have been blamed for their own condition. They have been charged with causing squalor. Hence, the research of the 1960s has been rendered compatible with the prevailing ideology of capitalist countries with only a few minor modifications of the crude formulations of earlier centuries to make the ideology more palatable to a supposedly more enlightened populace. In this context, the research has performed an important stabilizing and obfuscating function; it has received wide acceptance precisely because it has been conveniently supportive of existing social arrangements and our prevailing social ideology.

Theories of Poverty

Examined from a perspective of radical political economics, poverty is the result of the normal functioning of the principal institutions of capitalism—specifically, labor markets, social class divisions, and the state.

An individual's class status—his or her relationship to the means of production—provides the point of departure for an analysis of income inequalities and low incomes in an absolute sense. If an individual possesses both labor and capital, his chances of being poor or in a low income percentile are substantially less than if only labor is possessed. For individuals earning incomes under $10,000, nearly all income comes from labor. However, for individuals earning between $20,000 and $50,000 (in 1966), only slightly more than half comes from labor; while for individuals with incomes between $50,000 and $100,000 only a third comes from labor. And if you are rich—earning in excess of $100,000—only 15 percent comes from wage and salary earnings while two thirds comes from capital returns (the balance is composed of "small business" income).[3]

More important than the magnitude of capital income is its unequal distribution in our economy. Were we to redistribute this income, we could alleviate the purely financial aspects of low incomes. A direct transfer of income that would bring every family up to the Bureau of Labor Statistics' "Moderate but Adequate" living standard in 1966 (roughly $9,100) would have required $119 billion.[4] This comes to about 20 percent of total personal income, slightly *less* than the proportion of personal income derived from ownership of capital.

Consequently, any meaningful discussion of the causes of income inequalities or low incomes must start with a discussion of Marx's class categories. The plain fact is that the probabilities of being both a capitalist and poor are slim compared with the opportunities for poverty if labor forms the principal means of acquiring income. And under capitalism, there is no mechanism for sharing the returns from capital—it all goes to the private owners of capital.

The individual's relationship to the means of production is only the starting point in the analysis. The labor market is the next institution of capitalism which must be analyzed to understand the causes of poverty. Given the fact that workers have no capital income, the chances of becoming poor are increased. However, not all workers are poor in any sense of that ambiguous term. This leads us to our next concept in the analysis— *social stratification*. Social stratification refers to the divisions within a social class as distinct from the class itself. In this context, the divisions among workers in the labor market lead to social stratification among the class of workers which has had important implications for the cyclical and secular movements in class consciousness.

The functioning of labor markets, interacting with individual characteristics of workers, determines the wage status of any particular individual in stratified labor markets. The labor market causes poverty in several important ways. Contrary to conventional wisdom, nearly every poor person is or has been connected with the labor market in some way. Poor individuals sift into several categories. First, there are enormous members of *working poor*—individuals who work full time and full year, yet earn less than even the government's parsimonious poverty income. These people earn their poverty. Of all poor families attached to the labor force in 1968, about one-third (1.4 million) were fully-employed workers. Of the more than 11 million families with incomes under $5,000 in 1968, nearly 30 *percent* were headed by a full-time wage earner. The incidence of the working poor is greater among black poor families and families with female heads. About 22 *percent* of all black poor families were headed by an individual working full time in 1968. And a *third* of all black families with incomes under $5,000 worked full time. The Department of Labor reports that 10 million workers in 1968 (nearly 20 percent of the private nonsupervisory employees) were earning less than $1.60 per hour—the wage rate that yields a poverty income if fully employed.[5]

A second significant proportion of the poor are attached to the labor force but are not employed full time. Some of these individuals suffer intermittent periods of employment and unemployment, while others work for substantial periods of time and then suffer severe periods of long-term unemployment.

A third significant portion of the poor are handicapped in the labor market as a result of an occupational disability or poor health. However, these occupational disabilities are themselves related to a person's earlier status in the labor force. There are greater occupational hazards and opportunities for poor health in low wage jobs. Low incomes can contribute significantly to poor health, especially in the American markets for health care where enormous incomes or proper health insurance are an absolutely essential pre-condition for the receipt of medical care. Disabilities are widespread throughout the economy. In 1966, nearly *one-sixth* of the labor force was disabled for a period longer than *six months*. Only 48 percent of the disabled worked at all in 1966, while 12 percent of the employed disabled workers were employed only part time. As a consequence of disability, many households with disabled heads are poor—about 50 percent.[6]

Thus we see that nearly all of these poverty phenomena are endogenous to the system—they are a consequence of the functioning of labor markets in the economy. This argument can be extended to birth defects as well. There is a growing body of evidence which suggests that many forms of birth defects are related to the nutrition of the mother which, in turn, is related to family income (itself dependent upon the class status of the family and the labor market status of the family wage earners). Even with the evidence as tentative as it is, we can say that the probability of birth defects is greater in families with low incomes and the resultant poor nutritional opportunities.[7]

Another category of the poor are not presently attached to the labor market—the aged, the prison population, members of the military, the fully handicapped, and those on other forms of public assistance (principally women with dependent children). Though these individuals are not presently attached to the labor force, in many instances their low income is determined by past participation in the labor force.

For example, the ability of aged persons to cope with their non-employed status depends upon their wealth, private pension income, savings and public pension income (social security). Each of these, in turn, is related to the individual's status in the labor force during his working years. The one partial exception is social security which is typically cited as an income equalizing program where payments are only partially related to contributions. But even in this case, the redistributive effects of social security are not as great as they have been advertised, as we shall see later in this paper. This point aside, the payments for social security are so small that retired people, dependent solely on this source of income, end up in the government's poverty statistics.

The important elements of income for retirees are all associated with past labor force status and with the class status of the individual. High paid professional and blue-collar jobs typically provide private pension supplements to social security, while low paid jobs do not. Individuals with income from capital can continue to earn income from capital beyond the years they are attached to the labor force, while wage earners cannot. High income workers and owners of capital have vehicles for ensuring their security in old age, while medium and low wage earners have only social and financial insecurity to contemplate in their old age.

To a somewhat lesser extent other poor nonparticipants in the labor force attain their poverty as a result of their (or their spouse's) past association with the labor force. Even for the handicapped, the prisoner, or the welfare mother, the labor market is not a trivial determinant of their poverty status.

If labor force status provides such an important and inclusive explanation of poverty among individuals, the next question is: what determines an individual's status in the labor force? For simplicity, we will take occupation as an imperfect proxy for labor force status, bearing in mind that there is substantial variation in wage status within occupational categories as well as among occupational categories.

In broad terms, an individual's wage is dependent upon four types of variables:

1. Individual characteristics over which the individual exercises no control—age, race, sex, family class status, and region of socialization.
2. Individual characteristics over which the individual exercises a degree of control—education, skill level, health, region of employment, and personal motivation.

3. Characteristics of the industry in which the individual is employed—profit rates, technology, product market concentration,
relation of the industry to the government, and unionization.
4. Characteristics of the local labor market—structure of the labor
demand, unemployment rate, and rate of growth.[8]

One observation is immediately apparent: there are very few variables that lie within the individual's control that affect his labor market
status. Even the individual characteristics placed in category two are not
completely within the control of the individual. For example, as Coleman,
Bowles, and others have shown, education is heavily dependent upon the
socioeconomic status of the family, an attribute which lies outside of individual control.[9] Health is partially endogenous to the system as discussed
above. Geographic mobility depends upon income and wealth.

This classification scheme is a useful starting point, but a more
formal analysis is needed to understand the way in which these several
categories of variables interact in the labor market to yield low incomes.

The occupation an individual enters is *associated with* individual
characteristics: educational quantity and quality, training, skills, and health.
These attributes are normally defined as the *human capital* embodied in an
individual. The differences in these variables among individuals, which influence their entry into occupations, are dependent upon race, sex, age, and
class status of the family. Although human capital is *defined* by the set of
characteristics associated with the individual, the *determinants* of the differing levels of human capital among individuals are found in the set of individual characteristics that lie outside of the individual's control.[10]

The story does not end here; the wage is not solely dependent upon
the occupation of an individual. The fact that one person is a janitor, another a skilled blue-collar worker, tells us something about the wage that
each will receive but not everything. There is a substantial variation in wage
within each of those occupations that is dependent upon the industry and
the local labor market in which an individual works. There are a variety of
industrial and local labor market characteristics which yield different wages
for essentially the same occupation and level of human capital. The wage
will be higher for a given occupation in an industry with high profit rates,
a strong union, highly productive technologies, a high degree of product
market concentration, and a favorable status with the government.[11] A
similar type of analysis holds for the impact of local market conditions.

In sum, the individual has very little control over his or her labor
force status. If you are black, female, have parents with low socioeconomic
status, and dependent upon labor income, there is a high probability that
you will have relatively low levels of human capital which will slot you
into low-paying jobs, in low-wage industries, in low-wage labor markets.
With this initial placement, the individual is placed in a high-risk category,
destined to end up poor sometime during her working and nonworking
years. She may earn her poverty by working full time. Or she may suffer

either sporadic or long periods of unemployment. Or she may become disabled, thereby reducing her earning power even further. Or when she retires, social security payments will place her in poverty even if she escaped this fate throughout her working years. With little savings, wealth, or a private pension income, the retiree will be poor.

In contrast with this radical political-economic theory of the causes of poverty, both conservative and liberal political-economic theories look for the cause of poverty in terms of some individual characteristic over which the individual is presumed to exercise control. The conservative theory of poverty relies upon markets in labor and capital to provide sufficient mobility either within a generation or between generations to alleviate poverty. If one does not avail himself of the opportunities for social and economic mobility through the market, the individual is to blame. The poor cause their own poverty and its continuation. The individual is presumed to be master of his own destiny, and individualism will lead any deserving person out of poverty. (Of course, the people who posit these notions are the nonpoor.) For the undeserving poor, only institutionaliza- tion of one form or another will do.[12] These people are trapped by their lower-class life styles which prevent them from escaping poverty. If the poor would only work, there would be no poverty. The Elizabethan Poor Laws and their American counterpart considered unemployment a crime for which the penalty was work. Gilbert and Sullivan were appropriate when they said "let the punishment fit the crime."

The liberal (and dominant) theory of poverty grants some recogni- tion to institutions as partial causes of poverty as well as social class as an intergenerational transmitter of poverty. But rather than seeking remedies by altering these social institutions or searching for ways to break class rigidities, liberals concentrate their energies on trying to find ways to use government either to ease the burden of poverty or assist the individual in adapting to prevailing institutions. The liberals reject exclusive reliance upon the market to foster social mobility and attempt to use government to equalize opportunities within the market or assist individuals in coping with their poverty status by direct income transfers. Nonetheless, their commitment to "alleviating" poverty without systematic changes is as deep as any conservative's. Manifestations of this orientation abound. The entire social work profession, borne out of liberal social reform, exists principally to help people cope with a rotten personal or family situation. Hungry people are given nutritional advice rather than access to food, which would involve structural changes in agricultural markets.

The objective of liberal social policy is equal opportunity—a random distribution of poverty—though we are far from that goal today. The radical challenge goes as follows: if you start from a position of inequality and treat everyone equally, you end up with continued inequality. Thus the need to create equality in fact rather than in opportunities.

Manpower programs, educational assistance, and the like are the principal policy results of the contemporary liberal human capital approach to social mobility. All of these programs are based on an essentially *untested* view of the labor market: namely, that personal characteristics over which the individual has control are the major causes of unequal and low incomes. These programs are quite similar in their ideological premise to virtually all the poor laws of capitalist society, starting with the Elizabethan Poor Laws. Poverty is associated with the absence of work for which work is the cure. The poor are incapable of managing their own affairs so they must be "social worked" to adapt to the rigor and needs of an industrialized and urbanized society.

This view of poverty is wrong in theory, in fact, and in social values. The causes of poverty lie outside the individual's control in markets for labor and capital and class backgrounds. Equally important, something happens both to the people seeking to help the poor and to the poor themselves when we take as our starting point the premise that people are poor because of some manipulatable attribute associated with the person.

Corresponding to the several political-economic theories of poverty are *theories of the state*, that is, theories which discuss the origins and the role of government in eliminating poverty.

The *conservative* theory of the state views the origins of government as emerging from the consent of the governed. The proper economic role of the state is to leave things alone—*laissez faire*. The state exists solely to protect the basic institutions of capitalism—private property, markets in labor and capital, and markets in goods and services. It does this by providing both a domestic and a foreign military and by providing a system of courts to protect property and adjudicate disputes arising out of private property conflicts. The deserving poor will attain social mobility in this generation or the next via the normal functioning of markets. Any efforts by the state to interfere in this process will only distort these opportunities for mobility. Hence, the role of the state is simple: do nothing about the poor but protect their means to social mobility—free markets and capitalism.[13]

Liberals view the state as a mediator between conflicting interest groups in a pluralistic society. Since market institutions work imperfectly at best, the role of the state vis-à-vis the poor is to compensate for these shortcomings of the market by providing the opportunities denied to individuals by markets. "Where *opportunities* are free, the poor will disappear," might be a good liberal slogan. While the conservative would retort: "where markets are free, the poor will disappear." Liberals also recognize the existence of a residual population for whom no amount of indirect compensation will prevent their poverty. For these people, public welfare—direct payments—is the only solution.[14]

Radicals view the origin of the state in terms of a class of people who exercise dominant decision-making power in state institutions and who transmit their class power intergenerationally.[15] One's relationship to the means of production is an essential, but not exclusive, determinant of power, and the education system is an intergenerational transmitter and legitimator of this power. This is not the place to probe deeply into this complicated subject, but ask yourself this question: who is powerful in your local community? Are these people workers or owners (and managers) of capital?

Given this view of power in the state, as distinct from the liberal pluralist view or the conservative consent-of-the-governed view, the role of the state is to ensure the continued survival and perpetuation of its class of decision makers. If this analysis is valid, then the state becomes part of the problem rather than part of the solution. This does not mean that the same individuals or their inheritors have power in perpetuity, though this occurs—merely ponder the name Lodge, Harriman, or Rockefeller for awhile. This is why the term class is used, analytically distinct from a ruling elite or conspiracy theory of the state. In fact, liberals rather than radicals are the major proponents of conspiracy theories—witness the interest among liberals in a "military-industrial complex" conspiracy rather than a class analysis of the power of the military and its camp followers.

Several hypotheses flow from the radical theory of the state. First, government as a totality will reinforce the disequalizing tendencies of the market through its support of basic capitalist institutions even though liberals for the past 40 years have been attempting to do precisely the opposite. Second, programs to assist the poor will perhaps have some impact in the short run, but in the long run will either atrophy, become anemic in their impact, or become distorted in their purpose. Third, only those public programs that are compatible with the basic institutions of monopoly capitalism will see the light of day in the first instance and will survive to suffer the fate outlined above in the second hypothesis.

In contrast, liberals assume that the state intervenes on behalf of the underclass to redistribute wealth, opportunity, and privilege. In fact, the term used to characterize collective decision making in economics is the *social welfare function*. By pointing to some doubtful consequences of state intervention, I hope to show that the possibility of illfare as the outcome of state intervention cannot be dismissed.

Since 1789 there have been many administrations but only one regime.

Edward Lutwack, "Scenario for a Military Coup D'Etat in the United States," *Esquire* (July 1970), p. 60.

The State and the Poor

The basic problem is: Who benefits from state intervention? What is the distribution of the benefits of state intervention by socioeconomic class? Unfortunately, the question is easier to pose than it is to answer.

One point is clear, however. When analyzing the role of government, one must look at the *totality* of government activity, not just its anti-poverty activities. Subsidies to rich farmers, to the airlines, railroads, and maritime industry, to suburbanites via housing and highway programs, to rich defense contractors, and so on, must be considered against so-called poverty programs.[16] Even if poverty programs, broadly construed, benefited the poor, the analysis of the impact of state intervention should not end there. These *welfare* effects must be tallied along with the *illfare* effects of other government programs to determine whether the net effect of state intervention is to enhance the welfare or illfare of the people. It is inappropriate to simply analyze the *progressive* redistributional aspects of transfer payments without analyzing the *regressive* redistributional aspects of other government programs as well.[17]

When analyzing the purpose of any public programs, one must probe beneath the rhetoric of the program to analyze its actual operations. Public programs have what the sociologist Robert Merton describes as *manifest* and *latent* functions.[18] Manifest functions are normally contained in stated legislative objectives and announced administrative missions. Invariably, these manifest functions are stated in ideologically and socially acceptable terms. On the other hand, programs also have hidden or latent functions. At times the latent functions reflect the true objectives of public programs; in other instances, the latent effects of public policy may be unintended, though no less important. In the present discussion, this means that many programs with a *manifest function of poverty reduction* also have latent functions which at times lead to *unintended consequences*. A radical analysis must deal with both of these functions.

With this framework in mind, let us examine three major anti-poverty programs—the social security system for the aged poor, the various New Deal farm programs for the rural poor, and contemporary manpower and anti-poverty programs.

Poverty and Old Age—The Social Security System   Today, the aged constitute one of the largest segments of the poor even though the New Deal Social Security Program was supposed to deal with this problem. Many reformers consider the Social Security System our greatest welfare achievement. But in 1968, 24 percent of all the poor (classified by the government's definition) were over 65; about one-third of all persons in that age group are poor.[19]

The radical theory provides us with an interesting group of variables to isolate for investigation—especially, the question of class as it relates to the Social Security Program. The Social Security System is supported by a regressive tax system, while its benefits are graduated somewhat with higher wage earners receiving higher benefits; low earners receive benefits which are a higher percentage of their earnings but less in absolute amounts than higher earners. An individual earning between $4,000 and $5,000 (in 1967) paid an effective tax rate of *9.3 percent* while an individual earning over $25,000 paid only *1.5 percent* because only the first $7,800 of wage and salary income was taxable in that year.[20] The system is class biased against labor since only wages are taxed, leaving income from property (rent, interest, dividends, capital gains) untaxed.

Individuals receiving social security payments are restricted as to the amount of money they can earn in wages (up to age 72) or they lose their payments. Presently, an individual may earn only $1,680 before she begins to lose her social security payments. However, this restriction only applies to earnings from employment or self-employment, not income from capital. An individual can acquire unlimited amounts of income from rent, interest, dividends, private pensions, personal trusts, or capital gains with no reduction in social security payments. These two aspects of the program reveal its class bias. In both instances the program discriminates *against the working class* and in favor of *the owners and managers of capital.* Moreover, the shorter life expectancies of poor people (especially blacks) reduce the benefits received by that strata.

An important, but neglected, unintended consequence of the Social Security System is the latent function of the Social Security Trust Fund as a *war chest.* The Social Security Trust Fund (OASDI) is one of the three trust funds associated with social welfare programs. The size of these trust funds between 1959 and 1969 is contained in Table 1. Between 1965 and 1969—the period of the Vietnam build-up—the public debt increased by $50.3 billion. Essentially, all of this was for the Indo-China War since the debt had increased by much less between 1960 and 1964. During the 1965–69 period, the investments of social welfare trust funds increased by $16.1 billion. In short, the *increase* in social welfare trust funds accounted for nearly one-third (32 percent) of the net increase in the national debt incurred to finance the Indo-China War. The increase in social welfare trust funds was due to the initiation of new programs, increases in taxes, and increases in payrolls. I am not suggesting that the manifest function of the increase in social welfare trust funds was for war financing. However,

TABLE 1
Investments in U.S. Government Securities of Social Welfare Trust Funds, Selected Years 1959–1969
(Millions of Dollars)

Fiscal year	OASDI Trust Fund	Hospital Insurance Trust Fund	Unemployment Insurance Trust Fund	Total
1959–60	21,848.6	*	6,668.5	28,518.1
1964–65	20,641.3	*	7,819.3	28,640.6
1965–66	19,371.2	785.7	9,278.2	29,435.1
1966–67	23,596.7	1,776.9	10,601.0	35,974.6
1967–68	25,584.0	1,651.6	11,602.6	38,838.2
1968–69	29,710.9	2,359.3	12,624.1	44,694.3

* Program did not exist.
SOURCE: *Social Security Bulletin,* vol. 32, no. 12 (December 1969), p. 52, Table M-5; p. 53, Table M-6; p. 54, Table M-7; and p. 88, Table Q-18.

at a time when the government was desperately trying to find ways to camouflage the financing of the Vietnam War, the increase in trust funds provided a convenient means for the long-term financing of the war.

The failure to provide adequate benefit levels in the Social Security System has led to the growth of a vast exploitative private insurance industry, feeding on individual and group pension plans. These vast sums of money are a major prop to the stock market. Additionally, these vast concentrations of money have led to enormous concentrations of economic and political power.[21] In 1968, there were over 9 million individuals covered by private pension plans and close to $35 billion in reserves were held by private insurance companies.[22]

The question is not whether the aged are "better off" with the present Social Security System. That is a trivial formulation; obviously they are. But this is similar to the argument that blacks are better off as freemen after the Civil War, and therefore we should not criticize our society for being racist. These are not the only alternatives—as other less rich societies have demonstrated. Compared with any vision of a decent system for the aged, America's Social Security System must be judged a failure. America has made old age synonymous with insecurity and poverty. This insecurity, in turn, is one of the levers used to discipline us in the workplace—make us seekers after individual protection from old age—so that we can avoid the social *insecurity* created by the state's failures to deal with the basic economic failures of capitalism.

Rural Poverty—The Farm Program   The New Deal placed great hopes on farm programs to eliminate rural poverty. Radicals, like Henry Wallace, helped design the farm program. But today, the rural poor live at starvation levels while large corporate farmers dig into the government trough to line their pockets. The farm program, like the Social Security System, is class biased. The state pays the *owners* of farm property not to produce, but pays virtually nothing to *farm workers* who become unemployed as a result of this dole to property owners. Even the payments to farm owners are not equitably distributed. The larger farmers get higher subsidies. Of the 10 major crops under price supports, the top 10 percent of farm owners (in terms of income) received from 36 percent (tobacco) to 72 percent (sugar cane) of all price support payments. The lowest decile received from 0.1 percent (rice) to 1.9 percent (sugar beet).[23] But the story does not end there. Agriculture extension services have fostered technological change which has led to the displacement of farm workers and the concentration of farm ownership. The government's agricultural program, originally designed to alleviate rural poverty, has led to subsidized concentrations of wealth and power for *property owners* at the expense of *farm workers*.

Contemporary Anti-Poverty Programs—Manpower Programs and the War Against Poverty   But the farm program is an effort at poverty reduction from another decade. What about more contemporary efforts? An important component of the government's total poverty program is contained in the various manpower programs initiated in the 1960s. The program has grown from an expenditure of *$245 million* in 1961 to *$2.2 billion* in 1968.[24] Although this program had undoubtedly benefited some of those trained, other groups in the economy have not let this opportunity pass without dipping into the public trough. The government's efforts at training have certainly reduced private expenditures on training, thereby transferring a private cost onto the public. In effect, these programs constitute training subsidies to business.[25]

Evidence in support of this contention is found in the composition of training programs in the 1960s. In the mid-sixties the Department of Labor shifted its training programs away from *institutional* training—where the worker is given general skill training which enables him to achieve some flexibility and mobility in the labor force—to *on-the-job training*. The latter is more beneficial to employers since it trains the worker for a specific job associated with a particular firm.[26] On-the-job training as a percent of MDTA programs increased from 5 percent in 1964, to 20 percent in 1966, to 41 percent in 1968.[27] However, the General Accounting Office found, even in the case of on-the-job training, that monies were essentially being used to subsidize training that would have otherwise taken place. In their words:

> OJT Contracts had served primarily to reimburse employers for OJT which they would have conducted even without the Government's financial assistance. These contracts were awarded even though the intent of the program was to induce *new or additional training efforts* beyond those usually carried out. (Emphasis in original.)[28]

In addition, special programs developed in "cooperation" with private industry were supported by public funds. The JOBS program was given $60 million in 1968 to work with the National Alliance of Businessmen to hire and train the hard-core unemployed.[29] What is wrong with this, one may ask? The government did not provide job training for the development of collective enterprises or for neighborhood control of economic development in the inter cities. Instead, the training monies were direct subsidies to the very corporate interests whose power has thwarted the abolition of poverty in America.

No doubt, the programs of the War on Poverty per se assisted some of the poor. However, the evolving purpose of the programs became one of integrating the poor into the American mainstream to avoid extreme social disorder. For those who resisted in the early years of the War on poverty, more intense socialization programs were developed. For example, the Job Corps was created to prepare the disaffected young, in the legislation's words, "for the responsibility of citizenship."[30] Two eminently authoritative sources close to the poverty program frankly admit that "The

assumption underlying this mission was that many youths from impoverished homes should be removed from their home environment before they
could be rehabilitated through training and education."[31] One of the most
persuasive arguments used to achieve enactment of the legislation was the
high rejection rate of the poor among potential draftees for the military
revealed in a Defense Department funded study called One-Third of a
Nation.

Large contracts were given at high profit mark-ups to defense contractors seeking to diversify their operations in anticipation of a deteriorating
defense budget. (This activity begin before the Vietnam War rectified
the situation in the defense industry.) Unused military bases became Job
Corps Centers—apparently these installations had the needed environment
for rehabilitation.[32] Job Corps members were subjected to military-type en-
vironments—even down to the wearing of uniforms. John H. Rubel, Vice-
President of Litton Industries (one of the contractors) viewed his function
accurately:

> I think of the Job Corps as a complex transforming machine
> with many internal parts. The input—the raw material—that
> is fed into this machine is people. The output is people. It is
> the function of this machine to transform these people.[33]

Other poverty programs, though not as explicitly designed for social
control, had, as part of their latent function, behavioral engineering—for
example, the attempt to create better work discipline through manpower
training. Headstart programs for preschoolers, the Job Corps for teen-agers,
and a variety of community programs for adults were all designed to make
the poor adapt to the society to prevent large social disaffection with its
attendant potential for insurrection.

But somewhere the effort failed—witness the extensive urban insurrections of 1966 and 1967. The Kerner Commission concluded that the
urban insurrections were the consequence of unrealized expectations and
blocked opportunities attributable to the racist nature of American Society.[34]

They pointed to the failure of civil rights legislation. It was an easy
step for Nixon to blame these unrealized expectations, in part, on the War
on Poverty. At this juncture public policy shifted toward police repression—
an anti-poor program that cannot be neglected. Agnew-type attacks on
fuzzy-thinking social scientists sounded the end of the pernicious, but more
subtle, experiments at social control and signaled a new period of public
policy which may lead to an attempt to eliminate the poor instead of
poverty.

There is some evidence for this. For example, the surprisingly insightful analysis of racism and poverty of the Kerner Commission produced
several dozen policy proposals. But only one has been implemented—vast
sums of money and armaments for riot police and riot-trained National
Guard. We have witnessed the work of these people in the last several years.
The manifest function of these police programs—originally proposed by

liberals—was to fight street crime. This is ideologically and socially accept-able. However, the *actual allocations* of these vast sums have not been against street crime but against political opposition and radical anti-poverty groups (National Welfare Rights Organization, Black Panthers, Young Lords, and so on) as well as other anti-racist and anti-imperialist movements. The police do not need helicopters, M-16 rifles, armored personnel carriers, riot-equipped civil disorder squads and the like to stop street muggings! The Urban Coalition reports that 58 percent of all federal grants to police were for equipment which bore little relation to street crime.[35]

In the last two years, the fastest growing area of government re-search and instructional grants to universities has been for this effort at "Vietnamizing" the United States. Expenditures for "academic assistance" by the Justice Department's Law Enforcement Assistance Administration (LEAA) was planned at $18 million in fiscal 1970 and $21 million in 1971, a threefold increase over the $6.5 million spent in 1969.[36] In 1968, close to 50 colleges and universities were given grants by the Justice Depart-ment for research and instruction.[37]

The newest anti-poverty scheme, not yet enacted into law, is rep-resented by the various income maintenance programs under considera-tion. Nixon has proposed giving every urban family of four a generous $1,600 a year, less than one-half of the subsistence government poverty level and less than all but a handful of states presently pay in public welfare. The National Welfare Rights Organization (NWRO) has proposed $6,500. The BLS "Moderate But Adequate" standard would call for $9,100. All of these programs would involve redistribution of income—especially the NWRO and BLS standards.

Critics of the Nixon Family Assistance Plan have raised a funda-mental question which bears on our earlier discussion. Who will perform the many low wage jobs if roughly equivalent sums of money can be obtained by not working? My prediction is that no income maintenance system will be introduced unless it can be made compatible with the struc-ture of the labor market and its large number of low wage jobs. This is the explanation for the Administration linking the receipt of social welfare and social services to work, a social ideology deeply ingrained in Western societies since the Industrial Revolution. Nixon wants to turn the federal government into a national company store!

In sum, there is supportive evidence for the several hypotheses which flow from a radical theory of the state and the poor. Government expenditures, as a totality, are not as progressive as liberals have presumed, and, indeed, they may be regressive. Even poverty programs, per se, benefit groups beside the poor. Programs have been distorted in their implementa-tion—witness the farm program. Programs have been introduced only when rendered compatible with the structure of the economy and the prevailing ideology.

More important, none of these public programs has been based on a serious analysis of the causes of poverty. Nearly all are in the tradition of the Elizabethan Poor Laws which assume that poverty is the result of some manipulatable personal attribute. This explains why more money is spent each year on poverty programs (broadly defined) than is required to close the poverty income gap! Poverty persists because it derives from a low-wage labor market, which benefits the nonpoor by providing essential goods and services at lower prices than would prevail if we eliminated this low-wage labor market. But this is the essence of capitalism, and therein lies the contradiction.

The failure to construct public programs based on an analysis of the causes of poverty is the reason for the ambiguous accomplishments of public policy in the 1960s. Completers of manpower training programs have become members of the working poor. The median wage for all trainees between 1962 and 1967 was $1.74 per hour—$1.60 for blacks. Job Corps trainees received only about $1.45 per hour.[38]

Our earlier analysis suggests that poverty flows from the structure of the economy, but policy does not recognize this reality. George Schultz, former Secretary of Labor, candidly admitted this in his testimony on the Nixon Family Assistance Plan:

> I hasten to add that the labor market itself must be recognized as a constraint . . . It is a fact that our economy has a lot of jobs that pay low wages. We are not going to be remaking the economy in this program. (Family Assistance Plan) We can only put people in the jobs that exist . . . We will have to thread our way between our goals of providing good jobs . . . and the qualities of the kinds of jobs that are available.[39]

Recapitulation

The argument of this paper is that poverty is endogenous to our society and a logical consequence of the basic institutions of capitalism—class, labor markets, and the state. The interaction of these institutions is both a breeding ground and a perpetuator of poverty. Public policy to combat poverty has failed precisely because, under present arrangements, it is incapable of challenging the supremacy of these "institutions."

Problems of a fundamental nature require an equivalent response. Non-radical social scientists and non-radical policy have failed to comprehend this. The result has been the persistence of poverty amid affluence.

Notes

1. This question is examined in Sam Bowles, "Contradictions in U.S. Higher Education" (Mimeographed, January 1971).
2. Even some of the more "sophisticated" statistical work has merely measured the differential importance of various personal characteristics while

providing minimal insights into the causes of poverty. For example, see Lester C. Thurow, *Poverty and Discrimination* (Washington: The Brookings Institution, 1969) chap. 3.

3. Frank Ackerman, Howard Birnbaum, James Wetzler, and Andrew Zimbalist, "Income Distribution in the United States" (mimeographed, 1970), pp. 14–16.

4. Donald Light, "Income Distribution: The First Stage in the Consideration of Poverty," (appearing elsewhere in this publication).

5. A few lone researchers have been trying to alert us to the plight of the working poor. The most comprehensive studies are: Barry Bluestone, "The Tripartite Economy: Labor Markets and the Working Class," *Poverty and Human Resources* (July–August 1970), pp. 15–35, and Barry Bluestone, "Lower-Income Workers and Marginal Industries," in Louis A. Ferman, Joyce L. Kornbluh, and Alan Haber (eds.), *Poverty in America* (Ann Arbor: University of Michigan Press, 1968), rev. ed., pp. 273–302.

6. The President's Commission on Income Maintenance Programs, *Background Papers* (Washington: Government Printing Office, 1970), pp. 139–142.

7. See Leon Eisenberg, "Racism, the Family, and Society: A Crisis in Values," *Mental Hygiene* (October 1968), p. 512; and R. L. Naeye, N. M. Diener, W. S. Dellinger, "Urban Poverty Effects on Prenatal Nutrition," *Science* (November 21, 1969), p. 1,026.

8. This classification of variables is used to analyze low-wage employment in Howard M. Wachtel and Charles Betsey, "Employment at Low Wages," (mimeographed, 1971). In this study, industrial attachment was the most important determinant of wage earnings.

9. See Bowle's, in the work cited, and James S. Coleman, and others, *Equality of Educational Opportunity* (Washington: Government Printing Office, 1968). Data pertaining to this is contained in David Gordon (ed.), *Problems in Political Economy: An Urban Perspective* (Lexington, Mass.: D. C. Heath & Co., 1971), pp. 178–181.

10. This model is borrowed from the work in progress of Barry Bluestone and Mary Stevenson.

11. Barry Bluestone, "Lower Income Workers and Marginal Industries," pp. 286–301.

12. Edward C. Banfield, *The Unheavenly City* (Boston: Little, Brown and Co., 1968).

13. A recent statement of this view is in Milton Friedman, *Capitalism and Freedom* (Chicago: University of Chicago Press, 1962), especially chap. 2.

14. For an exposition and critique of the pluralist theory, see Jack L. Walker, "A Critique of the Elitist Theory of Democracy," *The American*

Political Science Review, vol. LX, no. 2 (June 1966), pp. 285–295 and the reply in the same issue of the APSR by Robert A. Dahl, "Further Reflections on the 'Elitist Theory of Democracy,'" pp. 296–305. Democratic pluralism has been integrated into economic literature by John Kenneth Galbraith, *American Capitalism: The Concept of Countervailing Power* (Boston: Houghton Mifflin Co., 1952).

15. For a recent exposition of this theory, see Ralph Milliband, *The State in Capitalist Society* (New York: Basic Books, 1969).

16. This novel approach is taken by Stephen Michelson, "The Economics of Real Income Distribution," *Review of Radical Political Economics*, vol. *II*, no. 1, (spring 1970), pp. 75–86.

17. The redistributive effects of transfer payments are substantially less than most social scientists have assumed. See Irene Lurie, "The Distribution of Transfer Payments Among Households," in the President's Commission on Income Maintenance Programs, *Technical Studies* (Washington: Government Printing Office, 1970), pp. 143–158.

18. See Robert K. Merton, "Manifest and Latent Functions," in N. J. Demerath III and Richard A. Peterson (eds.), *Systems, Change, and Conflict* (New York: The Free Press, 1967), pp. 10–76.

19. U.S. Department of Commerce, Bureau of the Census, *Poverty in the United States, 1959–1968* (Washington: U.S. Government Printing Office, 1969), p. 4.

20. Joseph A. Pechman, Henry J. Aaron, and Michael K. Taussig, *Social Security: Perspectives for Reform* (Washington: The Brookings Institution, 1968), p. 307. These calculations are based on the assumption that employer taxes are shifted "backward" to the employee.

21. These questions are discussed in the fascinating, but little-known work of Robert Tilove, *Pension Funds and Economic Freedom* (New York: The Fund for the Republic, 1959); and Joint Economic Committee, *Investment Policies of Pension Funds* (April 1970).

22. Institute of Life Insurance, *Life Insurance Fact Book, 1969* (New York: Institute of Life Insurance, 1969), p. 39.

23. The President's Commission on Income Maintenance Programs, *Background Papers*, p. 290; and John A. Schnittner, "The Distribution of Benefits from Existing and Prospective Farm Programs" (mimeographed, 1969).

24. Sar A. Levitan and Garth L. Mangum, *Federal Training and Work Programs in the Sixties* (Ann Arbor: Institute of Labor and Industrial Relations, 1969), p. 11.

25. There is a growing body of evidence in support of this contention, for example: U.S. General Accounting Office, *Improvements Needed in Contracting for On-The-Job Training Under the Manpower Development and Training Act of 1962* (Washington: General Accounting

Office, 1968); and U.S. General Accounting Office, *Need to Enhance the Effectiveness of On-The-Job Training in Appalachian Tennessee* (Washington: General Accounting Office, 1970).

26. The differential utility to a firm of general and specific training is analyzed in Gary Becker, *Human Capital* (New York: Columbia University Press, 1964), pp. 11–29; and Michael J. Piore, "Public and Private Responsibilities in On-The-Job Training of Disadvantaged Workers," (mimeographed, 1968), p. 1.

27. U.S. Department of Labor, *Manpower Report of the President, 1969* (Washington: U.S. Government Printing Office, 1969), p. 238.

28. U.S. General Accounting Office, *Improvements Needed in Contracting . . .*, p. i.

29. Corporate abuses of the JOBS program are discussed in United States Senate, Committee on Labor and Public Welfare, *The Jobs Program* (Washington: Government Printing Office, 1970).

30. Quoted in Levitan and Mangum, p. 163.

31. *Ibid.*

32. This discussion is based on the analysis of two economists close to the program, see *Ibid.*, pp. 163–210.

33. Quoted in *Ibid.*, p. 173.

34. *Report of the National Advisory Commission on Civil Disorders* (New York: Bantam Books, 1968), p. 204.

35. National Urban Coalition, *Law and Disorder II* (Washington: U.S. National Urban Coalition, 1970), p. 5.

36. *Ibid.*, p. 3.

37. Office of Law Enforcement Assistance, U.S. Department of Justice, *LEAA Grants and Contracts, Fiscal 1966–1968* (Washington: U.S. Government Printing Office, 1968), pp. 61–86.

38. Levitan and Mangum, pp. 51 and 206.

39. George Schultz, "The Family Assistance Act of 1969" (Statement before the Committee on Ways and Means, House of Representatives, October 16, 1969).

PART III

POLITICAL CHANGE: APPROACHES TO ANALYSIS AND ACTION

The selections in these last two parts address two separate but related topics—the ways in which change *is* defined and sought, and prescriptions about how it *should be* defined and sought. In prior sections, we have presented a number of selections which deal with changes in institutional forms or practices, or with changes in public policies intended to solve problems. Here, we approach change from a different perspective, that of groups which are seeking as yet unfulfilled goals. Some of these goals appear compatible with the existing social structure and the basic values of the society, and yet have not been realized; as we shall see in Part III, a variety of means have been taken to try to achieve them. In part because of failure to realize their goals by various actions so far, and in part because the nature of some of their goals is *not* consistent with the existing society, several groups have had to develop entirely new strategies to gain their ends. In Part IV, we shall see some of the latter type of goals and the prescriptions developed to achieve them.

What are some representative approaches to analysis and action? Implicit in many of our earlier selections is the assumption that social problems are or should be solved through a process in which the nature of the problem is made known to government decision-makers, who then develop the means and provide the resources to solve it. We have seen that there are many difficulties in the way of such direct communication, and many reasons why decision-makers do not or cannot act to try to solve problems. We are about to encounter another major obstacle: *in many instances, decision makers simply will not or cannot understand the problem as it appears to the people who actually experience it.* Coming from totally different class levels, with totally different life experiences and expectations, there is often a complete failure of understanding of how things look from the perspective of the poor, black or Chicano, unemployed, or economically-marginal working-class person.

This obstacle is made more formidable by the fact that decision-makers have often relied on the analyses of social scientists to tell them about the nature of problems. But social scientists are normally middle-class professionals like themselves, who use the same standards of judgment—and who have therefore frequently misunderstood problems or in effect blamed the poor or minority groups for not struggling hard enough to raise themselves up. The conventional wisdom of social science, for example, has long interpreted voter apathy and withdrawal as signs of health in the political system—on the grounds that if people really had grievances, they would complain loudly at the ballot box. Not considered were the possibilities that such people were too busy trying to survive economically to engage in politics, or that they knew from experience that their needs would not be served through electoral means. Instead, social science tended to view this electoral nonparticipation as "functional," for participation by the lower-class elements might mean "extremism" and be undesirable.

Another reassuring element of conventional wisdom is that the political system operates on a "pluralistic" basis, in which all groups have full opportunity to have their demands heard through the open political process, and that a group has only to engage in the standard bargaining, competitive process to be able to achieve its goals. This belief, often reiterated, can serve as a rationale for insisting that change-seeking groups be satisfied with whatever they obtain through such activities and refrain from any other. If it is not correct, however, it is really just a means of telling such groups that they should not seek anything that arouses serious opposition from other established groups, and that in any event they should abide by all the rules that those same other groups have laid down for the manner in which change may be sought.

The first three articles here take up key aspects of how we look at change, and whether such conventional wisdom of social science is correct. Michael Parenti offers a view of change that does not start with a series of benevolent assumptions about the democratic qualities of the American political system. Instead, he argues, this may be a system much like many others—that is, one organized to prevent many types of change, particularly those which challenge existing values or privileges. His analysis asks in effect whether there is realistic reason to hope that what he sees as necessary change can be attained. Lewis Lipsitz takes up the issue of voter apathy and nonparticipation, showing that it is not because of a lack of grievances about their lives. He finds many unfulfilled aspirations and needs, but a helplessness and sense of powerlessness about achieving them. In the final selection in this first series, Michael Parenti turns to some specific experiences in Newark, N.J., to show that the "pluralist" image of the decision-making process may be more illusion than fact. He demonstrates that more unified structures of power exist, and operate to determine results in politics. Taken together, these three selections may show a shift in the understanding of social science about problems; at least some researchers have begun to ask whether, *if viewed from the perspective of the people involved*, the American political system has been sufficiently perceptive and responsive to peoples' needs.

The next series of selections show several approaches actually taken by different groups in search of their goals. From the perspective of each group, government was not acting to help them, but rather in many cases to prevent them from achieving what they sought. They were therefore forced (in their eyes) to employ a variety of private resources, most of which were ultimately unsuccessful. Brenda Mull captures the grim determination of a group of women workers to improve their wages and working conditions. Bobby Seale's description of the Black Panther Party's Breakfast for Children Program represents an entirely different approach. Finally, the assumption of responsibility for ecology by an individual steelworker is used as a case study of industry's resistance to change in pollution practices. Taken together, these selections are intended to give a sense of the many ways that groups and individuals have sought to achieve rather modest and lawful goals, in circumstances where there appeared to them to be no other ways to gain them.

19.
THE POSSIBILITIES FOR POLITICAL CHANGE

Michael Parenti

A question pressing upon us with increasing urgency is, what are the possibilities for political change in America? More specifically, can the political system serve as a means for effecting the substantive reallocations needed to solve the enormous problems created within and by our economic system? What can we hope will be done about the continued plunder and pollution of our natural resources, the growth of a titanic military-industrial establishment, the massive concentration of corporate wealth and all its ensuing abuses, and the widespread infestations of rural and urban poverty? What kinds of solutions are in the offing, and, indeed, what kinds of definitions do we bring to the idea of "solution"?

I

Before considering the possibilities for political change, let us give some critical attention to the usual ways of approaching social problems. Social scientists and lay commentators alike have commonly assumed that solutions are arrived at by a process of systematic investigation. By identifying all the salient variables and then constructing paradigms which unravel the complex interactions of these variables, we can equip ourselves with inventories of causes and resources and develop strategies for solution. The remaining task would be to convince the decision makers to push the buttons provided by the social scientists. It is expected that the human stupidity and inertia of political actors would deter the implementation of certain proposals, but decision makers are thought to be as hungry as anyone else for viable programs and sooner or later would not be unresponsive to the promises of science.

This scientistic, technocratic view of social problems presumes that decision makers are as immune to the pressures of power and interest as

From Michael Parenti, "The Possibilities for Political Change," *Politics and Society*, vol. 1, no. 1 (November 1970), pp. 79–90. © 1970 by Geron-X Inc. Reprinted by permission of the publisher.

scientists are, or as scientists think they are. What is missing from this sci-entism is the essence of politics itself, an appreciation of the inescapability of interest and power in determining what solutions will be deemed suitable, what allocations will be thought supportable, and, indeed, what variables will even be considered as interrelating and salient. The presumption that there is a scientifically discoverable "correct" solution to problems overlooks the fact that social problems involve conflicting ends and often irreconcilable value distributions; thus one man's "solution" is often another man's dis-aster. A "correct" proposal for some political actors may be one which re-solves the threat of an opposing interest without causing any loss of profit or status to oneself. Hence the first instinct of established interests is so often toward halfhearted reform and wholehearted repression ("law and order"). For other advocates, a "correct" program is one calling for nothing less than momentous reallocations in the substance and process of the entire productive system (a remedy which offers the kind of paradigm that usually escapes the serious attentions of most liberal middle-class social scientists).

Unlike mathematical problems which might be resolved by pro-cedures exogenous to the life subjectivities of various mathematicians, the solutions to social problems cannot be treated except in the context of vested and conflicting interests which give vested and conflicting definitions to the problem. This is true whether the question is rebuilding the ghettos or withdrawing our troops from Vietnam: the solutions are potentially "at hand" or "nowhere in sight," depending on the ideological priorities and commitments of various proponents.

The scientistic approach presumes that problems exist because of the prevailing ignorance of the would-be problem solvers rather than because of the prevailing conditions of power among social groups. But, again, unlike mathematical problems which begin and end on paper, it goes without say-ing that social problems are never resolved by study but by action. Many of the social ills we live with have been studied repeatedly, but since they have not yet been resolved it is assumed by the proponents of scientism that they need further study. Here we have an uncharacteristic instance of social scientists pretending to an *ignorance* they do not really possess. For the last thing some of our problems need is further study. Witness the hundreds of studies, reports, surveys, and exposés done on Appalachia by a variety of commissions, committees, economists, and journalists, extending back more than half a century.[1] Neither history nor the historians have "bypassed" or "neglected" the people of Appalachia. The material forces of history, in this case the timber and mining companies that swindled the Appalachians of their lands, exploited their labor, and wreaked havoc with their lives, were all too attentive to the destinies of that region even though they were never held accountable for the social costs of their actions. The plunder and profit which is the history of the region has been duly documented; yet Appalachia is still treated today as a kind of historical mishap, an impersonal and presumably innocent development of "changing times," a "complex situation" needing our concerted attention.

Similarly, the plight of the urban poor in various Western industrial societies has been documented by official and unofficial sources for more than a century, and in recent decades we have traced the web of interests, the private and public forces, North and South, at the national and local levels, which have contributed to, and perpetuated, the black ghettos. The story is well known to us, but our discoveries have brought forth no solutions.

To be sure, the first step toward remedy is to investigate reality. But, eventually, if no second step is taken, no move toward action, then the call for "a study of the problem" is justifiably treated as nothing more than a symbolic response, an "appropriate reciprocal noise," designed to convey the impression that decision makers are fulfilling their responsibilities.[2] The commissioned "study" becomes an act which violates its own professed purpose: rather than inducing change, it is designed to mitigate the demands for change. Appearing before the Kerner Commission, the psychologist Kenneth B. Clark noted:

> I read that report . . . of the 1919 riot in Chicago, and it is as if I were reading the report of the investigating committee on the Harlem riot of '35, the report of the investigating committee on the Harlem riot of '43, the report of the McCone Commission on the Watts riot.
>
> I must again in candor say to you members of this Commission—it is a kind of Alice in Wonderland—with the same moving picture reshown over and over again, the same analysis, the same recommendations, and the same inaction.[3]

By incorporating Clark's admonition into its pages the Kerner Report may have achieved the ultimate in co-optation, for it, itself, is a prime example of that kind of official evasion and obfuscation designed to justify the very status quo about which Clark was complaining. The Kerner Report demands no changes in the way power and wealth are distributed among the classes; it never gets beyond its indictment of "white racism" to specify the forces in the political economy which brought the black man to riot; it treats the obviously abominable ghetto living conditions as "causes" of disturbance but never really inquires into the causes of the "causes." It does not deal, for instance, with the ruthless enclosure of southern sharecroppers by big corporate farming interests, the subsequent mistreatment of the black migrant by northern rent-gouging landlords, price-gouging merchants, urban "redevelopers," discriminating employers, insufficient schools, hospitals, and welfare, brutal police, hostile political machines and state legislators, and, finally, the whole system of values, material interests, and public power distributions from the state to the federal capitols which gives greater priority to "haves" than to "have-nots," servicing and subsidizing the interests of private corporations while neglecting the often desperate needs of the municipalities. The Kerner Report reflects the ideological cast of its sponsor, the Johnson administration, and in that sense is no better than the interests it served.[4]

To treat the *symptoms* of social dislocation (for example, slum conditions) as the *causes* of social ills is an inversion not peculiar to the Kerner Report. Unable or willing to pursue the implications of our own data, we tend to see the effects of a problem as the problem itself. The victims, rather than the victimizers, are defined as "the poverty problem." This is what might be described as the "VISTA approach" to economic maladies: a haphazard variety of public programs are initiated, focusing on the poor and ignoring the system of power, privilege, and profit which makes them poor. It is a little like blaming the corpse for the murder.

II

In looking to the political system as a means of rectifying the abuses and inequities of the socioeconomic system we are confronted with the inescapable fact that any political system, including one which observes democratic forms, is a system of power. As such, it best serves those who have the wherewithal to make it serviceable to their interests,—those who own and control the resources of money, property, organization, jobs, social prestige, legitimacy, time, and expertise, and who thereby command the attentive responses of political decision makers. Indeed, our political system works well for those large producer and corporate interests that control the various loci of power in the state and federal legislatures and bureaucracies. One can find no end to the instances in which public agencies have become the captives of private business interests.[5] Economic power is to political power as fuel is to fire, but in this instance the "fire" actually feeds back and adds to the fuel; for political power when properly harnessed becomes a valuable resource in expanding the prerogatives of those economic interests which control it. To think of government as nothing more than a broker or referee amidst a vast array of competing groups (the latter presumably representing all the important and "countervailing" interests of the populace) is to forget that government best serves those who can best serve themselves.

But the material advantages of the owning classes are supposedly offset by the representative forms of a democratic system which make explicit and institutionalized provision for the power of numbers and if the non-elites have nothing else they at least have their numbers. But numbers are not power unless they are organized and mobilized into forms of political action which can deliver some reward to or punishment upon decision makers. And the mobilization of potential numerical strength requires the use of antecedent resources. Just as one needs the capital to make capital, so one needs the power to use power. This is especially true of the power of numbers, which, to be even sporadically effective, requires large outputs of time, manpower, publicity, organization, knowledgeability, legitimacy, and—the ingredient that often can determine the availability of these other resources—money. The power of numbers, then, like the power of our representative institutions, is highly qualified by material and class considerations.

Consider those agencies which are specifically intended to mobilize and register the power of numbers, the political parties. The image of the political party as an organization inclusive of and responsive to the interests of rank and file voters does not find ready confirmation in the experiences of dissenters who have sought entry into the party system. To be sure, new voters in both rural and urban counties are usually welcomed onto the party roles especially if they are white and if their loyalties promise to fit into the established spectrum of political choices, but new ideas and issues, new and potentially disruptive interests, are treated most unsympathetically by the county bosses and district captains whose overriding concern is to maintain their own positions in the ongoing "equilibrium"; more often than not, the instinct of the local clubhouse, that "cogwheel of democracy" is to operate with exclusive rather than inclusive intent.[6]

In general, the two-party system throughout the local and national levels *avoids* rather than confronts many of the basic social problems of our society, or, when confrontation materializes, the electoral stances are usually reiterations of conventional formulas rather than invitations to heterodox ideas and choices. One need only recall how liberals and conservatives, Democrats and Republicans, spent 25 postwar years demonstrating their anti-Communist militancy on almost all domestic and foreign policy issues, thereby driving public debate on the question of "America's role in the world" to new levels of impoverishment. In an earlier work, I suggested: "The American political system has rarely been able to confront fundamental images, or serve as an instrument of creative discourse, or even engage in public discussion of heterodox alternatives. The two-party competition which supposedly is to provide for democratic heterodoxy, in fact, has generated a competition for orthodoxy [on most important questions]. In politics, as in economics, competition is rarely a certain safeguard against monopoly and seldom a guarantee that the competitors will produce commodities which offer the consumer a substantive choice."[7]

Offering itself as the voice of the people, as a measure of the polyarchic will, the representative system becomes one of the greatest legitimatizing forces for the ongoing social order and all its class abuses. A closer study of the "eras of reform" seems to support rather than refute this view. If the political system has done anything in the nineteenth and twentieth centuries, it has kept the populace busy with symbolic struggles while manfully servicing the formidable appetites of the business community. To take one instance among countless ones: the legislation of 1887 marking Congress's "great" reform effort in transportation gave the people their railroad regulation law and gave the business magnates their railroads complete with risk-free investment capital (compliments of the U.S. taxpayer), free land, and many millions of dollars in profits.[8] Similarly, the history of who got what during the New Deal has still to be written. There yet may emerge an American historian who will spare us his description of the inspirational rhetoric, the colorful personalities, the electoral ballyhoo, the 100 days of legislative flurry, the Brain Trust, the court-packing fight, and so on, and get down to a systematic and, I suspect, startling study of the New Deal's dealings with the political economy, revealing what classes carried the burdens of public finance, what ideologies prevailed at the operational level, what interests were left out and what interests actually got what magnitude of material outputs.[9] *Symbolic allocations to public sentiment and substantive allocations to private interests—such has been the overall performance of our political system even in times of so-called social reform.*

Speaking about the late nineteenth-century American political life, Matthew Josephson refers to the "contradictions between ideology and interest, between 'eternal principles of truth and right' and class-economic necessities . . . between the mask and parade—the theatrical duelings of prejudice, associations of thought, patriotic sentiment, illusions—and the naked clash of different conditions of existence, different forms of property and economy. . . . Behind the marching songs and slogans of the Ins and the Outs . . . we must grasp at the pecuniary objects, the genuine, concrete interests, the real stakes being played for, as in every historic social conflict."[10] For Josephson, the captains of industry were the "men who spoke little and did much" in determining the shape of our society and the quality of our lives, while the political leaders were "men who, in effect, did as little as possible and spoke all too much."[11] Together, the "robber barons" and the "politicos" represented the difference between substantive and symbolic politics.

Indeed, one might better think of ours as a dual political system: first, there is the *symbolic* input-output system centering around electoral and representative activities including party conflicts, voter turnout, political personalities, public pronouncements, official role-playing and certain ambiguous presentations of some of the public issues which bestir presidents, governors, mayors, and their respective legislatures.[12] Then there is the *substantive* input-output system, involving multibillion dollar contracts, tax write-offs, protections, rebates, grants, loss compensations, subsidies, leases, giveaways, and the whole vast process of budgeting, legislating, allocating, "regulating," protecting, and servicing major producer interests, now bending or ignoring the law on behalf of the powerful, now applying it with full punitive vigor against heretics and "troublemakers." The symbolic system is highly visible, taught in the schools, dissected by academicians, gossiped about by newsmen. The substantive system is seldom heard of or accounted for.

The have-nots who hope to win substantive outputs by working their way through the symbolic input-output system seldom see the light at the end of the tunnel. The crucial function of the electoral-representative process is to make people believe there is a closer connection between the symbolic and the substantive than actually exists. But those dissidents and protestors who decide to make the long march through primaries, fund-raising, voter registration, rallies, canvassing, and campaigning soon discover the bottomless, endless qualities of electoral politics. They find out that the political system, or that visible portion of it they experience, absorbs large quantities of their time, money, and energy while usually leaving them no closer to the forces which make the important substantive allocations of this society. On those infrequent occasions when reform candidates do win elections, they discover still other absorbent, deflective, and dilatory forces lying in wait. They find themselves relegated to obscure legislative tasks; they receive little cooperation from party leaders or from bureaucratic agenies. To achieve some degree of effectiveness in an institution whose dominant forces can easily outflank him, the newly arrived dissenter frequently decides that "for now" he must make his peace with the powers that be, holding his fire until some future day when he might attack from higher ground; thus begins that insidious process which lets a man believe he is fighting the ongoing arrangements when in fact he has become a functional part of them. Many of the accounts of life in Congress are studies in the methods of co-optation, the ways would-be dissenters are socialized to the goals and priorities of a conservative leadership.[13]

There are, of course, less subtle instances of co-optation: reformers have been bought off with promotions and favors from those who hold the key to their advancement. Having tasted the spoils of victory, they may reverse their stance on essential issues and openly make common cause with the powers that be, much to the shock of their supporters.[14] Well-meaning electoral crusaders who promise to get things moving again by exercising executive leadership, upon accession to federal, state, or local executive offices soon discover that most of the important options involving jobs, property, money, and taxes are dependent upon resources controlled by large corporations capable of exercising an influence extending well beyond the political realm as it is usually defined. When local, state, and federal officials contend that the problems they confront are of a magnitude far greater than the resources they command, we might suspect them of telling the truth, for in fact the major decisions about how the vast resources of our society are used are made by the private sector of the economy, and the economic institutions of a capitalist society are rarely, if ever, held accountable for the enormous social costs of their profit system.

III

Contrary to the gradualistic vision of America, things are getting worse, not better. As opposed to a decade ago, there are more, not less, people living in poverty today, more substandard housing, more environmental pollution and devastation, more deficiencies in our schools, hospitals, and systems of public transportation, more military dictatorships throughout the world feeding on the largesse and power of the Pentagon, more people from Thailand to Brazil to Greece to Chicago suffering the social oppression and political repression of an American-backed status quo. The long march through the American electoral-representative process has not saved the Vietnamese; it has not even saved the redwoods; nor, if our ecologists are correct, will it save the environment. Nor has it put a stop to the aggrandizements of American imperialism and its military-industrial complex. Nor has it brought us any closer to a real "war on poverty." Nor has there been any revision of priorities, any reallocations of resources away from the glut of a private commodity market and toward essential public needs and services. It is a small wonder that as social dissenters become increasingly aware of the limitations of debate, petition, and election for purposes of effecting substantive changes, they become less dedicated to election rituals and less attentive to the standard public dialogues heard within and without representative assemblies. For the same reason, those who oppose change become more dedicated to dialogue and symbolic politics, urging protestors to place their faith in reason, in free, open (and endless) discussion, and in the candidate of their choice.

In a system that responds only to power, what do the powerless do? Consider, once more, the problem of poverty: the people most needful of sociopolitical change, in this case, the poor, are by that very fact most deprived of the resources needed to mobilize political influence and least able to make effective use of whatever limited resources they do possess. If the poor controlled the values and goods needed to win substantive pay-offs, they would not be poor and would have less need to struggle for outputs which the economic and political systems readily allocate to more favored groups. This is the dilemma of lower strata groups: their deprivation leaves them at the low end of any index of power and their relative powerlessness seems to ensure their continued deprivation.

Lacking control of the things that would make decision makers readily responsive to them, and, therefore, lacking the specialized, organized, persistent, and well-financed forces of influence needed to function successfully in the substantive area of our dual political system, the dispossessed are left with the only resources they have: their voices, their bodies, their buying power and their labor; denunciations and demonstrations, sit-ins and scuffles, boycotts and strikes, the threat of disruption and actual disruption. The effectiveness of their protest actions, of course, is handicapped by the same scarcity of resources and consequent instability of organization that limits their opportunities for standard political influence. Nevertheless, the last decade has witnessed a growing tendency among aggrieved groups to heed the old Populist dictum to "raise less corn and more hell," to embark upon actions which inconvenience the normal arrangements of middle-class life and often upset middle-class sensibilities.

That is the idea—to inconvenience and upset. By increasing their nuisance value, the protestors hope to achieve a greater visibility for themselves and a greater sense of urgency in the public mind for the problems at hand. The nuisance and disruption caused by direct actions also become a leverage for those of little power, the withdrawal of the disruption being used as a negotiable resource. Thereby do dispossessed groups such as workers, blacks, students, and the poor attempt to induce through crude means a responsiveness from officialdom which the business community accomplishes through more effective and less strenuous channels.

But many of the demands put forth by protestors might be described as "transitional revolutionary." That is, they are essentially reformist and non-revolutionary in appearance *yet they are impossible to effect within the present system if that system is to maintain itself.* Students demand, for instance, that the university cease performing indispensable services for the corporate-military economy, including various kinds of vital research and personnel training, and that it withdraw its investments in giant corporations and devote a substantial portion of its resources to the needs of the impoverished, many of whom live within a stone's throw of its ivy-covered walls. And they demand that the multibillion dollar system of domestic and international service and armed protection given to the corporate elites be ceased on behalf of a multibillion dollar public investment against domestic and international poverty (one that would pre-empt some important private producer interests at home and abroad). While sounding enough like the reformist, peaceful-change-within-the-system policies of the gradualist, these demands are essentially revolutionary in their effect in that they presuppose a dedication to interests which deny the essential interests and power of the prevailing elites.

It becomes understandable, then, why appeals to reason and good will do not bring reforms: quite simply, the problem of change is no easier for the haves than for the have-nots. Contrary to the admonitions of liberal critics, it is neither stupidity nor opaqueness which prevents those who own and control the property and the institutions of this society from satisfying the demand for change. To be sure, the established elites suffer from their share of self-righteous stubbornness, but more often than not, meaningful changes are not embarked upon because they would literally undercut the security and survival of privileged interests, and it is in the nature of social elites that they show little inclination to commit class suicide.

In the early stages of particular social conflicts neither the haves nor the have-nots are fully appreciative of the systematic contradictions and limited options they face. An "Upward Bound" plan here, a "Head Start" program there, and an outpouring of rhetoric everywhere—such are the responses of the ruling interests, believing as they do that an abundance of symbolic outputs should sufficiently placate the malcontents. America was not built in a day, they remind us, and only time and patience will—through unspecified means—rectify our "remaining" social ills.

At the onset, protestors operate under somewhat similar assumptions about the basic viability of the system. There are "pockets" of poverty, "discrimination" against blacks and a "senseless" war in Southeast Asia: social problems are seen as aberrant offshoots of a basically good, if not great, society, rather than as endemic manifestations of the prevailing forms of social privilege, power, and property. The first soundings of dissent are accompanied by anticipations of change. There is often a kind of exhilaration when people, finally moved by that combination of anger and hope which is the stuff of protest, take to the streets: the handclapping, slogan shouting, the signs, the crowd are all encouraging evidence that many others share one's grievances. But, as time passes, as the symbolic dramatizations of protest produce little more than the symbolic responses of politicians (along with the free-swinging clubs, mace, tear gas, and guns of the police) dissent begins to escalate in tactics—from petitioning one's congressman to marching in the streets to "trashing" stores to the burning and bombing of draft boards, banks, and corporation offices, to sporadic armed encounters.

Just as significantly, dissent begins to escalate in the scope and level of its indictment. Increasingly convinced that the political system is not endowed with the responsible, responsive, creative, and inclusive virtues its supporters ascribe to it, dissenters begin to shift from incrementalist pleas to challenges against the fundamental legitimacy of the established economic and political elites. There is evidence of a growing militancy among deprived racial minorities, of a consciousness which begins with pleas for equal treatment in the ongoing society and soon evolves into a sweeping condemnation of white America's "power structure." A visible number of blacks, Mexican-Americans, Puerto Ricans, Indians, Orientals, and others have made the journey from civil rights "moderation" to radical militancy, from Thurgood Marshall and Roy Wilkins to Malcolm X and Eldridge Cleaver.

The white student movement has undergone similar transitions in both tactics and ideology. Many of those who pleaded for a cessation of the bombing of North Vietnam in 1966 were urging that we "bring the war home" in 1970; the V-sign of peace has been replaced by the clenched fist of resistance; "staying clean with Gene" has less appeal today than more direct and more radical forms of action. And in May 1970, the sporadic peace parades were replaced by a national student strike, the first of its kind in American history, affecting over 400 college campuses and at least an equal number of high schools.

Even among those who are described as "the silent majority" one finds some signs of a leftward discontent. White workers suffering the deprivations of their class as laborers, taxpayers, and consumers have experienced the contagion of protest. More often than not, the experiences of their own oppression are expressed in resentment toward "pampered" and "subversive" students and an almost obsessive animosity toward blacks who are seen as "getting everything" while they, themselves, must bear the costs. Yet there are indications that this picture is oversimplified. Labor has not reacted toward the protestors with one voice. The Vietnam War, the tax burden, inflation, and other such things could not be blamed on students and blacks. Discontent with "the establishment" can be found among small but growing numbers of working whites, and there is clear indication that important elements in the labor movement, especially in the ALA, look upon the national student strike and upon student militancy in general with something other than disfavor. There are indications, in places like Detroit with its "Black-Polish Alliance" and Chicago with its "Unity Coalition," that blacks and whites are beginning to join forces in protest action.[15] With increasing frequency students have been moving off campus, both individually and in organized moves, to join picket lines and to draw bonds of common action and interest with workers. Meanwhile, there has begun to emerge among the more literate segments of professional, middle-class America a spirit of protest which began as an anti-war expression and has since become an indictment against the whole quality of life in America. Finally, one should not overlook the increasingly widespread problems of morale and disaffection found in that most crucial of all power institutions, the U.S. Army, problems which, if they continue at the present rate, may have real revolutionary potential.

Yet neither should we overestimate the potential strength of radical protest nor underestimate the coercive, repressive, and pre-emptive capacities of the established politico-economic powers. From election laws to property laws, from city hall to federal bureaucracy, from taxation to welfare, government helps those who can best help themselves and this does not mean those wanting and needing fundamental changes in the class structure and in the ways in which the wealth of this nation is produced, distributed, controlled, and used. To deal with the protestors, the elites still have a variety of symbolic outputs as close at hand as the next election or the next press conference. Along with this they have the ability to discredit, obfuscate, delay, and "study" (what Richard Neustadt calls the "almost unlimited resources of the enormous power of sitting still").[16] Furthermore, elites are rarely hesitant to use the systemic rewards and punishments, the jobs, wealth, and institutions they control for the purpose of encouraging political conformity. And should all else fail, they have at their command that most decisive of political resources—the one the pluralists rarely talk about—the forces of obedient and violent repression: the clubbing, gassing, beating, shooting, arresting, imprisoning, rampaging forces of "law and order."

In sum, it is no longer a certainty that we will be able to solve our social ills by working with the same operational values and within the same systematic structures that have helped to create them. It does seem that we have seldom appreciated the extent to which the political system responds to, and indeed, represents, the dominant interests of the socio-economic system, and also how frequently political structures are simply bypassed by a corporate economy which significantly shapes the quality of our lives while in most respects remaining answerable to no one. A more realistic notion of how power is allocated and used in the United States should leave us less sanguine about the possibilities for political change. As of now we have no reason to hope that the "guardians of the public trust" will stop behaving like the servants of the dominant private interests, and no reason to presume that our political institutions will prove viable in treating the immense problems of this unhappy society.

Protest of a radical or potentially radical nature has arisen in a great many sectors of the American public. But the growth in protest has not brought forth a commensurate move toward needed changes from the powers that be, and the reason for this unresponsiveness, I have suggested, lies not in the technical nature of the problems but in the political nature of the conflicting interests, specifically in *the inability of the dominant politico-economic elites to satisfy the demands for structural changes while maximizing and maintaining their own interests*. Radical protest, then, is both a cause of and a response to the increasingly evident contradictions of the social system. Given the "Three R's" of politics—reform, repression, and revolution—it can no longer be taken as an article of faith that we are moving toward the first.

Notes

1. See Harry M. Caudill, *Night Comes to the Cumberlands* (Boston: Little, Brown, 1962), for the best recent study of Appalachia.

2. Murray Edelman, *The Symbolic Uses of Politics* (Urbana, Ill.: University of Illinois Press, 1964), offers a most provocative discussion of the ritualistic and control functions of political acts.

3. Clark's testimony is quoted in the *Report of the National Advisory Commission on Civil Disorders* (The Kerner Report) (New York: Bantam Books, 1968), p. 29.

4. See Andrew Kopkind's excellent critique of The Kerner Commission "White on Black: The Riot Commission and the Rhetoric of Reform," *Hard Times*, 44, September 15–22, 1969, pp. 1–4.

5. See Grant McConnell, *Private Power and American Democracy* (New York: Alfred A. Knopf, 1966), for a good discussion of the public powers of private interest groups.

6. For two studies of the ways local political parties work to defeat and exclude the dissident poor, see Philip Meranto, "Black Majorities and Political

Power: The Defeat of an All-Black Ticket in East St. Louis," in Herbert Hill (ed.), *The Revolt of the Powerless* (New York: Random House, 1970), and Michael Parenti, "Power and Pluralism, A View from the Bottom," in Marvin Surkin and Alan Wolfe (eds.), *The Caucus Papers* (New York: Basic Books, 1970).

7. Michael Parenti, *The Anti-Communist Impulse* (New York: Random House, 1969), p. 101.

8. Many of the rail lines built were overextended and of dubious use to American communities, but pecuniary gain rather than public service was the primary consideration. See Matthew Josephson, *The Robber Barons* (New York: Harcourt, Brace & World, 1934), pp. 306–307.

9. At least one American historian, in a very brief study, does note how the New Deal serviced the corporate owning class while devoting its best rhetoric to the common man: see Paul K. Conkin, *The New Deal* (New York: Thos. Y. Crowell, 1967). See Gabriel Kolko, *Wealth and Power in America* (New York: Frederick Praeger, 1962), pp. 30ff. for a discussion of New Deal taxation policy.

10. Matthew Josephson, *The Politicos, 1865–1896* (New York: Harcourt, Brace, & World, 1938), pp. 8–9.

11. Ibid., p. v.

12. See Edelman, *The Symbolic Uses of Politics,* for the best discussion of these components of the political system.

13. See Donald R. Matthews, *U.S. Senators and Their World* (Chapel Hill: University of North Carolina Press, 1960). For a discussion of how protest organizations and left-wing parties become co-opted into established parliamentary system, see Ralph Miliband, *The State in Capitalist Society* (New York: Basic Books, 1969), chap. 7.

14. This is a common enough occurrence in local politics but also not unknown at the national level where the symbolic appearances developed during the campaign soon collide with the substantive interests of the powers that be. Within four years, the American people elected two presidents who promised to end the Vietnam War and who, once in office, continued to pursue that conflict with full force.

15. See William Greider, "Poles, Blacks Join Forces in Detroit," *Chicago Sun-Times,* October 12, 1969, p. 10.

16. Richard Neustadt, *Presidential Power* (New York: John Wiley, 1960), p. 42.

20.
ON POLITICAL BELIEF: THE GRIEVANCES OF THE POOR

Lewis Lipsitz

When men are politically silent, what should we make of it? Perhaps it indicates a sort of satisfaction: the gourmet's quiet, his mouth full of life's peach flambée. Or perhaps the silence of some men tempts us to consider them politically irrelevant: misplaced IBM cards that don't show up in any of the totals. Or perhaps we should conclude that those who are silent are too transfixed, confused, ignorant, busy, tormented, or afraid, to know what to say or how to say it—stutterers who cannot get the first word out; people ducking into an alley away from the police; moviegoers who have lost their breath.

Whether we intend to or not, we have to deal with those who are politically silent, even if we do so only through our failure to consider them. When we confine a study of foreign policy making to a discussion of elite decisions, we have probably made the implicit judgment that on these matters the mass of men are usually silent followers. But we have also learned that silence is not necessarily a lifetime occupation. We have learned that when a society evidences a "domestic tranquillity," the "domestics" may not really be tranquil.[1] Protest may suddenly emerge where before there was only acquiescence, fear, and inner conflict. Then rage, envy, and repression may flourish where before there was only deference and orderliness. We have learned that there are dangers and possibilities in mass politics, as in all politics.

Some writers have become preoccupied with the fear of mass

From Lewis Lipsitz, "On Political Beliefs: The Grievances of the Poor," pp. 142–172 in *Power and Community Dissenting Essays in Political Science*, edited by Philip Green and Sanford Levinson. Copyright © 1969, 1970 by Random House, Inc. Reprinted by permission of Pantheon Books, A Division of Random House, Inc.

The author is especially indebted to David Tabb who helped to design the study, carry out the interviews and interpret the findings. I also wish to thank the Social Science Research Council for the initial grant that made this work possible; the Political Science Department of the University of North Carolina for its assistance along the way, Richard Hamilton of the University of Wisconsin for his helpful criticism, and Skip McGaughey who put in the time.

politics—the vision of previously silent people barging into the political arena, threatening civil liberties, supporting demagogues, and scapegoating. Such anxieties have commonly inhibited the perspectives of political scientists when they come to grips with the significance of political silence. But other writers have argued that mass movements hold out a democratic promise: changing society's agenda; creating new leaders; shaping articulate voices from the explosive and hesitant cries of the powerless. In any particular situation, writers disagree about the degree of danger and promise involved when people once silent begin to take on the burden of speech.

For those interested in the meaning and functioning of "democracy," political silence has to be an important concern. Democracy ought to have some connection with men's needs and desires—and that includes all men, whether they are politically articulate or not. We have seen theories elaborated which praise mass apathy or indifference, but even such defenses of democracy have to be understood with reference to a political system meeting the needs of the many and hopefully of all. The hidden assumption in many of these "theories" is that the kind of political arrangements we now have actually *do* meet the needs of the many—though the nature of these needs and their satisfaction is rarely brought up.

We have to decide about political silence. If we can understand it, we can gain a perspective on our society. It is important to know if the quiet we often hear is the sound of the gourmet or the stutterer, the hum of other enterprises, the muteness of the inchoate, or some combination of these. We have to grasp the nature of the political ideologies of ordinary people, or the nature of the absence of such ideologies. We have to see how people focus or fail to focus on "politics" in the usual sense, and how this is related to the rest of their life situation. A man may, for example, feel deep grievances about his position in life and yet be unable to connect such grievances with any social criticism, even of the most conventional sort. Perhaps this makes sense; perhaps his grievances are purely personal; perhaps not. A man may not be able to speak about politics in the ideological terms usual in his day, but the political significance of his grievances or opinions may be considerable, at least from the point of view of democratic theory. A man may be able to tell you that the shoe pinches but may have a difficult time figuring out exactly where and why, how things got that way, how the pinching is related to the structure of the shoe, and what he can do about it.

Marx, Burke, and Mass Ideology

The very events and vicissitudes of the struggle against capital, the defeats even more than the victories, could not help bringing home to men's minds the insufficiency of their favorite nostrums and preparing the way for a more complete insight into the true conditions of working-class emancipation.
—Friedrich Engels, 1888

The occupation of a hairdresser, or of a working tallow-chandler, cannot be a matter of honour to any person. . . .

Such descriptions of men ought not to suffer oppression from
the state; but the state suffers oppression, if such as they, either
individually or collectively, are permitted to rule.

—Edmund Burke, 1790

Marx and Burke present us with radically conflicting views about
the nature of mass belief systems. If we have a look at these opposed analyses,
it will help us understand more recent conclusions about mass publics and
also help us to gain some perspective on the general question of the connection between ideology and grievances. We might characterize Burke's
analysis as emphasizing the statics of "prejudice," while Marx is concerned
with the dynamics of grievance. Burke is obsessed with authority structures
and historical continuities. C. Wright Mills said about himself that he
worried "with" the Cuban Revolution, not "about" it; so, fundamentally,
Burke worried "with" the established institutions of his time, not "about"
them. For Marx, the legitimacy of existing institutions is a temporary
phenomenon, and revolutionary discontinuity is characteristic of Western
historical development.

Marx and Burke agree, however, on the enormous role of the past
in shaping men's perception of the present and future. When Marx says
in the *Eighteenth Brumaire*, "The tradition of all the dead generations
weighs like a nightmare on the brain of the living," he is referring to a
process that Burke recognized and elaborated upon. But Burke saw not the
past's nightmarish "weight," but rather the "weightness" of inheritance.
Reflecting on the French Revolution, Burke asserts triumphantly of the
English: "We fear God; we look up with awe to kings; with affection to
parliaments; with duty to magistrates; with reverence to priests; and with
respect to nobility."[2] Burke goes on to explain that the mass of the British
are what he calls "men of untaught feeling." They are the sort who "instead
of casting away all . . . old prejudices, . . . cherish them to very considerable degree, and, to take more shame . . . cherish them because they are
prejudices." Burke argues repeatedly for the importance of such "prejudices," including as they do the ordinary man's relationships to those in
authority. For Burke, as for many conservatives, man is a religious animal,
needing such prejudices, habits, unconscious affiliations, to help him deal
with his own feelings and to orient himself in an otherwise confusing and
embittering world. Speaking of the philosophers of reason who would
destroy the French monarchy, Burke talks of the need for illusion: "But
now all is to be changed. All the pleasing illusions, which made power
gentle, and obedience liberal, which harmonized the different shades of life,
and which, by a bland assimilation, incorporated into politics the sentiments
which beautify and soften private society, are to be dissolved by this new
conquering empire of light and reason. All the decent drapery of life is to
be rudely torn off. . . . On this scheme of things, a king is but a man. . . ."

What then is the nature of mass belief systems, according to
Burke? Under a settled constitution, the mass of men will tend to private

affairs, deferring to their betters in political matters. They will exhibit a tenacious attachment to established procedures, rituals, and authorities—and never raise fundamental questions about the legitimacy of a regime. Government does not derive from the consent of the governed, in any conscious, articulated sense, but maintains its solidity through behavioral inertia and successful socialization plus that modicum of ameliorative governmental remedies clearly required by considerations of prudence. Ideology, from Burke's point of view, is alien to the normal condition of most men. It is true that partisan questions must come up in political life, but the mass public will rarely have a part or want to have a part in such quarrels. The mass of men, then, accept their place in the scheme of things, and together with this fundamental acquiescence accept the places assigned to others. The emphasis in Burkean politics must fall upon ritual and proper procedure, rather than upon mass organization and struggle.

Reading such a discussion of mass beliefs, Marx might say to us: "The demand to give up the illusions about its condition is the demand to give up a condition which needs illusions." He is speaking here of religion and the social conditions which he believes give rise to it and which it helps to perpetuate. The Marxist critique of religion would apply equally to the other "decent drapery of life" so significant for Burke. All of these "illusions" share religion's "ideological" quality, serving to mask from men the real nature of their condition as historical actors. Marx's expectation is that systemic contradictions within the capitalistic political economy will slowly awaken the working class from the "nightmare" of the past. Workers will begin by experiencing their grievances separately, each worker within the chamber of his individual life. But the factory system will provide a communal context for these grievances. Slowly the workers will become enlightened, connecting personal grievances with group grievances, group grievances with social concerns, and social concerns with a scientific knowledge of social change. At each step, the workers will gain subtlety in their appreciation of the connection between their personal conditions, the condition of their fellows, and the nature of the system in which they play a part. Their grievances then acquire a dynamic quality, leading them on in a problem-solving manner into social struggle and organization building. The worker class becomes the agency of its own liberation because ordinary men and women have acquired a nose for reality, a clear-sighted and determined appreciation of the "true conditions for working-class emancipation." Marx's discussion of the Paris Commune shows his expectation that once in power, the workers would continue to exhibit the problem-solving scientific orientation they developed in the struggle. The workers are men who can dispense with illusions because they are dealing with the real problems of life from a historical perspective they have successfully internalized.

It is possible to overdo Marx's ideas about the democratization of history making. I am not asserting that Marx regarded leadership as unnecessary or dangerous, though he certainly seemed to credit leaders with a somewhat different significance in different writings. He clearly thought that some form of ideological and organizational leadership was essential to building a mass movement. Leaders help to define issues, structure priorities, and plan strategy. What Marx does emphasize, however, is that history making involves mass action and mass enlightenment. It involves struggles which grow more or less naturally out of the grievances of the mass of men. To paraphrase Burke, for Marx "a leader is but a man," yet one who can articulate mass grievances.

A Marxist explanation of political silence then would coincide in large part with Burke's ideas of "prejudice" but would see this inertia as a victimization of men. In the Marxist vision, ordinary people are capable not only of understanding social conditions, but, at the appropriate time, of participating in altering them decisively. If, for a time, most men are silent, this is because they have grown numb to the pinching of their shoes and cannot imagine any better fit. For Marx, man is a religious animal only for the time being; as a species he remains capable of becoming critic, organizational activist, and social theorist.

For Marx, once men see that no divine sanction infuses the social order, they begin to free themselves from idolatry. Social life then is essentially a world of practical questions. For Burke, however, the issue of rebellion is an unnatural one, since where institutions are held to be sacred, all the answers have already been provided. Burke's analysis would lead us to believe that most men will lack broad political ideas except customary "prejudices" and those notions supporting the legitimacy of the regime. They will not bring an independent, critical perspective to bear on the existing order. Their knowledge will be limited to matters immediately connected with their own little "platoon," and their interests will be similarly limited. Marx, on the other hand, foresees the development of a coherent political perspective that connects those grievances close to home with a system-level analysis. In the Marxist world, the leaders and the masses will increasingly share a common perspective; in the Burkean world, many of the concerns of the political elite will be remote from the day-to-day ideas of the mass of men.

Some Contemporary Political Science Ideas About Mass Beliefs

Robert Lane told us that the "common men" of Eastport lacked a utopian vision, a well-defined sense of justice that would provide them with a conscious and powerful instrument for scrutiny of their social order.[3] Jack Walker then argued that these men "share this disability with much of the American academic elite."[4] But perhaps Walker accepted Lane's testimony about the common man too readily; after all, the terms of the argument are rather vague—can't a man have a sense of grievance, if not a conception of justice? a few hopes, if not a utopian vision? When do we pass from one into the other? Walker's own critique of what he named "the elitist theory of democracy" called attention to mass-based movements of social protest. The very existence of such movements must testify to the presence of some grievances and some hopes, however ill-defined. Clearly, not all of the common men are deeply satisfied with the existing order, though they may have considerable difficulty articulating their criticisms.

Yet Lane's picture of the "ideology" of America's common men has much that is persuasive about it. It helps to explain what seems to be the relative "conservatism" of most working-class Americans. Discussing the fear of equality Lane tells us, "Lower-status people generally find it less punishing to think of themselves as correctly placed by a just society than to think of themselves as exploited or victimized by an unjust society." Such a generalization explains a great deal: a lack of interest in ideology; hostility toward the "left"; sensitivity to status concerns; a lack of political activism. This helps us understand why the American working class has been called the "least revolutionary proletariat in the world." But perhaps such a generalization, vague as it is, tells us too much—like a TAT picture into which we project our own inner lives. Perhaps it was not only that Lane's analysis was persuasive, but that it seemed to suit the temper of the times, that it was a convenient sort of analysis to believe. It implied that the world was probably about as acceptable as it could be and that ordinary men, sensibly enough, accepted it.

Stretching things a bit, we can see in Lane's analysis a sort of liberal Burkeanism. His study of the ideology of the common man, broad-gauge and deep as it was, failed to focus on the grievances these men felt. It emphasized instead how fully they had accepted both their own place in the social system and the workings of that system itself. It showed how nonideological they were (in the normal, more specialized sense of "ideological"). They, like Burke's common men, were guided by "prejudice," not grievance.

Lane interviewed 15 men, and these were all white, New Haven residents—the time was the late 1950s. Accepting what Lane describes, we can still see his conclusions as valid only for white Connecticut residents who are upper working class. Yet, the nonideological quality Lane found is to be found again in the American electorate as a whole. It is the conclusion of Philip Converse that the vast majority of American voters do not have any cohesive "ideology" that guides their views on the controversial social issues of the day.[5] Converse finds that only a small fraction of Americans can speak substantively about the meaning of a "liberal-conservative" dimension in relation to political parties. The best most voters can do is to discuss parties in terms of the social groups these parties supposedly favor. Converse also finds that individual views on specific issues appear to vary widely over time, indicating the lack of personally coherent political perspectives. The picture Converse conveys of the nature of mass belief systems is this: a sharp divorce between the ideological conflicts among elites and the vague, nonspecific, contradictory views of the mass public.

Between these two, Converse suggests the presence of issue publics, attuned to questions in some specific area.

Converse draws sensible and sobering conclusions from the American survey data of the 1950s, on which his analysis is based. Yet the article has a startlingly unreal quality about it. He seems to be describing to us a mass public that has few issue-related views except perhaps on matters concerning race. We get the image of people with certain traditional "prejudices" (such as an inherited party affiliation), but with little evidence of political grievances, opinions, or perspectives. This public orients itself in terms of its "prejudices" and for the rest appears to change its mind from time to time about "controversial" questions. No doubt, there is much truth in this image, perhaps particularly as drawn from the America of the 1950s. Yet it leaves us with too vacant a picture of the nonviews of the mass public. Most Americans may not evidence ideological "constraint" of the sort Converse is looking for; yet at the same time, they may harbor serious grievances and hopes which they may or may not be able to relate to politics. The lack of constraint in the beliefs of the mass public requires some explanation: is it that most people know very little; that they care very little; that they care, but don't understand; that they hold a good many views but don't make them cohesive; that there are underlying perspectives that individuals have trouble relating to the political system—exactly what? Are most people really "silent"—that is, without serious political grievances? Lane tacitly maintains that this is so, and it appears that Converse has only documented it more broadly, if in less depth.

Looking at Some of the Political Grievances of the Poor

If we turn to the American poor, then, what would we expect to find? We encounter here the least educated, least knowledgeable, and probably the most politically apathetic segment of the population. We would expect, then, to find an absence of ideological constraint, a vagueness about politics, a failure to see that politics are personally relevant, a skepticism, and a feeling of futility. Other studies have given us strong indications of these things. Yet, in the general silence of the American poor, a few voices have made themselves heard. We have seen some of the poor mobilized for political goals. We have seen some poor people gaining a bit of political sophistication. And we have, if we are honest, been educated by them. Political silence, then, is sometimes a relative matter, sometimes a temporary matter—related to the circumstances in which people find themselves and the way in which they comprehend those circumstances.

But how ideological or nonideological are the poor? Would Converse's generalization hold with them, or must we make some revisions? Let me examine these questions in the context of a study of poor whites and poor Negroes in a southern city; a survey made in the mid-1960s. This survey attempted to combine some of the features of Lane's depth-interviewing with more typical survey styles. Each of the 82 men (53 white, 29 black) who were selected by street address, randomly, from a low-income census tract, completed a three- to four-hour interview, much of which was open-ended. This kind of interview cannot make any pretense of obtaining real "depth"—it is mostly "breadth," rather, that is achieved.

To begin with, we find among these men the same absence of meaning in the liberal-conservative dimension that Converse shows in the American population as a whole. Eighty-six percent of the men could say nothing about this dimension at all in relation to the political parties; and of the other 14 percent, a good many had only a vague notion. One of the most articulate men saw the liberal-conservative dimension in primarily racial terms. "Conservative is to me just another word for not liking somebody. Talking about clinging to the old ways. That's what makes me mad. They cling to the old ways. The race thing is the only thing they want to cling to the old ways on. They're modernizing everything else. So if you're conservative, to me you're prejudiced." We have to be a bit cautious here, since at the same time that we find this absence of an ideological perception of the parties, we also find that 35 percent of the men would like to see a new political party get started, and of this 35 percent, most favor a party oriented toward labor and the poor.[6] On the question of a socialist or labor party, most of the men feel such a party would be more in touch with the need for better jobs and wages. One man brings a comparative perspective to bear: "It would be interesting to see a Labor Party like in England. They have a Labor Party over there and they seem to be doing fairly well. I always wondered how it would work here in America." Not all the men who are interested in a "labor" party emphasize economics, however. Consider the following exchange between interviewer and respondent:

> —Well, socialists wouldn't be too bad if they would get the right man in head there.
> —Why?
> —Well, they'd be more equal about some of the things they do there. Any damn thing would be a change to beat what's there.
> —What would a socialist President do that Johnson wouldn't?
> —Well, if he was gonna fight a country he'd fight it and if he wasn't gonna fight it he wouldn't. He'd more equalize each one than Johnson.

Some of the men explicitly rejected the idea of another party, and a common reason for doing so was that we had enough trouble as it was—another party would just make a bad situation worse.

Yet when we turn to other questions, we find that these men do have political opinions, in many cases fairly specific ones, and are often critical of government action and inaction. Taken as a whole, their views lend support to the idea that poor people do find ways to orient themselves to the political arena and develop points of view which we would expect to be fairly consistent over time. The views outlined below show that many of the American poor are anxious for the government to help them with their own problems and that their concern with their own economic well-being plays a significant role in orienting the poor politically. It may be true to argue, as Converse does, that Americans lack ideological clarity; but where the poor are concerned, we should not mistake this absence of clarity for a total absence of views. Many views are deeply felt; many grievances grow out of personal life and affect men's politics. Lacking a way of talking about the liberalism and conservatism of the political parties, a man may still think he smells something rotten in the state and (rightly or wrongly) be able angrily to point his finger at what he means.

To begin with, we find that these men show a hostility toward spending money on space exploration and foreign aid.

TABLE 1
Opinions Concerning Space Programs and Foreign Aid

	Space		Foreign aid	
	Percent	N	Percent	N
Favor and in-between	15	(12)	45	(37)
Oppose	75	(62)	50	(41)
Don't know	10	(8)	5	(4)

In both cases, a majority of the critics felt that there were better uses for this money here in the United States, and many cited the need to aid the poor. Several men mentioned specific "earthly" uses for these funds: "They should cut down on this mess about trying to beat the Russians to the moon. That is the main thing. It is the most senseless and the most useless thing I've ever heard tell of. That money they spend for that could be putting up a lot more hospitals and housing projects and schooling facilities."

"I think you better take care of your problems right here on earth. Everybody talking about a poverty program, making everybody equal and giving a poor family a fair share and making it better for the children to go to school; better homes for everybody to live in. Where are you going to get all this money from if you keep putting it into rockets and ships and things trying to get to the moon?"

The specificity of these statements is, however, unusual. It was common for opinions to be somewhat vaguer and frequently to emphasize a religious prohibition. For example: "The Lord wanted you up there, he'd have put one up there. I don't see no point in shooting to the moon. The Lord put that moon up there to stay. I don't think man should play with the moon and the sun. The Lord put that there to give us a little light at night."

The tendency to emphasize welfare issues is shown again in the responses to the question, Do you think the government in Washington spends too much money or not enough money? A majority of the men say "too much." But what is perhaps more important is that almost 80 percent of those who say "too much" specify that it is space expenditures, foreign aid, and Vietnam and military spending that should be cut. Of those who say the government does not spend enough, over 90 percent call for more government spending in nondefense areas, such as aid to the poor, housing, food, and education.[7]

TABLE 2
Does Government Spend Too Much, Not Enough,
Or About Right?

	Percent	N
Too much	52	(43)
Too much on some, too little on others	12	(10)
Not enough	12	(10)
About right	6	(5)
Don't know	17	(14)

TABLE 3
What Does Government Spend Too Much Or Not Enough On?

On What?	Too much*		Not enough*	
	Percent	N	Percent	N
Space, foreign aid, military	79	(41)	5	(1)
Domestic welfare state programs	0	0	95	(18)
Miscellaneous (e.g., highways)	21	(11)	0	

* The numbers in each column include responses from people who offered various responses as categorized in Table 2. For example, the "too much" column in Table 3 includes people from "Too much on some," and so on.

These sorts of inclinations find expression in another way. The men were asked which of three items was most important for good government:[8]

TABLE 4
Most Important for Good Government

	Percent Saying	N
Enough jobs to go around	48	39
Freedom of speech	36	30
A powerful army, navy, and air force	12	10
Don't know	4	3

On another set of three alternatives, there was a similar pattern of choices:[9]

TABLE 5
Most Important for Good Government

	Percent Saying	N
Equal treatment for all	60	49
Fighting communism	17	14
Lots of aid to the poor	15	12
Don't know	8	7

Questions of equality and employment are foremost, with military and anti-Communist options chosen by relatively few. This appears in accord with the previous findings which show the "domestic" politics, bread-and-butter orientation of the poor.[10]

Many of the men brought the Vietnam War up spontaneously during their interviews, emphasizing that they felt the cost of the war was hurting the chances for aid to those who need it at home. One man makes this point very emphatically:

> The only way to help the poor man is to get out of that war, in Vietnam. They're spending so much money the poor man—I mean—like social security—that goes up all the time. I don't mind paying social security if the old people going to get it. 'Cause some day I might be old. These taxes—high taxes—it's going over yonder to kill people with and I don't see no cause in it.

Another man can't understand why America can't end the war after having invested so much in powerful armaments.

> . . . And another thing I can't understand is this war in Vietnam. They send billions and billions of dollars for missiles and atomic warfare and stuff like that and now this war's going on there for a right good while and I read in the paper how many Americans have been killed. I can't see no use in that if they're going to have this war and spend money for these things and have that kinda power if they're not gonna use it. . . .

Here we see an implicit connection established between a concern with the government's wasting money and a desire for an escalation of the war.

But we can approach the question of grievance in another fashion: by asking people about the problems of daily life and finding out how they think government might relate to these problems. We went about this in two ways. First, we asked a set of questions about matters such as rent, prices, and interest rates that we thought might concern poor people. Second, we asked people what they found to be their biggest personal problem. In both cases, we then followed up by trying to find out if the person saw any role for the government in helping him to deal with what he perceived as a problem.

It turns out that most of the people we spoke to felt, first, that there were things they needed day-to-day but couldn't afford; second, that things cost too much these days; and third (for that half of the sample which had borrowed money), that interest rates were too high. Asked about their biggest personal problem, approximately 75 percent spoke of troubles that would come under the heading of health, money, education, and housing. Twenty percent said they had no big problems, and a few simply didn't know.

While 96 percent of the sample say that things cost too much these days, 77 percent say they favor governmental price controls (20 percent don't know). When asked whether the government should help them with things they can't afford, 75 percent (of those who say they need things they can't afford) say yes. On the question of interest rates, 94 percent of those who have had to make a loan feel that the government should help people like themselves borrow money. (And 76 percent of these people feel that interest rates are not fair.)

On the question of personal problems, 32 percent feel they are already receiving some assistance from the government, and all are able to specify what that assistance is.[11] Less than half, however, feel that the government is helping them enough, and most of those who complain can particularize their demand for additional aid. When we turn to those individuals who say that the government is not helping them with their biggest personal problem, 61 percent feel that it ought to be helping, and many of these people can spell out what sort of help they mean.

Speaking about their personal problems and the government's relationship to those problems, these men show four tendencies. First, many call openly and explicitly for government assistance and, in addition, make specific recommendations. One man, who states that he needs milk and meat and other proper food for his family (instead of dry beans), responds in the following way to a question about whether the government is helping him now:

> —I don't see where it helps—they taking money away from us.
> —Why don't they help?
> —They just ain't worried about the man. I mean the average man. The men up in Congress and all, they got money. They know their family going to eat. . . .
> —Should the government help?
> —I think they ought to . . . they ought to have a store, some kind of store where clothes is not as high as they are in other places . . . I think they ought to have stores set aside for a man with a certain income . . . when you file your income tax, if your income is so low, they send you like an ID card and you go in that store, that grocery store, and buy foods. . . . Have stores in each town set up and let you buy your food, clothes, maybe a man could make it.

Other men have other remedies to suggest, which focus on increasing present benefits and services and instituting controls on costly items. A second tendency is ambivalence in regard to government assistance: some men seem to want additional help but cannot bring themselves actually to ask for it or demand it. Complaining that he has trouble buying medicine and food, one man says the government ought to let him draw more money.

> —Does the government help in this way now?
> —Yes, they help some.
> —What do they do?
> —Well, they give me $71 and something or other, or somebody's giving it to me. Anyway, it comes.
> —Do you think anything else should be done?
> —I wouldn't say that, because the government is spending a lot of money now, and I tell you I can make out with what I'm getting but I would *love* to have more. But if it's going to end with the war, or end with—I wouldn't want to—in fact, the more you give people, the more they want. But I'm talking about people who need it and just aren't able to work. . . .

A third pattern might best be called bewildered resignation. For example:

> —Does the government help with your personal problems?
> —No.
> —Why not?
> —I don't know. I guess they go down the line, and I'm at the bottom of the line.

The expression of ignorance about why the government fails to provide help or to take proper action is extremely common. When pressed on the question of why the government does not do what they would like it to do, very few of the men can even begin to provide an answer. One man, who begins by endorsing what the government is doing, concludes with an unusually open expression of personal bewilderment:

> Oh, they going to provide better jobs. There ain't no use to even get in an argument in politics about that. 'Cause the government is doing a good job as it is. I don't see a thing wrong with the way government is doing things. The government is set up all right. They're doing a good job and everything. But there could be a lot of changes made which there should be changes made. The onliest way they'll get this world out is to change things. But I don't know what to tell 'em to change 'cause I don't know. I don't know what the trouble is and I don't know what the set-up is.

A few men argue against government assistance with their personal problems or feel that the government is already providing enough help. Drawing on a metaphor of moccasined individualism, one man maintains:

> I believe in each man carrying his own canoe.

We approached the question of grievance in another fashion—this time more abstractly, by asking questions about America and the American government. We wanted to see if poor people saw the government as benevolent or malevolent; if they saw the society as free or oppressive. Beyond these questions of mood, we wanted to see if people could speak in specifics, to what degree they could particularize their grievances. The results are set out in the tables below.

Sometimes people say this is a "free country." Does that mean anything to you?

	Percent	
Yes, free country	45	(The major meaning assigned to freedom was in personal terms—"doing what you want to do." A very few people mentioned religious freedom and equal rights.)
No, not free	44	(The answers here included nine different meanings. The major ones were: discrimination against Negroes; the cost of things and taxes; government regulation; the powerlessness of the poor; foreign involvements, and forcing integration. A plurality of responses focused on racial questions.)
Don't Know	11	

The question about "freedom" often evoked easily understandable responses, such as the one from a man who argued this way:

> There's not but two free people in this country, and that's a Negro woman and a white man . . . because a Negro woman can go anywhere she pleases and so can a white man. A white woman cannot go in the colored neighborhood . . . and a Negro man better not be caught in a white neighborhood.

But in many cases, responses seemed to refer to deeply felt but unfocused feelings—whether of anger or relief.

> If this is my home, I can go in and out. There are some places where you don't have the privilege of going out at night. If they tell you to go in you have to.
> It's free to a certain extent and then it's not. . . . There's a lot of ways it's not free. You about pay your way for everything

> you do. . . . You gotta right to go when you want to and do
> what you want to as long as you don't break the law. But there
> are a lot of laws. You can't hardly go down the street that you
> don't break a law.

Such statements are hard to interpret. Behind them, perhaps, stands a fear
of powerlessness, a sense that the world is beyond one's control. The
privilege of going in and out of one's house can mean a great deal to someone who feels excluded from most aspects of a society's life. It is also probably worth noting the association of "freedom" with the idea of paying-your-
way. This severe limitation on "freedom," as the poor experience it, finds
more complete expression in another man's response to this question:

> . . . you can't ever go out here and work and make a living.
> You got to pay taxes on what salary you make. That's buying
> your job. . . . Your food's taxed. You got to pay the grocery
> man's price and a tax on top of that . . . the water that God
> made for everybody—you got to pay for that. You can't even
> go fishing or hunting—you got to have a license. . . .

Now some people say that the government in Washington mostly takes away
people's freedom, but others say that the government helps to make people
free. How do do you feel about it? (People were allowed to choose both
responses if they wanted to.)

Percent

Takes away freedom	45	(Most responses focus on government regulation and forcing racial contact. But others include the draft, laws favoring the rich, and the role of police.)
Helps freedom	58	(Again a plurality of the responses assign meaning in terms of race—in this case, the government promoting integration and upholding rights; other responses cite help for the poor, the need for laws and regulations, and protection provided by the military.)

Do you feel the government ever really hurts (helps) the
ordinary person these days?

Percent

Hurts, yes	64	(There are three main specifics here: the government's failure to do enough for the ordinary man, high prices, and taxes—the last being most common.)
Helps, yes	72	(Nine different specific areas are mentioned: social security, welfare, housing, poverty programs, highways, mental-health programs, civil-

rights laws, education, government jobs. A
majority mention as "help" something in the
social security-welfare-housing category.)[12]

Many of those who agree that the government does supply some
help to the ordinary man maintain there is more it could be doing. The
following quotes are from men all of whom thought that the government
did help already:

> . . . I drew $54 social security and I drawed $27 welfare
> and health.
> —Are there other ways the government could help?
> —Well, I look at it this way—if every man in America I'd say
> 73 years old or the ones at the proper age—I think if he drawed
> $100 a month I don't think it would be too much.
> . . . the country's in such a shape. The only way to help the
> poor man is to get out of that war in Vietnam. They're spend-
> ing so much money, the poor man—I mean like social security,
> that goes up all the time. . . .
> . . . they're too busy spending money on roads and abroad.
> . . . The government is looking out for, shall I say . . .
> they're taking money building up the rich areas, people that
> have the money. And the other, they're sending it to people
> in Europe when they should be keeping some money over here
> to help their own people.

But when we move from a discussion that can focus on grievances
to questions related to particular programs and to linkages between grievances and public action, we see that a considerable number of these people
have not formulated opinions. For example, we saw earlier that more than
90 percent of these men feel day-to-day items cost too much, and more
than 75 percent of them favor price controls. We then asked them why
price controls were not in effect right now. Our expectation here was that
in attempting to explain the absence of a government action they felt was
important, these men would spell out the dynamics of the political system
as they saw it. We might even encounter a certain degree of "ideological"
analysis here. It didn't turn out that way. On the question of why there
weren't price controls, 73 percent couldn't respond at all. A few (7 percent)
argued that price controls were in effect; another 21 percent offered the sort
of answer we expected would be more common—an answer, vague though it
was, that placed blame for unresolved grievance. They said, the leaders don't
try. The same pattern prevailed on other questions about the "why" of
political events. And few of the men could name groups that believed as
they did or opposed their beliefs.[13]

Conclusions

A recent survey finds that poorer Americans (under $5,000) are far
less likely to favor a race to the moon than are wealthier Americans (over

$10,000). The figures are 22 percent compared with 56 percent.[14] This is in accord with what we saw of poor people's attitudes in Durham. Richard Hamilton, in a recent discussion of mass support for "tough" military initiatives, found that poorer people were less likely to favor American involvements in Korea and Vietnam and were more likely to support negotiations and de-escalation.[15] This also finds some support in the Durham interviews.[16] The content of those interviews gives us some idea of why poorer people should react in this fashion. The dominant theme is the sense of being cheated: one's government is not concerned enough with one's well-being; one's government is willing to spend money on what appear to many of these men as frivolous or illegitimate enterprises while it fails to meet their own deeply felt day-to-day needs.

In keeping with this sense of deprivation, we also found a desire among the poor for some sort of assistance from the government, and a series of dissatisfactions with the kind of work the government was engaged in. It is interesting to reflect that Herbert McClosky, in his article "Consensus and Ideology in American Politics,"[17] found that mass attitudes were far more favorable to economic equality than were the attitudes of political elites. Oddly, McClosky took some pains to show the greater agreement on democratic "essentials that existed among political activists as compared with the mass public: essentials such as censorship, procedural due process, academic freedom. McClosky, curiously, chose to ignore in his analysis his own data on economic equality. He refused to allow this set of findings to disturb his conclusions and brushed it off by arguing that economic welfare was not so clearly a component of what democracy meant. But to whom? It was, he argued, a matter of opinion. Yet he failed to acknowledge that censorship, due process, and Fifth Amendment rights were also controversial matters—this was precisely why he had investigated opinion about them.[18] More recently, Form and Rytina[19] have found that poorer people are more likely to support an image of politics in which no one group has predominant power, while wealthier people are more likely to support business dominance. They also find, in keeping with the Durham interviews and many other attitude surveys, that poorer Americans are more likely to favor government involvement in helping the disadvantaged in our society.

Discussions of ideology have frequently overlooked or slighted the obvious preference of poorer Americans for an increased degree of economic well-being. In particular, if we reflect now on the analyses of "ideology" offered by Converse and Lane, we can draw the following conclusions:

1. The particular questions asked and the manner in which they are asked will probably have decisive effects on the findings, particularly among the poorer, less educated respondents. Converse bases his discussion of the lack of ideological "constraint" in the American public on responses to questions administered in survey style and based upon political issues, such as public ownership of utilities, that were of concern to elites at the time.

He is probably right when he questions the reliability of such questions and methods in getting at the concerns of much of the American population.[20] A failure to respond to such questions in a consistent way does not imply, as Converse concludes, that large portions of the electorate do not have meaningful beliefs about politics. We have seen, for example, that within certain limits people can reflect meaningfully on what they expect of government within the context of their own personal problems. One would expect such responses to show considerable consistency over time—depending both on life circumstances and on the strategies of various political groupings.

More specifically, we should acknowledge that poor people have many grievances concerning both what the government does and what it does not do, ranging from taxation to racial integration to space programs and foreign wars. In addition, we should expect that poor people, again within certain limits, will be able to speak meaningfully about what they want to see government do or stop doing.

2. Ideology must be thought of in a manner more subtle than either Lane or Converse allowed for. First, grievances and issues must be distinguished. Significant portions of a population may have grievances without those grievances being shaped into issues by political activists. The reverse is also true: issues which many portions of the population neither understand, nor care much about, may be debated among elites. Beyond this, latent grievances may exist which people are themselves unaware of and which can only be grasped or defined through unusually sensitive interviewing. These latent grievances are important if we are to understand the potentialities of a situation and some of the deeper emotions people feel. Neither Lane nor Converse makes these sorts of distinctions.

Second, politically relevant views have to be distinguished from concepts of how political systems work. A man may have grievances without knowing exactly who his friends and enemies are. The global concept of ideology as a utopian vision or a well-developed sense of justice encompassing a thorough world view should not obscure more common, mundane concerns. Lane's failure to deal with latent grievances, in the absence of what he regarded as a radical ideology, led him to conclude too quickly that because there were no revolutionaries there was also no bitterness.

One way to restructure the concept of ideology is to see it as an expression of concern about the distribution of resources —as the individual sees that distribution.

We would expect constraint among those issues an individual perceives as immediately relevant to himself. Among poor whites, for example, the race issue will be important because these people feel what they experience as the "bite" of equality.

3. The most vaguely developed aspect of poor people's (and most people's) political views is likely to be the area of explanation— why things happen and don't happen; who opposes what and why; how things can be changed. It is in this area that the linkage is made between personal grievances and political action. Without such a link, the grievances may remain inchoate or feebly articulated. This is where mass movements function: setting agendas, ordering priorities, communicating what is possible. Such movements have the most meaning for the creation of democracy where established institutions and parties have not been in touch with the latent sentiments of portions of the population. Such movements also serve as a focus for rage and resentment—such as the civil-rights movement does for many whites.[21]

I have not attempted here a thorough elaboration of the ideology of the poor, either black or white. I have tried to suggest, instead, that the poor have politically meaningful ideas and that it would be easy to miss this when reading some contemporary political science.[22] I have tried, implicitly, to argue for a focus on "grievance" when investigating the political ideas of poor people, rather than accepting the Burkean focus on legitimacy. Such an approach has importance for democratic theory, for it helps us to distinguish among the various "silences"—to differentiate between the bitter and the complacent. It will help us identify more clearly which people feel their needs are not being met and to identify grievances which have not been formulated as issues by political activists. If the political scientist is to be the physician of the body politic, he will first have to remove his own cataracts.

Notes

1. This insightful pun is Howard Zinn's.

2. All quotes are from Burke's *Reflections on the Revolution in France*.

3. Robert E. Lane, *Political Ideology* (New York: The Free Press, 1962), esp. chap. 21.

4. Jack L. Walker, "A Critique of the Elitist Theory of Democracy," *American Political Science Review*, LX (June 1966), pp. 285–95.

5. Philip E. Converse, "The Nature of Belief Systems in Mass Publics," in David E. Apter, (ed.), *Ideology and Discontent* (New York: The Free Press, 1964), pp. 206–61.

6. Here racial differences seem significant. Among whites, of the 47 who responded, about a third (16) favored a new party. Of these 16, eight spoke of a socialist or labor party, and six of the Dixiecrat-type party. Among the Negroes, 25 of 29 respondents commented on the new party issue, and of these 25, 12 favored a new party. Of these 12, nine looked toward a party oriented toward labor, the poor, or the Negro. From this point on, a note will elaborate on those findings on which racial differences are significant. If no such note is found, this indicates that racial differences were relatively trivial.

7. There are sharp racial differences here. Three whites out of four say the government spends too much, whereas less than a third of the Negroes argue this way. The responses here show clearly the general tendency among whites to see government aid as going to other groups, particularly Negroes. Taking such a view, the best they can hope for is lower taxes, rather than imagining an improvement in the way government assistance is distributed.

8. Racial differences here are fascinating:

	Percent Saying	
	Whites	Negroes
Enough jobs	51	38
Freedom of speech	26	55
Powerful army, etc.	17	3
Don't know	6	3

The Negro emphasis on free speech probably reflects the problem of demonstrations and voting rights, which were important at the time.

9. Both whites and Negroes choose "equal treatment" about 60 percent of the time. But whites are more likely to choose "Fighting communism," and "Negroes," "Aid to the poor."

	Percent Saying	
	Whites	Negroes
Equal treatment	59	59
Fight communism	21	10
Aid to poor	11	21
Don't know	10	10

This emphasis on equal treatment has different meanings to different men. For Negroes its meanings are obvious; for whites it represents a preference for what they regard as a fair shake from the government, as well as the notion that poorer people ought to receive more attention. The "Aid to the poor" alternative may have been chosen by relatively few because of the widespread sense among these men that poor people ought to receive only the aid they really need to get started: the word "lots" therefore could be interpreted as meaning excessive aid. Equal, not preferential, treatment is what most of these men favor, at least verbally.

10. Overall, the picture on domestic vs. military priorities is a confusing one. The two previous tables have indicated a strong emphasis on welfare-state priorities, but other evidence is not as clear-cut. For example, asked if America should build additional military power, 46 percent were in favor, 27 percent against, and 27 percent didn't know. Sixty-six percent favor the Test Ban treaty, with 15 percent opposed. Twenty-nine percent favor the Bay of Pigs, with 24 percent opposed. On questions concerning the Vietnam War, the picture is also mixed, but on the whole, the Durham sample is more dovish than the national sample reported in S. Verba, and others, "Public Opinion and the War in Vietnam," *American Political Science Review*, June 1967. The Durham sample is less likely to favor escalation and less likely to favor additional expenditures involving tax increases or cutting welfare state payments. On the other hand, this sample is less likely than the national sample to favor a coalition government and slightly more likely to favor atomic war with China. These issues will be explored more fully in a future article.

11. Of those who say they have serious problems, a somewhat larger percentage of Negroes is receiving government assistance.

12. On these questions, racial issues become prominent, and the differences between Negro and white responses are marked. On the question of a "free country," Negroes are less likely to respond negatively than are whites, 31 percent to 57 percent. On the question of taking away or helping freedom, whites are more than twice as likely (53 percent to 24 percent) to see the government taking away freedom, but only a little less likely to see it helping freedom (38 percent to 45 percent). When it comes to specifics, the racial issue is clearly dominant on this question—a plurality of the answers in terms of taking away freedom cite forced racial integration; a plurality of those in terms of helping freedom concern racial integration. On the question of the government helping or hurting the ordinary man, the pattern is somewhat similar. Four whites say the government hurts for every three who say it helps, where two Negroes say it helps for every one who says it hurts. Yet the racial issue itself does not loom large in the substantive responses to this question.

13. Of the 22 whites (42 percent) who named a group they felt was against the things they favored, seven spoke of business and the "rich," while 10 named civil-rights groups. Among the Negroes, nine of the 10 (34 percent) who named a group named business and the "rich."

14. Harris survey, *Washington Post*, July 31, 1967.

15. Richard F. Hamilton, "A Research Note on the Mass Support for 'Tough' Military Initiatives," *American Sociological Review*, XXXIII (June 1968), pp. 439–445.

16. Harris has also reported on the greater reluctance of poorer Americans to support the sending of U.S. troops to aid Israel. Those in favor were: Under $5,000, 17 percent; $5–10,000, 23 percent; $10,000 and up, 32 percent. *Washington Post*, June 10, 1967.

17. Herbert McClosky, "Consensus and Ideology in American Politics," *American Political Science Review*, June 1964.

18. There are other serious problems with McClosky's interpretations of his findings. See my "Communication," *American Political Science Review*, December 1966, pp. 1,000–1,001. Unfortunately, McClosky's data have not thus far been analyzed further in class or other terms.

19. William H. Form and Joan Rytina, "Ideological Beliefs on the Distribution of Power in the United States," *American Sociological Review*, XXXIV (February 1969), pp. 19–31.

20. The full passage in which Converse expresses his doubts goes this way: ". . . the discouragingly large turnover of opinion on these issues in the total mass public might be taken as evidence that the questions were poorly written and thus extremely unreliable and that the main lesson is that they should be rewritten. Yet the issues posed are those posed by political controversy, and citizens' difficulties in responding to them in meaningful fashion seem to proffer important insights into their understanding of the same political debates in real life. More crucial, still, what does it mean to say that an instrument is perfectly reliable vis-à-vis one class of people and totally unreliable vis-à-vis another. . . ." Converse, "Nature of Belief Systems," p. 244.

21. Goldwater was a popular candidate among whites. Forty-seven percent reported voting for him, 28 percent for Johnson, and 25 percent didn't vote. Johnson received the votes of 83 percent of the Negroes, 17 percent not voting. The conflicts within whites about race versus class orientation will be explored more fully in a future article.

22. See, for example, the discussion in Walter Dean Burnham, "The Changing Shape of the American Political Universe," *American Political Science Review*, March 1965, and A. Campbell and H. Valen, "Party Identification in Norway and the United States," *Public Opinion Quarterly*, Winter 1961.

21.
POWER AND PLURALISM: A VIEW FROM THE BOTTOM

Michael Parenti

In the absence of its natural defenders, the interest of the excluded is always in danger of being overlooked.
John Stuart Mill

Was he free? Was he happy? The question is absurd!
Had anything been wrong, we should certainly have heard.
W. H. Auden

It is said we live in a pluralistic society, and indeed a glance at the social map of America reveals a vast agglomeration of regional, class, occupational, and ethnic associations all busily making claims upon state, local, and national governing agencies. If by pluralism we mean this multiplicity of public and private interests and identities, then America—like any modern society of size and complexity—is pluralistic. Used in this broad sense, the term is not particularly arresting for those political scientists interested in determining the extent to which power is democratically operative in America. However, if by "pluralism" we mean that the opportunities and resources necessary for the exercise of power are *inclusively* rather than exclusively distributed and that neither the enjoyment of dominance nor the suffering of deprivation is the constant condition of any one group, then the question of whether ours is a pluralistic society is not so easily resolved.

From Michael Parenti, "Power and Pluralism: A View from the Bottom," *The Journal of Politics*, vol. 32, no. 3 (August 1970), pp. 501–530. © 1970 by the Southern Political Science Association. Reprinted by permission of the publisher.

The author would like to thank Darryl Baskin, Robert Dahl, Edgar Litt, Douglas Rosenberg, and Kenneth Sharpe for their helpful comments. This is a revised and expanded version of a paper given at a panel sponsored by the Caucus for a New Political Science at the annual convention of the American Political Science Association, Washington, D.C., September 1968.

The protracted debate between "pluralists" and "anti-pluralists" is testimony to the difficulties we confront. After investigating "concrete decisions" at the community and national levels, the pluralists conclude that participation in decision making is enjoyed by a variety of competing groups operating in specific issue-areas often in response to the initiatives of democratically elected officials. No evidence is found to support the claim that a corporate "power elite" rules over an inarticulate mass. If there are elites in our society, they are numerous and specialized, and they are checked in their demands by the institutionalized rules of the political culture and by the competing demands of other elites, all of whom represent varying, if sometimes overlapping, constituencies.[1] Conflict is multilateral and ever-changing, and the "bulk of the population consists not of the mass but of integrated groups and publics, stratified with varying degrees of power,"[2] and endowed with "a multitude of techniques for exercising influence on decisions salient to them."[3]

Not long after this theory became the accepted view in American political science, anti-pluralist critics began voicing certain reservations. The anti-pluralists remain unconvinced that influence and benefits are widely distributed, and that political and administrative officers operate as guardians of the unorganized majorities and as the controllers, rather than the servants, of important interest groups.[4] While not defending the idea of a monolithic power elite, they question whether elites are mutually restrained by competitive interaction, observing that many of the stronger elites tend to predominate in their particular spheres of activity more or less unmolested by other elites.[5] Not only are elites often unchecked by public authority on the most important issues affecting them, but in many instances *public* decision-making authority has been parcelled out to *private* interests on a highly inegalitarian basis.[6] The anti-pluralists further criticize the pluralists for failing to take notice of the "powers of pre-emption"; is it not true, for instance, that corporate leaders often have no need to involve themselves in decision-making efforts because sufficient anticipatory consideration is given to their interests by officeholders?[7] Attention, therefore, should be directed to the "nondecision," "non-issue" powers such as the power to predetermine the agenda and limit the scope of issue conflict, and the power to define and propagate "the dominant values . . . myths, rituals and institutions which tend to favor the vested interests of one or more groups relative to others."[8]

The pluralists respond to these last few criticisms by noting that theories about unuttered anticipatory reactions, invisible participants, and hidden values cannot be scientifically entertained. We may conjure an "infinite regress" of imaginary powers operating behind the observable decision makers, the pluralists say, but we can study empirically only what is visible, and only those who can be observed making decisions or engaging in activity bearing directly upon decision making can be said to share power.

Now I, for one, have no quarrel with the dictum that we observe only the observable, but it may be suggested that what the pluralists have defined as "observable" is not all that meets the eyes of other researchers. Particularly troublesome to me is the relative absence of lower-strata groups from most community-power studies and the ease with which their absence is either ignored or explained away.

Let me begin with a fundamental pluralist proposition, namely, only those who participate in the decision process share in the exercise of power. If true, then it would follow that those who do *not* participate in decision making do *not* share power. This latter proposition, however, is treated rather equivocally by most pluralists. If the non-participants are of the upper classes, it is concluded that they are non-influential. But if the non-participants are from the lower income groups, it is usually maintained that they exercise "indirect" influence.

The New Haven investigation conducted by Robert Dahl and his former student, Nelson Polsby, represents one of the most important of the pluralists' community studies and, for the moment, I shall concentrate on what is revealed in that work. Dahl and Polsby discover that New Haven's active decision makers consist primarily of civic and political leaders centering around the mayor; only a few of these participants are members of the "economic elite." For one to argue that municipal authorities are under the power of the economic elite one must demonstrate, according to Polsby, that upper-class members "customarily give orders to political and civic leaders" which are obeyed, or that they regularly and successfully block policies, or that they place "their own people in positions of leadership." Finding to his own satisfaction that none of these conditions obtain in New Haven, Polsby concludes that the upper class is not preponderantly influential.[9] The only way to determine whether actors are powerful, he says, is to observe a sequence of events demonstrating their power: "If these events take place, then the power of the actor is not 'potential' but actual. If these events do not occur, then what grounds have we to suppose that the actor is powerful? There appear to be no scientific grounds for such an assumption." Those who assign "a high power potential to economic dominants" are therefore "indulging in empirically unjustified speculation."[10]

What, then, of the lower-strata groups that do not participate in decision making? The New Haven study shows that only a miniscule fraction of the citizenry engage in any activity bearing directly upon community decisions and that none of the decision makers are drawn from lower-income groups, white or black.[11] The non-participant, however, exercises "a moderate degree of indirect influence" through his power to elect officials or—if he does not vote—through his "influential contact" with those who do vote, presumably relatives and friends.[12] The vote is an effective popular control because "elected leaders keep the real or imagined preferences of constituents *constantly in mind* in deciding what policies to adopt or reject."[13] Most people, Dahl observes, "use their political resources scarcely at all," some not even bothering to vote; hence they never fully convert their "potential influence" into "actual influence."[14] They do not exert themselves because they feel no compelling need to participate. To assume that citizens, especially of the lower class, should be politically active is, Polsby says, to make "the inappropriate and arbitrary assignment of upper and middle-class values to all actors in the community."[15] There are "personally functional" and habitual reasons for lower-class withdrawal having nothing to do with political life. Polsby further assures us that "most of the American communities studied in any detail seem to be relatively healthy political organisms which means that there are bound to be considerable conservatism and self-preservation rather than innovation and demand for change within the system."[16]

Here it seems we are confronted with a double standard for the measurement of power. (1) Despite the fact that large corporation leaders and other economic notables control vast resources of wealth and property that affect the livelihoods, living standards, and welfare of the community, it cannot be presumed that they exercise indirect or potential influence over political leaders. Furthermore, it is unscientific to speak of political leaders as having anticipatory reactions to the interests of these economic elites. There must be discernible evidence of upper-class participation and victory in specific policy conflicts. But (2) it may be presumed that the unorganized, less-educated, lower-income voters exercise an indirect influence over decisions to which they have no easy access and about which they often have no direct knowledge. They accomplish this by evoking in the minds of political leaders a set of "constant" but unspecified anticipatory reactions to the voters' policy preferences, preferences that are themselves frequently unspecified and unarticulated.

If it may be postulated, without the benefit of empirical research that ordinary voters exercise indirect controls over decisions, then we can conclude that any community in America that holds elections is, by virtue of that fact, pluralistic. We have thereby presumed to know precisely the things that need to be empirically determined: to whose needs and imperatives do elected officials respond, as measured by which actual decisions and outcomes?

If, however, lower-class groups do not participate in decision-making activities, how can we determine the extent of their influence, if any, over actual decisions? And what meaning can we ascribe to their nonparticipation? I would suggest that instead of declaring them to be an unknown but contented entity, we should directly investigate the less privileged elements of a community to determine why they are not active, and what occurs when they attempt to become active. Studies of policy struggles involving lower-strata groups are a rarity in the literature of American political science partly because the poor seldom embark upon such ventures[17] but also because our modes of analysis have defined the scope of our research so as to exclude the less visible activities of the underprivileged.

"The case study approach to power location should not be discredited," Todd Gitlin reminds us, "but why are only certain cases studied?"[18]

What I shall attempt to do in the following case studies of three "issue-areas" is to observe power "from the bottom up." I shall not attempt any detailed analysis of the maneuvers and interactions within official circles normally considered a central part of the "decision-making process"; rather the focus will be on actors who try to influence decisions from afar, the active non-elites who attempt to overcome the social distance that separates the subject of politics from the object by trying to participate both in the creation of an issue-agenda and in issue-decisions. Any assessment of non-elite influence should take into account actual outcomes: that is to say, to determine whether the protest group does or does not prevail we need to look at the effects of the contested decision. A view from the bottom requires a shift in emphasis away from studying process as an end in itself divorced from substantive effects (who governs?) and toward some empirical consideration of substantive effects (who gets what?). The presumptions are that substantive effects are, after all, what make the decision process a meaningful and important topic of study, and that they are certainly an essential variable for political actors whose efforts otherwise cannot be properly understood.

Many questions of broad theoretical import might be entertained when investigating the limits and realities of lower-class power and participation. Attention in the present study will be directed primarily to the following theoretical considerations: Is the present political system, as pluralists contend, responsive to the interests of all groups that seek to exercise influence through legitimate channels? And do the protest groups that represent the more acutely deprived strata suffer liabilities within the political system of a kind not usually accounted for in the pluralist theory?

II

Early in the summer of 1964, at the invitation of a private welfare group, 13 members of the Students for a Democratic Society went into the lower Clinton Hill neighborhood in Newark's South Ward and in cooperation with local residents formed the Newark Community Union Project (NCUP), an organization intended to assist ghetto people in the building of a social-protest movement.

The lower Clinton Hill area was turning into an all-black area whose outward appearance of greenery and trees did not quite hide the underlying conditions of overcrowding, poverty, underemployment, and insufficient public services.[19] The already strained housing conditions were further aggravated by the influx of displaced persons whose previous neighborhoods were being obliterated by urban-renewal projects. Nevertheless, as is the case with many large ghettos, the population was somewhat heterogeneous, including in addition to the very poor some relatively comfortable wage earners, semi-professional and even professional people who remained in the South Ward because of racial discrimination or personal preference.

The NCUP organizers began making contacts with the poorer residents, hoping to find specific issues that would bring people together and involve them in community action.[20] The people who came to NCUP meetings, numbering from 25 to 80 on different occasions, and others interviewed in their homes or on street corners, almost invariably expressed anger and distress about such problems as job discrimination, job shortages, poor wages, garbage- and snow-removal services, inadequate schools, rent gouging, police brutality, merchant overpricing, etc. "I am mad," said one, "I am angry when I see my people living the way they do." Coupled with these feelings was the widespread conviction that protest efforts would meet with frustration, and that the voices of the poor would not be heard, and if heard, not heeded. "What's the use?" "Nothing can ever get changed." "Why get your hopes up?" were some of the more common remarks. Nevertheless, some 15 residents and seven white students were resolute enough to give almost full-time efforts, staying with NCUP for the duration of its existence. ("This time the poor man's going to do something for himself," said one resident.) Another 25 blacks were intensely active for periods extending from several months to half a year, and still scores of others involved themselves intermittently. It may be roughly estimated that as many as 150 residents participated in some major or minor way over a two-and-a-half year period in public demonstrations, rent strikes, meetings, and other organizational activities.[21]

The problems to which organizers could address themselves were varied and enormous. Several considerations determined priorities: first, what did the people themselves feel most strongly about; second, were there visible targets and goals; third, was there some chance of success? During a period extending from 1964 to 1966 efforts focused primarily on the following issues.

Issue #1 Housing   The poor in the South Ward area paid monthly rents ranging from $115 to $135 for the privilege of living without benefit of proper heating and water facilities in small sub-divided apartments in deteriorated, ill-lit, unpainted, rat-infested buildings. Groups of tenants organized by NCUP made several trips to municipal housing authorities to complain of conditions, winning nothing more than promises to "look into things." Subsequent visits to the Human Rights Commission induced that agency to send inspectors to the buildings in question. The inspectors found evidence of widespread building-code violations (as many as 125 in one apartment house), filed reports, and sent copies to the landlords in question. Lacking enforcement powers of its own, the Commission took no further actions. After two months had passed without any response from the building owners, NCUP began organizing rent strikes in some of the worst buildings in an eight-block area. This action led several of the landlords, including South Ward City Councilman, Lee Bernstein, to make minor repairs in a few buildings. But most owners did not respond during the first month of the strike and none attempted any major improvements.[22] A visit by protestors to the mayor's office in turn produced a visit by Mayor Addonizio to one of the apartment houses; the rent-strike issue had by now won some passing attention in the local press. After taking due note of conditions, the mayor and his team of observers returned to city hall where, in the words of one tenant, "They made us a lot of promises but they didn't carry any out." NCUP protestors, joining forces with a local anti-poverty group, resorted to picketing the suburban home of one of the worst slumlords, an action taken over the protests of Councilman Bernstein who described the peaceful picketing as "disgraceful behavior."

After two months, the landlords whose buildings were affected by the rent strike began issuing eviction notices. One tenant, Mrs. Ida Brown, a mother of five children, was forcibly barred from her apartment by her landlord and two city detectives. When Mrs. Brown protested and attempted to enter her apartment, she was arrested and charged with assault and battery.[23] Her arrest was sufficient to persuade a number of other tenants that they had better withdraw from participation in the rent strike. Still other tenants, with the threat of eviction hanging over them, eventually moved out—their places quickly taken by other poor families—or complied with the law and resumed rent payments. Fear of arrest, forceful eviction, and legal prosecution, combined with a growing realization that nothing was being won except promises from public officials and threats from landlords, eventually proved effective in breaking the momentum of the rent-strike campaign. "There is," a resident accurately concluded, "no way us tenants, no legal way we can fight a landlord."[24] The ghetto residents learned what many always had suspected: some laws, such as those dealing with the collection of rents, the eviction of tenants, and the protection of property, were swiftly enforceable, while other laws, such as those dealing with flagrant violations of building and safety codes and the protection of people, were unaccountably unenforceable.

The rent strikes ebbed in Newark as in other cities without winning improvements in living conditions, without creating a permanent tenant's movement, and without getting the city and the courts to change their methods of dealing with slumlords. With nothing to show for their months of strenuous organizing, NCUP volunteers turned to a smaller and ostensibly more manageable issue.

Issue #2 A Traffic Light   Given the ghetto's immense needs, the desire for a traffic light on Avon Avenue might have seemed almost frivolous, but neighborhood feelings were surprisingly strong on this issue: too many children had been maimed and killed by speeding vehicles, and people found it hazardous to cross the avenue. For most residents the traffic light was literally a matter of life and death. In a few weeks NCUP collected 350 signatures on a petition, held a block rally, and waged call-in and letter-writing compaigns directed at the mayor and the City Council. Such efforts eventually earned the residents an audience with Mayor Addonizio who, confronted with a strong and well-organized community demand, agreed that a traffic light would be installed forthwith, contingent only upon City Council approval. The residents departed from the meeting in a hopeful spirit. But after another month of inaction NCUP sent another delegation to city hall this time to be told that a traffic light would cost $24,000 and was therefore too expensive, an argument that even the municipal authorities soon discarded as untenable. The protestors took to blocking traffic and picketing at the Avon Avenue intersection. On several occasions police dispersed the demonstrators with little difficulty, because most participants were hesitant to force a confrontation and expose themselves to arrest. A few "Stop" signs were installed on the side streets leading into Avon Avenue, a gesture that did nothing to slow down the main artery traffic, although it served to forestall further demonstrations as people awaited the impending light. Municipal officials gave repeated assurances that a traffic light would soon be placed, as one said, "If only you'll just be a little patient." After several more months of inaction and several more visits to city hall, it was revealed that the mayor had no authority to install a traffic light; the matter fell under state jurisdiction and had been referred to Trenton.

The protestors took to the streets again; this time attempts to block traffic led to the arrest of a few demonstrators. Municipal traffic officials continued to send assurances that the permit was "going through." But it remained for the State Bureau of Motor Vehicles to demonstrate how best to thwart the petitioners. State authorities informed NCUP organizers that they could not install a light until they had undertaken an extensive study of traffic conditions at the intersection. Data would be needed to demonstrate that a certain number of accidents—only of a kind that a light could prevent—occurred on Avon Avenue over a given period. Since no one in the community, including police and medical authorities, had kept complete records of vehicle and pedestrian mishaps, there was no proof that a light was needed; only an independent study of forthcoming fatalities and injuries could decide the matter. Despite this professed commitment to empirical research, state traffic authorities seemed unable to indicate when they might initiate the requisite survey. (Soon after this position was enunciated, white residents in a nearby middle-class neighborhood were able to get a traffic light installed 28 days after submitting a petition of approximately 50 signatures.)

Three years later, at the time of this writing, there is still no light, children are still hit by speeding vehicles at the intersection, and state officials have yet to begin their exhaustive study. More than 10 months of intensive protests by lower Clinton Hill residents had produced another defeat.

Issue #3 Electoral Contest   "Why didn't you go to the local politicians for help on the rent strike and the traffic light?" I asked a number of the neighborhood organizers. "Are you kidding! They hate us! They call us troublemakers," exclaimed one. "They are whites, Toms, and heavies. They want to run us out of town," said another, "What could they have done?" a white student conjectured in retrospect. "They knew cooptation in the Democratic Party wouldn't silence us. We couldn't be bought off. So they were out to defeat us—even on a little thing like a traffic light." The Democratic party regulars were viewed as either indifferent or unsympathetic to ghetto needs. On the few occasions when they showed themselves responsive to the poor, it was in the performance of petty favors. They might "look into" a complaint by a mother that her welfare checks were not arriving, but they would not challenge some of the more demeaning and punitive features of the welfare system nor the conditions that fostered it. They might find a municipal job for a faithful precinct worker, but they would not advance proposals leading to a fundamental attack on ghetto unemployment. They might procure an apartment for a family, but they would not ask the landlord, who himself was often a party contributor, to make housing improvements, nor would they think of challenging his right to charge exhorbitant rents. The party regulars, whether white or Negro, seemed prepared to "look into" everything except certain of the more harrowing realities of slum life.

An opportunity to challenge them seemed to present itself in the autumn of 1965 when the United Freedom Ticket (UFT), a coalition of dissident blacks, Puerto Ricans, and "civil-rights oriented whites," asked NCUP to support the insurgency candidacy of George Richardson, a black man and a former Democratic assemblyman who had broken with the party because of its unwillingness to confront the problems of slum housing and police brutality. Richardson was "sort of a politician" to some NCUP people, and "no great prize in his political views," but he compared most favorably to his Democratic opponent whom one UFT supporter described as "the ultimate Uncle Tom." After some debate, NCUP decided to support the United Freedom Ticket which, in addition to Richardson, was running two other black candidates for State Assembly offices. After the failure of the rent-strike and traffic-light campaigns, a frontal assault at the polls seemed the only recourse: "We are tired of protesting and losing, so we're going right into politics," explained one organizer who hoped that NCUPs coalition with the UFT would increase the efficacy of both groups. Even if the Democratic incumbents were not defeated, a serious electoral challenge might make them somewhat more responsive to reformist pressure.

It was anticipated by some of the NCUP people that the campaign would provide an opportunity for creating a community-wide dialogue on fundamental issues. "Organizing the people" was, first of all, a matter of devising means of reaching and talking to persons who had never been reached before; the campaign seemed to offer just such an occasion. But faced with the necessity of swiftly reaching large numbers of people, and equipped with only limited resources, the challengers soon found themselves resorting to the traditional techniques of sound track, leaflets, and slogans. Even so, not more than one-third of the contested area was covered and less than one-third of the voters were actually approached by UFT volunteers.

"We've got that one thing that can take it away from [the bosses]," Candidate Richardson said, "the vote." Not many residents believed him. Campaigning for "decent housing," "more and better jobs," and "freedom," the UFT found itself burdened by the very sins it was trying to fight: too many years of unfulfilled pledges by too many candidates had left people immune to political promises. Some residents felt threatened by appeals for direct involvement: "I don't know anything about politics. I don't want to have anything to do with it," was a typical response. Many had never heard of the UFT and were hesitant about an unknown ingredient. Still others indicated their sympathy for the third party's goals but were quick to voice their skepticism: "We've had our people in there before and they couldn't do nothing." The many expressions of cynicism and distrust reported by UFT canvassers might be summarized as follows: (1) Reformers were politicians, and therefore were as deceptive and insincere as other politicians. (2) Even if sincere, reformers were eventually "bought off" by those in control. (3) Even if not "bought off," reformers remained helpless against the entrenched powers: what could the UFT do even if it won all three contested seats? The conviction that "politics" could not deliver anything significant left many of the poor unresponsive, even if not unsympathetic, toward those who promised meaningful changes through the ballot box.

Of the blacks who voted, the greater number were the "better-to-do" elements—ministers, funeral directors, small businessmen, postal and clerical workers, and some skilled workers. A sizable number were beholden to, or related to those beholden to, the Democratic organization for jobs or for positions within the party that brought a modicum of social prestige. Often both resented and respected by poorer residents, the local ward politicians cultivated a wide range of acquaintances and traded on "friends and neighbors" appeals. They repeatedly stressed that a vote for the UFT might bring a Republican victory, and while many voters entertained no great expectations about the Democrats, they did fear that the Republicans might in some nameless way create still greater difficulties for blacks.[25] For some middle- and lower-middle-class blacks the act of voting was valued as a manifestation of civic virtue comparable to saluting the flag or singing the national anthem, a mark of good citizenship status reflecting well upon those Negroes who achieved it.[26]

Both the Democratic and Republican organizations provided substantial funds for neighborhood workers who saturated the black and white precincts with posters, party literature, and door-to-door canvassing, and who manned the fleet of cars to transport voters to and from the polls on election day. Even with these efforts, less than half of the registered blacks bothered to vote (as against almost two-thirds of the whites in the contested areas). The UFT ticket was thoroughly defeated, running well behind both major parties and polling less than 5 percent of the vote.

This description of events in Newark cannot be concluded without some mention of the role played by community officials. In statements to the press and sometimes to the protestors themselves, municipal officials voiced a dedication to the best interests of the people. It would have been remarkable had they professed anything else, but their behavior sometimes did betray their words. The methods they utilized to defeat NCUP on the rent-strike and traffic-light issues were familiar ones—the insistence that the problem in question needed elaborate investigation, the claim that the issue was not within a given authority's jurisdiction, the posing of rigorous and time-consuming legalistic procedures, the ritualistic appearance of a public official to investigate the question—followed by disingenuous promises that a solution was at hand, and the constant admonition that the protestors should exercise restraint and patience. "They just moved to go through the motions, to make us think they were moving," said one black man. "The city," concluded a white youth, "did a masterful job of destroying us. After awhile we didn't know who was the target. . . . we were always promised something to take the steam out [of us]. . . . They just wore us down with a run-around."[27]

The protestors also were subjected to a series of unsavory harassments. A replica of the *NCUP Newsletter*, printed by unknown individuals and containing what purported to be admissions of perverted sexual practices and communist affiliations falsely attributed to NCUP volunteers, was mailed to some 500 *NCUP Newsletter* subscribers. NCUP was infiltrated by at least one undercover agent who was ejected from the organization after admitting to being in the pay of an unnamed municipal personage. It was apparently through his efforts that the newsletter subscription list was obtained. A black detective, who quit the police force out of disgust for the racism he had encountered, confirmed the strong suspicions of NCUP workers that their telephone was being tapped by the police. On one occasion three NCUP girls were evicted from their three-bedroom apartment on charges of maintaining an unsanitary premise, sleeping on the floors, and conducting sex orgies. The landlord's letter containing these accusations was reprinted by a City Councilman and circulated among members of the Council and other municipal authorities. NCUP itself was evicted from its original storefront office, without being given a reason for the action. On another occasion threatening calls on the telephone by unidentified voices were followed by the breaking of NCUP office windows. Police repeatedly entered the office and arrested NCUP workers on disorderly conduct or loitering charges. A municipal judge once instructed one organizer brought before him to "go back to Russia." Other workers were arrested without cause while lawfully picketing a local food store accused of overpricing. Within a period of a few days, six black teen-agers who assisted in routine NCUP tasks and who were planning a youth organization were arrested coming to and from the NCUP office. When Jesse Allen, a mild-mannered black leader of NCUP, went to the fifth precinct station to inquire on their behalf, he, too, was placed under arrest. Two of the youths who were arrested were convicted of breaking probation, and each was made to serve two years in prison.

The only conceivably friendly gesture directed toward NCUP in the several years of its existence came in the late spring of 1967 when Mayor Addonizio and Police Chief Spina sent letters asking the organizers to help "keep a cool summer" in the ghetto. The ensuing summer riots sent a number of NCUP people into hiding because, as two of them testify, a highly placed state official gave warning that police would be "out to get the radicals." These precautions did not prevent several NCUP workers from being arrested soon after the disorders and charged with conspiracy to riot and arson, charges that were subsequently dropped for lack of evidence.

By the end of 1967 NCUP ceased functioning. Several of the whites moved on to SDS organizing or to community action programs in other cities; others got jobs in Newark. Some of the activist blacks became involved in running a community center set up by the Union Community Corporation, an anti-poverty group under OEO sponsorship. They now found their energies absorbed in minor administrative tasks and were no longer involved in protest action. NCUP dissolved without ever coming close to achieving its central objective: the building of a viable local social movement that could exercise influence and win changes in community conditions and in the system that fostered those conditions.

In his study of young radicals, Kenneth Keniston made an observation that might serve as a summary description of the white and black activists in Newark: "What is most impressive is not their secret motivation to have the System fail, but their naive hope that it would succeed, and the extent of their depression and disillusion when their early reformist hopes were frustrated."[28] Some of the people who were engaged in NCUP have long since discarded their earlier hopes about the viability of the system, thereby recalling to mind an observation made by Christian Bay in 1965: "If budding western-democracy-type pluralist institutions turn out to benefit only the middle and upper classes—as in many Latin American countries— then we should not be surprised if idealistic students and others with a passion for social justice . . . become disposed to reject the forms of pluralist democracy altogether."[29]

III

The events in Newark provide us with a view of community power that qualifies the pluralist picture in several important respects. The following discussion attempts to summarize the findings and analyze some of the wider implications of this study.

1. For the urban blacks of Newark who had the temerity to fight city hall there exists the world of the rulers and the world of the ruled, and whether or not the first world is composed of a monolithic elite or of intramurally competing groups does not alter the fact that the blacks find themselves inhabiting the second. What impresses them and what might impress us is that the visible agents of the ruling world, a "plurality of actors and interests"—as represented by the municipal and state housing officials, motor vehicle and transit authorities, the landlords and realty investors, the mayor, the City Council, the political machines, the courts, and the police—displayed a remarkable capacity to move in the same direction against some rather modest lower-class claims.

It is one thing to conclude that power is not the monopoly of any one cohesive power elite and another to contend that it is broadly distributed among countervailing and democratically responsive groups. The belief that lower-strata groups exercise a constant, albeit indirect, power remains an article of faith rather than a demonstrated proposition at least with regard to the issues investigated in this study. Banfield's assertion that community decision makers operate "on the principle that everyone should get something and no one should be hurt very much," and Dahl's view that "all active and legitimate groups in the population can make themselves heard at some crucial stage in the process of decision," do not seem to be borne out.[30] Nor were we able to detect the "multitude of techniques for exercising influence on decisions" that Polsby believes are readily available to any group willing to engage in political competition.[31]

It may be that decision makers are responsive to lower-class pressures that are less visible than those observed in this study, but, as the pluralists would warn us, we should not embark upon an infinite regress of conjectures about covert influences. If Newark's officials were favorably influenced by the ghetto poor it must have been in ways so subtle as to have escaped the attention of both the researcher and the poor themselves. Since the data indicate that a lower-class group exercises no successful influence when *active*, I find no compelling reason to entertain the conclusion that the group wields power through unspecified means when *inactive*.

The data on Newark are consistent with the suggestion, offered by Edelman and Lipsky, that students of power and protest make a distinction between symbolic reassurances and substantive goods; the former are almost always more readily allocated to protesters and are usually designed for the purpose of deflecting the protest.[32] The few "positive" responses made by Newark's officials cost little in time, energy, and support; they were the appropriate "reciprocal noises," to use Dahl's term, intended primarily as substitutes for more tangible allocations. The familiar delaying tactics used by public officials are, Lipsky observes, "particularly effective in dealing with protest groups because of [the group's] inherent instability."[33] And the group's instability is, he adds, due to its dependence on the political resources of "third parties." This study of Newark shows, however, that even when a group demonstrates unusual durability— the NCUP persisted for three years—it still may be unable to outlast the decision makers. The latter can, so to speak, wait forever, and on many issues they would prefer to do so, while the protest group, no matter how organizationally stable, must start producing results if it is ever to attract a stronger following.

The idea that nothing succeeds like success is well understood by the challenged authorities. Often their unwillingness to make tangible allocations is due less to any consideration of immediate political expenditure than to their concern that present protests are but a prelude to more challenging and more costly demands. The traffic light (unlike the housing issue) hardly represented an appropriation that would have strained municipal resources or threatened the interests of more powerful groups, but a victory for the protestors might have strengthened precisely the kind of oppositional activity that Newark's officials wanted to discourage.

2. One of the most important aspects of power is the ability not only to prevail in a struggle but to predetermine the agenda of struggle, that is, to determine whether certain questions ever reach the competition stage. Assertions about the impossibility of empirically studying these "nondecisions" need to be re-examined. Many "nondecisions" are really decisions of a sort, specifically to avoid or prevent the emergence of a particular course of action.[34] Much of the behavior of Newark's officials can be seen as a kind of "politics of prevention," to use Harold Lasswell's term, a series of decisions designed to limit the area of issue conflict. More extensive study of the attitudes, actions, and inactions of municipal authorities toward lower-strata claims might reveal a startling number of instances in which office-holders avoid politically difficult responses to lower-class pressures. "The problem of politics," according to Lasswell, "is less to solve conflicts than to prevent them." Too much inclusiveness of "all the interests concerned arouses a psychology of conflict

which produces obstructive, fictitious and irrelevant values," a situation best avoided when social administrators and political leaders learn to dampen by skillful tactics those issues that they judge to be detrimental to the public interest.[35] Newark offers an example of how "the politics of prevention" is practiced in the less than antiseptic world of a municipality.

Direct observation of lower-class groups may bring to light other instances of "nondecisions" and "non-issues," specifically those resulting from the actual and anticipated discouragements suffered by people at the lower level of the social structure. In classic democratic theory and in much of the pluralist literature attention has been focused primarily on the presumed capacity of political leaders to anticipate the interests of various constituencies, but perhaps a more significant determinant of the conflict agenda can be found in the anticipatory reactions of lower-strata groups toward those who govern. In Newark, for instance, no attempt was made to organize protest around a number of real grievances. "If we couldn't even get a lousy traffic light with half the neighborhood out there screaming for it," explained one NCUP worker, "how could we hope to fight the corporations and the unions . . . or even the school system?" Protest groups remain inactive in certain areas because, given the enormity of the conditions needing change and the strength of the interests opposing change, they see no opportunity for effective protest.[36] For them the agenda is predetermined by preferences and powers other than their own.

The same might be said of isolated individuals. Only a small percentage of the lower Clinton Hill residents were active in the various NCUP projects. According to one view, most sternly enunciated by Polsby, there is no reason to assume that politically quiescent people suffer deprivations unless they express actual grievances. But this ostensibly empirically-minded position harbors an a priori assumption, for, in fact, individuals may remain politically quiescent (1) because they feel no deprivation or (2) because they feel real and urgent deprivations but are convinced that protest is futile and, hence, give no political expression to their grievances. One can decide which is the case only by empirical investigation of the social group in question.[37] Any widely felt deprivation discovered by the investigator that fails to become an issue because the deprived don't have the ability to force a confrontation may be considered a "non-issue"; these "non-issues" (or anticipatory reactions) are empirically visible even if, by their nature, they tend to be politically invisible.

The unwillingness of so many people in Newark to make

any kind of political commitment can be partly attributed to the limitations on the time and energy of the poor.[38] Working long hours for low pay, deprived of a host of services that middle-class whites take for granted, many residents have neither the physical nor psychic energy to engage in the demanding tasks of community organizing. Many do not feel personally capable and confident enough to ask their neighbors or themselves to participate actively. In a way that most white people cannot appreciate, fear is a palpable ingredient in the lives of the black poor; many are deterred by fear of eviction, legal harassment, prosecution, police assault, and by a more diffuse and ubiquitous fear of the powers that be.

If I were to offer any one explanation for non-participation it would be the profound and widespread belief of so many ghetto residents that there exist no means of taking effective action against long-standing grievances, and that investments of scarce time, energy, money, and, perhaps most of all, hope serve for nought except to aggravate one's sense of affliction and impotence. In this case, non-participation is an expression of what Kenneth Clark describes as "the psychology of the ghetto with its pervasive and total sense of helplessness,"[39] a pattern of anticipatory reactions that attempt to avoid direct exposure to, and competition against, unresponsive and unsympathetic authorities.

The contention that the poor are not really discontent else they would register a protest vote at election time presupposes among other things that the poor share or should share the middle-class belief that the ballot is an effective and meaningful means of changing the condition of their lives and their community. But, recalling Polsby's warning, we must guard against "the inappropriate and arbitrary assignment of upper and middle-class values to all actors in the community." We might also avoid treating lower-class non-participation as a self-generated entity, a manifestation of some innate subcultural habit or lack of civic virtue, and allow ourselves the notion that attitudes of defeatism and withdrawal are fostered by conditions within the socioeconomic system and to that extent are accurate representations of the systemic realities and everyday-life conditions faced by the black poor.[40]

With that in mind, we might question the consistency and ease with which public-opinion surveys report that lower-strata individuals are more apathetic and less informed than citizens from better educated upper-income groups. If by "apathy" we mean the absence of affect and awareness, then many ghetto blacks, while non-participants in the usual political activities, can hardly be described as "apathetic." Apathy should not be confused with antipathy and alienation.[41] As to the finding that lower-class people are "less informed," what impressed me most about the poor, often semi-literate, blacks I talked to (residents of Newark and also of New York and more recently New Haven) was the extent to which they had a rather precise notion of what afflicted them and certainly a better sense of the difficulties and deprivations that beset the black community than the whites have in the same cities, many of whom refused to accept the legitimacy of black complaints.[42]

Whether a group appears apathetic and ill-informed depends on the kinds of questions it is being asked. Perhaps survey research, not unlike I.Q. testing, inadvertently reflects the cultural and class biases of the dominant society by focusing on those questions that are defined by the white middle-class world as "public issues." Something of the same criticism can be made of community power research of the last 15 years. That researchers have been able to study so many American cities and find so few deep-seated grievances tells us more about their research models than about urban reality. By confining themselves to issues pursued by politically visible interests they have rarely reached the muted lower strata.[43] "Rigid adherence to a conceptual schema," Charles McCoy notes in his critical appraisal of pluralism, "restricts the range of the political scientist's observable data so that he may fail to see what is taking place outside his frame of reference."[44]

3. If "inequalities in political resources remain, they tend to be *noncumulative*," some pluralists believe, since no one group either monopolizes or is totally deprived of the attributes of power.[45] Even if lacking in money and leadership, the lower strata still have the power of numbers. Thus it may be argued that the failure of NCUP and the UFT to mobilize sufficient numbers of poor people tells us only that they were unable to tap the ghetto's power resources and not that such resources are nonexistent.

The contention that the slum constituency is ineffective because it fails to mobilize its numerical strength is something of a tautology. It is to say that the poor will have power if and when they act in such a way as to have power—presumably in sufficient numbers with sufficient energy. But the only way we can determine "sufficiency" is by noting that the poor prevail on a given issue. By that approach, they can never be judged powerless. If they win on any issue, then they have power; if they lose, they still have power but sufficient numbers have not made sufficient use of it. One cannot imagine a situation in which sufficient numbers have acted and lost; the proposition is established by definition rather than by observation and is non-falsifiable.

Moreover, to contend that the lower strata have a potential power that would prevail should they choose to use it presumes that their non-participation is purely a matter of volition. The volition argument is given its more familiar and vulgar expression by those who dismiss the inequalities of opportunity in economic life: "Anyone can make his fortune if he puts his mind and effort to it." The antecedent conditions that are crucial determinants of performance merely become a matter of self-willed doggedness.[46] The argument overlooks the fact that the ability to take effective advantage of an opportunity, the ability to convert potentiality into actuality, is itself a crucial power. The actualization of any potential power requires the use of antecedent resources, and just as one needs capital to make capital, so one needs power to use power. This is especially true of the power of numbers insofar as the opportunity to achieve political effectiveness by activating large numbers of people, especially lower-class citizens, within the normal channels of group politics, necessitates a substantial command of time, man-power, publicity, organization, legitimacy, knowledgeableness, and—the ingredient that often can determine the availability of these resources—money. Aside from its more circumspect influences, money is needed for the acquisition of elected office. "Probably the most important direct contribution" to political leaders, according to Dahl himself, "is money." The "most important indirect contribution is votes . . ."[47] The power of numbers, then, is an influence that is highly qualified by material and class considerations.

For the poor of Newark, the situation closely approximates one of "cumulative inequalities," to use Dahl's term. If the poor possessed the material resources needed to mobilize themselves, they would not be poor and would have less need to organize their numbers in a struggle to win services that the economic and political systems readily grant to more favored groups. Can the dispossessed who desire inclusion in the decision process gain access to political office without the capital needed to mobilize and activate their numbers? There seems no easy answer to this question. The problem of "political capital accumulation" is compounded by the fact that, unlike the indigent in many other countries, the poor in America are a minority and therefore even when mobilized for electoral participation may have only a limited impact. The power of numbers can be employed with countervailing efficacy by the majority that identifies itself with the "haves" and against the "have-nots."

Furthermore, in places like Newark, the one institution theoretically designed to mobilize and respond to the demands of the unorganized lower strata—the local political party—fails to do so. One of the hallowed teachings of American political science is that the political party is the citizens' means of exercising collective power; the stronger the party system, the more ably will it affect the polyarchic will. But the party organization in Newark is less a vehicle for democratic dialogue and polyarchic power than a pressure group with a rather narrowly defined interest in the pursuit of office, favor, and patronage. Moved to collective activity only at election time, local politicians seem most possessed with the overriding task of securing and advancing their own positions and maintaining the ongoing equilibrium.

Party politicians are inclined to respond positively not to group *needs* but to group *demands*, and in political life as in economic life, *needs* do not become *marketable demands* until they are backed by "buying power" or "exchange power" for only then is it in the "producer's" interest to respond. The problem with most lower-strata groups is that they have few political resources of their own to exchange.[48] NCUPs protest action failed to create the kinds of inducements that would have made it in the political leaders' interest to take positive measures. The withholding of rent payments, the street-corner demonstrations, the momentary disruptions of traffic and the feeble electoral challenge were treated by the politicians of Newark not as bargaining resources but as minor nuisances that were not to be allowed to develop into major threats. Concessions to the troublemakers might have led to demands for even greater reallocations and eventually would have challenged the interests of groups endowed with far more political "buying power."

4. Not only do party regulars have little inclination to entertain the kinds of issues that might incur the wrath of higher political leaders or powerful economic interests, but they also try to discredit and defeat those reformers who seek confrontations on such issues.[49] Questions about poverty, urban squalor, unemployment, the tax structure, and the ownership, control, and uses of private and public wealth do not win the attention of most urban political organizations. But the sins of the politician are more than personal ones, for the forces that limit him also circumscribe most of political life. The very agenda of legitimate conflict is shaped by widely accepted and unquestioned belief systems and power distributions that predispose the decision maker to view the claims of certain groups as "reasonable" or "essential" and the claims of other groups as "questionable" or "outrageous." The systemic norms and rules governing political

procedures operate with something less than egalitarian effects. To say that the political system is governed by "the rules of the game" is to apply an unfortunate metaphor. In most games the rules apply equally to all competitors, but in political life the symbolic norms, standards, and practices that govern traditional forms of political competition are themselves part of the object of competition. Rules that regulate procedures and priorities in any social system cannot be extricated from the substantive values and interests that led to their construction. Rather than being neutral judgments, they are the embodiment of past political victories and, as such, favor those who have "written" them. Many of the past struggles of dispossessed groups have involved actions that, until legalized as part of the rules, were treated as crimes against property and against the Constitution; these actions have included collective bargaining, boycotts, strikes, sit-downs, and the demand to legislate standards for wages, hours, and other working conditions. Many of the earlier efforts in the labor movement were directed toward legalizing certain methods of protest and competition, thereby changing the rules so as to allow for more effective participation in future competitions.[50] Those who contend that a commitment to the rules is a precondition for democratic politics[51] overlook the fact that for some groups such a commitment is tantamount to accepting a condition of permanent defeat since certain of the rules as presently constituted (for example, the rent laws) are, in fact, the weapons of a dominant interest.

We can conclude that the existence of protest activity should not be treated as a sure manifestation of a pluralistic influence system. Even if the thought is incongruent with the pluralist model, it should come as no surprise to political scientists that the practices of the political system do not guarantee that all groups will have accessibility to the loci of decision making, and that the ability to be heard in a debate, even when achieved, is not tantamount to the sharing of power. If American communities are governed democratically, then let it be said that democracy, like any other form of government, is a power system that allocates its values and priorities most favorably to those who have the most power, to those who have the wherewithal to take best advantage of systemic arrangements. The political order that emerges may prove to be "functional" and "workable" without contributing to the well-being of large segments of the population. Those who are most needful of substantive reallocations are, by that very fact, usually farthest removed from the resources necessary to command such reallocations and least able to make effective use of whatever limited resources they possess.

Notes

1. Robert Dahl's, *Who Governs?* (New Haven: Yale University Press, 1961) remains the most intelligent and important pluralist statement, one that can still be read with profit even by those who disagree with it. Other pluralist views may be found in Arnold Rose, *The Power Structure* (New York: Oxford University Press, 1967); Edward Banfield, *Political Influence* (New York: The Free Press, 1961); David Riesman and others, *The Lonely Crowd* (Garden City, N.Y.: Doubleday Co., 1955); Nelson Polsby, *Community Power and Political Theory* (New Haven: Yale University Press, 1963); David Truman, *The Governmental Process* (New York: Alfred A. Knopf, 1953).

2. Rose, *Power Structure*, p. 6.

3. Polsby, *Community Power*, p. 118.

4. For data and critical analysis supporting the anti-pluralist position see Grant McConnell, *Private Power and American Democracy* (New York: Alfred A. Knopf, 1966) and the many studies cited therein; see also, Paul Baran and Paul Sweezy, *Monopoly Capital: An Essay on the American Economic and Social Order* (New York: Monthly Review Press, 1966); Ralph Miliband, *The State in Capitalist Society* (New York: Basic Books, 1969); Henry Kariel, *The Decline of American Pluralism* (Stanford: Stanford University Press, 1961); Theodore Lowi, "The Public Philosophy: Interest-Group Liberalism," *American Political Science Review*, 61 (March 1967), pp. 5–24; Philip Green, "Science, Government and the Case of RAND," *World Politics*, 20 (January 1968), pp. 301–326. For a collection of the best analytic critiques of pluralism, see the articles reprinted in *Apolitical Politics: A Critique of Behavioralism*, Charles McCoy and John Playford (eds.) (New York: Thomas Y. Crowell, 1967).

5. See Peter Bachrach, *The Theory of Democratic Elitism* (Boston: Little, Brown, 1967), p. 37. Some anti-pluralists such as G. William Domhoff, *Who Rules America?* (Englewood Cliffs, N.J.: Prentice-Hall, 1967) conclude that a power elite rules at the national level even if there may be more pluralistic elites at the community levels.

6. See Kariel, *Decline of American Pluralism*, especially chaps. 5 and 6 for a development of this point; also Lowi, "Interest-Group Liberalism."

7. Even the pluralist Banfield seems to support the above idea. In *Political Influence* he observes (251): "When Mayor Daley took office, he immediately wrote to three or four of the city's most prominent businessmen asking them to list the things they thought most needed doing. . . . He may be impressed by the intrinsic merit of a proposal . . . but he will be even more impressed at the prospect of being well regarded by the highly respectable people whose proposal it is."

8. Peter Bachrach and Morton Baratz, "Two Faces of Power," *American Political Science Review*, 56 (December 1962), p. 950, reprinted in McCoy and Playford, *Apolitical Politics*. For a detailed development of

the effects of myth and ritual in political life, see Murray Edelman, *The Symbolic Uses of Power* (Urbana, Ill.: University of Illinois Press, 1964); also Thurman Arnold, *The Symbols of Government* (New Haven: Yale University Press, 1935). For a detailed analysis of the structure and content of a prevalent belief system, see Francis X. Sutton and others, *The American Business Creed* (Cambridge: Harvard University Press, 1956).

9. Polsby, *Community Power*, pp. 88–89. Yet Polsby goes on to say, "Mayor Lee's achievement in generating support from New Haven's economic and social elite should not be underestimated. . . . Economic and social leaders, who had originally been reluctant to support the urban redevelopment program, became so firmly committed to the program and to Lee that many of these lifelong Republicans found themselves actively supporting Lee for the U.S. Senate and contributing heavily to his re-election campaign against the Republican candidate. At least one businessman even suggested that the *Republican* party nominate Lee for Mayor." (Emphasis in the original.) It seems not to have occurred to Polsby that Lee's unusual popularity with businessmen was due less to his personal seductiveness than to his having proven himself so repeatedly responsive to business interests. For a more critical study of Mayor Lee's urban renewal program and his dealings with the economic elite, see John Wilhelm, "The Success and Tragedy of Richard Lee," *The New Journal*, 1 (October 15, 1967), pp. 5–9.

10. Polsby, *Community Power*, p. 60. By this approach, considerations of historical, class, cultural, and structural factors are relegated to an incidental or even non-scientific status. Here indeed is "behaviorism" in its Pavlovian-Watsonian sense.

11. Dahl, *Who Governs?*, pp. 180–181. Other community studies similarly find that active participants are almost invariably drawn from professional, business, and better-income strata.

12. *Ibid.*, pp. 164 and 100–103.

13. *Ibid.*, p. 164; the italics are mine.

14. *Ibid.*, 270 ff.

15. Polsby, *Community Power*, p. 116–117; see the critical comments in Jack L. Walker, "A Critique of the Elitist Theory of Democracy," *American Political Science Review*, 60 (June 1966), p. 289.

16. Polsby, *Community Power*, p. 134.

17. Actually, political activities involving the dispossessed occur more frequently than we have assumed. In recent years migrant workers, sharecroppers, ghetto blacks, rural whites, American Indians, indigent elderly, and others have made scores of attempts to effect specific changes in various communities and institutions. Most of these activities have yet to be studied systematically as situations that tell us something about the dynamics and distributions of power in America. Most studies of conflict and discontent within the political system are written from the

perspective of those concerned with channelizing or reducing the challenges of competing groups; see, for example, Neil J. Smelser, *Theory
of Collective Behavior* (New York: Free Press, 1963). Note the discussion in William Gamson's *Power and Discontent* (Homewood, Ill.:
Dorsey Press, 1968), pp. 11–19.

18. Todd Gitlin, "Local Pluralism as Theory and Ideology," *Studies on the
Left*, 5 (Summer 1965), reprinted in McCoy and Playford, *Apolitical
Politics*, p. 143.

19. More than one-half of Newark's 400,000 residents are black. A third of the
city's housing is substandard. Unemployment in the ghetto is "officially
set at 12 per cent, unofficially as high as 20 per cent"; some 17,000
households try to exist on annual incomes of less than $3,000. See Paul
Goldberg in the *New York Times Magazine*, September 29, 1968,
p. 117. The conditions in Newark are bad but hardly atypical. In
municipal governmental structure, political-party system, racial makeup,
population density, housing conditions, occupational and income distributions, and the incidence of riot and civil disturbances Newark is
fairly representative of most good-sized American cities in the Northeast.

20. Many of the events described herein occurred before I began my research.
My information is based on protracted interviews and less structured
conversations conducted in the autumn of 1965, the winter of 1966,
and the spring of 1968 with black activists and whites involved in
NCUP, and with other Newark residents. In most instances the information reported here has been corroborated by two or more
respondents. A less detailed but helpful history of the events described
above has been recorded in the documentary film, "The Troublemakers," produced and distributed by Newsreel, Inc. New York, N.Y.
The direct quotations in these case studies are from my interviews and
field observations, except for a few taken from the documentary film.

21. One of the black leaders, Jesse Allen, a former union shop steward, exhausted his life savings in order to support himself while working for
NCUP. Other black activists included youths, welfare mothers, house-
wives, and working and unemployed men.

22. In a number of instances it was difficult to determine who owned what
building. Some owners found it advantageous to use "fronts." Occasionally a building might change hands several times in quick succession only to return to the hands of the original owner.

23. The detectives charged that Mrs. Brown threw one of them down a flight
of stairs. Eyewitnesses gave a contrary account, testifying that it was
Mrs. Brown who was thrown down the stairs. The jury chose to believe
the police and Mrs. Brown was convicted and given three years probation. A subsequent grand-jury investigation of her countersuit led to
the conviction of one of the detectives for assault and battery. The conviction against Mrs. Brown, however, was never repealed.

24. This also seems to be the case in other communities. In Mount Vernon,
N.Y., in 1965, 15 welfare mothers submitted a petition to housing
authorities protesting conditions in their apartment building. Within a

week all had been served eviction notices. In New York and other cities, rent strikes when "successful" often produce results of dubious value to the tenants. After laborious legal proceedings on the tenants' parts and after the numerous delaying tactics and appeals available to the landlord have been exhausted, the city usually takes the building into receivership, uses the rent money to make repairs and then returns the building to the landlord while allowing him to charge substantial rent increases because of the improved conditions. Frequently, the repairs are so extensive that the tenants are evicted by the city only to be relocated in slums elsewhere, far from their neighborhood friends, their jobs, and their children's schools. Today most community organizers have few illusions about the efficacy of rent strikes. See Stanley Aronowitz, "New York City: After the Rent Strikes," Studies on the Left, 5 (Winter 1965), pp. 85–89.

25. The South Ward might be considered as having a "modified two-party system": the Republicans are always strong enough to raise a serious electoral challenge but seldom strong enough to win.

26. Compare with Howard Swearer's explanation of electoral participation in the Soviet Union in his "The Functions of Soviet Local Elections," Midwest Journal of Political Science, 5 (May 1961), p. 149.

27. Those who insist that more militant protest tactics should not be employed until all legitimate legislative and administrative channels for redressing grievances have been exhausted, might consider whether such channels are not, by their very nature, inexhaustible.

28. Kenneth Keniston, Young Radicals, Notes on Committeed Youth (New York: Harcourt, Brace and World, 1968), p. 127.

29. Christian Bay, "Politics are Pseudopolitics: A Critical Evaluation of Some Behavioral Literature," The American Political Science Review, 59 (March 1965), pp. 39–51; reprinted in McCoy and Playford, Apolitical Politics.

30. Banfield, Political Influence, p. 272; Robert Dahl, A Preface to Democratic Theory (Chicago: University of Chicago Press, 1956), p. 137, but see the qualification Dahl offers on p. 138. Another pluralist, Merelman, goes so far as to argue that those who are defeated nevertheless share in power because they have been able to induce the prevailing group to expend the effort needed to vanquish them! "Even if those planning to initiate policies hostile to an 'elite' become subject to its power and are constrained to desist, they still have exerted power of their own. The elite has been forced to anticipate them and exert power in return." Richard Merelman, "On the Neo-Elitist Critique of Community Power," The American Political Science Review, 62 (June 1968), 455. It is impossible using Merelman's model to imagine any situation, even a suppressive one, as not being somewhat pluralistic: both conqueror and conquered, victimizer and victim, share in power. In contrast, the model offered by Dahl and Polsby defines power as the ability to prevail in a given issue conflict.

31. Polsby, *Community Power*, p. 118.

32. See Edelman, *Symbolic Uses of Power*, 2 and *passim*; and Michael Lipsky, "Protest as a Political Resource," *American Political Science Review*, 62 (December 1968), pp. 1148 and 1155.

33. Lipsky, "Protest," pp. 1156–1157.

34. Here I am not referring to that category of nondecisions that Bachrach and Baratz see contained in the norms and beliefs of the socio-political culture and that are less frequently or less obviously the objects of deliberate manipulation. But even such "unconscious," "implicit" belief systems are not inaccessible to analysis. See Sutton and others, *American Business Creed* and Edelman, *Symbolic Uses of Power*. Few political scientists have begun to think of belief systems as resources of power comparable to the other resources commonly identified in decision conflicts.

35. Harold Lasswell, *Psychopathology and Politics* (Chicago: University of Chicago Press, 1930), pp. 196–197; also the critical comments in Kariel, *Decline of American Pluralism*, 117 ff., and Bachrach, *Democratic Elitism*, pp. 66–67.

36. Compare with E. E. Schattschneider's remark: "People are not likely to start a fight if they are certain that they are going to be severely penalized for their efforts. In this situation repression may assume the guise of a false unanimity." *The Semi-Sovereign People* (New York: Holt, Rinehart and Winston, 1960), p. 8.

37. Painstaking field work may no longer be necessary if one simply wishes to establish the fact that lower-class grievances exist. Expressions of ills have become so explosive and riotous as to have won even the glaze-eyed attention of the mass media. In the summer of 1967 there were 75 major outbreaks of disorder and in the spring of 1968 over 100 cities suffered some kind of riot and disorder.

38. Non-participation can also be ascribed in part to conditions that are hardly exclusive to the poor. Thus it may not be clearly within the interest of individual members of large groups to make the kinds of personal expenditures needed to win goals beneficial to the entire group unless there are more particularized rewards or coercions that act as personal incentives. To some extent this is a problem confronting all collective action. See Mancur Olsen, Jr., *The Logic of Collective Action* (New York: Schocken Books, 1965). One might still observe that economically deprived groups are unusually wanting in the resources that allow for particularized incentives and hence they suffer unusually severe difficulties of organization and leadership.

39. Kenneth Clark, *Dark Ghetto* (New York: Harper and Row, 1965), p. 156.

40. Contrary to an accepted notion, the great majority of the poor families of Newark, New York, New Haven, Chicago, Washington, D.C., and Watts—to mention a few of the places that have been studied—are

stable, self-respecting, and hard-working, headed by fathers, or in the absence of a male, by working mothers who care deeply and labor hard for their children, but they face substandard housing, inhumane hospitals and schools, poor work conditions, low pay, high rents, over-priced stores, and so on. They find themselves trapped not by "a matriarchal slave-family cultural heritage" but by the socioeconomic system. See Studs Terkel, *Division Street: America* (New York: Pantheon Books, 1967); Paul Jacobs, *Prelude to Riot* (New York: Random House, 1966); Charles Willie's "Two Men and their Families," in *Among the People*, Irwin Deutscher and Elizabeth Thomson (eds.) (New York: Basic Books, 1968), pp. 53–66; and Clark, *Dark Ghetto.*

41. Many of the black poor of Newark fit Robert Lane's description of the "alienation syndrome": "I am the object, not the subject of political life. . . . The government is not run in my interest; they do not care about me; in this sense it is not my government. . . ." *Political Ideology* (New York: Free Press, 1962), p. 162.

42. A similar conclusion is drawn by Terkel, *Division Street*, after extensive interviews with whites and blacks in Chicago. See also the findings on black attitudes concerning the 1964 riots and the comparison to white responses in J. R. Feagin and P. B. Sheatsley, "Ghetto Resident Appraisals of a Riot," *Public Opinion Quarterly*, 32 (Fall 1968), pp. 352–362; and the "Kerner Report" on the 1967 riots: *Report of the National Advisory Commission on Civil Disorders* (New York: Bantam Books, 1968), chap. 5 and *passim.*

43. Thus neither Dahl nor Polsby have much to say about the reactions of slum dwellers displaced by the New Haven urban renewal program. Polsby observes: "Who wanted urban redevelopment? By 1957, practically everyone who had anything to say in public strongly favored this program." *Community Power*, p. 71. Dahl makes a passing reference to those who did not have "anything to say in public": "several hundred slum dwellers without much political influence" and a handful of small businessmen. Nothing more is heard about those who suffered from urban redevelopment. *Who Governs?*, p. 244. (See comments by Gitlin, "Local Pluralism," pp. 141–142.) Polsby (*Community Power*, pp. 96–97) further assures us that in regard to goals that are "in some way explicitly pursued by people in the community, the method of study in New Haven has a reasonable chance of capturing them." Whether that claim is true or not, his method of study will tell us nothing about those goals desired by large segments of the population but not "explicitly pursued," or goals that, if pursued, fail to achieve political visibility because of the organizational weakness of the deprived group or the unresponsiveness of community leaders. Similarly, Harold Lasswell's contention that "it is impossible to locate the few without considering the many" is highly questionable. Lasswell's own work repeatedly demonstrates that a student of power can focus on the activities of the few without finding it imperative to consider the well-

being of the many. See his *Politics: Who Gets What, When, How* (New York: World Publishing Co., 1936), p. 309 and comments by Bachrach, *Democratic Elitism*, p. 66.

44. McCoy in the introduction to McCoy and Playford, *Apolitical Politics*, p. 5.

45. Dahl, *Who Governs?*, p. 85; italics in the original.

46. In fairness to Dahl it should be said that his view of "potential power" is not as simple as that held by other students. In *Who Governs?*, p. 275, he notes that there are important "objective differences" among constituents that limit their potential power: ". . . being poor or rich, well-educated or uneducated, a professional man or an unskilled laborer, living in a slum area or a middle-class neighborhood—these are differences in objective situations of a most persistent and general sort that are likely to show up in a variety of different ways over a long period of time." It is our loss that Dahl did not see fit to develop these observations.

47. *Ibid.*, p. 97.

48. See the analysis in James Q. Wilson, "The Strategy of Protest: Problems of Negro Civic Action," *Journal of Conflict Resolution*, 3 (September 1961), pp. 291–303; and Lipsky, "Protest," pp. 1145–1146.

49. Newark is not the only city in which the party regulars manifest either indifference or antipathy toward the issues raised by reformers. Describing Negro politicians in Chicago, Banfield notes: "Like all politicians, they had to consider their political futures. Only one or two were 'race men.' The others had accommodated themselves to a situation in which whites held the upper hand." The man who dominated Negro political life for so many years, Congressman Dawson, is described as one who does small favors for constituents, "takes care" of his precinct workers, and remains "indifferent to issues and principles including those of special importance to the race." Banfield, *Political Influence*, pp. 41, 260. A year as participant-observer in New Haven politics (1967–68) leads me to the same conclusions about the Negro ward leaders in that city; they say and do nothing that might earn the disapproval of Democratic Town Committee Chairman Barbieri, raise no issues of racial or economic content, and oppose those white reformers and black activists who do—as on the issue of the black boycott in the spring of 1968.

50. See Michael Walzer, "Civil Disobedience and Corporate Authority," forthcoming in a book of readings edited by Philip Green and Sanford Levinson.

51. Thus Truman notes that the rules of the game are part of "the substance of prevailing values without which the political system could not exist." *Governmental Process*, p. 348; and James D. Barber writes: "To a large degree, a successful democracy depends on agreement as to how the system is to be used, on the rules of the game." *Citizen Politics* (Chicago: Markham Publishing Company, 1969), pp. 93–94.

22.
BLUE RIDGE: THE HISTORY OF OUR STRUGGLE AGAINST LEVI-STRAUSS

Brenda C. Mull

Levi-Strauss came to Blue Ridge, Georgia, in 1956. The people who were first employed were told by the company, "If and when you prove to us that this plant and area can be a productive and profitable one, we will build a new plant and expand." To me this is like me saying to someone, "Show me a profit and I will expand and make more. I don't take any chances of losing money."

It only took between three and four years for a crew of totally untrained and unskilled people to prove they were a profitable and progressive group of workers. This may not seem like a great feat to people who know nothing of plant progress, but take my word for it as a worker of this type, it is just short of a miracle.

There are, however, several facts that should be known and told about the conditions the employees of Levi had to work under during the first three years: the kind of wages earned; the entire picture of how the operation of the plant went.

The girls would come to work at regular working time, only to clock in and then turn around and clock out (completely out as though they weren't on the job). They weren't allowed to go home though. Several of the women were paying a baby sitter while sitting at work and not drawing pay. To cover up for this the company (the upper crust) gave this poor excuse: They had no knowledge of how the employees were being cheated on their pay or how the plant was being run. However they only paid back the amount that could be proved by the poorly-kept books and time records. Practically all of the girls lost a large sum of money. All this took place when the new management took over and the old clique was ousted and blamed for things wrong in the plant.

Now to get back to the beginning of the plant while the old clique was in. To humiliate everyone and to prove himself to be a man of little

From Brenda C. Mull, *Blue Ridge: The History of Our Struggle Against Levi-Strauss* (Boston: New England Free Press, no date). Reprinted by permission of the author.

thought to others, the manager hung an old timey bath tub and a bar of soap on the wall. There was a sign by it saying, "If anyone does not have a bath at home, they may borrow this one." My people are not like the tub presented them to be. The manager must have just felt inferior to the workers, thus doing all he could to prove it. There were people from close by and from California coming and going, but the tub still hung. It seems to me he pushed sanitation in some ways while disregarding it in others. The bathrooms would tear up and run over onto the floor, but nothing was ever said about this.

The women would go to work and carry an extra sweater along with their regular winter coats, because they never knew if there would be heat or not. They were made to stay and work with their coats and sweaters on until the fuel man arrived. This might be three hours after starting to work or after dinner. Nearly every time the fuel ran out, they had to wait until the company was called and could find time to come and fill up the tank.

It was so in the old building and in the new one, that is, partiality in who was fired and who was hired. I and others have heard the workers say:

> I had a job and drew a small weekly pay each week, but I was afraid to go in debt or be dependent on my job. I never knew from day to day if I had a job or would be fired.

One woman put it like this:

> I went to work at the Levi plant in Blue Ridge. One of the supervisors there did not like me. I was fired shortly after going to work. I went to the Levi plant in Murphy, N.C. I said nothing of working at the plant in Blue Ridge, Ga. I worked there for several months and was placed on the floor as supervisor simply because I was qualified. Shortly afterwards, the supervisor from Blue Ridge plant came to Murphy and seen me working. In less than a week I was fired.

This is the kind of job security poverty people have.

Equality was an unheard of thing at Levi-Strauss. We sat there slaving and sewing, while others who catered to the boss walked the floor and made no pretense to do their job. The slavers were the ones who were fired, not the lazy. Why? Because we were the independent ones and did not cater to the boss.

Between the time of moving from the old building into the new one, the style of pants was changed. Also with the change of style the productions were raised on practically every operation. The girls had proved their speed and accuracy to be superior to other Levi employees throughout the country, and the company was beginning to take advantage of it. The piece-rate work is supposed to be set by an average worker's production, not by the fastest hand in the line being timed; but suddenly, the piece-rate was based on the fastest.

There was to be an eight-week training period program for all new employees. If they were progressing slower than Levi liked, they were fired. As usual, people were employed and fired in less than a week. Why, I don't know. Some say they tried for more than a year to get an interview at Levi's plant without success. Then they would later be called. I don't know why this happened when they were always needing hands.

The new plant was built around 1960, on property donated in part by the business people of Blue Ridge. During the change-over from the old building to the new one, some of the workers were laid off as long as nine months. They did draw unemployment, but a lot of them weren't called back in rotation as they should have been. The favored individual went back first. Also, some of them weren't called back at all, even if their work was satisfactory.

As you read this and think, "Oh, that isn't much," you must keep in mind, it is the day to day things that make up the industrial worker's life. Also, it is these "little" things that can knock a girl's payday. First to prove that all wasn't well in the plant, go to the old saying, "Figures do not lie." During the time Levi has been here, they have employed over 3,800 just to get a work force of 560 employees. These people came from a three-county area.

In an area where there is little work and people only have a grade school or high school education, a big company feels it has the right to exploit the people. All unorganized plants pay just what the law requires of them. If you are on production, an employer must pay a few cents according to the wage law. This is exactly what Levi and others do.

There is nothing better than a Merry Christmas with Levi and a free dinner while you are exploited by the company. One year the company gave a dinner for the employees. During this the employees sat and listened to records from the main office in San Francisco praising them highly on their quality and quantity. We heard how Levi was expanding all over the world. The people, knowing this, also asked, "Why then, do we not get a small raise? Why, then, must our production be so high? Why must we have untrained mechanics?" This costs the workers when a mechanic doesn't know how to fix a machine, and it doesn't work.

We also wondered why they couldn't lower production on the more difficult materials to sew. One woman remarked:

> I sat there listening to the record of praise with my hands cracked and peeling, nearly to the point of bleeding, from handling the new stiff material on the old high production rate and could have cursed, to think a company would brag of such success and could not at least be fair about production. It seems to me as if Levi just tried to rub it in.

There was always a lot of overtime to be worked, especially during the summer months. It seemed as though it did not matter to the company that people would not baby-sit on Saturday or disliked keeping children nine hours a day every day. The company has told many of the women that not having baby sitters was no excuse for being out of work. It did not matter to the company if you had worked nine hours a day 5 days a week and four to eight hours on Saturday. You were expected to do the same the following week.

At one point, in the old building, the women were asked to work all day, go home for supper, return and work three or five hours, and then return and do the same the next day.

When a machine tears up (which is pretty regular) you might wait at least a half day to get it fixed and when the undertrained mechanic came and worked on it, the machine still would not sew half the time. Then the supervisor would sew on it and declare that the fault was with the operator. The way our pay was set up, machine trouble could cost the girls much money. We had to average 100 percent five days a week if we drew production pay. You could make 100 percent of your production every day and miss it by one pair of pants on the last day and you would lose your production pay for the entire week. Then you would just get the minimum wage and the company had an excuse to get angry at you. Of course, if you began to always make your production, the company would just raise it, but you can see how important it was when a girl lost time for machine repair. Sometimes it meant a whole week's effort down the drain. Sometimes your machine tore up and you had to sew on a broken spare instead of clocking out and you lost a lot of money and the time you gained for that day.

As I said, we were paid a flat $1.25 per hour if we could not meet the high production. When we met it, we received a few cents over. If you were lucky enough to do a bundle over, you were paid a little over the average pay. However, if you had your quota for the day a little early (10 or 15 minutes before time to quit work) you could not quit until the bell rang.

One woman was an excellent operator. She was fast with her hands and accurate in her work. She did well over her production (which is unusual in the first place for a Levi worker) and when she quit five minutes before the bell rang, her supervisor told her to sew another bundle, although she did not have time to finish it before leaving that day. Being a good union person, she stalled until quitting time. The high production on the majority of the operations helped to keep the girls from making production pay, although they produced enough work to make and clear a big profit for the company, they still didn't get fair pay.

When you got sick on the job, the company would ask you to leave work and see a doctor and then return to work—even if you were very sick. This was worked by the company calling the doctor to see at what time he would be able to attend to your problem. Then the doctor's office called the plant to let you know they could see you. Also if your children were sick, the company said you should try and take them to the doctor on a Saturday, or send them by someone else.

There seemed to be absolutely no feelings for the employees' problems, large or small. There was one employee whose work record was excellent and who never asked for time off unless it was absolutely necessary. Her mother lived about 200 miles away from Blue Ridge. Her mother had been sick for a long period of time. The employee only went for visits with her mother on long weekends and holidays because the company kicked so about being out of work. The mother was already bedfast and then she had to have her leg amputated. The employee asked off to be with her during the operation and a couple of days later to see if she was going to be all right. The doctor doubted that her mother would make it off the operating table. Since the operation was to be on Monday, the lady would need to stay at least until Wednesday morning to be able to tell how things were going. The company asked her to go and stay Monday and come back Tuesday, although there were only three full working days in that week, due to a holiday.

To me these are some of the real problems of southern labor today. Also the things that helped to bring on the strike. People being thought of as animals, and being treated like them. Why does this sort of thing happen? Probably because people are uninformed of these problems and don't really understand. It is, however, each and every citizen's responsibility to make things like this (as well as national problems) their business too. If we do not, things will never be any different.

At the very beginning of the organizing, the people who first started the wheels to rolling knew that the element of surprise would help to bring a victory. There had been a meeting called and some cards signed before the company realized what was happening to them. Although during the debate about Levi coming to Blue Ridge, Levi said they were not anti-union—probably meaning United Garment Workers, the company union in three or four of their sweatshops—upon knowledge of ILGWU's presence, they began to do everything they could to prevent a union victory. The people were quizzed like this: "There are union cards being signed, aren't there? Do you know what union it is? Have they got far enough along to get cards signed? Do you know anyone who has cards in the plant to sign?" Then one woman said to another, "The boss said if you all want a union, to let this all die down, and he will bring one into the plant then." I am sure it would have been nothing short of a company union to keep a good one from coming in. That is the way we were thought of—ignorant and totally unable to know better than that type of thing. To me, this is one of the most insulting things a boss could do to me. Like children in school.

One of the men helping to organize had a wife working in the plant as a floor lady (supervisor or straw boss). Of course, when the company discovered this situation, they went out to get her. During the meetings held between management and supervisors each morning, her husband was talked about in her presence and in the presence of others. I cannot say what went on exactly, but I can say what the girl was told in her section by the boss. After a slew of tales flew through the plant and every section was angered, and she was laid off, the girls in her section were called into the office in a group. The girls were told by the area manager, "We have gone as far as we can with your supervisor. I think you girls can understand the company situation. Besides, we feel the strain on her working on the floor under the circumstances, and then going home and not being able to discuss things with her husband (organizer), is a big strain. We feel it would be to her interest not to work now. But we hope to have her back when things settle down. We don't feel we should ask her to work now, as it would jeopardize her home life this way."

Some of the girls showed by expression or speech how they felt. We went back to our jobs, and in less than five minutes the ones showing their disapproval were called back to the office for another session like the first one. Of course, when the case was arbitrated, she was reinstated with full back pay. This sounds good, and is, but all our cases did not go this way, and all employees could not withstand the tension from day to day. The constant picking through her work. Some of them broke down and said "I quit," and of course this was fine for the company, which planned such things.

There was one case where this happened, and the girl was advised to return to work the next morning and explain what happened, and ask for her job back. She did not get it. The labor board did rule that she should receive two weeks' pay, because the company refused to give her the regular two weeks' notice. Some of the employees did not get that much. I have watched grown women sit and cry as they sewed. Some just plain quit and gave Levi up as a bad thing. While all this was going on in the plant, there was all sorts of talk flying about how a union would ruin the workers and all belonging to it. About this time in the game, the company had placed pictures of a baby crying on the bulletin boards, with slogans indicating that the employees were babies and could not take it.

After I had decided to forget anything the company did and totally ignore it, they came up with a shocker. They took $5 from the original pay check and wrote a separate one for $5 with a note attached indicating that this would be our union dues and there would be all kinds of assessments and raises in dues that we would not have any way of doing anything about. Then the company took us back to grade school days by having us ask their supervisor before going to the rest room.

Another woman's husband was helping to organize the plant while she was working there. The manager called her to his office. While she was in the office, the management began to talk about her husband in her presence. Naturally, this provoked her into saying things that weren't becoming to a woman; after all, we had lived in a nervous strain for weeks, and the boss knew this and depended on it to do the trick. This gave the company a cause to fire her. She won her case in the labor courts. There was also a petition passed around in the plant for the employees to sign, saying, "We do not need a union to represent us, and we do not want a union." Naturally, this went off so poorly that it disappeared and wasn't seen anymore.

The word got out that the ILGWU was nothing short of "Fink Agitators and trouble makers all the way around." I can't say where the word started. All I know is that tales like this went on all during the organizing and after the union was voted in. At one time, a tale was out that the company said, if the union was voted in, Levi would move out. We wish it had.

To add to the tactics used by a company like Levi, a system was set up where three or four girls called "quality line checkers" went through each individual's work every day to catch errors and point them out to each worker. If there were more than three repairs in a bundle (60 pairs to a bundle), the operator got a yellow slip turned in against her. If you received a number of these, you could be fired. Anyone wanting to find fault with a person's work could do so. This is how sewing piece-rates are in all factories.

Also, there was a system where, if an operator surpassed the already high production, there was a flag placed on her machine to show she was producing above her production. If she went further upward, her picture was placed out in the lobby as being a high percentage operator. At one point of organizing, the company played "I spy" to see who attended the meetings. And once again the company showed how much respect it had for the workers by asking that you attend work half a day and then leave to attend a funeral, unless it was someone in the immediate family.

I feel that you can see now, after reading the real facts and figures on my people's lives, why the union was voted in by a vote of two to one. Before the election, the plant manager had agreed to announce the outcome over the speaker system. After he learned the results, he refused to do so. The votes were counted and totaled just before quitting time. We learned the results from a union man outside the plant as we left. It was passed on to others still coming out of the plant. Everyone was jumping up and down and hollering, blowing their horns and all. One girl who had been forced into saying "I quit" before the election, was out on the lot dancing a jig. The people were so excited that two of our own people bumped each other's cars. One woman was so excited that she backed over a cross tie which separated and marked the places to park, then she proceeded to go back over it before ever getting out of the lot.

What sticks with me the most, at this point, is the morning after the election. It was like a funeral all over the plant. You could almost hear a pin drop, even with the machines going. No one was talking; everyone was doing her work the very best she could. All the excitement had left everyone and had been replaced by fear and worry. We all knew trouble was on its way, more than ever, now that the union was voted in and that we would have to stick in there and fight with everything we had to stay alive and to keep the union going.

I should point out here that we were more determined to keep the union alive than the union was. This was our biggest disappointment. After we had fought so hard, it was shocking to realize what some International Unions were like. I will just say a few honest words about our union, but I never want to be taken as anti-union. (1.) ILG signed a terrible contract for us which gave Levi power to crush us and our Local union; (2.) They did not back us up, even where they could have, because of their policy that "You take what you can get and hope for better next time." This let the company think our union was not behind us. (3.) Even when we had taken so much that we warned the company and the union we would have to walk out if it continued, the union took no solid stand. They say they couldn't support our "wildcat" because of the no-strike clause. But, they let the company violate their end of the agreement every day. If this is union policy in the South, we say it should be changed, or unions will lose the support of the people that make them rich. Somehow I look back on our victory with regret. Not of organizing, but of learning just how unjust things are here in America and in our laws. It still gives me the feeling of being in bondage. We were a group of people fighting for justice and our rights, not knowing all that was against us. We learned it wasn't just Levi-Strauss. I see that the blame has to be shared with our lawmakers and politicians, plus some hard-headed businessmen that are out for the dollar and that is all that matters to them. Not the people who make it and spend it to make them rich.

I learned that all business people seem to have a code that says, "Come South; Labor is cheap; the people are hard workers. They're poor and will even be grateful to work hard. Their towns are all hungry for a payroll." I am of the opinion that the business people of Blue Ridge go along with this code. I also feel that they don't have to be this way—there is good opportunity for towns who consider their people first. They say that some of us are getting lazy. Ask yourself this question: "If I cannot get a decent place to work, which do I want—to work long hours and hard, only to spend half of what I make on Doctor bills and die young; or do I rather want to have less, live longer, and have some time to spend and enjoy the children I am working to support?"

Naturally, after the election and after the sorry contract was signed, the company set in with the same old things only harder and more directed to specific persons—along with a few new added tricks. One such case was a woman who is very timid about taking up for herself and was so scared she preferred to quit rather than fight for her job. The company realized this and set in to get rid of one more union member without firing her. She was out sick for three days. She had reported in each day saying she was too sick to work. She heard from one of the girls she worked with that the company had hired a new girl and placed her on her machine. She called the plant manager to ask about it and he said it was true. We finally convinced her to go ahead and report to work on Monday morning; that he could not do this to her. The company figured she would not push the issue and they would be rid of her. However, she did, with the committee's help, report back to work. She was put back to work on the same day. The company did not give up though. They began to pick through her work day after day with a fine-toothed comb. Of course, they found something to nag her about. The operation she was on is like that. You could do the same thing to any one on the same operation. She became a nervous wreck, lost weight, and went to the doctor continually. Finally she found a job out of town and had to move to work there. Then she quit Levi. Now she is healthy and gaining weight.

There was one girl that worked on the union every spare minute she had. Even though she was on one of those jobs where no one outside of one or two exceptional people made and held their day to day quota, and there was always something wrong with a bundle of work if you looked at it enough. She knew that eventually she would be fired, but she felt that the union could get her job back under this kind of circumstance. She did as well as any hand on her job. She was fired and the union bargained for her job back like this: "We have several arbitration cases that we could win if we take them to court and you know this. We will drop this and this against you if you put these few people back to work." As soon as the time limit on the arbitration cases ran out by law, and the union could no longer hold them over the company's head, those girls were fired again. Their case the last time was as good as it was the first, but the union never pressed it, and the girls lost their jobs. Wonder why. Oh well, we are used to being kicked by all sides. Maybe we learned our lesson this time. I hope the union learned a good one too. But it's us who suffer.

I will never forget the case of a woman whose husband had cancer, and she quit her job to take care of him and the children. They could live better on the disability check than they could if she worked and paid a baby sitter and someone to come in and take care of her husband. He had to be looked after all during the day. However, there was a delay in the disability checks and in desperation she went back to Levi and explained what happened and asked for her job back. At least she could depend on the little she got at Levi. The company refused to return her to work, even though they were in bad need of operators to do the job she was trained to do. Everyone practically begged them to give her job back. It did not gain a thing, although the company knew that the family had no income and that the finance company had already taken the kitchen utilities out of the house. This made no difference. You see, she was a good union member, and she refused to take things from her supervisor. A price for rights as a human being.

To me, another inhuman thing was when a woman was laid off for a month because she stayed out of work and went out of town to bring her father home from the hospital. She had mentioned this time off to her supervisor and gotten her permission to be off. But the boss said she did not come by the office, and he laid her off for a month as a punishment.

The company started requiring the employees to bring a doctor's statement each day they were absent from work. Three days' absence without a statement would allow the company to fire you, especially if you were a good union member. Not having a baby sitter wasn't considered a reasonable excuse for being out from work—even if it was overtime work.

Somehow, the union never grasped the idea of how bad we were discriminated against, or else they did not want to understand anything about the members of their union at the Levi-Strauss plant in Blue Ridge, Georgia. During organizing some of the out-of-town organizers stayed in town. Some people say there were threats made to those who kept them over night. This is freedom in America. Is this what our boys are fighting for in today's wars? Their parents can't even join a union.

The Walk-Out

The last straw, that brought things to a head in the plant and caused the walkout on August 10, 1966, was an incident about seniority on machines. The company had started changing machines any way possible in order to raise production so high that half of the girls—especially the union members—could not make production. By this I mean that they would give a girl a production rate she could make on a new machine but not on her old one. Then they kept her on her old one. This happened mostly to union members. Their job became very difficult and tedious, and was a big strain. New machines would have taken the strain off. We warned the company a month before the strike that unless any new machines that came in were given to the girls with the most seniority, we would walk out. Both the company and the union were warned at the same time—that we just weren't going to take any more. Our contract did cover this problem. Although the contract was weak and practically everything ended or started with the clause, "If in the opinion of management . . . ," we felt that the union could have taken a stand for us. This was our greatest disappointment.

On the very day of the walk-out, our shop steward, Mrs. Darlene Davis (whose house was later burned down) went to the office and told the manager we were walking out if the new girls weren't taken off the new machines. The manager called the side-seamers into the office and tried to talk the anger down. After this, the shop steward again reported to the manager and told him we would walk out. He said "Go Ahead." The walk-out occurred at five minutes after noon. The irony of it all is the number of people who came out with the union members and never returned to work. A large number of the non-union members came around asking if it would be all right to walk out with us. That they knew we were right and they just could not sit there and work. They left that day and did not return the next day. Only a few people on the evening shift went to work that evening.

It was once said among the people that the supervisor and assistant manager actually talked anti-union to people and let it be known that to be union was to be fired. Things were so bad at one point before the walk-out that there was a vote to walk out. At that time, we had little hope left that we could ride the sorry contract out. It would mean another year of harassment and firing before a new contract could be negotiated. There was a chance, however, that the company would have already accomplished their goal of busting the union and getting rid of a large majority of the union members before negotiations came. There was also the thought of having another bad contract to ride out. Just one more example of company cruelty before I describe our lives during the strike. One occasion toward the end was a good union member whose baby had a twisted foot and was about to have corrective surgery. She told the company she had to be with him at the hospital. The company suggested, "Why don't you get a neighbor to stay with him?" The child was only nine years old. And Levi forgot all our neighbors are out slaving in sweatshops like we are.

On the Picket Line

The strike started out with a lot of violence and trouble from the town. A truckdriver pulling a load out of Levi pulled a gun on us to get safely across the picket line. There was a fight in the shopping plaza between two or three anti-union people and two or three strikers. Several of us went to see what was happening. When warrants were served, all the women who weren't involved got them, too. When it went to court, seven witnesses, including the sheriff, said they weren't involved. But they were all fined. While we pleaded our case, the judge looked out the window. This is the justice we're dying for.

On September 31, 1966, one of the picketers was hit by a car. She was picketing lawfully. Everyone feels it was no accident the car went so far out of its way. The picketer went to the hospital with a fractured vertebra. The case was taken to court, but all charges against the scab who hit her were dropped and dismissed. When the scab accused the same girl she hit of throwing a rock at her car, the striker was fined. Justice, justice in Blue Ridge, Georgia.

Even though we have been let down by the union and by our town and neighbors around us, by all of them not taking a stand for what they know is right, WE WILL CARRY ON THE BATTLE AS A GROUP OF PEOPLE WHO BELIEVE WHAT IS RIGHT IS WORTH ANY STRUGGLE; RIGHT IS RIGHT, AND WRONG IS WRONG AND CAN BE PUT TO RIGHT IF WE STAND UP AND FIGHT WITH A TRUE DESIRE TO GET JUSTICE.

The company called in the Southern Detectives to "guard" the plant while we were large in number on the picket line. The guards were turned loose on the lot at Levi with guns. That isn't so bad, but it is when they are about half-drunk and wearing a gun isn't my idea of a guard.

During the time our girls were picketing at night, they were harassed, and one time even shot at. The pellets from the blast fell on top of the tent they were using for shelter. Blue Ridge police pretended they were too busy to do anything about it. Gordon Ware, an officer of our local, had his house shot into one night. Another striker's house was shot into and the walls outside were brick and the inside was panelled. The bullets went through the brick and the inside wall and right into the mattress of his children's bed. There was nothing done about these crimes against our people.

Our strikers went to work at other plants as far as 50 miles from home to earn enough money to keep up the fight and to help support other strikers. Many times they were fired because someone found out they were active in the Levi strike.

Two more incidents during the strike. A man and his wife were holding night shift picket. One night they had just settled down and about half asleep when a car passed real fast and a thud against the side of the trailer alarmed them. He ran out to see what was going on. Someone had thrown a coke bottle full of kerosene and fire against the trailer. They knew people were inside the trailer asleep. If they had been sound asleep, they might have burned up.

Mrs. Darlene Davis, our shop steward, was a very active member of the union. One night about 2:00 A.M. her husband woke the family up saying "Get out, the house is burning down." Somehow they managed to get the fire out before it destroyed the house. They stayed with relatives the rest of that night. On the following night, the house caught fire again and burnt to the ground. No one was inside. Mrs. Davis' son, who was in a cast from his waist down, had nightmares for a long time after that fire.

What We Are Doing Now

After a year of picketing, without the support of our union or our town, Levi has called a decertification election and won. We have no one left to depend on, but ourselves.

Not long after we lost the strike, we met some organizers from Atlanta, and we began to talk about a community organization for all the workers in our county. Its purpose would be to pressure companies like Levi out through boycotts, and so on, and also to work for more decent local government. We called it Southern Labor Association. But we all knew after a year of struggle and going hungry, we better start thinking of ways for people to earn a living too. The idea of a co-op factory of our own came up. Since then we have organized our own factory, employing 64 people, mostly strikers, and most of us have been working for nothing for a long time to get it off the ground. But it is going now, and we are all very proud. Naturally, we have a lot of problems to iron out, but we are working full time on them. From here, we're going to build our community organization. We proved to everybody we could do what we said, and now we're going to do something else we said: "Make Fannin County a decent place for working people to live!"

23.
PARTY PROGRAMS—SERVING THE PEOPLE

Bobby Seale

In 1969, the Black Panther Party tried to reach millions of people, both to organize resistance to fascism and to find out about, and receive service from, the basic community programs that we have already set up and will be setting up in the future. This is what we call a broad, massive, people's type of political machinery. It developed out of the rising tide of fascism in America, the rapid attempt on the part of the power structure to try to wipe out the Black Panther Party and other progressive organizations, and the use of more troops and more police forces to occupy our communities.

The cops in Los Angeles and several other places have walked in on the Free Breakfast for Children Program to try to intimidate the children and the Party. They come down there with their guns, they draw a gun or two, say a few words and walk all over the place, with shotguns in their hands. Then the little kids go home and say, "Mama, the police came into the Breakfast for Children Program." This is the power structure's technique to try to destroy the program. It's an attempt to scare the people away from sending their children to the Breakfast Program and at the same time, trying to intimidate the Black Panther Party.

Meanwhile, through the politicians and the media they try to mislead the people about the value of such a program and the political nature of such a program. We say that we want that program, not just right now for some political purpose—we say that the program should survive right into the future for years and years. The Party's community programs are the peoples' programs that we define as revolutionary, community, socialistic programs.

A lot of people misunderstand the politics of these programs; some people have a tendency to call them reform programs. They're not reform programs; they're actually revolutionary community programs. A

From *Seize the Time* by Bobby Seale, pp. 412–22. Copyright © 1968, 1969, 1970 by Bobby Seale. Reprinted by permission of Alfred A. Knopf, Inc.

revolutionary program is one set forth by revolutionaries, by those who want to change the existing system to a better system. A reform program is set up by the existing exploitative system as an appeasing handout, to fool the people and to keep them quiet. Examples of these programs are poverty programs, youth work programs, and things like that which are set up by the present demagogic government. Generally they're set up to appease the people for a short period of time, and then are phased out and forgotten about.

The objective of programs set forth by revolutionaries like the Black Panther Party is to educate the masses of the people to the politics of changing the system. The politics are related to people's needs, to a hungry stomach, or to getting rid of the vicious pigs with their revolvers and clubs. The revolutionary struggle becomes bloody when the pig power structure attacks organizations or groups of people who go forth with these programs.

We started the Free Breakfast for Children Program by asking businessmen in the black community and outside of it, to donate food and money. We also moved to get as many other people in the community as possible to work on these programs and take over running them. The programs are generally started off in churches. In one case we actually got a Free Breakfast for Children going in the school itself, which was very, very good, because the school cafeteria facilities and everything were used; this was over in Marin County, north of San Francisco. We generally work out of churches, because the churches all have facilities, like a large hall, a kitchen, tables and chairs, and so on. Members of the Party get up early in the morning, at 6:00 A.M. to get down and begin preparing the food so when the kids start coming at 7:00 and 7:30, everything is ready. We also try to get as many people from the community to schedule themselves, for one or two days out of the week to come in and work on the Breakfast for Children Program. It has to be a very organized thing so that it's speedy and at the same time the children get good, wholesome breakfasts.

There are millions of people in this country who are living below subsistence; welfare mothers, poor white people, Mexican-Americans, Chicano peoples, Latinos, and black people. This type of program, if spread out, should readily relate to the needs of the people. Donations of food and money can be gotten from churches, stores, and companies. When the stores and milk companies don't donate, people should leaflet the community. Any particular chain food stores that can't donate a small, small percentage of its profits or one penny from every dollar it makes from the community, to Breakfast for Children and other community programs, should be boycotted. We don't ever threaten or anything like that, but we tell the people in the community that the businessman exploits them and makes thousands and thousands of dollars, and that he won't donate to a Breakfast for Children Program that's actually tax deductible. This is exposing the power structure for what it is, the robbery of poor oppressed people by avaricious businessmen. Black, brown, and red people, and poor whites can all have the same basic program, and that means we're breaking down racism and focusing in on the power structure.

Another program that we're setting up is free medicine and free medical care. We'll be setting those up in community centers. If we start off with nothing more than a doctor and his bag, and some aspirin, this is the beginning of a free health clinic, the beginning of free medicine for the people in the communities. We work to serve the people in the communities on a very practical level.

Right in the Bay Area we have some 25 doctors and medical students who've pledged their time to be scheduled in different community centers that we're putting up and this will be free of charge. We have free health clinics all over the country and we are putting more up, just as fast as the people can work with NCCF.

In addition, Charles R. Garry is contacting a lot of lawyers who are opening their eyes and beginning to see that the black community needs more legal aid. So we're putting together free legal services, which will also be set up in the community centers. The poverty programs that have free legal service are always told that they can't get funds if they're at all political. That's done so they won't expose the power structure and the injustices of the system. They only handle civil cases. Our legal aid will handle both civil and criminal cases.

Another thing we'll be doing is heavy voter registration. The purpose of this registration will be to get more black and poor people on the juries so we can really be tried in courts by juries of our peers. The DAs will try to get all white racist juries or maybe to put one jive Uncle Tom on them, but it'll be much harder if a lot of blacks are registered and are on the jury panel that they pick from. Black people have to understand the experience of serving on juries because black people are railroaded in these courts. Poor oppressed people are railroaded in courts because they don't have funds to obtain lawyers. A lot of the older people are frightened or allow themselves to be frightened away from being jury members, and a lot of black people move around so much that they don't bother to re-register. It's a real problem, but we've got to educate the people to the fact that they should be on the rolls for jury duty. Then we can begin to get some revolutionary justice. Right now the type of so-called justice that's being meted out to a majority of the poor oppressed people is the "injustice" of racism and capitalistic exploitation.

The Black Panther Party has black caucuses, Black Panther caucuses in a number of unions, and we definitely are working with the union people. We're not putting in Black Panther caucuses as racist groups. We're talking about a caucus that works in conjunction with the union to help educate the rest of the members of the union to the fact that they can have a better life, too. We want the workers to understand that they must control the means of production, and that they should begin to use their power to control the means of production to serve all the people.

Workers have high taxes taken away from their wages, but they should begin to understand that they have to move not only for a 15 or 20 percent wage raise, because taxes have gone up, and not only for better working conditions, but also because they have to realize the need to use their working power for the benefit of all the other poor oppressed people.

They should use their union power to create employment for more of the poor people throughout the country. We're advocating that workers begin to move to control the means of production by first demanding 30-hour work weeks with the same 40-hour pay. By doing this, they will automatically open up more jobs. These jobs can be filled by poor, unemployed people. This would be part of the program of educating the masses of the workers to be a political force against the three levels of oppression—the avaricious, big-time, greedy businessmen, the demagogic politicians who lie and use the unions, and also the facist pig cops who have been used in the past and are used today to break up the workers' constitutional rights to strike and redress their grievances.

Employed or unemployed, workers must unite with each other and with the community. They should be registered voters, too, and serve on jury panels and circulate the community control of police petition, too.

Another Black Panther Party program is the Liberation Schools. These schools are held in the afternoons, along with the free breakfasts and free lunches. They're held in churches and the community centers. We see the Liberation Schools as a supplement to the existing institutions, which still teach racism to children, both white and black. The youth have to understand that the revolutionary struggle in this country that's now being waged is not a race struggle but a class struggle. This is what the Liberation Schools are all about.

We are working to show children that a person's skin color is not important, but in fact it's a class struggle against the avaricious businessman and the small ruling class who exploit us and perpetuate the racism that's rampant in our communities. When we teach Black American History, we teach it in terms of the class struggle, not in terms of a race struggle.

In New York we also started a free clothing program. Black Panther Party members went out and asked businessmen to donate sets of clothes, for school children on up to teen-agers. We tried to get brand new clothing, because black people are tired of hand-me-downs. Some of the clothing was very good clothing that people never came back and picked up from dry cleaners. We got all kinds of clothing together, but our primary objective was to get free clothing for the people by asking the businessmen to donate two complete changes of clothes for children. This is especially important before school begins in September and in mid-term around January. When this free clothing program got kicked off, some 500 or 600 black people in Harlem, mothers and welfare people, came down and got the clothing for their kids.

It takes a lot of work, and a lot of people donating time and funds to run these programs. The programs are not run by the fascist government at all. Naturally, these programs spread and as they begin to reach more and more people, the Party is moving closer and closer to implementing the 10-point platform and program of the Black Panther Party. When we have community socialistic programs such as these, and move them to a real level where people actually begin to receive help from them, it shows the people that by unity, by working and unifying around such programs, we can begin to end the oppressive conditions.

The Black Panther Party is not stupid at all in understanding the politics of the situation. We understand that the avaricious, demagogic, ruling class will use racist police departments and mass media to distort the real objectives of the Black Panther Party. The more we're successful with the programs, the more we'll be attacked. We don't take guns with us to implement these programs, but we understand and know from our own history that we're going to be attacked, and that we have to be able to defend ourselves. They're going to attack us viciously and fascisticly and try to say it was all justifiable homicide, in the same manner they've always attacked black people in the black communities.

We also go forth to advocate the right to self-defense from unjust attacks by racist, fascist pigs. Even when the policemen come into our communities with guns and tanks and the National Guard, we have the right to self-defense. Brothers and sisters shouldn't riot in large numbers. They should work in small groups of three, four, and five, to fight back when they attack our communities with tanks and start blasting buildings away and killing people. When they come and occupy our community and start killing people, those brothers running in threes, fours, and fives are going to have to know how to stop those tanks and those guardsmen from brutalizing and killing and murdering us.

We aren't hungry for violence; we don't want violence. Violence is ugly, guns are ugly. But we understand that there are two kinds of violence: the violence that is perpetrated against our people by the fascist aggression of the power structure; and self-defense—a form of violence used to defend ourselves from the unjust violence that's inflicted upon us. The power structure metes this violence upon the Black Panther Party because we've implemented programs that are actually exposing the government, and they're being implemented and put together by a revolutionary political party.

The freeing of political prisoners is also on the program of the Black Panther Party, because we have now, at this writing, over 300 Black Panthers who have court cases that are pending. In addition there have been hundreds of arrests, unjust arrests of Party members, who were exercising their constitutional rights. We believe in exercising our constitutional rights of freedom of assembly, of freedom of the press (the Black Panther Party newspaper), our constitutional right to bear arms, to be able to defend ourselves when attacked, and all the others. So we've been arrested.

What has to be understood is that they intend to destroy our basic programs. This is very important to understand. The fact that they murder Black Panther Party members, conduct attacks and raids on our offices, arrest us and lie about us, is all an attempt to stop these basic programs that we're putting together in the community. The people learn from these programs because they're clear examples, and the power structure wants to stop that learning.

We do not believe in the power structure controlling these programs, but we do believe in making the power structure admit that it has to change the system, because we, the people, united and together, can begin to change our conditions ourselves. We have to move with the power of the people, with the workers and the laboring masses of the people, to have control of the means of production and make the power structure step back. We're going to have to defend ourselves with guns because we know we're going to be attacked and we know they're going to attempt to make more political prisoners.

Community control of police is the key. We've got to have community control of the police in every city where there exists police brutality, in every metropolis in America where black people, Latino people, and Chinese people live in large numbers. In all these cities, and where there are progressive and liberal white people who are protesting, police forces have been doubled, tripled, and quadrupled, and fascist oppression has been meted out upon the heads of all of us. The workers too are attacked and threatened by police when they strike and protest over their conditions.

Our community control of the police campaign is a petition drive. Registered voters will sign the petition and will vote into their city charters a new legal structure for the police department. The people will be voting in a law that says that all policemen who patrol the community, must live in the community. They will be voting in a decentralized police department.

We will have neighborhood divisions with neighborhood councils, who are duly elected in the particular neighborhoods. We'll have two, three, four, and five police departments that work in conjunction together through the commissioners of particular neighborhood divisions, so there will not be a single police chief. These commissioners can be removed by the duly elected neighborhood councils. The 15-man neighborhood councils will be able to appoint and fire a commissioner, will be able to discipline police officers who are unjust, or who get out of hand, and will be able to set salaries and pay the police officers. The people throughout the city will control the police, rather than the power structure, the avaricious businessmen, and demagogic politicians who presently control them. The point of community control of police is that those people living in those neighborhoods will actually do the hiring and firing of the policemen who patrol that area, and those policemen will be people from those neighborhoods—black police for a black neighborhood, Chinese for a Chinese neighborhood, white for a white neighborhood, and so on. The tax money which used to be given to the central police department will be divided up among the neighborhood divisions. All the facilities, all the cars, all the equipment for the police that the city now owns, will be in the hands and in the control of the people in the community.

Now when this begins to move, the pig power structure is gonna say, "O.K., you can have civilian review boards." But all that does is allow the same old fascist power structure to keep control of the police while you have a front civilian review board, and this is not what we're talking about at all. What we're talking about is righteous community control, where the people who control the police are elected by the people of the community. Those people who are elected have to live in the community. They can be removed by circulating petitions for re-elections if they go wrong. We know that such a program is very positive and necessary in order for the people to have power in this country and to stop the avaricious businessman from ruling us with guns and violating our constitutional rights.

Everybody knows that they lied about the way they murdered brother Fred Hampton, and then tried to justify it. Mitchell, Agnew, and Nixon are running an operation to wipe out the Black Panther Party behind the scenes, when they send the Civil Rights Division of the Justice Department in to investigate the slaying of brothers Fred Hampton and Mark Clark. We don't want them to investigate anything. We want the civilian and people's investigation to come forth. Thousands of people went in to the brother's apartment and investigated, and found out that it was outright murder; that there was no shoot-out, but the brothers in fact, were shot in their bedrooms while they slept. This is outright murder; this is outright fascism. The next attack was on the Los Angeles office, a few days later. Community control of police is where it's at. The only other choice is guerilla warfare.

Guerilla warfare is going to exist if the power structure is not stopped with community control of the police. One of the reasons the people have to work on the community control of police campaign is to curtail civil war in America, because it's at that point right now. Community control of police is one of the most functional and most necessary programs to make all the other basic community programs work.

24.
CONSCIENCE OF A STEELWORKER

Barbara and John Ehrenreich

When steelworker Gilbert Pugliese was suspended from his job for disobeying a foreman's order on July 14, his local union officials were off in Washington, entering their second week of industry-wide negotiations with the steel industry. President Nixon had just met with United Steelworkers' President I. W. Abel and other union and industry representatives to plead for "moderation." In the spotlight of national attention the union appeared a well-matched opponent to the giant steel corporations. But it is a tired and troubled union—a generation older than it was in its organizing heyday, 12 years older than it was during its last nationwide strike. Caught between rising inflation and the steady decline of the American steel industry, the union has barely held its own on bread-and-butter issues. It has little energy left for such noneconomic issues as health, safety, pollution, and job security.

To steelworkers, there is probably no better measure of their union's helplessness than job security. Any step out of line—a sarcastic remark to a foreman is sometimes enough—can bring down disciplinary actions ranging from informal harassment to a formal reprimand to suspension, or even to firing. The union big shots can bluster in Washington; the man in the mill has learned to keep his mouth shut and follow orders.

Gilbert Pugliese's crime was a trivial one in Jones & Laughlin Steel Corporation's scale of priorities. He had not interrupted production, damaged equipment, or advocated control by the workers. It was just an irritating breach of discipline. At the beginning of the morning shift at J&L's Cleveland plant, Pugliese was ordered to press a button which would send several hundred gallons of waste oil into the Cuyahoga River. This was not an unusual order: the oil, waste from steel rolling operations, collects in sump holes under the mills and must be disposed of frequently, and pushing the button came within Pugliese's line of duties as a millwright. Pugliese, J&L steelworker for 28 years, knew all this, but he nevertheless refused to carry out the order. He was summarily marched to the front office and handed a

From Barbara and John Ehrenreich, "Pugliese vs. Jones & Laughlin: Conscience of a Steelworker," *The Nation*, September 27, 1971, pp. 268–71. © 1971 by Nation Associates, Inc. Reprinted by permission of the publisher.

five-day suspension. In normal J&L practice, a five-day suspension is an all but automatic prelude to being discharged.

J&L is a major Cleveland polluter. The emissions from its blast furnaces, coke plant, sintering plant, powerhouse, and other facilities, along with those from Republic Steel and U.S. Steel nearby, hang in a cloud over the downtown area. Its liquid wastes—oil, phenols, ammonia, and so on—have helped make the Cuyahoga River literally a fire hazard; they flow on from there to contribute to the slow poisoning of Lake Erie. Like the other steel companies, J&L is on the defensive. "The quality of our environment has become an issue of critical concern throughout the country," says the 1970 annual report. "J&L is pledged to meet all government standards. Our objectives and those of the various regulatory agencies striving to achieve clean air and water are one and the same. Any misunderstanding that may exist is in regard to the time required to achieve the objectives, not the objectives themselves."

Compared to the rest of J&L's insults to the environment, oil dumping is a minor affront. It is a violation of the 1899 Refuse Act, but it isn't central to the plant's operation and it's relatively inexpensive to correct. When the federal government stepped up pollution abatement proceedings against J&L in 1969, the company could easily have complied on this particular form of pollution by pumping the oil into drums for proper disposal. But it was more convenient to continue dumping the oil into the river. According to several J&L millwrights, the company's major concession was to order the workers to confine oil dumping to the night shift. "During the day the coast guard patrols. But at night, the water's black, the oil's black; no one can tell," one steelworker told us. "When the inspectors come around, the company diverts the flow and puts the oil into barrels for disposal."

When we met Pugliese on the day after his suspension, the first thing he wanted to make clear to us was that he had not acted on impulse. He had a history of resistance, he told us, and the company was out to get him:

> It's common practice to dump pollution into the river without any pressure from the authorities. Now you've got this serious situation and this pollution consciousness. Anyone with a conscience, who is concerned about the health and welfare of himself and his family, is concerned about this. They [the companies] just keep on stalling, polluting the waterways and air. So one day you take a stand. I took my stand on June 5, 1969. I refused to pump any more oil into the water. I suggested that they pump it into drums and throw out the drums. . . . This would mean more work for me. Dumping it into the river only involves pushing a button. Pumping it into drums is much more difficult. You have to get the drums and find a hand pump. I said I would do this, but they ordered me to pump it into the river.

Luckily for Pugliese, the company was then under considerable pressure from federal water pollution agencies. After first threatening to suspend him, the company higher-ups quietly dropped the case:

> They were afraid other men would start refusing to dump the oil. So for two years they didn't ask me to do it. They got other men to do it. . . . The foreman or someone would do it at night, or they'd pick on someone who wouldn't argue. . . . But they [the foreman and the supervisor] started harassing me, they ridiculed me, they said they'd like to fire me. They said, "Sometime you're going to do it [dump the oil]—you've got to do it." It turned into a personal vendetta against me.

Other millwrights confirm Pugliese's story. One told of "the time the foreman pointed at [Pugliese] and said, 'We don't need guys like Pugliese around here.' "

We asked Pugliese why his bosses took his 1969 refusal so personally. Did they have a guilty conscience about pollution? Pugliese doubted that this was the reason:

> You see, I set a precedent among the men. I showed that big industry can be made to obey the law. . . . They think I hampered their authority to give orders. Where it used to be ordinary procedure to pump out the floors every two hours [after the 1969 incident], the men would just let it go until they were pressured. Consequently we would have flooding conditions with up to 48 inches of pollution in the basement. . . .
>
> Like you say, I became kind of a legend. I'm a little older than a lot of the others. Most of the older men won't do anything. They're weary, just riding along. I feel like that, too, a lot. But I claim that they're violating my civil rights—in the first place by polluting the atmosphere and the waterways and causing a condition which is detrimental to everyone, and then they are asking—ordering—me to be a partner in violating the law. Even if they want to break the law, they have no right to order me to break it, too.

For two years, the company humored Pugliese. As long as he wasn't directly ordered to dump oil, he was all right. If he was ordered, he knew he'd refuse. When the order came, at 7 A.M. on July 14, it was in a tone of deliberate provocation. "Who's going to do this?" the foreman asked. "I think *Pugliese* would be a good man to do it." "I said, 'What are you trying to do?' " Pugliese told us. " 'We went through this two years ago.' He told me, 'I'm telling you to pump it into the river or go home.' I offered to get a portable pump and pump it into drums, but he said, 'You're refusing an order to work. Either you do it or you go home.' "

From the company's point of view, Pugliese thinks, the order was well timed, because the local union leadership was away in Washington and a grievance on Pugliese's part could not get immediate top-level attention. Pugliese knew this, knew he had 18 years' seniority behind him (10 of his years with J&L don't count toward seniority because of a technicality) and only six years to hold out for retirement with a pension. Of course, he refused.

Going to meet Pugliese, we were half prepared for some kind of oddball—a middle-aged freak, a paranoid conservationist, a sectarian hold-out from the union's more turbulent days. We were not prepared for a man who, except for his single aberration, would be chiefly interesting as a prototype millwright, homeowner, and father. He is an ordinary looking man; compactly built, brown-haired, wearing glasses and sports clothes, a little young looking for 59. He comes from a family of 22, raised in the factory town of Ashtabula, Ohio; his wife is from Youngstown, where her four brothers still work in the steel mills. For the last 37 years, the Puglieses have lived in their own home, a two-story frame house in a "mixed" (white Eastern and Southern European and Appalachian) neighborhood on Cleveland's near West Side. They put their four children through college and thence to good marriages, good jobs, and homes in the suburbs. At the time of our first visit, Mrs. Pugliese's chief concern (after the job and the pension) was about the effect of the publicity on the oldest son, a successful dentist. "I don't know how he's going to explain this to his patients."

Pugliese's career as a steelworker cannot have left much time for hobbies or politics. He quit school at 16 to start work at Otis Steel (later incorporated into J&L) and, except for jobs in defense plants during World War II, has been a steelworker ever since. During the postwar readjustment, he was laid off from three consecutive steel jobs, finally settling down at J&L in 1953. After hours he likes to read—"sometimes till morning," his wife said—and this, rather than any formal education, accounts for his articulateness and wide range of information. Other than that, he likes to be as active as he can in the union.

Even in his concern about pollution, Pugliese is not stridently different from his neighbors or fellow workers. Another J&L millwright told us:

> If they had to close down the J&L plant to fix it so it wouldn't pollute, there'd be a lot of people out of jobs while they were fixing it. But if they don't fix it, then twenty years from now no one will have any jobs at all.

Like other Clevelanders of his age, Pugliese has watched the gradual destruction of the area's beaches, parks, and fishing spots. "During the 1956 [steel] strike, we found fish coming back up the river because the steel mills weren't running," he told us. "Just from the steel alone stopping. The same thing again in the 1959 strike. Just think about that." And, like many other old-time steelworkers, he lives on the shallow hills overlooking the Cuyahoga Valley's industrial flatland. "You can scrub and scrub and never keep up," Mrs. Pugliese told us of the air pollution. In her immaculate rooms, she did seem to be keeping up, but the outside surface of the house, like those of the others on the block, was a corroded, peeling gray.

Pollution hounds a steelworker all day, everywhere. In the plant, Pugliese told us, "the pollution is terrible. It's dirty, greasy, full of fumes and smoke. The floors are always wet and slippery." With the outside pollution, it's as if the company were following you home, spoiling everything. Gesturing to the smoke-filled Cuyahoga Valley, Pugliese said:

> What gives them the right to monopolize the whole valley, the whole river and even the air? To take over complete control? This could be a beautiful valley for recreation. Now you can't even go down there without a badge. It's a prison camp atmosphere.

Another steelworker who had dropped in to visit the Puglieses agreed: "They [the companies] act like they own everything."

What is different about Pugliese is not how he *felt* but that he *acted*, and he seemed to take no special pride in this distinction:

> Of course, all the guys feel the same. They've been calling up and coming over. They're with me 100 per cent. . . . I guess most of the men are afraid of losing their jobs, taking a risk. The only thing different about me is I had to take a stand somewhere.

But once Pugliese had taken his stand on July 14, he found himself essentially alone. There was no immediate response from other workers; no rush to put down work and accompany Pugliese en masse to the front office. The union's initial response was no more encouraging. The only local official on hand, the assistant chief grievance man, tried to persuade Pugliese to back down, follow the order for the time being, and register his principles by filing a regular grievance. Pugliese told us:

> I said to him, "I respect your view but I'm going through with this. Are you going to represent me?" He said, "I will." I said, "O.K., represent me. Get in there. You're my attorney now. . . ." The union's on my side, of course. It's limited, though. They're taking it through channels. If I'm not satisfied with the results I'll retain an attorney and take this to the civil courts.

Pugliese said he had acted for "the health and welfare of the general public," and it was to this amorphous constituency that he appealed after he left the plant. His own calls to whatever pollution agencies, public and private, he could think of, and to the local television stations netted a series of polite but indifferent responses. It took a few calls by a sympathetic ex-*Plain Dealer* reporter to get the media interested in the story. By the afternoon of Thursday, July 15, Pugliese was being swept into the public's attention a little too fast for his own comfort. He saw his story on the front page of the *Cleveland Press*, complete with a picture of himself holding up a sample of J&L's oily wastes. He watched himself on the television news, sitting on his porch and responding gravely to the same modish young newscaster who gave the news on the phone strike and the closing of the U.S. Steel plant in Youngstown. "There's no rehearsal. They don't even tell you what they're going to ask you. Just like that—you're on the spot," he told us. By evening the Pugliese story was spreading beyond the northeast Ohio region. "If I get nothing else out of this I got my pound of flesh," he admitted. "I've got nothing personal against the company, but I don't mind seeing them squirm."

In the union and the plant, the impact of the Pugliese "story" quickly surpassed that of the event itself. Another millwright told Pugliese:

> The guys think it's the best thing that could have happened. This puts the union on the spot and they've got to do something now after all the publicity. They got your picture out of the paper and put it up all over the plant today.

By Friday, July 16, Pugliese's fellow workers were planning a wildcat strike if J&L tried to fire Pugliese at the end of the five-day suspension. Probably more concerned about the possibility of a wildcat than about the suspension itself, the union quickly dispatched the local's chief grievance man back from Washington. By late afternoon Friday, Pugliese could see his case moving smoothly through the regular union channels.

Meanwhile, the Pugliese case had put the pollution agencies on the spot as much as the union. The state government, it turned out, had given J&L a permit to discharge "normal sewage" into the river, on the condition that the company submit an abatement plan for treating the sewage. But the deadline for submitting the plan had already passed, with no action by the Ohio state attorney. As for the oily waste at issue, the local office of the Federal Environmental Protection Agency hastened to announce that it had noted "unusual" liquid discharges from the J&L plant on the morning of July 14. (They were probably unusual only by virtue of having occurred in the daytime.) A few days later, the EPA confirmed that these discharges did indeed contain high concentrations of oil, and "recommended" that J&L install alternative disposal facilities.

Under fire from the union, the press, and the pollution agencies, and faced with a possible wildcat, J&L had little choice but to back down on the Pugliese issue. Their only option lay in what tone to take, and they chose to be as ungracious as possible. On July 15, at the height of the publicity, the company's Pittsburgh headquarters told the press, "J&L does not publicly discuss any disciplinary action involving an employee," and went on to refute the pollution charges as if they were a separate issue:

> In regard to the control of water discharges from the finishing mill at the Cleveland works, we have taken a number of interim measures to minimize the discharges of oil and other substances into the river pending the completion of a $2 million pollution control system which is now under construction.

On Friday afternoon, July 16, J&L officials met with union representatives and "conceded" a two-day reduction in Pugliese's suspension. The union representatives got up and walked out. A few hours later, J&L called Pugliese to tell him he was being reinstated with full back pay. But true to its principles to the bitter end, J&L is insisting on giving Pugliese a formal reprimand.

On Saturday, July 17, Pugliese reported back for work. The company was installing drums and pumps to dispose of the oil in the sump holes. But nothing else had changed since Wednesday. Heavy smoke and filthy water still poured out of the plant. Inside, there were the same thick fumes, slippery floors and overpowering heat, the same long uncorrected safety hazards. On Wednesday, July 21, one week after taking his stand, Pugliese was helping load a roll (the cylinder which actually rolls out the steel) onto a high truck. The crane operator was inexperienced and under pressure to meet a schedule. He hoisted the crane before the roll was securely fastened and the 10-ton roll swung down on Pugliese. Jumping off the truck to avoid being crushed, he broke his leg. When we last saw Pugliese, he was at home again, facing an eight-week convalescence. "Production's the god," he said:

> That comes first. Regardless of what they say about safety, equality or anything, production is first. That's the almighty word. Machines cost money, so they spend money to repair them, to maintain them. But men are free, so who cares? If a machine overheats, they put in a fan. But we could die of heat prostration. We can't get a fan. Men are expendable.

PART IV
POLITICAL CHANGE:
GOALS AND PRESCRIPTIONS

In this section, we present several illustrations of recent thinking on the part of some—though hardly all—major social movements currently seeking change in the American political system or its policies. Several things should be noted about these selections. First, the authors are not necessarily completely representative of the movements involved; each movement naturally has many differences of emphasis on goals and tactics within its membership, and one spokesman cannot embody all of these. Each selection does, however, reveal the basic outlines of the movement's position. Second, perhaps the most important point to see in each selection is the frame of reference of the author. By this, we mean the way in which the author (and presumably many others within the group for which he or she is speaking) understands the position of his or her group with respect to the rest of the world, the kinds of goals the author has for the group and the larger society, and the tactics the author sees as appropriate to get there. One of the most serious problems in coming to grips with contending prescriptions for change is to identify the assumptions and images of the world that lie behind a change-seeker's demands. In many cases, failure to understand such premises leads to total lack of communication.

The first two selections reflect two potentially far-reaching movements of quite different sorts. Caroline Hennessey's *Strategy of Sexual Struggle* excerpt captures much of the character and determination of the women's liberation movement. First it indicates the depth of the sometimes unconscious male domination ethic, and then it sets forth ways of combating such views and practices. It should be noted that there are many different levels of political sophistication and purpose involved in the women's liberation movement, ranging from agitating for the elimination of degrading sexual advertising and discriminatory laws, to withdrawal into self-

359

developing encounter groups, to active participation in socialist revolutionary politics. Hennessey's position includes many shared dimensions and is roughly typical of the political views of many members of the movement. The Pearls' article represents the major issue-based movement (as distinguished from status-based) of the 1970s. The ecology-environment movement in effect succeeded the Vietnam War as a focus for orthodox political effort by many people, particularly including middle-class persons. The Pearls' article shows the scope of concern for aspects of pollution, the impact of technology, and so on, that are characteristic of this movement. They go further than others, however, in raising ecology to the level of a basic organizing principle for societal change.

The next two selections show how differently minorities may address themselves to achieving change against the reluctance or outright opposition of the dominant society. Armando Rendón, speaking as a Chicano, emphasizes cultural uniqueness and racial pride; his message may be directed as much to Chicanos themselves as to others, of course, but it does not seem calculated to gain many allies for the cause he espouses. The basis of Chicano demands, and their long-standing origins, are made clear, however, as is the distinctiveness of their values from those of the surrounding Anglo society. Robert Allen, by contrast, emphasizes economic causes and remedies in his prescription for a black program. He pays careful attention to the particular economic and social conditions of blacks and the larger society today, and erects a specific program to deal with those environmental circumstances and achieve black goals. The goals he holds, as distinguished from those held by blacks who emphasize cultural or nationalist goals much in the manner of Rendón, are goals which ultimately apply to many groups within the society; although his first concern is with the well-being of blacks, it is clear that his argument carries beyond blacks as a distinctive group.

The last two selections are intended to stand for a large group of movements and political tendencies that have developed after the apparent demise of the New Left in its original form. The New American Movement is an effort by several persons once active in the civil rights, anti-war, and student power movements to draw together again with a focus on the working class. Its leaders seek to unite the many local groups which regularly form and recede around specific local issues such as neighborhood improvements, health services, local elections, and so on and to give these groups a national tie. The ultimate goal is democratic socialism, and the route is seen as through engaging the working class in locally-developed groups of ever-increasing size and issue-emphasis. The National Caucus of Labor Committees is a national group of longer standing which emphasizes the careful application of Marxist analytic principles to the evolution of American society. Focusing on developments within the world and American economies, and particularly on the (previously predicted) monetary crisis of 1971, the NCLC foresees a major depression in the United States in the near future, and seeks to build broadly shared consciousness of the need for radical social change among all working peoples.

The quite different positions taken by these six selections are, quite naturally, the result of highly variant understandings of the nature of the present social and political systems, of what goals should be given highest priority, and of what ways there are to achieve such ends. Some of these authors appear to have considered the obstacles in the way of achieving their goals, and some do not. All of them can and should be challenged, not only in terms of the validity of their assumptions and images of how change might be attained, but also in terms of the desirability of the prescriptions and goals they put forward.

25.
THE STRATEGY OF SEXUAL STRUGGLE

Caroline Hennessey

The President of the United States is a male.

The Vice-President of the United States is a male.

So are virtually all the nation's rulers, decision and policy makers and implementers, bureaucrats, power-players, manipulators, financiers, industrialists, business executives—in short, all those whom Ferdinand Lundberg has called the "Pubpols" and "Finpols."

That is the picture in the United States today, in the Year of Our Patriarchal Lord One Thousand Nine Hundred and Seventy One.

Strange.

Less than two centuries ago, our Forefathers brought forth upon this Continent a government dedicated to the proposition that there shall be no taxation without representation, and that if they could not have Liberty For All, they much preferred Death.

Why, when more than one-third of the nation's labor force consists of women (who pay the same taxes—and more—than men), is not one-third of the United States Congress female?

Is it because as Frederick Lewis Allen claimed, few women have been able to "rouse themselves to even a passing interest in politics?"

Or is it because the lip-servers of the American Constitution who have iron control over the nation's political parties and machinery are entirely male and continue to practice their exclusion policies against women?

Common sense alone—never mind the mountains of evidence everywhere around us—says it is discrimination, exclusion, that prevents women from being selected and endorsed as candidates.

That same discrimination and exclusion also bars them from holding responsible positions in most sectors of American commerce and industry. Vance Packard (no Bachofen, he!) summed it all up in his incisive study of American business manners and mores, *The Pyramid Climbers.* Packard cites a Harvard Business School report which says:

Very few women were found to be holding top executive jobs in the sense of corporate officers or senior executives.

Packard adds:

The prevailing sentiment was expressed by the head of a Chicago management-consulting firm in these terms: 'The highest position that women are going to reach in the foreseeable future in any large numbers is that of assistant to a top executive. This will be primarily an expansion of the secretarial function!

Vance Packard was led to the conclusion that:

(Women) are perhaps the most discriminated-against of all minority groups in industry.

Which contention Shirley Chisholm, for one, verified from her own personal experience—and from her heart—when she said: "I have been more discriminated against because I am a woman than because I am black."

The discrimination extends beyond industry into the sciences and professions—and there are more than faint echoes of the ordeals faced by Elizabeth Blackwell in 1849 in the situations that prevail in American medical schools today. As recently as October 1970, *Newsweek* magazine published an article headed "The Medical Sexists." The magazine—probably the fairest and most objective of all the country's weekly newsmagazines—cited a report by Dr. Harold I. Kaplan of the New York Medical College, saying:

In the U.S. . . . women comprise only 9 percent of the total supply of physicians. On the other hand (Dr. Kaplan) adds, two out of three doctors in Russia and nearly one of four physicians in Great Britain are females.

To which it might be added that in France—a country which the conventional wisdom holds to be a stronghold of the Feminine Woman and Femme Fatale—the proportion of women doctors is four times greater than that in the United States.

According to *Newsweek* Dr. Harold Kaplan "queried the administrators of all U.S. and Canadian medical schools on their attitudes toward women students." To quote further from the article:

Some of the replies he got, says Kaplan, "were too outrageous to be published." (Among those) fit to print (was that of) the administrator of one Western school (who said) "I think that (women) ordinarily have so many emotional problems that we have not been particularly happy with their performance."

Shades of the frail and emotionally unstable Eve! No wonder Dr. Kaplan was moved to conclude:

> While no school in the U.S. overtly or officially refuses to accept women, prejudice does seem to manifest itself.

Political sexists, industrial sexists, medical sexists—the list could be continued indefinitely. Eight years after the publication of Betty Friedan's book, *The Feminine Mystique*, and despite the apparent gains made in the interim, American women are still second (or third or tenth) class citizens. And even that presupposes they are considered to be citizens at all by men and the Male Establishment.

The Faustian legend had Woman as Marguerite, willing to barter herself and all that she held dear for flattery, baubles and the pleasures of the pudenda. The Faustian Age—as pontificated by Oswald Spengler—relegated her to that "sole ordained vocation," to wit: "To experience Man and his Sons."

In the post–World War II Freudian Age, the Transfigured Marguerite was held to be ready at an instant's notice to barter herself and all that she held dear in return for the possession of a penis of her own. It was, according to Freudian Theology, her envy of man's possession of a penis that made Woman so weak, frail in morality and spirit, unreliable, unworthy, inferior. Her attempts to gain human status in a man-ruled world were nothing more than symbolical searches for a penis she could attach to her own body.

The Dawn of the Friedan Age should have demolished Freudian Theology for once and all, making clear (as Sofie Lazarsfeld stated it) that:

> Actually, what women desire is not the possession of a penis in their own organism, but the power and privileges which the possessors of a penis have secured for themselves by way of over-compensation for the physiological inadequacy of that organ.

To men, these were dangerous, subversive concepts that menaced the very foundations of the Masculine Mystique. They could not possibly accept them when first enunciated. Nor have they accepted them to any discernible degree. Instead, they have recoiled—and reacted. The reaction has been in the form of continuing attempts to rely on their time-honored techniques of doling out sops, pacifiers, and bribes and seeking by every conceivable means to divert and distract. The one encouraging variation on the ancient theme is that, so far, men have been unable to take back more than the few inches of ground they have yielded.

It must be admitted that many women have been unable to accept the implications of the Friedan Age. Brainwashed, conditioned, they see their servile dependence on the male as their sole source of safety and security in a hostile world. Thus, eight years after the first awakenings, millions of American women are still docile, submissive wives. It is impossible to estimate how many of them still trot off each morning to menial jobs, return at night to cook and sew and perform housework, and uncomplainingly turn their pay checks over to their husbands who "know how to manage money and keep checkbook balances straight." These are also the women who continue to foal children, Pristeening their vaginas between deliveries, dumping Axion into their washers, and filling their mortgaged homes with more and ever more overpriced and gaudy junk.

Nevertheless, the response of American women to the call for action has been astounding. Innumerable organizations sprang up—spontaneously, without any central direction, or even coordination, of efforts. True, that some of these organizations have been more flamboyant, noisy, and even sophomorically exhibitionistic than effective. Some of the women who organized groups and joined them have been more interested in attracting cheap publicity (and offering themselves as targets for the derision and scorn of the communications media) than in making any genuine contributions to the movement. These "somes" have been very much in the minority, though—albeit that the kept-media have given them insanely disproportionate exposure. By far the greatest majority of organizations are serious, sincere—and their members honestly dedicated.

Withal, where are we women now—RIGHT NOW, in 1971?

First of all, American women are very far ahead of where they were even a few years ago—if for no other reason that they have finally begun to awake from their long sleep. American women by the many millions have become conscious, aware of themselves and of their degraded condition as women in our male-dominated society. They have also begun to understand clearly the problems they—and all women—face in that society, and have made positive moves to ameliorate the condition and resolve or solve the problems.

These are gains—no less great and significant because they cannot be measured with calibrated gauges or expressed in terms of absolutes. There are uncounted numbers of "Women's Lib" organizations and groups—formal and informal—scattered across the country, each having little direct communication with the next. It is therefore impossible to estimate with any degree of accuracy how many American women are active members.

The Male Establishment media typically make a great issue out of this. They use it wherever and whenever possible in an effort to derogate the "organizational ability" and "efficiency" of the movement (and therefore, of women). After all, the argument runs, what sort of organization fails to count its members, take a census? The statistical report is a fetish of American's punchcard-produced males.

What is completely overlooked is that—as has been emphasized elsewhere in this book—"Women's Lib" is a social phenomenon, *not* a monolithic organization. No one who is active in it has time to count heads—there is far too much to be done that is more important. In any event, and this is what frightens the male chauvinists most, the fact remains that—whether leaping from 2,000,003 to 3,000,009, or from 5,123,456 to 6,987,654 in a day, a week, a month or a year—the Women's Lib movement is growing, expanding, attracting (and, what is even more important, *holding*) new and active members.

Ten years ago, the militant neo-feminists in the United States were but an unheard tiny handful. Today, they are an army—a steadily increasing army—and they are being heard, loudly and clearly, everywhere in the country.

The movement—and the pressures created by it—can certainly be said to have brought about many tangible, positive results, as a rather random selection of examples will show.

As early as 1964, Congress added "sex" to the Civil Rights Bill passed that year to prevent discrimination in employment practices. That some Congressmen later tried to pretend it was a sort of joke (on whom?), means little—if anything. The fact is that Congress was already feeling the pressure of aroused and bitterly resentful women. The joke proved to be on Congress—and the Male Power Structure that the male majority of both Houses represents. The insertion of the word was intended as a sop, a pacifying gesture over which much noise could be made, but which would not change anything. Instead, the red-faced lawmakers have since realized that they opened a floodgate.

Women have taken advantage of their newly guaranteed rights under the 1964 Civil Rights Law. They have sought—and obtained—jobs in fields and areas previously barred to them. Furthermore, they have not shown fear or hesitation about invoking the Law, making it stick. The Federal Equal Employment Opportunity Commission—established under that law to hear and act upon complaints of discrimination on grounds of race, color, national origin, religion or sex—has received a total of some 46,000 complaints since it was established. Of these, almost 8,000 were filed by women, charging discrimination on grounds of sex.

No, there are no women on the General Motors Board yet, and the Male Establishment will fight to the last gonad to prevent one from ever being on the Boards of the great corporations and conglomerates. Of that, we can be sure. However, those 8,000 complaints and all that they symbolize and imply are proof that women are finally beginning to fight for their rights—and a reasonable indication that they will continue to fight even harder in the future.

The law passed in New York permitting doctors to perform abortions legally is another victory. A large share of the credit for its passage—against bitter opposition from Male and Religious Establishments—must be given to the Women's Lib movement, at least in the sense that participation in the movement, the inspiration provided by the very existence of the movement, spurred women to campaign vigorously for passage. (It might also be reasonably supposed that these same factors worked to force reluctant male legislators to vote for the law.)

Other random straws in the wind have been the ordination of the first woman rabbi, the admission of women as voting delegates to the Episcopal Church's House of Deputies, increasing demands on the Roman Catholic Church to open all liturgical functions to women.

These are particularly significant developments. They strike at the very foundations of the Judaeo-Christian doctrines that bear so much responsibility for the repression and degradation of women in the Western World. For Christian dogmatists, they are a turning of the world upside down—a revolt against the words of Paul, who (in Timothy 2:11–14) ordered:

> But I permit not a woman to teach, nor to usurp authority over the man, but to be in silence. For Adam was the first formed, then Eve. And Adam was not deceived, but the woman, being deceived, was in the transgression.

All these—and the many other—gains, large and small, registered in recent years reflect the indisputable fact that women are no longer content to "be in silence." At long last, they have made a start. They are showing—openly, courageously—that they will no longer submissively accept downgrading to the status of nonentities. More to the point, they refuse to be cowed and intimidated by traditions and conventions.

The awakened and aware American woman has freed herself of the Faust legend, emerged from the Faustian Age—and is even disentangling herself from the *nouvelle blague* bonds of the Freudian Age. The neo-feminist of the Friedan Era sees herself as a person, an individual, a creature with an identity—and rejects all outmoded concepts of Woman as an Eve, a Marguerite, a chattel or a sexual object, as anything but a human being entitled to the same rights, privileges, and prerogatives purportedly guaranteed to all by the Constitution and its amendments.

The women of America are rapidly learning—again to the consternation of their male masters—that promises and tokens are meaningless. They have been down the dismal road of disappointment and disillusion much too often. They will not be led down it again. They have been swindled by promises of reforms and surface shows of sympathy from the Male Establishment too many times in the past. Their prevailing mood is that reflected by Bulwer-Lytton when he wrote:

> A reform is a correction of abuse; a revolution is a transfer of power.

Not even genuine "reform" will satisfy women. It cannot, for mere reform implies nothing more than the correction of certain abuses within the framework of the existing social organization. And that, in turn, implies that men—despite their numerical inferiority in the population—will retain the power within the social organization.

If women are to have equal rights, then it follows that—in our democratic form of government—each of them shall have a vote equal in weight to that of each male. But there are more women than men—by some millions, according to Census figures. Thus, solely by exercising their Constitutional right to vote, women can amass the electoral plurality necessary to obtain a commensurate degree of power. That, if our vaunted democratic principles are allowed to govern, as a natural consequence means the balance of power will tip in their favor. As the majority, they are entitled to the majority voice in our affairs—and whether or not men like it, the revolution as a transfer of power will be an accomplished fact.

Such are the positions the feminine liberation movement has reached in its few short years of spectacular growth. That is where we are in 1971.

Where do we go next—why and how?

Bill of Particulars

Sigmund Freud, in between his muckings about with theories of penis-envy, once wrote:

> The great question that has never been answered and to which I have not yet been able to answer despite my 30 years of research into the feminine soul is: What does woman want?

Herr Doktor Freud could have saved himself an immense amount of research had he but bothered to ask any aware, enlightened woman. He would have had to look no farther than to Dr. Sofie Lazarsfeld, who was a pupil of his own erstwhile colleague, Dr. Alfred Adler.

In the mid-1930s—when Sigmund Freud was still very much alive and presumably sufficiently literate to read—Dr. Lazarsfeld spelled it all out carefully, unmistakably. She stated this fundamental and unarguable premise:

> Owing to their training to rely on their helplessness, women have renounced the complete development of their personalities.

Then, she declared:

> It is essential to disprove the hypocritical argument concerning biological inferiority of women which is so glibly used to support the tendency of suppressing the development of the female personality.

There it is, all of it. Women want that which has been stolen and withheld from them. They want their identity, personality, individuality as equally human human beings, their human self-respect. They want to be free of their servile dependence on men. They are not helpless. They do not want to be treated as though they are.

WOMEN DO NOT WANT PATRONIZING CONDESCEN-SION.

They want to be free of the oppression and subjugation that are the male's and man-ruled society's cynical, amoral over-compensation for the male's unconscious knowledge—and his conscious fear—of his sexual inadequacy.

Women want the opportunity to achieve complete development of their personalities:

Sofie Lazarsfeld wrote:

> Modern science has definitely destroyed the argument (concerning biological inferiority of women), and has proved that there is no 'feminine biological tragedy,' and that women can be independent. Nor is there any doubt that women could make themselves independent.

No, Dr. Freud, none of this indicates that women want a penis all their own. Far—oh, so very far—from it. A woman desires to be a female, NOT a man-surrogate. Women have absolutely no wish to step into the shoes or the standup urinals of men.

Penis-envy, indeed!

(It would not be too unreasonable to suppose that rather than women having any such sort of envy, it is the impotence/sexual inadequacy-fearing male chauvinist who suffers from a gnawing, pernicious form of cunnus-envy.)

Women want their personalities, identity, independence, and equality as women. They yearn to be whatever they are, or whatever they are capable of becoming, in their own right, of their own volition, by their own efforts, as members of their sex.

They want no special favors, preferred treatment, extraordinary consideration because they are women. No, thank you, they most certainly do not. They have been stifled, subjugated, exploited much too long by the "gallantries" and "courtesies" that have been among the most insidious weapons used against them by men.

Women want—they demand—precisely the same starting-line opportunities and advantages as have been, and are, enjoyed by men in our society. Furthermore, whatever road they may choose to follow in their lives or careers, women want the lanes they travel to have neither more nor less obstacles strewn along them than are normally found along the lanes traveled by men.

Women—unlike males—are not afraid of competition, provided the competition does not rig the game against them.

(It should certainly be added that the capacity of women to meet even the most unfair and vicious male competition has been proven time and time again by those women who have succeeded in making names for themselves in fields traditionally monopolized by men. For example, a woman who has made it through Law or Medical School has battled her way through not only studies and examinations, but through the even more formidable barriers of male prejudice and discrimination.)

Sigmund Freud to the contrary, there should be no doubt in any-one's mind what it is that women "want." Their "wants" have been stated clearly and unequivocally for well over a century.

It may come as Revelation to men, but the answers to the question, "What do women want?" have not been withheld from them, or whispered secretly, or communicated only in undecipherable codes. If men have failed to get the message earlier, it has been solely because they refused to see, hear and heed. Now, it is no longer what women "want," but what they DEMAND, and will take for themselves.

The demands of "neo-feminists" do not differ greatly from those of the "original" feminists. They are, at most, updated refinements of—rather than departures from—the changes called for by the delegates to the first Woman's Rights Convention held in Seneca Falls in 1848. (This should, in itself, demonstrate conclusively to any uncommitted or skeptical American woman just how very short a way you've really come—baby.)

Here, then, is a Bill of Particulars spelling out what it is that women "want"—what they demand and will obtain. The nation's penis-proud, impotence/sexual inadequacy-fearing male chauvinists are welcome to view it as a Manifesto, an Ultimatum, a Declaration of Independence or a Declaration of War. It is all of these—and more.

1. There must be a complete restructuring of sex-relationships in our society.

    There must be an end to the concept of the submis-siveness and servility of women. They must have the right and freedom to develop their own personalities. They must be rec-ognized as human beings equal in all rights and privileges to men. They must be entitled to their self-respect as women—and to respect as equal human beings and independent in-dividuals.

    It follows that all forms and manifestations of male chauvinism must be eradicated. The mythic dogmas and con-cepts that hold the male to be superior need to be expunged from our society.

2. Women demand the abolition of inequalities in law and social custom and usage between females and males which exist or are imposed on the basis of difference in sex.

Women must be granted complete equality before the law and by the social customs, attitudes, and codes prevailing in our society. There can no longer be one set of rules for men, another for women. Whatever inequities exist must be eliminated.

Three random, diverse but sharply illustrative examples of women's inequality under our present laws:

The noted legal authority, Samuel G. Kling, tells us:

> Generally speaking, it is the *duty* of the wife to live where her husband desires. Even a promise before marriage not to take her away from (a given neighborhood) is not binding. (Emphasis added.)

In other words, according to law, the wife must follow her husband wherever he decides to move or go if he insists that she accompany him.

A husband cannot be convicted of rape for having sexual intercourse with his wife against her will.

The woman who is a prostitute or call-girl is a criminal offender under our laws, subject to arrest, prosecution and fine or imprisonment (to say nothing of constant hounding by the authorities and the opprobrium of society). But the men who patronize—who use—her have nothing to fear from the law or from society.

Many sexually based or oriented inequities in law and social usage *ostensibly* favor women at the expense of men. They seem to offer women certain protections, advantages and benefits not granted to men. When examined closely, however, they prove to be cleverly crafted devices for keeping women in their dependent and degraded condition. Nevertheless, it is invariably to these laws and customs that men point when they hear women demand equality.

Men sneeringly demand to know if women are willing to have these abolished, too. The reply that all aware women give is yes, certainly—abolish away. Unlike men, who have created and maintained double standards for their own convenience, benefit, and profit, women have but a single standard of equality. It applies to and for all.

3. We call for an elimination of all patterns of child training and education which tend to perpetuate sexual stereotyping. There must be no teaching of the female child that she is weaker and inferior because she is a female. Most certainly, she cannot be conditioned to accept her subjugation and to look forward to no other future or reward than that of housewife. The male child must not be taught and conditioned to consider himself the superior of the female.

4. Women demand an end of all educational programs which assume different orientations, emphases or characteristics for the different sexes. There must be absolutely equal educational opportunity at all levels for both females and males. The female student must be afforded precisely the same types and quality of education as male students. Any form of discrimination, exclusion or prejudice against female students must be eliminated.

5. There must be a final and complete end to any and all discrimination in employment on grounds of sex. There must be complete parity of employment opportunity, pay, and opportunity for advancement and promotion.

   We demand that there be no field or endeavor, no job or profession, from which women are excluded by virtue of their sex provided they are otherwise qualified. Determination of their qualifications should be made according to criteria identical with those used for men. If there is any doubt on the part of a female applicant that any determination was not impartial and objective, she must have the right of appeal. Employers showing discrimination on grounds of sex should be subjected to appropriate penalties.

   It is imperative that the same principles apply in regard to assignment of tasks and responsibilities, to promotions and advancement. The practice of excluding women from holding higher supervisory, management and executive posts must be outlawed, and laws prohibiting such practices must be stringently enforced.

6. Identical principles and policies of non-exclusion and non-discrimination must be adopted by political parties and organizations. There must be an end to the male monopoly of the nation's political machinery at all levels.

   More than half the population—and more than half the nation's voters—are women. A concerted effort by unified women voters can break the male stranglehold on American political machinery and politics, force political organizations and parties to cease their policies of exclusion and give women their proportionate voice and permit them to present a proportionate number of candidates.

7. An end to the sexual exploitation of women.

8. The absolute guarantee of freedom of choice and decision to women.

   Although it might seem that the demand for this guarantee is covered—or at least implied—in preceding paragraphs, it deserves separate and special mention.

   Unfortunately, large numbers of women fail to appreciate how severely their freedom of choice and decision is circumscribed in all areas of their lives and activities.

For instance, there are relentless social, economic, and other pressures brought to bear on women so that they will marry—and preferably at a very early age. The "single woman" of 25 is practically a pariah in our society. At 30, she is an object of pity or scorn.

The most barbaric and insidious restrictions of woman's freedom of decision in our society are those which concern her choice of whether or not to have children or a particular, as yet unborn, child.

Women demand the repeal of any and all laws prohibiting or inhibiting the distribution and use of contraceptive devices and drugs that pose no proven threat to the physical health of the user.

They also demand the repeal of any and all laws prohibiting or restricting abortions performed by qualified medical practitioners. The right to have abortions should be extended to all women, whether married or single.

Furthermore, since it is known that the overwhelming majority of unwanted children are born to mothers in the lower economic brackets, we demand free, government-sponsored programs that will provide instructions on the use of contraceptive drugs and devices, the drugs and devices themselves and abortions free for women who are unable to pay.

A corollary of this demand is one for the abolition of all laws and social-usage prejudices which in any way discriminate against a child born out of wedlock. In short, this calls for the total elimination of any and all concepts of "legitimacy" versus "illegitimacy" of any child.

10. Women demand governmentally sponsored and financed free child-care centers for the children of working mothers.

(It is, indeed, a sad commentary on the vaunted American Way of Life that such centers exist in many other countries—even in such countries as Italy, where there is strong Church influence.)

That is the Bill of Particulars. Implicit in its points are such often-voiced specific demands as that housework and child-care be shared equally between mother and father and that laws or social customs prohibiting or discouraging consenting adults from engaging in sexual intercourse or from living together as man and wife should be abolished.

The Bill of Particulars provides all the answers Sigmund Freud or anyone else could possibly need for the question of what it is that women want.

There now remains only the question of how women can obtain what they want, achieve their goals.

Women's Strategy for Victory

We know our goals: "The power and privileges which the possessors of a penis have secured for themselves by way of over-compensation for the physiological inadequacy of that organ."

We have identified our opponents, our enemies: "It is not only the individual man, but the male sex as a whole . . . it is a matter between the entire male sex and the entire female sex."

Women's struggle for complete liberation, for the achievement of complete equality, must be directed against the entire male sex, and thus against a society despotically ruled by males—and, therefore, against the institutions of that society. But women must first thoroughly understand the nature of those institutions, for it is in them that the great force of their male opponents is concentrated. The institutions are the focal points of power, the seats of privilege. They operate to perpetuate that Masculine Mystique and to keep women subjugated and degraded. To understand them is to know the strength—and the fundamental weakness—of the enemy. The great weakness is glaringly revealed by Thurman Arnold, who writes:

> Institutional creeds such as laws, economics or theology must be false . . . This paradoxical statement means that they must express contradictory ideals, and must authoritatively suppress any facts which interfere with those ideals.

Women must first awaken completely from their mesmerized, conditioned slumber and realize fully the utter falseness of the "Institutional creeds" that prevail in our male-dominated society. The laws, economics, and theologies that have been—and are being—used to maintain the superiority of the male over the female are bogus, artificial, baseless. They are empty myths that have been fashioned into weapons for employment against women.

To recognize a lie is to free oneself from fear of the lie. When women recognize the falseness—the lie—of institutional creeds, those creeds can no longer suppress the facts that not only interfere with, but will destroy, the whole-cloth "ideals" inherent in the great myth of male superiority.

But what is involved in the destruction of established institutional creeds, an attack on a social organization, a struggle to seize control of an entire existing power-structure for the purpose of changing its composition and its fundamental principles?

In a word, it is revolution.

The term, "revolution," requires definition.

According to *Webster's*, a revolution is:

A complete change of any kind (or) the overthrow of a government or social system with another taking its place.

The *Oxford* Dictionary describes revolution as:

Complete change, turning upside down, great reversal of conditions, fundamental reconstruction, especially forcible substitution by subjects of new ruler or polity for the old.

Readers may take their choice. I prefer the *Oxford* version.

However—and unfortunately—we cannot rest on simple definition. The Establishment, fearful of losing any of its prerogatives, has conditioned the minds of the majority so that the word revolution now has extremely negative connotations. The fact that the right to revolt is a basic American— a basic *human*—right has been largely blanked out of the American group-unconscious. Perhaps these words of Abraham Lincoln may help re-establish some degree of perspective:

This country, with its institutions, belongs to the people who inhabit it. Whenever they shall grow weary of the existing government they can exercise their constitutional right of amending it, *or their revolutionary right to dismember or overthrow it.* (Emphasis added.)

Let me reiterate once again what I have repeatedly stressed. The Women's Liberation movement is not an organization. It is a social phenomenon, a widespread upheaval, the rapidly and steadily growing—and increasingly impatient and violent—reaction of women grown weary of their repression and suppression by a man-ruled society and its institutions.

Women's Liberation is a spontaneous revolution, an exemplification of the sort of social phenomenon described by Wendell Phillips when he said: "Revolutions are not made; they come."

Further to the point are the words of Nikolai Lenin:

It is impossible to predict the time and progress of revolution. It is governed by its own more or less mysterious laws. But when it comes, it moves irresistibly.

The revolution of women against men, their sexist polity, and sexist institutions, has come. It is moving—irresistibly and inexorably as a phenomenon, as a movement without central organization or central direction.

Hundreds, perhaps thousands, of small groups and millions of individual women are seeking, working toward, the same general goals. They are weary not only of their own condition under the existing chauvinistic male autocracy. They are no less weary of the overall incompetence and ineptitude shown by ruling males in all areas of human endeavor. No amount of token reform will satisfy women. Edward Bulwer-Lytton said:

A reform is a correction of abuses; a revolution is a transfer of power.

The ultimate aim of Women's Lib is to effect nothing less than a transfer of power. This is the aim and goal of women's revolution. Women have no reticence to be revolutionaries; their attitude was stated long ago by Thomas B. Reed, Speaker of the House of Representatives 1889–91 and 1895–99, when he declared:

The only justification of rebellion is success.

Long suffering, all too often duped in the past, women will no longer settle for half—or any other fractional—gains. They are determined to justify their rebellion fully, with complete success. It does not matter that the Women's Liberation movement is not tightly organized, that it consists of independent groups and unaffiliated individuals. Eventually a process of coalescence will begin, but each woman can contribute greatly to the progress of the movement through individual initiative, her own strategy, her own action.

Strategy—like charity and many other things—begins at home. This is particularly true now, while the majority of actual social, political, legal, and economic power still remains in the hands of their opponents, men.

Any and every woman qualifies as a militant neo-feminist the moment her individual development has passed through these three phases:

1. The awakening of her consciousness of herself as Woman.
2. The expansion of that consciousness to the point of commitment.
3. The transformation of the potential of commitment into the kinetic of involvement.

The next step is for the individual woman to adopt the mentality and tactics of the Resistance fighter, the guerrilla. In his authoritative book, *Irregulars, Partisans, Guerrillas* (Simon-Schuster, 1954), Irwin R. Blacker states:

The tactics of guerrilla warfare require cunning and imagination. The guerrilla (lacking strength) to meet an enemy openly . . . must compensate for weakness with surprise. This becomes a weapon of incalculable strength when well used. (Guerrilla) tactics, well and suddenly sprung on an enemy, keep him off balance and confused. At this point the guerrilla has won much of the battle.

History demonstrates that revolutions, once they come, move irresistibly and inexorably. History also demonstrates that hidebound, inflexible Established Orders are incapable of long coping with or defending themselves against the imaginative, unpredictable, innovative and punishing attacks launched against them from all directions by guerrillas and partisans. Although it is powerful, the Male Establishment is rigid, unimaginative, the trapped victim of its own dogmatic codes and credos. Its patterns of action and reaction are fixed, repetitive, predictable. It is at a total loss for defense against subtlety, surprise.

Furthermore, each individual male is vulnerable, fragile. His two principal sources of strength are his over-compensating sense of male superiority and his sense of economic domination over women. The first is entirely false, being a most tenuous and frangible defense against his own fear of sexual inadequacy and impotence—and the woman who recognizes these truths can readily attack and destroy. The second is valid only in steadily diminishing part—but, even so, when viewed by an aware woman with expanded consciousness of herself and the relationships between the sexes, it becomes a weakness rather than a strength.

Women must bear in mind that there are no rules of warfare, no limitations or restrictions in the struggle for liberation. Men have never deigned to show women any quarter in the millennia-long one-sided campaigns of subjugation and degradation they have waged against women. It is necessary to fight them in the same manner; women can—and should—use any and all tricks and stratagems with clear and easy consciences.

Subversion, sabotage, deceit, coercion, intimidation—all and more are entirely permissible (indeed, highly recommended) weapons. Each individual woman can register important gains—for herself and for all women—by undermining, boring, and chipping away at men, their masculine sense of security and superiority, at both the facades and foundations of sexism and the Masculine Mystique.

It is this simple: the fundamental strategy for the women's revolution is personal, individual. It begins with each individual woman exerting and maintaining unrelenting pressure in every sphere of activity, in all situations requiring interaction with men and their sexist institutions.

Strategy begins "at home" in such ways as these:

- Women must renounce all traditional patterns of passivity, submissiveness, docility. They must avoid at all times retreating into hurt or helplessness. They must assert themselves and their demands. Among those demands must be one for the application of exactly equal standards in any and all relationships with men.
- The average housewife and mother can begin her guerrilla warfare on the most immediate battleground of all—in her own home—by insisting that her husband share equally in the work of housekeeping and child-care. When one wife in a neighborhood has succeeded, others will swiftly follow suit. From there, it is a short—and usually automatic—step to group commitment

and involvement in concerted efforts toward the achievement of broader goals. Multiply the results that will be obtained by a few thousand neighborhoods—and the entire edifice of male supremacy begins to crumble.

- Women should bring pressure on local schools to eliminate all policies, courses, or classes that tend to create or emphasize a "difference" between the sexes as they perpetuate the myths of male superiority/female inferiority. School administrators and school boards have extremely low thresholds of resistance to such pressure. A few dozen mothers can turn prevailing policies and curricula upside down and inside out if they are sufficiently vocal and persistent.

- The woman who is gainfully employed outside the home has particularly tempting opportunities for waging guerrilla warfare and performing acts of sabotage. Most working women are employed by firms owned, controlled, and managed by men who clearly demonstrate discrimination against women in hiring and promotion policies. But even the lowliest female employee can cause work slowdowns, purposely make costly errors, undermine efficiency, and hinder production. Misdirected telephone calls, mislaid messages, misfiled documents—such acts of sabotage can wreak havoc in any plant or office.

  A clever worker, stenographer, switchboard operator, receptionist —or whatever—can cost a firm fortunes through such sabotage and have little fear that her actions will be detected. In fact, a smart woman can always make it appear that the fault and blame are those of a male superior, thereby adding further to the confusion and damage.

- Another super-powerful weapon in women's armory is the boycott. Stores and firms that practice exclusion, discrimination policies, or are engaged in activities tending to exploit women sexually should be openly—and noisily—boycotted. It does not take a very big drop in sales or profits before money-oriented males begin to weasel and make concessions. Once a concession has been gained, it is just that much easier to obtain another and another—until, at last, the board has been swept clean.

- Of immense value at both practical and symbolic levels is the growing tendency of women to reject male criteria of "femininity" and "womanliness." This takes its most direct and immediately evident form in the widespread—and steadily increasing—refusal of women to heed the blandishments of the purveyors of cosmetic junk. The American "beauty-aid" industry rakes in billions of dollars annually. Most of the income is pure profit, for guck that costs the profiteers 10 cents a jar to produce is sold to brainwashed women for 10 or 20 or even more dollars in retail stores. Herein, of course, is one of the most glaringly evident and cynical manifestations of the Male Establishment's eternal drive to degrade women and force them to conform to standards established by men.

The Women's Liberation movement hardly suggests mastectomy or vulvectomy to prove women's case. But it does most certainly insist that "femininity" and "womanliness" are human qualities—not quick smears and globs of insanely overpriced guck or sprays of 57-flavored vaginal deodorants.

- Women should join and participate actively in groups—formal or informal—that are dedicated to the cause of women's liberation. There are large numbers of these. Many have widely varying political orientations. Presumably, each individual woman will want to associate herself with a group whose orientation is consonant with her own. If none such is available, then the individual may very well form her own with like-minded friends.

- Every chance that presents itself for obtaining some benefit or advantage through applying pressure to political organizations, parties, or candidates must be exploited to the utmost. The neo-feminists who style themselves as liberals will, no doubt, be content with obtaining certain reforms, making a gain here, another there. But women who (like this author) prefer a radical approach should not disdain working through traditional "democratic" channels and processes—for the time being and with carefully pre-planned motives.

- Men and their institutions should be used in every manner possible. It is a shrewd move for women with radical orientations to insinuate or force themselves into political organizations—quite literally infiltrate them. No woman should ever overlook the opportunity of using that much-maligned but highly effective technique of boring from within. I, personally, would love to see the day when several *thousand* radical women formed a fifth column *inside* our existing political parties and political machines. When the time was ripe, they could cause endless mischief and harm to the sexist male leadership of the organizations.

These are but a very few typical means for spreading the disruption, dislocation, and dismay that will go a very long way toward destroying the male chauvinist structure of our society. That structure must be attacked at every level and from every direction—and each and every aware woman is naturally an organizer, leader, strategist, guerrilla fighter for women's freedom.

It—and here, with apologies to Karl Marx, I borrow from myself— it must always be remembered that:

The history of all hitherto existing society is the history of male chauvinism, of the exploitation and depersonalization of the female.

Our present epoch possesses this distinctive feature: it has simplified the sexual antagonisms. Society as a whole is more or less splitting up into two great hostile camps facing each other: Female and Male.

The Male, historically, has played a most reactionary, repressive part. Obtaining the upper hand, it has ever put an end to equal and honorable relationships, torn asunder what naturally should be the mutual bonds between women and men, who conferred upon themselves the title of "natural superiors" and left no other nexus between man and woman than the naked self-interest of the former.

The Male has drowned the life-spark of the Female in the icy water of egotistical calculation. The Male has resolved the personal worth of the Female into exchange value as an object and, in place of numberless indefeasible chartered freedoms, has set up this single unconscionable freedom—the freedom to be completely submissive. In one word, for exploitation, veiled by religious and political illusions, it has substituted naked, shameless, direct, brutal exploitation.

Now, suddenly, men, the Male Establishment and man-ruled society find themselves put back.

Why?

Because there is
- too much civilization . . .
- too much means of subsistence . . .
- too much industry . . .
- too much commerce . . .
- and too much of an awakening among the oppressed.

The forces at the disposal of male-dominated society no longer tend to further the oppression of the subjugated females.

On the contrary, the females have discovered themselves too powerful for the conditions by which they are fettered . . .
- and as soon as they overcome these fetters . . .
- they will bring disorder into the whole of the Male Establishment . . .
- and write finis to male chauvinism, the Masculine Mystique, and male supremacy in our society.

Therein lies the key to women's strategy for victory.

Whatever is necessary will be done—and will be worth the final prize.

Women will take back what has been withheld, stolen, swindled, robbed, and raped from them. They will achieve freedom and independence. They will win back the right to be individuals, equal human beings.

Women declare openly that their ends can be attained only by the forcible overthrow of all existing sexist institutions, creeds, and canons—of the existing man-ruled social organization.

Let the male rulers tremble at a feminist revolution.

Women have nothing to lose but the chains of their subjugation, of the demeaned and degraded molds and roles into which they have been forced by men.

Women have a world to win—a world in which they can be for once human beings, individuals, capital-P Persons.

And we *shall* win that world.

Soon.

Very soon.

26.
TOWARD AN ECOLOGICAL THEORY OF VALUE

Arthur Pearl and Stephanie Pearl

Debate and discussion about the need to radically reorganize society are so common nowadays and so far from a practical framework for action that they tend to get lost in refinement rather than resolution. What is required is not more analysis, but a pragmatic focus for action—a focus rooted in political and economic reality and incorporating both social theory and social policy.

It seems to me that the so-called ecology crisis that besets us—pollution, the erosion of the earth's resources, and the threat of overpopulation—is the immediate, real-world focus demanding the attention of those of us who are profoundly dissatisfied with our social order, disappointed with its economic priorities, and disgusted with its human costs. After all, when looked at in political and economic terms, the ecological question must inevitably lead us to a full consideration of what the social, economic, and political world should look like. It most certainly will look very different both from what we have now and from what the popular superficial discussions of ecology might lead one to think.

Piecemeal changes will not do. We are going to have to come to grips with changes of much greater scope than population control and pollution, namely, the profound questions that come with having to learn to live with a state of economic equilibrium in an increased-scarcity society —a society of depleted, exhaustible resources—rather than put our eggs in the basket of limitless technological solutions or the intensity of a post-scarcity consumption syndrome.

The ecology crisis is the logical outcome of long-standing, accumulating crises. Ecology is a term descriptive of the give-and-take relationship among all organisms and the importance of each living thing in maintaining the delicate balance of the environment. Man, as a biological entity, functions as a vital link in this ecological chain; but at the same time, through his political and social extensions, he is threatening the very balance upon which his life—and all life—depends.

Ecology Spells Basic Human Issues So when one speaks of ecology one must, for any real understanding, include all things that affect man's ultimate survival and his ability to enjoy life. In this context, racism, poverty, and war are ecological problems. Analysis of the ecological crisis that doesn't include concern for these overwhelming national and international problems is dangerous, not just because it is shallow, but because it misses the overwhelming fact that rising consciousness of ecological deterioration offers a powerful chance to redeem a very long history of antidemocratic triumphs.

Meanwhile, in its current, piecemeal, Madison Avenue form, the ecology crisis threatens to divert us from potentially radical change by ignoring the political realities and vested interests that co-opt ecological anxiety through rhetorical flourishes, leaving the essentially destructive nature of the world much as it is and making campaigns for ecological sanity a huge hoax.

The ecology hoax is different from most hoaxes, however, in that hoaxes generally involve phony issues. With ecology the issue is very real; it is the leaders who are suspect. Infatuation with ecology, the pollution craze, has been attacked by blacks as a diversion from concern with race and poverty and by the New Left as a "cop-out"; and it has been treated by business as little more than a public relations problem. Unfortunately, some of the ecology warriors have given grounds for such attitudes.

The "experts" have displayed little expertise in approaching the problems of environmental deterioration. They reveal enormous gaps in basic scientific understanding, and their political approaches to the crisis seem to be either extraordinarily naïve or completely lacking. They have been too single-issue minded, have put forth approaches that are little more than melioristic, and have failed to offer a vision of and plan for an ecologically sound society. The "clear water" people ignore the "clean air" folk, to say nothing of the clean-up-the-slums advocates. The "overpopulation" people view population control as the one and only step. And few have seen the opportunity presented by the concern for ecology as a way to shape social policy, to increase significantly and in new ways public control over the private sector, or to move toward a new, humane, less acquisitive and exploitative society.

Although we have been treated to a variety of dire predictions concerning the fate of our planet—our spaceship, if you will—we have not been shown realistic means to alleviate what is, indeed, a critical situation. The visions range from flaming holocaust to computerized utopia; but we have yet to encounter any realizable, step-by-step, political (and it must be political) way to salvation. Few seem to understand that it will take a lot more than a letter to a congressman to get things going.

Thoroughly oversimplified, these serious and vital problems have been presented to the American people as a kind of Sesame Street for adults, a Smokey-the-Bear approach to a situation so severe that its resolution will require re-examination both of distribution of wealth, even of the indices that are used to determine wealth, and of all our political processes: governmental accountability and assessments of the legitimate and illegitimate uses of power must take place within an environmental framework, through evidence and logic formulated in environmental terms.

Currently, government functions primarily through proscription; even activities generated to provide support for people end up controlling their behaviors through sanctions and punishments. The rights to air, water, and a livable environment must be translated into forms that make possible the specific assignment of government accountability.

Judicial, legislative, and executive priorities must be recast in the context of a struggle for survival. Our codes of ethics and laws must be revised. Clearly, property rights now regarded as sacrosanct must be reconsidered in the light of ecological imperatives. Some people will have to be removed from free society (for their own protection or for the protection of others), but ecological society cannot be based on punishing offenders. The kind, duration, and nature of the confinement must be based on potential threat to the physical and social environment.

In an ecologically oriented society a person who persists in despoiling the environment is a far more dangerous criminal than a person who engages in petty theft. A person who betrays a public trust is far more dangerous as a criminal than a person who writes a worthless check. A military officer or cabinet minister who fabricates an external threat as a device to obtain larger defense appropriations is a far more dangerous criminal than even a psychopathic murderer, because of the number of people affected by his act.

Changes this far-reaching are not going to be accomplished by returning pop bottles.

Probably the most tragic misconception of those concerned with ecology is the notion that individuals or small groups can slip quietly away and live in harmony with nature. Those who adhere to this philosophy feel that by not polluting, by not overpopulating or overconsuming, they will, by example, set in motion a giant reaction of change. So they organize rural communes and form food cooperatives, isolate themselves and attempt to live an ecologically sound existence. Unfortunately, they are deluding themselves. They are not living in harmony with nature: they are living in harmony with the overconsumers, the overpopulaters, and the polluters. Their opting out is copping out, taking the heat off the system. And where will these scattered little Waldens be in a decade or so when a dying world gasps for breath and violently struggles for food and clean water?

A Real and Present Danger   The threat to man's existence is in three interrelated areas—population, pollution, and consumption of resources.

In order of importance, the most severe of these is the consumption of nonreplenishable resources. At an ever-increasing rate, man is using up the earth. It is impossible to unthinkingly drain the earth and expect to continue to have an enjoyable style of life. Plunder on this scale, with no regard for the ultimate results to our habitat, cannot go on indefinitely.

As an example of the interrelatedness of the various areas, this geological rape will inevitably lead to an even greater lack of stability in international relations than we know now. The United States, in the role of villain, with its 6 percent of the world's population using more than half of the world's resources, cannot be expected, simultaneously, to play an effective role as peace-keeper in a world in which the lack of equity between population and consumption causes periodic re-eruption of unresolved international tensions.

The present automated production of food, while efficient in producing more food in the short run, is poisoning the atmosphere and the water. Unless farming alters its approach to the pesticide and inorganic fertilizer business, we will have an enormous agricultural crisis within the next 25 years. Unless the form of transportation changes radically from one dominated by a car culture locked into exhausting the earth's unreplenishable resources, we will utterly spoil the atmosphere. Until we use far less electrical and nuclear power, we will draw fatally closer and closer to the erosion of our land, to the destruction of the earth.

The issue of overpopulation has been given considerable attention. But endless descriptions notwithstanding, the analyses and suggested solutions have consistently ignored the questions of war, racism, and poverty, which are the most overt manifestations of our ecological amorality. The solution of these problems on any significant scale rests entirely with the reordering of our economic values within a static rather than an expansive frame of reference, that is, developing mores that reflect humane rather than productive, competitive, destructive goals. Our guilt and impatience with the depravities of war, racism, and poverty, if honest, must act as both anchor and compass for the depth and breadth of ecological sanitation. Thus far this has not been the case, so that the honesty of our guilt and impatience is seriously impugned; and proposals offered to solve the dilemma have failed to generate an integrated strategy and to connect feasible tactics with that strategy. As a consequence, population control is reduced to little more than subscription to Zero Population Growth and various graffiti attached to bumper strips.

The problems of pollution are also well publicized. Every polluter in the nation has pledged his untiring support to cleaning up the environment—some time in the not-too-distant future. But still the poisoning goes on. Air, water, and space are contaminated daily; but the remedies heard are no more than an intellectual pollution of half-truths and outright lies. Those who have produced the most garbage are demanding the responsibility to do the housecleaning, and for a number of reasons that make about as much sense as giving the Mafia the task of administering justice.

Ecological Cost-Benefit Analysis   The new struggle in society is man versus nature, not labor versus capital; and only a workable ecological theory of value can resolve it.

We over-eat (the World Wildlife Fund estimates that we over-eat by 30 percent and produce 100 pounds of garbage annually per person); we are clothed in highly wasteful ways in which annual "model" changes have become as required as in the automobile industry; we are transported about via land-gobbling freeways in air-polluting private cars with enormous wasted energy; our technology is oriented toward producing goods rather than producing services and improving the quality of life.

The drive for accumulation of enormous personal or private corporate wealth threatens ecology above all else. Private wealth acquired primarily from devastation of the environment must sustain itself through continued devastation. What is required is a new type of ecological cost-benefit analysis, on a world-wide basis, in which planning must move us from a goods-oriented society to one oriented toward quality of life and human service. Unless we move from a military-dominated society and space research, we will gut the earth. The tremendous technological advances in both the socialist and capitalist worlds are threatening us with a new type of scarcity as the world's resources are rapidly being used up. New technology is leading to the rapid depletion of food, minerals, land, fuel, and sea life. The "Triple Revolution," which promised a new quality of life with high levels of leisure and new levels of consumption, may ultimately produce just the opposite. Advances in technology directed at reducing scarcity threaten to produce a new type of scarcity.

Paul Ehrlich has pointed out, "Each American has roughly 50 times the negative impact on the earth's life-support system as the average citizen of India." Or putting it another way, Ehrlich states that the addition of 75 million Americans (current projections for the year 2000), "from the standpoint of consumption of ever scarcer nonrenewable resources . . . will be the equivalent to more than 2 billion Colombians, 10 billion Nigerians, or 22 billion Indonesians!" (*The New York Times*, November 4, 1970.)

An ecological theory of value must be viewed in contrast to a labor theory of value, which in one form or another influences price structures, government fiscal and monetary policies, labor-management relations, and so on. A labor theory of value argues that the manpower required to produce the service or commodity determines its worth. The natural consequence of concern for saving manpower has inevitably been more and more reliance on technology, which has led to depletion of the earth's resources, because the more sophisticated the technology, the more iron, glass, fossil fuels, or electrical power has been consumed to run it. Look at the rationalization process that has taken place in goods-producing industries. The men who lugged and toted cargo were replaced by lift trucks. The saving in labor was enormous: one lift truck did the work of a dozen or more men. But there was an inverse cost in terms of environment. The lift truck consumed far more of the environment than did the labor done by man while, at the same time, contributing significantly to pollution. This trivial example multiplied manyfold gives some indication of the cost of technology to the environment.

An ecological theory of value implies a far different interpretation of inflation from that which stems from a labor theory of value. In a labor theory of value inflation is hypothesized to be due to the cost in man-power of producing a commodity in contrast to the demand for such a commodity. In an ecological theory, inflation would be the ratio of demand to the environment's ability to produce the commodity.

Ecological value must alter the state of relations between labor and management. Labor's demands for ever-increasing wages will result in profligate wasting of the environment unless labor's concerns for security and an opportunity to live the good life are successfully incorporated into labor-management relations. The guarantee of employment of choice to every-one, health and other services, a secure old age, quality education for all youth, access to enjoyable leisure—the motivations that stimulate aggressive labor organization—would be markedly reduced under an ecological theory of value.

Simply stated, an ecological theory of value would fix the worth of goods or services in terms of units of the environment required to create them. The law would be this: the value of any activity would be high either if very little of the environment were used or if the resources required for it were easily replenished. At the root of all economic policy based on an ecological theory of value would be both the use of little and the creating of more.

Political Strategy: The Only Way   The ecological dilemma is soluble only through political means. In order to avoid a calamity, there must be coherent and coordinated attacks in all four political arenas: (1) electoral (supporting the election of candidates who know the score and are willing to act, not expecting much concern for ecology from candidates whose campaigns are heavily financed by economic interests that despoil or pollute); (2) confrontational (meeting those who destroy the environment head-on, through boycotts and similar efforts); (3) educational (making the public *truly* aware of the seriousness of the environmental crisis through description, analysis, and prescription); and (4) influential (maintaining pressure on principal policy-making bodies through lobbying and petition).

The ecological crisis boils down to a political problem, because only through action on a governmental scale is there any possibility that man will survive. And it is going to take a lot of dedicated action to set the giant bureaucratic sloth known as government into motion. At present, the government is aggressively un-ecological. It subsidizes industrial activity that depletes the earth of its nonreplenishable resources, destroying rather than preserving and paying for this destruction by allocating the majority of government funds for war and defense. It supports manpower and social service policies that deplete our natural wealth while refusing to support work activities compatible with and necessary for survival.

The present attack on the problem of drug abuse, for example, is even more indefensible than the behavior itself in that it leads to the destruction of a sense of community (indispensable in an ecological world), stirs up unnecessary controversy, and requires persons in the nonproductive roles of inmates and caretakers. Many behaviors now treated as criminal must be reassessed and placed in the context of education, medicine, or social service.

Current approaches to shelter must change; they must be discarded, in fact, if ecological balance is to be achieved. Housing now wastes materials, space, and energy. The shelter of the future must offer privacy, but economize on building materials. What can be shared with others without inconvenience must be shared. Current inducements to home ownership could be halted, and instead there should be encouragement of less permanent attachment to places of residence.

An Ecologically Sound Utopia   I am not in any way suggesting a return to the past, based upon scarcity, a low level of technology, primitive demands, and so on. I am suggesting, rather, that we organize our resources very carefully to produce a high level of culture, esthetics, and new qualities of living that are not based on a "thing culture," waste, built-up (advertised) demand for things that exhaust the world's resources and pollute the air. Thus, in transportation, I see monotrains with cars that include games, interesting foods (but a lower level of caloric intake), art work, participatory education, movies, drinking, and so on. I envision a society in which $800 billion of human services are produced with 120 million jobs, eliminating 50 million jobs in goods production (10 million in automobile-related industries alone). I see a system of policing technology by limiting production to only those things that are necessary for a desirable quality of life.

Recognition of ecological factors would lead to a 180-degree flip in urban living and development. Currently the megalopolis is ecologically indefensible, and the ever-increasing trend toward urbanism is only worsening the situation, requiring more and more miles of auto travel, highway construction, and so on, which persistently drain depletable energy sources. In place of this helter-skelter growth, model communities of a maximum size of 250,000 residents must be planned. The cities would be so arranged, logistically, that only rarely would people be required to move outside them. For the United States and, with modifications, for the world at large, ecological living would amount to a revitalization of rural sectors and a reverse of migration patterns—pioneering in the twentieth century.

There can be no unemployment in an ecologically balanced economy. Unemployment cannot be permitted because of the needs of a world with scarce resources, because the insecurity that unemployment brings contributes to unecological hoarding impulses, and because enforced idleness contributes to unecological, anti-social behavior. But only work compatible with nature can be tolerated in the future. This means that all activity that does not contribute to quality of life or that contributes at too great a cost in natural resources must be abolished. More and more, man-power must be employed in health, education, welfare (particularly in activities that would enable people to cope with their environment), leisure, conservation, and resource development.

Indeed, the expansion of social services is basic to an ecologically defensible economy. Reflect that the world of tomorrow will require people to adjust to even more demanding living arrangements. There will be more of us in the world; and we must learn to work cooperatively in smaller expanses of space with persons of many tempos, styles, and values if Spaceship Earth is to survive. The essence of ecological citizenship will be personal accountability. Every person must be prepared to justify his style of life. To be accountable, a person must not only be willing to conform to legitimate constraints but also be able to distinguish between legitimate and illegitimate demands made of him; and, probably most important of all, he must be able to play a leader role in shaping the world in which he has to live. The ecological citizen must possess qualities far different from those of the non-thinking, passive conformist who today has made the optimal adjustment as a respected member of the silent majority.

Social service must be thought of in a continuum of support that stands between education and medicine. Given an ecologically based education and relieved of the unecological contradictions of an unecological economy, a great many people will probably be able to meet the new challenges. But some few will be devastated by these challenges and will require medical assistance. Between these extremes will be those experiencing trouble and discomfort. The social worker of tomorrow must be prepared to assist that struggling group.

The areas that ecological social workers must be competent in will be those that historically have been difficult to resolve. The social worker will attempt to ease the pains of generational conflict, marital conflict, ungratifying work, racial, class, and ethnic tensions, ethical and social value problems, lack of community synergy, and so on. The goal of tomorrow's social service is to assist every person to a productive and satisfying life. That goal must be sought because the threat to man's survival (1) does not permit the luxury of many persons in nonuseful roles, and (2) does not allow the relegating of others to serve as caretakers for the non-productive.

A society based on the notion that every person is active, productive, and sensitive to the needs of others—in an even more complicated, crowded, interdependent world—must be committed to an adequately trained social service force organized so as to be maximally helpful. It is impóssible to estimate accurately how many people will be needed to help others to cope, but it is not unreasonable to hazard a guess that one in every 100 citizens will need extensive assistance and that one in 10 will require some kind of help. Given a population of over 200 million, a commitment of 1 million persons in the area of social service careers does not appear to be excessive, though even this figure represents an enormous increase over the number of those now in social service.

Despite the finite quantity of many elements of life—food, oil, iron, water, space, air—many life concerns are not finite. Only a small percentage of the world's population receives adequate services devoted to health, education, welfare, and the pursuit of leisure. Consider the United States as an example. We are a society in which only 77 million persons work (and many of them at totally useless jobs) out of almost 120 million people who are of work age. Manpower resources, it is clear, have not been effectively tapped. Politics is also an arena without limits. Although there is only one president at a time (and some observers insist that this is more than actually serves), everyone can participate in government if that government is organized to encourage participation.

The infinite aspects of life are individually determined. There is no fixed amount of belonging, usefulness, or competence. These attributes can be the driving force to energize reform in the use of the world's finite resources. So, we have the way. The unprecedented and obvious threat to our planet that accompanies our continued subservience to expansive economic mores should give us the will—if only we risk enough.

An Ecological Rationale for a Human Services Society

In a number of responses to Arthur Pearl and Stephanie Pearl's "Toward an Ecological Theory of Value" (*Social Policy*, May/June 1971), readers asked for clarification of a number of issues. The key points raised were:

1. What is wrong with GNP as a yardstick of where we are?
2. How does the notion of an ecological theory of value relate to the differences between goods production and services?
3. Would not the problems raised be solved in a socialist society?
4. Are there not basic conflicts between the goals of ecologists and those concerned with poverty and racism?
5. Is the society that is being sought anything more than an expansion of the present health, education, and welfare activities?

Arthur Pearl Replies
1. GNP does what it does well. It is a global measure of the exchange of goods and services and as such allows for some gross

economic statements and comparisons. Unfortunately, it high-lights much that is second-rate in our society. It does not indi-cate that we are on a course to ecological disaster. The real prob-lem is that it affects national policy.

GNP measurement pushes toward emphasis on produc-tion, particularly of a capital-intensive nature. The deleterious consequences of productive activities are not measured. That is, the environment-destructive consequences of manufacturing are not subtracted from the GNP; in fact, the reverse occurs when manpower and resources that are extended to "clean up" the waste are also counted as part of the GNP.

When GNP is used as the prime criterion in the measurement of economic well-being, any cooling down of the economy means cutting back on economic activity. This cutting back has come to mean a drastic reduction of publicly funded human services, which seriously reduces the number of people employed in providing those services. It must be obvious to everyone by now that the chief casualties of the current govern-ment-inspired recession have been in the areas of health, educa-tion, welfare, recreation, and conservation.

The tragedy is that of all work activities, the human services, from an ecological point of view, are the least destruc-tive of nature. Conversely, heating up the economy in a fashion designed to expand GNP stimulates goods-producing industries that devastate the earth of its scarce nonrestorable commodities. Because GNP is solely a measure of quantity, not quality, it becomes a force that undermines ecological balance. Any true concern for the environment must stress quality and must de-emphasize growth in terms of sheer size.

More specifically, a society that, for instance, measures its commitment to education by calculating the proportion of its GNP that is devoted to teacher and administrative salaries and school construction is deceiving itself. The gain to the pupil is in no way assessed: more or less pay to the teacher seems to have little or no effect upon pupil learning, and thus it is misleading to imply that increased dollar investment has a salutory effect on the service. This quantitative thinking is dangerously uneco-logical. We must develop measures of quality, not quantity. Clearly, these will be more difficult to construct, but we need them badly nonetheless.

2. Confusion still reigns about the significance of an ecologically healthy world. People continue to call for the growth of the private sector in our society at the expense of the quality of life. The kind of growth that is necessarily related to the private sector is *capital intensive and therefore resource depleting*. The

more we continue growth as it has been traditionally defined by both capitalist and socialist societies, the more rapidly will we use up the earth's resources, particularly those of the developing countries. This is the basic reason for the threat of continued wars and new forms of imperialism in which the developed nations fight to control the resources of the poorer nations.

Only through a human-services-oriented society, in which the predominant expenditures in the public sector are not for hard services and military goods, can we promote human development toward a higher quality of life. It is only in a human services society, which is labor intensive rather than capital intensive, that the resources of the earth will be conserved and human resources be expended for the benefit of human beings. Such a society is less likely to breed war, racism, and poverty; these are necessary concomitants of a capital-intensive society.

In essence, we have a surplus of human beings and a shortage of nonrenewable materials; thus we have to reverse our historical view of efficiency. Heretofore, efficiency has been calculated by the introduction of labor-saving, capital-intensive activity. Now we must have ecological efficiency, replacing machines wherever possible with human beings and, at the same time, offering the worker a gratifying experience, a feeling of competence, belonging, and usefulness, which once again leads us back to a human services society that is labor intensive and environment saving. We can no longer continue to use the public sector to prop up the private sector via tax benefits, subsidies, and fiscal and monetary policies that contribute to the maldistribution of wealth and income.

3. We need a sound, ecologically based, cost-benefits formula different from both the socialist and the capitalist perspectives. The two crucial variables are quality of life and environment. Our cost-benefits analysis must ask how much nonreplenishable nature is expended in relation to the benefit side of improved quality of life.

   It must be remembered that socialist society is rooted in the belief of an infinitely expanding technological base in which growth continues infinitely and there is no awareness of overutilization of resources. The Marxist formula was "From each according to his ability, to each according to his needs." The ecological credo must be: "To each an improved quality of life; from each a respect for nature"—which in essence says we can't rip off the earth.

4. Those who cry that the ecological crisis is diverting us from a war on poverty, although correct about the ways in which environmental approaches are being commercially manipulated,

fail to recognize that a genuinely ecological strategy is the only fundamental anti-poverty approach possible in the present and future world. Unless there is enough food, shelter, and clothing for all, there must be poverty, racism, and war. Unless there is enough available quality education, health services, opportunity to enjoy leisure, clean air to breathe, and unpolluted water to drink, there must be poverty, racism, and war. The goods-producing emphasis detracts from the mobilization of world resources to meet both basic needs and human quality needs. A state that gives highest priority to basic life support and quality human services will create enormous numbers of real jobs in the human services and in environmental development and control, jobs for millions of unemployed and underemployed people. It will lead to greater redistribution of wealth and the destruction of the capital-intensive basis for the expansion of profit. Right now we have neither a war on poverty nor a war on pollution. To talk about reducing poverty without recognizing that before long there will be an increasing shortage of food and water in the world becomes indeed ridiculous. Conversely, to talk about solving ecological problems without discussing career opportunities for the downtrodden and the oppressed is equally absurd.

A basic ecological strategy is also fundamental for reducing the deep alienation that pervades most of the world. Despite the fact that we have a great many more goods and gadgets, the needs for which have been grossly overstimulated, people are deeply alienated and unhappy, and therefore turn to drugs, alcohol, and so on. An ecologically oriented society will have to educate against gluttony and provide monetary and fiscal controls and other forms of regulation to reduce our absurd consumption patterns.

But the human services society of the future is, of course, not a world-wide commune. It is too late to de-institutionalize and to turn our backs on technology and our institutions in the service of human growth and environmental conservation. Unless ecological controls are instituted, there will be no post-scarcity society; in fact, there may be no society at all.

It is important at this juncture to recognize the crunch that the blue-collar worker is in. The environmentalists by and large have asked him to sacrifice for conservation by paying increasing taxes for cleaning up the society and surrendering employment and comfort. He is also asked to pay for the human services, but these in no way serve his needs. He has reason to be unhappy with the education his children receive and his low-quality and expensive health services. A true environmental approach would offer quality services and place the burden of cost on those most able to pay.

5. We want to see a society in which there are vastly expanded, reorganized, and highly efficient human services, basically directed toward an improved quality of life. This clearly does not mean simply health, education, and welfare, or the usual ways that the human services are defined and inefficiently offered in the present period; nor is it synonymous with the "public sector." We see human services including art, recreation, communications, research, group development, human potential development, architecture, religious and philosophic experiences, rehabilitation, the development of alternative life styles, environmental improvement, and so on. We mean a higher education that really expands knowledge and consciousness.

Human services have been narrowly defined in the current bureaucratic approaches to mean health, education, and welfare, usually in the interest of the professionals who provide services to the exclusion of the clients. More money for the expansion of these services is important—it always is—but expansion alone is not enough. The institutions currently entrusted with determining adequacy of service must be opened up to include clients as participants in decision making—no longer as dependent subjects. An ecological theory of value would require the qualitative changes that can be generated by increased accountability and would consider the expansion of services to dependent recipients grossly unecological.

The measure of social progress to which we must move must be grounded in a theory of value that makes it perfectly clear that the status and self-image of "recipient" in all major social activities deplete individual human resources, reduce the individual's power to act on his environment, and, finally, eliminate all possibility of social control in the interest of a more human and sanitary environment—or, in the long run, of any habitable environment at all.

27.
CHICANO MANIFESTO: NEW STRATEGIES FOR THE SEVENTIES

Armando B. Rendón

When the national magazines, newspapers, and electronic media offered their traditional end-of-the-decade reviews in January 1970, a people who had begun an awful struggle to free themselves from the gringo world and establish a unique identity in the Americas merited not one mention. The Chicano people should not permit this indifference to continue in the 1970s. The seventies should become the decade of the Chicano.

Not that the Anglo media are the bench marks of success, but they reflect the national thinking, or, rather, the lack of concern of the dominant society for the Mexican American. A Chicano once described to me a visit he paid to an Eastern newspaper editor's office: on the wall behind the news executive was a long sheet of paper with about 20 categories, beginning with inflation, Vietnam, crime, and so on, with blacks and urban decay nearly last; the Chicano had not even impressed the editor as deserving of a place on the scroll. Whenever an "interpretative" news article, that is, an article by an Anglo about Chicanos, has appeared in recent months, one or another of the various aspects of the liberation movement is given emphasis to the detriment of the overall effort under way. Gringo books and articles about Chicanos tend to create new stereotypes as much as they seek to catch the "color" of, say, the Tijerina-led, land grants movement or Chavez' unionization drive. Articles will emphasize Chavez sitting in a rocking chair (like President Kennedy's) due to ailments that developed from his long fast; or another will dwell on Tijerina's being called King Tiger, which is only very slightly derived from his name. A recent book about *la raza* was reviewed in the syndicated *Book World* section under the title, "I Am Not a Boy," which is the way in which the reviewer defined the word *Chicano*. And when a news article does try to tell the full story, it is squelched: for example, a story by Associated Press features writer Dave Smith, on Chicano power, was withdrawn from publication after it had been wired to subscribers for August 13, 1967, release. The follow-up wire from AP killing the story read: "Focus questioned. It may be reinstated in another form in the future." Smith merely considered the Chicano's deliberation of the "rewards for rioting" which Negroes had gained recently and what alternatives that left the Chicano. Could there have been some fear that the story might spread the idea among the *barrios*? Or was the article just too blunt about the fact that Negroes did get rewarded for the riots?

The U.S. Information Agency (USIA) quashed an article about Cesar Chavez titled, "New Voice in the Vineyard," from appearing in its August 1970 photo bulletin, sent monthly to USIA officials in 118 countries overseas. The man responsible for killing the story was R. Kenneth Towery, USIA assistant director for press and publication and a former aide to Senator John Tower of Texas, where Chavez' union organizers have been very active.

Never has the full impact or the full meaning of the Chicano movement been appreciated, but, then, Chicanos have never had the opportunity to communicate their deepest feelings and aspirations to the world. Gringo control of the media has seen to that. One artful piece in the *Washington Post* early last year dealt with the student unrest in South Texas, and was headlined, "The Chicanos Want In." The writer managed to suggest just the opposite of what most Chicanos intend. We want out:

- Out of a cultural milieu which desensitizes man and woman into profit-producing machines, devoid of humanity and soul.
- Out of a country which poses a military answer to every foreign issue; and despite having been born in revolution against Old World oppression, seeks to deny the same right to nations who reject Brave New World oppression.
- Out of gringo patterns of injustice and prejudice which have suppressed the best talents and minds of our people and accepted only those few willing to gringoize themselves to achieve a measure of fulfillment.
- Out of a system of government which is controlled by economic and social influence to reap its benefits at the expense of the poor and minority peoples.

To put this in positive terms, the Chicanos in essence desire three things:

- To fulfill our peoplehood, Chicano;
- To reclaim our land, Aztlán;
- To secure the future for ourselves and our countrymen.

To achieve these goals Chicanos must have political, social, and economic freedom. We know that none of these basic freedoms will be achieved merely by wishing or asking for them. Therefore, Chicanos are confronted with the realities of devising new methods, perhaps techniques never tried before, of developing the resources to support those techniques, and of establishing, in some cases, new systems to supplant the worn-out and harmful gringo ones. How do we accomplish this? Outright revolution —that is, armed insurrection, appears to be only a devise of the rhetoricians. Our revolt may cause violence, but we will be the chief victims of it if it occurs. The events of August 29, 1970, in East Los Angeles bear out this truth. I believe in fighting against the political structures and social practices which have suppressed us but not in a violence that endangers lives. If our revolt should lead us further toward violence, the police, the National Guard, and the armed forces are at the beck and call of the oppressive forces in the United States—that way lies the destruction of our people. The gringo reacts with excessive force against the Black Panthers, against the Young Lords, and against the Brown Berets. We must find means of revolution which accomplish the same goals that armed insurgence might.

What has been begun by Cesar Chavez, Corky Gonzales, José Angel Gutiérrez, and Reies Tijerina must be carried forward. The priority of the *huelga*, the spark of the Chicano revolution struck by Delano farm workers, should remain a primary goal for Chicanos to achieve. The shameful fact is that Chicanos in many cases have allowed the Anglo to pre-empt the stage in this struggle, which is so deeply rooted in our past. The success of the *huelga* is *la raza*'s success; there must be a new surge of interest by all *raza* in changing the National Labor Relations Act and assuring other civil guarantees for farm workers and migrant laborers. In a very real sense, the predicament of the *campesino* underscores the predicament of all *raza*, for if we cannot free the Chicano of the fields, how can we free the Chicano of the *barrio*? They are one and the same.

The strongest current among our people is the youth force struggling for recognition and liberation. While generational discrepancies persist among young and old Chicanos, there is a cross section of Chicanos who speak and think in similar terms about their aims and aspirations, which is quite broad as to age and economic and educational background. Nevertheless, generational breakup is one of the Anglo social norms that Chicanos have to combat vigorously. It sometimes seems, as a consequence of some Chicanos gaining middle-class status, that there is a greater commonality of thought between the very old and the very young; the middle aged are still too tied up with making it as Anglos, with being agringados or *blanqueados*. But these, too, can be made to come around to their senses. *Si no, que se chingan.*

The Chicano community is undergoing one of the most rapid changes of any people of the Americas. We can point to many causes— racial and cultural prejudice, labor exploitation, educational deprivation, and political disenfranchisement—to explain, up to a point, why Chicanos have taken so long to pull themselves together and to assert that identity and unity of purpose which would clearly manifest our peoplehood. In many ways, we have inner strengths to accomplish communion among ourselves; but we have been distrustful, unfaithful, and weak among ourselves as well. That negative aspect of our experience in Anglo America, which has taught us many of its worst traits, must now become a lesson of the past. Chicanos have to look to their own resources to accelerate the change we will effect in the seventies. If the resources do not lie in the community, we must learn how to bring them in from outside the barrio.

The upward and increasingly sophisticated evolution of Chicanismo can be even more rapid and contributive to sanity in the United States than the black movement. Chicanos can approach the crisis of races that torments America as the single group in the nation which represents, with our brother raza, broad racial and cultural integration. Chicanos must explore the multicultural and multiracial wellsprings of la raza Chicana. We must study it, write about it, speak out to the nation. We are a modern people. While the nonraza nations are dying or dead as cultural entities, the mestizo people, la raza, are but a few hundred years old. "We are a big baby," Reies Tijerina has put it in referring to the mestizos, who number some 200 to 250 million people in the Western Hemisphere today. By the year 2000, we will be twice as many as the Anglo American.

We must explore and exploit the heritage of the Spaniards, a thousands-of-years-old history and culture, with ties going back to the Phoenicians, the Greeks, the Romans, and the Arabs. We must give honor to the Spanish father, as Wilfredo Sedillo insists, and I with him. We have hardly begun to investigate the fathomless inheritance that is ours from our Indian forebears, the Nahúas, the Toltecs, the Aztecs, and the North American Indians. José Angel Gutiérrez once spoke of the Indian heritage as "our better half," that is, our Indian mother. We are the offspring, the mestizo, who finds himself in an alien culture, but who is finding himself able to adapt to both culture sources and become the modern Chicano.

Because we are interiorly integrated, the integration syndrome of black-white America has no relevance to the Chicano. For example, we do not believe that our Chicanitos must attend classes with Negroes and Anglos in order to attain an adequate education. If there must be integration, we say, let it be in terms of cash, curriculum, and control. Let the Chicano enjoy a just share of funds so that his barrio schools can hire the most qualified teachers, purchase the best equipment, and give young people the finest education possible. Integrate the history books, the literature books, the languages spoken in the classroom, so that the Chicano can identify himself there and feel pride in his being Chicano. The Anglo must let go of the total control he has maintained over the educational system, the curriculum, the hiring and firing, the discipline, and the decision making so that Chicanos will have a say in the schooling of their children. Of course, the Anglo or black will not bow to this prescription for change. Chicano communities will have to force this change, this brand of integration. Because of the Anglo society's resistance, Chicano take over of educational systems, not everywhere, but in many places in the Southwest and Midwest, may be that much more complete when they occur. Chicanos in Houston conducted a weeklong boycott in September, with 3,000 to 4,000 raza children kept out of school by their parents. The protest of the Chicano Community won a reversal of an HEW integration order which put Chicanos and blacks together, while Anglo schools remained segregated.

In the educational context, an exemplary effort is being made in Mercedes, Texas, to build a Chicano university from the ground up. (An Indian-Chicano institution is also developing in Davis, California, near Sacramento, under the name, Deganawidda-Quetzalcoatl University.) Jacinto Treviño College, named after a Chicano whose reputation for killing los *rinches cobardes* (cowardly Rangers) is celebrated in *corridos* (Chicano songs), began classes in the fall of 1970.

Founded as an extension of Antioch College of Yellow Springs, Ohio, and financed by foundation and government moneys, Treviño College is in the first phase of certifying 15 masters degree candidates, who will in turn become the undergraduate school faculty. The director is Dr. Leonard Mestas, a Coloradoan who completed his doctoral studies in education at the University of Colorado.

There are also 22 GED students ranging in age from 18 to 45 years old who will themselves form the core of the first year undergraduate student body. According to Narciso Aleman, a MAYO founder, now the college's administrator and a masters candidate himself, Treviño anticipates collaborating with Crystal City schools in bridging the whole community's educational needs.

Eventual site of the college is an abandoned Oblate Fathers monastery in Mission, a few miles from McAllen, where MAYO held a crucial organizational conference in December 1969. A dispute among the Oblate Fathers has withheld final liberation of the "mission" for Chicano use. Located on a slight elevation above the Rio Grande Valley floor, the mission could be no better situated for it overlooks both the United States and Mexico across the Rio Grande. In fact, the site reflects the history of the *colegio's* namesake, Jacinto Treviño. Treviño was born in the United States. In 1910, one part of his family was living in Mexico and the other part on this side of the border. A gringo beat up his brother. Jacinto heard that his brother had been killed by this certain gringo, the son of a rich Texan. In his grief and anger, Jacinto killed the young *gringo de veras*. Jacinto escaped across the border, but later was induced to return by a cousin named Pablo. Rangers ambushed him. As he and another brother Joaquin fought their way out, they shot Pablo and one of the Rangers. The story has since been perpetuated in El Corrido de Jacinto Treviño.

The 24-year-old Aleman clarifies the deeper reasons for choosing

Treviño's name: "The Treviño family signifies what has happened because of an artificial boundary. Jacinto himself was not a violent man but he defended his family and himself. And the local populace identified with him." Aleman stresses the point.

"We wish to dedicate Treviño College to this spirit, to this history," Aleman says. "We would like to believe that the *colegio* will dedicate itself through its students and faculty to *los de abajo*, to the poor."

With time and good fortune, for the Chicanos who created Treviño College certainly have the will, a truly Chicano institution could develop. In a sense, Chicanos have been hampered by not having had their own segregated colleges; blacks at least have had some 50 schools they could attend for a degree. We Chicanos were fooled into believing that we were white, Caucasian and thus integrated into the United States melting pot, while all the time we were actually being segregated and set apart in "Mexican" schools. But the privilege of education was withheld beyond the elementary grades. It was useful to maintain us at a certain level of ignorance so that we could not operate or compete on a level with the Anglo, thus forcing us into a worker class and a soldier class. Those are categories we still suffer for the sake of "integration," gringo style.

The Chicano brand of integration can be carried into every area of life: in economics, whether related to the workingman or the businessman; in civil rights related to voting, housing, the institutions of justice; and in politics. Events of the past five years demonstrate that the greater the resistance Chicanos meet in achieving an equitable role or a share in jobs, housing, education, and politics, the more complete and total their eventual assumption of these powers will be. This is the pattern that will manifest itself more and more in the seventies. There are regions or cities in the Southwest, and even in the Midwest and Northeast, where Mexican Americans or *raza* can take over the functions and power of government, where school systems can be controlled by the *barrios*, and where the economic life of the *barrios* or *pueblos* can be placed in the hands of the Chicanos who live there.

Coalition is one of the first avenues of action for Chicanos. The brief experience in the Poor People's Campaign demonstrated that on certain issues based on common needs, there can be coalition. In 1968 Reies Tijerina convened with black activists in California and pledged with them a black and brown coalition. Chicanos have many things in common with the black people of the United States. We can do much together and still maintain our own identity. In fact, there may be greater sense of community among the two groups than we have yet seen, simply because not enough Chicanos and blacks have taken the time to correspond and plan together. We have been pitted against each other for 120 years by the white man. It is time that we turn the tables.

But because of our Indian inheritance, Chicanos should begin to communicate with the Indian brother. Our historians and scholars should research the intermingled roots of our history and culture. The Yaqui Indians, for example, have maintained certain modes of life that are distinct from the *mestizo* culture, but they still are a relevant link with the Chicano past. They have endured the pressures from Mexican and Anglo governments, and have revolted against the Mexican government several times as late as the 1920s, with some tribesmen escaping across the Sonora-United States border and settling in communities near Tucson and Phoenix. These people have an embattled history which is characterized by a fierce rejection of the white man. Still, along with their tribal customs they have retained many Spanish influences in a kind of synthesis of both the Indian and Spanish heritage. One such settlement represents about a third of the population in Guadalupe, a small unincorporated community just on the edge of Phoenix. Descendants of the Sonoran tribesmen, they are Mexican Americans in terms of identification, but they represent one extreme of the spectrum of the Mexican American people. At the opposite extreme of the spectrum are those who emphasize their Spanish origins. The Yaquis have their own customs, quite separate from their Mexican American neighbors. They retain the customary *el capitan*, a ceremonial leader who presides at annual celebrations, as well as other customs and dances. The Yaqui has somehow withstood many generations of the Anglo presence to preserve his tribal ways. They have even set limits on the extent of Spanish-Mexican influence. How have they done this? Is there something in their personality and way of life that Chicanos can adapt as we struggle to cope with the pressures of a dominant society which we cannot reject entirely but from which we must learn to extract its best features? Can we learn from the Yaqui experience how the fusion of Spanish-Mexican culture has occurred?

North American Indian tribes have suffered a kind of cultural shock from their discovery, an unplanned one, in March 1966, of the presence of the Tigua Indian tribe of Isleta, Texas. Vine Deloria, Jr., describes the event in his book, *Custer Died for Your Sins.* "The modern era of Indian emergence had begun," he writes, when representatives of the tribe appeared before the National Congress of American Indians' executive committee meeting in El Paso. The Tiguas had been forced to transport the goods of the Spaniards (who had been driven out of New Mexico in 1688) back to El Paso. Assigned a piece of land at what is now Isleta, down south about 10 miles from present-day El Paso, the little tribe was virtually forgotten for centuries. After their appearance before the NCAI, they obtained formal recognition as an Indian tribe in early 1968 from the United States Government. "Discovery of the Tiguas rocked Indian people in several respects," Deloria relates. "Indians had been brainwashed into accepting the demise of their tribe as God's natural plan for Indians. Yet the Tiguas plainly demonstrated that Indian tribal society had the strength and internal unity to maintain itself indefinitely within an alien culture."

Haven't we Chicanos also a discovery to make, perhaps a mutual discovery, among our Yaqui brothers? Are there not other tribesmen in the Southwest with whom we have cultural and psychological bonds that could result in a mutual effort to reclaim a way of life that the gringo has nearly destroyed? One person who has expressed his affinity is Mad Bear Anderson, one of the Indian leaders in the repossession of Alcatraz Island in San Francisco Bay. At the December (1969) Moratorium Day in San Francisco, Anderson declared, "The only people who have a right to live on Alcatraz are the Indians and the Chicanos."

The realities of black urban strength will necessitate political coalitions with black organizations, but, also, Chicanos have an obligation, much like a family duty, to collaborate with Indian tribes in their struggles. The Indian mother—that side of our past that binds us to the earth, inspirits our hands and minds with the esthetic, and colors our vision with sensitivities for the humanity in man—has been neglected by many of us Chicanos. It must be one of our objectives to return to that nurturing mother in order to revitalize those values and insights which Chicanos need to achieve more profound levels of thought and motivation.

Reclamation of the *barrio*, from within, must be an objective of Chicanos in the seventies. For this purpose, again, Chicanos must investigate what cultural traits and side-by-side economic and political realities can be converted into specific programs for rehabilitation of the pueblo, which is both the Chicano people and where they live. Take the issue of housing. Mexican American people tend to exist in substandard housing five or seven times more often than Anglos. Somehow our people survive in living conditions that are as bad as any in the country. There is no competition as to who lives in the worst conditions—it's a fact of Chicano life. One of the cultural traits that has been adulterated by gringo social mores (suburbanismo) is *la raza's* propensity for communal living as a survival technique and a social function. The 1968 Housing Act provides for the purchase by tenants of public housing. Suppose a *barrio* community organization working with a public housing tenants group were to effect such a purchase; the tenants would become owners of their own units and would be bound together in community ownership of the whole project. Responsibility for upkeep and maintenance, for payments on the loan, and for management would be in the hands of the tenant-owners. In effect, rents would be loan payments, and if the project were handled as a shareholding operation, the tenant-owners might expect a dividend at the end of the year or some return on their investment, should they move. The cooperative and communal nature of such a housing project corresponds to the interdependence for survival among Mexican American families which we have experienced throughout our entire history.

The phrase "black capitalism" was in vogue as an answer to the problems of the black ghetto until blacks realized that very few black businessmen would actually benefit and that by and large, ghetto enterprise would remain an extension of the white corporations, another form of

Anglo colonialism. Because the Chicano's predicament is set within the *barrio*, often an isolated community, it follows that in order to rehabilitate the *barrio*, entrepreneurship must be established *barrio*-wide. Chicanos have to engage in cooperative enterprises that benefit as many people as possible.

A situation might develop thus: a *barrio* organization scratches up the financing for a wholesale produce outlet. An adjunct of the outlet would be an open-air market, a typical *raza* form of commerce. Stores in the *barrio* could buy from the outlet at reduced prices, or a block group could form a buying cooperative. Perhaps a few aspiring entrepreneurs might be encouraged to set up their own *tiendas*. Meanwhile, small farmers in the area, attracted to the produce outlet, would organize themselves into a farmers' cooperative so that they could get the best price. The Chicano outlet can still offer the lowest possible prices to the *barrio* consumer, while larger produce houses will be forced to compete on retail prices but maintain the farmers' level of payments. In various *barrios* of the Southwest, Chicano organizations are developing cooperative ventures of this kind. An organization need only observe what services are brought into the *barrio* and controlled by Anglos to know what services they can begin to offer, thereby undercutting the Anglo's influence in the *barrio*. These are the kinds of enterprises that should be high priority in the plotting for economic turnovers by Chicano organizations. Restaurants are being opened by Chicano groups. Home delivery of Mexican foods, a mattress factory, and a publishing house are other efforts that have developed out of *barrio* unification and *barrio* needs. The Tierra Amarilla farming co-op is only the first of many more to come. The people's clinic in Tierra Amarilla, bombed out once already but reopened, is an example in the health field. Churches, foundations, or unions could well afford to supplement these most relevant efforts, not to dictate how they are to be run or how the funds are to be allocated, but to support what is one of the most fundamental developments in Chicano action.

For some time, I've had the idea that a *barrio* union might be a concept worth exploring for implementation in certain areas. The idea might not be feasible in some *barrios*, but might be quite practical in others. Basically, the *barrio* union would develop out of already existing organizations or simply from *barrio* people coming together to pool their resources. Much like a labor union, *barrio* members would pay dues; they would meet regularly, once a week or once a month, or whenever necessity demanded, and elect officers and bargaining representatives. They would have basically the same weapons that labor unions have (except for the Taft-Hartley Act): the strike, walkout, boycott, picketing, threats of any of these, plus withholding of taxes and the vote. The *barrio* union's representatives would bargain collectively with city, county, or state authorities to remedy *barrio* citizens' possible complaints, such as: street lighting, paving of streets, sewer improvements, improved police and fire protection, as well as controversies over police misconduct, court injustices, increased representation in government, zoning laws, and the distribution of job resources in businesses or industries relocating near the *barrio*. The *barrio* union could also establish its own community agencies, such as a crime-prevention unit, which would maintain surveillance of the neighborhoods to hold down all crime but also to keep down *chota* crimes. Such a union might advise that taxes be withheld until street lights or sewers were allocated for the *barrio*, for, in the event of complete cutoff of services by the city or county, the notoriety that would befall such a city administration would be highly undesirable. Besides, in some *barrios*, the difference between services rendered and complete cutoff is very slight.

Such an approach could work, I believe, because some of the fundamental features required to carry it out are deeply ingrained in the Chicano experience. The concept of union dues is well known, if not a common experience, among Chicano communities. The necessity for the people to pool their resources to help each other is well grounded in the Beneficencia societies which still operate in a few *barrios*. The concept also depends on cultural bonds that are being more strongly and openly asserted in the barrios; a *barrio* union falls right into the *raza* cultural mode. Membership in the *barrio* union could have immediate benefits for joining. A small dues payment per month would entitle a member immediately, for example, to membership in a buying cooperative, free medical and dental services, a subscription to a *barrio* newspaper published by the union, and, most importantly, to a voice and a vote in the determination of *barrio* union programs and policies.

An urban project that seems on the threshold of realizing the *barrio* union concept is The East Los Angeles Community Union (TELACU), a multifunded operation in East Los Angeles. Its director is Esteban "Ed" Torres, an organizer for the United Auto Workers. "Essentially, TELACU is directed toward a membership form of organization, dues paying or share holding," says Torres. TELACU is an urban version of the rural model for organizing the Chicano that the United Farm Workers Organizing Committee demonstrates in Delano, more than 100 miles north of Los Angeles. Each is involved in a credit union, economic development, job improvements, housing, and health. TELACU, Torres suggests, is a kind of reception center for the workers displaced by farm automation: "Someone has to meet the problem of the increased influx of unemployed from the farms and rural areas."

TELACU is also interested in developing a business-industrial complex in the East Los Angeles area that would include already established Chicano entrepreneurs, the creation of new firms, and the recruiting of non-Chicano firms on a lease basis to a central, *barrio*-controlled corporation. Along with provisions for training and hiring of Chicano *barrio* residents by outside firms, a business-industrial complex would also be geared to include health facilities, child-care, schools, and motels. While the basic framework and rationale of the union organism could undergird the *barrio* union, I do not suggest that unions attempt to establish *barrio* locals, as it were.

Delano represents the nearest thing to a *barrio* union among Chicanos, or in the nation, for that matter, because the *barrio* community and union members are in large part the same. However, because of its affiliation with AFL-CIO, the *barrio*-community element has lost a degree of autonomy that it had until the original Filipino-Chicano UFWOC affiliated with AFL-CIO in 1966. The *barrio* union, at its best, would establish a self-sufficient organism, as independent as possible from outside controls and resources but attuned to the techniques for utilizing consultant and technical assistance. The achievement of self-sufficiency is all-important to the fulfillment of the Chicano nation. The *barrio* union is a potential method for rehabilitating the *barrio* from within. Only the Chicano himself can accomplish this. The economic and political barriers to implementing this concept are unquestionably enormous; they are also unknown, and this may be the greatest barrier, a fear of trying something that hasn't been tried before.

An imperative to establishing the *barrio* union or any form of *barrio* organization that utilizes the cultural and psychological strengths of the Chicano *pueblo* is political activism. One might lead to the other, but certainly where a *barrio* is isolated by the encroachment of Anglo domination, the only recourse is to organize the *barrio* totally. The organizational effort for this to be accomplished must be ingenious and prolonged, but unless Chicanos act to revitalize the *barrio*—the most immediate resource we have for a land base—internally and soon, the more difficult it will be to enkindle the sense of peoplehood and protect the political advances we may achieve.

The stress in *barrio* organization must be on cooperative action, whether it is in social action or in business enterprise. When profit-producing businesses of one kind or another are established in the *barrio*—that is, businesses which are essentially outgrowths of *barrio* entrepreneurial and *barrio* manpower resources—the structure under which they are incorporated should be on a profit-sharing basis for the employees. The workers should have an opportunity to become partners in the enterprise, in this way gaining a greater share of the *barrio* profits from the development of businesses or industries, rather than having all profits go to a few entrepreneurs. The idea of employee ownership of companies is a relatively new concept, but one that is being tried in several places. One of the few companies totally independent of major corporation boards of directors for its profits and direction is a black manufacturing firm in Portland, Oregon's Albina ghetto. Blacks manage the company, type on the typewriters, work the lathes, push the brooms; and each is building up a share ownership in the business. The blacks who spearheaded the development of the corporation intend to implement a new form of corporate structure—a radical departure from the usual top-heavy profiteers of the major corporations—to motivate workers by providing the opportunity to share in owning and guiding the future of the company, and to establish a second-income source based on a form of stock investment in the company. The Second Income Plan—as it is called by its most prominent promoter, Louis Kelso, a San Francisco corporation lawyer—develops as follows:

A deferred-compensation trust (essentially a retirement plan until the company achieves a profit margin, in which case it could pay dividends) is established in behalf of employees. The trust program is administered by both the trust and the corporation, both of which are comprised of a board of directors, as broadly representative of the company and the community as possible. The individual employee, at the end of each year of employment, is vested or assigned 15 percent of his total income in shares; his regular income has not been touched. The 15 percent is predicated on the expected corporate growth of the company. After the first three years of employment, the worker will own outright 30 percent of the number of shares he has built up. Gaining an added 10 percent each year, by the end of 10 years he will have complete ownership of his shares. He can sell his shares at any time, of course, according to the percentage of value they represent.

The Portland ghetto corporation is a complex interrelation of many factors: hard-core job trainees, hard-nosed and experienced black specialists in contracting, managing, and product development; community involvement; white consultants; and government (SBA and OEO) subsidization. It is not a proposition which can be easily capsulized; but because of its most notable features of employee ownership, capital-sharing, and community involvement, it falls right into line with the strengths and needs of the *barrio*. Capital investment is considered a luxury for the more affluent to indulge in. As long as it remains the fundamental means of the production of wealth, minority people should also be in on the receiving end of the profits which they help produce. And there is "progressively more of it each year," according to Kelso, who asserts that equality of economic opportunity should also connote "opportunity to produce affluence." Even Chavez stresses this point of view in regard to farm workers sharing in the benefits that automation brings to the farmer. *Barrio* organizations should investigate the potential of this second-income plan approach; it may become a prerequisite to permitting companies to set up in the *barrio* or to utilize *barrio* manpower.

Kelso's theories, which go beyond the basic income-investment proposal, are spelled out in his book, *The Two-Factor Theory*. In this slender volume, which must be read with due caution by the noneconomist, Kelso points out that less than 1 percent of American households are capitalist, that is, make at least half their income from capital investments. A concomitant fact is that in the past 11 years, U.S. corporations generated new capital internally rather than from newly issued stock. This was done in such a way that ownership of these corporations was more concentrated rather than broadened. These facts refer to the corporations that produce most of the goods and services of the U.S. economy.

While capital investment has far outdistanced land as a source of wealth in the United States, land still has a permanence and productivity beyond stock-market quotations that appeals to many Chicanos. Land has been the life of northern New Mexicans. Land held in common for many years formed the economic and social buttresses of life. Historians, law analysts, and the Alianza alike can prove that fraud and violence robbed the Spanish, the Mexican, and the *mestizo* forebears of the Chicano people of the life-giving foundation of the land. We maintain that there exist blood bonds and cultural bonds to the land of the Southwest; we do not deny the Indian peoples' claims to the land. We believe we have had at least a share in its perpetuation through the hands of those who originally worked the land and who have historical claims to it. This issue of land and its relationship to the Chicano should be discussed with Indian tribesmen. An understanding must be reached on the viability of pursuing a land strategy aimed at recovering lands once held by the Indians or the Spanish. Chicanos have a blood relationship to our Indian forebears. Descendants of early Spanish colonists who reject such an alliance with the Indian natives of the Americas also reject the most obvious claim to retribution for the misdeeds committed by the Anglos who stole the land, the United States Government in particular. The only feasible program is to demand retribution; the land itself will simply not be returned. We Chicanos can assume control politically over an area—whether it is a section of a city, the city itself, a county, or a state, but we cannot completely reclaim the land that was taken from our ancestors.

The Treaty of Guadalupe Hidalgo, of course, is the ethical and legal basis for the retribution demands that Chicanos will make. But the United States Government should not be the only target; the churches, the foundations, the corporations, and the unions should be reminded that they, too, have a debt to repay. The churches, especially the Catholic Church, have helped the Anglo-American to rob us of our pride. They have told us, "Have patience, *mi hijo*" (and don't forget to put something in the collection basket); and we have learned to bide our time.

Catholic bishops have sided with the growers in California in their efforts to break the farm labor strike. They have remained silent lest the growers withhold their annual pledges. The bishops have silenced young priests who have attempted to implement the teachings of Pope Leo XIII and Pope John XXIII. Catolicos por La Raza, a new group which sprang up in Los Angeles, vigorously protested the million-dollar expenditure for a cathedral by the former Los Angeles archbishop and cardinal, James McIntyre. Money that dioceses or archdioceses spend for buildings these days, whether in Los Angeles or in Washington, D.C., is tainted by racist attitudes when it is spent to house the glittering ceremonies for the middle-class and upper-class Roman Catholics. The poor, the blacks, and the

Chicanos invariably wind up with the financially failing parish plants, ill-financed schools, shabby churches, and mediocre pastors who can't finagle anything better for themselves.

The Catholic Church has been criticized for ignoring the black people of the United States, or for segregating them when they do convert. What does the church owe to Chicanos who are traditionally the mass base for the church's erection of edifices and the unpaid or underpaid manpower for their construction as well? How would the Catholic Church like to make up for the repression of our people it has caused by its concentrating on patience and penance rather than justice and freedom? We do not need preachers among the *pueblos* of *la raza*; we need a Hidalgo and a Camilo Torres.

Chicanos have to liberate themselves from guilt feelings or fears about telling the church where it stands now. When Chicanos deliberate about taking over institutions, they should not forget the churches. The churches belong to us, the people; so do the school buildings and the diocesan newspapers. The church bureaucrats can no longer operate their fiefs without regard for the needs of the poor.

It does appear that churches were planned to serve the rich. Recently, when Bishop Fulton Sheen tried to turn ownership of a parish plant in Rochester over to the black community, to fill its particular needs, church officials, clergy, and rank-and-file Christians criticized the move so strongly that the former television homilist was forced to withdraw the offer. Never have I known a rich parish to freely share its resources with a poorer parish. Every diocese in the country should have a pool of money to be shared with less affluent parishes; on the national level, more affluent dioceses should willingly combine funds to assist poorer dioceses.

Chicanos have given much to make the Catholic Church a living presence in the Western Hemisphere. Our forefathers absorbed the Christian doctrine—it was similar to theirs in many respects—and eventually Catholicism became the pervasive top layer of Mexican-Indian religiosity. It was the Mexican Indians who made the expeditions of the *adelantados* and *padres* possible; it was the Indians who built the missions; it was the Chicanos who labored and sacrificed to build the churches of the Southwest. Thus it should not be a matter of debate as to whether the Chicano and Indian peoples deserve outright financial support from the churches; the only question is how much and how fast will the churches invest in helping the people whom they have spiritually enslaved for generations.

The churches trespass on our land and our lives; so, too, the corporations with their tax loopholes, the foundations, and the unions owe their wealth and influence to the Chicano's work-bent back and straining muscles. In March 1969, the Inter-Agency Committee invited 36 foundations to meet with its staff to ascertain how these resources of program and research funds could aid Mexican Americans. Only two of the smaller foundations demonstrated interest, the rest, including the major ones in the United States, were too busy or did not believe that their funding interests related to Mexican American needs.

To recoup land losses, especially for those *raza* who believe they have legal claims to the land, and to exact retribution from the United States Government, which may be more desirable and more feasible than actually reclaiming the land, *la raza* must establish a new relationship with Anglo America. *La raza* must make the concept of nationhood a living reality. We can look toward someday convening a national congress of Chicanos that would deliberate and arrive at a consensus as to the forms of retribution that must be made to our people. Why could we not elect representatives to such a congress from the various *pueblos* in the nation? Why could we not establish a framework of autonomous, democratic *pueblos* which would not relate to political parties or class distinctions? Why could we not petition as a nation for at least an elected, nonvoting delegate in both the House and Senate? Puerto Rico has such a representative, Jorge Cordova, for its 2.7 million *puertorriqueños*. We deserve at least one, if not two, who could represent the Chicano. Obviously, I doubt that the Spanish surnames in Congress adequately represent the Chicano. We could lead the way through such a procedure to unify (not absorb or lead) the Third World forces which at present are at the threshold between life and death. We must do something as a people to change the United States, to change the Americas. Perhaps such a conversion could take place in the seventies; perhaps it is an impossible dream. But regardless, Chicanos must create for themselves, if we are to survive as a people, a new form of existence. It can come from the *barrios*, from the colleges, from the *colonias*, from the fields, from everywhere Chicanos live. We have a very personal stake in altering the attitudes and conduct of the Anglo-American and the black American. These two can destroy themselves and with them us and the *raza* of Latin America. Yet, we have not begun to speak out against the atrocities that the United States is committing in Bolivia, in Santo Domingo, in Cuba, in Mexico, as well as in East Los Angeles, Denver, San Francisco, Delano, Phoenix, Albuquerque, Tierra Amarilla, San Antonio, Chicago, and Rio Grande City. Where are the Chicano legislators and leaders to speak out against the murders of Chicanos by gringo *chotas*, against the deaths of Chicanos in a gringo war against another oppressed people, and against the assassinations of *raza* in Mexico, Santo Domingo, Bolivia, and Colombia through counterinsurgence meddling by the United States?

Increasingly, the Chicano will discover that the social and economic revolution in which he is involved in the United States is a part of the revolution that is developing in Latin America. Senator J. William Fulbright addresses the issue of U.S. attitudes toward Latin America in *The Arrogance of Power* (1966) as if North American foreign policy affected *raza* only beyond the U.S. borders. The Arkansas senator need only have observed U.S. "foreign" policy toward the Chicano to understand somewhat more rudimentarily why the United States is a counterrevolutionary force in the Americas as well as in the world. "America forced on Spain a war," ostensibly to liberate the Cuban people, "that [Spain] was willing to pay almost any price short of complete humiliation to avoid," Fulbright says. But 50 years before the war with Spain, Anglo America had liberated a huge expanse of land from Mexico through a war which would never have occurred except for the gringo government's disdain for the Mexican people. Fulbright adds, "The movement of the future of Latin America is social revolution. . . . Paternalism is no longer a workable basis for our relations with Latin America." That is obviously correct, but he is far from correct when he asserts that the United States "has already come to terms with one great social revolution in Latin America," meaning Mexico. The United States has yet to comply fully with an agreement made 123 years ago with Mexico, and with the Mexican American (as a silent, third party). The United States has meddled in some way with Latin America's social and political development ever since it could turn its attention away from its own revolution of 1776. In April 1965, to cite a recent instance, the United States violated the Charter of the Organization of American States when Marines were sent into the Dominican Republic. The history of North American impertinence and impudence toward Latin America is astounding. Chicanos should have something particularly insightful to say about U.S. policy because we are as much victims of the U.S. attitude as la raza in South America. We are treated as foreigners; Spanish is taught as a foreign language although it predates English in the Americas. Revolutionary forces in South American countries, from the Mexican students to Brazilian insurgents, consider the United States—this includes the Chicano people—the worst enemy of their people. I wonder how many Chicanos have been trained as special forces or are used as instructors for CIA-sponsored counterinsurgent military units which infiltrate and combat revolucionarios. Do peoples of Latin America realize that a distinct Chicano community exists in the United States? Have Chicanos done anything to make our Latin American brothers aware of our existence? Chicanos can fulfill in part the desire for freedom of raza all over the Americas by making ourselves more aware of their history and struggle, of which we are so much a part.

One of the important means by which Chicanos will make known their collaboration with the peoples of Latin America is for more and more Chicanos to turn their minds and talents to an expression of their feelings and their ideas through the arts—writing, music, painting, sculpture, dance, and drama. Generations of Chicanos have come and gone and we are only now beginning to form a body of literature or fine arts that are distinctively Chicano. We have to create these works from our own hands and minds. Men and women of la raza, from Spain to South America, Central America and the Caribbean have contributed some of the greatest manifestations of literary and artistic talent, and philosophic and interpretative thought, in the world. Not many Chicanos know this reservoir of inspiration exists; or worse, through unfounded fears and timidity, they hold themselves back from emulating it and, I believe, surpassing it. Chicanos have told me that they want to paint, to carve and mold, to write novels, essays, and poetry; the esthetic swells within our people. As Abelardo Delgado, a 39-year-old Chicano poet, has said in a 1969 poem,

"stupid america"

stupid america, see that chicano
with a big knife
on his steady hand
he doesn't want to knife you
he wants to sit on a bench
and carve christfigures
but you won't let him.
stupid america, hear that chicano
shouting curses on the street
he is a poet
without paper and pencil
and since he cannot write
he will explode.
stupid america, remember that chicanito
flunking math and english
he is the picasso
of your western states
but he will die
with one thousand masterpieces
hanging only from his mind.

We are striving to formulate a new body of writings and art that will tell our story our way, that will preserve the Chicano esthetic for sight and sound and movement. The Chicano press newspapers, *barrio* publications that have paralleled the movement's pace and vigor, are a basic outlet for young and old writers of history, culture, poetry, and the graphic arts. Individuals have published slim volumes of poetry—including Rodolfo Gonzales of Denver and Delgado of El Paso. Quinto Sol Publications in Berkeley, California, is a young publishing house that prints *El Grito*, a literary magazine, and volumes such as *El Espejo*, a compilation of various Chicano writers' works. A handful of books by Chicano authors are in the works or just recently published by major companies. But efforts for more Chicano publishing firms are increasing, notably Barrio Press in Denver, Mictla Publications in El Paso, and Chicano Features Syndicate in Washington, D.C.

Teatros, small mobile drama-comedy troupes presenting satires and *Actos* (commentaries on Chicano life and experience) are quickly becoming a living art form of Chicanismo. First promoted by Luis Valdez in Delano with El Teatro Campesino (the Farm Workers' Theater), *teatros* have multiplied and become one of the freshest forms of expression for Chicanos. Lupe Saavedra and Augustin Lira are other prominent proponents of the *barrio* theater. Since literature, theater, and the other arts distill the essence of a people, the Chicano is on the verge of a renaissance.

Our own artistic creativity should be stimulated, but it is important also that Chicanos should themselves control the channels of communication that pipe information *into* the *barrio*, as well as direct the *barrio* media that informs the outside world about the *barrio*. Chicano newspapers and magazines must proliferate. Opportunities need to be provided for Chicano youth to learn basic skills, from writing to film-making. We need to take over local newspapers, radio and television stations, where possible; establishing publishing houses and our own news service—all such ventures are greatly needed by the Chicano community. But when certain institutions in or related to the *barrio* cannot be expropriated by the people, compliance with the demands of the *barrio* will have to be forced through some means. A newspaper, a radio or television station should publish or program Chicano activities and interests; certain federal regulations require community-wide programing of the electronic media. The key, of course, to such direct action is the foundation of a political and economic power base, either through fully organizing the *barrio* or through exerting a strong influence in the political sector.

Stemming from these avenues of action, which are but an overview of the kinds of things Chicanos will be doing in the next few years, the effects of the Chicano uprising on the international level can be limitless. In the past couple of years, I have known of only one interpretative article about Mexican Americans to appear in a foreign country—England, of all places. While the article itself contained several inaccuracies based on a limited understanding of the Chicano, it may have given the first inkling to other peoples of the world that something else besides the black movement was happening in America. The international branching-out of the table grape boycott also added weight to the emergence on a global scale of Chicano aspirations. The boycott, however, may be easily misconstrued as only a management-labor dispute while the cultural overtones go unnoticed. I believe that the Chicano does have an international origin, for he was a party, a silent third party, to an international agreement, the Treaty of Guadalupe Hidalgo. Therefore, he should be accorded certain international rights, such as the right to present, before such bodies as the United Nations or a world court, his cause in relation to lands stolen from him in violation of the treaty. He has the right to retribution owed him for the injustices of 120 years of peonage to the gringo. In this way, we might startle the world, and particularly the United States, if we were able to demonstrate that Chicanos must seek justice through world institutions, since we have been denied a hearing from our own government.

Until now, the Chicano has been forced to play the white man's game on the defensive side; the Anglo encourages and perpetuates division among minority peoples to maintain control over them. We Chicanos are now making this isolation work for us. In the future we should not undertake activities that would only divide us or separate us from other peoples in the United States. Incidents and words are used today that create artificial barriers and misunderstanding. However, Chicanos also realize that the character of our revolt against *gringoismo* will prevail through our being more positive and unified in our words and actions. We must not undermine, by seeking wholly separatist avenues of action, the distinctive role we can play in the future of the Americas. There is an overwhelming need for the Chicano to find himself and for Chicanos to find each other. He needs to fortify himself with tradition, language, history, and culture. The events of the past decade suggest the Chicano's sense of history, his longing to establish a modern tradition, and his hunger for dates of beginnings and culminations that are his to cherish. A parallel realization of these aspirations is the understanding of our duality of culture and insight that may very well be the most important factor in our relations with the non-Chicano world tomorrow.

We can look for Chicanismo to influence more mexicanos—that is, more of those persons of Mexican-Indian origins—including the return of many who previously disavowed their heritage. Chicanismo has that kind of redemptive force.

The essence of Chicanismo will become more deeply internalized through an ever-increasing identification by raza with each other. Also, through the Chicanos' expression of Chicanismo in almost every art form, the peoplehood we seek will clearly manifest itself.

The quest for Aztlán will never be fulfilled, for Aztlán is not just a thing or a place to the Chicano. Land and power will come into the Chicanos' hands, but Aztlán will remain an inspirational ideal and a goal ever drawing us forward.

Because Chicanismo is part of the raza revolution that encompasses the Americas, Chicanos should strive to influence international thought and action, particularly between the United States and Latin America. The Chicano is of key importance to future relations in the Americas; he is that latent bond between the peoples of the Western Hemisphere, because already he embodies the two worlds of the North and South American continents.

28.
BLACK AWAKENING: TOWARD A TRANSITIONAL PROGRAM

Robert L. Allen

Since the masses of black people are not going to be integrated into the economy in the foreseeable future, as the reformers would have one believe, and since there are few signs of an imminent revolution in this country, contrary to the hopes of some radicals, it is necessary for the black liberation movement to devise a transitional program, which will operate until such time as conditions develop that will make possible full liberation through social revolution. This program must be aimed at building a mass revolutionary organization, and it must facilitate community development and offer constructive interim reforms.

Black people cannot afford the social injustices of capitalism. They cannot afford a system which creates privileged classes within an already super-exploited and underprivileged community. They cannot afford a system which organizes community resources and then distributes the resulting wealth in a hierarchal fashion, with those who need least getting most. Neither can black people afford some half-hearted compromise which would make the black community in general, and its educated classes in particular, subservient to the expansionist needs of corporate capitalism. Of course, capital must be accumulated to make possible the economic development of the black community, but this must be done in a way that precludes the enrichment of one class at the expense of those below it.

One program for this sort of economic development was outlined three decades ago by W. E. B. DuBois. In his autobiographical essay, *Dusk of Dawn*, DuBois, then over 70 years old, succeeded in modifying and merging black nationalism with radical socialism. The outgrowth was a program for what he termed a "co-operative commonwealth" in black America.

DuBois had come to the realization that while it was necessary to agitate for equality, the struggle would be slow and painful, and genuine equality for blacks in America probably would not be forthcoming for many, many years. Racism, he concluded, was not due simply to ignorance or deliberate maliciousness on the part of whites. These played a part, but more fundamental were the deeply ingrained habits which sprang from (frequently unconscious) economic motives. To white America, black people were a resource to be exploited ruthlessly—and racism facilitated this exploitation by degrading blacks in the eyes of whites, thereby placing the former outside the pale of normal moral or humanistic compunction. DuBois believed that this deeper cause of racism could be changed only slowly, and in the meantime it was necessary to develop the inner economic and social strength of the black community.

At the same time, however, he refused to accept racial separation as the ultimate solution to the race problem. For this reason he opposed "back to Africa" and other emigration schemes. To the degree that segregation is a reality it must be dealt with in the most constructive manner possible, he felt, but this by no means implies that blacks should meekly submit to segregation.

DuBois advocated economic development, but he opposed any program of black capitalism on the grounds that this "will have inserted into the ranks of the Negro race a new cause of division, a new attempt to subject the masses of the race to an exploiting capitalist class of their own people."[1] Instead he insisted that the principle of democracy must be applied to economic relations.

> I had been brought up with the democratic idea that [the] general welfare was the object of democratic action in the state, of allowing the governed a voice in government. But through the crimson illumination of war [World War I], I realized and, afterward by traveling around the world, saw even more clearly that so-called democracy today was allowing the mass of people to have only limited voice in government; that democratic control of what are at present the most important functions of men: work and earning a living and distributing goods and services; that here we did not have democracy; we had oligarchy, and oligarchy based on monopoly and income; and this oligarchy was determined to deny democracy in industry as it had once been determined to deny democracy in legislation and choice of officials.[2]

What was required, DuBois contended, was careful planning of the inner economy and social structure of the black community so as to promote maximum development of that community in toto. Thus he called for "economic planning to insure adequate income" to the members of the community; establishment of consumer unions; elimination of private profit in merchandising operations; a planned system of black hospitals and socialized medicine; cooperative organization of black professionals so that they could provide service to all in need without regard to their own personal profit; and the establishment of a black-controlled educational system.

There were other details in DuBois' plan, but in substance what he proposed was to create a planned, communal social system in black America. Planned, in the sense that all important aspects of this system were to be thought out and analyzed in advance and then carefully guided in order to facilitate community development. Communal, in the sense that property relations would become social rather than private, thereby avoiding economically inspired class division, and making economic exploitation more difficult. Communal, in the sense also of strengthening family and group ties and building a stronger sense of community among black people so that all become dedicated to the welfare of the group rather than personal advancement.

The cost of such a program, DuBois maintained, must be borne by the black community itself, rather than by white people or white-dominated institutions. It can be objected, however, that the community does not possess sufficient resources to finance such a program. This objection cannot be ignored, but if neocolonialism is to be avoided, it is essential that control over the use of any outside aid must rest completely in the hands of the black community. This in turn demands thorough political organization of the entire community.

On this latter point DuBois had little to say, and this was a serious flaw in his plan. He did not explain how it was to be implemented. He did not describe a social agency then in existence, or to be created, which could adopt his plan as its program. Perhaps he still cherished hopes that the NAACP could be convinced of the viability of his program, despite the fact that his political thinking diverged dramatically from the politics of the NAACP, and he had split with that organization some years earlier.

Many years later, Harold Cruse, under the influence of DuBois, drafted a similar program for Harlem. Cruse, however, argued that black intellectuals and a new black middle class were to play an important part in implementing this program. There is certainly a role for members of the black middle class, but their past failures and current growing attachment to corporate imperialism raise serious doubts as to their leadership capabilities. The increasing militancy and spirit of independence exhibited among ordinary black workers, as seen in Detroit and other cities, strongly suggests that if the black community is to win real self-determination it must cultivate a militant leadership cadre drawn from its less-privileged classes. The danger of an irresponsible elite arising is far less acute if the leadership of a movement is organically related to the rank and file; that is, if leaders do not come from or otherwise form a social stratum with interests differing from those of their followers.

Implicit in DuBois' program was a vision of a separate and largely self-sufficient black economy. This was not possible in 1940, and it is not possible today. The black community does not have control over all of the essential goods and services which it requires for survival. Moreover, as long as corporate capitalism exists, the black community is not likely to acquire such control. This, however, should not automatically preclude a struggle to create an all-encompassing, planned communal social system on a national scale and with strong international ties. Such a struggle would begin to break down capitalist property relations within the black community, replacing them with more socially useful communal relations. Consequently, any benefits accruing from the planned economy could be distributed throughout the community according to individual or family needs, or income could be reinvested to increase the capital assets of the community. Furthermore, this struggle would aid materially in breaking black dependency on white society. Considerable capital and other white-owned resources within the community could be gradually freed and restored to the community. Many concrete reforms could be won in the course of the struggle and, as long as these reforms did not become ends in themselves and their relation to corporate capitalism were fully understood, this could be immensely helpful. The program of the Black Panther Party is a list of some such needed reforms and concessions.

The establishment of close working relationships with revolutionary forces around the world would be of great importance. The experiences of Third World revolutionaries in combating American imperialism could be quite useful to black liberation fighters. For the moment, mutual support between Afro-American and Third World revolutionaries is more verbal than tangible, but the time could come when this situation is reversed, and black people are well advised to begin now to work toward this kind of revolutionary, international solidarity. Imperialism is a worldwide force whose final defeat will require a united effort on the part of its victims, and other anti-imperialist nations.

Finally, the struggle to implement this program should increase the organization, and consequently the fighting ability, of the black community. What is called for is an independent black political party capable of providing militant leadership. To the degree that the proposed party is successful in implementing the program sketched above, it will grow in strength and experience, gradually establishing itself as the effective governing power of black America. This will require many years, but it is not an unreasonable projection, so long as the political party is solidly based upon the masses of ordinary black working people. This means that the popular masses must provide the rank and file and the leadership, and the party must always seek to extend itself among this segment of the black population. Here lies the great majority of black people, and they must lead themselves if self-determination is to be meaningful.

Of course, the party should seek also to encompass, insofar as this is possible, the entire black population. Black intellectuals and members of the black middle class should be encouraged to participate—as individuals. However, because of the inherent ambivalence of these classes, they must not be allowed, as *classes*, to assume leadership of the party. As classes, intellectuals and petty bourgeois blacks are as likely to be reactionary as they are to be revolutionary, and for this reason they must always be somewhat suspect.

The idea of a black political party is not particularly new. In 1904 the National Liberty Party was organized and ran George Edwin Taylor as its presidential candidate. The early 1960s witnessed the rise and demise of the Freedom Now party, and currently there exist the Lowndes County Freedom Party and the Black Panther Party. Both of the latter built solid community bases, and it is within the realm of possibility that one or the other of them will emerge as the kind of political instrument being discussed here.

With respect to encounters with white America, a black party should not rely on exclusively legal campaigns, nor should it restrict itself to all-out street warfare. Instead it must devise a strategy of calculated confrontation, using a mixture of tactics to fit a variety of contingencies. The object of this strategy should be to abolish, by any means possible, the real control of white society over the black community, and to extract needed reforms. Tactical innovation should be the order of the day, and anything workable goes—depending on specific conditions and the relation of forces —from legal struggle, to electoral politics, to direct action campaigns, to force.[3] In short, what is required is a coordinated, multifaceted, multilevel struggle which will enable black America to defeat corporate imperialism and free itself from the shackles of domestic neocolonialism.

Under the aegis of a militant political party—a party which acts not as an occasional vote-getting machine but as a continuously functioning governing instrumentality—diverse activities, from efforts to establish rank-and-file labor union caucuses to struggles for community control of local schools, can assume a cohesiveness and meaning, independent of their immediate success or failure. Within the framework of the party, these activities can become integrated into a unified strategy for winning black self-determination. Over the long run, they could well become the individual building blocks of social revolution in America.

Black liberation, however, will not come about solely through the activities of black people. Black America cannot be genuinely liberated until white America is transformed into a humanistic society free of exploitation and class division. The black and white worlds, although separate and distinct, are too closely intertwined—geographically, politically, and economically—for the social maladies of one not to affect the other. Both must change if either is to progress to new and liberating social forms.

It goes without saying that black people should not postpone their freedom struggle until white America rouses itself out of its lethargy. On the contrary, blacks should never desist from struggle and agitation. But neither should black people deceive themselves into thinking that simple separation from oppressive white society will solve the problem. Blacks and whites here have lived in separate worlds for four centuries, but this was hardly an economic or political boon to black people. In the quest for black liberation, white society cannot be ignored or cast aside with a sigh of relief. It must be changed. Otherwise, the racism and exploitative social relations which characterize that society will defeat even the best efforts of black freedom fighters. This is one of the clearest lessons of the black experience in America.

This raises for the nth time the thorny question of domestic allies. The black liberation movement needs allies. It needs allies who are capable both of aiding the black movement and of promoting social change in white America. In recent years a growing sense of unity has developed between Afro-Americans and Puerto Ricans, Mexican-Americans, American Indians, and Orientals. This is good, because all of these communities desire to abolish their present status of semicolonial dependency on white society. As to white allies, they are presently limited largely to militant students and white radicals. The value of these allies should not be underestimated. An advanced industrial society depends ever more heavily on its educated classes for their technical and managerial skills. The student revolt, which has surged across campuses throughout this country, can precipitate a movement to upset the delicate machinery of corporate capitalism. The student militants are demanding greater control over the educational process and, indeed, a redefinition of it. They seek to make education the servant of the best impulses in man rather than the servant of a base and twisted society. White radicals, too, are helpful, despite their small numbers, because they are what might be termed a "leading minority": they are capable of initiating skirmishes, which then mobilize thousands of non-radical whites. Witness the anti-war movement, which started with a handful and grew to include hundreds of thousands.

But black people must assemble a more powerful array of allies than these. Social change requires the active support, or at least benevolent neutrality, of the major part of society. Students, radicals, and minority groups are important, but they are not the majority that is needed. Whether this majority can ever be mustered is problematical. It is currently fashionable among black militants to write off the revolutionary potential of the bulk of the white working population because of its unreconstructed racism. The myopia of the labor unions is adduced as proof.

Two factors, however, may upset this reactionary status quo. First, the advance of mechanization and cybernation promises to undermine the security of even those who believe they are safely ensconced in suburbia. Not only does the industrial system require relatively fewer blue-collar workers, but automation is even making inroads into the ranks of white-collar clerical and middle-level employees.[4] This presents a great challenge to organized labor. The labor movement is in decline. Desperate but short-sighted labor leaders are making concessions to the rise of automation in a last-ditch effort to preserve their personal power and hold their unions together. This policy is bound to lead to the collapse of organized labor as a social force. The only alternative is for the labor movement to begin organizing the unemployed, white-collar, and government employees, and to move beyond traditional union issues and demand that working people as an organized body have greater say in the functioning of the total economy. This program probably transcends both the ability and narrowly perceived self-interest of America's labor bureaucracy, but the rise of rank-and-file militancy since 1966 and widespread organizing committees among white-collar workers point in a more hopeful direction.

The second factor is even more stark. The economic gap between rich and poor nations is widening at an alarming rate. At the same time the world's population is skyrocketing. Already it is estimated that there are 3.5 billion people on this planet, 55 percent of them in Asia alone. It is expected that by the year 2000 this figure could climb well above 6 billion. Most of these people will be ill-fed, ill-clothed, and angry. The standard solution offered by the American government is more birth control. But, as was suggested in Chapter V, there is, in many underdeveloped areas of the world, an equally pressing need for rational reorganization and redistribution of wealth and resources, which must be done on a national and international basis if a world-wide catastrophe of unprecedented proportions is to be averted. Many population experts agree that the world has the resource capability to support anticipated population growth in the foreseeable future. The question to be decided is whether anachronistic political forms will be allowed to obstruct rational utilization of these resources.

Today's generation of Americans, in the world's richest and most powerful country, have it within their power to make this decision. And some decision must be made soon. Either a fortress America will be established—in which case a bloody and protracted international conflict can be anticipated within 15 to 25 years—or America will take part in building a rational world order in which all men participate, and through which the planet's resources can be intelligently organized and distributed in accordance with need.

The first uncertain steps toward some kind of decision in this urgent matter already are being taken in this country. The Third World, the underdeveloped world, exists just as surely within America as it does across the seas. In the dialectic between black and white America, a preview of what may be in store for the world can be glimpsed. If black liberation is indeed emasculated and equated with corporate imperialism—if this country evinces no better understanding of the necessities of liberation and self-determination—then the hope that the United States will somehow transform itself into a welcome member of the community of humankind is further diminished, even extinguished. The script will have been written, the cast selected, and the stage set for yet another tragedy in man's tortuous ascent toward a just society.

Notes

1. W. E. B. DuBois, *Dusk of Dawn* (New York: Schocken, 1968), p. 208.

2. *Ibid.*, p. 285.

3. The use of organized force should not be discounted out of hand, nor should it be glorified. This is simply one of a host of tactical questions which will confront a militant party devoted to black liberation. The important thing to bear in mind is that the objectives of the black liberation movement are basically political and economic, rather than military, and every proposed tactic must be appraised according to whether it will bring these objectives nearer to realization.

4. See "Automation and the Work Force" by Ben B. Seligman in Robert Theobald (ed), *The Guaranteed Income.*

29.
TOWARD A NEW AMERICA

New American Movement

As far as the eye can see . . . desks. Women sitting behind them, backs straight and stiff, transferring from one sheet to another something someone else has written, and someone else will receive, but no one really needs.

Men and women on an assembly line . . . putting together a product that will fall apart, will blow up, will cost many times more than it is worth; men and women with no say in the building of the product, or where it will go.

In the factory and the field, in classrooms and coal mines, in hospital and home . . . Americans toil. For what? For the next meal, the next pay check, the next promise, for the shoddy goods and polluted air, for their children who will rebel at the prospect of being part of this meaningless and empty life? For the profit of the few, the many give their lives in this dull routine. Many people anxiously watching the clock at work, only to be so exhausted during their leisure, that TV becomes the only way to pass the time.

America is soaked with alienation; with people who can't afford to be sick and can't find a way to be healthy; with poverty and hunger, drudgery and boredom; with veterans returning from an immoral war who can't find jobs; with racism; with heroin; with despair.

That despair is not just the despair of the poor and those who toil endlessly. That despair extends to those whose basic material needs have been met as well. The vast majority of people are prevented from realizing their human potentials in freedom and creativity. The technology and wealth that could be used to liberate us from toil and allow us to meet everyone's basic human needs is used, instead, to enslave us to a life of drudgery. Nothing is more clear in America today than the huge distance between the actuality of America in the seventies and its potential. And

From "Toward a New America": (Draft Platform of the New American Movement).
New American Movement, September–October 1971.

nothing is more frustrating than the endless line of politicians and opportunists, some of whom recognize the existence of a problem, but none of whom dare offer any real alternative.

Why?—An Analysis

America is run by a small group of people whose economic power gives them political power. These people control all the basic decisions that affect the lives of most Americans, and through an elaborate system of military and economic arrangements, control the destinies of most people in the world. That control is exercised not for the benefit of the majority, but in order to increase the wealth and power of that small minority. We believe that power must be redistributed to all people so that they can control their own lives. In practical terms, this means putting most questions directly to the people. It means ending a phoney electoral system in which one gets to choose between personalities who agree on the basic questions. It means ending the advertising industry's job of creating needs in people for products that they would otherwise never buy. It means ending the manipulative techniques employed in the media to "engineer consent-manage elections." It means democratization of the economy, from the local level on up, and abolition of the power of the corporations. In short, we are for a totally democratic socialism.

Democratic socialism has little in common with the bureaucratic regimes of Eastern Europe or the welfare statism of Sweden. It is true that the advance of the welfare state and the advent of communist dictatorships have helped raise the material standard of living in many countries. But at the same time, the bureaucracies that have developed have taken on many of the features of previous class societies—using their special power to exploit workers and to create a sense of powerlessness and alienation that undermines the freedom and creativity that must be an essential part of human life. We do not want to substitute a new bureaucracy for the old—we want a totally new society in which the people control their own lives and are free to develop themselves in ways which they themselves choose. Hence, while we are concerned to eliminate the poverty and degradation of a society run by the capitalists, we want simultaneously to be preparing people to govern their society for themselves.

Socialism, then, is just the opposite of what has gone on in this country during the New Deal or in England or Sweden. It does not mean more power for the government but means total power directly to the people. The people who run this country have done a good job of confusing Americans about what socialism really is. The word conjures up visions of a vicious state bureaucracy taking away your car or stereo or your refrigerator. But when socialists talk about the elimination of property, they do not mean the property that you have to live on or the material comforts that people have worked hard to earn. Rather, they mean that private ownership of the means of production will end, that is, production will no longer be geared to making profits for a few, but instead toward producing goods that people actually need. It's the less than 1 percent of the population in this country that own the majority of stock in the majority of large factories who, afraid they are going to lose control, try to scare everybody else into thinking that everyone is going to lose control over their own homes and lives. But nothing could be further from the truth.

Socialism has also seemed a bit dubious because there are countries around the world that call themselves socialist that don't really give their people any control over their own lives. But before we discard the notion of socialism on this basis, we should ask ourselves how this happened and why. Remember, America calls itself a "democracy" and yet the only parties that can ever afford to buy newspaper ads and TV time are in exact agreement on virtually every fundamental question and only disagree on the *tactics* of how to best preserve the current maldistribution of power and wealth. We wouldn't want to throw away the concept of democracy just because the U.S. which calls itself democratic doesn't have real democracy. Similarly with socialism. The countries of the Third World and the Soviet Union had their "socialism" develop under extreme conditions of hardship which made any real socialism virtually impossible. For one thing, the capitalist countries, including the U.S., tried to encircle and starve to death each of these countries, from Russia to China to Cuba. Eventually the U.S. had to change its policies when they didn't work in destroying these countries, but still, the hardships that these countries faced made the question of democracy much less relevant than the question of mere physical survival. Even more important, all these countries were starting out from a basically feudal, agrarian economy. They had to go through a long period of industrialization before they could really be ready for socialism. It's a tragedy that they took that title to describe the process by which they went through industrialization, but if we consider the brutalization of black slaves in America and of tens of millions of peasants in Western Europe, we realize that the process of industrialization was just as brutal in the West though spread out over a longer period of time. In any event, socialism in an advanced industrial society would have very little in common with what happened in the so-called socialist countries of the Third World. In the United States it is possible to build a democratic socialism in which the vast potentials of this country can finally be applied to solving our problems instead of making a few men wealthy and powerful.

To remake American society along democratic socialist lines will take a very hard struggle. Not only must we undermine the tremendous military and economic power of the ruling class, but we must also combat the defeatism and feelings of powerlessness that keep many exploited groups from confronting their exploiters.

One of the main ways in which people are kept in line in America, is through the prevalence of false ideas that the system inculcates in the people to keep us passive. We are taught that we are incapable of running things for ourselves; that we cannot trust our own intelligence or our own feelings. The ideas that whites are better than blacks, that men are better than women, that Americans are better than foreigners, all divide working people among themselves and make us accomplices in the exploitation of others. We are taught that competition and mutual exploitation are indelible parts of "human nature." We feel an unhappiness and alienation and lack of fulfillment both in our work and in the general tenor of our lives. Yet we are made to believe that this is our own personal problem and not at all attributable to aspects of a social order that could be arranged differently. We want to change all of these ideas, and to show the majority of the American public that a just and fulfilling social order is possible if we will struggle for it. And we are intent upon recapturing the revolutionary spirit that was such a basic element in the American self-identity in the past, though always stunted and misdirected by the capitalist system of which it was a part.

The process of making a social revolution is not like a coup d'etat: it is not just a question of seizing state power out of the hands of the exploiters and putting power into the hands of the people. It is also a question of building institutions in the economic and political arena in which people are already exercising power or have some idea of how to do so. Our strategy is to begin this task by a series of struggles in which the people begin to force changes in the economy and the political order that serve their needs and in which they exercise some power.

Whenever possible, we will seek to build institutions that formalize a transfer of power from the rulers to the people. But since this will often be met with extreme resistance, we will build temporary institutions as well that prepare people to make the decisions that affect their lives and from which we can launch struggles against the established order. These institutions we shall call "people's councils," and we shall build them both at the places where people work and in the community at large.

A people's council at work will develop plans for how the factory or office should be run, what it should be producing, and how. A people's council around a school or hospital or police department or housing authority or transit authority, would develop plans about how these institutions should be run. And each will struggle to switch power from their current locus, to the councils themselves, or to otherwise institutionalize real power over decisions in the hands of the people. Not every struggle, however, will be a struggle for institutionalizing new power arrangements. For instance, if the people succeed in forcing the rulers to end the war in Vietnam and to stop financing future military adventures to support the American economic empire, that would be an important success even if it did not institutionalize some mechanism for popular control over foreign policy.

Our programs will be adopted in accord with one simple criterion:

we ask ourselves what changes are necessary in the American social system to allow people in this country and around the world to achieve for themselves a life of dignity, self-realization, self-determination, and adequate material goods. We must realize that America is not one homogenous society: what people need depends a great deal on their economic class and their sex, and race.

There are large numbers of young people who have "passed through affluence" and find the quality of life in America profoundly alienating. Programs designed for their needs will concentrate on maximizing their possibilities for self creation and for non-alienating social relations. While these needs will be shared by all other sectors of American society as well, the form in which these needs will seek expression is likely to be different.

For many working people, especially those who have received higher levels of education and training, the work situation is totally frustrating: their intelligence and creative talents are stunted in the interests of profits and a mystique of efficiency and professionalism and respect for authority. What they get in compensation for a life full of meaningless labor, is a bit of money, which is quickly taken away from them through a tax structure which benefits the wealthy, through a series of expenses for transportation, housing, medical care, and vital social services which have increased in cost as they have become more necessary; and through a desperate desire to escape the frustration of a seemingly meaningless existence in the frenzied consumption of goods. Increasingly, they are exposed to food and air that are poisoned, and to an environment made ugly and drained of its natural resources by the capitalists' endless search for profits.

Then there are those who live on the margins of society, the over 12 million Americans on the verge of physical starvation; the tens of millions who are hungry; those who live in squalor and physical misery; the aged who have been used and then tossed aside—all of whom need a higher level of material well-being, ways to get meaningful labor, health care, housing, and so on.

Although women and blacks are especially exploited economically, they are also exploited as women and blacks, regardless of their economic position, so that they have special needs for new human relations devoid of sexism and racism.

It is unlikely at this time, that an effective struggle against sexism can be waged without an independent, anti-capitalist women's and gay liberation movements. But we also need a larger anti-capitalist movement that continually raises and confronts the problem of sexism in the context of programs ranging over broader interests and includes both men and women.

It is important for us to realize and fully understand the sexism that permeates and helps maintain capitalist domination. The system would not be able to function nearly so efficiently if one section of the population were not taught to accept all the menial work of the home without wages; if there were not isolated family units to purchase the stream of useless products dreamed up by the producers to keep the economy running; if there were not an available and cheap reserve supply of labor; and if men and women were not divided against each other. Women are often the last hired and first fired, paid lower wages for equal work, taught to think that their "true" role is in the home as a mother, housekeeper, and husband-tender, and discouraged and often prevented by discriminatory practices from developing into full human beings.

From an early age, men and women are taught sex stereotypes—women are mentally and physically weak, to be governed by men; while men are taught to be aggressive, skilled, and dominating. Women are turned against one another as they compete for men and affection and security. Sexism continues to divide men and women. We must realize that we can never truly eliminate sexist institutions and ideologies until we have eliminated the exploitative domination of capitalism which continues to foster sexist attitudes for its own maintenance. But we must also understand that we will never achieve a full socialist society as long as sexist oppression exists. That is why the struggle against sexism is *integral*, not just a side effect, to the development of a socialist society.

One of the greatest weaknesses of past revolutionary movements in the United States has been their failure to confront racism. Blacks were brought to this country as slaves, and when they were finally freed legally, the ruling class still managed to use them as a source of cheap labor and a perpetual "underclass." The Kerner Commission in 1967, responding to a series of ghetto rebellions, certified that racist practices were still embedded in the economic and political structure, and many liberals hailed that report as a great turning point. But the fact is, that nothing has changed, except for the worse. As the economic situation has become less secure, and the fabric of American life torn apart by the war in Vietnam, racial tensions have increased as the rulers seek a scapegoat in their campaign for law and order.

Blacks, Chicanos, American Indians, Puerto Ricans all find that beyond the normal levels of deprivation, they are faced with escalated state repression. Meanwhile, racism divides the working class and makes it impossible to mount united actions against the bosses. Minority groups are right to refuse to lend their support to unions that have discriminated against them, but the end result is a battle amongst the working class for different sections of the small slice of the pie that the rulers have granted them. What is needed, instead, is united action so that the working class, as a whole, can get a fair share of the wealth that it has created and real control over their own lives. But this will never happen until whites make a conscious effort to combat the racist institutions of American society. In the meantime, blacks, Chicanos, and other groups will need to build their own political identity in institutions that they, themselves, totally control, and whites can unite with them around specific programs of mutual concern. Organizing against racism, we must stress, is not a matter of urging people to be moral: it is a matter of showing people concretely how their own survival and liberation depends on the destruction of racist institutions and attitudes, as well as the moral issue. There is no hope for serious change as long as the rulers of this country can manipulate white's fears of blacks; and no hope that blacks will work in joint struggles with whites until they have grounds to trust that whites will not sell out their interests and needs.

Social change cannot be based on every man having a woman as a slave in the home, existing primarily to serve male ego, male sexual needs, and male domestic services. Nor can solidarity be built in the work force if men accept arrangements in which women are discriminated against in any way. The struggle to end racism and sexism in our work places, in our unions, in our neighborhoods, and in our homes, is integral to the general struggle for human freedom and dignity.

Our programs must be directed at the needs of all these sectors of the population and must help them come to an awareness of the common source of their oppression in the American economic and political system, and their need to unite in struggle for radical change.

Vitally important also is the struggle of people around the world for self-determination unencumbered by the economic and political domination of the U.S. and its powerful multinational corporations. We are for the dismantling of the American empire not just because we want to stop squandering our resources on useless weapons of destruction, and use them instead to fulfill human needs, but also because we support the same right for self-determination for Vietnamese, Chileans, Bolivians, and so on, that we want for ourselves. These people are not our enemy.

The struggle against the war in Vietnam is one of the most important facts in the re-emergence of radical consciousness in the United States. The Pentagon Papers have conclusively shown what the left has been saying for the past seven years: that the government has been lying to the people, that the war was caused solely by the imperial ambitions of the United States, and that the only way for the war to end is for the United States to get out immediately and unconditionally. The anti-war movement through its marches, sit-ins, draft refusals, civil disobedience, rallies, and other forms of demonstrations, has succeeded in dramatizing the war in all of its stupidities and its planned and conscious evil. When the war ends, it will be the anti-war movement and the Vietnamese people who forced it to end, and not the various opportunists, from liberal Democrats to Nixon, who try to claim the credit for jumping on the anti-war bandwagon after 73 percent of the American people had resolutely demanded immediate withdrawal.

But the anti-war movement has been curiously inadequate in showing people how the war relates to the rest of the capitalist system. This is in part due to the reason that it has refused to link the anti-war struggle to the general struggle to build socialism. No one is fooled when a primarily anti-war constituency tacks on a poverty or racism demand to its rhetoric, but programmatically, still focuses on the war only. The meaning of anti-war demonstrations will be greatly transformed, and their power greatly enhanced, when they are seen as part of a left that is clearly fighting for the interests of the majority of the American people around programs that include, but go far beyond, the war. The struggles that emerge around such a program will have the consequence of severely weakening American imperialism and its ability to fight for its empire.

The irony of American imperialism is that it must attempt to manipulate American patriotism and use it, just as it did in every previous war, to defend the economic interests of a very small section of the population. We must stress that there is another side to the American patriotic tradition, the side that is rooted in revolution and that led Thomas Jefferson to proclaim: "God forbid that we should ever by twenty years without a rebellion." If life, liberty, and the pursuit of happiness are part of the American dream, then we can show people how that dream can only be fully realized by the development of a new economic and social structure that replaces American imperialism, racism, and sexism with a new democratic socialism.

The primary element that we orient toward in building an American socialism is the working class. But we reject any simple notion of who, or what, that working class is. While it is still true that millions of people fit into the category of the "industrial workers" who are super exploited on the assembly lines and in the mines, it is also true that a conception of working people must include the many who are exploited in offices and in sales positions, and even teachers, government workers, social workers, and many who like to hide beneath the title of "professional" to keep from themselves the fact that they, too, must sell their labor power in order to eat. One of the most important devices by which the working class is kept disunited is through that section of bourgeois ideology that teaches millions of people who live miserable lives that are totally powerless and alienated, that they are not really part of the working class, but rather part of some mystical middle class. We are told that the majority of people are really "middle class" and thus that the problems of American workers have largely been solved, or if they are not solved, they can't be solved because the vast middle class won't approve. The fact is that most people who believe this are still making profits for someone else, and coerced by the system to sell their labor power in ways which give them no human satisfaction.

We need a much more careful study of the working people of this country which recognizes the highly variegated nature of the working class and stops trying to generalize when there is no basis for the generalization but which also shows how much the interests of working people can be made to work together.

Saying that we orient to the working class does not mean, however, that we see the enemy as the upper middle class. While it is often true that upper professionals and store owners side with the interests of the ruling class against the people, our primary quarrel is not with these people, but with those whom they serve. The Vietnam War showed many of these people how very powerless they were as well: despite all their alleged influence, they found themselves powerless to stop the war that many of them opposed as long as it seemed to be in the interests of a powerful section of the ruling class. The power of the ruling class is not in its numbers, but in its ability to set people fighting against each other. Our strength will be in our ability to focus attention on the ruling class and on capitalism, not on the many people who serve as functionaries for the system, but who have no real power to control it. Anyone who joins with us in the struggle for socialism, regardless of class of origin, is our ally. At the same time, we should understand that some of our programs will certainly annoy some moneyed interests that are not yet ruling class. For instance, tax programs that relieve working people will certainly take some money away from the upper middle class, and there are likely to be squawks. Our general principle here is: is the program justifiable and explainable to most working people? To talk of working people does not just mean those currently employed. People on welfare and unemployed fit into our category of the working class, and so do most students who are simply being trained to accept the highly specialized and technological jobs that an advanced industrial society has produced.

Our tactics will include mass demonstrations, civil disobedience, boycotts, strikes, and electoral activity. They will be decided by the people who are actually working on a particular program. Our strength will be focused in our national presence, in the fact that each local group will know that it has the support of groups like it in every major area in the country. And it will grow from the adequacy of our programs to meet human needs. We reject the policy of lesser evilism: the notion that we should tailor our programs to what is likely then we could easily win. The syndrome of compromise has been one of the major reasons why American society is falling apart today—people settled for what the rulers told them was "realistic."

It seemed realistic in the past to just ask for wage increases and a few more social benefits, but never to struggle for real power for the people. The result was that the men with power would give in to a few demands— but always by making the people pay for it in some other way. "Sure you can have social security—if we tax the workers more." "Sure the unions can get recognition—if they don't make demands for anything more than wages," and then the companies simply raise prices for their goods without cutting into their super-high profits.

"Sure you can have a higher standard of living—if you're willing to send your children to die in foreign wars to protect our exploitative investments and not ask for any domestic redistribution of wealth."

And now, the same cynical logic is being used in the fields of ecology, health care, and racism: "Sure we can clean things up in the environment and provide better health care and hire more blacks—but the working people will have to pay for it with higher taxes and accepting more bureaucratic controls from the top."

We are not going to settle for any of this. The corporations and the wealthy have created many of the problems in this society—and they will have to bear the burden of straightening things out. Nor will people any longer settle for a few sops—people want real power to control their lives and real ways of realizing their human needs.

We will settle for nothing less. In this way, we are completely different from the left-liberals of the Democratic and Republican parties, who often mouth a good line, but who are always ready to compromise away the crucial parts of their programs at the moment they come into real conflict with the economic power structure.

The next few years will probably see the development of a new force in America, as sections of the rulers who have extensive investments in the cities will attempt to coalesce a political party around urban spending. We have seen the harbingers of this development in the programs of the Urban Coalition and John Gardner's Common Cause. It is even likely that in either 1972 or 1976 there will be a major third party if the liberals have not managed to take control of the Democratic Party. The base of this alliance will be the urban poor and blacks, together with some of the most important corporations on the American scene. To some degree, the program of this group will overlap with our programs, but to a larger extent, it will not. The corporate elite that finances this move will not support programs that shift financial burdens onto themselves, nor will they support genuine control by the people except in areas where they think it is totally non-threatening. They will be offering another New Deal, and we are the inheritors of an America that was kept together by the first New Deal.

Liberal measures will only demonstrate more clearly the need for something more radical—a democratic socialism that is not some compromise between the needs of the rich and the needs of the majority of the people, but is completely geared to fill the needs of the people even if that means radical revision of the economic and political institutions along truly democratic lines.

Instead of jumping on any bandwagon of these new forces in the hope that the Fords and the Carnegies and Wall Street investors will miraculously lose their own interests and solve everything once their candidates make it into public office, we will resolutely push forward around programs that genuinely deal with human needs, and if those human needs are not met by the existing social and economic arrangements, we will change those arrangements.

There is much good work being done on the local level in a few communities, and these local organizing projects often have avoided some of the worst mistakes of movement organizing. But pockets of radicals, and pockets of organizing projects, do not constitute a movement. Some people believe that this is not the right time to build an organization on the national level, and argue that the organization will emerge more organically in a few years from now. But our own experience leads us to a different conclusion.

Within many of the local projects there is a dynamic of initial enthusiasm and hard work, gradually giving way to feelings of frustration, isolation, and final dissolution of the project. The same energy, if coordinated nationally into a series of similar projects with a similar thrust would have much more political clout. For one thing, people would begin to take the project more seriously as they see that it was being organized all over and that there was a coordinated left force. No matter how much sense the local organizing project seems to make on the local scene, it will never be taken as a real alternative until people feel that there is a national left that is seriously contending for power around its programs. Further, local organizers often devise programs that only focus on those problems that actually can be solved locally, since they correctly assess that no one would take them seriously if they were organizing around programs that could only be instituted on the national level when they have no national organization.

The fact is that local projects have fallen apart at an alarming rate and the absence of any rational, national organization for the left has had the consequences of making local organizing harder in many instances. Large numbers of people who related to the left in some way in the past, are moving toward the Democratic Party not because they have suddenly lost their left analysis, but because they see no way of moving within the left (indeed, it is hard to find anything to move within). Unless you are a full-time organizer, willing to do full-time movement work, there is almost nothing to do, no place to go, that makes any sense. In building an organization nationally that is not aimed at revolutionary cadre, but in providing a place for the masses of Americans who have become radicalized in the past few years, we are not attempting to supplant any existing organizations, but only to build a form where none exists, and one is badly needed.

The New American Movement (NAM) is a mass membership organization of Americans committed to the struggle to rebuild America on democratic socialist lines, as explicated in the analysis. Our primary orientation is to reach the millions of Americans who have come to realize that America's problems are not peripheral and passing, but are basic and structural.

This organization does not conceive of itself as the final vehicle for working people to take state power, but as an interim institution, built for the next several years, that can move to consolidate and provide leadership for the marked trend to the left of recent years. Because our aim is to reach tens of millions of people in this country, and provide a focus through which they can fight for socialism, we will not sanctify any one life style as the only legitimate one, and will severely discourage the dynamic of "more-revolutionary-than-thou" inside our organization—a dynamic that always drives out just the people we want to be speaking to. We are not building a revolutionary vanguard party. Some of us believe that such a party will eventually be necessary, some do not, and some are unsure; but we are all agreed that if such a party is ever necessary, it is certainly premature at this point and that our organization will help to create the preconditions for such a party.

Because we are not building a sect group, there will be several ultimately important political questions we will not attempt to answer as an organization. We are building the kind of organization in which it must be possible not only now, but five years from now as well, for people to disagree on a number of important questions about how to make the revolution, and yet still feel comfortable in working with each other. The question that we must decide in this organization is not how to make the revolution, but how in the period ahead can we provide programs which will help unify large numbers of working people in a struggle against the ruling class and for socialism.

People will join the New American Movement primarily through local chapters which are formed around the analysis and around the programs that have been adopted as national priorities at annual national conferences. We anticipate that two or three such programs will be developed as national priorities at the first national conference over Thanksgiving weekend in November. Each chapter will work on the national priorities as well as on any other programs that the chapter develops for itself in its own area. Chapters are not, however, merely extensions of some top-down leadership, but will themselves be the basic units which decide what national policies and national programs deal with. But agreement on national programs is necessary both to give force and reality to those programs, and because many of the most pressing problems on the local level are problems that can only be solved at the national level.

The national organization would provide a source of strength for people in left caucuses and at the same time help them coordinate their activities. In no sense would a national organization of the sort we are building seek to subvert or take power over these caucuses or to get people to think them unimportant. Rather, they would be an excellent place for people to push for struggle around the programs we are developing. At the same time, the ideas that emerge in such caucuses might be integrated into newly developing programs on the national level.

In the course of the next few months at regional meetings, and finally at the national conference in November, a structure for the organization will be designed by those who participate in it. That structure will attempt to ensure that local groups are given full power to decide for themselves how best to implement national programs in their own area as well as to initiate their own activities consistent with the general politics of the organization. We would envision that such a structure would include regional and national coordinating councils elected both at large and from regional and local affiliates. And we envision that these bodies (democratically elected, representative, and responsible to a particular electorate that could hold it accountable and replace it) will have the power to provide leadership around the specific programs and analysis that have been mandated by the entire organization, and to help spread the message of the organization to areas and sections of the population not adequately covered by local chapters.

While the basic unit of the organization will be chapters, we also recognize the importance of providing for the affiliation of already-existing organizing projects and activities that are not focused around our national priorities but are nevertheless advancing the general socialist analysis that we hold. It should be possible for such groups to join as special chapters. But the exact form of such affiliation is yet to be worked out, and we welcome the cooperation of these groups in working out a form that would help us unite our strengths.

While our orientation is outward, to constituencies that have been previously unreached by the left, we also realize that during our first year or two, before we are generally well known, that it is likely that we will draw heavily from the university community and old movement people. In this transition period, we will reject both of two possible errors:

(a) The error of thinking that in the transition stage we are somehow illegitimate and not real yet because we have not yet become what we can become.

(b) The error of thinking that the initial constituency is the only possible one that will ever be attracted, and hence make that a self-fulfilling prophecy by developing programs that speak only to the people currently in NAM.

We have a very modest self-conception. NAM is not meant to be a substitute for the independent women's movement or the black liberation movement, but rather hopes to work with these movements on a variety of concrete programs. NAM is not a revolutionary party. And it urges people who are looking for any of these forms to join those other groups and work out a relationship through those other organizations. Nor do we view ourselves as a replacement for trade unions or professional associations, though we think that a strategy for working in these groups may be developed by people who work together in NAM.

What's Wrong?

To build a new American movement we must learn from some of the mistakes of the past. While the movement is too big and variegated to say that any particular error affected every part of it, there are certain trends that have become dominant among large sections of the movement that must be unequivocally rejected if we hope to really build something new. We recognize however, that there are several groups like the National Lawyers' Guild, MCHR, and sections of the women's movement who have avoided many of these mistakes.

Misuse and Over-Glorification of the Third World   The movement has been correct to reject the kind of national chauvinism which led many to support U.S. foreign policy even when they could plainly see that it was wrong. U.S. schools and colleges try very hard to convince people that the U.S. is an exception to every rule, that it can do no wrong, and that it is invincible! The understandable reaction was to reject all of this nonsense and to begin to show people that the U.S. was doing wrong in Vietnam and in many other places around the world, that it was acting just as every other imperialist power had acted in the past, and that in fact it was being beaten in the battlefield by the Viet Cong. The movement also stressed, correctly, the humanity and beauty of the Vietnamese people. But sometimes these tendencies have gone overboard, portraying Third World revolutions as the embodiment of all virtue and wisdom.

Instead of learning what was relevant, while carefully recognizing the differences between a revolution in a peasant society and a revolution in an advanced industrial society, many sections of the movement have attempted to mechanically transplant the messages of the Third World to this country. Hence, on the one hand, the development of quasi-Maoist sects who try to fit the American experience into a Chinese mold, and on the other hand, the more general new left glorification of the Vietnamese and Cubans. Such an approach leaves people totally confused when Mao's China suddenly makes co-existence overtures to the U.S. or when it supports a dictatorship in Pakistan which is engaged in genocide against a popular rebellion, just as it leaves them confused when Cuba is forced in order to survive (under conditions which could not foster genuine socialism) to make accommodations with the Soviet Union that limit internal democracy and self-determination.

The strategy for building socialism in a country with an educated working class and a fully developed technological and industrial base will be quite different from what is appropriate for Cuba or China or Vietnam. It will have to build from the problems, shared to some extent by other advanced industrial societies, that come from the maturation of capitalism.

Anti-Intellectualism and Following Every Fad   Partly in an effort to appear genuinely American, and partly as a real reflection of the anti-intellectualism of American life, many sections of the movement have tended to glorify spontaneity and feeling at the expense of (rather than alongside of) any intellectual life. There is very little serious scientific study of American life in the movement.

Feeling has often replaced thinking, with few people really coming to understand that those feelings themselves are products of an intricate process of education and socialization—not something pure and "natural" that has been polluted by thought and reflection. Instead of making a careful study of America, the movement has been quick to adopt slogans and fads that are not only implausible, but often mutually self-contradictory. One week, for instance, we are told that hippies are living off of their white-skin privilege and should be scorned; the next week a Weatherman communique tells us that "freaks are revolutionaries and revolutionaries are freaks." Inconsistency itself becomes a glorified principle, and mistakenly confused with "dialectical thinking."

The most destructive fad adopted in recent years has been that of the street-fighting urban guerrilla. Some sections of the movement have established a criterion of seriousness that revolves around how many crazy risks one is willing to take and how much one is involved in the street fighting. But the real areas where militancy is needed—the struggles for power in each community and each institution—are often seen as somehow reformist. The notion is that anything short of the final revolutionary battle is impure, so count us out until the golden moment arrives. In the meantime, we are urged to learn revolutionary skills, like karate and gun training. This approach must be rejected.

Rather, we need to carefully study the economic and political system at the community, state, and national level to find out where the critical contradictions are and bring people to a fuller understanding of how they can move. The real skills that we need are those that can get others to join us in political struggles against the institutions that oppress all of us. Only when we build a movement that understands in detail, institution by institution, how the capitalist system acts to oppress people, will we have a movement that can plausibly provide leadership in a struggle to build a new society.

This is not to suggest that the only way to learn about America is by abstract study—some, though not all, of our information about America will come through research and study, but some must come through engaging in concrete struggles to change these institutions. But very little will be learned by pretending that we are really romantic and heroic Third World guerrillas.

Inwardness   The impetus toward self-transformation that developed in the movement in the past few years was rooted in a justifiable reaction to some of the worst aspects of previous movement practice. The movement was almost as alienating as the rest of society in many respects. Competition for approval and power often seemed to be the dominant mode: and meetings often turned into furious ego-battles between aggressive males. Women were often relegated to doing the same kind of shit-work they were assigned in bourgeois society, and made to feel that their insights and understanding were too inferior to be worth mouthing to the "heavies." In a similar way, non-aggressive men were shoved aside if they had not mastered the same verbal skills that gave the "superstars" their visibility and power.

Everyone felt stifled and used, and as a result the movement had an even larger turnover in membership than even its essentially transient student population would have dictated. In this context, a basic rethinking of our internal operations and the way in which we related to each other was absolutely essential, and the emergence of the movement made that rethinking inevitable. The heightened consciousness that has developed both of the oppression of women and of the destructive ways in which men have been socialized to be aggressive, to deny their own feelings, and to need to have their ego gratified, has made it possible now for men and women to work together on a new and better basis than that which existed in the early years of the new left.

But some sections of the movement have become so concerned with the task of transforming the consciousness of their own members that the begin to ignore the plight of the rest of the population. Fantasies began to emerge that everyone could reject their whole conditioning immediately upon realizing the problem and beginning to struggle against it. The notion somehow developed that we not only could, but must, transform ourselves into socialist human beings before the revolution, and that we must do this before we start organizing others. Who are we, the argument runs, to try to organize others when we are so messed up ourselves? The answer is that we are people oppressed by this system whose only hope lies in a socialist revolution; that while we should do all we can to transform ourselves in the course of that struggle, there is little likelihood that socialist human relations can be created and sustained as long as the economic and political structures of the society we live in are controlled by the capitalist ruling class; and hence, that it is our own urgent need to move large numbers of other people to the same realization about this society so that, together, we can overthrow it.

We do not wish to overthrow this society merely to re-establish its same stifling features in a new society. That is why it is so crucial to struggle to transform ourselves in the course of the anti-capitalist struggle. But at any particular moment we must not become so harsh on each other that we set up utopian standards to judge ourselves and our progress. It is these utopian ideals that have often caused the reverse of what they alleged to create. In the name of making relationships in the movement more humane and less based on authority figures and male chauvinism, some sections of the movement have focused on fighting itself and have become more inhumane and less sensitive. Many intelligent and sensitive people see that they will be personally crushed in such a movement, and have decided that they don't want to subject themselves to the abuse that it requires, and so have withdrawn into their own private life or into political activity so isolated that no one can find them to trample on them.

Anti-Leadership   Part of the reason for the anti-leadership tendencies in the movement was the emergence of bad leadership: people who were not sensitive to the ways in which they trampled on others in their race to gain prominence and power in the movement. Another reason was the justified resentment of movement people against a leadership that often seemed incapable of developing programs or a vision that would move the movement out of its isolation from the majority of the American people and that seemed to become more sectarian every time a major breakthrough to mass dialogue and understanding became possible. Even more frustrating was the unresponsiveness of leadership to those whom it pretended to lead. It might be possible within SDS to elect a new national leadership every year (until the Weathermen dissolved the mass organization so as to eliminate any possible challenge to its leadership), but who could control the famous media stars in what they did and said? It was infuriating enough to have liberal Democrats pretend to be the leadership of the anti-war movement in order to gain votes, but to have uncontrolled superstars within our own movement was too much.

Unfortunately, the impetus to control leadership moved very quickly to a doctrine of anti-leadership in many sections of the movement. Anyone who attempted to provide leadership or vision was viewed with suspicion or even hostility.

The notion that leadership is illegitimate, or in itself elitist, must be rejected. No leadership can ever by itself create the conditions for socialist revolution when there is no objective crisis in capitalist society; but no spontaneous reactions to this crisis will be adequate for focusing political action in such a way as to really expose the contradictions and then put forward a coherent and attractive alternative that people will rally around. We need a left that has a program and a vision that speaks from and to American reality, and seeks to provide leadership in building a new society. Leadership is also necessary if a humane, democratic socialism is to evolve from revolutionary upheaval. The new society must be planned and organized. It won't happen by itself. We have to begin training people for these roles now.

Leadership should be followed when it is good leadership, and rejected from wherever it comes if it's not. One of the most irrational aspects of the past few years has been the way in which every oppressed group will provide the best revolutionary leadership—a notion which has no reasonable ground. So, for years, people looked to blacks for political leadership. This was an easy substitute for developing any real leadership in the white movement, and for what the blacks told us for years to do—organize the white movement ourselves. The disillusionment that followed the split in the Panthers only makes sense in this context—because whites had been living their revolution vicariously through blacks, rather than attempting to build an organization in the white community that could speak to the needs of the white community. The original impetus in this direction, of course, was extremely important: the long history of whites attempting to dominate mixed organizations had needed the corrective that the emergence of the black power movement provided. Young whites were right to stress the importance of respecting black leadership and not trying to co-opt it. But too soon this changed from respect to glorification. It seemed as if the latest phase of American racism was manifesting itself in the movement: whites can treat blacks as slaves or as gods, but not as human beings who have similar strengths and are allowed similar human weaknesses the same as whites.

What is good leadership? Whatever else, it must include the following:

a. Involving as many people as possible in political debate, decision making, and activity, rather than trying to hoard any of this for itself.

b. Attempting to impart to as many people as possible the skills of leadership, so that no one becomes absolutely indispensable.

c. Always trying to make its assumptions and activities explicit so that others may learn from them.

d. Always trying to articulate the relationship between any particular program, action, idea, and the more general visions that we hold.

e. Honesty.

f. Ability to keep in touch with the language, needs, and problems, not just of an organization's membership, but with those whom the organization ultimately hopes to attract or speak to.

g. A deep understanding of the American economic and political structure which is constantly increased through new study and new insights.

Having articulated these qualities, we can see how far we have to go before we can develop good leadership. This is not something people are born with, but rather takes long periods of nurturing.

Just as it is incumbent on any leadership in an organization to take great care to develop leadership in others and to use its talents, not as a ticket to stardom, but as a means of strengthening others, so it is incumbent on any organization that can ever hope to succeed, to give strong support to its leadership. Leadership must feel able to experiment, to make mistakes, and to fail in particular struggles, if it is ever to become really creative and imaginative. The notion that leadership is old leadership and must be replaced just because it has been around for awhile, was one of the most destructive aspects of SDS, and could only emerge in a transient student base. If it is to succeed, leadership must have something behind it—the confidence and dedication of a real organization. None of this is to suggest that leadership should be allowed to do whatever it wants despite the wishes of the membership. That would bring us back to traditional bourgeois leadership à la John Gardner's Common Cause. Leadership must be given latitude to lead, but must always act within the political guidelines set by the organization and must always be strictly accountable and replaceable by the membership. The complete powerlessness of people in the left today is shown by our inability to control those who allegedly speak in our name. The absence of a national organization does not mean that we don't have national spokespeople—we do, and they are quoted regularly. But we have absolutely no power over who they are and what they say. The creation of NAM will completely change that and force leadership to be responsive just as it will allow leadership to really lead because it will be able to speak for a real organization and not just for personal fantasy-trips.

We have put forward these criticisms of the movement not because somehow we had managed to escape from them ourselves in the past, and are simply looking down on everyone else with disdain. On the contrary, some of us were deeply involved in these mistakes and they are put forward as much as self-criticism as anything else. Some of us played very bad roles as leaders in the past, and we have been castigated for it and learned much through our mistakes and the ensuing criticism. None of us comes forward with the claim that we have such sterling practice in political activity that we should look to it as proof that what we say is right. The proposal for the New American Movement comes from those who have learned from past errors, have attempted to transform themselves and their ideas in the light of those mistakes, and who wish to work together with others who share their conception of what we can do in the future to build a real mass socialist movement that speaks to the American reality.

30.
STRATEGIES FOR SOCIALISM: TASKS AND PERSPECTIVES

National Caucus of Labor Committees

While dissonant parodies of Herbert Hoover's 1929–31 speeches are heard from today's White House, the U.S. economy has reached the fag-end of its postwar prosperity, and is lurching toward both a new world depression and the most brutal re-enactments of head-on struggles between capital and labor throughout the advanced capitalist sector.

Not Only in the Capitalist Sector   Except to imbeciles, who foolishly imagine that "socialism in one country" is really possible, it is obvious that the relatively backward economies of the Soviet Union and Eastern Europe are dependent upon prosperous conditions of the capitalist world market for successful development of the Soviet sector. Without finding a favorable capitalist market for exports, the Soviet sector cannot import those means of production which it requires from the capitalist sector. Economic conjectures in the capitalist market are thus almost direct causes for depressing material conditions of life in the less-developed Soviet sector, producing social crises in Eastern Europe at the same time as in Western Europe.

The objective possibility for socialist transformation of the entire world is within sight, provided that we in the U.S. succeed in engaging the "little wheel" of socialist program and leadership with the "big wheel" of massive, emerging struggles of the labor movement and its allies. The "if" is hardly of small significance. Did the world ever see so overripe an objective opportunity for socialist transformation as in France during late May 1968—with one of the largest Communist parties (CP) on the scene, with a massive following in the labor movement (CGT)? Repeatedly, mankind has seen overripe objective opportunities for socialism, but qualified socialist organizations either virtually did not exist or, like the CPs throughout most of the world since the late 1930s, the socialist parties on the scene have

From L. Marcus, *Tasks and Perspectives: 1971 Strategies for Socialism* (New York: National Caucus of Labor Committees), pp. 1–43. Reprinted by permission of the publisher.

actually proven to be a major subjective obstacle to socialism where the objective possibilities have been the greatest.

Recent history demonstrates that the two dominant socialist organizations on the scene in the U.S. (the Socialist Workers Party-Young Socialist Alliance/Communist Party-Young Workers Liberation League) are inferior in socialist potential to the Parti Communiste Française of 1963, and, despite the adequacy of program and orientation of the third U.S. socialist organization (our own), we have seen during 1970 that about one-third of our own membership has had to be dragged kicking and screaming, from its petit-bourgeois orientation toward the emergent political struggles of the U.S. working class. It is the subjective possibilities for socialism which have to be urgently matched to the accelerating objective opportunities.

It is to that purpose that the present statement of tasks and perspectives is published: immediately for the guidance of our own organization's members, but also for the education of otherwise rudderless socialists in the SWP-YSA, CP-YWLL, and other such organizations. Considering the poor level of political literacy in our opponent socialist organizations, it is necessary to say more in this document than if it were written for members of the National Caucus of Labor Committees alone.

The principles and main perspectives represented in this present statement do not differ in any essential respect from those expressed by draft resolutions of our organization's March 1969 (*Third American Revolution*) and September 1970 (*Emergency Draft Program, Tasks & Perspectives Resolution*) national conferences. In addition to the recurring need to update perspectives in matters of tactical detail, the following principal considerations demand this present, new resolution:

1. The unfolding of developments constantly confronts socialist organizations with new concrete forms of work to be accomplished, sometimes a qualitative shift like that of the past year: the death of the New Left.
2. The perspectives adopted as recently as September 1970, of an emerging change in political quality of labor struggles, has been advanced from a correct prediction of a changed situation to a manifest actuality.

Lessons must be drawn, and tasks for 1971 detailed accordingly.

Appearance Versus Reality

The absolute discrepancy between crude appearances and reality in the situation of the Young Socialist Alliance organization exemplifies the leading methodological difficulties in attempting to comprehend the present tactical situation.

From fall 1969 through spring 1970, the YSA grew at a rate which astonished its leadership most of all. From this short-term development, the YSA became more deluded than ever respecting the eternal merit of its opportunist, petit-bourgeois social orientation to Vietnam War issues and "nationalist" minority ferment. It attributed its organizational growth to the "positive" effect of such YSA policies, rather than facing the truth, that the YSA was simply fattening itself for the moment by carrion-eating. The illusory expansion of the socialist movement which the YSA saw in its own temporary growth, was actually a product of the shattering of an organization of tens of thousands of members (SDS), in which process a few hundred SDSers oriented to the nearest-available large piece of political flotsam—YSA.

The essential fact of the 1969–70 period is the total collapse of the Left of the 1960s, while the beginnings of political ferment among organized and unorganized labor are being felt.

Thus, all the pragmatic truisms developed during the 1958–68 decade of New Radicalism are now reduced to junk by the virtual evaporation of the radicalized social strata to which those opportunistic tactical recipes are applied. So the SWP-YSA and CP-YWLL have totally lost their intellectual moorings in what must seem to them to be a kaleidoscopic progression in tactical realities. It is just because the CP-YWLL has had such inferior success at the carrion-feast upon SDS (and thus less surfeit of gluttonous petit-bourgeois delusions) that the CP has been able to outflank the SWP on the left, responding to the emerging political ferment of the labor movement in at least a disgusting CP way where the SWP-YSA has been unable thus far to respond to the new situation at all.

It is therefore part of the intent of the present statement of tasks and perspectives, to show viable individuals and groupings within the SWP-YSA, CP-YWLL and other nominally socialist organizations a lighted pathway out of their present organizational and political muddles.

Membership in the NCLC   As we stated in the September 1970 resolution, the function of tasks and perspectives resolutions for socialist organizations flows from the problem of the role of the single socialist individual in history. Unless one has a conception of how one is intervening or can intervene, as an individual, to alter the course of human history, then the idea of socialist politics, or tasks and perspectives resolutions, would be self-socializing idiocy.

Thus, a principal cause of profound disorientation among well-intended contemporary socialists is that on this question (the individual in history) they are "Marxists" in name only. The relevant point is symptomized by the continuing efforts (especially since the 1930s) to set a "mature" Karl Marx into some degree of philosophical antagonism to the Marx of 1844–46. This baseless, attempted dichotomy is an effort by political semi-literates to save the appearances of their "Marxism" economic-determinist fatalism, a pseudo-Marxist view palpably based on hearsay acquaintance with *Capital* from an empiricist standpoint. Contrary to the views of such unfortunate persons, the essence of the Karl Marx of 1844–46, on which the entire "mature" Marx is directly based, is Marx's successful location of the basis for a real individual human identity in the developmental processes of social evolution.

Faced with the short span of individual biological existence, the individual can realize a permanent place in humanity only to the extent that his practice has permanent value for humanity. This aspiration, which distinguished human identity from that of lower animals, has been generally expressed in modern times only in the disguise of Judeo-Christian religious ideology (or cognates), in which one's humanity is located in an after-death spirit world or in a contemporary spiritual contemplative life parasitizing on secular reality.

The task of liberating humanity from such mere delusions is absolutely not accomplished by naive atheism. The solution to the aspirations of the human individual must be entirely situated within the real world. Human virtue must be located not within churchly canons, but in terms of a scientific comprehension of the order of nature. Not empiricist or positivist science, which are merely religious axioms covered with an opaque cloth. Rather, a science which takes human existence as its sole premise, axiom, postulate or what have you, and thus situates the criteria of scientific practice (whether in laboratory, classroom, workplace or streets) on the premise that the individual's understanding of nature is to be measured by his contributions to the qualitatively-improving mastery of nature for the purpose of improving the quality of species-existence. My identity does not reside in some fantastic "other world," but in humanity's permanent debt to my existence for that small, permanent contribution which flows from my conscious determination to act for such results.

This notion of positive individual identity within society could exist only in abstraction (for example, Spinoza's "extended being") until about the beginning of the nineteenth century in Europe and the U.S. Capitalism's profound contribution to humanity, however unintentional, has been that of lifting humanity out of "the idiocy of rural life," and replacing the fragmentation of humanity by socialization of human existence (objectively speaking) through the growing, deepening interdependence of the world's productive forces. Today, no individual person within the advanced capitalist sector (or, "workers' economies" sector) can biologically survive as a potentially productive human being without the at least indirect contributions to the production of everything he consumes by the interdependent efforts of almost every person throughout the world. No individual human being in any part of the world has the prospect of emerging beyond his present state of misery except by the collective productive efforts of society on a world scale. Spinoza's quasi-religious view—to achieve humanity for the individual through understanding one's place as an "extended being" in the causal sequence of a totality of human events—is now a practical, immediate reality of everyday life in even the most obscured and backward nooks of our society as a whole.

What each individual contributes or fails to contribute to the advance of culture and production of means of existence has rather immediate material consequences for the world as a whole. The deliberate, materially-realized achievement of real humanity is now within the practical grasp of every *potentially-socialist* individual within society. Individual man cannot be thus lifted from the alienated state of quasi-bestiality, from the pit of anarchist despair—of each individual living for himself—into the condition in which every human individual achieves real humanity—living self-consciously as a person of importance to the entire human species present and future. An individual must see in himself or herself the "brick" on which the foundations of future humanity are laid. An individual must find and realize in reality that nobility which religious ideology fantastically disguised in order to deny man humanity in real life and locate the hope of being human only in the deluded "immortality" of spiritual life.

The activity of becoming such a human being under conditions of capitalist social-productive relations is socialism. Socialism is primarily a philosophical world-outlook on the whole of human history and one's Self, which drives one without "remedy" to bring immediately into being those new modes of socialist productive relations in which each individual comes to play a conscious, determining part in shaping the productive and related policies of his entire society. Socialism is a philosophical world-outlook which drives one without "remedy" to establish the beginning of true humanity in a democratic, deliberative process through which every member of society contributes to the formulation of the policies and "plans" by which society collectively administers its own existence, a society in which every individual can secure such human rights by becoming a part of the political working class for itself.

Socialism thus necessarily begins to become actual socialism as socialists develop their world-outlook in terms of a systematic or scientific world-view of the progressive, evolutionary reproduction of man as a self-changing species. In this view, the successive forms of human society have, in effect, superseded the task of simple biological evolutionary differentiation among lower animal species as the form of the evolution of life to higher forms. Thus actual, but still abstracted socialism becomes practical socialism (socialist practice) as the philosophical world-outlook developed by Karl Marx during the 1844–46 period is applied to understanding and mastering the potentialities of the available productive forces of capitalist society, and on the basis of that understanding formulates "economic programs" for the establishment of a socialist state and management of means of production. An "economic program" through which existing productive capacities are employed to increase total social accumulation of wealth at the most rapid rate: the necessary material process-condition for qualitative improvements in the condition of life of every member of the human species.

The socialist does not foolishly imagine that such "economic programs" by themselves will win a majority of society to socialism. The irony of capitalism is that while it socializes objective productive relations on a world scale, it simultaneously fragments the same humanity into small groupings somewhat replicating man's bestial, primitive past—bitterly-contending local "community" and other parochialist forms. Even the working class under capitalism does not (usually) see itself as a class, but each section of the class is divided into competing groupings along national, ethnic, regionalist, trade-union parochial, "local community," and other quasi-bestial lines. Thus, the fragmented forms of working-class organization secrete hegemonic ideologies which are absolutely irreconcilable with the socialist view. Thus, the precondition for winning masses of working people to the socialist program is the supercession of parochialist forms of self-organization of the working class and its potential allies. Socialist consciousness, the ability to recognize the need for socialist economic program, is a product of successful subordination of localist forms of class organization to mass forms representative of common class interests. To win a majority to socialism it is first necessary to begin to qualitatively change the way working people think; to accomplish that, it is necessary to change the forms of self-organization.

This kind of transformation of consciousness is accomplished under those conjunctural circumstances in which it is uniquely possible to catalyze alliances against capitalists among previously-antagonistic sections of what Marxists term "the political class for itself." The "united front" (absolutely not the "Popular Front"!) of masses of working people and their allies against *all* capitalist political formations (for example, Democratic, Republican, Liberal, "New Priorities," and so on), or—the same thing—the Soviet form, or "strike support" alliances which bring together trade unionists, professional socialists, unorganized and unemployed working people, oppressed minority groups, radical youth as such, on the basis of *anti-capitalist* programs addressed to the *positive* material interests of the class (wages, working conditions, conditions of productive development, enlarged productive employment, and so on), are each various approximations of the political (working) class for itself forms through which the people's philosophical world-outlook is qualitatively changed, in a socialist direction.

The form of self-consciousness of one's Self as a member of an anti-capitalist political class, a class which rejects nationalism, trade-union narrowness, "local community" parochialism, and so on, is what Marxian socialists mean by "class consciousness." Trade-union militancy, for example, is absolutely not a form of class consciousness, although the conditions for trade-union forms coincide with "united front" forms of political organization.

Nor is it enough to simply work to bring such class-conscious political formations into being. The development of a competent socialist economic program demands years of intensive intellectual effort by persons who accept the responsibilities of Marxian economics as a profession. It is impossible for masses of workers and others suddenly brought together under conditions of struggle to "spontaneously" develop an economic program any more than they might "spontaneously" solve the riddles of medicine or atomic physics. The conditions for mass political formations are conditions demanding immediate and profound alternatives, and such conditions do not permit us to contemplate extended periods of education and professional development of the sort which must come immediate after successful socialist transformation. The task of the socialist is to interconnect the practical organization of alliances with the development and propagation of "economic" program, attempting to bring the two elements of socialist practice (consciousness and organization) together exactly as the advances in philosophical world-outlook (class consciousness) among masses of people suddenly make socialist programs agreeable to them.

The task of socialists' mass practice is to connect the "little wheel" of socialist theoretical consciousness to the "big wheel" of a political class for itself movement. It is in that process that every potential Marxian socialist has the opportunity to play a decisive role as an individual in the making of future human history.

The principal functional disorders affecting well-intended socialists are summed up in the synonymous terms, "pragmaticism," "empiricism," or "opportunism." On the scale of day-to-day "ego needs," considering the short span of biological existence, and the brevity of the span of one's most active, formative years of adult life, the connection between cause and effect does not seem to correspond in practice to that of the Marxist theoretical world-view except at the most extraordinary moments of development. The need of the "ego" to justify its activity in terms of "organizational success" by philistine, "business-like" standards, compels socialists to waver, to dabble in organizational "short cuts." Thus, the tendency among socialists to degrade practice to a succession of tactical "fads," to attempt to predict current developments only in the short run, and to orient to current political breezes—to play down socialist perspectives in the interest of getting in "on the inside" of anything of possibly larger notoriety as a short-term, popular-radical manifestation.

This is not to suggest that the actual socialist must not reckon with short-term movements. However, the socialist sees the short-term and local within the longer-range and holistic. As for Hegel and Marx, the particular by itself is purely "negative," alienated. The positive significance of the particular can only be dialectical, within the whole and as the particular directly subordinates itself to and services the whole.

"Sectarianism," abstention from developments, is simply the reverse side of opportunism. The sectarian socialist opportunist, recognizing his own proclivity for such opportunism, withdraws himself from the sphere of temptation in consoling, self-righteous contemplation of his "purity of essence."

The central problem, therefore, in maintaining the continuity of socialist development of cadre-forces through successive periods of ebb and flow of radical ferment, is that of developing individual and collective mastery of Marxian theory to the extent that this represents actual knowledge and understanding of the subject rather than the sophomoric gloss-making we usually encounter among spokesmen for various socialist organizations. Without a real assimilation of the Marxian philosophical world-outlook to that extent, no professed socialist can withstand the disorienting and morally debilitating effects of short-term ebb and flow or of sharp turns in the tactical situation.

That, in sum, is the premise for the existence and membership within the National Caucus of Labor Committees: To reproduce a "hard core" of developed Marxian socialist cadres within the U.S. socialist movement, cadres who have attained the degree of intellectual and moral development to withstand the kind of debilitating vicissitudes of ebbs and flows which have previously destroyed the revolutionary potential of organizations such as the Communist and Socialist Workers' parties.

Our perspective for the left-hegemony of our programmatic views, which might seem wildly pretentious to a naive viewer of present arrangements, is based on an understanding of the way in which various philosophical world-outlooks are determined among various strata of the population, and of the special circumstances under which large numbers of working people and others are susceptible of almost "suddenly" being won over to our sort of programmatic outlook and organizational proposals.

The ability of our organization to function as a "task-oriented" deliberating body, to function so that we may be assured in advance that our decisions will actually represent an essentially-correct socialist decision, is based on the limiting assumption that our membership is governed by the founding principles of our organization, as summarized here. A *homogeneous philosophical world-outlook, realized as a coherent body of materialized practice.*

Understanding Current History The developments of the past half-century can be competently understood only as a vindication ("with a vengeance") of the overview of Marx's dialectical method and economic theories represented in Rosa Luxemburg's *The Political Mass Strike* and *The Accumulation of Capital.* It is in significant part a testament to the extent of actual male chauvinism in the socialist movement that leading socialist figures have "gotten by with" deriding the overwhelmingly-vindicated theoretical achievements of a "mere woman."

Of all leading socialist figures since Karl Marx and F. Engels themselves, only Rosa Luxemburg has comprehended the ABCs of Marx's dialectical method and economic theories. Where, for example, most self-styled Marxists have explicitly or implicitly identified *Capital* as a collection of empirical constructs from a study of a capitalist "closed economic model" of "nineteenth century competitive capitalism," only Luxemburg of all leading literary figures recognizes the actual significance of Marx's dialectical method in this work. She uniquely comprehends that the essential contradiction of capitalism is located not as an "internal contradiction" of a "closed economic model," but as a contradiction between the subjective and objective side of capitalist society, between the capitalist market valuation of capitalists' (paper) capitals (property-titles in investment) and the underlying, objective social productive "use-value" relations—as Marx emphasizes in the concluding, summary section of the Volume III (*Capital*) chapter on "Internal Contradictions."

Consequently, because of the prevailing, blundering understanding of Marx's economics by such leading figures as Lenin, the Marxist-Leninist movement (in particular) has treated capitalist value-relations as essentially matters of a closed, mechanical system, and they have foolishly denied that the development of capitalism has been dependent largely on material resources exogenous to capitalist production as a "closed system." On such mistaken premises, Lenin's *Imperialism* was written, containing a most un-Marxian (actually, Lassalleian) explanation of the so-called "aristocracy of labor," and attempting (after Hilferding) to explain imperialism simply in terms of the export of capital. Consequently, Lenin's *Imperialism* has been discredited *in fact* by developments of the past half-century, while Luxemburg's analysis of the breakdown of imperialism and the emergence of imperialist, statist war-economy has been entirely vindicated.

It is the anti-Luxemburgist frauds and delusions of self-styled Leninist organizations which have inevitably played so large a part in accomplishing the total abandonment of serious studies of Marx's economics in the leadership and ranks of these groupings. The overwhelming majority of such groupings, Communists, "Trotskyist," or "Maoist," have absolutely no theoretical apparatus for unraveling the processes of current economic and related developments, and are thus compelled to limit themselves to a few mere glosses on the economic situation, generally deriving their "best estimation" of the current economic situation from (at best) the *London Economist* and (at worst) the financial columns of the *New York Times*.

The essential feature of capitalist society *as an historically delimited* "stage" of human development is that the accumulation of capitalists' capitals depends upon massive looting of natural and non-capitalist forms of wealth. Capitalism emerges as capitalism from the looting of (mainly) the feudalist countryside, and depends today upon ravishing non-capitalist populations, natural resources, and even the depletion of potential productive labor-power in the most advanced subsector (depressing levels of existence of "poor" below that required for modern productive labor-power). Thus, in its own *specific* fashion (thus, analogous to every pre-capitalist society) capitalist production exhausts those natural and man-improved resources on which continued production of the means of existence of the entire population depends. The so-called "ecological crisis" is simply and essentially a reflection of capitalist production coming into

confrontation with the results of its unpaid looting of the natural preconditions for continued production and even human existence.

Once the national resources for such looting (primitive accumulation) dropped below the rate of potential looting required by national
capitals (about 1870), capitalism perpetuated its economic existence by
imperialism, a new form whose essential feature was "international loans."
Through the development of centralized banking and related institutions,
purely-fictitious capitalists' capitals as well as unsold production and idle
capacities were converted into credit-debt capital. These forms of capitaliza-
tion of fictitious capitals were then used as means of purchase of heavily-
discounted loan-capital advanced to the account of native economies as a
massive, self-perpetuating foreign debt upon those subject sectors. The
"hard" part of the original capital ("unsold inventories" and idle capacity)
were indeed exported as part of this process, which neither Hilferding nor
Lenin comprehended, is the way in which the metropolitan capitalists
realized real values to substantiate the purely-fictitious portions of the principal amount and debt-service of the international loans. Masses of use-
values (natural resources and unpaid native labor) were simply "stolen" to
become capitalist commodities securing the fictitious valuation of the principal amount of paper capital advanced in such international loans. The
characteristic feature of imperialism (1870–1913) was not overseas capitalist
investment in expanded production of surplus value, but looting of existing
non-capitalist and natural wealth.

By approximately 1913, the rate of capitalist looting of the "underdeveloped" sectors had reached the proportion that the possible rate of
looting was insufficient to satisfy the engrossed appetites of all the imperialist nations *simultaneously*. The inevitable and most logical resolution
of this technical difficulty was World War I, in which the game of "survival of the fittest imperialism" was played out in a manner agreeable to
capitalist morality. However, World War I solved nothing. Apart from the
dynamic of continued U.S. internal development and Latin-American looting during the early to middle 1920s, and apart from U.S. propping up of
the toppling credit structures of Europe during that period, the entire
capitalist world was in a perpetual near or actual depression from the end
of World War I to the onset of the Great Depression in 1931. When the
credit-expansion capabilities of the U.S. sector were virtually exhausted during the 1929–31 period, the entire edifice of the old imperialism came
toppling down in the form of *the imperialist breakdown crisis which
Luxemburg had foreseen*. (With a delayed reaction in a French economy
too rotten to immediately detect the fact of its demise.)

The final break with the old form of imperialism began to develop
in the U.S. and Germany in the 1933–34 period. Roosevelt's NRA and
Hitler's *ultimately*-analogous programs in Nazi Germany represented the
establishment of statist war-economies as the new form of imperialism—
*exactly as Luxemburg's correct application of Marx's economic theories had
forewarned*.

The differences between the U.S.A. and Nazi Germany developments were ultimately located in the differing strategic situations of the two imperialist economies. Germany as a "have-not" nation in the imperialist sense, was compelled by lack of colonies and satrapies to proceed immediately and directly to looting neighboring capitalist (even fascist—Poland) populations and means of production as well as the Soviet Union, as the only means for most-urgently shoring-up the value of the Deutschemark as the autonomous monetary basis for the Third Reich's autarky. The U.S., as the emerging hegemonic imperialist power, was able to loot its neighbors by more "democratic" means.

Thus, in Nazi Germany, the ideology employed for mass-liquidation of European Jewry was essentially the wedge-end of the liquidation of tens of millions of Europeans in Krupp's (and other smokestack baron's slave-labor) system of converting the broken, bled bodies of slave-labor into a source of capital. Looted plants of French and other capitalists replaced the simple imperialist looting of non-capitalist wealth. The more general result of the emergence of statist war-economy was World War II, through which the U.S. conquered every former enemy and ally alike (excepting the Soviet sector). The paper capital of Germany and Japan was conveniently liquidated, and the real productive forces of those countries integrated into the U.S. dollar-based monetary system at bargain-basement prices. Postwar devaluations of the pound and franc exemplify the means by which the U.S. purchased its former allies (and their former colonial possessions) at the lowest, clearance-sale prices. Through the pioneering pragmatism of the American Military Government and auxiliary, ad hoc European recovery aid, culminating in the Marshall Plan and the Common Market—EFTRA arrangements, the postwar U.S. dollar based itself firmly on the cheaply-purchased material assets of both the advanced capitalist sector and its former colonies, clearing the decks for a relatively short-lived (approximately two decades) of postwar economic recovery of the U.S. statist war-economy.

This process came to an approximate end during the 1964–65 period, a development mediated by the 1957–58 recession in the U.S. itself.

The internal dynamic of the U.S. domestic postwar recovery was relatively depleted following the post-Korean War credit-expansion of 1954–57, precipitating the U.S. sector into a 1957–58 recession from which the economy has never essentially recovered. The ability of the U.S. sector to survive 1957–58 was mainly based on the continuing "Marshall Plan" development of Western Europe and Japan, a process which would and did continue up to the point that the super-profits made in Europe (by virtue of cheapness of European labor and currencies relative to the dollar) did not encounter the inevitable contradictions of this one-time solution to U.S. economic problems. Once Europe itself was confronted with the rising costs of actually reproducing a modern labor force (as opposed to capitalizing on productive wealth left over from World War II resources and potentials), and once the development of Western Europe began to depend upon expanding markets for international loans and investments, the entire world monetary system would have begun plunging toward a new general breakdown crisis.

The imminence of breakdown began to be manifest during the 1964–65 period. The events of 1964–68 in Britain, France, and Italy, less directly the developments in Greece, the demonetization of the dollar in March 1968, and subsequent conditions in Italy and elsewhere, bespeak the downward spiraling of the monetary process toward a new conjuncture more profound in its implications than that of the 1930s and May 1971.

Either socialism, or fascism and nuclear holocaust, are the unique historical alternatives for humanity throughout the world during the 1970s. There is no "middle ground."

The Rise and Collapse of the New Left   The effect of the 1957–59 period in the U.S. itself was to abort the process of expanded reproduction (in real terms) within the national sector. To the extent that productive employment continued and even expanded to approximately 1953 levels (!) under the Kennedy and Johnson administrations, this modest growth was mainly dependent upon supplying real wealth for means of production and consumption demanded by expansion of the "new Frontier" to broader and more distant realms of military spending and outer space itself.

Despite continued absolute growth in the size of the working class and some increase (based largely on military aerospace) in employed workers, productive employment as productive employment has essentially stagnated in the U.S. since 1957–58! Increasing employment during the 1961–69 period has been based on not only the expansion of military-aerospace forms, but upon the proliferation of other categories of nonproductive activity, exemplified by governmental and related bureaucracies and office-building construction.

This has meant that increasing proportions of those dependant upon expanded productive employment were pushed out of the productive labor force into the ranks of the "poor" and unemployed youth, or into thinly-concealed forms of imminent unemployment. The masses of black and Hispanic internal migrants to urban centers, new generations of ghetto youth, had virtually no real opportunities for progressive assimilation into productive roles (and incomes) within the U.S., but were chiefly relegated either to virtual "slave labor" categories of marginal employment, or to a lumpenized scrap-heap of persons denied the material level of existence and culture to become potentially productive in terms of modern productive technology.

With the majority of youth in general, the process was sometimes more subtle. In significant part, the massive expansion of university enrollments during the 1958–68 period was essentially a form of disguised youth unemployment.

The irony of this expansion in university enrollments is that the development of a modern productive labor force demands an "open admissions" program aimed at training the virtual entirety of youth not only according to the technological requirements of the most advanced forms of production, but more emphatically to foster exactly that creative concept-forming potential which tends to be destroyed by present norms of family and institutionalized educational life. In general these were not the goals or content of expanded academic enrollments of the recent period.

The pseudo-employment was concealed in part by the growth of non-productive governmental and service employments, and in a very large part by the need of an expanded educational process for more instructors. Most sociologically and politically significant was the multiversity's revealing degradation of the quality of higher education, a development which in several ways unconsciously communicated to the student, the emptiness of this expansion of youthful leisure forms.

Thus, the after-effects of 1957–58 were immediately the disaffection of increasing numbers of youth in general and oppressed minorities in particular. The way in which this disaffection became radicalism—the New Radicalism of the 1960s—was partly and significantly molded by dissimilar social reactions to post-1959 within the ranks of the organized working class. As youth and oppressed minorities became more radicalized, organized labor became—for a time—more decidedly politically conservative.

Trade unions as "economist" forms, naturally tend to be breeding places for not socialism but political conservatism of a certain kind. This general tendency of trade unions in Europe and the U.S. during the past century has been exacerbated during the past quarter century as the cumulative effect of the shaping of legalized trade-union institutions under the politically-treacherous leadership of the Lewises, the Hillmans and (least heroic of the trio) Reuther . . . to say nothing of so obvious a type as Meany. In periods of expanded capitalist employment of productive labor, this conservative tendency of organized labor tends to be offset by recruitment into the plants from "outside" strata of youth, proletarianized ex-farmers, immigrant national-minority strata, and so on. In the process of recruiting new social strata of the political working class forces into trade unions and imminent trade-union organization, the new recruits become the social basis for a social and potentially political orientation of hard-core "older" unionists to the other layers of the political class. A "normal" process which was attenuated during the 1960s.

Thus, all the circumstances of stagnation of the early 1960s tended to make unions more distinctly politically conservative.

This combination of social tendencies provides the determining setting for the emergence of the New Radicalism—or, "New Left"—of the 1958–65 period (especially), and indirectly but definitely accounts for most of the idiotic notions which were the leading convictions among most New Lefters during those and subsequent years.

The immediate, domestic origins of the New Radicalism of 1958–65 are located in the interrelations between the two social strata who made up that movement's loosely-defined ranks: petit-bourgeois youth and lumpenized poor.

The petit-bourgeois suffers a double alienation. Where the member of the working class has an immediate social identity in his comprehension of society's dependence upon his production and productivity, and the capitalist is able to identify himself as a member of society's ruling class, the petit-bourgeois does not represent a real class in any true sense, does not represent a social formation potentially capable of reorganizing society as a whole, and is, furthermore, atomized into a mere collection of the most viciously parochialized functions (administrative appendages) of capitalist political and economic institutions. To find his "Self," to gain a "soul," the petit-bourgeois radical must attach himself either to the ruling class (fascism) or to the working class (socialism). Sufficiently exasperated, and lacking a working-class social orientation, the petit-bourgeois radical easily degenerates into a "political terrorist" or becomes an actual fascist or proto-fascist.

For most of the radicalized youth of the 1958–65 period, the sole available source of "soul" was the oppressed stratum of lumpenized blacks (later, Hispanic and other oppressed groups were added to this repertoire). The strata to which the petit-bourgeois radical turned was itself the victim of vicious alienation from real productive life, and thus a stratum susceptible to petit-bourgeois-like social value-judgments.

These radical youth were pronounced in their anti-working class moods. Not only was the organized working class politically conservative, but the most influential stratum of New Radical youth, including numerous "red diaper babies" steeped in their parent's political demoralization, was recruited mainly from that layer of students and younger faculty who were freed of the need to qualify themselves to become productively employed. It was the radicalized youth of leisured suburbia, a youth whose delusions were subsidized by parental remittances (actual or available on call), who expressed their own social outlooks in favor of a society based on persons who rejected working for a living. This stratum was the most glibly mis-educated, and combined thus the leisure and the capacity for passable double-talk to become the influential cadres of the New Radical "counter culture."

It was this underlying, permeating social orientation of the New Left, its dominant anti-working class moods, which inevitably found their appropriate expression in the epidemic mental-political disease of U.S. "Maoism." Beginning with the "Bay of Pigs" incident, when significant numbers of these youth began to go beyond ultra-militant liberalism toward anti-capitalist politics, the anti-working-class philosophy of these youth found in first Cuba and then Mao Tse Tung a rationalization for a "cultural revolution" without the working class. Mao Tse Tung's empiricist ravings and Mao's image as the leader of a world-wide peasant revolution, set increasing numbers of radicalized youth (and later, sections of the black minority radicals) into a search for a U.S. "domestic" peasant constituency, a "new working class" of professionals, social parasites, and unemployed. The happily-defunct "May Second Movement," the earliest organized expression of such political insanity, was not accidently the breeding place for the political factions at the head of proto-fascist/political terrorist (anti-working class) cults such as "Weatherman" today.

The 1965 developments of the Vietnam War became the "Bay of Pigs" on an extended scale. This phenomenon, indirectly linked to conjunctural economic developments then emerging, became for masses of radicalized youth the transmission belt from impatient liberalism into anti-capitalist moods and postures.

On two counts 1965 represents a breaking-point in the development of New Radicalism. The first basis for dividing the development into a 1958–65 and 1965–68 period (or, 1965–69 development period) is obvious enough on premises already stated: 1965 marks the transition of SDS and similar impatient-liberal groupings of youth into mass anti-capitalist institutions. More subtle, but of more lasting importance is the emergence of the beginning of a pro-socialist current within the New Left after 1965.

This initially small portion of the New Left development was immediately prompted into existence by the failure of the liberal "community" and "poor" schemes of Tom Hayden and other apostles of engaged liberalism, a development embodied in the split of the old *Studies on the Left* editorial board after a prolonged factional feud in 1966. Despite the lag in ridding the movement of pre-1965 liberal tactical recipes, recipes which came cropping up afresh wherever the radical ferment attempted to relive the past, those who had experienced and studied the bankruptcy of Hayden's liberal schemes were convinced of the need for an anti-capitalist approach to the economic issues of life of the oppressed (and other) sectors of the working class forces. The dissolution of the M2M potfreak society by PLP reflected PL's opportune shift from anti-working class toward pro-working class orientations in response (in part) to the new turn in the most advanced stratum of radicalized youth.

The culmination of the post-1965 pro-working class (pro-socialist) development within the New Left was the 1968 Columbia Strike. It was this development which produced the forerunners and present organization of the National Caucus of Labor Committees, an organization which represents the socialist faction of the 1968 split between pro-working class and anti-working class factions of the fractured New Left.

The way in which the hegemonic socialist groups responded to Columbia and its aftermath has much to do with the unfortunate sides of the past two years' developments and also illustrates in telling fashion the constitutional incapacity of the SWP-YSA, CP-YWLL and other such groups to play a meaningfully positive role in current history.

Had cadres from the Communist and Socialist Workers' parties intervened on the side of the socialist factions against the anti-working-class factions at Columbia (and afterward) the political situation among campus radicals would not be the dismal shambles it had become, and the revolutionary-socialist forces in the U.S., instead of being generally disgraced as they are, would number in tens of thousands of committed cadres with a substantial working-class composition having developed in the wake of labor ferment since late 1969. The present, less fortunate state of things essentially reflects the very nature of the CP-YWLL and SWP-YSA, which prevents them from playing a positive political role at any crucial turn in the political situation.

The role of the CP and SWP, during the week of the sit-ins, was to collaborate with a Praxite "double agent" within the Columbia Strike, using muscle forces to prevent support for the Columbia strike from being organized during the morning of the "Sheep's Meadow" festivities. Later, during the late spring, summer, and fall of 1968, the CP and SWP-YSA critically supported the anti-working-class factions at Columbia (and throughout national SDS) against the pro-working class factions. Considering the stupidity of the other pro-working class faction within national SDS, the burden of presenting and defending a socialist perspective within SDS (an actual socialist perspective, based on a working-class orientation) fell on what were (during 1968) about 50 members of the Labor Committees' (LC) organization! Considering the several successful and other near-successful factional struggles of the LC's against all their opponents (PLP included) during that period, it is obvious that critical support from any socialist organization would have to suffice to give the anti-working class anarchist factions a crushing defeat and thus direct the development of SDS toward pro-working class, actual socialist views instead of the moral imbecility which became hegemonic in that organization during 1969.

The critical developments leading to the self-destruction of the last vestige of the New Left in the summer of 1969, and the last gasp of the whole 1968–70 student-radical process in the May (Cambodia) demonstrations, were the dissolution of the Columbia Strike Committee in June 1968 and the New York City Teachers' Strike of the fall of 1968.

From April 23 to about May 15, the Columbia Strike was conducted on the basis of the program developed and advanced by the Labor Committee faction of the strike leadership (Papert, Komm, Dillon). This faction proceeded explicitly from studies of Luxemburg's *The Mass Strike* (Papert, Dillon) and Trotsky's "Germany" pamphlets (Komm), proposing on that theoretical basis a political mass-strike or united front approach to the imminent social eruptions *around* Columbia. The programmatic approach, of a common-interest anti-capitalist program in the interests of students, faculty, campus employees, neighboring tenants, and black working-class forces "down the hill" in Harlem, was that of the Labor Committee faction, and the organization of the Strike Committee as a "Soviet" on the basis of one delegate for 70 members from every group supporting the program anywhere in the city, was the Labor Committee's social-political proposal and perspective.

This shifted the Columbia Strike potential away from the parochialist perspectives of the right-wing SDSers (The "Praxis-Axis"), the impotent "single-issuers" around the YSA, into the nucleus of a socialist movement which aimed at uniting the various elements of the potential political working class under a common interest, anti-capitalist programs.

The well-advised counterinsurgency tactic of New York City and Columbia University officials (who stated their fear that Columbia would become a "model" for emulation around the world) was to attempt to split the Strike Committee into a collection of parochialist, contending social groupings. The leading black "domestic CIA" official on hand, the Ford Foundation's Dr. Kenneth Clark, intervened during the sit-ins, to split a section of the Black Columbia students from the strike forces. A Ford Foundation grant was given as a reward to a group calling itself "Students for a Restructured University," who attempted to wreck the Strike Committee over the issue of allying to off-campus forces. During mid-May, counterinsurgency advisors led the university into a clever provocation as a way of expediting a split from faculty forces from the Strike organization. Liberals contributed generously (from certain quarters) to strengthen the anarchist factions bent on dissolving the Strike Committee into a federation of politically-autonomous "radical action projects" (RAPs).

The most effective assistance to the "CIA" was given by the radical forces within the Strike Committee around M2M and PLP-dropout, John Jacobs, a notably, viciously anti-working class "red diaper baby." The alliance of Jacobs (and Jacobs' stooge, Rudd) with David Gilbert of the anti-socialist "Praxis-Axis," managed to assemble a narrow majority among a rump of strike supporters remaining after the majority of participating students had left campus that June. Using the rump vote (and a seizure of mimeograph machines for exclusive use by Jacob's cronies) Jacobs and certain of the most morally-depraved anarchist types hanging around the strike (bumming dimes and quarters as well as generally scrounging) the Rudd-Praxis group (which controlled the strike funds) dissolved the strike committee and destroyed the established program of the Summer Liberation School, degrading most of the "classes" to illiterate ranting-sessions by potheads reciting from Mao's little red book.

This criminal sabotage of the Strike Movement was rationalized by Rudd-Jacobs-Gilbert on two political premises:

1. That the working-class forces (with which the Labor Committees insisted on allying the strike movement) were an organic part of the "establishment," and therefore the "main enemy" of "revolution."
2. That the "cultural revolution" was based on parochialist ultra-

militant "struggles" by separate local-interest groups as autonomous communities. That blacks, students, and others, should
each be organized in separate constituency groups, each developing their own "thing."

On this set of premises, the strike organization was destroyed in favor of
a federation of "radical action projects" (RAPS)—a loose collation which
quickly evaporated down its hard core of petit-bourgeois bathless anarchists.

This anarchist faction of the strike was shrewdly played up by the
leading press and by various publishing concerns which got immediately
into the profitable business of circulating fraudulent inside accounts of the
strike. Rudd and his fellow-factioneers toured U.S. campuses, spreading
their infantile recipes for "total revolution" which credulous militant youth
and opportunistic PLPers applied with such generally-disastrous outcomes
during the fall of 1968 and spring of 1969. This public relations campaign
by the leading bourgeois institutions involved served the double purpose of
presenting the nakedly anti-working-class side of the strike to working-class
readers and of conning gullible radical readerships into associating themselves with the self-destructive factions of the student upsurge.

The response to the New York City Teachers' Strike of 1968 was
the "clincher."

Ironically, the United Federation of Teachers (UFT), for all its
faults and weaknesses, was one of the most democratic unions in the nation,
and had played a leading role in efforts to upgrade educational opportunities
for ghetto victims in NYC. The UFT had pushed the More Effective
Schools program in the New York City system, a plan for provided enriched services to ghetto students, and local UFT leaders in Brownsville
had helped make possible the very Ocean-Hill-Brownsville "community
control" project which became the so-called issue of that strike.

During 1967 and 1968, a handful of "black bourgeois" opportunists,
typified by Reverend Galamison, Herman Ferguson, and Ralph Poynter,
as well as a handful of well-intended but duped black ghetto parents had
been encouraged by counterrevolutionary "braintrusters" around Kenneth
Clark's MARC office to launch an attack on the United Federation of
Teachers as a way of obtaining funds and patronage jobs for local Black
Tammany-Hall-type political organizations. Clark's vicious attacks on black
children were revealed by his lying insistence that ghetto material conditions
of life, lack of job opportunities, and so on, had nothing to do with the poor
educational performance of black children—that only "racist" attitudes of
teachers were to blame.

The astonishing fact about the prevailing myth of the 1968 New
York City Teachers' Strike today is that the Ford Foundation faction
behind bureaucrat Rhody McCoy and others had virtually no support
within the city's black community at the start of the attack on the UFT by
a mere handful of "domestic CIA" types in black faces. The illusion of a

massive struggle between the UFT and black parents was first established by outright lies circulated as reporting by City Hall, the *New York Times* and the Columbia Television Network's flag-station, WCBS-TV. The immediate effect of this bourgeois propaganda was to mobilize every white-radical political prostitute in New York City (Communist Party, Socialist Workers Party, Progressive Labor Party, and others) to put on a mask of black rhetoric and mobilize themselves and their followers as finks, goons, and strike breakers in general. These handfuls of white-radical (and very few black) "enraged community forces," followed by a WCBS-TV camera crew and *New York Times* reporters, sufficed to create the illusion of a mass "community control" movement against which a "racist" UFT was mobilized. The campaign of lies succeeded so we have some actual white-radicals manifestations from that quarter before the strike was finally ended.

This teachers' strike became for the most morally-imbecilic strata of SDS leaders the absolute proof of the need to regard the working class as the "main enemy." It was that "big lie" which led directly into the emergence of the "Weatherman" group as an openly protofascist organization during the summer-fall 1969 period, and accomplished, with the assistance of critical support against pro-working class forces by the YSA, the destruction and demoralization of SDS by June 1969.

Thus, the New Radicalism of the 1958–68 period is dead; the New Left is dead, and new campus-radical ferment can emerge only on the new foundation of an orientation to the exasperated class struggles of capital and labor throughout the advanced capitalist sectors.

The Labor Movement Today   A statist war-economy produces a shallow, short-lived (historically) capitalist prosperity by increasing non-productive expenditures (such as war production, welfarism, and so on) while holding the number of the labor force engaged in production of useful commodities relatively fixed or diminishing. A war-economy accomplishes its purpose in part by taxing all capitalists and pooling the accumulating funds so obtained to sustain some capitalists in war-production. This permits the capitalist to have the essential, technologically-advanced "edge" of Department I production, essential to the very existence of capitalist economy, without suffering the countervailing effects of employing the major portion of this technology in competition with existing capitalist commodity production. The profitability of this useless production of military-aerospace goods is obtained by adding to the laundry-swapping among capitalists the margin of profit provided by taxation on incomes of wage earners. In general, provided that other props (primitive accumulation) are sufficient, this war-economy arrangement permits a capitalist economy to survive *with stagnating productive labor forces* for a decade or so, while increasing the proportion of total capital associated with pure social waste!

The result of such an arrangement must be, ultimately, a deflationary inflation. The pressures of inflation on the capitalist monetary system produce deflationary pressures against the production of useful commodities. This very pressure against expansion of useful production increases the cost of overall waste and debt-service per productive worker employed in producing useful commodities, so that deflationary measures exacerbate the rate of apparent "cost inflation."

The analytical powers of pro-capitalist economists respecting this paradoxical phenomenon are truly wonderful to contemplate.

Since the valuation of capitalists' capitals (property titles in investment) is based on a multiple of profit-earnings, the capitalist system is prevented by monetary collapse only by increasing profits now at the expense of real incomes of wage earners. Capitalism thus responds to the new monetary crises of today by attempting to increase the mass of profits at the expense of wages (real wages). Reducing real wages contracts the internal market for useful production, thus weakening the profitability of useful production, thus compelling the capitalists to gouge real wages more deeply.

The capitalist press echoes the White House's assertion that the problem of inflation is caused by rising costs. The fraud in this assertion is the failure to distinguish between productive and non-productive costs. Obviously, if one reduces the proportion of wage-earners engaged in useful production of useful commodities, while maintaining war production and other forms of waste activity, the non-productive costs to be applied as an "overhead burden" to the employment of every productive worker increases. Thus, although productivity of productive workers actually gallops ahead at rates in the vicinity of 7 percent per annum, the non-productive burden on each of these productive workers is growing even more rapidly, so that the apparent overall costs per productive worker are, in fact, rising. Since all of this must be paid for out of either the price of useful commodities or taxation on wages, we have the results manifest in the U.S. economy today. Inflationary deflation under conditions of rapidly-rising productivity, while real wages rapidly decline!

This economic situation undermines the objective basis for continuation of the labor-Democratic Party alliances in the U.S. as it tends to break apart other forms of alliances with working people and capitalist political parties in every advanced capitalist sector.

The break develops unevenly. The initial effect of pressures against real wages is to make many workers initially more politically conservative in the U.S., a conservatism exemplified by the worker's determination to keep up his mortgage and consumer credit payments, to cling to "legal" trade union forms, such as the "legal" company-union contract and the state legal and administrative machinery which is the formal basis for union contracts today. Fringe benefits, in the tradition of Bismarck's "labor reforms" of the nineteenth century, also make the worker initially more conservative as he becomes more militant *in defense* of what he has. More generally, he is inclined to depend more "loyally" on his union leadership (which is organically tied to the Democratic and Republican machines) at the same time he is cursing it and moving beyond it in his intentions.

For such and other reasons, there has been no *notable* rise in union "rank and file" caucuses during the recent period. A slight increase in general caucus ferment, larger formations tied to one faction of the bureaucracy against another faction in certain notable and exceptional cases, but no burgeoning trend in truly independent "rank and file" caucuses with significant mass support.

The "other reasons" for the lag in caucus formation within unions are more important than those already cited. The fact is, local rank and file caucuses have no credible basis for coming into being *as mere within-union oppositional groupings*. Making existing unions "more militant" is mainly a self-consoling delusion of those activists schooled in the socialist tactical traditions of the late 1930s and early 1940s. Making existing unions "more militant" is absolutely no *competent* alternative to what is loosely described as the "sell-out" proclivities of existing union leaderships *generally*.

Union leaderships of the CIO type do not "sell out" the membership because they are wretched in general. On the contrary, union leaderships sometimes seem to "sell out" because they, like the majority of "rank and file" members, refuse to undertake the sole alternative to accepting a poorer settlement. Union leaders of the CIO-type generally go as far as they think the majority of members' union militancy will carry the union in gaining additional benefits. Tiny minorities of "rank and file" professional insurgents are often more militant on these questions precisely because they enjoy the speculative luxuries of being out of office. The isolated militant can imagine all sorts of wonderful gains which would absolutely not seem credible to him were he faced with the responsibilities of union office, were he faced with the tactical realities which the incumbent union leadership has to face as long as it accepts existing legal forms of labor struggle and as long as the membership is unwilling to go beyond mere legal forms.

To obtain larger economic gains than are generally obtained under CIO-type union leadership today, to break through on all the important working conditions and related issues, it is essential to go beyond mere trade-union forms. Admitting that existing CIO-type union leaderships often miss a widespread upswing on members' militancy, that they fail— even within trade-union terms—to provide the quality of leadership which could mobilize labor's subjective as well as material trade-union potentials, and so on, what a union can win is brutally circumscribed by shifting policies and practices of government administration, legislatures and courts at the federal, state, and local levels. The margin of contractual wage-gains and working conditions gains needed to maintain a real-wage level today tends to go beyond what the capitalist class (conscious policy of government and leading employers) will permit to be awarded. Every strike which seriously aims at maintaining real wages is no longer a simple trade-union struggle; it is already a political strike against both government and employers.

For reasons to be considered a space ahead, it is possible for some sections of the labor movement to secure exceptional concessions, like

Rockefeller's overriding of Lindsay's political blunder in the famous Sanitation Workers' strike. The question of risking a political break with a significant section of the working class before the capitalist class is prepared or forced to risk such a break will sometimes cause government and employers to pull back from a head-on collision. These pull-backs, used to sustain vestiges of the labor-capitalist party alliances, will in general be less and less possible for the *capitalists* and politicians in the period immediately ahead.

Thus, a caucus based on the narrow perspective of solving problems of workers by changing the guard at the top is plain self-delusion or outright fraud. The only viable form of "rank and file" caucus within the shop is a local caucus organized for the purpose of linking the union membership directly to "cross-union caucuses" of various sections of the political working class, like the Strike Support Committee organized in Baltimore this past fall. The only viable basis for "rank and file" caucuses within unions and shops is a policy of shifting the basis of struggle from unions by themselves into the domain of emerging approximations of political class-for-itself forms, as proposed in the Labor Committees' September 7 and September 25, 1970 "calls" in connection with the General Motors strike.

The relative success of the Baltimore Strike Support Committee, organized at the instigation of the Labor Committees, illustrates several important and interrelated points for work in the months immediately ahead.

Firstly, the success of the Baltimore Strike Support committee was possible because it was immediately focused on a local strike of (mainly oppressed minority) bakery workers. The margins of support added by the work of the Strike Support Committee was a decisive contribution to winning that and other connected strikes.

Secondly, the UAW local in Baltimore County began to respond seriously to the Strike Support Committee at the point the General Motors strike (if it had continued) would have gone into a second, and more political stage. UAW members around the nation showed little interest in "strike support"—serious or "soup pail" varieties—as long as it appeared that the strike was proceeding successfully along lines which have become traditional during the past quarter-century in the U.S. It was only at the point that a continued strike meant a changed political overtone for the struggle that unionists who were prepared to continue began to think in terms of "outside support" and more political forms than mere pure-and-simple militant trade-unionism.

The second point vindicates the estimation spelled out in the Labor Committees' September 25, 1970 analysis and "call." It also implies that the formation of Strike Support Committees must not be delayed until a large union's membership suddenly decides to make a turn in its strike orientation; if no strike support formation exists, to precisely what can the union so suddenly turn? Obviously, the existence of the very sort of strike support groups we instigated in Baltimore, the sort of strike support the

CP and SWP-YSA refused to assist in organizing—the progress of political-social developments in the labor movement will tend to be aborted, precisely in the way that the CP and SWP-YWLL (among other socialist groupings) literally sold out the working class by abstaining from the Labor Committees' September 7 and September 25 call, as those socialist organizations literally sold out the General Motors UAW workers.

The first point shows how strike support organization is to be built generally, focusing on those strikes and related labor struggles in which the mobilizable amount of material assistance to the struggle is a possible margin for success over defeat. This "less spectacular" focus of work provides a nation-wide strike support movement with the roots, the growth, the increased cadres through which to become a major factor in major strikes.

We emphasize that to the extent the so-called socialist movement responds to today's labor struggles at all, it and its campus-radical peripheries show an understandable but misguided tendency to "take a position" only on strike campaigns by national unions against large corporations or large employer associations. This amiable blunder by such socialists reflects their mechanistic state of mind, identifying a national movement only with actions by national labor institutions, and so on. We are, contrary to such mechanistic outlooks, in a period of generalized and escalating class struggle, with limited socialist forces on hand to intervene. The possibility of national political class for itself formations depends significantly upon establishing "smaller precedents" for such formations on a larger scale through numerous smaller, more local successes and partial successes. The point is to mobilize support on the broadest scale for each local struggle of the form proposed in the September 7 and September 25, 1970 General Motors' strike calls by the National Caucus of Labor Committees (NCLC).

The proposal to "bite off what one can chew" would itself lead to folly if we approached such work in terms of each local Labor Committee attempting to establish its own local, autonomous strike-support organization. Wherever such a formation is established, this formation must be immediately supported with telegrams and other forms of support-declarations from around the nation. A dozen persons in this group here, a score in that group there, a half a hundred on a certain campus—taken nation-wide, it adds up to thousands or tens of thousands declaring solidarity with a struggle—under conditions in which the greatest subjective danger to work is a feeling of isolation. Such forms of token mobilization must of course be supplemented by material support, as feasible and appropriate. The tactical objective of such work, beyond the immediate situation under scrutiny, is that of laying the basis for a nation-wide organization, an organization based largely on those small groupings brought together through support of several such local struggles around the nation.

Strike support does not mean setting up a calendar of "glorious festivities" based on when the railway workers or steel workers are due to begin walking picket lines. National strike-support organization is a permanent, continuing undertaking for this entire period, a form of growing self-organization of the nation-wide political (working) class for itself, a process of focusing the support of everyone we can mobilize at each juncture for every strike-support effort of the "Baltimore" form in every locality they develop. *National strike support organization of the "Baltimore" form is the unfolding of a process leading directly into the creation of a mass-based socialist party capable of becoming the government and management of the U.S. economy during the present new decade.*

Our approach to trade union work must be principally oriented to creating caucuses within unions which are mainly premised on the perspective just stated.

This tactical and organizing work is not limited by any means to bargaining issues of local or nation-wide unions. Issues of housing and other "consumer" issues of working people are just as much a part of the working class's political struggle as union struggles. Strike support organization means welding union members, unorganized, unemployed, welfare victims, and political socialist organizations into a united front which addresses itself to meeting all working-class working conditions, employment and real income demands at capitalist expense, whether by means of appropriating incomes of capitalist employers or through shifting tax burdens from wage-earners to capitalists, or by eliminating capitalist waste projects of all sorts in favor of useful production and construction in the interests of the working class.

The Labor Committees' *Emergency Reconstruction Program* for a socialist U.S. government during the 1970s represents a guide for the development of positive class demands leading toward the programmatic measures to be taken by socialist government.

The critical task in this work is that of creating united fronts which are *self-consciously* simultaneously representative of white and black trade unionists (notably), unorganized and unemployed workers, oppressed-minority strata as such, and socialist political forces. It is a matter of the dividing line between socialist principles and pro-capitalist or merely reformist pseudo-socialism that the socialist be opposed to parochialist struggle formations which exclude other sections of the political class, or which propose, as anarchists do, a mere federation of autonomous parochialist groups, each with its own autonomous "program." The program of the united front subordinates the parochial interest to the political class interest, and the organization of the united front explicitly denounces or repudiates exclusion of rights of membership in the united front to any section of the political class which accepts the united front's program.

The immediately opposed formula for strike support is that which is usually offered by most U.S. socialist groups (whenever they elect to concretize their technical affiliation to the working class). These groups insist that "strike support" means supporting the demands of a particular union. The only admissible variation on this subordination of one's support to a union's "autonomous" program is the legalism termed "critical support," in which one notes one's exceptions to particular features of either the union itself or its program of demands or proposed tactical approaches. This is the notorious "soup pail" theory of "strike support" endorsed by the SWP-YSA and CP-YWLL, the centrist or "Menshevik" conception of "strike support." What they reject is the notion developed by Karl Marx that the political class for itself is a superior body of the class forces respecting any mere class-in-itself grouping. In strike support work by Marxists, it is the strike-support organization, the united-front organization, which establishes the program and tactical approach for the forces involved, not the union itself. A "strike support" organization as the "local socialist soup-pail auxiliary" of a union is an abomination, which has nothing in common with the serious strike support organization the Labor Committee is proposing.

While the Labor Committees may collaborate with such disgusting "soup pail" associations under certain circumstances, the reasons for and limitations upon such uneasy associations of revolutionaries with fools will be plain enough in each case.

It is essential that capitalist political organizations not be included in united front organizations. Individual capitalist politicians and factions of capitalist parties may join united fronts provided that those individuals' first accept the anti-capitalist programmatic features of the united front organization. That they agree first to tax capitalist rather than wage-earners' incomes as a general method of funding needs, that they repudiate the class treachery of "ability to pay" introduced to the labor movement like a hari-kari knife by the late Walter Reuther. A "united front" which negotiates a program of strike support with a faction of the Republican, Democratic or Liberal parties is no united front at all, but an exercise in prima facie class betrayal.

Political anti-capitalism is social, and programmatic content is essential. It is not essential that the united front be organized around the specific term, "anti-capitalism"; it is indispensable that the united front be constituted of social elements of only the political working class and that the program of this formation counterposes the programmatic interests of the political working class to the political capitalist class, which means rejecting out of hand all capitalist political parties and their factions.

It will, of course, be argued that such a "sectarian" posture may preclude auspicious strike support formations for certain strikes where capitalist political factions are willing to support the strike on certain (reasonable) conditions. A practical approach to getting the best compromise under such circumstances is like sharing the costs of a shared suit of clothes with a horse; the garments that represent the results of such a compromise between a two-legged and a four-legged creature will fit neither.

The objectives of the united front organization are two. Firstly, obviously enough, it is a way of assembling sufficient masses of the political working-class forces to permit a victory in local strikes, housing struggles, employment struggles, and so forth, where the forces and friends of those immediately involved in the issue would not suffice. Secondly, the tactical urgency of just such formations is what makes the united front possible and the real purposes of united-front formations practicable. The united front is for its participants a qualitatively new kind of social process, in which they are forced to "relate to" dissimilar sections of their own political class in a positive way *for the first time*. It is this qualitative change in relationship of man-to-man within the class forces which produces those changes in consciousness we term class consciousness, the suddenly-developed capacity for understanding man and nature with a depth and scope way beyond what one has probably dreamed of in ones' earlier life, the increased mental power to comprehend socialist program and the need for socialism as the alternative. The united front is not merely a tactical tool, although it has that purely tertiary importance; it is a way of transforming the consciousness of its participants to become socialists.

During 1970, organizations of the unemployed became a root question in many parts of the U.S.A. for the first time since the 1930s. Barring full war-economy regimentation of the U.S., or a rate of inflationary expansion certain to set off an inflationary explosion in short order, unemployment will grow rapidly during 1971, with many areas experiencing the 12.5 percent unemployment rates seen in Seattle this fall.

The early 1930s demonstrated the important role unemployed organizations can play in the mobilization of political mass strikes. The bringing together of unemployment inevitably forms organizations representative of every sector of the potential political class for itself. Thus, the positive features of such organizations ought to be obvious enough.

The difficulties become clearer once the question is posed: *What to organize the unemployed to do in their own, immediate behalf?* A person faced with protracted job loss has immediate problems which are not so easily resolved under present conditions of bankrupted state and local treasuries! *Massive organizations* of unemployed and trade unionists for extended and augmented unemployment and welfare benefits become essential to pry loose from capitalist pockets the immediate funds needed to meet the immediate needs of the unemployed and those immediately threatened with unemployment. *Who pays for unemployment? No layoffs of those presently employed!* These become immediate tactical questions, immediate concrete questions during a period of capitalist recession or depression. Demands for new productive jobs in housing, school, medical facilities, transit-system construction, paid for by taxation of capitalist incomes (incomes, not "profits"), have sharpened importance. Moratoria on rent payments and mortgage payments of wage earners on their homes while unemployed, moratoria on taxation of wage earners' homes during unemployment, no evictions, and related campaigns are obvious sorts of rear-guard struggles.

It is most important among unemployed not to promise un-employed (or present welfare victims) more than is within reach with the forces at hand. Organizers must maintain a strict distinction between *agitation*, on the one hand, and propaganda and education, on the other. Those being organized must be clear concerning what the immediate action is aimed at gaining, as distinct from what we propose to gain by the further actions we take with larger forces, and so on. Every socialist must con-tinually make the difference between *agitation* and *propaganda* clear to those being organized, especially in unemployed and welfare work. It is criminal to play "fast and loose" with the struggles of persons in such desperate personal situations.

In general, the programs for all struggles are to be *derived from* immediate applications of our *Emergency Reconstruction Program*. The program we propose for socialist government in the U.S. in the 1970s represents a set of historic principles *toward which* we work in terms of approximations which fit the agitational situation in which we are working.

In concluding this section, we summarize the organizational goals of the process we see embryonically represented in the fall 1970 Baltimore Strike Support coalition work.

The leading role in the formulation of program and in catalyzing the formation and development of political-class-for-itself forms is the socialist vanguard organization, like the organization of the National Caucus of Labor Committees and socialist organizations allied with the Labor Committees in such undertakings. These vanguard organizations have a somewhat direct connection to broader masses of working people through propaganda (newspapers, magazines, and so on), but, in practice, the con-nection of the socialists to larger numbers of working people is mediated through several social strata. The most immediate such stratum is the organization of the Baltimore "cross-union caucus" type, which represents the most advanced stratum of the potential political-class-for-itself. The more advanced working people who play an active role in such cross-union caucuses are, in turn, embedded in whatever actual or nascent local caucus formations tend to exist within unions and other parochialist institutions of the class. These caucuses within parochialist formations like the union are, in turn, the connection of the more advanced ("cross-union caucus" member) to the broader organized masses, and to the unorganized masses around the organized strata.

These four tiers of organized forces are not fixed social categories, but are determinate stages of a process leading every member of the political working class (in principle) to socialist affiliations and world out-looks. This process-relationship is demonstrated by considering the way in which "cross-union caucus" forces are assembled and dispersed in the suc-cessive flows and ebbs of united front activities. As the result of a productive struggle along "Baltimore" lines, a certain proportion of those engaged are won to or toward a socialist world outlook, while others are in varying degrees becoming more sympathetic to the socialist world outlook. When the action ebbs, the cross-union caucuses tend to disperse; a handful joining socialist organizations, others return to day-to-day life of a more ordinary sort. When the next call for united-front action develops, the socialist cadre-organizations intervene with augmented forces, as a result of previous recruitments in united-front work, and (during a rise in social ferment) they more easily assemble the forces of an active "cross-union caucus," which now penetrates more deeply into the various stratifications of class forces than during the preceding actions.

As the numbers of working people developing approximations of a socialist philosophical world-outlook increases in this way, the capacity of the movement to act on more advanced programmatic conceptions is increased; the movement is broadened in its penetration and deepened in its penetration of the consciousness of every social stratum of the working class involved.

It is in this sort of process, on the ascending scale of social ferment in the working class, that the socialist vanguard organization is transformed into a mass-based socialist party, and acquires its proper authority to speak for the broad masses of working people.

The Organized Socialists   In the U.S. today, there are three principal organized groupings of the type which terms itself revolutionary socialist, plus two organizations limited in membership to "national minorities." The first three are the Socialist Workers Party-Young Socialist Alliance, the Communist Party-Young Workers Liberation League, and the National Caucus of Labor Committees. The latter two are the Black Panther Party and the "Young Lords."

In addition to this there are, of course, numerous professed "Marxist-Leninist" groupings, ranging in numbers of members from a few hundred individuals (Progressive Labor Party, International Socialists), through several of between 50 to 100 members, and, finally assorted grouplets of telephone-booth dimensions. None of the organizations have any historic relevance to the question of which socialist tendency will gain left-hegemony over emerging labor forces during the 1970s—except as members of these doomed organizations may end up in one of the three principal organizations through the process of splits and fusions throughout the movement. It is the three principal organizations and their relationship to the Black Panthers which will determine the course of future U.S. history in the most immediate way.

However "irrelevant" the factional struggles among the three leading socialist organizations may seem to be at times, considering the minute fraction of the U.S. population directly engaged, if one understands the social process by which a revolution is organized, in such seemingly irrelevant disputes the future history of mankind is being rather directly settled.

As to the question of the irrelevant socialist groupings, the decline of Progressive Labor Party (PL) from "third place " exemplifies the questions involved. As we noted in assessing the rise and fall of the New Left, "Maoism" ran amuk among U.S. campus (and other) radicals during the 1960s because Mao Tse Tung exemplified for U.S. suburbanite radicals and lumpenized strata the notion of an anti-capitalist revolution without the working class. Progressive Labor flourished because its ultra-left former trade union colonists had turned, out of "unrequited love," to punish the ungrateful workers, accomplishing this by publicity consorting with the U.S. "peasantry," which they located in the persons of anti-working-class radicalized youth and, wherever possible, labor-hating black militants. The radicalized youth, in turn, saw in PLs ultra-left tantrum a means of giving socialist "legitimacy" to suburbanite hatred of working people generally.

Or, to be more exact, during the 1958–68 period, PLs ambivalence toward the working class made it a suitable halfway house for radicalized youth of two species. PL became, as for John Jacobs and other subsequent protofascists, a way-station which was half-way to the more virulent forms of petit-bourgeois anarchism and "political terrorism." To the extent that PLs ambivalence represented an orientation (of sorts) toward the working class, it also became a transmission belt for saner radicalized youth into the Labor Committees. Now that both the protofascists and their opposites, the Labor Committees, exist independently of PL, there is no longer any reason for PL to continue existing, except for the inertial commitment of that organization's proprietors.

The International Socialists (IS), the only other association numbering hundreds of members, is actually not a socialist organization in the sense that the SWP, CP, NCLC or PLP are. IS is principally a confederation of distinct and fundamentally-irreconcilable tendencies bound together by fear of independent existence—a collection of irreconcilable factions huddled together for "warmth." The organization is a product of its times, emerging by stages from the SP during the 1965–67 period under the impulsion of emerging labor ferment of that time, and briefly flourishing under the borrowed charisma of Eldridge Cleaver during the 1968 "Peace and Freedom" campaign, the IS has since then demonstrated nothing so much as an incapacity to act in a serious, sustained way in any form of "outside work." Its serious internal problems are reflected in its recent device for copping-out of New York Strike Support work during the General Motors strike. The New York IS group entered into public cohabitation with the infinitesimal Spartacist organization on the United Automobile Workers of America (UAW) strike, an engagement which is best described as a united-front with the graveyard.

The remainder of the irrelevant groupings are sufficiently detailed in paragraph for all. The Workers' League flourishes in irrelevance by means of its single technical accomplishment, a weekly 12-page tabloid of 5,500 circulation by one of the smallest socialist organizations in the U.S., an actual accomplishment it embellishes by grossly-exaggerated representations of a British co-thinker group, the Socialist Labour League. There is, next, Sam Macry's personal cult, a schizophrenic affair with one ectoplasmic foot in the labor movement (Workers' World) and a youth organization whose sympathies vacillate between anti-working-class socialism and outright proto-fascism. Then, including several recent splits from the decayed Socialist Labor Party, there are post-office box organizations whose political-theoretical pretensions to absolutely-distilled purity of "essence" are in inverse proportions to membership rosters.

The Socialist Workers Party

During L. Trotsky's lifetime, the U.S. Trotskyist organization never exceeded a few hundred members, but was nonetheless able to exert a significance way beyond such numerical forces mainly because of Trotsky's stature as the most heroic revolutionary figure of his time, and, in part, because of the relatively exemplary role played by a handful of Trotskyists in Twin Cities, in Auto, and other locations. The "failure" of the Trotskyist organization to achieve greater relevance during that period does not reflect relative weaknesses in quality of organizational leadership vis-à-vis the Community Party in the United States of America (CPSUA) but the hegemonic appeal of the Soviet Union for radicalized U.S. workers. To have become a significant force during the late 1930s or early 1940s, the SWP would first have had to split off a significant section of the CP worker-cadres.

During the 1937–40 period, the SWP, like the CP, underwent a sharp degeneration in political quality, reflecting the lack of political-theoretical competence of its leading cadres and the pressures of depoliticization in the masses of U.S. workers. Like the CP, the SWP tended to function as a group of *militant trade-unionist leaders first and as politicals second*. Under the sway of this political retreat, the SWP leadership became generally infected with "Stalinophobia." This moral disorder, which was not lacking in abundant empirical foundation in certain important respects, reflected an adaptation to "anti-collectivist" moods among rank-and-file trade-union militants who were becoming increasing apolitical and socially parochialists.

Trotsky himself had denounced both SWP tendencies in 1940, pointing to the wretched, apolitical trade-union opportunism of the "Northwest Organizer" publication, and the "Stalinophobia" rampant in the Cannon leadership which had just split from Schachtman!

Following Trotsky's assassination, the SWP carried its errors to the point of a wild, postwar delusion, to the effect, that it, the SWP, having achieved the magnificent dimensions of about 3,000 members (against tens of thousands of CPers!) was now situated to ignore the CP (!) in the process of directly leading a postwar American socialist revolution! From the combined effects of such soft politics with wild delusions the SWP has never recovered.

Aggravating those difficulties in more recent years, the SWP leadership, like the CP from which the U.S. Trotskyist organizations were formed, has always been deeply infected with the same sort of anti-intellectualism one is otherwise accustomed to expect from a wretch like Stalin or some trade-union bureaucrat of the lower orders. The Cannon-Foster faction of the 1920s reeked with this social chauvinism and a correlated tendency to degrade itself before the AFL bureaucracy of that time—translating Lenin's prescriptions in *Left-Wing Communism* into a catechatical repudiation of the horrors of "dual unionism." The SWP leadership after 1938–40 *equated trade-union militancy with "class consciousness,"* and generally emulated the centrist Bebel on both the organizational question (bureaucracy) and in equating parochialist trade-union caucus leadership with the qualities of "distilled class consciousness"—a pretext for systematically suppressing the development of an actual revolutionary intelligentsia within the SWP. ("Intellectuals" within the old SWP were expected to "fawn upon" "worker-leaders" to "ask permission to speak.") Consequently—and it remains the case today—the SWP is organized *not* to resist petit-bourgeois social influences; on the contrary, it has been virtually taken over by the worst sort of petit-bourgeois Menshevik youth during the past five years! It is organized to prevent the development of a viable revolutionary intelligentsia within its ranks, and is thus incapable of becoming revolutionary again by internal means.

From 1948 to 1958, the Trotskyist movement (so-called) clung to a precarious organized existence, on the basis of continuing to represent the political literary heritage of Leon Trotsky vis-à-vis the lies of the Moscow Trials. Three developments coming to a head in the 1957–58 period offered the SWP the long-awaited opportunity to challenge the CP for left-hegemony. Firstly, the Khrushchev "revelations," which destroyed the myth of the Moscow Trials for every CPer who had a modicum of judgment. Secondly, Hungary, which destroyed the myth of the Stalinist monolith. Thirdly, the 1957–58 recession, which called into question the demoralizing myth of neo-capitalism. It was the third development which made the first two worth-while.

Almost as a reflex, two SWP leaders, Murry Weiss and James P. Cannon, turned all of their organizational talents toward a "regroupment" with whatever parts of the CP and its peripheries could be snagged into the project. Unfortunately, 1958 was not 1938; the SWP of 1958 had nothing but programmless warmth to offer the CPers. The "regroupment" failed because the SWP was constitutionally incapable of offering anyone (including itself) a programmatic perspective for socialism in the U.S. for the foreseeable historic future.

Then and immediately afterward, the SWP leadership did respond to political and social manifestations flowing from the 1957–58 recession (all the while denying, emphatically that that recession had had much importance). They aimed themselves at the hindside of Civil Rights, radical-youth ferment, Cuba and Elijah Muhammad; they adopted the policy of attempting to get at the head of whatever procession passed the SWP headquarters, so to speak, and represented such exertions as theoretical leadership!

Until 1957–58 the SWP had maintained a formal pretense of conjunctural orientation toward a renewed working-class political struggle in the U.S.A. This pretense evaporated in the evolution of the "regroupment" tactic. The abandonment of that formal yardstick for measuring principled political differences within the organization destroyed the only premise for *principled* factional life within the organization. During the 1958–60 period, the leading social formations around the SWP leadership formally degenerated into cliques pure-and-simple, the bitterest "factional" struggles mobilized within the organization without a shred of systematic political differences offered by any of the several sides involved. The result was the purge of 1961–65, which destroyed the last vestige of democratic life within the organization in the *formulation* of political policies—democratic discussion was degraded into a mere exercise of tongues after the policy had been decided elsewhere.

The first flagrant manifestation of this overt political degeneration was Joseph Hansen's rationalization of the experience of the Cuban Revolution as a "new model" for socialist revolution for the entire period ahead. The issue is not whether Cuba became a workers' economy in the 1960–61 period; it did. The issue is that Hansen and others, covered up the most essential feature of the Cuban Revolution—*its absolutely exceptional circumstances*, of a sort not likely to be repeated—and abstracted from a most fortunate contingency a general "new model" for socialist revolution during an entire historic period. Since Hansen is usually consulted by other SWP leaders whenever a literary precedent is required, it is relevant to observe that Trotsky debated the problem of such "exceptional circumstances" with E. Preobrazhensky during 1929, in which Trotsky conceded that the Chinese might make a revolution along the lines of the Chinese Revolution as later did occur, but that the person who generalized from such "exceptions" to a "new model" was guilty of attempting to cut the throat of the revolutionary movement. As one can observe in the case of those noble, misguided youth who attempted to naively repeat the "Cuban model" everywhere on instant notice, some literal revolutionary throats did become literally cut following the advice of Hansen and similarly gifted prophets of the accomplished fact.

As U.S. socialist organization's gate-receipts from the influence of the Cuba Revolution ebbed during late 1961 and early 1962, the SWP found a substitute for the Cuban Revolution in a brilliant *empiricist* study of "black nationalism" presented by Robert Vernon. Malcolm X then emerged in late 1963 and early 1964 to save the SWP-YSA from total inactivity.

The strict interpretation of Black Nationalist tailism policies ("white folks keep out") had certain contradictions for the SWP-YSA. The obvious predicament was represented in a resolution of the fall 1964 YSA

Plenary session: The only movement in the U.S. is the black nationalist movement, from which white socialists must abstain; therefore, except for a handful of black YSA members, the YSA must restrict itself to selling the Militant and supporting the presidential ticket of DeBerry and Shaw.

SDS "fortunately" appeared to rescue the YSA from such a horrible self-imposed death. Jack Barnes, then chief YSA huckster, went on a national sniffing-tour during late 1964, during the course of which he discovered the existence of SDS, returning (via a visit to Cannon in Los Angeles) to propose a new turn for the YSA. This led, following a rubber-stamp endorsement by the winter 1965 SWP Plenum, to the SWP-YSA intervention in the SDS anti-war movement.

For the SWP-YSA 1965 was a fateful year. The 1965 SWP National Convention rationalized the slow purge of 1961–65, effectively destroying all internal political democracy within the SWP and YSA and casting off all control of the organization's political lines by working-class political criteria. The fall 1965 Convention also embraced the single issue anti-war tactic line in its first official version. These developments not only determined the persistent line of the organizations since that time, but have transformed the organization sociologically. As a result of its non-working-class political orientation, its opportunism, the SWP-YSA has destroyed itself politically by constituting a cancerous mass of petit-bourgeois Menshevik youth as the overwhelming majority of its organizations!

This organizational fact was politically demonstrated at the Oberlin conference of the SWP-YSA during the past summer. The pressure of anti-working class Menshevik forces within the SWP-YSA was manifestly so great that *the SWP responded to a new eruption of the working-class struggle by turning absolutely away from it, on the premise that the "nationalist" struggle is the working-class struggle!*

Thus, while there are undoubtedly numerous valuable cadres and potential cadres within the SWP-YSA, it is a hopeless undertaking to attempt to reform the organizations from within. Should a principled factional struggle erupt within those organizations, it is of course desirable that cadres within the organizations conduct a principled struggle to the end of its course, not because they might win, but because in the course of such a principled struggle they themselves can develop. There is no hard and set rule to be applied. A revolutionary goes where he can to do what has to be done the best.

The Communist Party

Numbers of persons around the socialist movement made strong criticisms of our report in *The Campaigner* that the CPUSA was a "sleeper: in the U.S. movement." Since that report was both written and published, the prediction has been well borne out. The Young Workers Liberation

League is admittedly off to a very late start as a youth organization, but its recruiting since its formation has been at least as significant as that of the YSA. The parent organization, the CP, has seemed to come alive, as we predicted, under the impulse of a resurgence within the labor movement to which the CP tends to respond as the CP. Otherwise, that organization has material resources and reactivable cadres and peripheries in many strata, including the labor movement, which make it the first force to be reckoned with in the U.S. movement today.

The most conscious weakness of the CP as an organization engaged in reproducing itself is the loss of large sections of "red diaper babies" to other socialist currents as well as to petit-bourgeois anarchism and even protofascism ("Weatherman"). Not that organizations of this sort reproduce themselves biologically, but the loss of the "red diaper babies" reflects a cutting-off of the CP from the majority of radicalized youth.

As the revival of the CP recently shows, the CPs situation is not impossible because of these difficulties. The SWP-YSA was, without doubt, relatively hegemonic to the CP in 1968–69. It was the SWPs failure to respond positively to the new ferment in the labor movement which created a virtual vacuum in which even the moribund CP flourished. The anti-working-class bias of the YSAs anti-war and "nationalism" lines impels the sort of youth being radicalized today in increasing proportions toward the CP. It may be generally stated that the SWP-YSA are presently the main recruiters to the CP-YWLL.

Except on one notable count, the CP has all the vices of the SWP in their worst possible form, adding to that repertoire of centrist betrayal the one monstrous crime of which the SWP-YSA is not yet overtly guilty: "intervention" within the Democratic Party and similar machines.

The sole favorable distinction of the CP—vis-à-vis the SWP—is that the CP has responded far more quickly and significantly to the class struggle, even if in a disgusting way. This is a virtue only to the extent that this issue marks the CP-YWLL as suitable recruiting-ground for the National Caucus of Labor Committees.

Counterrevolutionary Roles of CP and SWP

When the term, "counterrevolutionary," is employed to describe a working class oriented, nominally socialist organization, the meaning is by no means the same as when the same term is applied to capitalist political parties, police agencies, and so on. In the present usage, the term signifies systematic sabotage of absolutely necessary forms of socialist work and drawing invaluable masses of socialist cadres away from urgent self-development and activities into demoralizing and useless or worse activities. Such sabotage of socialist work, when it involves a significant proportion of socialist cadres is objectively counterrevolutionary, as the French CP of 1968 was so obviously counterrevolutionary.

Three recent counterrevolutionary crimes are sufficient to warn us of this trait in both the CP and SWP. Firstly, as in the attempt to sabotage a Saturday morning demonstration in support of the Columbia Strike, and the CP and SWP in the anti-war movement have intervened to oppose connecting the anti-war issue to the issue of socialist reconstruction, or the issues of the war-economy to the issues of the working-class struggle. Secondly, the New York Teachers' Strike, where both organizations contributed their entire resources in support of a "domestic CIA" maneuver to set black minorities and trade-unionists into head-on collision; in this connection the CP and SWP behaved as virtual "CIA" agents—which is otherwise instructive on how the CIA succeeds in certain operations abroad—it finds dupes like the CP and SWP in those countries to assist in setting one national minority against another (for example, would the SWP have supported Gorbes Burnham against Cheddi Jagan?), as Ernest Mandel supported exactly such a criminal enterprise in Belgium! Thirdly, when they respond to the labor movement, they respond with "soup pail" strike support gimmickry, acting as virtual goons of the labor bureaucracy within the socialist movement to keep support movements subordinated to the demands of particular unions, and so on, and prevent a political class for itself form of struggle from developing. This was their wretched joint role during the GE strike, the Postal workers' strike, and during the UAW General Motors Strike.

If either the SWP-YSA or CP-YWLL secures hegemony over the Left in the U.S. in the immediate years ahead, the socialist movement in this country is doomed, and the human race is thereby virtually doomed. "Counterrevolutionary" thus seems rather too mild an epithet to apply to those organizations.

The U.S. Political Capitalist Class Capitalist parliamentary governments and parties depend for their existence upon certain kinds of favorable conditions of capitalist economic development. The essence of the "pluralist" system on which parliamentary machines are built, through which various sections of the ruled are assimilated into such machines, is the ability of the ruling class to dole out measured doses of material and related concessions to each of these assimilated "constituencies." What we come to know as capitalist democracy is thereby limited to a very narrow range of relatively advanced capitalist sectors under conditions of relative prosperity—at least, capitalist prosperity.

When a capitalist sector is in an age to accumulate at the maximal rate by virtue of relative economic backwardness or because of other problems of national development of a conjectural urgency, there is virtually no latitude for democratic largesse to the broad masses. Even in advanced sectors, under conditions of actual or imminent general breakdown crisis, the same rule of iron-fisted regimentation applies. Democracy is possible only for sectors of capitalism in which the productive forces have developed to a certain extent and in which political democracy is imposed upon the ruling class as a necessary correlative of a relatively skilled and mobile working class. Once a breakdown crisis faces the capitalist economy, the narrow span of democratic life erodes.

Where the material conditions favorable to measure concessions to all major sections of the ruled no longer exist, the parliamentary system persists only in a state of perpetual crisis until the economic situation is either restabilized or the parliamentary system is replaced either by socialism or some form of capitalist police-state, such as fascism.

The deepening crisis of the capitalist world monetary system since 1964–65, reflected in the galloping state and local budgetary crises in the U.S., and in general, rising inflationary-deflationary crisis in the economy generally, has destroyed the real basis for the persistence of the traditional "parliamentary" party machines of the Republican and Democratic parties. The labor Committees and their antecedent organizations have predicted and analyzed this process of breakup of the "two party" system since 1966, expressing views which have been more recently replicated in a more superficial way by capitalist analysts and some socialists outside our organization. A 40 percent President (Nixon) and a 40 percent New York City Mayor (Lindsay), accompanied by a galloping growth of the cancer of Conservatism and the increasing objective basis for significant socialist electoral formations, is the Italian state of U.S. political life.

This erosion of the parliamentary system of government during the past five years is a world-wide phenomenon of the advanced sector and its immediate political appendages. Italy has been essentially ungovernable since 1968. Capitalist government in France rests mainly on the mortal aromas emanating from the PCF-CGT. Great Britain has been ungovernable for almost the entire half-decade; the illusion of the German Federal Republic's "economic miracle" is about to be punctured. The Trudeau government's application of the "War Measures Act" is the appropriate inaugural act of the 1970s.

Interpenetrating this general tendency are a variety of shifting policy positions within the political capitalist class and its intelligentsia.

From the last years of the Eisenhower Administration until about 1968, the basic policy of the leading capitalists was as follows: (A) temporarily stabilize a statist war-economy within the U.S.A.; (B) develop the economic integration of Western Europe as the main, immediate prop of the sagging U.S. dollar; (C) begin applying the "Third Stage of Imperialism" policy (Development Decade) in the most serious way to Southeast Asia, Latin America, Africa, the Near East; (D) develop a détente with the Soviet Union, involving Soviet contributions to the imperialist "Development Decade" program. Under this general fourfold thrust of U.S. policy, it was proposed to begin applying to the U.S. itself some of the infrastructural-developmental policies (for example, O.E.O.) which the CIA and allied agencies were applying to the "underdeveloped sector" generally.

During the last quarter of 1967 and the beginning of 1968, there were several manifestations of sharp turns in the world economic situation, undermining the possibility for immediate application of the basic long-range developmental policies to which leading capitalists were committed.

These included the devaluation of the British pound, which itself set off a series of shock-waves threatening to topple the entire world monetary system *within months!* By March of the following year (1968) the U.S. dollar itself had been virtually demonetized, a development followed by collapse of the French franc and revaluation of the German mark. By the end of 1968, inflationary forces had already threatened to explode the U.S. dollar into a new world-wide convulsion that must surely usher in a depression, a general breakdown crisis.

Under these conjunctural circumstances, the long-term policies of the leading capitalists and their intelligentsia tend to be subordinated and even seemingly pushed to one side in behalf of contradictory short-term expediencies. The "Third Stage" policy progresses in Latin American countries in its various forms as "developmental" juntas in Peru and Bolivia or the Allende regime in Chile, and Robert McNamara is the most active agent of this policy at the World Bank—but there is yet no unified thrust of imperialist resources behind this "last-chance" policy of the imperialist system, since to act upon a "last-chance" tomorrow the capitalist system must first survive today—or, so it seems to them.

All of the short-term programs orbit about the extremely-difficult undertaking, of stabilizing capitalist property-titles for a year or more by direct assaults on the real wages and established legal rights of existing trade union forms throughout the advanced capitalist sector. The ruling circles are reluctant to go as far in this as economic self-interest dictates, since they as yet have no political machinery capable of governing without working-class cooperation. They would prefer to destroy the trade-unions' rights by "inches," a process which proceeds too slowly now from the standpoint of accelerating economic pressures for head-on collision with major sectors of the working class.

Short-term capitalist "recovery" in the U.S. is not absolutely excluded, even during the present secular thrust into a new depression. Such variants merely become increasingly unlikely every day. If such an upturn occurs for a brief period, it can only occur by means of either massive regimentation or inflationary stoking, both of which would catalyze more-explosive social crises and make the ensuing collapse more violent in economic and social effects. Short-term increases in employment and superficial forms of prosperity are not excluded; they are unlikely, could only be very short-lived, and would result only in accelerating and deepening the general breakdown crisis.

The fundamental contradiction in policy for the capitalists remains the issue of labor policy. Economic interests, taken by themselves demand an immediate, all-out effort to break the labor movement and crush real wage-levels. Since capitalists' capital is a political form, rather than wealth for itself, the existence of capitalists' capital as capital depends upon the political stability of the capitalist state, the stability of governmental debt and credit, and stability of the various governmental sectors abroad which are essential, satrapal pillars of the U.S. world monetary system. The immediate political stability of the democratic capitalist states depends to a major extent on continued cooperation of large sections of the working class into political machines of the capitalist parties—as we see in the past two years of Italy, a situation which has been tolerated by the U.S. rulers of Italy only because those rulers have as yet no alternative to center-left-*left* parliamentary cretinism as the basis for some semblance of stable government in that country.

Here, thus, politics and economics interpenetrate in the most immediate way. A sharp, head-on collision with working people, when the capitalists have not yet mustered a large right-wing, anti-union machine independent of working-class forces, will tend to bring into being the political mass strike formations which are the social foundation for mass working-class parties and successful socialist revolutions. To the capitalists it is politically preferable to administer economic and political repression by "inches" or perhaps "feet," keeping each new progress an atrocity contained to one or another isolated sector of the political working-class forces, avoiding the clear sort of attack which would be taken as a general provocation even by trade-union bureaucrats and "hard hats." This policy of measured assaults depends, obviously, on the lack of socialist forces capable of catalyzing a mass response to an attack on one isolated sector of the class—the anti-labor policy in the U.S., for example, depends upon the continued hegemony of such "socialist organizations" as the SWP-YSA and CP-YWLL. However, this more cautious tactic (again) fails to produce the rate of profit-gains from reduced real wages which the situation of spiraling deflation demands. Thus, on the latter grounds, the capitalist class is impelled to undertake social confrontations for which it is not really prepared and, conversely, for fear of such poor correlation of social-political forces, to dally, permitting the pressures of inflation-deflation to advance more rapidly—up to the point the desperate situation plunges the ruling circles into totally-irrational desperation.

Under these circumstances, it would be the height of insanity for socialists to imagine that some more liberal section of the political capitalist class will rally to halt the attack on labor by means of some new "New Deal" turn. There is absolutely no economic basis for such a new "New Deal." However, wherever large socialist organizations develop, it is almost inevitable that the capitalist parties will include a proposal (for a brief period) of "Popular Front" government (for example, the Communist or Socialist Workers' Party grown sufficiently large, of a sudden, to be offered a minor piece of an electoral slate, and so on). The sole purpose for such an offer is to induce potentially-dangerous socialist (organized) forces to demoralize their own following and to totally disgrace themselves publicly.

This is not the same issue as that of the role of certain liberal strata in opposing the systematic destruction of civil liberties. The working class comes to political power normally with the support of large sections of the petit-bourgeoisie, including peasants and professionals, the characteristic representatives of this class. While the liberal politicians are customarily mere appendages of the political capitalist class, they may be momentarily shaken loose from leading capitalist circles during a sharp political turn, and can be won—as surface reflections of the petit-bourgeois to support of working class formations, provided that socialist parties move decisively and quickly at each appropriate moment for action. Socialist organizations must put themselves in the lead in the defense of civil liberties generally, not only because we are for civil liberties, but because we must create the political movement of socialists on this question which will tend to draw the viable strata of petit-bourgeois into the support of the revolutionary-socialist movement. This work must not be *directly* connected to nor subordinate independent political class for itself formations and work; it is a purely auxiliary, secondary aspect of the process.

Thus, given the capitalist postures and vacillations which flow from the general economic and political situation, what the capitalists do will be determined by what we do. If and only if socialists succeed in creating mass-based political class for itself formations through "strike support" organizations along "Baltimore" lines, the capitalists may well offer a "popular front" tactic to us, if we are gullible and criminal enough to seek such an "opening." In sum, what the capitalists do will depend upon what the working class does in the way of political self-organization along class lines; and what the working class does in that respect is determined by the potentially-hegemonic organized currents within the socialist movement. In that sense, the secret to the future zigs and zags of capitalist policy is located not behind the governmental and corporate boardroom door, but in the dynamics within socialist organizations such as our own.

We have already stipulated the optimal course of action for the working-class forces: it is necessary, in assessing capitalist policies to concentrate immediately on the most likely and deadly blunder which might be committed by a relatively hegemonic socialist force under conditions of political working-class upsurge in the months and years immediately ahead.

It is absolutely essential to educate all working people against any participation in either the Democratic or Republican parties or in "Popular Front" organizations (coalitions of socialist and capitalist political organizations). Wherever we intervene in the electoral field (as we must where possible), our intervention is in behalf of the clearest presentation of our full program and immediate tactical objectives. We must explain the dangers of all programmatic opportunism by socialist and labor organizations, and insist on a workers' government as the only acceptable governmental coalition at the very juncture (above all) that "Popular Front" coalitions are offered. The point at which a capitalist party seriously offers a coalition government with socialist organizations is almost invariably the point at which the socialists must move directly toward the establishment of a workers' government as such.

It must be made clear, as through the work of historians in exposing the lessons of the past to masses of working people through our journalism and forums, that the "Popular Front" offer, provided it is made, will be an offer to socialists to enter new political forms of the "New Priorities" type (immediately, anyway), and requires that socialists submit their programs to the "hopper" of mutual, selected governmental platform-program formulation. By negotiating compromises with capitalist political factions of that sort, the socialist program is degraded to farce to the extent that it is represented in the coalition slate platform; otherwise the capitalist political faction would become a revolutionary-socialist formation in fact! Thus, the only purpose of including socialists in "New Priorities" type organizations is to induce the socialist movement to totally discredit itself.

It is under such circumstances that the traditions of the CPUSA become the most virulent, counterrevolutionary danger to the future of the world's humanity. The socialist movement must expose as "class traitors" all those who propose to intervene within "New Priorities" movements at any stage of those "movements" development, except from the outside for raiding and exposure purposes—absolutely no merger of socialist forces with capitalist political factions, left or otherwise.

A more subtle, but equally dangerous form of class treachery is already formulated by the SWP-YSA in those organizations' present view that the "national" struggle is the highest form of the working-class struggle at this juncture. The SWP-YSA, seeking to attach its mouth firmly to the posterior of whatever new Pilsudski appears in black-face, has simply offered the old Stalinist "theory of stages" "pop-front" lines in the thinnest of rhetorical disguises.

As we can readily document from token cases of SWP-YSA class treachery to date, their version of the old Russian Menshevism is that of entering "Popular Front" formations based on national minorities, or on a colonial national liberation movement. In that "Popular Front," *they already propose to function* as a "principled" political "loyal opposition" to pro-capitalist currents within such political capitalist formations. They might, to give them the best of it, strongly object to obvious class treacheries of the most undisguised forms. That display of threadbare conscience would have little practical value; by leading socialist cadres into the swamp of petit-bourgeois nationalist political parties, the SWP-YSA and its co-thinkers would have already sabotaged the possibility of any alternative, and their expressions of political protest against "betrayal" would be nothing more than empty, self-consoling rhetoric, a harmless, disgraceful spectacle to amuse the "CIA" types running such nationalist parties.

The National Caucus of Labor Committees   How can a mere few hundred persons, mostly less than 25 years of age, mostly recruited from campus-radical strata, propose to intervene in the situation in the U.S.

today to bring about a socialist transformation within this decade? That is the question now to be answered: nothing else is worth considering at this juncture.

Our organization has some token empirical demonstration of the validity of certain relevant, scientific principles in our role in the 1968 Columbia Strike, the 1969 University of Pennsylvania Strike, and in the recent Baltimore Strike support work—among a variety of similar and less-notable experiences of the same general sort during the past two years. The principles we have applied to those situations are, in general, those identified at the outset of this resolution, also identifiable with Rosa Luxemburg's analysis of the Political Mass Strike process. In that application we have demonstrated that a mere handful of persons, armed with an appropriate conception of transitional socialist program and Marxian sociology, can become a leading force in movements hundreds of times more numerous than the initiating group. These recent proofs are less proof of the principles themselves than demonstration that our mastery of the lessons of previous history have been real and practical rather than simply literary.

The principal question for us is how to connect numerous such embryonic mass-strike developments to one another to produce a nation-wide political mass-strike movement in a matter of a few years at most.

Provided that such a small group as ours has the essential program necessary for socialist state power, which we do, and provided that this small group can catalyze into being social formations of trade-unionists, un-organized and unemployed, oppressed minorities, radicalized youth, and professional socialist cadres, this fusion of program and political class for itself forms results in the creation of mass organizations of socialists in a short historical time. That, provided that the struggle has sufficient continuity to sustain advances from one forward tactical moment to another, so that the conscious experience of increasing numbers of participating masses is progressively connected as a general process of changing consciousness, of emerging socialist class consciousness.

That was our perspective at Columbia in the spring of 1968, at the University of Pennsylvania in the winter of 1969, and in every other tactical undertaking which local Labor Committees have approached in collaboration with our organization's national leadership. Those are the premises for our seemingly-pretentious foresight of left-hegemony for our organization.

The immediate tasks of our organization during the next six months in particular are thus as follows:

1. To accomplish a number of internal developments in organization of business meetings and other internal functions which make our internal organizational life more agreeable to cadres recruited from the working class through the mediation of "cross-union caucus" work.
2. To concentrate, through "cross-union caucus" work, on recruit-

ing significant numbers of cadres of workers, notably including special emphasis on cadres from black and Hispanic minorities, thus increasing our immediate penetration of the working class as a whole.

3. Of increasing the frequency and circulation of our newspaper, *New Solidarity*, with increasing usage of materials of reference which provide more effective communication of advanced theoretical and programmatic conceptions to workers in shops and in communities of oppressed minorities. Not to dilute the level of political thought to a condition of "popularization," but to employ terms of reference through which advanced conceptions are more immediately communicable to advanced working-class strata.

4. Of creating intermediates forms of organization, including regular forums for workers and students, regional conferences of workers and others on urgent theoretical and tactical problems, through which broader strata of the working class can find agreeable ways of associating with the peripheries of our organization.

5. Of developing pedagogical forms for education of workers in Marx's dialectical method and economic theories, and constituting regular classes for such education of workers.

6. Opening up new Labor Committee locals in the industrial "heartland" bordering the Great Lakes and in those regions of the South where industrial development has created new opportunities and immediate needs for organizing unorganized workers.

7. Bringing every politically-significant local "strike support" effort along "Baltimore" lines into national focus through every means available to our national organization. Organizing support on whatever level possible, ranging from telegrams of solidarity on up, from small groups to whole larger organized working-class forces, for struggles of this form in one area from every possible other area. Thus, to create the favorable subjective conditions for building toward national "strike support" organizations along "Baltimore" lines.

8. Of envisaging political class for itself approximations developing during 1971 as the social basis for possible electoral interventions during 1972.

9. Continually pressing members of all socialist organizations for "united front" work on the same general basis we pressed for such joint efforts in our September 7 and September 25, 1970 appeals.

10. Developing the membership of the NCLC as a centralized task-oriented organization respecting both tactical undertakings

and the quality of deliberative processes required to comprehend and solve problems of "sharp turns" in the tactical situation. The principal emphasis accompanying centralized deliberative and action processes is in education in the Marxian dialectical method, as that method has been represented in the courses on which our organization was first established and in the literature we have already published on this subject.

11. Increasing the scope and depth of coverage of international socialist developments in *New Solidarity* and the *Campaigner*, thus giving a means for raising the notion of political class for itself consciousness and actions above parochialist national lines.

12. Developing a sustained and scholarly program of educating workers and others in the history of the socialist and labor movements as those histories bear on understanding the tasks and problems before us today.

Education Within the NCLC The National Caucus of Labor Committees is the first revolutionary socialist organization of this present century to actually be formed on the premise of a vanguard revolutionary intelligentsia. Only in the nineteenth century, in such instances as represented by the close circles around Karl Marx or the peer-group of the Polish revolutionary organization around Rosa Luxemburg, do we find a direct comparison.

At the other extreme, the more "normal" form of establishment of a self-styled revolutionary-socialist organization has been the emergence of some new expression of "apostolic succession" of alleged "true prophets" and canonical literary "Marxist" doctrine. "Marxism-Leninism," "Marxism-Leninism-Stalinism," "Marxism-Leninism-Trotskyism," and "Marxism-Leninism-Stalinism-Maoism," are the representative self-designations of these groupings. Each of them has come into existence either as replications of some socialist organization of the same apostolic profession in another country or as factional spin-offs from a larger socialist organization of the "apostolic" form within the same country.

In each of these instances, particularly today, the new self-styled revolutionary-socialist grouping is absolutely not premised on the assimilation of Marx's actual method and economic theories, or the application of that method and theories to concrete materials. Rather, the member of the "apostolic succession" bases himself on what he regards as a sufficient interpretation of Marx's "sacred texts" in the form of official catechism of his particular organization; the "original," "divine revelation" within Marx's thought is esteemed as comprehensible only to certain, selected "true prophets" or in the resolutions and legalistic precedents of action of selected party congresses of certain forerunner organizations of the supposed apostolic succession.

The usual exhibition of this religious scholastic or Talmudist procedure reminds one of Saul-turned-Paul on the Damascus Road. One finds in each distinct sect the arguments that certain figures became filled with the Holy Ghost of revolutionary socialism at a certain date and, in most cases, that the Holy Ghost abandoned those same mortal premises at some later date, to be superseded in tenancy by some spiritual manifestation of bourgeois Satan. The same scholastical procedures are applied to entire parties.

In this way so-called "socialist theory" has been degraded to various sequences of canonical precedents and sacred Talmudic marginal notations, all based on the working assumption that the identified popes and organizations were perfect embodiments of the Holy Spirit's influence between two more or less precisely-located dates. Thus, it represented that the utterances of those persons and organizations during such intervals are thus regarded as "true revelations" of the Divine Will, just as the Chinese Communist leadership has elevated Mao Tse Tung into a new living Buddha and located the mediation of spiritual virtue in the turning of a prayerwheel on which is pasted various selections from Mao Tse Tung's "Little Red Book."

This procedure is the means employed to argue for the currently exclusive tenancy of the same Holy Spirit in this or that particular sect today. As in the most notorious case, Healy's Socialist Labour League in Britain, the most hair-raising replications of medieval scholasticism are employed to "prove that" Healy (for example) is the only true Pope of Socialism, involving a meticulous tracing of the alleged laying on of hands, to document the migration of the Spirit of Infallibility from one Pope to the next.

This dismal, scholastic practice is itself sufficient proof that the organization so afflicted with self-deceptions is nothing better than a counterrevolutionary centrist socialist formation within the socialist movement. The habit of representing revolution theory as a body of religious like doctrine and socialist leadership qualifications in terms of a Kantian or worse explanation of the embodiment of the Divine Will within certain leaders, is sufficient demonstration that such "theory" is merely self-consoling religious rhetoric, whose function is thus to disguise the contrary (non-socialist) content of the organization's day-to-day practice.

The Labor Committees, by contrast, have come into being as a result of a predetermined effort to evade precisely such miserable "apostolic" degradation of socialist cadres. The Labor Committees were founded as more or less an intellectual peer-group of revolutionaries whose common denominator has been some degree of actual personal mastery of Marx's dialectical method and economic theories. The organization is essentially the outgrowth of classes in Marx's method and economic theories, and of propaganda, education, and agitational work by groups formed from participants in those classes. Thus, conceding the short-comings of comprehension inevitable among any body of students new to any field of study, the NCLC is based on the scientific verifiability of Marx's method and economic theories as such, rather than any set of "historical," "legalistic" or "canonical" precedents of "Marxism-Leninism."

Where weakness has been manifest in the organization, these difficulties have been attributable in each case to a lack of self-education premised in assimilation of Marx's actual dialectical method. Invariably, where economic-theoretical and political errors have become the basis for factional life in the organization, the obvious root of such blundering political conceptions has been a lack of comprehension of Marx's method, a deficiency demonstrated by the persons' sympathy for outrageous slanders against Marx's method by certain logical positivists within our organization's ranks.

These difficulties are inevitable for any socialist organization which develops itself even on the best basis. While the hard core of our organization's membership has been assembled on the basis of the educational process identified above, the NCLC has also appealed to certain strata from former campus radical ferment simply because ours is the only organization within which the individual is encouraged (as well as permitted) to pursue an active, serious intellectual life in connection with the formulation of the national organization's policies. Thus, serious, critical work by mere academic standards of undergraduate or graduate competence in social "sciences" has sometimes been regarded as a substitute for scientific comprehension premised on Marx's method and actual theories. The essential weaknesses, around the fringes of our organization, have been associated with a lag in assimilating Marx's actual dialectical method, and a resulting tendency under conditions of ebb in campus-radical ferment and a turn in the social situation toward the labor movement, to substitute mere forms of intellectual accomplishment for the actual content of the work of the revolutionary intelligentsia.

This weakness has been manifest during 1970 as a tendency of some members to accommodate to petit-bourgeois moods in the surrounding campus milieu, to divorce the abstracted form of our socialist reindustrialization program from its social setting in the emergence of actual political (working) class-for-itself forms. There has been a potentially-dangerous tendency to imagine that the mere brilliance of our programs, analyses, and predictions, addressed to almost any radical or even liberal milieu, would win over large strata by the sheer power of reason. Not accidentally, those who have succumbed to such petit-bourgeois social tendencies have failed miserably in every single prediction they offered during the past year!

This tendency, in which our organization suffers only far, far less acutely than the predominantly petit-bourgeois Menshevik SWP-YSA, reflects (again) ignorance of the ABC's of Marx's method, that the intellectual power to assimilate and comprehend the NCLC program depends upon the active social form of relations peculiar to approximations of political-class-for-itself formations, not individual reason per se. The attempt to divorce the issue of program and the form of propagation of form from working-class social-political forms is absolutely not understanding nor agreement with our program, but the degradation of that program to a hollow shell, a mere glitter without social substance. Program for us is the subjective side of work in building political-class-for-itself forms.

We seem, admittedly, to have stipulated an exception to this fundamental rule in the case of the revolutionary intelligentsia. However, that exception exists only for those persons who totally misunderstand the social basis for the revolutionary intelligentsia itself. The revolutionary intellectual is distinct from mere academic intellectuals as he, first of all, is situated to develop an overview of social productive relations on a world scale, and to situate this overview on the social basis of what the productive working class is capable of becoming, provided that that class is transformed from a class in itself to a political class for itself. It is the revolutionary intellectual's dialectical contempt for compartmentalization, which makes him immediately a ruthless factional opponent of most mere academic intellectuals, and his location of his personal identity in a future political class for itself, which distinguishes him.

Like all working-class socialists, we start from the productive working class as such. Unlike all other socialist currents in the U.S. today, we do not stop there. We do not attempt to view the working-class-in-itself as the potential repository of "class consciousness." We stipulate, in opposition to the SWP, CP, PLP, IS, and others, that the working class must be first transformed into itself by breaking open trade-union formations and other parochialist forms to include membership by which chauvinistic trade unionists (for example) regard as "outsiders," providing these "outsiders" represent elements of the political class for itself.

The centerpiece of this unique tactical approach of our organization is comprehension of the dialectic of the production of consciousness, understanding the social processes determining the production of concepts and entire philosophical world-outlooks among specific kinds of social formations. This comprehension demands de facto comprehension of the essential features of Hegel's *The Phenomenology of Mind*, and of Ludwig Feuerbach's corrections of Hegel, provided that Feuerbach's *Principles of the Philosophy of the Future* is interpreted from the standpoint of Marx's critique of that work, in the "Theses on Feuerbach," and in the first section, "Feuerbach," of *The German Ideology*.

Without that understanding, it is impossible to understand the relationship between socialist program and class for itself formations, except as compartmentalized, almost-mechanistic categories, and for lack of such comprehension, to seek to connect such mechanistically-rectified categories by a desperate search for a "middle tactic"—not accidentally, such "middle tactics" invariably prove to be some version of "Popular Front" treachery if not even more wretched forms of class betrayal.

This problem, which has been the characteristic difficulty of the old German Social-Democracy and the old Communist parties, has inevitably and repeatedly led those who failed to master the dialectical method into Menshevism, whether of the Russian form, the centrist forms of the 1907–1914 SPD or CP-CGT formations, or the betrayals of socialism in Western Europe during the immediate post–1944 period by Stalin and by Western European Communist parties. Without a dialectical comprehension that the relationship of political class for itself formations and socialist program is direct, needing no middle tactic, every socialist organization must tend to fall into the empiricist's trap of seeking that "middle tactic," which lies only in the betrayal of the socialist struggle within adaptation to "broad," "popular" movements of a class-conciliationist form.

Thus, the capacity of the NCLC to recruit and actually assimilate new members, to absorb whole factions of the socialist movement in fusions, and so on, depends upon energetically remedying the theoretical weaknesses which have been manifest within our membership during 1970.

This problem will take a special form in the process of assimilating workers as cadres. Since recruits from the working class, especially its oppressed strata, do not have the educational backgrounds to assimilate Marxist dialectical method and economic theories in the same way, with the same glib facility as student-derived revolutionary intelligentsia, there is a misguided temptation to degrade Marxian conceptions to "popularized" forms, thus degrading the education of workers to a shallow, hearsay acquaintance with a "few facts" about "Marxian theory."

The actual pedagogical problem to be solved demands precisely the opposite approach. The task of educating workers involves developing a pedagogy through which politically-advanced workers can become masters of the most advanced theoretical conceptions. Unfortunately, as we turn to this indispensable task, we are confronted with a general failure of the entire past socialist movement to provide even mediocre precedents upon which we might draw.

Our national organization must therefore establish a system of "night schools" for worker-socialists in every location in which we have the physical means, penetration, and available qualified instructors for this purpose. The curriculum for this school program must be essentially the same in content and pedagogical objectives as the Marcus course in Elementary Marxist Economics, but the presentation must be expanded in numbers of sessions and in scope of detailed content, so that the instructors can thereby engage workers' attention at the level of their present educational developments, providing such students with the necessary prerequisites to master the subject on the same level as the Marcus course for college graduate and undergraduate students.

This demands creative insight into the pedagogy of concept formations, to the point of building actual comprehension in the student by successive steps of development of his self-consciousness. The first thing the instructors and courses must accomplish is that of making the student aware of the problem of concept-formation, of his (or her) initial starting-point of bourgeois-ideological philosophical world-outlook, as Gramsci has appropriately identified this important pedagogical problem of workers' education. The course will depend for its effectiveness on destroying the student's faith in his naive, common sensical view at a very early point in the curriculum. It is on this establishment of the importance of developing an entire new philosophical world-outlook, of therefore mastering the problems of philosophy per se, that comprehension of Marxian method and concepts depends.

It is necessary, from observations of past experience, to warn against instructors who content themselves with parading a mere superficial grasp of the subject as a matter of social posturing before a class. Admittedly, and even emphatically, a class has criteria which make it selective; any "lowest common denominator" approach will result in a pedagogical abortion. The point here is that the business of presenting Marxian economics is not a matter of reciting a series of canonical glosses plus several paraphrases of such glosses, nor disgusting homilectic rhetorical methods. Weak comprehension of the subject by the would-be instructor invariably produces all these and other, related disorders. The education of the educators is one of our principal problems in this undertaking.

There should be an expansion of *New Solidarity* for this same purpose. Without reducing the more-advanced theoretical-conceptual treatments addressed to existing socialist cadres, it is essential that the pages of our newspaper address the consciousness of working people from the standpoint of the foregoing educational policy. No bowdlerized "truisms," and so on, but rather using the literary devices of irony to assist readers in reaching a state of mental crisis respecting their present concepts, in which provoked state of mind our writing in *Solidarity* should assist them in reaching the needed new conceptions.

Such ironies are feasibly if not easily developed by our writers and editors provided the essential irony of capitalist life is kept in view. Where the parochialized subjective life of working people causes them to develop conceptions which are appropriate to parochialized or individual-qua-individual pseudo-reality, reality is actually determined in whole processes. The elementary rule of thumb for socialist literary irony is thus as follows. First, marshall all of the most powerful (commonsensical) arguments for the parochialist delusion, and then destroy all of these premises and their associated conceptions by introducing the contradictory reality of the whole process. That is the exemplary tactic for our organization's educational work in formal classes and journalism during the months immediately ahead.

1 2 3 4 5 6 7 8 9 10